The Complete Guide to

America's National Parks

ELEVENTH EDITION

The Official Visitor's Guide
of the National Park Foundation

Fodor's Travel Publications
New York • Toronto • London • Sydney • Auckland
www.fodors.com

The Complete Guide to America's National Parks

Project Editor: Pamela Wiesen
Design: Guido Caroti
Research Assistance: Research assistance provided by the National Park Service: Office of Public Affairs; Division of Park Planning and Protection; Harpers Ferry Center Publications Division; and Karene Grad
Photography: Stone: *Daniel J. Cox,* cover; PhotoDisc, xvii, xli, 413, 445; PictureQuest, iii

Copyright

Eleventh Edition
ISBN: 0-679-00769-5
ISSN 1532–9771

Special Sales

Fodor's Travel Publications are available at special discounts for bulk purchases for sales promotions or premiums. Special editions, including personalized covers, excerpts of existing guides, and corporate imprints, can be created in large quantities for special needs. For more information, contact your local bookseller or write to Special Markets, Fodor's Travel Publications, 280 Park Avenue, New York, NY 10017. Inquiries from Canada should be directed to your local Canadian bookseller or sent to Random House of Canada, Ltd., Marketing Department, 2775 Matheson Boulevard East, Mississauga, Ontario L4W 4P7. Inquiries from the United Kingdom should be sent to Fodor's Travel Publications, 20 Vauxhall Bridge Road, London SW1V 2SA, England.

PRINTED IN THE UNITED STATES OF AMERICA

10 9 8 7 6 5 4 3 2 1

CONTENTS

THE NATIONAL PARK FOUNDATION

Every year millions of Americans travel to national parks like Yosemite and Yellowstone, which incorporate some of the most stunning landscapes on Earth. The National Park Service, which preserves and protects these areas, also cares for several hundred other areas, including not only forestlands studded with unique natural features but also coastal areas and historic sites and landmarks.

Chartered by Congress in 1967, the National Park Foundation is the official nonprofit partner of the National Park Service. The National Park Foundation honors, enriches and expands the legacy of private philanthropy that helped create and continues to sustain America's National Parks.

This book, as the Official Visitor's Guide, helps support the national parks. So when you take it home, you'll be helping to preserve and protect some of the most fascinating and most beautiful parts of the United States.

Another way to help the parks is by purchasing a National Parks Pass. The National Parks Pass costs $50 and is valid for one full year from month of purchase for admission to all National Parks that charge an entrance fee. The Pass comes with a special National Park Pop-Out™ map, a Proud Partner vehicle decal, and an offer for a free *GoParks* newsletter.

The image on the National Parks Pass is chosen through an annual nationwide photo contest. The National Parks Pass *Experience Your America* Photo Contest is sponsored by the National Park Foundation and the National Park Service with Kodak, a Proud Partner of America's National Parks. For more information, please visit www.nationalparks.org, home of the National Park Foundation.

Officers

Chairman
The Honorable Gale A. Norton
U.S. Secretary of the Interior

Vice Chair
David Rockefeller Jr.
Director, Rockefeller & Co., Inc.

Secretary
Denis P. Galvin
Acting Director, National Park Service

President
Jim Maddy

Members of the Board

HOW TO USE
THIS BOOK

The national parks are the focus of this guide, and you'll find a thumbnail sketch of each along with information about what you'll see and do there. It should help you immeasurably as you plan your travels.

In these pages the alphabet rules. Parks are grouped by states, and both the states and the parks they contain are arranged in alphabetical order. Some parks straddle state lines, or have units in more than one state; you'll find the text for these in the chapter devoted to the state in which the headquarters are found. Affiliated areas, which are not federally owned or administered by the National Park Service but that draw on technical or financial aid from the Park Service, are listed in the Other National Parklands section at the end of the book, along with the couple of dozen national trails, national heritage areas, and national rivers that are not adminstered by the park service. At the end of each chapter are cross-references to all affiliated areas and multistate parks found within the boundaries of the state covered by the chapter. Regional maps at the front of the book pinpoint locations of the parks (or, in the case of multistate entities, that of their headquarters).

Programs & Events

In addition to opportunities for outdoor or cultural pastimes, many parks also sponsor special programs, which operate either year-round or seasonally. We've spelled out those you'll find year in and year out and noted when others are available. These may be orchestrated when demand warrants and when manpower and funding permit—and that's often not more than a few months in advance.

Sometimes programs are cut and hours scaled back at short notice. So, although you can rest assured that all information in this book was checked thoroughly by the parks themselves at press time, it's always a good idea to confirm information when it matters—especially if you're making a detour to visit a specific place.

Types of Parks

There are a variety of parks, and each type is indicated by an icon, as follows:

National Parks contain a variety of resources protected by large areas of land or water. **National Preserves** also protect specific resources but allow activities not permissible in national parks, such as hunting, fishing, and the extraction of minerals and fuels, so long as they do not jeopardize natural values. **National Reserves** are like National Preserves, but are managed not by the Park Service proper but instead by local or state authorities.

National Memorials are primarily commemorative of a historical subject or person.

National Monuments, usually smaller than national parks and lacking their diversity, preserve at least one nationally significant resource.

Parks designated as **National Historic Sites** preserve places and commemorate persons, events, and activities important in the nation's history. **National Historical Parks** are similar but are larger and more complex.

National Military Parks, National Battlefield Parks, National Battlefield Sites, and **National Battlefields** are all associated with American military history.

National Recreation Areas are set aside purely for recreational use. **National Lakeshores and National Seashores** preserve shorelines and islands while providing water-oriented recreation. **National Rivers and Wild and Scenic Riverways** protect ribbons of land bordering streams that have not been dammed, channelized, or otherwise altered. Besides preserving rivers in their natural state, these areas provide opportunities for outdoor activities. **National Scenic Trails** are long-distance footpaths that wind through areas of natural beauty. **National Parkways** include a roadway and the ribbons of land flanking them, offering leisurely drives through areas of scenic interest.

OTHER TERMS USED IN THIS BOOK

The section of the guide entitled "Other National Parklands" also discusses Affiliated Areas and National Heritage Areas. An **Affiliated Area** is a significant property preserved in the United States or Canada that has not been designated by Congress as one of the 384 units of the National Park System but that draws on the financial or technical expertise of the National Park Service. Some of these sites have been recognized by Acts of Congress; others have been designated National Historic Sites by the Secretary of Interior. (Some National Historic Sites are part of the park system proper, while some are Affiliated Areas.) There are also a number of **National Heritage Areas** around the country, which conserve the nation's natural and cultural heritage and make it accessible to visitors. These regions, mainly private property, are managed by partnerships among federal, state, and local governments and private nonprofit organizations.

National park areas may also have additional designations assigned by the United Nations Educational, Scientific, and Cultural Organization (UNESCO) in accordance with the World Heritage Convention. **World Heritage Sites** are irreplaceable properties of outstanding international significance; **Biosphere Reserves,** exemplifying some of the world's varied ecosystems, provide a field for research and education, serve as repositories of genetic diversity, and provide baseline data for monitoring global environmental change.

ABOUT YOUR VISIT

More than ever, our national parks are being discovered and rediscovered by travelers who want to spend their vacations appreciating nature, watching wildlife, and taking adventure trips. But as the number of visitors to the parks increases, so does stress on wildlife and plant life. Tourism can drum up concern for the environment, but it can also cause great physical damage to parks. As you visit the parks, please keep in mind that these lands will not thrive without your care, nor will they last without your support. And use common sense, to keep your visit as safe as it will be enjoyable.

Entrance Fees

The entrance fees charged by many national park areas are noted in the text. If your travels will take you to many national parks, consider purchasing the **National Parks Pass** ($50), which admits you and your 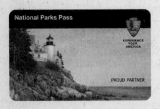 companions to all parks that charge entrance fees for one year at no additional charge. (Camping and parking cost extra.) A percentage of the proceeds from sales of the pass helps to fund important projects in the park. The **Golden Age Passport** ($10), for those 62 and older, and the **Golden Access Passport** (free), for travelers with disabilities, both entitle holders to free entry to all national parks, plus 50% off fees for the use of many park facilities and services. You must show proof of age and of U.S. citizenship or permanent residency (such as a U.S. passport, driver's license, or birth certificate) and, if requesting Golden Access, proof of your disability. You must get your Golden Access or Golden Age passport in person; the former is available at all federal recreation areas, the latter at federal recreation areas that charge fees. You may purchase the National Parks Pass by mail or on the Internet. For information, contact the National Park Service (Department of the Interior, 1849 C St. NW, Washington, DC 20240-0001, 202/208–4747, *www.nps.gov*). To buy the National Parks Pass, write to 27540 Ave. Mentry, Valencia, CA 91355, call 888/GO–PARKS, or visit www.nationalparks.org.

New Parks

Regularly, sites important to the country are designated as national parks to protect them and inspire future generations. As we go to press, a number of parks have just been named.

Rosie the Riveter/World War II Home Front National Historical Park in Richmond, California, was established to commemorate the mobilization of the workforce on the home front during World War II, while specifically recognizing the contributions of women and minorities to this effort. Established on October 24, 2000, the park is made up of several sections that extend along the waterfront of Shipyard #3 and in Richmond. Contact: National Park Service Pacific West Region, 600 Harrison St., Ste. 600, San Francisco, CA 94107, tel. 415/427–1320.

Governor's Island National Monument, on Governor's Island, New York, at the confluence of the Hudson and East rivers, once protected New York City from sea attack. Part of a 1985 National Historic Landmark District, it contains Castle William and Fort Jay, constructed between 1806 and 1811 as part of the First and Second American Systems of Coastal Fortification. The monument played important roles during the War of 1812, the Civil War, and World Wars I and II. Contact: Northeast Region Office, U.S. Custom House, 200 Chestnut St., 5th floor, Philadelphia, PA 19106, 215/597–7989.

First Ladies National Historic Site in Canton, Ohio, was authorized on October 11, 2000, to preserve and interpret the role and history of First Ladies in American history. The site consists of two properties: 331 Market Avenue South, the home of First Lady Ida Saxton McKinley, and 205 Market Avenue South, the City National Bank Building. The site will be managed through a cooperative agreement with the National First Ladies' Library, a nonprofit corporation. Contact: Pat Krider, National First Ladies' Library, 331 Market Ave. S., Canton, OH 44702, tel. 330/452–0876.

Virgin Islands Coral Reef National Monument preserves submerged lands off St. John in the U.S. Virgin Islands, part of a platform that extends several miles from shore to the deepest part of the Atlantic. Many species—among them whales, dolphins, brown pelicans, terns, and sea turtles—exist in a delicate balance here, interlinked through complex relationships developed over tens of thousands of years. Contact: National Park Service Southeast Region Office, 100 Alabama St., SW, NPS/Atlanta Federal Center, 1924 Bldg., Atlanta, GA 30303, 404/562–3182.

Staying Safe

Motor-vehicle accidents, drownings, and falls are among the leading causes of death in the national parks. These are accidents that common sense can help you avoid. If you find yourself in an emergency situation, call 911; there are telephone booths at the visitor centers and other locations throughout the parks. Some parks have their own emergency numbers as well.

Before you go, be sure to pack a first-aid kit, including a first-aid manual. Keep in mind that even in summer the weather can change unexpectedly—especially in mountainous parks. Temperatures can rise into the 90s during the day and drop into the teens or lower at night. Always have warm clothing and rain gear handy, no matter how promising the day.

WILD ANIMAL ENCOUNTERS

As human development shrinks wildlife habitats, animal encounters are increasingly common in national parks. To avoid attracting bears, raccoons, and other scavengers, be sure to animal-proof your food supplies. At developed campsites, animal-proof containers are available; in the backcountry, hang food in a bag or container at least 15 ft above ground and as far away from the trunk of the tree as possible. Stay away from bears and their cubs, and try not to hike at dawn or dusk, when encounters with mountain lions are most common. If you do see one, inch away steadily without turning your back or bending down.

Staying Healthy

ALTITUDE SICKNESS

One of the most common problems for hikers is altitude sickness, which results when you ascend above 8,500 ft without proper acclimitization. To help prevent altitude sickness, spend a night or two at a higher elevation before attempting any strenuous physical activity, and if you have a history of heart or circulatory problems, talk to your doctor before planning a visit to areas at high altitudes.

Symptoms of altitude sickness include headache, nausea, vomiting, shortness of breath, weakness, and sleep disturbance. If any of these occur, retreat to a lower altitude. Altitude sickness can develop into high-altitude pulmonary edema (HAPE) and high-altitude cerebral edema (HACE), both of which can be permanently debilitating or fatal.

ANIMAL AND SNAKE BITES

Some animals, especially rodents, carry dangerous diseases. If you are bitten by a wild animal, see a doctor as soon as possible. Many animal bites require a tetanus shot and, if the animal could be rabid, a rabies shot.

Snakes do everything to avoid you, but in the event that you have a run-in and are bitten, act quickly. If it's a harmless snake, treat as you would any other puncture wound. If it is poisonous, have the victim lie down and remain as still as possible so as to minimize the spread of venom through the body. Keep the wound below the rest of the body, and have another person seek medical help immediately.

GIARDIA

You can't see giardia, but these tiny water-borne organisms can turn your stomach inside out. Carry bottled water for day trips; drinking water is available at many campgrounds. If you're hiking into the backcountry and can't carry enough water, you must purify all spring or stream water, no matter how clear. The easiest way to purify water is to drop in a water-purification tablet or to filter it through a water-purification pump, available at camping equipment stores. Boiling water, another method, takes time and uses fuel. But if it is the only method available, allow the water to boil for at least 10 minutes, longer at high altitudes.

HAZARDS OF HIKING, PRECAUTIONS TO TAKE

Always choose hiking trails suitable to your physical condition and the amount of weight you plan to carry. Consider the length of the trail, its steepness, and how acclimated you are to the altitude at the start and finish. Always be aware of the possibility of altitude sickness. Every hiker planning multiday backcountry trips, particularly those traveling solo, should leave their intended route, planned length of trip, and return date with a park ranger before setting out.

Proper clothing is essential, especially on more rigorous hikes. Hiking boots should be well broken in and sturdy, with good traction and ankle support. On less demanding trails, athletic shoes are fine. Wear thick wool socks, and always bring a second pair in case one gets wet. Rain gear is a good idea, since the weather in most of the national parks can change drastically within moments. Always carry at least two quarts of water per person per day, even more if you are staying overnight or are hiking in hot weather.

HYPOTHERMIA AND FROSTBITE

It does not have to be below freezing for hypothermia to strike: This potentially fatal decrease in body temperature occurs even in relatively mild weather. Symptoms are chilliness and fatigue, followed by shivering and mental confusion. The minute you spot these signs, seek shelter, remove wet clothing, and wrap the victim in warm blankets or a sleeping bag—if possible get into the sleeping bag with him or her. High-energy food and hot drinks also aid recovery.

Frostbite is caused by exposure to extreme cold for a prolonged period of time. Symptoms include the numbing of ears, nose, fingers, or toes; white or grayish yellow skin is a sure sign. Take frostbite victims into a warm place as soon as possible, and remove wet clothing. Then immerse the affected area in water that's warm—not hot—or wrap the area in a warm blanket. Do not rub, as this may permanently damage tissues. When thawing begins, have the victim exercise the area to stimulate blood circulation. If bleeding or other complications develop, get to a doctor as soon as possible.

LYME DISEASE

This potentially debilitating illness is caused by a virus carried by deer ticks, which thrive in dry, brush-covered areas. Before walking in woods, brush, or through fields in areas where Lyme disease has been found, spray yourself thoroughly with tick repellent and wear pants tucked into socks, and long sleeves. When you undress, search your body for ticks and remove them with rubbing alcohol and tweezers. Watch the area for several weeks. Some people develop a rash or flulike symptoms; if this happens, see your physician immediately.

Lyme disease can be treated with antibiotics if caught early enough.

PLANT POISONS

Learn to recognize poison ivy, poison oak, and poison sumac, and avoid them. If you accidentally step into a patch, wash exposed skin immediately with soap and water, and do not touch clothing that has been in contact with the plants. If a rash and blisters develop, use calamine lotion or cortisone cream to relieve itching.

SUNBURN AND HEAT STROKE

Always protect yourself from the sun. At higher altitudes, where the air is thinner, the ultraviolet rays are stronger. Sun reflected off snow, sand, or water can do special damage, even on overcast days. Liberally apply a sunscreen of SPF 15 or higher before you go out, and wear a wide-brimmed hat and sunglasses.

If you are exposed to extreme heat for a prolonged period, you run the risk of heat stroke (also known as sunstroke), a serious medical condition. It begins quite suddenly with a headache, dizziness, and fatigue but can quickly lead to convulsions and unconsciousness or even death. If someone in your party develops any of the symptoms, have one person go for help, move the victim to a shady place, wrap him or her in wet clothing or bedding, and try to cool him or her down with water or ice.

Leave No Trace

FIRE PRECAUTIONS

When it comes to fire, never take a chance. Always build them in a safe place (away from tinder of any kind) and use a fireplace or fire grate if one is available. Clear the ground in the immediate area so wind cannot blow sparks into dry leaves or grass, keep your fire small, and never leave it unattended. Throw used matches into the fire, and always have a pot of water or sand next to your campfire or stove. Don't build fires when you're alone. When you are finished with your fire, be sure it is out cold—you should be able to touch it with your bare hands. Never cook in your tent or a poorly ventilated space.

MINIMUM-IMPACT CAMPING AND HIKING

The little extra effort it takes to use the parks responsibly goes a long way toward ensuring the future of North America's natural beauty. Do not leave garbage on trails or in campgrounds. If you hike in the back-country, carry out what you've carried in, including all your trash. Bury human waste at least 100 ft from any trail, campsite, or water source in a hole at least 8 inches deep; some parks and many environmental organizations advocate packing out even human waste. Do not wash dishes or clothing in lakes and streams. If you must use soap, make sure it is biodegradable, and carry water in clean containers 100 ft away from its source before using it for cleaning.

In national parks that include dunes and barrier islands, walk on marked pedestrian paths. Over time, climbing on the dunes causes erosion and weakens the primary dune system. Never pick dune grasses, which also help ensure the preservation of the dunes.

RESPECTING WILDLIFE

Have respect for the creatures you encounter: Never sneak up on them, don't disturb nests and other habitats, and don't touch animals or try to remove them from their habitat for the sake of a photograph. Never stand between animal parents and their young, and never surround an animal or group of animals. To help protect endangered species, report any sightings.

PETS IN THE PARKS

Generally, pets are allowed only in parks' developed areas, including drive-in campgrounds and picnic areas, but they must be kept on a leash at all times. With the exception of guide dogs, pets are not allowed inside buildings, on most trails, on beaches, or in the backcountry. They also may be prohibited in areas controlled by concessionaires. Some parks have kennels, which charge a small daily fee. Be sure to inquire about restrictions on pets before leaving home.

VOLUNTEERING

Air pollution, acid rain, wildlife poaching, and encroaching development are among the threats to America's national parks. These problems are being addressed by the National Park Service, but you can help by donating time or money. The National Park Service's Volunteers in the Parks program welcomes volunteers to do anything from paperwork to lecturing on environmental issues. To participate, you must apply to the park where you would like to work, or visit the Web site at www.nps.gov/volunteer. To contribute money, contact the National Park Foundation, the official nonprofit partner of the National Park Service (1101 17th St. NW, Suite 1102, Washington, DC 20036-4703).

Overnight Stays in the Parks

CAMPING

Most drive-in campsites in the national parks are run on a first-come, first-served basis. If you are traveling during peak summer months, arrive as early as possible or have standby reservations at a nearby public campground. For 25 of the most popular parks, you can make reservations in advance through the National Parks Reservation Service (tel. 800/365–2267) or via http://reservations.nps.gov; these include Acadia, Assateague, Cape Hatteras, Channel Islands, Chickasaw, Death Valley, Everglades, Grand Canyon, Great Smoky, Greenbelt, Gulf Islands, Joshua Tree, Katmai, Mount Rainier, Rocky Mountain, Sequoia and Kings Canyon, Shenandoah, Sleeping Bears, Whiskeytown, and Zion. A second telephone number (tel. 800/436–7275) takes reservations for Yosemite. Reservations are available up to five months in advance; not all campgrounds may be available. Fees, ranging from $4 to $18, are payable by MasterCard, Visa, and Discover.

RVING

Most national park campgrounds are equipped for RVs, although you will usually find only basic facilities. Electrical hookups, water pumps, and disposal stations are available only at a handful of locations.

HOTELS, MOTELS, AND CABINS

Accommodations in and near national parks range from chain hotels and motels with modern appliances to rough and rugged wilderness camps with kerosene lamps instead of electricity. Cabins with housekeeping facilities are popular, as are small, family-owned bed-and-breakfasts and the occasional grand old hotel. If you're traveling in high season—roughly between Memorial Day and Labor Day—make reservations three or four months in advance or more, if you can. At some of the most famous hostelries, some people reserve for the next summer as they check out. Bear in mind that prices are higher in summer, and drop as much as 25% when the season comes to a close.

On the Web

A visit to the Web site of the National Park Foundation, **www. nationalparks.org,** can greatly enhance your experience. You can add a photo to the National Park Foundation's Photo Quilt, send a National Park postcard, contribute your park story to the NPF Park Journal, or enter the National Parks Pass *Experience Your America* Photo Contest. You can also learn about National Park Foundation programs, find out how you can give something back to the parks, and buy an annual parks pass on-line. In addition, in the site's Meet at the Lodge section, you can trade park tips with other travelers, and in the Visitor Center section, you can link to the National Park Service's own site, **www.nps.gov,** where you will find complete information about each park.

Maps

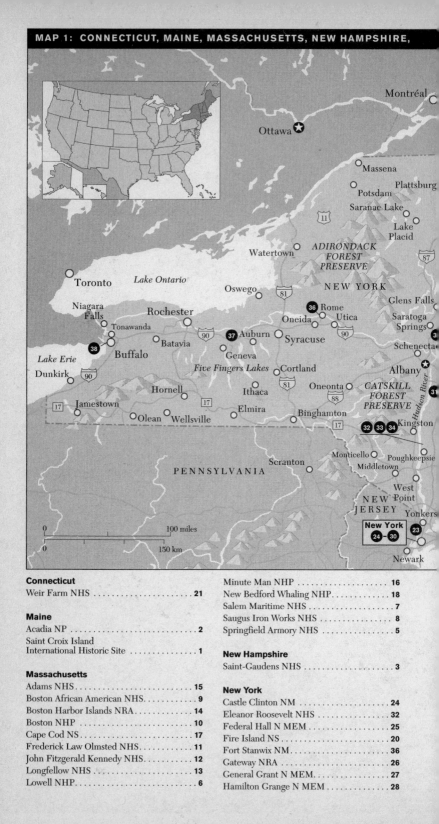

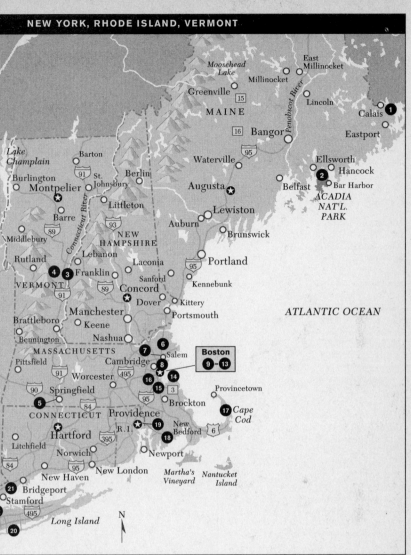

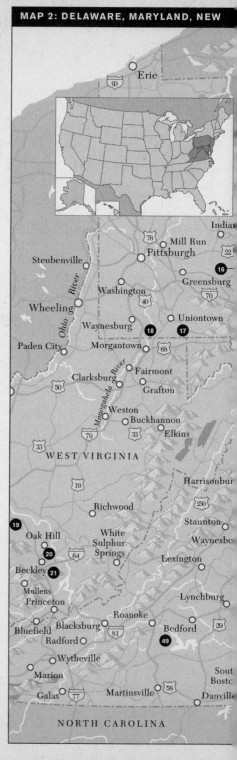

MAP 2: DELAWARE, MARYLAND, NEW

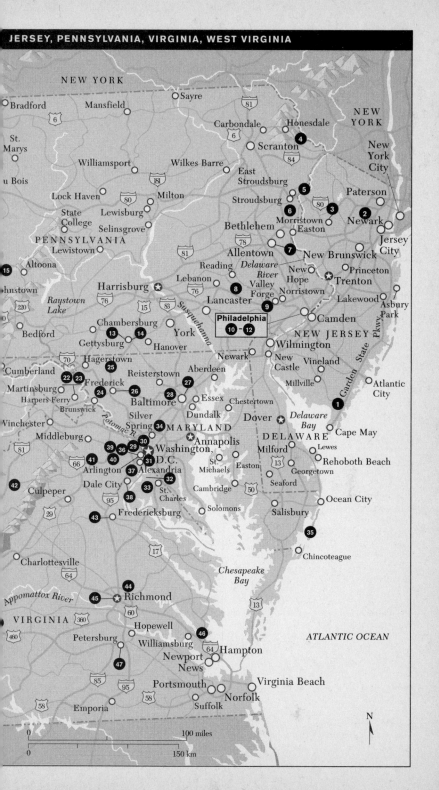

NEW YORK

Bradford   Mansfield   Sayre

St.   Carbondale   Honesdale   NEW
Marys   YORK

u Bois   Williamsport   Scranton   New
                                                                    York
          Lock Haven   Milton   East   City
          State   Lewisburg   Stroudsburg
          College   Selinsburg   Stroudsburg   Paterson
PENNSYLVANIA   Bethlehem   Morristown   Newark
          Lewistown   Easton
                                                              Jersey
Altoona   Allentown   New Brunswick   City
hnstown   Harrisburg   Reading   Delaware   New   Princeton
          Raystown   Lebanon   River   Hope   Trenton
          Lake   Valley   Norristown
                                        Forge   Lakewood   Asbury
          Chambersburg   York   Lancaster   Park
          Gettysburg   Hanover   Philadelphia   Camden
Bedford   NEW JERSEY
                      Hagerstown   Newark   Wilmington
Cumberland   Reisterstown   Aberdeen   New   Atlantic
Martinsburg   Frederick   Essex   Castle   Vineland   City
Harpers Ferry   Baltimore   Chestertown   Millville
Brunswick   Dundalk   Delaware   Cape May
Vinchester   Silver   MARYLAND   Dover   Bay
Middleburg   Spring   Annapolis   DELAWARE   Lewes
                      Washington,   Milford   Rehoboth Beach
Arlington   Alexandria   D.C.   St.   Easton   Georgetown
Dale City   Charles   Michaels   Seaford
Culpeper   St.   Cambridge   Ocean City
              Fredericksburg   Charles   Solomons   Salisbury
Charlottesville   Chincoteague
                                        Chesapeake
                                        Bay
VIRGINIA   Richmond
              Hopewell   ATLANTIC OCEAN
Petersburg   Williamsburg   Hampton
              Newport
              News   Virginia Beach
              Portsmouth   Norfolk
Emporia   Suffolk

0   100 miles
0   150 km

N

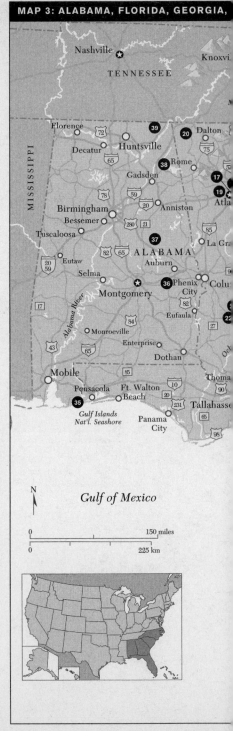

MAP 3: ALABAMA, FLORIDA, GEORGIA,

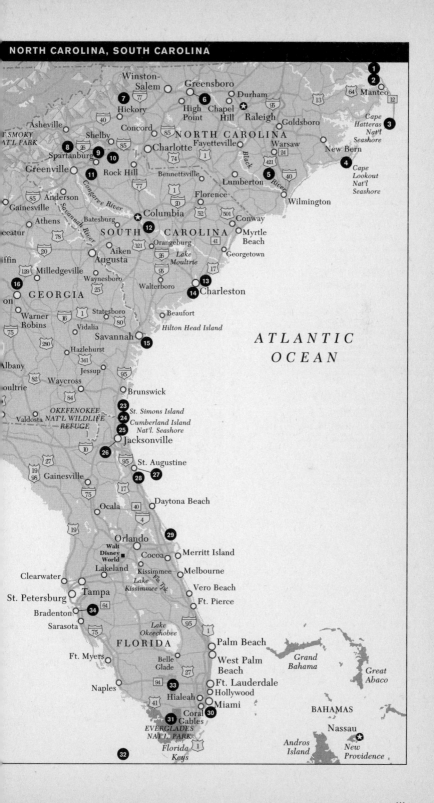

MAP 4: ARKANSAS, KENTUCKY,

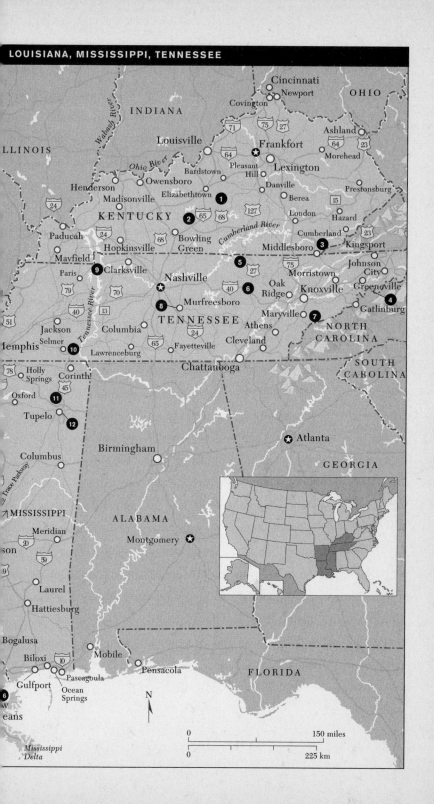

LOUISIANA, MISSISSIPPI, TENNESSEE

OHIO

Cincinnati
Newport
Covington

INDIANA

71 75 27

Louisville

Ashland
64 23
Morehead

ILLINOIS

64

Frankfort

Lexington

Ohio River

Bardstown Pleasant
Hill Danville

Henderson Owensboro Elizabethtown ① Berea Prestonsburg
Madisonville

24 KENTUCKY ② 65 68 127 London 15 Hazard

Paducah 24 68 Bowling Cumberland River Cumberland 23
Green Middlesboro ③ Kingsport
Hopkinsville

Mayfield Johnson
City
Paris 79 ⑨ Clarksville ⑤ 27 75 Morristown Greeneville

70 Nashville 40 ⑥ Oak Knoxville ④
Ridge Gatlinburg

51 40 13 ⑧ Murfreesboro Maryville ⑦
Jackson TENNESSEE Athens NORTH
Selmer Columbia 24 CAROLINA
Memphis ⑩ 65 Fayetteville Cleveland

78 Holly Lawrenceburg Chattanooga SOUTH
Springs Corinth CAROLINA
45
Oxford ⑪
Tupelo ⑫

Columbus Birmingham Atlanta
GEORGIA

MISSISSIPPI

Meridian ALABAMA
30 Montgomery
son
9 59
Laurel
Hattiesburg

Bogalusa

Biloxi 10 Mobile
Gulfport Pascagoula Pensacola FLORIDA
⑥ Ocean
w Springs N
eans

Mississippi
Delta

0   150 miles
0   225 km

Wabash River

Tennessee River

Trace Parkway

MAP 6: IOWA, KANSAS, MISSOURI,

MAP 7: ARIZONA, NEVADA, NEW MEXICO

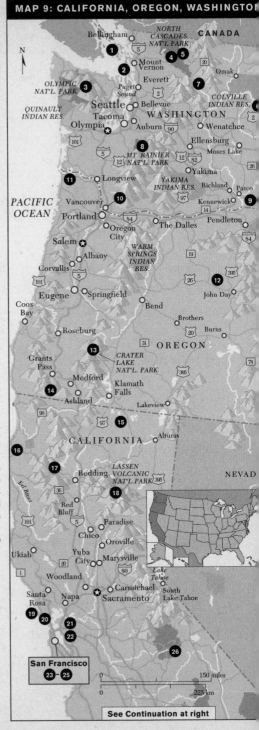

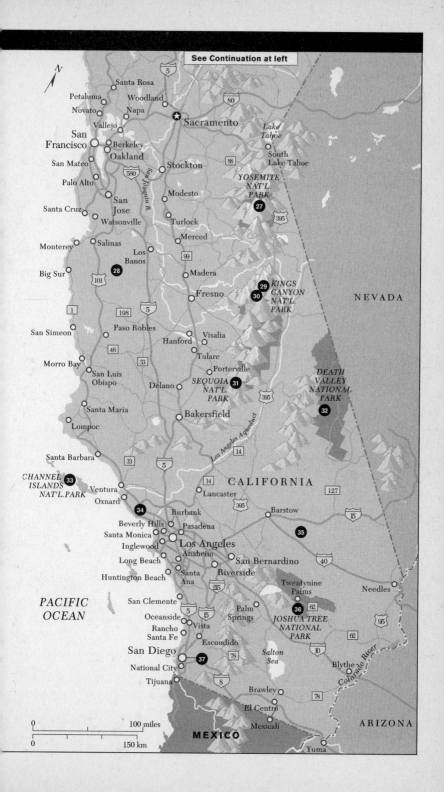

See Continuation at left

PACIFIC
OCEAN

CALIFORNIA

NEVADA

ARIZONA

MEXICO

Santa Rosa
Petaluma
Novato
Woodland
Napa
Vallejo
San
Francisco
Berkeley
Oakland
San Mateo
Palo Alto
San
Jose
Santa Cruz
Watsonville
Monterey
Salinas
Los
Banos
Big Sur
San Simeon
Paso Robles
Morro Bay
San Luis
Obispo
Santa Maria
Lompoc
Santa Barbara
CHANNEL
ISLANDS
NAT'L. PARK
Ventura
Oxnard
Burbank
Beverly Hills
Santa Monica
Pasadena
Inglewood
Long Beach
Huntington Beach
Santa
Ana
San Clemente
Oceanside
Rancho
Santa Fe
Vista
Escondido
San Diego
National City
Tijuana

Sacramento
Stockton
Modesto
Turlock
Merced
Madera
Fresno
Hanford
Visalia
Tulare
Porterville
Delano
Bakersfield
Lancaster
Los Angeles
Anaheim
Riverside
San Bernardino
Palm
Springs
Barstow
Twentynine
Palms
Needles
Brawley
El Centro
Mexicali
Yuma
Blythe

Lake
Tahoe
South
Lake Tahoe
YOSEMITE
NAT'L.
PARK
KINGS
CANYON
NAT'L.
PARK
DEATH
VALLEY
NATIONAL
PARK
SEQUOIA
NAT'L.
PARK
Salton
Sea
JOSHUA TREE
NATIONAL
PARK

San Joaquin R.
Los Angeles Aqueduct
Colorado River

27
28
29
30
31
32
33
34
35
36
37

5
80
88
395
99
101
1
198
5
46
33
305
14
14
395
127
15
40
95
62
62
10
78
8
78
580

0   100 miles
0   150 km

XXXV

MAP 10: ALASKA AND HAWAII

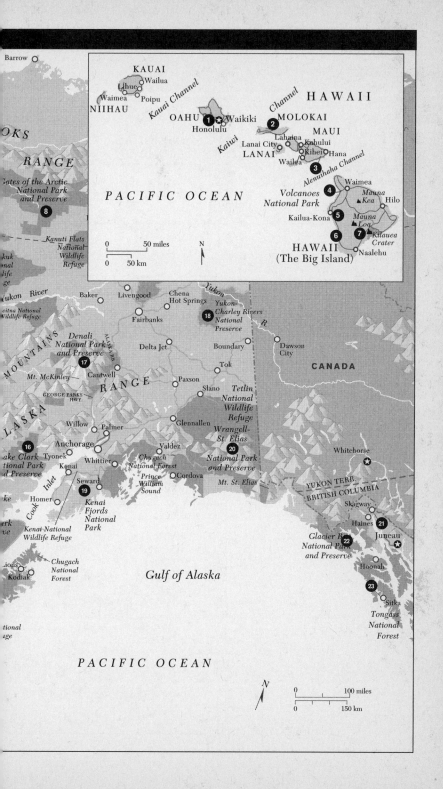

KAUAI
Wailua
Lihue
Waimea
Poipu
NIIHAU

Kauai Channel

HAWAII

OAHU
Honolulu
Waikiki

Kaiwi

Channel

MOLOKAI

Lahaina
Lanai City
LANAI
Wailea

Kahului
Kihei
MAUI
Hana

Alenuihaha Channel

PACIFIC OCEAN

Volcanoes
National Park

Kailua-Kona

Waimea
Mauna
Kea
Hilo
Mauna
Loa
Kilauea
Crater
Naalehu

HAWAII
(The Big Island)

0   50 miles

0   50 km

N

Barrow

OKS

RANGE

ates of the Arctic
National
and Preserve

8

Kanuti Flats
National
Wildlife
Refuge

kuk
nal
life
ge

Yukon River

vitna National
Wildlife Refuge

Baker

Livengood

Chena
Hot Springs

Yukon

Fairbanks

Yukon-
Charley Rivers
National
Preserve

18

R.

Dawson
City

Denali
National Park
and Preserve

17

Delta Jct.

Boundary

CANADA

Mt. McKinley

Cantwell

Tok

George Parks
HWY.

RANGE

Paxson

Slano

Tetlin
National
Wildlife
Refuge

MOUNTAINS

ALASKA RGE.

Willow

Palmer

Glennallen

Wrangell-
St. Elias

ALASKA

16

Anchorage

Valdez

20

National Park
and Preserve

Whitehorse

ake Clark
tional Park
d Preserve

Tyonek
Kenai

Whittier

Chugach
National Forest

Cordova

Mt. St. Elias

YUKON TERR.

ke

Seward

19

Prince
William
Sound

BRITISH COLUMBIA

Cook

Homer

Kenai
Fjords
National
Park

Skagway

ark
ve

Kenai National
Wildlife Refuge

Haines

21

Juneau

ions

Chugach
National
Forest

Glacier B
National Park
and Preserve

22

Kodiak

Hoonah

tional
ge

PACIFIC OCEAN

Gulf of Alaska

N

0   100 miles

0   150 km

23

Sitka

Tongass
National
Forest

MAP 11: AMERICAN SAMOA, NORTH

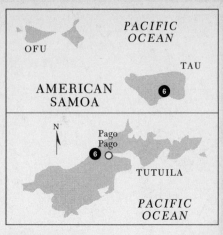

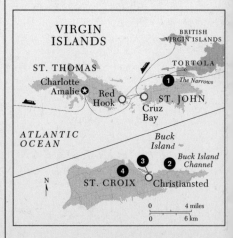

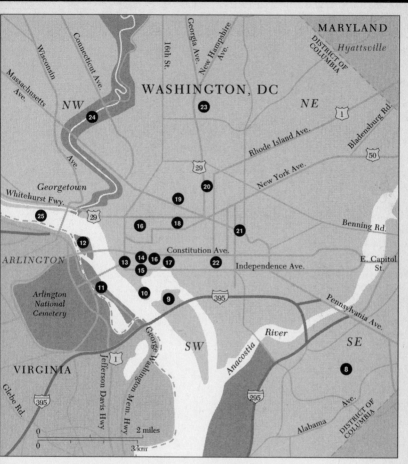

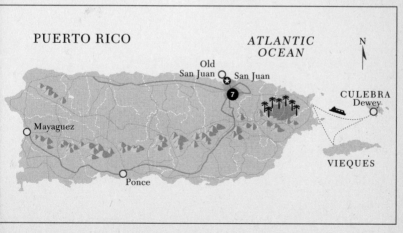

America's National Parks

ALABAMA

Horseshoe Bend
National Military Park

Near Dadeville

On March 27, 1814, General Andrew Jackson's Tennessee Army of 3,000 regulars, militia, and Native American allies crushed 1,000 Red Stick Creek Indians led by Chief Menawa. The bloody defeat ended the Creek Indian War, broke the tribe's power over the Southeast, and added Creek lands comprising three-fifths of present-day Alabama and one-fifth of Georgia to the United States. The park was authorized in 1956.

WHAT TO SEE & DO

Picnicking, touring museum and battlefield, watching slide program and electric map presentations. **Facilities:** Visitor center with interpretive exhibits, interpretive trail, tour road. Boat ramp, book and map sales area, grills, picnic pavilions and tables. **Programs & Events:** Living-history programs with encampments and demonstrations of soldier life, flintlock black-powder musketry, and native culture, camp cookery demonstrations, evening campfire and lantern programs, musket drill (monthly, Sat.). Battle anniversary encampment (last weekend, Mar.), park anniversary encampment (Aug.).

PLANNING YOUR VISIT

⛺ **Camping:** Available at Wind Creek State Park near Alexander City; none in park. 🛏 **Lodging:** Available in Alexander City, Dadeville; none in park. ✕ **Food & Supplies:** Available at Alexander City, Dadeville, New Site; none in park. ☞ **Tips & Hints:** Go in spring and fall for better weather and more living-history programs. Busiest in May and June, least crowded in December and January. 🎫 **Fees, Permits & Limitations:** Free. No hunting or firearms. Leashed pets only. Pedestrian traffic only on trails. Park open daily 8–4:30. Closed Thanksgiving, Dec. 25, Jan. 1. Visitor center open daily 8–4:30.

HOW TO GET THERE

12 mi/19 km north of Dadeville on AL 49. Closest airport: Atlanta's Hartsfield International (100 mi/160 km).

FOR MORE INFORMATION

Horseshoe Bend National Military Park (11288 Horseshoe Bend Rd., Daviston, AL 36256, tel. 256/234–7111; Web site www.nps.gov/hobe). Dadeville Chamber of Commerce (185 S. Tallahassee St., Dadeville, AL 36853, tel. 256/825–4019).

Little River Canyon
National Preserve

In the northeast, near Fort Payne

The nation's longest mountaintop river and the Southeast's deepest canyon create an awe-inspiring backdrop for the preserve. Formed by river waters that are among the nation's purest, the canyon's cliffs tower up to 600 ft/182 m and enclose vast biodiversity, including rare and endangered species. Recreational opportunities abound, including hiking, rock climbing, hunting, and fishing. The preserve was authorized on October 24, 1992.

WHAT TO SEE & DO

Canoeing, fishing, hiking, horseback riding, hunting, mountain biking, picnicking, rock climbing, wading, walking. **Facilities:** Interpretive centers at Canyon Mouth Park and Little River Falls, DeSoto State Park, Canyon Rim Drive, overlooks. Gift shop, grills, pavilion and picnic tables. **Programs & Events:** None. New park under development.

PLANNING YOUR VISIT

Camping: Campground (DeSoto State Park, reservations required, tel. 256/845–5075). Backcountry camping available (permit required, *see below*). Group campsite available (DeSoto State Park, no reservations). Private campgrounds available in Cedar Bluff, Centre, and Fort Payne. **Lodging:** In the park: DeSoto State Park Lodge (tel. 256/845–5380). Lodging also available outside the park in Cedar Bluff, Centre, Collinsville, Fort Payne, Leesburg, Mentone, and Valley Head. ✕ **Food & Supplies:** In the park: meals at DeSoto State Park Lodge (tel. 256/845–5380), country store. Food and supplies also available in Centre, Fort Payne, Leesburg, and Mentone. ☞ **Tips & Hints:** Be prepared for challenging rapids and rock climbing. Watch footing on scenic bluffs and cliffs. Go between late October and early November for fall colors, spring and summer for wildflowers. ▣ **Fees, Permits & Limitations:** Free. Alabama state fishing and hunting licenses required. Backcountry permit required (free, Little River Canyon, tel. 256/845–9605; DeSoto State Park, tel. 256/845–5075) for all backcountry camping. Permit required for rock climbers to add or remove bolts. Leashed pets only. Hunting restricted to wildlife management area in season only. No vehicles off roads. No bikes in DeSoto State Park. No collecting rocks or plants. No weapons, alcohol, or fireworks. Park open daily. Canyon Mouth Park open daily 8–8.

HOW TO GET THERE

From Chattanooga, TN, take I–24W to I–59S to Fort Payne exit 222 and follow signs to the preserve. From Birmingham, AL, take I–59N to Fort Payne exit 215 (SR 35). Take SR 35 to the Preserve. Closest airports: Chattanooga (45 mi/72 km), Birmingham (100 mi/160 km), Atlanta (100 mi/160 km).

FOR MORE INFORMATION

Little River Canyon National Preserve (2141 Gault Ave. N, Fort Payne, AL 35967, tel. 256/845–9605, fax 256/997–9129; e-mail LIRI_superintendent@nps.gov; Web site www.nps.gov/liri). DeKalb County Tourist Association (1503 Glenn Blvd. SW, Fort Payne, AL 35968, tel. 256/845–3957, fax 256/845–3946; Web site www.hsv.tis.net/~dekbtour). Fort Payne Chamber of Commerce (Box 680125, Fort Payne, AL 35968, tel. 256/845–2741).

Russell Cave National Monument

In the northeast, near Bridgeport

Russell Cave was inhabited for almost 10,000 years, from at least 7000 BC to AD 1650. Virtually no other place in the region offers so many clues to how the "First Americans" fed, clothed, and protected themselves. The monument was proclaimed on May 11, 1961.

WHAT TO SEE & DO

Touring cave, watching film and slide programs. **Facilities:** Information center with interpretive exhibits, museum, trail. Bookstore. **Programs & Events:** Conducted programs and guided cave walks, demonstrations of prehistoric tools and weapons (daily by request).

PLANNING YOUR VISIT

Camping: Available locally; none at monument. **Lodging:** Available locally; none at monument. **Food & Supplies:** Available locally; none at monument. **Tips & Hints:** Plan to spend at least one hour in the museum area and cave mouth. Add one hour for conducted programs. Busiest in July and October, least crowded in December and January. **Fees, Permits & Limitations:** Free. Permit required for wild caving and other off-trail activities. Monument open summer 8:30–5:30, winter 8–4:30. Closed Thanksgiving, Dec. 25, Jan. 1.

HOW TO GET THERE

7 mi/11 km northwest of Bridgeport via County Rds. 75 and 98. Closest airport: Chattanooga, TN (45 mi/72 km).

FOR MORE INFORMATION

Russell Cave National Monument (3729 County Rd. 98, Bridgeport, AL 35740, tel. 256/495–2672; Web site www.nps.gov/ruca).

Tuskegee Airmen National Historic Site

In Tuskegee

This site will commemorate and interpret the actions of the Tuskegee Airmen during World War II. The Airmen included African American pilots, navigators, bombardiers, and others trained by the Army Air Corps program to fly and maintain combat aircraft. The Tuskegee Airmen overcame segregation and prejudice to become one of the most highly respected fighter groups during the war. Their achievements, together with those of the men and women who supported them, paved the way for full integration of the U.S. military. The site was established on November 6, 1998.

WHAT TO SEE & DO

This is a new site under development.

PLANNING YOUR VISIT

⚠ **Camping:** Available in Chewakla State Park, primitive camping at Tuskegee National Forest; none at site. ▥ **Lodging:** Available locally; none at site. ✕ **Food & Supplies:** Available locally; none at site.

HOW TO GET THERE

Headquarters is on the campus of Tuskegee University in Tuskegee. The University is on Old Montgomery Rd., 1.5 mi/2.4 km northwest of downtown Tuskegee, 35 mi/56 km east of Montgomery, and 20 mi/32 km west of Auburn. From I–85, take Exit 38 and travel north on Hwy. 81 for 6 mi/10 km to Tuskegee. Follow signs to site. Closest airport: Dannely Field (Montgomery, 50 mi/80 km).

FOR MORE INFORMATION

Tuskegee Airmen National Historic Site (Drawer 10, Tuskegee Institute, AL 36087, tel. 334/727–3200; Web site www.nps.gov/tuai).

Tuskegee Institute National Historic Site

In Tuskegee

In 1881, at the age of 26, Booker T. Washington became the first principal of a newly formed Normal School for Negroes in Tuskegee. George Washington Carver joined the faculty in 1896 and revolutionized agricultural development in the South in the early 20th century. Preserved here are the brick buildings the students constructed, Washington's home, and the George Washington Carver Museum. The site was authorized on October 26, 1974.

WHAT TO SEE & DO

Touring the Historic Campus District, touring the Chappie James Exhibit (by appointment), visiting Carver Museum and The Oaks. **Facilities:** Carver Museum; The Oaks, home of Booker T. Washington; Chappie James Museum; walking trail through Historic Campus District. Bookstore. **Programs & Events:** Ranger-led tours of The Oaks; Black History Month Program and Exhibit (Feb.), Annual Carver Crafts Festival (May), Annual Carver Sweet Potato Festival (Oct.), Open House (Dec.).

PLANNING YOUR VISIT

⚠ **Camping:** Available in Chewakla State Park, primitive camping at Tuskegee National Forest; none at site. ▥ **Lodging:** Available locally;

none at site. ✗ **Food & Supplies:** Available locally; none at site. ☞ **Tips & Hints:** Plan to spend at least two hours at the Carver Museum and The Oaks. Busiest February through May, least crowded September through December. ✉ **Fees, Permits & Limitations:** Free. Site open daily 9–5. Closed Thanksgiving, Dec. 25, Jan. 1.

HOW TO GET THERE

The site is on the campus of Tuskegee University in Tuskegee. The University is on Old Montgomery Rd., 1.5 mi/2.4 km northwest of downtown Tuskegee, 35 mi/56 km east of Montgomery, and 20 mi/32 km west of Auburn. From I–85, take Exit 38 and travel north on Hwy. 81 for 6 mi/10 km to Tuskegee. Follow signs to site. Closest airport: Dannely Field (Montgomery, 50 mi/80 km).

FOR MORE INFORMATION

Tuskegee Institute National Historic Site (Drawer 10, Tuskegee Institute, AL 36087, tel. 334/727–3200; Web site www.nps.gov/tuin).

See Also

Natchez Trace Parkway, Mississippi. *Natchez Trace National Scenic Trail,* Mississippi. *Selma to Montgomery National Historic Trail,* National Trails System in Other National Parklands. *Trail of Tears National Historic Trail,* National Trails System in Other National Parklands.

ALASKA

Alagnak Wild River

In south Alaska, near King Salmon

The 69 mi/110 km of federally designated Alagnak Wild River runs out of Kukaklek Lake in the Katmai National Preserve. It offers outstanding white-water floating, as well as abundant wildlife and sportfishing for five species of salmon. The wild river was established on December 2, 1980.

WHAT TO SEE & DO

Fishing, float trips, wildlife watching. **Facilities:** Visitor center—King Salmon.

PLANNING YOUR VISIT

⚠ **Camping:** Primitive camping available (permits recommended, *see below*). ▥ **Lodging:** Available in King Salmon; none in park. ✖ **Food & Supplies:** Available in Anchorage, King Salmon; none in park. ☞ **Tips & Hints:** Bring rain gear, waterproof foot gear, and wool clothing. Busiest in July and August, least crowded in December and January. ▦ **Fees, Permits & Limitations:** Free. Permits recommended (free) for all primitive camping. Alaska state fishing license required.

HOW TO GET THERE

Charter flights are available from Anchorage and King Salmon.

FOR MORE INFORMATION

Katmai National Park and Preserve (Box 7, King Salmon, AK 99611, tel. 907/246–3305; Web site www.nps.gov/alag). Alaska Public Lands Information Center (605 W. 4th Ave., Suite 105, Anchorage, AK 99501, tel. 907/271–2737).

Aniakchak National Monument and Preserve

On Alaska Peninsula

The Aniakchak Caldera covers 10 square mi/26 square km and is one of the great dry calderas in the world. Located in the volcanically active Aleutian Mountains, the Aniakchak last erupted in 1911. Inside the crater are lava flows, cinder cones, and explosion pits, as well as Surprise Lake, the source of the Aniakchak River, which cascades through a 1,500-ft/457-m gash in the crater wall. The site also contains the Aniakchak Wild River. The site was proclaimed a national monument in 1978 and established as a national monument and preserve in 1980.

WHAT TO SEE & DO

Fishing, float trips, wildlife watching.

PLANNING YOUR VISIT

⚠ **Camping:** Primitive camping only available in park. ⌂ **Lodging:** Available in Anchorage, King Salmon; none in park. ✕ **Food & Supplies:** Available in Anchorage, King Salmon; none in park. ☞ **Tips & Hints:** Plan to be self-sufficient. Bring wool clothing, rubber boots, and good rain gear. Bring all food if camping, and be sure tents can withstand bad weather: the caldera is subject to violent wind storms. Busiest in August and September, least crowded in January and February. ✉ **Fees, Permits & Limitations:** Free. Backcountry permits available from Aniakchak office in King Salmon. Alaska state fishing license required. Park open daily.

HOW TO GET THERE

Regular flights are available from Anchorage to King Salmon. Regular and charter flights are available from King Salmon to Port Heiden, a 10-mi/16-km hike over open tundra from the monument. Closest airport: Port Heiden.

FOR MORE INFORMATION

Aniakchak National Monument and Preserve (Box 7, King Salmon, AK 99613, tel. 907/246–3305; Web site www.nps.gov/ania). Alaska Public Lands Information Center (605 W. 4th Ave., Suite 105, Anchorage, AK 99501, tel. 907/271–2737).

Bering Land Bridge National Preserve

In the west, near Nome

The preserve is a remnant of the land bridge that connected Asia to North America more than 13,000 years ago. The land bridge is now beneath the Chukchi Sea and the Bering Sea. During the glacial epoch, whenever ocean levels fell enough to expose the land bridge, people and animals migrated into the area. Archaeologists agree that it was across this Bering Land Bridge, also called Beringia, that humans first passed from Asia to Northwest Alaska. The preserve also is home to paleontological and archaeological resources, large populations of migratory birds, wildlife (including brown bear, moose, caribou, reindeer) and ash explosion craters and lava flows. The preserve was proclaimed a national monument in 1978 and established as a preserve in 1980.

WHAT TO SEE & DO

Arts and crafts, backpacking, bird-watching, canoeing, coastal boating, cross-country skiing, dogsledding, exploring ancient Eskimo and gold rush–era remains, fishing, hiking, hunting, observing Eskimo reindeer herding, river floating, snowmobiling. **Facilities:** Visitor center (240 Front St., Nome). **Programs & Events:** Seasonal activities and special events available.

PLANNING YOUR VISIT

⚠ **Camping:** Primitive camping only available in park. Camping also available at the north end of Salmon Lake, 38 mi/61 km north of Nome. ⛺ **Lodging:** In the park: shelter cabins and bunkhouse-style cabins in Serpentine Hot Springs. Lodging also available in Kotzebue and Nome. ✕ **Food & Supplies:** Food and supplies available in Kotzebue and Nome; none in preserve. ☞ **Tips & Hints:** Be prepared to be self-sufficient. Exposure and hypothermia are threats throughout the year. Temperatures in summer are usually 50°F/10°C on the coast and 65°F/18°C–75°F/24°C inland. Snow, freezing temperatures, and long periods of clouds, rain, and wind are possible year-round. Summer days are long, almost without darkness. Average January lows are -15°F/-26°C on the coast and -50°F/-46°C in the interior. Winds average 8–12 mph but can reach 70 mph in storms. Winter days are short, with only a few hours of light. Go in May and June for rare migratory bird viewing. Busiest June–August, least crowded in January and February. ▣ **Fees, Permits & Limitations:** Free. Alaska hunting and fishing licenses required. No helicopters or all-terrain vehicles. Preserve open daily.

HOW TO GET THERE

Accessible only by foot travel, small aircraft, and boats in summer and fall, by snowmobile, dogsled, cross-country skis, or small plane on skis in winter and spring. Closest airports: Kotzebue, Nome.

FOR MORE INFORMATION

Bering Land Bridge National Preserve (Box 220, Nome, AK 99762, tel. 907/443–2522; Web site www.nps.gov/bela). Nome Convention & Visitors Bureau (Box 240 HP-N, Nome, AK 99762, tel. 907/443-6624, fax 907/443-5832; Web site www.nomealaska.org).

Cape Krusenstern National Monument

In the northwest, near Kotzebue

Archaeological sites along a succession of 114 lateral beach ridges illustrate every known Eskimo cultural period in Alaska over 4,000 years. Older sites are located inland along the foothills. The monument includes a representative example of the Arctic coastline along the Chukchi Sea. The monument was proclaimed on December 1, 1978.

WHAT TO SEE & DO

Backpacking, beach walking, bird-watching, hiking, kayaking, wildlife viewing. **Facilities:** Park Headquarters (Kotzebue), Kotzebue Public Lands Information Center.

PLANNING YOUR VISIT

⚠ **Camping:** Backcountry camping only. ⛺ **Lodging:** Available in Kotzebue; none at monument. ✕ **Food & Supplies:** Available in Kotzebue; none at monument. ☞ **Tips & Hints:** Be prepared to be self-sufficient. Rugged terrain is subject to harsh weather, high winds, rain, and snow. Guard against hypothermia, giardiasis, wild animals, mosquitoes, and biting flies. Don't interfere with subsistence camps, fishnets, or other equipment. Respect property and privacy. Go in summer for wildflowers and migrating birds. Busiest in July and August, least crowded in September, October, and November. ▧ **Fees, Permits & Limitations:** Free. Reservations recommended for most visitor services from commercial vendors. Open daily. Park Headquarters (Kotzebue) open weekdays 8–5. Kotzebue Public Lands Information Center hours mid-May–mid-Sept., daily 8–6.

HOW TO GET THERE

Accessible by plane from Fairbanks or Anchorage to Kotzebue; scheduled flights available from Kotzebue to the villages of Noatak, Kivalina, Shungnak, Ambler, Kobuk, Kiana, and Noorvik; summer access to and through the monument via motorized and nonmotorized watercraft and aircraft and on foot; air taxis and snowmobiles can be used in winter.

FOR MORE INFORMATION

Cape Krusenstern National Monument (Box 1029, Kotzebue, AK 99752, tel. 907/442–3890; Web site www.nps.gov/cakr).

Denali National Park and Preserve

In the south-central part of the state, near Denali Park

Denali, the "High One," is the name Athabascan native people gave to Mount McKinley (20,320 ft/6,164 m), the massive peak that crowns the 600-mi/960-km Alaska Range. The park's 6.1 million acres include countless other spectacular mountains and large glaciers. Denali encompasses a complete subarctic ecosystem that is populated with grizzly bears, wolves, Dall sheep, caribou, and moose. Mt. McKinley National Park was established in 1917 and designated an international biosphere reserve in 1976. Denali National Monument was proclaimed in 1978 and both were incorporated into Denali National Park and Preserve in 1980.

WHAT TO SEE & DO

Backpacking, bicycling, bus touring, cross-country skiing (backcountry permit required; *see below*), dog mushing, hiking (backcountry permit required; *see below*), mountaineering (permit required; *see below*), snowmobiling, snowshoeing, stargazing, wildlife viewing. **Facilities:** 2 visitor centers with interpretive exhibits—Denali (mile 237 George Parks Hwy.), Eielson (mile 66 Denali Park Rd); ranger station—Talkeetna Mountaineering Center (Talkeetna). Bookstores. **Programs & Events:** Ranger and naturalist programs (mostly June–August). Seasonal activities and special events available.

PLANNING YOUR VISIT

⚑ **Camping:** 7 campgrounds (reservations required, tel. 907/272–7275 or 800/622–7275). Backcountry camping available (permit required, *see* *below*). Group campsites available (reservations required, tel. 907/683–2294). ⊞ **Lodging:** In the park: Denali Park Hotel (tel. 907/683–2215). Lodging also available in Cantwell, Healy, McKinley Village, and in the canyon near the park entrance. ✗ **Food & Supplies:** In the park: restaurant and snack shop in Denali Park Hotel (tel. 907/683–2215). Convenience store nearby. Food and supplies also available in Cantwell and Healy. ☞ **Tips & Hints:** Go between late May and early September for main visitor season. Plan to spend at least one day to tour the park road by shuttle or tour bus, several days for day or backcountry hikes. Get reservations for camping and shuttle to avoid one- to two-day wait for bus availability during peak season. Bring rain gear and hiking boots in summer when weather is cool and damp. Bring specialized cold-weather gear for winter visits, when temperatures drop to -40°F/-40°C or lower. Read *Mountaineering: Denali National Park and Preserve* to begin planning mountain climbs in the park. Busiest in July and August, least crowded in January and February. ▦ **Fees, Permits & Limitations:** Entrance fee: $10 per family, $5 per person. Fees vary for shuttle (reservations available, tel. 907/272–7275 or 800/622–7275, fax 907/264–4684) and tour bus service (tel. 800/276–7234). Backcountry permits required (free) for backcountry camping, hiking, and skiing (no permit required for day use). Camper bus pass ($15.50) needed to reach most backcountry. Mountaineering permit registration packets must be submitted 60 days in advance ($150). No snowmobiling in wilderness core area of park and preserve. Park open daily. Visitor center hours: Denali—late May–mid-Sept., daily 7 AM–8 PM; winter headquarters—mid-Sept.–early May, daily 8–4:30; Eielson—June–mid Sept., daily 9–7.

HOW TO GET THERE

Denali is accessible by car or the Alaska Railroad (tel. 907/265–2494 or 800/544–0552) from Anchorage and Fairbanks. In summer, a variety of private bus and van services and the railroad operate daily from Anchorage and Fairbanks. The park and preserve is on AK 3 (George Parks Hwy.), 240 mi/384 km north of Anchorage, 125 mi/200 km south of Fairbanks, and 12 mi/19 km south of Healy, AK. The Denali Park Rd. is accessible by private vehicle for 15 mi/24 km to the Savage River Bridge. Shuttles and tour bus services are available at the bridge for travel farther into the park. Mountaineering headquarters is in Talkeetna, 100 mi/160 km north of Anchorage. Closest airport: Fairbanks.

FOR MORE INFORMATION

Denali National Park and Preserve (Box 9, Denali Park, AK 99755, tel. 907/683–2294, fax 907/683–9612; Web site www.nos.gov/dena). Talkeetna Mountaineering Center (Box 588, Talkeetna, AK 99676, tel. 907/733–2231). Healy Chamber of Commerce (Box 437, Healy, AK 99743, tel. 907/683–4636).

Gates of the Arctic
National Park and Preserve

In central Brooks Range, near Bettles, in the north

This park and preserve may be Alaska's ultimate wilderness park. The National Park Service manages this 8.4-million-acre park and preserve and maintains the land's wild and undeveloped character. There are no roads, trails, or visitor services here. In this, the park system's northernmost park, visitors experience the natural world much as it was when wilderness advocate Robert Marshall visited it more than 60 years ago. The area was proclaimed a national monument in 1978 and established as a park and preserve in 1980.

WHAT TO SEE & DO

Dogsledding, fishing, hiking, hunting, kayaking, mountain climbing, rafting, snowmobiling. **Facilities:** Visitor contact station with displays (Bettles); interagency visitor center (summer only, Coldfoot). Book sales outlet (Bettles, Coldfoot). **Programs & Events:** Backcountry orientation and limited interpretive programs available at a park ranger station in Bettles. Interpretive programs (Bettles: by request; Coldfoot: summer, daily).

PLANNING YOUR VISIT

Camping: No public or private campgrounds. Backcountry camping available. Backcountry orientation required but no permit or reservations needed. **Lodging:** In the park: Peace of Selby (Box 86, Manley Hot Springs, AK 99756, no phone). Lodging also available outside the park in Anaktuvuk Pass, Bettles, Coldfoot. **Food & Supplies:** Available in Anaktuvuk Pass, Bettles, Coldfoot; none in park. **Tips & Hints:** Plan to be self-sufficient in the park and preserve, where contact with other visitors is rare. Be knowledgeable about camping and hiking in bear country. Contact park staff in Anaktuvuk Pass, Bettles, or Coldfoot for updated information before going into the park or preserve. Bring plenty of insect repellent and head nets. Biting mosquitoes and gnats during the summer can make a stay unbearable. Insect numbers decline by late August. Go between May and September to avoid snow. Winter temperatures between October and March usually are subzero, and can drop to as low as -60°F/-51°C. Busiest in July and August, least crowded in October and January. **Fees, Permits & Limitations:** Free. Alaska state fishing, hunting, or trapping licenses required. Commercial guide required for nonresidents hunting in preserves for certain species of wildlife. Hunting in preserve areas only. No motorized vehicles. Pets must be under control at all times. No rest rooms. Park and preserve open daily. Visitor center in Bettles open daily 8–5; in Coldfoot, May–Sept., daily 8–5.

HOW TO GET THERE

The park and preserve are accessible on foot, by small aircraft, or by boat. Bettles and Anaktuvuk Pass, 160 mi/256 km and 240mi/384 km north of Fairbanks, are nearest to the center of the park. Neither has road access. Scheduled air service from Fairbanks is available daily. Coldfoot, which provides access to the east section of the park and preserve, is 250 mi/400 km north of Fairbanks via the Elliot and Dalton highways.

FOR MORE INFORMATION

National Park Service (Box 26030, Bettles, AK 99726, tel. 907/692–5494; Web site www.nps.gov/gaar). City of Bettles (General Delivery, Bettles, AK 99726, tel. 907/692–5191).

Glacier Bay National Park and Preserve

In the southeast, near Gustavus

Glacier Bay is a 3-million-acre wilderness park accessible only by boat or plane. Just 200 years ago a solid sheet of ice covered what is now the bay. In two centuries, the glacial ice has retreated 65 mi/104 km and left a newly barren landscape to be recolonized by plant and animal life. You can travel by boat from a lush green rain forest up to the impressive tidewater glaciers and, perhaps, see wildlife along the way, including bears, mountain goats, whales, seals, eagles, and puffins. The site was created as a national monument in 1925 and designated a national park in 1980. The park was designated a Biosphere Reserve in 1986 and a World Heritage Site in 1992.

WHAT TO SEE & DO

Fishing, hiking, kayaking (rentals, Bartlett Cove, Gustavus), viewing glaciers by boat. **Facilities:** Visitor center with interpretive exhibits— Glacier Bay Lodge (Bartlett Cove). Book and map sale area. **Programs & Events:** Ranger-guided hikes, walks, evening programs (mid-May– mid-Sept.).

PLANNING YOUR VISIT

⚠ **Camping:** Primitive campground (no reservations). Backcountry camping available (camper orientation, bear-resistant food canisters, and permit required, *see below*). Group camping available (no reservations). ⊞ **Lodging:** In the park: Glacier Bay Lodge (tel. 800/451–5952, mid-May–mid-Sept. only). Lodging also available outside the park in Gustavus. ✕ **Food & Supplies:** In the park: meals and sundries at Glacier Bay Lodge (mid-May–mid-Sept. only). Restaurants, hardware shop, small store in Gustavus. ☞ **Tips & Hints:** Bring rain gear: Glacier Bay gets more than 75 inches per year. Busiest in June and July, least crowded in November and December. ▤ **Fees, Permits & Limitations:** Free. Glacier Bay Lodge (reservations, tel. 800/451–5952) offers daily boat trips to the glaciers. Backcountry permits (free), camper orientation, and bear-resistant food canisters (free) required (tel. 907/697–2627, summer only). Permit required for pleasure boat operators to enter Glacier Bay or dock at Bartlett Cove (June–Aug.). Permit applications are available through the park and should be returned no earlier than 60 days prior to the proposed date of entry. Because the number of permits is limited, planning ahead is strongly advised. Permits can be issued for up to seven days. Alaska state fishing and hunting license required. No firearms in park. Hunting in preserve only. No pets onshore except in Bartlett Cove. Leashed pets in restricted areas only in cove. Park open daily. Visitor center open mid-May–mid-Sept., daily 12:30–9.

HOW TO GET THERE

60 mi/96 km northwest of Juneau. Flights are available from Juneau, Skagway, or Haines to Gustavus, which is 10 mi/16 km by road from Bartlett Cove, the park headquarters.

FOR MORE INFORMATION

Glacier Bay National Park and Preserve (Box 140, Gustavus, AK 99826, tel. 907/697–2230, fax 907/697–2654; e-mail GLBA_Administration@nps.gov; Web site www.nps.gov/glba). Gustavus Visitor Association (Box 167, Gustavus, AK 99826, tel. 907/697–2245).

Katmai National Park and Preserve

In the southeast, near King Salmon

Variety marks this vast land, where lakes, forests, mountains, and marshlands abound in wildlife. The Alaska brown bear—the world's largest carnivore—thrives here, feeding upon red salmon that spawn in the many lakes and streams. Wild rivers and renowned sportfishing add to the attractions of this subarctic environment. In 1912, Novarupta Volcano erupted violently here, forming the ash-filled "Valley of Ten Thousand Smokes" where steam rose from countless fumaroles. Today only a few active vents remain. The park-preserve also contains part of the Alagnak Wild River. The site was proclaimed as Katmai National Monument in 1918 and established as a national park and preserve in 1980.

WHAT TO SEE & DO

Backcountry camping, bear viewing, boat touring, bus touring, fishing, hiking. **Facilities:** 2 visitor centers—King Salmon (next to the airport terminal in King Salmon); Brooks Camp (open early June–mid-Sept.). Bear viewing platforms, bookstore. **Programs & Events:** Ranger-led cultural walks, interpretive programs, evening slide programs (June–mid-Sept., Brooks Camp).

PLANNING YOUR VISIT

Camping: Campground: Brooks Camp at the Brooks River area (reservations required, tel. 800/365–2267). Backcountry camping available (permit recommended, *see below*). **Lodging:** In the park: lodging available at Grosvenor Lake and Brooks Camp (June 1–mid-Sept., reservations required, tel. 907/243–5448 or 800/544–0551). **Food & Supplies:** In the park: meals at Brooks Lodge (tel. 907/243–5448 or 800/544–0551). Brooks Lodge Trading Post sells white gas, fishing gear, some snack foods, souvenirs, and other limited supplies. ☞ **Tips & Hints:** Be prepared for cold, rainy weather as well as some warm, sunny days in summer. Temperatures usually hover around 60°F/15°C. Cool, overcast days with strong winds are common. In spring and fall, temperatures are cool and nights are cold. Winters are cold and receive six hours of sunlight. Get bear-resistant canisters at visitor centers. Be prepared for bears in vicinity of Brooks Camp. Very close encounters with bears are common and require visitors to move briskly. Go in July and September for best bear viewing. Expect waits and time limits on bear viewing platforms in July. Busiest in July and August, least crowded in January and February. ▨ **Fees, Permits & Limitations:** Free. $10 day use fee at Brooks Camp. Reservations recommended for daily bus tour ($79) from Brooks Lodge to the Valley of 10,000 Smokes (tel. 907/243–5448 or 800/544–0551). The trip starts at Brooks Camp and includes a day hike to Ukak Falls. Backcountry permits (recommended) available at Brooks Camp and King Salmon. No capsicum bear spray allowed on commercial flights. Park open daily. Park Service and concession services offered at Brooks Camp early June–mid-Sept.

HOW TO GET THERE

290 mi/464 km southwest of Anchorage on the Alaska Peninsula, just west of King Salmon; no road access. Daily commercial flights run between Anchorage and King Salmon. Charters, air taxis, and boat tours available from King Salmon, Anchorage, Homer, and Kodiak. Scheduled service into Brooks Camp available from King Salmon by floatplane and boat. Many area lodges provide their own transportation to the park.

FOR MORE INFORMATION

Katmai National Park and Preserve (Box 7, King Salmon, AK 99613, tel. 907/246–3305; Web site www.nps.gov/katm). Katmailand (concessioner, Web site www.katmailand.com). Alaska Public Lands Information Center (605 W. 4th Ave., Suite 105, Anchorage, AK 99501, tel. 907/271–2737).

Kenai Fjords National Park

In the south-central part of the state, near Seward

Harding Icefield—300 square mi/777 square km in size and one of four major ice caps in the United States—is one of the attractions in this coastal mountain park. Tens of thousands of birds breed in the park's rich, varied rain forest, and sea lions, otters, and seals inhabit the park's waters. The 669,500-acre site was proclaimed a national monument in 1978 and established as a national park in 1980.

WHAT TO SEE & DO

Bird and wildlife viewing, boat touring, fishing, flightseeing, hiking, kayaking. **Facilities:** Visitor center with interpretive exhibits (Seward), trails. Bookstore. **Programs & Events:** Ranger-led walks (Memorial Day–Labor Day).

PLANNING YOUR VISIT

⚠ **Camping:** Campground (no reservations). ▦ **Lodging:** In the park: 3 backcountry coastline cabins (summer), accessible by boat, kayak, or small plane; 1 Exit Glacier cabin (winter). Cabin reservation required (tel. 907/271–2739). Full-service lodging available in Seward. ✕ **Food & Supplies:** Available locally; none in park. ☞ **Tips & Hints:** Weather is usually overcast and cool in this maritime climate, and it rains often. May is the driest month, following months see increasing precipitation, and the wet, stormy fall begins in September. Expect summer daytime temperatures between 45°F/7°C and 70°F/21°C. Bring wool or synthetic clothing and sturdy rain gear, including pants, coat, and a hat. Stay on the glacier trail and off the ice. Commercial guides provide camping, fishing, and kayaking services. Get bear-resistant canisters at visitor center. Air charters provide flightseeing and fjord access. Boat tours and charters are available in Seward. In summer, boat tours ply the coast, observing calving glaciers, sea birds, and marine mammals. Boat charters offer overnight fjord trips and fishing trips to the fjords and Resurrection Bay. Busiest in July and August, least crowded in November and January. ▦ **Fees, Permits & Limitations:** $5 vehicle fee at Exit Glacier. Park open daily. Visitor center open daily Apr.–Sept. Park headquarters open weekdays 8–5.

HOW TO GET THERE

The park is 130 mi/208 km south of Anchorage on the Seward Hwy. The park's headquarters and visitor center are in Seward's small boat harbor. Bus and commuter flight service link Seward and Anchorage. The Alaska Marine Highway (ferry) System connects Seward with Homer and Seldovia via Kodiak and provides service to Valdez and Cordova. The Alaska Railroad serves Seward from Anchorage during the summer months. Exit Glacier can be reached in summer by car on a 9-mi/14-km gravel road and a short trail. The Harding Icefield is accessible by air or trail. Air and boat charters provide access to the fjords.

FOR MORE INFORMATION

Park Headquarters, Kenai Fjords National Park (Box 1727, Seward, AK 99664-1727, tel. 907/224–2132 for park information or 907/224–3175 for headquarters, fax 907/224–2144; Web site www.nps.gov/kefj). Seward Chamber of Commerce (Box 749, Seward, AK 99664, tel. 907/224–8051 or 907/224–3094).

Klondike Gold Rush National Historical Park

In Skagway and in Seattle, WA

The park has two units: one in Skagway, Alaska, and the other in Seattle, Washington. The Skagway unit includes 15 buildings in Skagway, plus the Chilkoot and White Pass trails. Miners used the trails in 1897 and 1898 to reach the rich Yukon gold fields. Hikers can retrace the miners' footsteps on the Chilkoot Trail. The White Pass and Yukon

Route Railway, constructed between 1898 and 1900, runs a train through the pass to Fraser, British Columbia, each summer. News of the gold strike in Canada's Yukon Territory spread from Seattle across the country, and most prospectors left for the northern gold fields from Seattle. Today, the Seattle unit has a visitor center in the Pioneer Square Historic District, the center of gold rush activity. The park was established on June 30, 1976.

WHAT TO SEE & DO

Skagway: Attending slide programs, fishing, hiking (backcountry permit required, *see below*), touring the historic districts and museums. Seattle: Touring Pioneer Square, watching movie and slide show and gold-panning demonstration. **Facilities:** Skagway—visitor center with interpretive exhibits (2nd and Broadway), hiker information center (Trail Center across from visitor center), exhibit area in the Railroad Building (2nd Ave.), Mascot Saloon (Broadway and 4th), Moore House (5th and Spring St.), interpretive displays (town of Dyea), wayside exhibits (Alaska Marine Highway Ferry Terminal, Broadway), and Klondike Highway; Seattle—visitor center with interpretive exhibits, historic district. Bookstores at both units. **Programs & Events:** Skagway—gold rush film (by request); film (May–Sept., hourly), guided walking tours of historic district (May–Sept., twice daily), ranger-led tours of Dyea (June–Aug.), tours of Moore House (May–Sept.), reading of poetry by Robert Service (June–Aug., Mon. and Tues. evenings); presentations and special events subject to staffing. Seattle—movie and slide program; Pioneer Square walking tour and gold-panning demonstration (summer).

PLANNING YOUR VISIT

⚠ **Camping:** Skagway—Campground in Dyea (no reservations). Campgrounds also available in Skagway. Seattle—Available locally; none in park. 🏨 **Lodging:** Available in Skagway or Seattle areas; none in parks. ✗ **Food & Supplies:** Available in Skagway or Seattle areas; none in parks. ☞ **Tips & Hints:** Skagway—Tours and buses pick up and drop off hikers at both ends of Chilkoot Trail. Go in May or June for best weather, mid-July for blooms, August for salmon run. Seattle—Allow 2½ hours for exhibits, movies, and gold-panning demonstration in summer. Busiest in June and July, least crowded in December and January. 🎫 **Fees, Permits & Limitations:** Skagway—free. Moore House tour fee: $2 per adult, $1 under 16 and over 62. Backcountry permits required to hike the Chilkoot Trail (free on U.S. side, available from Trail Center, June–Aug.; call 800/661-0486 for Canadian side fees and permits). Alaska state fishing license required. No hunting on Chilkoot Trail. No motorized or mechanized equipment on trail. No pets on trails. Visitor center open May–Sept., daily 8–6; June–Aug., extended hours until 8. Trail Center open daily 7:30–4:30. Moore House open May–Sept., daily 10–12, 1–5. Mascot Saloon exhibit open May–Sept., daily 9–5. Seattle—free. Visitor center open daily 9–5. Closed Thanksgiving, Dec. 25, Jan. 1.

HOW TO GET THERE

Skagway—80 mi/128 km north of Juneau by air or water and 110 mi/176 km south of Whitehorse, Yukon, by road. Closest airport: Skagway. Seattle—From I–5 or I–90, exit on 4th Ave., make a left on Main to 117 S. Main. Closest airport: SeaTac.

FOR MORE INFORMATION

Skagway—Klondike Gold Rush National Historical Park (Box 517, Skagway, AK 99840, tel. 907/983–2921, fax 907/983–9249; e-mail KLGO_ranger_activities@nps.gov; Web site www.nps.gov/klgo). Skagway Convention and Visitors Bureau (Box 415, Skagway, AK 99840, tel. 907/983–2854, fax 907/983–3854). Chamber of Commerce (Box 194, Skagway, AK 99840, tel. 907/983–1898, fax 907/983–2031). Seattle—Klondike Gold Rush National Historical Park (117 S. Main, Seattle, WA 98104, tel. 206/553–7220, fax 206/553–0614; e-mail KLSE_Ranger_Activities@nps.gov; Web site www.nps.gov/klgo).

Kobuk Valley National Park

In the northwest, near Kotzebue

Located 26 mi/42 km above the Arctic Circle, this 1.8-million-acre park preserves the central Kobuk River valley, the Great Kobuk Sand Dunes, and the Little Kobuk and Hunt rivers. Here are the northernmost limit of the boreal forest, as well as caribou, wolf, fox, and grizzly and black bear. The site was proclaimed a national monument in 1978 and redesignated in 1980.

WHAT TO SEE & DO

Backpacking, boating, canoeing, hiking, kayaking, rafting, wildlife watching. **Facilities:** Information center and park headquarters in Kotzebue. No facilities in park. Sales area. **Programs & Events:** Interpretive programs (Kotzebue). Seasonal activities available.

PLANNING YOUR VISIT

⚠ **Camping:** Available in Ambler, Kiana, Kotzebue, Noatak; none in park. ▣ **Lodging:** Available in Ambler, Kiana, Kotzebue, Noatak; none in park. ✕ **Food & Supplies:** Available in Ambler, Kiana, Kotzebue, Noatak; none in park. ☞ **Tips & Hints:** Prepare to be self-sufficient. Wear sturdy hiking boots and waders for wet terrain. Expect high winds throughout the year and short, cool, and sunny summers with 24 hours of daylight for one month. Winters are long, severe, harsh, and extremely cold, with one hour of daylight by December 1. Guard against hypothermia, giardiasis, wild animals, mosquitoes, and biting flies. Don't interfere with subsistence camps, fishnets, or other equipment. Respect property and privacy. Busiest in July and August, least crowded in December and January. ▨ **Fees, Permits & Limitations:** Free. Park open daily. Information center open mid-May–mid-Sept., daily 8–6.

HOW TO GET THERE

Kotzebue is 26 mi/42 km north of the Arctic Circle in northwest Alaska. Access to Kotzebue (headquarters and information center) is by Alaska Airlines. To reach the park, air taxis and scheduled and charter flights are available. In summer, access is by motorized and nonmotorized watercraft, aircraft, and foot. In winter, access is by snowmobiles, aircraft, and foot.

FOR MORE INFORMATION

Park Headquarters (Box 1029, Kotzebue, AK 99752, tel. 907/442–3890 for headquarters or 907/442–3760 for Kotzebue Public Lands Information Center; Web site www.nps.gov/kova).

Lake Clark National Park and Preserve

In the south-central part of the state, near Port Alsworth

Covering 4 million acres, this spectacular park and preserve stretches from the shores of Cook Inlet across the Chigmit Mountains to the tundra-covered hills of the western interior. The Chigmits, the junction of the Alaska and Aleutian ranges, are an awe-inspiring array of jagged mountains and glaciers that include Mt. Redoubt and Mt. Iliamna, two active volcanoes. The 50-mi-/80-km-long Lake Clark and other waters in the park are vital salmon habitats for the Bristol Bay salmon fishery, one of the world's largest sockeye salmon fishing grounds. Anglers find trophy fish; hikers explore high tundra slopes; river runners thrill to the Tlikakila, Mulchatna, or Chilikadrotna wild rivers; and campers find lakeshore sites inspirational. The site was proclaimed a national monument in 1978 and established as a national park and preserve in 1980.

WHAT TO SEE & DO

Backpacking, bird- and wildlife watching, fishing, flightseeing (charters, Port Alsworth, Kenai, Anchorage), hiking, hunting (preserve), kayaking, mountaineering, river running (rentals, Anchorage, Kenai, Port Alsworth). **Facilities:** Visitor center with interpretive exhibits (Port Alsworth), backcountry patrol cabins (Telaquana Lake, Twin Lakes, Crescent Lake and Chinitna Bay), trails. Book sales area, post office. **Programs & Events:** Slide shows and presentations (on request as staffing permits). Slide presentations (June–Sept.), guided hikes (on request).

PLANNING YOUR VISIT

⚑ **Camping:** Backcountry camping available. 🏠 **Lodging:** Lodging available on Cook Inlet, along Lake Clark, and in Port Alsworth. Minimal facilities available in park interior. ✗ **Food & Supplies:** Lodges provide food. Café in Port Alsworth (May 15–Oct.). No groceries or camping supplies in park. ☞ **Tips & Hints:** Go in summer for best fishing, September for fall colors. Prepare to be self-sufficient for backcountry travel. Stay away from game trails and fresh signs of bears. Bring extra food and cooking fuel. Expect 50–65°F/10–18°C temperatures from June to August, with considerable precipitation. Plan for frost and snow as early as August. Plan for strong winds any time and winter temperatures to -40°F/-40°C. Respect private property within park boundaries. Weather changes can delay scheduled pickup by aircraft by several days.

Busiest June through September, least crowded in January and February. ✉ **Fees, Permits & Limitations:** Free. Alaska state fish and hunting licenses required. Hunting and trapping in preserve only. No gathering of plants or live trees. Leashed pets only. No rest rooms available. Park and preserve open daily. Visitor center open summer 8–5.

HOW TO GET THERE

150 mi/240 km southwest of Anchorage on the west side of the Cook Inlet and the north end of the Alaska Peninsula. Access to the Lake Clark region is by air only. A one- to two-hour flight from Anchorage, Kenai, or Homer provides access to most points within the park and preserve. Scheduled commercial flights between Anchorage and Iliamna, 30 mi/50 km outside the boundary, also provide access. Floatplanes may land on lakes. Wheeled planes land on open beaches, gravel bars, or private airstrips in or near the park.

FOR MORE INFORMATION

Lake Clark National Park and Preserve (1 Park Pl., Port Alsworth, AK 99653, tel. 907/781–2218; Web site www.nps.gov/lacl).

Noatak National Preserve

In the northwest, near Kotzebue

One of North America's largest mountain-ringed river basins with an unaltered ecosystem, the Noatak is home to many Arctic plants and animals and offers superlative wilderness float-trip opportunities. The 6.6-million-acre preserve also includes the 65-mi-/104-km-long Grand Canyon of the Noatak. The Noatak was proclaimed a national monument in 1978, established as a national preserve in 1980, and designated a Biosphere Reserve in 1976.

WHAT TO SEE & DO

Backpacking, boating, canoeing, hiking, hunting, rafting, wildlife watching. **Facilities:** Information center and park headquarters in Kotzebue. No facilities in park. **Programs & Events:** Interpretive programs (Kotzebue). Seasonal activities and special events available.

PLANNING YOUR VISIT

⛺ **Camping:** Backcountry camping available (check in with park rangers at Park Headquarters). Private campgrounds available in Ambler, Kiana, Kotzebue, Noatak. ▥ **Lodging:** Available in Ambler, Kiana, Kotzebue, Noatak; none in park. ✕ **Food & Supplies:** Available in Ambler, Kiana, Kotzebue, Noatak; none in park. ☞ **Tips & Hints:** Prepare to be self-sufficient. Wear sturdy hiking boots and waders for wet terrain. Expect high winds throughout the year; short, mild, cool, and sunny summers with 24 hours of daylight for one month; and long, severe, harsh, extremely cold winters with one hour of daylight by December 1. Guard against hypothermia, giardia lamblia, wild animals, mosquitoes, and biting flies. Don't interfere with subsistence camps, fishnets, or other equipment. Respect property and privacy. Busiest in July and August, least crowded in November and December. ✉ **Fees,**

Permits & Limitations: Park open daily. Kotzebue information center open mid-May–Sept. 30., daily 8–6.

HOW TO GET THERE

Kotzebue is 26 mi/42 km north of the Arctic Circle in northwest Alaska. Access to Kotzebue (headquarters and information center) is by Alaska Airlines. To reach the park, air taxis and scheduled and charter flights are available. In the summer, access is by motorized and nonmotorized watercraft, aircraft, and foot. In winter, access is by snowmobiles, aircraft, and foot.

FOR MORE INFORMATION

Park Headquarters (Box 1029, Kotzebue, AK 99752, tel. 907/442–3890; Web site www.nps.gov/noat). Kotzebue Public Lands Information Center (Box 1029, Kotzebue, AK 99752, tel. 907/442–3760).

Sitka National Historical Park

In the southeast part of the state, near Sitka

Sitka was the cultural and political hub of Russian America in the early 19th century. In 1867, Russia ended its 126-year New World enterprise with the sale of Alaska to the United States for $7.2 million. Set aside in 1890, this park's 107 acres commemorate the Battle of 1804 between the local Tlingits and the Russians. The park was placed into the National Park System in 1910, making it the oldest and smallest national park in Alaska. The temperate rain-forest park consists of the fort site, a sizable totem-pole collection, the Southeast Alaska Indian Cultural Center (housed in the visitor center), and the restored Russian Bishop's House, which was built in 1842. The site was proclaimed in 1910 and designated a national historical park in 1972.

WHAT TO SEE & DO

Bird- and wildlife watching, picnicking, touring the restored living quarters in the Russian Bishop's House, viewing exhibits and salmon-spawning stream, walking, watching slide show and local artisans at work in the cultural center. **Facilities:** Visitor center with interpretive exhibits, Russian Bishop's House, cultural center, trails, interpretive signs. Bookstore, picnic area. **Programs & Events:** Russian Bishop's House tours (mid-May–Sept. 30, daily; Oct. 1–mid-May, by appointment only), slide show (upon request). Tours of the Bishop's House and battle walks (June–Sept.), other programs (depending on staff availability). National Park Service Week (usually 1st week in Apr.), Alaska Day (Oct. 18).

PLANNING YOUR VISIT

Camping: Available in Sitka; none in park. **Lodging:** Available in Sitka; none in park. **Food & Supplies:** Available in Sitka; none in park. **Tips & Hints:** Bring rain gear and rubber boots. Visit between June and August, but rain is a certainty at any time. Busiest in July and August, least crowded in December and January. **Fees, Permits & Limitations:** Entrance fee: $3 for Russian Bishop's House. Fishing restricted to Dolly Vardens only. Alaska state fishing license required. Leashed pets only. No bike riding. No camping. No fires outside grills. No motorized vehicles on trails. Park grounds open summer, daily 6 AM–10 PM; fall–spring, daily 6 AM–8 PM. Visitor center open mid-May–Oct., daily 8–5; Nov.–mid-May, weekdays 8–5. Closed on major holidays. Russian Bishop's House open late May–Sept., daily 9–1, 2–5; Oct.–late May, by appointment only. The park will be closed to the public through May 2001.

HOW TO GET THERE

0.3 mi/0.5 km from downtown Sitka. The Bishop's House is downtown. Closest airport: Sitka (1.5 mi/2.4 km).

FOR MORE INFORMATION

Sitka National Historical Park (106 Metlakatla St., Sitka, AK 99835, tel. 907/747–6281, fax 907/747–5938; Web site www.nps.gov/sitk). Sitka Convention and Visitors Bureau (303 Lincoln St., Box 1226, Sitka, AK 99835, tel. 907/747–5940, fax 907/747–3739).

Wrangell–St. Elias National Park and Preserve

In the southeast part of the state

This 13.2-million-acre park and preserve, the largest in the U.S., is a pristine wilderness encompassing towering mountains, glaciers, meandering rivers, and volcanoes. Here the Chugach, Wrangell, St. Elias, and Alaska mountain ranges converge to form what is considered the "mountain kingdom of North America." The park and preserve contains the continent's largest assemblage of glaciers and greatest collection of peaks above 16,000 ft/4,853 m. Mount St. Elias (18,008 ft/5,462 m) is the second highest peak in the United States. The site was proclaimed a national monument in 1978, a World Heritage Site in 1979, and a park and preserve in 1980.

WHAT TO SEE & DO

Backpacking, fishing, flightseeing, hiking, hunting, kayaking, mountain biking, mountaineering, river floating, sea kayaking, wildlife viewing. **Facilities:** Visitor center with interpretive exhibits (Copper Center); ranger stations at Yakutat, Slana, and Chitina; trails. Bookstore. **Programs & Events:** Slide program. Park programs available (summer).

PLANNING YOUR VISIT

⚠ **Camping:** Primitive campground. Backcountry camping available. Group camping available. Campgrounds also available in Chitina, Glennallen, Kenny Lake, McCarthy Road, Nabesna Road, Slana. 🏨 **Lodging:** Available in Chistochina, Chitina, Copper Center, Gakona, Glennallen, Kennicott, Kenny Lake, McCarthy, Nabesna, Slana; none in park. ✗ **Food & Supplies:** In the park: meals at Kennicott Glacier Lodge (tel. 907/554–4477), McCarthy Lodge (tel. 907/554–4402). Food and supplies also available in Chitina, Copper Center, Glennallen; supplies only in Kenny Lake. ☞ **Tips & Hints:** Thoroughly research your visit to the Wrangells.

This is a vast expanse of rugged wilderness with few services. Develop map- and compass-reading skills for backcountry travel. Be prepared for unpredictable weather, dangerous stream crossings, and grizzly and black bear encounters. Road access to park is via Nabesna and McCarthy Roads, both gravel-surfaced. Take an air taxi to view the park's mountain wilderness. Visit between mid-May and October for best weather. Busiest in July and August, least crowded in December and January. ▧ **Fees, Permits & Limitations:** Free. Alaska state fishing and hunting license required. ATVs in designated areas only, permit required. Park open daily. Visitor center open in Labor Day–Memorial Day, weekdays 8–4:30, Memorial Day–Labor Day, daily 8–6. Ranger stations open Memorial Day–Labor Day.

HOW TO GET THERE

The park visitor center is 199 mi/318 km east of Anchorage via Hwy. 1, 258 mi/413 km southeast of Fairbanks via Hwys. 2 and 4, and 105 mi/168 km north of Valdez via Hwy. 4. Air service available between Glennallen and Anchorage.

FOR MORE INFORMATION

Wrangell–St. Elias National Park and Preserve (Box 439, Copper Center, AK 99573, tel. 907/822–5234, fax 907/822–7216; e-mail WRST_Administrator@nps.gov; Web site www.nps.gov/wrst). Greater Copper Valley Chamber of Commerce (Box 469, Glenwallen, AK 99588, tel. 907/822–5555).

Yukon-Charley Rivers National Preserve

In east-central Alaska, near Eagle

On the Canadian border in central Alaska, the 2.5-million-acre preserve protects 115 mi/184 km of the 1,800-mi/2,880-km Yukon River and the entire Charley River basin. Numerous rustic cabins and historic sites are reminders of the importance of the Yukon River during the 1898 gold rush. Peregrine falcons nest in bluffs overlooking the river, and the preserve's rolling hills are home to an array of wildlife. The Charley, an 88-mi/141-km wild river, is considered to be the most spectacular river in Alaska. The site was proclaimed a national monument in 1978 and established as a national preserve in 1980.

WHAT TO SEE & DO

Bird- and wildlife watching; exploring historic trapping, mining, and woodcutter sites; fishing; hunting; river running. **Facilities:** Visitor center with interpretive exhibits (Eagle). Book and map sale area. **Programs & Events:** Video presentations. Yukon Quest dogsled race (Feb.).

PLANNING YOUR VISIT

⚠ **Camping:** Backcountry camping available. Private campgrounds in Circle, Eagle. ⌂ **Lodging:** In the park: 4 cabins—along the Yukon River corridor at Kandik River mouth, Nation Bluff, Glenn Creek, and historic Slaven's Roadhouse at the mouth of Coal Creek (no reservations). Lodging also available in Circle, Circle Hot Springs, and Eagle. ✕ **Food & Supplies:** Available in Circle, Eagle; none in park. ☞ **Tips & Hints:** Be prepared to be self-sufficient. Winter temperatures are as low as -60°F/-51°C, and summer highs can reach 90°F/32°C. Busiest in June and August, least crowded in November and December. ▥ **Fees, Permits & Limitations:** Free. Alaska state hunting and fishing license required. No artifact collecting. Preserve open daily. Eagle field office open mid-May–mid-Sept., daily 8–4:30; mid-Sept.–mid-May, weekdays 8–4:30.

HOW TO GET THERE

The preserve is in east interior Alaska, 150 mi/240 km east of Fairbanks. Air taxis serve Eagle, located upriver, and Circle, downriver of the preserve. Eagle is at the end of the Taylor Hwy., and Circle is on the Steese Hwy. The preserve is reached by either river or air travel along the Yukon or by flying in to upper Charley River.

FOR MORE INFORMATION

Yukon-Charley Rivers National Preserve Headquarters (Box 74718, Fairbanks, AK 99707, tel. 907/456–0593; Web site www.nps.gov/yuch). Yukon-Charley Rivers National Preserve Field Office (Box 167, Eagle, AK 99738-0167, tel. 907/547–2233).

See Also

....

Alatna Wild River, Wild and Scenic Rivers System in Other National Parklands. *Aleutian World War II National Historic Area,* Affiliated Areas in Other National Parklands. *Aniachak Wild River,* Wild and Scenic Rivers System in Other National Parklands. *Charley Wild River,* Wild and Scenic Rivers System in Other National Parklands. *Chilikadrotna Wild River,* Wild and Scenic Rivers System in Other National Parklands. *Iditarod National Historic Trail,* National Trails System in Other National Parklands. *John Wild River,* Wild and Scenic Rivers System in Other National Parklands. *Kobuk Wild River,* Wild and Scenic Rivers System in Other National Parklands. *Mulchatna Wild River,* Wild and Scenic Rivers System in Other National Parklands. *Noatak Wild River,* Wild and Scenic Rivers System in Other National Parklands. *North Fork of the Koyukuk Wild River,* Wild and Scenic Rivers System in Other National Parklands. *Salmon Wild River,* Wild and Scenic Rivers System in Other National Parklands. *Tinayguk Wild River,* Wild and Scenic Rivers System in Other National Parklands. *Tlikakila Wild River,* Wild and Scenic Rivers System in Other National Parklands.

ARIZONA

Canyon de Chelly National Monument

In the northeast part of the state, near Chinle

At the base of sheer red cliffs and in caves inside canyon walls are ruins of Native American villages built between AD 350 and 1300. The monument presents southwestern Native American history from the earliest basket makers to the Navajo Indians who currently live and farm here. The monument was authorized on February 14, 1931.

WHAT TO SEE & DO

Auto touring (permit required in canyon, *see below*), hiking (permit required in canyon, *see below*), horseback riding (rentals), Jeep touring (rentals, Chinle), picnicking, pictograph viewing. **Facilities:** Visitor center with interpretive exhibits, auto and hiking trails.

PLANNING YOUR VISIT

Camping: Campground (no reservations). Backcountry camping allowed with authorized guide. Group campsites available (no RVs; reservations available, tel. 520/674–5500). Private campground also available on South Rim. **Lodging:** In the park: Thunderbird Lodge (tel. 520/674–5841/5842, or write Thunderbird Lodge, Box 548, Chinle, AZ 86503). Lodging also available in Chinle and Window Rock, AZ, and Gallup, NM. **Food and Supplies:** In the park: meals at Thunderbird Lodge (tel. 520/674–5841 or 520/674–5842). Food and supplies also available nearby in Chinle. **Tips & Hints:** Beware of quicksand, deep dry sand, cliffs, loose rocks, and flash floods. The inner canyons are impassable in winter and at certain other times of the year. Busiest in May and August, least crowded in December and January. **Fees, Permits & Limitations:** Entrance fee: free. Hiking within the canyon requires a Park Service permit, fee, and an authorized Navajo guide, except along the 2.5-mi/4-km White House Ruins Trail. To drive on the canyon bottom, you must have a four-wheel-drive vehicle, a Park Service permit, and an authorized Navajo guide. Fees apply. Concession Jeep tours (tel. 520/674–5841 or 520/674–5842 or write Thunderbird Lodge, Box 548, Chinle, AZ 86503). Drive on paved roads only. No vehicles over 32 ft/10 m at park campground. Visitor center open Oct.–Apr., daily 8–5; May–Sept., daily 8–6. Closed Dec. 25.

HOW TO GET THERE

3 mi/5 km east of U.S. 191, near Chinle, via Exit 333 off I–40. Closest airport: Farmington (150 mi/240 km).

FOR MORE INFORMATION

Superintendent, Canyon de Chelly National Monument (Box 588, Chinle, AZ 86503, tel. 520/674–5500; Web site www.nps.gov/cach).

Casa Grande Ruins
National Monument

In the south-central part of the state, in Coolidge

Among the 60 prehistoric Native American sites preserved at Casa Grande Ruins National Monument, Casa Grande, the four-story caliche building built 650 years ago, is the most prominent. Its purpose in the Hohokam culture, which flourished for 1,000 years in the Sonoran Desert, never has been determined. The site was established as a federal reservation in 1892 and a national monument in 1918.

WHAT TO SEE & DO

Picnicking, touring the archaeological sites. **Facilities:** Visitor center with interpretive exhibits, museum, self-guided trail, observation platform. Bookstore, picnic area. **Programs & Events:** Interpretive programs (Nov.–Mar.).

PLANNING YOUR VISIT

Camping: Available in Casa Grande, Coolidge (RV camping only), Eloy, Florence, Phoenix, Picacho State Park, and Tucson areas; none in park. **Lodging:** Available in Casa Grande, Coolidge, Eloy, Florence; none in park. **Food & Supplies:** Available in Casa Grande, Coolidge, Florence; none in park. **Tips & Hints:** Summer temperatures can reach 115°F/46°C, and there is little shade. Go from mid-October to early May for mild weather. Busiest January through March, least crowded in July and August. **Fees, Permits & Limitations:** Entrance fee: $2 per person (children under 16 free) or $4 per car. Only Compound A (Casa Grande ruin) and picnic area (with observation platform) open to the public. Monument and visitor center open daily 8–5. Closed Dec. 25.

HOW TO GET THERE

On the north edge of the city of Coolidge 60 mi/96 km southeast of Phoenix and 70 mi/112 km northwest of Tucson. Closest airport: Phoenix.

FOR MORE INFORMATION

Casa Grande Ruins National Monument (1100 Ruins Dr., Coolidge, AZ 85228, tel. 520/723–3172, fax 520/723–7209; Web site www.nps.gov/cagr). Coolidge Chamber of Commerce (Box 943, Coolidge, AZ 85228, tel. 520/723–3009).

Chiricahua
National Monument

In the southeast part of the state, near Willcox

A volcanic eruption 27 million years ago, 1,000 times greater than the eruption at Mount St. Helens, laid down 2,000 ft/607 m of ash and pumice that fused into rock and later eroded into the huge balanced rocks, towering spires, and massive stone columns present in the monument today. Now the intersection of two deserts and mountain ranges, Chiricahua's 12,000 acres represent one of the premier areas of biological diversity in the Northern Hemisphere. Also on site is the Faraway Ranch, originally the homestead of Swedish immigrants and later a working cattle and guest ranch. The monument was proclaimed in 1924 and transferred to the Park Service in 1933.

WHAT TO SEE & DO

Auto touring, bird-watching, hiking, picnicking, touring ranch, wildlife watching. **Facilities:** Visitor center with interpretive exhibits, ranch, trails, amphitheater. **Programs & Events:** Faraway Ranch tours (year-round, times vary). Interpretive programs (Mar.–Nov., days and times vary), evening programs (Fri. and Sat. at 7 or 7:30 PM).

PLANNING YOUR VISIT

Camping: Campground: no hookups or reservations. Camping also available in surrounding Coronado National Forest. **Lodging:** Available in Bisbee, Tombstone, Willcox; none in park. **Food & Supplies:** Available in Bisbee, Tombstone, Willcox; none in park. **Tips & Hints:** Get gas in Willcox. Watch for rattlesnakes. Drive carefully on winding scenic road. Bring light clothing in summer, when temperatures range from 50°F/10°C to 95°F/35°C each day; rain gear during thunderstorm season (July–Sept.); warm clothing during winter, when temperatures range from 50°F/10°C–60°F/16°C to 10°F/-12°C–20°F/-8°C each day, with wind chills possibly below zero. Busiest in March and April, least crowded in June and July. **Fees, Permits & Limitations:** Entrance fee: $6 per vehicle, $3 per motorcycle, bicycle, or walk-in. Visitor center open daily 8–5. Closed Dec. 25.

HOW TO GET THERE

120 mi/192 km east of Tucson via Exit 340 (Willcox) off I–10, Rtes. 186 and 181. Closest airport: Tucson.

FOR MORE INFORMATION

Superintendent, Chiricahua National Monument (13063 E. Bonita Canyon Rd., Willcox, AZ 85643, tel. 520/824–3560; Web site www.nps. gov/chir). Willcox Chamber of Commerce & Agriculture (1500 North Circle I Rd., Willcox, AZ 85643, tel. 520/384–2272).

Coronado National Memorial

On United States–Mexico border

The 4,750-acre memorial commemorates the first major exploration of the American southwest by Europeans. The scenic overlook at Montezuma Pass offers sweeping views of the San Pedro River Valley, which is believed to have been the expedition route of Vasquez de Coronado in 1540. The natural environment typifies the "Sky Island" mountains of southeast Arizona, with desert grasslands and oak woodlands. The site was authorized as an International Memorial on August 18, 1941, and redesignated on November 5, 1952.

WHAT TO SEE & DO

Caving, hiking, picnicking. **Facilities:** Visitor center with interpretive exhibits, trails, wayside exhibits, cave. Book and map sales area, picnic areas. **Programs & Events:** Interpretive talks and walks (Feb., Mar., weekly).

PLANNING YOUR VISIT

⚠ **Camping:** Private campgrounds available in Bisbee, Sierra Vista. U.S. Forest Service campgrounds available at Parker Canyon Lake and upper Carr Canyon. ⊞ **Lodging:** Available in Bisbee, Sierra Vista; none in park. ✗ **Food & Supplies:** Available in Bisbee, Sierra Vista; none in park. ☞ **Tips & Hints:** Go in spring and fall for best hiking, bird migrations. Busiest in February and March, least crowded in November and December. ▣ **Fees, Permits & Limitations:** Free. Flashlights (1 per person, 2 if traveling alone) and permit required (free) to visit Coronado Cave. No hunting. No pets on trails or backcountry. No bikes or motorized vehicles on trails. Memorial open daily dawn–dusk. Visitor center open daily 8–5. Closed Thanksgiving, Dec. 25.

HOW TO GET THERE

50 mi/80 km south of I–10 off AZ 92. The turnoff from AZ 92 onto Coronado Memorial Rd., which leads to E. Montezuma Canyon Rd., is 16 mi/26 km south of Sierra Vista and 21 mi/34 km west of Bisbee.

FOR MORE INFORMATION

Coronado National Memorial (4101 E. Montezuma Canyon Rd., Hereford, AZ 85615, tel. 520/366–5515 ext. 23, fax 520/366–5705; e-mail CORO_Interpretation@nps.gov; Web site www.nps.gov/coro). Sierra Vista Convention and Visitors Bureau (21 E. Wilcox Dr., Sierra Vista, AZ 85635, tel. 520/458–6940 or 800/288–3861, fax 520/452–0878; E-mail chamber@c2i2.com or www.arizonaguide.com/sierravista). Bisbee Chamber of Commerce (Box BA, mail) or 31 Subway St. (for visitors), Bisbee, AZ 85603, tel. 520/432–5421).

Fort Bowie
National Historic Site

In the southeast part of the state, near Bowie

Fort Bowie commemorates the bitter conflict between the Chiricahua Apaches and the U.S. military. For more than 30 years Fort Bowie and Apache Pass were the focal points of military operations that culminated in the surrender of Geronimo in 1886 and the banishment of the Chiricahuas to Florida and Alabama. It was the site of the Bascom Affair, a wagon train massacre; and the Battle of Apache Pass, where a large force of Chiricahua Apaches under Mangus Colorados and Cochise fought the California Volunteers. The remains of Fort Bowie, the adobe walls of post buildings, and the ruins of a Butterfield Stage Station are carefully preserved. The site was authorized in 1964 and established in 1972.

WHAT TO SEE & DO

Bird-watching, hiking, picnicking, touring fort ruins. **Facilities:** Visitor center with interpretive exhibits, trails, fort and ruins. Bookstore, picnic areas.

PLANNING YOUR VISIT

⚠ **Camping:** RV camping available in Bowie, Willcox; none at site. ⛺ **Lodging:** Available in Willcox; none at site. ✗ **Food & Supplies:** Available in Bowie, Willcox; none at site. ☞ **Tips & Hints:** Plan at least a two-hour hike to fort and back. Busiest in January and February, least crowded in September and March. ☰ **Fees, Permits & Limitations:** Free. Visitor center open daily 8–5. Closed Dec. 25. Ruins Trail open sunrise–sunset.

HOW TO GET THERE

116 mi/186 km east of Tucson and 227 mi/363 km from Phoenix via I–10. From Willcox, off I–10, take AZ 186 to the Fort Bowie turnoff, then drive 8 mi/13 km on unpaved road to Fort Bowie Trailhead. Closest airport: Tucson.

FOR MORE INFORMATION

Fort Bowie National Historic Site (Box 158, Bowie, AZ 85605, tel. 520/847–2500; Web site www.nps.gov/fobo).

Glen Canyon
National Recreation Area

In Page, Arizona, and south Utah

The 1.2-million-acre recreation area lies in the midst of the country's most rugged canyon country and some of the most scenic backpacking country on the Colorado Plateau. Lake Powell, the second largest man-made lake in the United States, stretches for 186 mi/301 km along the old Colorado River channel with a shoreline of 1,960 mi/3,136 km. The park also contains the world's largest natural bridge (Rainbow Bridge National Monument, *see separate entry*); Lees Ferry, which contains two historic district properties; and the Orange Cliffs unit next to Canyonlands National Park. The recreation area is administered under cooperative agreements with the Bureau of Reclamation, U.S. Dept. of the Interior, signed April 18, 1958, and September 17, 1965, and was established on October 27, 1972.

WHAT TO SEE & DO

Backpacking, boating (rentals at park marinas, Page, AZ; Big Water and Ticaboo, UT; tours at Bullfrog, Halls Crossing, Wahweap), fishing, four-wheel driving, hiking, hunting, mountain biking, picnicking, swimming, waterskiing. **Facilities:** 4 visitor centers with interpretive exhibits—Carl Hayden, Bullfrog, Navajo Bridge Interpretive Center, and Escalante Inter-agency Center; 2 contact stations—Halls Crossing and Hite; pedestrian walkway over Colorado River (Navajo Bridge, Hwy. 89A, near Lees Ferry), trails, historic districts, outdoor exhibits. Book and map sale areas, gas stations, gift shops, picnic facilities. **Programs & Events:** Interpretive programs (on request). Ranger programs (Memorial Day–Labor Day).

PLANNING YOUR VISIT

⚲ **Camping:** 9 campgrounds: 3 with hookups (reservations available at Bullfrog, Halls Crossing, and Wahweap, tel. 800/528–6154), 6 primitive. Backcountry camping available (permit required in Orange Cliffs district, requested for Escalante district, *see below*). Group campsites at Wahweap (tel. 800/528–6154). Private campgrounds in Page. ▣ **Lodging:** In the park: ARAMARK (tel. 800/528–6154). Lodging also available in Page, AZ. ✕ **Food & Supplies:** In the park: groceries at all marinas; restaurants at Wahweap and Bullfrog (summer); snack bar at Dangling Rope (summer). Food and supplies also available in Page and Greenehaven, AZ, and Ticaboo, UT. ☞ **Tips & Hints:** Know and follow all boating-safety and water-quality regulations. See park's Web site for information. Visit between April and October. Busiest in July and August, least crowded in January and February. ▨ **Fees, Permits & Limitations:** Entrance fee: $5 per vehicle or $3 per pedestrian, bicyclist, or motorcyclist. Boat launch fee: $10 for first vessel, $4 for each additional. Backcountry camping permit required for backcountry camping in Orange Cliffs district (available from Canyonlands National Park, *see separate entry*), requested for backcountry camping in Escalante district (available from Escalante Inter-agency Visitor Center). Arizona or Utah state fishing or hunting license required. Leashed pets only in developed areas. No pets at Rainbow Bridge. Mountain bikes on established roads only. Hunting allowed in restricted areas. Park and roads open daily, except The Chains and Sunset Hill overlooks, which are open daylight hours only. Visitor center hours: Carl Hayden—daily 8–5 with extended summer hours, closed Thanksgiving, Dec. 25, Jan. 1; Bullfrog—opened intermittently in Mar.; Apr.–Oct, daily 8–5; closed Nov.–Feb.; Escalante—mid-Mar.–mid-Oct., daily 7:30–5:30, mid-Oct.–mid-Mar., weekdays 8–4:30; Halls Crossing and Hite—intermittently; Navajo Bridge Interpretive Center, mid-Apr.–Oct. daily 9–5.

HOW TO GET THERE

Glen Canyon Dam and the Wahweap Marina are near Page, AZ, on Hwy. 89. North sections of the area, Bullfrog, Halls Crossing, and Hite and the Orange Cliffs may be reached from Hwys. 95 and 276. Escalante is on UT 12. Lees Ferry and the Navajo Bridge Interpretive Center are off Hwy. 89A near Marble Canyon. Closest airport: Page (3 mi/5 km).

FOR MORE INFORMATION

Glen Canyon National Recreation Area (Box 1507, Page, AZ 86040, tel. 520/608–6404; Web site www.nps.gov/glca).

Grand Canyon National Park

In the north part of the state, near Tusayan

One of the most spectacular examples of erosion anywhere in the world is the Grand Canyon, which has incomparable vistas. The Colorado River snakes its way through the 277-mi-/443-km-long park, which reaches a depth of 1 mi/1.6 km and a width of 18 mi/29 km in places. The canyon's walls are 1.8-billion-year-old rock layered in pink-and-brown sandstone, granite, shale, and limestone. Grand Canyon was proclaimed as a forest preserve in 1893 and a game preserve in 1906, a national monument in 1908, transferred to the Park Service and established as a national park in 1919, and declared a World Heritage Site in 1979.

WHAT TO SEE & DO

Air, auto, and bus touring (rentals); hiking; horseback riding (rentals); mule riding (rentals); rafting (rentals). **Facilities:** Information Center with interpretive exhibits—Canyon View Information Plaza (South Rim south of Mather Point), 4 visitor contact centers—Yavapai Observation Station, Tusayan Museum, Desert View, and North Rim; Kolb Studio; overlooks; Bright Angel Trail and South Kaibab Trail (South Rim); North Kaibab Trail (North Rim); other trails; IMAX theater (Tusayan). ATM, bank, bookstores, car repair, gift shops, laundry, pet kennels, photo processing, post office, religious services, showers. **Programs & Events:** Ranger-led walks, talks, and evening programs; air tours; mule trips; horse rides; Kolb Studio art exhibits (year round). Grand Canyon Field Institute seminars, backpacking trips, and river trips (Mar.–Nov., tel. 520/638–2485). Grand Canyon Music Festival (Sept.). Check *The Guide* on arrival for schedule of additional seasonal activities and events.

PLANNING YOUR VISIT

Camping: 4 campgrounds: 3 tent campgrounds (reservations available at Mather and North Rim, tel. 800/365–2267), 1 RV campground with hookups (tel. 303/297–2757). Backcountry camping available (permit required, *see below*). Camping also available in Tusayan and Kaibab National Forest. **Lodging:** In the park: Bright Angel Lodge, El Tovar Hotel, Kachina Lodge, Maswik Lodge, Phantom Ranch (canyon floor), Thunderbird Lodge, and Yavapai Lodge (tel. 520/638–2631 for same-day reservations or 303/297–2757 for advance), Grand Canyon Lodge (North Rim, mid-May–late Oct., tel. 520/638–2611 front desk, 303/297–2757 advance reservations). Lodging also available in Cameron, Chinle, Flagstaff, Fredonia, Gray Mountain, Jacob Lake, Kaibab Lake, Kayenta, Keams Canyon, Marble Canyon, Page, Red Lake, Second Mesa, Tsegi, Tuba City, Tusayan, Valle, and Williams, AZ, and Kanab and Monument Valley, UT. **Food & Supplies:** In the park: meals at Arizona Steak House, Bright Angel Restaurant, and El Tovar Dining Room (reservations available at El Tovar, tel. 303/297–2757), Canyon Village Marketplace, cafeterias at Maswik and Yavapai, snacks at Bright Angel Fountain and Hermits Rest Snack Bar. Groceries and supplies at Canyon Village Marketplace (Grand Canyon Village and Desert View); camper store at North Rim. Food and supplies also available in Tusayan. ☞ **Tips & Hints:**

Plan ahead for lodging, backcountry permits, and mule trips. Write the park in advance to request a trip planner or backcountry trip planner if you are planning to backpack. Be prepared for a variety of climates. Expect snow in winter and cool nights in summer at South Rim (7,000 ft/2,123 m) and snow almost any time of year at North Rim (8,000 ft/2,427 m). In summer, inner canyon temperatures can reach 120°F/49°C on canyon floor. Arrive early in the day because parking is limited. Expect crowds during winter holiday weekends and all summer. Avoid midday. Busiest in July and August, least crowded in December and January. ▨ **Fees, Permits & Limitations:** Entrance fee: $20 per vehicle, $10 per bicyclist or walk-in. Permit required ($10) for all backcountry camping. Hermit Rd. and Yaki Point closed to private vehicles Mar. 1–Nov. 30. Free shuttle service available in Grand Canyon Village to South Kaibab Trailhead and on Hermit Rd. Mar. 1–Nov. 30. Bus tours available (tel. 520/638–2631 or 303/297–2757 for advance reservations). Mule trips into canyon available (tel. 520/638–2631 or 303/297–2757 for advance reservations). Horse rides available (tel. 520/638–2891). Air tours available (contact Canyon View Center for tour operators). Rafting available (tel. 520/638–2631 or 800/528–6154, 303/297–2757 for advance reservations or contact visitor center for list of river trip operators). The park's South Rim open daily; North Rim Road closed late Nov.–mid-May. Canyon View Information Plaza, Kolb Studio, and Yavapai Observation Station open early fall–late spring, daily 8–5; late spring–early fall, daily 8–7. Desert View open Mar.–Oct., daily 9–7. North Rim Visitor Center open summer, daily 8–6. Tusayan Museum open spring–fall, daily 9–5; winter, daily, hours vary.

HOW TO GET THERE

Grand Canyon Village on the South Rim is 60 mi/96 km north of I–40 at Williams via Hwy. 64 and 80 mi/128 km northwest of Flagstaff via U.S. 180. The North Rim is 44 mi/70 km south of Jacob Lake via Hwy. 67. Bus service available from Flagstaff and Williams via Nava-Hopi Bus Tours (tel. 800/892–8687). Historic steam train service available from Williams (tel. 800/843–8724). Shuttle from Tusayan to Grand Canyon Village available (tel. 520/638–0871 or 520/638–0821). Taxis available from Grand Canyon National Park Lodges, tel. 520/638–2631 ext. 6563. Closest airports: Grand Canyon Tusayan (8 mi/13 km); Flagstaff, AZ (80 mi/128 km); Phoenix, AZ (220 mi/352 km); Las Vegas, NV (291 mi/466km).

FOR MORE INFORMATION

Trip Planner, Grand Canyon National Park (Box 129, Grand Canyon, AZ 86023, tel. 520/638–7888; Web site www.nps.gov/grca). Flagstaff Chamber of Commerce (101 W. Rte. 66, Flagstaff, AZ 86001, tel. 520/774–4505). Grand Canyon (Tusayan) Chamber of Commerce (Box 3007, Grand Canyon, AZ 86023, tel. 520/638–2901). Kane County (Utah) Chamber of Commerce (78 E. 100 S, Kanab, UT 84741, tel. 435/644–5033). Kingman Chamber of Commerce (120 W. Andy Devine, Kingman, AZ 86401, tel. 520/753–6106). Page Chamber of Commerce (Box 727, Page, AZ 86040, tel. 520/645–2741). Williams Chamber of Commerce (200 W. Railroad Ave., Williams, AZ 86046, tel. 520/635–4061). Flagstaff Visitor Center (1 E. Rte. 66, Flagstaff, AZ

86001, tel. 520/774–9541 or 800/842–7293). Arizona Office of Tourism (2702 N. 3rd St., Suite 4015, Phoenix, AZ 85004, tel. 800/842–8257).

Hohokam Pima National Monument

In the south-central part of the state, south of Phoenix

Preserved here are the archaeological remains of a Hohokam village that was occupied between AD 300 and AD 1100. Hohokam is a Pima Indian word meaning "those who have gone."

WHAT TO SEE & DO

The site is closed to the public.

FOR MORE INFORMATION

Hohokam Pima National Monument (c/o Casa Grande Ruins National Monument, Box 518, Coolidge, AZ 85228, tel. 520/723–3172; Web site www.nps.gov/pima).

Hubbell Trading Post National Historic Site

In the northeast part of the state, near Ganado

This site, located in the Navajo Nation, commemorates the distinctive role of the Native American trader in the American Southwest. The post has a preeminent place in the history and ethnography of the Navajo people. It still functions much the way John Lorenzo Hubbell operated it in the late 1800s and is internationally renowned for authentic and high-quality Native American arts. The site was designated a National Historic Site in 1965 and transferred to the National Park Service in 1967.

WHAT TO SEE & DO

Buying arts and crafts, jewelry, and rugs; picnicking; touring the post and Hubbell homestead; watching Navajo weavers. **Facilities:** Visitor center with Navajo weavers, trading post, Hubbell homestead. Bookstore, picnic areas. **Programs & Events:** Homestead walks, Navajo culture and rug talks, tours of the Hubbell family home. Pueblo Colorado Wash walking tour (May–Sept.), Native American Arts Auction (Apr., Aug.), Old Time Trading Days (one weekend, Aug.), Luminaria Night (Dec.).

PLANNING YOUR VISIT

⚠ **Camping:** Available in Canyon de Chelly National Monument (*see separate entry*) and Gallup, NM; none in park. 🛏 **Lodging:** Available in Chambers, Chinle, Window Rock; none in park. ✗ **Food & Supplies:** At the post: grocery store. Food and supplies also available in Ganado.

☞ **Tips & Hints:** Because the Navajo Nation observes daylight saving time but the State of Arizona does not, Navajo Nation time is one hour later than time in the State of Arizona from April to October. Busiest in June and July, least crowded in December and January. ▦ **Fees, Permits & Limitations:** Free. Site and visitor center open Oct.–Apr., daily 8–5; May–Sept., daily 8–6. Closed Thanksgiving, Dec. 25, Jan. 1.

HOW TO GET THERE

On AZ 264, ½ mi/1 km west of Ganado. Closest airports: Gallup, NM (60 mi/96 km); Albuquerque, NM (180 mi/288 km).

FOR MORE INFORMATION

Hubbell Trading Post National Historic Site (Box 150, Ganado, AZ 86505, tel. 520/755–3475, fax 520/755–3405; e-mail hutr_interpretation@nps.gov; Web site www.nps.gov/hutr). Gallup Convention and Visitors Bureau (Box 600, Gallup, NM 87301, tel. 505/863–3841 or 800/242–4282, fax 505/863–2280). Gallup Chamber of Commerce (103 W. Hwy. 66, Gallup NM 87301, tel. 505/722–2228).

Montezuma Castle National Monument

In the central part of the state, near Camp Verde

Montezuma Castle is one of the best-preserved prehistoric structures in the Southwest. Sinagua farmers began building the five-story, 20-room dwelling in the 12th century. Early settlers marveled at the structure and thought mistakenly that it was Aztecan in origin. A detached unit of the monument, known as Montezuma Well, is a limestone sink that measures more than 400 ft/121 m across and supplied irrigation water to the prehistoric people. The monument was proclaimed in 1906.

WHAT TO SEE & DO

Hiking, picnicking, viewing castle and well. **Facilities:** Visitor center, castle, well, interpretive trails. Book sales area, picnic tables. **Programs & Events:** Ranger talks (as staffing permits).

PLANNING YOUR VISIT

⚠ **Camping:** Available in Camp Verde area; none at monument. ▣ **Lodging:** Available in Camp Verde area; none at monument. ✕ **Food & Supplies:** Available in Camp Verde area; none at monument. ☞ **Tips & Hints:** Avoid summer heat. Go in spring or fall. Busiest in March and April, least crowded in December and January. ▦ **Fees, Permits & Limitations:** Entrance fee at press time: $2 per person 17 and older. Leashed pets only. Monument and visitor center open Sept.–May, daily 8–5; June–Aug., daily 8–7.

HOW TO GET THERE

3 mi/5 km north of Camp Verde on Montezuma Castle Hwy., off I–17. Closest airport: Flagstaff (50 mi/80 km).

FOR MORE INFORMATION

Montezuma Castle National Monument (Box 219, Camp Verde, AZ 86322, tel. 520/567–3322; Web site www.nps.gov/moca). Camp Verde Chamber of Commerce (Box 3520, Camp Verde, AZ 86322, tel. 520/567–9294).

Navajo National Monument

In the northeast part of the state, near Kayenta

Well-preserved ruins of villages abandoned around AD 1300 by prehistoric Pueblo peoples are the attractions in this park. Built and occupied for only 50 years, the ruins represent the final settlement of farmers who adapted to the area's scarce rainfall to grow crops, build houses, and raise families. Betatakin, Keet Seel, and Inscription House (closed since 1968 because of its fragility) are three cliff dwellings at the site. The monument was proclaimed on March 20, 1909.

WHAT TO SEE & DO

Hiking, picnicking, viewing ruins. **Facilities:** Visitor center with interpretive exhibits, trails, overlooks, ruins. Arts and crafts store, bookstore, picnic area. **Programs & Events:** Ranger-led tours (Memorial Day–Labor Day), evening campfire programs (as staffing permits).

PLANNING YOUR VISIT

Camping: Campground: no hookups (no reservations). Backcountry camping available at Keet Seel (permit required, *see below*). Group campsites (reservations available, tel. 520/672–2366). **Lodging:** Available in Kayenta, Page, Tsegi, and Tuba City, AZ, and Monument Valley, UT; none in park. **Food & Supplies:** Available in Black Mesa, Kayenta, Tuba City; none in park. **Tips & Hints:** Busiest in July and August, least crowded in January and February. **Fees, Permits & Limitations:** Free. Access to ruins by ranger-guided tour only. Backcountry permit covers camping at Keet Seel only in conjunction with a visit to Keet Seel. Surrounding backcountry land is Navajo property and off limits to visitors. No collecting. No wood or charcoal fires. Campstoves only. Monument closed Thanksgiving, Dec. 25, Jan. 1.

HOW TO GET THERE

The visitor center turnoff at Black Mesa on SR 564 is 50 mi/80 km northeast of Tuba City and 19 mi/30 km southwest of Kayenta off US 160. Turn north on SR 564 and travel 9 mi/14 km to the visitor center. Closest airport: Page (88 mi/141 km).

FOR MORE INFORMATION

Navajo National Monument (HC-71, Box 3, Tonalea, AZ 86044-9704, tel. 520/672–2366/2367, fax 520/672–2345; Web site www.nps.gov/nava).

Organ Pipe Cactus National Monument

In the southwest part of the state, near Ajo

An extraordinary collection of plants and animals of the Sonoran Desert is displayed in this monument, including the organ pipe cactus, a large cactus rarely found in the United States. Gila monsters, rattlesnakes, and scorpions are among the creatures that have adapted to the region's extreme temperatures, intense sunlight, and infrequent rainfall. The monument was proclaimed in 1937 and designated a Biosphere Reserve in 1976.

WHAT TO SEE & DO

Auto touring, backpacking, bird- and wildlife watching, hiking, mountain biking, picnicking. **Facilities:** Visitor center with interpretive exhibits, self-guided nature trail, amphitheater, scenic drives. Bookstore, picnic areas. **Programs & Events:** Guided hikes, interpretive talks and evening programs (mid-Dec.–mid-Apr., daily). O'Odham Day Celebration (mid-Mar.).

PLANNING YOUR VISIT

Camping: 2 campgrounds: 1 with dump station, freshwater spigots at main campground by visitor center and rest rooms, no hookups (no reservations), maximum vehicle length: 35 ft/10.6 m; 1 primitive campground (no reservations; permit required, *see below*). Backcountry camping available (permit required, *see below*). Group camping available (reservations required, tel. 520/387–6849). Primitive camping also at Alamo Canyon. Private campgrounds in Ajo, Lukeville, and Why. **Lodging:** Available in Ajo and Lukeville, AZ, and Sonoyta, Mexico; none in park. **X Food & Supplies:** Available in Ajo, Lukeville, Why; none in park. **☞ Tips & Hints:** Beware of the cactus and six varieties of rattlesnakes, as well as Gila monsters and scorpions. Be prepared for desert walking. Carry one gallon of drinking water per person per day. Best time to camp and hike is between mid-November and mid-March. Go between mid-March and mid-April for flowers, and in April and September for migrating birds. Busiest January through March, least crowded in July and August. **☒ Fees, Permits & Limitations:** Entrance fee: $2 per person on bike or foot, $4 per vehicle. Backcountry and primitive camping permits required. No collecting. No hunting. No off-road vehicles. No pets in backcountry. Leashed pets elsewhere. Special trails marked for pet use. Mountain bikes on maintained roads only. Maximum vehicle length recommended on scenic drives: 25 ft/7.6 m. Monument open daily. Visitor center open daily 8–5. Closed Dec. 25.

HOW TO GET THERE

The monument headquarters is 22 mi/35 km south of Why via Hwy. 85. Closest airports: Phoenix and Tucson (150 mi/240 km).

FOR MORE INFORMATION

Organ Pipe Cactus National Monument (Rte. 1, Box 100, Ajo, AZ 85321, tel. 520/387–6849, fax 520/387–7144; Web site www.nps.gov/orpi). Ajo

Chamber of Commerce (400 Taludro St., Ajo, AZ 85321, tel. 520/387–7742).

Petrified Forest National Park

In the northeast part of the state, near Holbrook

Petrified Forest has one of the world's largest and most colorful concentrations of petrified wood. The park's 93,533 acres also include the multihued badlands of the Painted Desert, archaeological sites, and displays of 225-million-year-old fossils. This tableland is also one of the last pristine vestiges of "high desert" and its inhabitants. The park was designated a national monument in 1906 and a national park in 1962.

WHAT TO SEE & DO

Backpacking, hiking, viewing film, walking, wildlife watching. **Facilities:** Visitor center—Painted Desert; Painted Desert Inn National Historic Landmark with archaeology displays, Rainbow Forest Museum, trails, interpretive signs and guidebooks. Covered picnic tables, gas stations, gift shops, post office. **Programs & Events:** Ranger-led interpretive talks, walks, and hikes (year-round). Summer Solstice at Puerco Pueblo, a prehistoric solar calendar at work (June 14–28, 8:30 AM). Special events available.

PLANNING YOUR VISIT

Camping: Backcountry camping available (permit required, *see below*). Private campgrounds in Holbrook. **Lodging:** Available in Holbrook; none in park. **Food & Supplies:** Cafeteria and travel store (north entrance, tel. 520/524–3756), snack bar/soda fountain (south entrance, tel. 520/524–3138). Food and supplies also available in Holbrook. **Tips & Hints:** Prepare for summer temperatures near 90°F/35°C, high elevation (5,100/1,547 m–6,235 ft/1,891 m), and high winds. Visit in spring and fall. Busiest in July and August, least crowded in December and January. **Fees, Permits & Limitations:** Entrance fee: $10 per private vehicle or $5 for walk-ins and bicyclists. Backcountry permits required (free, visitor center or Rainbow Forest Museum). No collecting. Gift shops sell petrified wood that has been legally obtained from private land outside the park boundaries. Motorized vehicles and bicycles on paved roads only. No four-wheel-drive vehicles or mountain biking. No pets in buildings, in backcountry, or on Giant Logs Trail. Leashed pets elsewhere. Park, visitor center, and museum open mid-May–early Sept., daily 7–7; Sept.–May, daily 7:30–5. Closed Dec. 25. Park gates are locked at night.

HOW TO GET THERE

The park stretches between I–40 and U.S. 180. From the west, enter the south end of the park off U.S. 180. Travel through the park and exit I–40E. From the east, enter at exit 311 of I–40. Travel through the park to U.S. 180 on to Holbrook and I–40W. The north entrance is 25 mi/40 km east of Holbrook on I–40. The south entrance is 19 mi/30 km east of Holbrook on U.S. 180. Closest airports: Holbrook or Flagstaff (125 mi/200 km); Gallup, NM (60 mi/100 km).

FOR MORE INFORMATION

Superintendent, Petrified Forest National Park (Box 2217, Petrified Forest, AZ 86028, tel. 520/524–6228; Web site www.nps.gov/pefo). Holbrook Chamber of Commerce (100 E. Arizona St., Holbrook, AZ 86025, tel. 520/524–6558 or 800/524–2459).

Pipe Spring National Monument

In the north part of the state, near Fredonia

Pipe Spring's waters allow plant and animal life to thrive in this desert region north of the Grand Canyon. Beginning at least 1,000 years ago, ancestral Puebloans and later Paiutes raised crops in the area. In 1871, Mormon pioneers built a fort over the main spring and established a cattle-ranching operation. The monument commemorates western pioneer settlement and American Indian–pioneer interactions on the frontier. The monument was proclaimed on May 31, 1923.

WHAT TO SEE & DO

Hiking ½-mi trail, touring the "Winsor Castle" fort and grounds. **Facilities:** Visitor center with interpretive exhibits, castle, audio stations on grounds, trail. Bookstore and gift shop. **Programs & Events:** Ranger-guided tours of castle (daily, 8–4:30 every half hour). Ranger talks (June–Sept., 2–3 times a day), cultural demonstrations (June–Sept., 3–6 times a week).

PLANNING YOUR VISIT

Camping: Kaibab-Paiute Tribe campground just outside monument (full hookups, rest rooms, and showers); private campgrounds in Fredonia, AZ, and Kanab, UT; none at monument. **Lodging:** Available in Fredonia, AZ, and Kanab, UT; none at monument. ✗ **Food & Supplies:** Food and supplies available near monument and in Fredonia, AZ, and Kanab, UT; none at monument. ☞ **Tips & Hints:** Watch for rattlesnakes in summer. Stay on sidewalks. Go in March, April, September, or October for bird migrations, May and September for flower blooms. Busiest in July and August, least crowded in December and January. **Fees, Permits & Limitations:** Entrance fee: $2 per person 17 and up. No bikes or motorized vehicles. No pets in historic buildings. Leashed pets only on trails. Monument open daily 8–5. Closed Thanksgiving, Dec. 25, Jan. 1.

HOW TO GET THERE

15 mi/24 km west of Fredonia, AZ, via AZ 389: 60 mi/96 km east of Hurricane, UT, via UT 59 and AZ 389. Closest airport: St. George, UT (65 mi/104 km).

FOR MORE INFORMATION

Pipe Spring National Monument (HC 65 Box 5, Fredonia, AZ 86022, tel. 520/643–7105, fax 520/643–7583; Web site www.nps.gov/pisp). Kane County Travel Council (78 S. 100 E, Kanab, UT 84741, tel. 435/644–5033).

Saguaro National Park

In the south-central part of the state, near Tucson

The saguaro cactus, which can grow 50 ft/15 m tall in a 200-year life span, was the primary reason for creating the park, which has districts on each side of Tucson. But the park is home to many other wonders as well. More than 1,000 species of plant life dot the lower elevations of the 91,453-acre park. Douglas fir and Ponderosa pine are common forests at 8,000 ft/2,427 m. Nearly 320 km/200 mi of hiking trails challenge visitors. Numerous historic structures blend into the vistas, and ancient Hohokam petroglyphs abound in this predominantly wilderness park. The site was proclaimed a national monument in 1933 and redesignated a national park in 1994.

WHAT TO SEE & DO

Auto touring, biking, hiking. **Facilities:** 2 visitor centers—East District (Old Spanish Trail at Freeman Rd. east of Tucson), Red Hills West District (Kinney Rd. west of Tucson); cactus gardens, hiking trails, scenic drives, bike paths. Bookstore, picnic areas with shade ramadas. **Programs & Events:** Interpretive walks and talks (mostly in cooler months).

PLANNING YOUR VISIT

⚠ **Camping:** Backcountry camping available (permit required, *see below*). Private campgrounds available in Tucson area. ⛺ **Lodging:** Available in Tucson area; none in park. ✕ **Food & Supplies:** Available in Tucson area; none in park. ☞ **Tips & Hints:** Go between late March and early April (usually) for desert plant blooms, March through May for saguaro blooms. Busiest November through March, least crowded in June and July. ▦ **Fees, Permits & Limitations:** Entrance fee: $6 per vehicle for scenic loop drive in East District only, $3 for pedestrians and bicyclists. Backcountry permit for camping required (free, East Side visitor center). No pets on trails. Leashed pets on roads. East District road open daily 7 AM–sunset; West District road open daily 6 AM–sunset. Visitor centers open daily 8:30–5. Closed Dec. 25.

HOW TO GET THERE

Reach East District and park headquarters from Tucson by driving east on Speedway, Broadway, or Old Spanish Trail; reach West District via Speedway Blvd. W. Closest airport: Tucson.

FOR MORE INFORMATION

Saguaro National Park (3693 S. Old Spanish Trail, Tucson, AZ 85710, tel. 520/733–5153, fax 520/733–5183; Web site www.nps.gov/sagu). Tucson Chamber of Commerce (465 W. St. Mary's Rd., Tucson, AZ 85701, tel. 520/792–1212).

Sunset Crater Volcano National Monument

In the north-central part of the state, near Flagstaff

A volcano that erupted in the winter of 1064–1065, when molten rock sprayed high into the air out of a crack in the ground, is protected here. Periodic eruptions that may have lasted as long as 200 years formed a cinder cone 1,000 ft/304 m high. Lava that flowed from the base of the volcano appears now as a stark, jagged landscape. The site was proclaimed a national monument in 1930 and transferred from the Forest Service in 1933.

WHAT TO SEE & DO

Auto touring, hiking, picnicking, touring museum, walking. **Facilities:** Visitor center with interpretive exhibits and movie (2 mi/3 km east of Hwy. 89 on Forest Rd. 545), wayside exhibits, trails, self-guided walks, overlook, scenic loop drive. Book and map sales area, picnic tables. **Programs & Events:** Ranger-guided walks in morning and afternoon (daily, June–Aug.), evening programs (Fri., Sat., and some weekdays, June–Aug.).

PLANNING YOUR VISIT

⚠ **Camping:** Available in Coconino National Forest's Bonito Campground (tel. 520/526–0866) near visitor center; none in park. 🏠 **Lodging:** Available in Flagstaff; none in park. ✗ **Food & Supplies:** Available in Flagstaff; none in park. ☞ **Tips & Hints:** Watch for deep, narrow cracks in the earth and razor-sharp lava when hiking. Drink water and moderate activity at high elevation (7,000 ft/2,123 m). Use caution on unpaved roads because vehicles can become stuck in soft cinders (in dry weather) or mud (during flash floods). Come between June and October for best weather. Busiest in June and July, least crowded in January and February. ✉ **Fees, Permits & Limitations:** Entrance fee: $3 per person over 16. Sunset Crater Volcano closed to hiking but other nearby volcanoes can be climbed. No pets on trails. Leashed pets only in parking lots and picnic areas. No bicycles or motorized equipment on hiking trails. No hunting. Park open daily sunrise–sunset. Visitor center open fall–spring, daily 8–5; summer, daily 8–6. Closed Dec. 25.

HOW TO GET THERE

Reach park from Flagstaff via Hwy. 89 for 13 mi/21 km and Forest Rd. 545 for 2 mi/3 km. Closest airport: Flagstaff.

FOR MORE INFORMATION

Sunset Crater Volcano National Monument (Rte. 3, Box 149, Flagstaff, AZ 86004, tel. 520/526–0502, fax 520/714–0565; e-mail FLAG_-_Sunset_Crater@nps.gov; Web site www.nps.gov/sucr). Flagstaff Visitor Services (1 E. Rte. 66, Flagstaff, AZ 86001-5754, tel. 520/774–9541 or 800/842–7293, fax 520/556–1308).

Tonto National Monument

In south central Arizona, near Roosevelt Lake

Well-preserved cliff dwellings here were occupied during the 13th and 14th centuries by the Salado culture, which farmed the Tonto Basin Valley. It is the only Salado site in the park system. The monument was proclaimed in 1907.

WHAT TO SEE & DO

Hiking to cliff dwellings (permit required, *see below*), picnicking, touring museum, watching video program. **Facilities:** Visitor center with interpretive exhibits (1 mi/2 km off Hwy. 88), trails. Bookstore, picnic area. **Programs & Events:** Upper Cliffdwelling tours and guided hikes (Nov.–Apr.); Lower Cliffdwelling interpretive talks, self-guided tours (on request). Open House to Upper Cliffdwelling (1st weekend, Nov.; 1 weekend, Mar.).

PLANNING YOUR VISIT

Camping: Available in Globe, Miami, Payson, Punkin Center, Roosevelt Lake; none at monument. **Lodging:** Available in Globe, Miami, Payson, Punkin Center, Roosevelt; none at monument. **Food & Supplies:** Available in Globe, Miami, Payson, Punkin Center, Roosevelt, Roosevelt Marina, Tonto Basin; none at monument. **Tips & Hints:** Watch for snakes and cactus. Stay on trail. Permit required for hiking. Visit in November–April. Busiest January through March, least crowded June through August. **Fees, Permits & Limitations:** Entrance fee: $4 per vehicle or $2 per person on bikes, walking, or on bus. No hunting. No resource gathering. Leashed pets only at Visitor Center and Lower Cliffdwelling trail. No pets on Upper Cliffdwelling trail. Stay on trails. No fires. Park and visitor center open daily 8–5, Lower Cliffdwelling trail open daily 8–4. Closed Dec. 25.

HOW TO GET THERE

65 mi/104 km northeast of Phoenix via Hwy. 88E; 30 mi/48 km northwest of Globe; and 55 mi/88 km south of Payson. Closest airport: Phoenix.

FOR MORE INFORMATION

Tonto National Monument (HC02, Box 4602, Roosevelt, AZ 85545, tel. 520/467–2241, fax 520/467–2225; Web site www.nps.gov/tont). Greater Globe/Miami Chamber of Commerce (1360 N. Broad, Globe, AZ 85501, tel. 520/425–4495). Payson Chamber of Commerce (100 W. Main, Payson, AZ 85541, tel. 520/474–4515).

Tumacacori
National Historical Park

In the southern part of the state, near Nogales

Tumacacori was established in 1691 by Father Eusebio Francisco Kino, an Italian-born Jesuit priest. At that time, Tumacacori was the northern frontier of the Spanish colonial empire. The Jesuits, and later the Franciscans, attempted to convert the native population to Christianity and incorporate them into Spanish society. The conversion of these native people, known as the Pima, was only partly successful. At Tumacacori, you will find the stabilized ruins of the Franciscan church, a cemetery, and other outbuildings. The park was proclaimed a national monument in 1908 and redesignated in 1990.

WHAT TO SEE & DO

Picnicking; self-guided and ranger-led tours of the museum, church, and other historic structures. **Facilities:** Visitor center with interpretive exhibits, video, historic structures, trail, interpretive signs. Bookstore, picnic tables. **Programs & Events:** Ranger-led tours (Oct.–Apr., generally at 11 and 2 daily and by special arrangement); crafts demonstrations such as tortilla, paper-flower, and pottery making; glass painting; and basket weaving (Oct.–Jan. and Apr.–May, weekends; Feb.–Mar., daily). Fiesta (1st weekend, Dec.); Latin High Mass (twice yearly, usually May and Oct.); Full Moon and special night tours with musicians and crafts demonstrations (occasionally); Photo Scavenger Hunt for children (upon request).

PLANNING YOUR VISIT

Lodging: Available in Amado, Green Valley, Nogales, Rio Rico, Tubac, Tumacacori; none in park. **Food & Supplies:** Available in Amado, Green Valley, Nogales, Rio Rico, Tubac, Tumacacori; none in park. **Tips & Hints:** Allow two hours to see the park. Prepare for 100°F/38°C temperatures in summer and below-freezing temperatures on winter nights. Busiest January through March, least crowded June through September. **Fees, Permits & Limitations:** Entrance fee: $2 per person 17 and older or $4 per car. No hunting, bicycling, or collecting historic or natural artifacts. Park open daily 8–5. Closed Thanksgiving, Dec. 25.

HOW TO GET THERE

Tumacacori is 45 mi/72 km south of Tucson and 18 mi/29 km north of the Mexican border in Nogales via Exits 29 or 34 off 1–19. Closest airport: Tucson.

FOR MORE INFORMATION

Tumacacori National Historical Park (Box 67, Tumacacori, AZ 85640, tel. 520/398–2341, fax 520/398–9271; Web site www.nps.gov/tuma).

Tuzigoot
National Monument

In the central part of the state, near Cottonwood

Tuzigoot, an Apache word meaning "crooked water," is the remnant of a Sinaguan village built between 1125 and 1400. The original pueblo was two stories high in places and had 77 ground-floor rooms. The monument was proclaimed on July 25, 1939.

WHAT TO SEE & DO

Bird-watching, viewing ruins, walking the trails. **Facilities:** Visitor center, ruins, trails. Book sale area. **Programs & Events:** Interpretive programs (as staffing permits).

PLANNING YOUR VISIT

⚠ **Camping:** State campground nearby; none at monument. ⛺ **Lodging:** Available in Clarkdale and Cottonwood; none at monument. ✕ **Food & Supplies:** Available in Clarkdale and Cottonwood; none at monument. ☞ **Tips & Hints:** Visit in spring and fall. Busiest in March and April, least crowded in December and January. ✉ **Fees, Permits & Limitations:** Entrance fee at press time: $2 per person over 16 years. Leashed pets only. Visitor center and Monument open Labor Day–Memorial Day, daily 8–5; Memorial Day–Labor Day, daily 8–7. Closed Dec. 25.

HOW TO GET THERE

2 mi/3 km east of Clarkdale along U.S. 89A and 50 mi/80 km south of Flagstaff via U.S. Alt. 89. Closest airport: Flagstaff.

FOR MORE INFORMATION

Tuzigoot National Monument (Box 219, Camp Verde, AZ 86322, tel. 520/634–5564; Web site www.nps.gov/tuzi). Cottonwood Chamber of Commerce (1010 S. Main St., Cottonwood, AZ 86326, tel. 520/634–7593).

Walnut Canyon
National Monument

In the north-central part of the state, near Flagstaff

Cliff dwellings built by Pueblo Indians between 1100 and 1250 are preserved in this monument. Using existing limestone alcoves, the Native Americans built side and front walls and nature provided the roof overhang. The presence of water at the time the Sinaguans lived in the canyon probably made this a very desirable place to live. The Sinagua (Spanish for "without water") were dry-land farmers who grew crops on the canyon rims and supplemented their diet by hunting and gathering. Their departure around 1250 is a subject for speculation, but archaeologists think that Hopi people who live on mesas in northern Arizona today are probably the descendants of the Sinagua. The park was proclaimed on November 30, 1915.

WHAT TO SEE & DO

Hiking, picnicking, touring cliff dwellings. **Facilities:** Visitor center with interpretive exhibits, self-guided 0.75-mi/1.2-km and 0.9-mi/1.4-km interpretive trails, interpretive display boards. Bookstore, picnic areas. **Programs & Events:** Ranger-guided hikes, interpretive talks (June–Sept., when staffing permits).

PLANNING YOUR VISIT

⚠ **Camping:** Available in Flagstaff area; none in park. ⊞ **Lodging:** Available in Flagstaff area; none in park. ✕ **Food & Supplies:** Available in Flagstaff area; none in park. ☞ **Tips & Hints:** The Island Trail may be strenuous: it descends 240 steps at an elevation of 6,800 ft/2,063 m. Borrow baby backpacks from visitor center for Island Trail hikes because strollers aren't allowed. Limited parking space for large vehicles. Busiest in June and July, least crowded in December and January. ▱ **Fees, Permits & Limitations:** Entrance fee: $3 per person over 16. No pets on trails or in visitor center. Stay on trails. No hunting or firearms. No open fires. Gas stoves only. No collecting potsherds, rocks, pinecones, flowers. Park and visitor center open Dec.–Feb., daily 9–5; Mar.–May and Sept.–Nov., daily 8–5; June–Aug., daily 8–6.

HOW TO GET THERE

10 mi/16 km east of Flagstaff, off I–40 via Exit 204. Closest airport: Flagstaff.

FOR MORE INFORMATION

Walnut Canyon National Monument (Walnut Canyon Rd., Flagstaff, AZ 86004, tel. 520/526–3367, fax 520/527–0246; Web site www.nps. gov/waca). Flagstaff Visitor Services (1 E. Rte. 66, Flagstaff AZ 86001–5754, tel. 520/774–9541 or 800/842–7293, fax 520/556–1308).

Wupatki National Monument

Near Flagstaff

The monument preserves the ruins of red sandstone pueblos built about 1100 by farming Sinagua and Anasazi people. Made from slabs of sandstone, limestone, and basalt and held together with clay-based mortar, the dwellings were inhabited until about 1225. Wupatki was the largest pueblo of its day in the Flagstaff area. The modern Hopi are believed to be partly descended from these people. The monument was proclaimed on December 9, 1924.

WHAT TO SEE & DO

Self-guided walking to four sites. **Facilities:** Visitor center with interpretive exhibits, interpretive signboards. Book and map sale area. **Programs & Events:** Discovery hikes (June–Aug., Sat. for 3–4 hrs).

PLANNING YOUR VISIT

⚠ **Camping:** Available in Cameron, Flagstaff, Coconino National Forest Bonito Campground (tel. 520/526–0866); none at monument. ⊞ **Lodging:** Available in Cameron, Flagstaff, Gray Mountain; none at monument. ✕ **Food & Supplies:** Available in Cameron, Flagstaff, Gray Mountain; none at monument. ☞ **Tips & Hints:** Busiest in June and July, least crowded in December and January. ▨ **Fees, Permits & Limitations:** Entrance fee: $3 per person, free under 17. No pets or bikes on trails. No off-trail hiking. Monument open daily sunrise–sunset. Visitor center open June–Sept., daily 8–6; Oct.–May, daily 8–5. Closed Dec. 25.

HOW TO GET THERE

40 mi/64 km north of Flagstaff via U.S. 89 and Forest Rd. 545, a 35-mi/56-km loop road that connects Wupatki with Sunset Crater Volcano National Monument (*see separate entry*). Closest airport: Flagstaff (46 mi/74 km).

FOR MORE INFORMATION

Wupatki National Monument (HC 33, Box 444A, Flagstaff, AZ 86004, tel. 520/679–2365, fax 520/679–2349; Web site www.nps.gov/wupa). Flagstaff Convention and Visitors Bureau (211 W. Aspen Ave., Flagstaff, AZ 86001, tel. 520/779–7611, fax 520/556–1305).

See Also

Juan Bautista de Anza National Historic Trail, National Trails System in Other National Parklands. *Lake Mead National Recreation Area,* Nevada.

ARKANSAS

Arkansas Post
National Memorial

In the southeast part of the state, near Gillett

This memorial on the banks of the Arkansas River commemorates the site's complex history, which began when Frenchman Henri de Tonty established the "Poste de Arkansea" in 1686 at a Quapaw village near the confluence of the Mississippi and Arkansas rivers. After a century of struggle among the French, Spanish, and English for control of interior North America, the United States bought the area in 1803 from the French as part of the Louisiana Purchase. The post thrived in the first half of the 19th century but fell into decline after the Union Army destroyed much of a Confederate fort located here. Activities include fishing, watching wildlife, and exploring remnants of the town site and Civil War earthworks. The memorial was authorized on July 6, 1960.

WHAT TO SEE & DO

Fishing, hiking, picnicking, touring museum, watching film. **Facilities:** Visitor center with interpretive exhibits, scenic drive, trails, wayside exhibits. Bookstore, grills, picnic areas. **Programs & Events:** Self-guided tours of town site and nature trails. Special events and historical reenactments.

PLANNING YOUR VISIT

⚲ **Camping:** Available in Pendleton, Lake Merrisach parks; none at memorial. ⬚ **Lodging:** Available in DeWitt, Dumas, Gillett; none at memorial. ✕ **Food & Supplies:** Available in DeWitt, Dumas, Gillett; none at memorial. ☞ **Tips & Hints:** Watch for alligators. Busiest in May and June, least crowded in November and December. ▣ **Fees, Permits & Limitations:** Free. Arkansas state fishing license required. No hunting or firearms. Fires in grills only. Leashed pets only. Park open daily 8–dark. Visitor center open daily 8–5. Closed Thanksgiving, Dec. 25, Jan. 1.

HOW TO GET THERE

On State Rd. 169 9 mi/14 km south of Gillett via U.S. 165 (Great River Rd.); 17 mi/27 km northeast of Dumas via U.S. 165. Closest airport: Little Rock (100 mi/160 km).

FOR MORE INFORMATION

Arkansas Post National Memorial (1741 Old Post Rd., Gillett, AR 72055, tel. 870/548–2207, fax 870/548–2431; Web site www.nps.gov/arpo).

Buffalo National River

In the north-central part of the state, near Harrison

Totaling about 95,700 acres, this unpolluted national river encompasses 135 mi/216 km of the 150-mi-/240-km-long Buffalo River, which begins as a trickle in the Boston Mountains, 15 mi/24 km above the park boundary. Following what is likely an ancient riverbed, the Buffalo cuts its way through massive limestone bluffs and travels east through the Ozarks and into the White River. The national river has three designated wilderness areas totaling 36,000 acres within its boundaries. The national river was authorized on March 1, 1972.

WHAT TO SEE & DO

Canoeing (rentals), fishing, hiking, horseback riding, picnicking, swimming. **Facilities:** Tyler Bend visitor center (Middle District, 11 mi/18 km north of Marshall on U.S. 65), Park Headquarters (Walnut and Erie Sts., Harrison), Pruitt Upper District Ranger Station (5 mi/8 km north of Jasper on Hwy. 7), Buffalo Point Lower District information stations (17 mi/27 km south of Yellville on Hwys. 14/268); over 100 mi/160 km of trails. Bookstores, picnic areas. **Programs & Events:** Ranger-led hikes, canoe trips, and evening programs (Memorial Day–Labor Day).

PLANNING YOUR VISIT

Camping: 14 campgrounds, 12 primitive, 1 with hookups (no reservations). **Lodging:** In the park: 5 rustic and 8 modern cabins (reservations available, tel. 870/449–6206 or write Buffalo Point Concession, Buffalo National River, HCR 66, 2261 Hwy 268E, Box 388, Yellville, AR 72687). Lodging also available in Harrison, Jasper, and Yellville. **Food & Supplies:** In the park: meals at Buffalo Point Restaurant (Memorial Day–Labor Day, tel. 870/449–5900). Food and supplies also available in Harrison, Jasper, and Yellville. **Tips & Hints:** Allow an hour for visitor center. Bring a wet suit if you plan to canoe between December and February, rain gear March–May, shorts and T-shirts June–August. For best floating, go to Upper District March–May, to Middle District May–June, and to Lower District June–August. Park busiest in June and July, least crowded in January and February. **Fees, Permits & Limitations:** Free. Park open daily. Visitor center daily 8–4:30. Park headquarters open weekdays 8–4:30. Pruitt Ranger Station open Memorial Day–Labor Day, daily 8–4:30; spring, limited basis. Buffalo Point Upper Ranger Station open daily 8–4:30, Campground Station open Memorial Day–Labor Day, daily 8–4:30.

HOW TO GET THERE

Middle District: U.S. 65S from Harrison for 31 mi/50 km; Upper District: Hwy. 7 or 43 from Harrison; Lower District: Hwy. 65S out of Harrison 5 mi/8 km, then Hwy. 62/412E and Hwy. 14S. Closest airports: Harrison, Fayetteville, or Little Rock, AR (150 mi/240km); Springfield, MO (80 mi/128 km).

FOR MORE INFORMATION

Buffalo National River (Box 1173, Harrison, AR 72602, tel. 870/741–5443; Web site www.nps.gov/buff).

Central High School National Historic Site

In the center of the state, in Little Rock

Little Rock High School, now Central High School National Historic Site, is a national emblem of the often violent struggle over school desegregation and represents the federal government's commitment to eliminating separate systems of education for blacks and whites. It is the only operating high school to be designated a national historic site. The site was designated on November 6, 1998.

WHAT TO SEE & DO

Touring the school, viewing videos and exhibits. **Facilities:** Visitor center with interpretive exhibits and two audiovisual presentations, school building. Bookstore. **Programs & Events:** Year-round guided tours of visitor center. Guided tours of Central High School (Oct.–Mar., Tues and Thurs, 9:30–10:15). Reservations required for guided tours, tel. 501/374–1957.

PLANNING YOUR VISIT

Lodging: Available in Little Rock; none at site. **Food & Supplies:** Available in Little Rock; none at site. **Tips & Hints:** Visitor center is a restored Mobil gas station. **Fees, Permits & Limitations:** Free. No pets. Site open daily, Mon.–Sat. 10–4, Sun. 1–4. Visitor center closed Thanksgiving, Dec. 25, Jan. 1.

HOW TO GET THERE

Take I–630 to Martin Luther King Drive exit, left on Martin Luther King Drive, right on Daisy L. Gatson Bates Dr. Site is at the intersection of Daisy L. Gatson Bates Dr. and Park St. Closest airport: Little Rock (7 mi/ 11 km).

FOR MORE INFORMATION

Central High School National Historic Site (2125 Daisy L. Gatson Bates Dr., Little Rock, AR 72205, tel. 501/374–1957; Web site: www.nps.gov/cehi).

Fort Smith National Historic Site

In downtown Fort Smith, in the western part of the state, on the Oklahoma border

The site commemorates a significant phase of America's westward expansion and stands as a reminder of 80 turbulent years in the history of Federal Indian policy. It includes the remains of two frontier forts and the 19th century Federal Court of the Western District of Arkansas. The site was authorized on September 13, 1961.

WHAT TO SEE & DO

Touring renovated historic buildings and grounds, viewing video, walking river trail with wayside exhibits. **Facilities:** Visitor center (Historic Barracks/Courthouse/Jail) with interpretive exhibits, restored courtroom, 1888 jail cells, restored gallows, historic Commissary Building. Bookstore, fort site, trails. **Programs & Events:** Year-round guided tours (by appointment) of courtroom, jail, gallows, and grounds; living history programs, Civil war encampments, artillery demonstrations.

PLANNING YOUR VISIT

▥ **Lodging:** Available in city of Fort Smith; none at site. ✕ **Food & Supplies:** Available in city of Fort Smith; none at site. ☞ **Tips & Hints:** Busiest in June and July, least crowded in December and January. ▨ **Fees, Permits & Limitations:** Entrance fee: $3 per person, $6 family rate, free 16 and under. Site open daily 9–5. Closed Thanksgiving, Dec. 25, Jan. 1.

HOW TO GET THERE

From Garrison St. (U.S. 64) turn south on 4th St., west on Garland Ave. to Rogers Ave. Closest airport: Ft. Smith (8 mi/13 km).

FOR MORE INFORMATION

Fort Smith National Historic Site (Box 1406, Fort Smith, AR 72902, tel. 501/783–3961, fax 501/783–5307; Web site www.nps.gov/fosm).

Hot Springs National Park

In the west-central part of the state, near Hot Springs

The park's 47 hot springs, which lack the sulfur odor and taste of many hot springs, are at the heart of a great social and medical resort. In its heyday, between 1890 and 1920, the park's monumental bathhouses catered to crowds of health seekers. Today the park preserves the finest collection of historic bathhouses in the United States. Approximately 850,000 gallons of natural thermal water still flow out of the mountainside and into the beautifully landscaped Bathhouse Row area each day. Much of the water is still supplied to traditional spas and jug fountains for bathing and drinking. Hot Springs Reservation was set aside on April 20, 1832; dedicated to public use as a park on June 16, 1880; and redesignated a national park March 4, 1921.

WHAT TO SEE & DO

Auto touring, bicycling (rentals, Hot Springs), fishing, going up observation tower, hiking, picnicking, taking thermal baths, touring Fordyce Bathhouse, viewing springs. **Facilities:** Visitor center with interpretive exhibits and film (Fordyce Bathhouse, Bathhouse Row, 300 block of Central Ave./AR 7), amphitheater, trails, interpretive signs. Bookstore/gift shop, pedestal grills, picnic areas. **Programs & Events:** Guided tours of Fordyce Bathhouse. Thermal features tours (Apr.–Nov.), special programs and hikes (occasionally). Constitution Week (Sept. 17–23), Volksmarsch/Oktoberfest (one week in Oct., Hot Springs).

PLANNING YOUR VISIT

⛺ **Camping:** Campground: no hookups or showers (no reservations). Private campgrounds available in the Hot Springs area, state parks, Corps of Engineers lakes, and the Ouachita National Forest. 🏨 **Lodging:** Available in Hot Springs; none in park. ✕ **Food & Supplies:** Available in Hot Springs; none in park. ☞ **Tips & Hints:** Go in April for dogwood blooms and spring warbler migration, May–July for southern magnolias, October–November for fall colors. Busiest in June and July, least crowded in January and February. 🎫 **Fees, Permits & Limitations:** Free. Thermal water bathing prices available at the park visitor center and at the bathhouses. Thermal bathing inside the park: Buckstaff Bathhouse (tel. 501/623–2308), Hot Springs Health Spa (tel. 501/321–9664). Outside the park: Arlington Hotel (reservations required, tel. 501/623–7771), Austin Hotel (reservations required, tel. 501/623–6600), Downtowner Motor Inn (tel. 501/624–5521), Majestic Hotel (reservations required, tel. 501/623–5511). Physical therapy using hot spring water available at Libbey Memorial Physical Medicine Center (inside park, tel. 501/321–9664) and Leo N. Levi Arthritis Hospital (outside park, tel. 501/624–1281). Fee charged for Hot Springs Mountain Tower (tel. 501/623–6035). Arkansas state fishing license required. No vehicles or bicycles on sidewalks and trails. No vehicles over 30 ft/9.1 m on Hot Springs Mountain Dr. No hunting. Do not remove or disturb any plant, animal, rock, or other object. Leashed pets only. No pets in visitor center. Park open daily. Visitor center open daily 9–5, extended summer hours possible. Closed Thanksgiving, Dec. 25, Jan. 1.

HOW TO GET THERE

Take U.S. 70, U.S. 270, or AR 7 to the city of Hot Springs, which adjoins the park. Park visitor center is on AR 7, along Bathhouse Row. Closest airports: Hot Springs, Little Rock (55 mi/88 km).

FOR MORE INFORMATION

Hot Springs National Park (Box 1860, Hot Springs, AR 71902, tel. 501/624–3383, ext. 640, fax 501/624–3458; Web site www.nps.gov/hosp). Hot Springs Visitor Information (134 Convention Blvd., Hot Springs, AR 79101, tel. 800/772–2489). Arkansas Division of Parks and Tourism (Dept of Parks and Tourism, 1 Capitol Mall, Little Rock, AR 72201, tel. 800/828–8974). Hot Springs Advertising and Promotion Commission (Box K, Hot Springs National Park, AR 79101-1982, tel. 501/321–2277). Hot Springs Chamber of Commerce (Box 6090 Hot Springs, AR 71902, tel. 501/321–1700).

Pea Ridge National Military Park

In the northwest part of the state, near Rogers

The 4,300-acre park represents what might be the best-preserved Civil War battlefield in the country. The March 7–8, 1862, battle, which pitted Major General Earl Van Dorn's 16,000 Confederates against 10,500

Union soldiers under Brigadeer General Samuel Curtis, saved Missouri for the Union. The Confederate force included 800 Cherokees, and half the Union army were German immigrants recruited near St. Louis. The park includes a reconstruction of the Elkhorn Tavern, site of bitter fighting on both days. The park also includes a 2.5-mi/4-km segment of the Trail of Tears, the route used by the Cherokees between 1838 and 1839 when they were forcibly moved from their homeland in the South to the Indian Territories of Oklahoma and Arkansas. The site was authorized on July 20, 1956.

WHAT TO SEE & DO

Auto touring of battlefield, hiking, horseback riding, picnicking, touring museum, watching slide show, wildlife viewing. **Facilities:** Visitor center with interpretive exhibits, 7-mi/11-km tour road, 11-mi/18-km horse trail, 10-mi/16-km hiking trail. Bookstore, picnic area. **Programs & Events:** Living-history demonstrations and education programs (summer, weekends as staffing permits), tours of Elkhorn Tavern (Memorial Day–3rd week in Oct. as staffing permits). Battle anniversary (weekend nearest Mar. 7–8), Memorial Day remembrance.

PLANNING YOUR VISIT

Camping: Available at Beaver Lake; none in park. **Lodging:** Available in Eureka Springs, Rogers; none in park. **Food & Supplies:** Restaurants nearby and supplies in Eureka Springs, Garfield, Pea Ridge, Rogers; none in park. **Tips & Hints:** Busiest in May and July, least crowded in January and February. **Fees, Permits & Limitations:** Entrance fee: $2 per adult 17–61 or $4 maximum per car. No recreational sports. No hunting or trapping. Lock your vehicle. Park and visitor center open daily 8–5. Tour road open daily 8–4:30. Closed Thanksgiving, Dec. 25, Jan. 1.

HOW TO GET THERE

80 mi/128 km southwest of Springfield, MO, via U.S. 60, MO 37, and U.S. 62; 90 mi/144 km northeast of Fort Smith, AR, via I–44, I–540, U.S. 71, and U.S. 62E; and 120 mi/192 km east of Tulsa, OK, via the Cherokee Turnpike and U.S. 412, 71, and 62E. Closest airports: Northwest Arkansas (25 mi/40 km); Springfield, MO (82 mi/131 km).

FOR MORE INFORMATION

Pea Ridge National Military Park (Box 700, Pea Ridge, AR 72751, tel. 501/451–8122, fax 501/451–8635; e-mail PERI_Interpretation@nps.gov; Web site www.nps.gov/peri). Rogers Chamber of Commerce (317 W. Walnut St., Rogers, AR 72756, tel. 501/636–1240).

See Also

Trail of Tears National Historic Trail, National Trails System in Other National Parklands.

CALIFORNIA

Cabrillo National Monument

In the southwestern part of the state, in San Diego

The site commemorates Juan Rodríguez Cabrillo's 1542 expedition, the first European exploration of the west coast of the United States. The park is home to the Old Point Loma Lighthouse, one of the first lighthouses built on the West Coast, and preserves some of the best examples of the coastal sage scrub and tidepool communities of Southern California. The view of San Diego from the site is said to be the finest harbor view in the nation. The site was established on October 14, 1913.

WHAT TO SEE & DO

Attending ranger programs, bird-watching, hiking, visiting tidepools, watching film presentations, watching whales. **Facilities:** Visitor center with auditorium and exhibit room; wayside panels at visitor center along Bayside Trail, near tidepools and lighthouse; temporary and seasonal exhibits; radio information. Bookstore, educational materials, postcards. **Programs & Events:** Ranger-guided tours and programs and frequent costumed interpretive programs available year-round. Gray whale talks and watching (Dec.–Feb.), coastal sage-scrub and wildflower walks (Feb.–Apr.), tidepool walks (Nov.–May). Cabrillo Festival—traditional dances, food, costumed interpretation (Sun. closest to Sept. 28); Lighthouse programs, costumed interpreters, tower and catwalk open to public (Aug. 25, Nov. 15); Whale Watch Weekend—speakers, whale programs, children's programs (third weekend in Jan.).

PLANNING YOUR VISIT

Camping: Available in Pacific Beach, San Diego; none at the monument. **Lodging:** Available in Ocean Beach, Point Loma; none at the monument. **Food & Supplies:** In the park: snacks and drinks from vending machines. Food and supplies also available nearby in Ocean Beach, Point Loma. **Tips & Hints:** Go in winter for clearest weather, December–February for whale migration. Busiest in March and August, least crowded in October and January. **Fees, Permits & Limitations:** Entrance fee: $5 per vehicle, $2 per pedestrian, motorcyclist, and bicyclist. No pets except at tidepools or in vehicles. Leashed pets only. No bikes on trails. Park and visitor center open daily 9–5:15.

HOW TO GET THERE

At the end of Hwy. 209/Catalina Blvd., Point Loma, San Diego; 10 mi/16 km from downtown San Diego. Closest airport: San Diego (8 mi/13 km).

FOR MORE INFORMATION

Cabrillo National Monument (1800 Cabrillo Memorial Dr., San Diego, CA 92106, tel. 619/557–5450, TTY 619/222–8211, fax 619/557–5469;

Web site www.nps.gov/cabr). San Diego Convention and Visitors Bureau (401 B St., Suite 1400, San Diego, CA 92101-4237, tel. 619/232–3101, fax 619/696–9371). San Diego Visitor Information Center (2688 E. Mission Bay Dr., San Diego, CA 92109, tel. 619/276–8200, fax 619/276–6041).

Channel Islands National Park

Off the southern coast of California, in the Santa Barbara Channel

In this park are five islands (Anacapa, Santa Barbara, Santa Cruz, Santa Rosa, and San Miquel) and 125,000 acres of submerged lands that provide habitat for marine life from microscopic plankton to Earth's largest creature—the blue whale. The park was proclaimed a national monument April 26, 1938, and designated a Biosphere Reserve in 1976 and a national park on March 5, 1980.

WHAT TO SEE & DO

Bird-watching, boating (permit required, *see below*), camping, diving, fishing, hiking, kayaking, picnicking, snorkeling, swimming, whale-watching. **Facilities:** 3 visitor centers—Ventura (1901 Spinnaker Dr.), Anacapa and Santa Barbara islands. Book, map, and video sale area (Ventura). **Programs & Events:** Ranger programs (Ventura, weekends 11 and 3) and guided walks (islands, daily) available. Underwater video program (Memorial Day–Labor Day, Tues. and Thurs. at 2).

PLANNING YOUR VISIT

Camping: Primitive campgrounds on all five islands (reservations required, tel. 800/365–2267). **Lodging:** Available in Ventura; none in park. **Food & Supplies:** Available in Ventura; none in park. **Tips & Hints:** Visit January through March to see migrating gray whales, in spring to see wildflowers. Busiest in July and August, least crowded October through December. **Fees, Permits & Limitations:** Free. No pets. No mountain bikes. Park open daily. Visitor centers open daily, 8:30–5. Closed Thanksgiving, Dec. 25.

HOW TO GET THERE

The park is in the Santa Barbara Channel. Closest park island is 14 mi/22 km and farthest is 55 mi/88 km from Ventura harbor. Visitor center is in Ventura harbor. Transportation available through boat and airplane concessionaires, information available from park. Private boats permitted. Closest airport: Oxnard (5 mi/8 km).

FOR MORE INFORMATION

Channel Islands National Park (1901 Spinnaker Dr., Ventura, CA 93001, tel. 805/658–5700, fax 805/658–5799; Web site www.nps.gov/chis). Ventura Chamber of Commerce (785 S. Seaward Ave., Ventura, CA 93001, tel. 805/648–2875). Ventura Visitors and Convention Bureau (89 S. California St., Suite C, Ventura, CA 93001, tel. 805/648–2075).

Death Valley National Park

In Death Valley

Despite the severity of Death Valley, more than 1,000 species of plants and 98 species of animals live within the park's boundaries. Also in the hottest spot in North America are snow-covered peaks, rugged canyons, and beautiful sand dunes. In extremely wet years, perhaps once in a decade, spectacular wildflowers may be seen. The park was proclaimed a national monument in 1933 and redesignated a national park in 1994. It was designated a part of the Colorado and Mojave Desert Biosphere Reserve in 1984.

WHAT TO SEE & DO

Auto touring, biking, hiking, horseback riding, Jeep riding, picnicking. **Facilities:** Visitor center with interpretive exhibits (Furnace Creek, Rte. 190), Borax Museum (Furnace Creek Ranch), trails, wayside exhibits. Airport, book and map sales area, gas stations, general store, gift shop, golf course, laundry, picnic area, pool, post office, religious services. **Programs & Events:** Guided tours of Scotty's Castle (year-round). Ranger-guided talks, interpretive talks and evening slide programs (Nov.–Apr.). Forty-niner Encampment (2nd week of Nov.).

PLANNING YOUR VISIT

Camping: 9 campgrounds: no hookups (reservations available for Furnace Creek, tel. 800/365–2267). Backcountry camping available (permit recommended, *see below*). Group camping available (reservations available, tel. 800/365–2267). Private campgrounds available within the park at Stovepipe Wells Village and Panamint Springs Resort. Camping also available outside the park in Shoshone and Tecopa, CA, and Amargosa Valley, Beatty and Pahrump, NV. **Lodging:** In the park: Furnace Creek Inn (tel. 760/786–2361), Furnace Creek Ranch (tel. 760/786–2345), Panamint Springs Resort (tel. 775/482–7680), Stovepipe Wells Village (tel. 760/786–2387). Lodging also available outside the park in Amargosa Valley, Beatty, and Pahrump, NV; Death Valley Junction, Lone Pine, and Shoshone, CA. **Food & Supplies:** In the park: restaurants and bars at Furnace Creek Inn, Furnace Creek Ranch, Panamint Springs Resort, and Stovepipe Wells Village. Stores at Furnace Creek Ranch and Stovepipe Wells Village. Snacks at Scotty's Castle. Food and supplies also available in Amargosa Valley, Beatty, and Pahrump, NV; Death Valley Junction, Lone Pine, and Shoshone, CA. **Tips & Hints:** Be prepared for extremely hot summer temperatures. Always carry water in the car and on hikes. Dress warmly when visiting the mountains in the winter. Best time to visit: October through April. Go in March and April for wildflowers, between May and October to hike Telescope Peak. Busiest February through mid-April and in November, least crowded in December and January. **Fees, Permits & Limitations:** Entrance fee: $5 per person on foot, bicycle, or motorcycle; $10 per vehicle. Guided tours of Scotty's Castle: $8 for adults 16 and over, $6 for 62 or older, $4 children 6–15 years, children 5 and under free, $4 for adults with disability, $2 for children with disability. Backcountry permits recommended for all backcountry camping. No collecting or disturbing natural, historical, or archaeological features. Don't feed or disturb wildlife. All vehicles, including motorcycles, trail bikes, bicycles, and four-wheel-drives, must remain on established roads. No hunting or firearm use. Leashed pets only. No pets on trails or in wilderness. Park open daily. Visitor center open daily 8–6.

HOW TO GET THERE

From U.S. 395W, take Rte. 190, 136, or 178. From U.S. 95E, take Rte. 267, 373, or 374. From I–15S, take Rte. 127 at Baker and Rte. 190. Closest airport: Las Vegas (120 mi/192 km).

FOR MORE INFORMATION

Death Valley National Park (Box 579, Death Valley, CA 92328–0579, tel. 760/786–2331, fax 760/786–3283; Web site www.nps.gov/deva).

Devils Postpile
National Monument

In the east-central part of the state,
near Mammoth Lakes

Hot lava cooled and cracked to form fractured basalt columns 40 ft/12 m to 60 ft/18 m high that resemble a giant rock pipe organ. The 798-acre monument high in the Sierra Nevada also protects the 101-ft/31-m Rainbow Falls and Soda Springs, carbonated mineralized springs. The John Muir and Pacific Coast trails cross the monument. It was proclaimed in 1911 and transferred to the Park Service in 1933.

WHAT TO SEE & DO

Bicycling, fishing, hiking to springs and falls. **Facilities:** Ranger station, trails. **Programs & Events:** Ranger-led interpretive programs, campfire programs (July–Labor Day).

PLANNING YOUR VISIT

Camping: Campground (open mid-June–Oct.). Camping also available in Red Meadows and Inyo National Forest. **Lodging:** Available in Mammoth Lakes, Red Meadows; none in park. **Food & Supplies:** Available in Mammoth Lakes, Red Meadows; none in park. **Tips & Hints:** Stay back from cliff edges. Store food properly to avoid bears. Busiest in July and August, least crowded in October and June. **Fees, Permits & Limitations:** Free. Day-use visitors must use shuttle bus late June–early Sept., between 7:30 and 5:30, at Mammoth Mountain Inn to reach park. California fishing license required. No hunting. Leashed pets only. No bikes off road. Monument open mid-June–Oct.

HOW TO GET THERE

10 mi/16 km west from U.S. 395 on Rte. 203 to Minaret Summit, then 7 mi/11 km on a paved narrow mountain road. Closest airports: Mammoth (22 mi/35 km), Reno (181 mi/290 km).

FOR MORE INFORMATION

Devils Postpile National Monument (Box 501, Mammoth Lakes, CA 93541, tel. 760/934–2289; Web site www.nps.gov/depo).

Eugene O'Neill National Historic Site

Near San Francisco, in Danville

Eugene O'Neill, the architect of modern American theater and the only Nobel Prize–winning playwright from the United States, lived at Tao House from 1937 to 1944. Here he wrote his final and most successful plays: *The Iceman Cometh, Long Days Journey Into Night,* and *A Moon for the Misbegotten.* Since 1980, the National Park Service has been restoring Tao House and its courtyard and orchards. The site was authorized on October 12, 1976.

WHAT TO SEE & DO

Touring home, courtyard, and orchards. **Facilities:** Visitor center with interpretive exhibits, home. Bookstore. **Programs & Events:** Guided tours, interpretive programs. Theater (May–June).

PLANNING YOUR VISIT

△ **Camping:** Available in Mount Diablo State Park in Diablo; none in park. ⊞ **Lodging:** Available in Danville, San Ramon, and Walnut Creek; none in park. ✕ **Food & Supplies:** Available in Alamo, Danville, San Ramon, and Walnut Creek; none in park. ☞ **Tips & Hints:** Watch for uneven walking surfaces, stairs and downhill and uphill walking. Best time to visit is between March and May. Busiest April through June, least crowded in December. ▨ **Fees, Permits & Limitations:** Free. Reservations required for tours (tel. 925/838–0249). No bikes. No pets. No hunting. Site opens Wed.–Sun. at 10 AM and 12:30 PM for tours. Closed Thanksgiving, Dec. 25, Jan. 1.

HOW TO GET THERE

In Danville, 26 mi/42 km east of San Francisco off I–680. Closest airport: Oakland.

FOR MORE INFORMATION

Eugene O'Neill National Historic Site (Box 280, Danville, CA 94526-0280, tel. 925/838–0249, fax 925/838–9471; Web site www.nps.gov/euon). Danville Area Chamber of Commerce (117 E. Town and Country Dr., Danville, CA 94526, tel. 925/837–4400).

Fort Point National Historic Site

In San Francisco

Situated beneath the Golden Gate Bridge, Fort Point is a classic example of the coastal fortifications constructed by the U.S. Army Corps of Engineers during the mid-19th century. Built prior to the beginning of the Civil War, the brick and granite fort embodies the commercial and strategic military importance of San Francisco. Between 1933 and 1937 the fort was used as a base of operations for the construction of the Golden Gate Bridge. During World War II, Fort Point was occupied by 100 soldiers with searchlights and rapid-fire cannon as part of the protection of a submarine net strung across the Bay entrance. The site was established on October 16, 1970.

WHAT TO SEE & DO

Scenic viewing; self-guided and guided fort tours; viewing African American Soldier Experience and Women in U.S. Military History photography exhibits, Construction of the Golden Gate Bridge exhibit; watching videos. **Facilities:** Fort, exhibits. Bookstore. **Programs & Events:** Ranger-guided tours (daily), cannon drill demonstrations (daily), education programs. Crabbing program (Mar.–Oct.), Candlelight tours (Oct.–Feb.). Special events available.

PLANNING YOUR VISIT

Camping: Available in San Francisco area; none at site. **Lodging:** Available in San Francisco area; none at site. **Food & Supplies:** Available in San Francisco area; none at site. **Tips & Hints:** Allow at least one hour for your visit. Weather at Fort Point is cool and windy. Summer months can be cold, with fog rolling into San Francisco Bay. Winters are generally cold with variable precipitation. Go in spring and fall for best weather. Busiest in June and August, least crowded in December and January. **Fees, Permits & Limitations:** Free. Audio tour rental: $2.50 per adult, $1 per child. Fort will be open limited days due to construction. Closed Thanksgiving, Dec. 25, Jan 1.

HOW TO GET THERE

Beneath the south end of the Golden Gate Bridge, in the Presidio of San Francisco. Turn off Hwy. 101 at the bridge and turn left on Lincoln Blvd. Closest airport: San Francisco (15 mi/24 km).

FOR MORE INFORMATION

Fort Point National Historic Site (Box 29333, Presidio of San Francisco, San Francisco, CA 94129, tel. 415/556–1693; Web site www.nps.gov/fopo).

Golden Gate
National Recreation Area

*In the northern part of the state,
in San Francisco area*

This recreation area is the largest national park adjacent to an urban area in the world. The 76,500-acre park encompasses 28 mi/45 km of shoreline in San Francisco, Marin, and San Mateo counties, including ocean beaches, redwood forest, lagoons, marshes, former military properties, a cultural center at Fort Mason, and Alcatraz Island. The area also includes Fort Point National Historic Site and Muir Woods National Monument (*see separate entries for each*). The park was established in 1972 and designated a Biosphere Reserve in 1988.

WHAT TO SEE & DO

Attending cultural programs, biking, bird-watching, board sailing, golfing, hiking, off-road biking, picnicking, sailing, swimming, visiting museum, walking. **Facilities:** 7 visitor centers—Fort Mason, Presidio, Muir Woods (*see separate listing*), Alcatraz, Marin Headlands, Cliff House, Fort Point (*see separate listing*); Nike Missile Site; trails, fire roads. **Programs & Events:** Year-round programs available.

PLANNING YOUR VISIT

⚠ **Camping:** Backcountry and group campsites available at Marin Headlands (reservations and permit required, tel. 415/331–1540). 🏠 **Lodging:** In the recreation area: American Youth Hostels at Marin Headlands area and Fort Mason (reservations required, tel. 415/771–1065). ✗ **Food & Supplies:** Available locally; none at recreation area. ☞ **Tips & Hints:** Allow two or three days to see all areas of the recreation area. Expect windy, cool temperatures, fog in summer, and best weather in spring and fall. Busiest in July and August, least crowded in December and February. 🎟 **Fees, Permits & Limitations:** Entrance fee: $2 for Muir Woods; $1 daily use fee for Alcatraz Island (plus ferry transportation). Reservation required for Alcatraz (tel. 415/705–5555). Ferry transportation fee: $8.75 round-trip per adult, $7 per senior citizen, $5.50 for children 5–11. Audiotape tour: $3.50 per adult or senior citizen, $1.50 for children 5–11. Permit required for backcountry camping at Marin Headlands. Most facilities open daily 10–4:30. Visitor centers: Fort Mason open Mon.–Fri. 9:30–4:30, closed holidays; Cliff House open daily 10–5, closed Thanksgiving, Dec. 25, and Jan. 1; Fort Point open daily 10–5, closed Dec. 25 and Jan. 1; Marin Headlands open daily 9:30–4:30, closed Thanksgiving and Dec. 25; Muir Woods open daily 8–8. Nike Missile Site open at Marin Headlands weekdays and 1st Sun. of the month 12:30–3:30. Presidio visitor center open daily, 9–5.

HOW TO GET THERE

Much of the recreation area is within walking distance of San Francisco, with other areas up to an hour's drive away. The recreation area follows the city's north and west shoreline, extending down the peninsula. Across Golden Gate Bridge in Marin County, follow access roads off Hwy. 101, including Alexander Ave., Shoreline Hwy., and Sir Francis Drake Blvd., to the recreation area. The Municipal Railway (MUNI) bus system serves Rodeo Beach in Marin on Sun. Recreation area lands in San Mateo County are accessible via Skyline Blvd. In San Francisco, MUNI provides frequent service from downtown to shoreline destinations, especially Aquatic Park, the Cliff House, Ocean Beach, and Fort Mason. Limited MUNI transportation is available to the Presidio. Because traffic is sometimes heavy and parking is limited, public transportation is recommended. MUNI also connects from San Francisco to other Bay Area transit systems: Golden Gate Transit (GGT) in Marin County; Bay Area Rapid Transit (BART) and Alameda/Contra Costa Transit (AC TRANSIT) in the East Bay; and San Mateo Transit (SAM TRANS) in the peninsula area. The Blue & Gold Fleet ferries provide transportation to Alcatraz. Closest airports: San Francisco International, Oakland International.

FOR MORE INFORMATION

Golden Gate National Recreation Area Headquarters (Fort Mason, Bldg. 201, San Francisco, CA 94123, tel. 415/556–0560; Web site www.nps.gov/goga). Other visitor information centers: Presidio (Presidio, Bldg. 102, San Francisco, CA 94129, tel. 415/561–4323); Muir Woods (Muir Woods National Monument, Mill Valley, CA 94941, tel. 415/388–2595); Alcatraz (Fort Mason, Bldg. 201, San Francisco, CA 94123, tel. 415/556–0560); Marin Headlands (National Park Service, Marin Headlands Visitor Center, Bldg. 948, Fort Barry, Sausalito, CA 94965, tel. 415/331–1540); Cliff House (Golden Gate National Park Association, Point Lobos Ave., San Francisco, CA 94121, tel. 415/556–8642); Fort Point (Box 29333, Presidio, San Francisco, CA 94129, tel. 415/556–1693).

John Muir
National Historic Site

In San Francisco Bay area, in Martinez

Naturalist John Muir lived in this 14-room Victorian home from 1890 until his death in 1914. Also preserved are 325 acres of open space and 8.5 acres of the fruit ranch. Muir served as first president of the Sierra Club and advocated the creation of Yosemite, Sequoia, Mt. Rainier, and Grand Canyon national parks. He popularized the idea of preserving wild lands not for their commodities (timber, grazing, and water resources) but for their wildness, openness, and natural splendor. The site was authorized in 1964.

WHAT TO SEE & DO

Hiking, picnicking, touring the house and grounds, viewing film. **Facilities:** Visitor center, auditorium, house, grounds, trail. Bookstore, picnic area. **Programs & Events:** Guided tours, bird walks, wildflower walks, junior ranger programs. Full-moon walks (June, July, Sept.), Perseid

Meteor Shower viewing (Aug.). Muir's Birthday (early May), Ranch Days (Sept.), Victorian Christmas and Las Posadas (Dec.).

PLANNING YOUR VISIT

Camping: Available in Mt. Diablo State Park; none at site. **Lodging:** Available in Martinez; none at site. **Food & Supplies:** Available in Martinez; none at site. **Tips & Hints:** Busiest in May and June, least crowded in September and January. **Fees, Permits & Limitations:** Entrance fee: $2 per adult 17 and older. Leashed pets only. No smoking. No food in house. No mountain bikes on nature trail. Park and visitor center open Wed.–Sun. 10–4:30. Closed Thanksgiving, Dec. 25, Jan. 1.

HOW TO GET THERE

In the San Francisco metro area, on the East Bay in Martinez. Take Alhambra Ave. exit off CA 4 between I–80 and I–680. Closest airport: San Francisco.

FOR MORE INFORMATION

John Muir National Historic Site (4202 Alhambra Ave., Martinez, CA 94553, tel. 925/228–8860, fax 925/228–8192; e-mail JOMU_Interpretation@nps.gov; Web site www.nps.gov/jomu). Martinez Chamber of Commerce (620 Las Juntas St., Martinez, CA 94553, tel. 925/228–2345).

Joshua Tree National Park

*In the southeast part of the state,
near Twentynine Palms*

Geological formations, a beautiful and strange Joshua Tree forest, mining history, homesteading history, and peace and quiet are the attractions at this 792,750-acre park. Two different deserts meet at Joshua Tree: in the north and west portions is the Mojave Desert; and in the south and east portions is the Colorado Desert, a subsystem of the Sonoran Desert. The site was designated a national monument in 1936, redesignated a national park in 1994, and designated a Biosphere Reserve in 1984.

WHAT TO SEE & DO

Backpacking, boulder hopping, hiking, mountain biking, rock climbing (rentals, town of Joshua Tree), picnicking. **Facilities:** 3 visitor centers with interpretive exhibits—Twentynine Palms (Utah Trail), Cottonwood (47 mi/75 km east of Palm Springs off I–10), Black Rock Nature Center (Joshua La., Yucca Valley). Bookstore and sales areas, picnic areas. **Programs & Events:** Ranger-led hikes, interpretive talks, and campfire programs (mid-Oct.–mid-Dec. and Mar.–May).

PLANNING YOUR VISIT

Camping: 9 campgrounds: no hookups (reservations available at Indian Cove and Black Rock Canyon, tel. 800/365–2267). Backcountry camping available (self registration). Group campsites available (reservation required, tel. 800/365–2267). Private campgrounds available in

Twentynine Palms. ⊞ **Lodging:** Available in town of Joshua Tree, Twentynine Palms, Yucca Valley; none in park. ✕ **Food & Supplies:** Available in town of Joshua Tree, Twentynine Palms, Yucca Valley; none in park. ☞ **Tips & Hints:** Be prepared for all types of weather, including temperatures of 95°F/35°C–110°F/44°C between June and September. Bring plenty of water. Go between February and mid-May for flowers; between February and April and in fall for bird migrations; and in spring, fall, and winter for best weather. Busiest in March and April, least crowded in July and January. ▨ **Fees, Permits & Limitations:** Entrance fee: $10 per vehicle. No hunting. Leashed pets only. Pets may not be left alone and are restricted to campgrounds and dirt road areas. Mountain bikes only on designated trails and roads open to motorized vehicles. Park open daily. Visitor centers open daily 8–5.

HOW TO GET THERE

50 mi/80 km north of Palm Springs. From I–10, take Hwy. 62N to the town of Joshua Tree and turn south on Park Blvd. to reach west entrance. Park entrances also at Twentynine Palms (15 mi/24 km east of Joshua Tree) and from I–10 (47 mi/75 km east of Palm Springs). Closest airport: Palm Springs.

FOR MORE INFORMATION

Joshua Tree National Park (74485 National Park Dr., Twentynine Palms, CA 92277, tel. 760/367–5500, fax 760/367–6392; Web site www. nps.gov/jotr). Twentynine Palms Chamber of Commerce (6455A Mesquite Ave., Twentynine Palms, CA 92277, tel. 760/367–3445). Joshua Tree Chamber of Commerce (Box 600, Joshua Tree, CA 92252, tel. 760/366–3723). Yucca Valley Chamber of Commerce (55569 Twentynine Palms Hwy., Yucca Valley, CA 92284, tel. 760/365–6323).

Kings Canyon National Park

See Sequoia and Kings Canyon National Parks.

Lassen Volcanic National Park

In the northeast part of the state, near Mineral

Lassen Volcanic National Park is an oasis in a vast volcanic landscape. All four types of volcanoes in the world are found here. Lassen Peak, possibly the world's largest plug dome volcano, erupted in May 1914. Today the park has bubbling mud pots and steaming fumaroles, great lava pinnacles, lava flows, and jagged craters. Two great mountain ranges, the Sierra Nevada and Cascades, intersect with the Great Basin lava flows at the park, and flora and fauna from both ranges intermingle here. More than 700 flowering plant, 200 bird, and 50 mammal species grace the park. The park was established on August 9, 1916.

WHAT TO SEE & DO

Auto touring, cross-country skiing, fishing, hiking, picnicking, viewing volcanic landscape and thermal features. **Facilities:** Visitor center (Park Headquarters, Mineral); Southwest Information Station (next to Lassen Chalet near southwest entrance), Loomis Museum with interpretive exhibits (near Manzanita Lake), wayside interpretive signs, amphitheaters, trails. Book and map sale areas, gift shop, picnic tables, fire pits and grates. **Programs & Events:** Talks, walks, and evening programs (late June–Labor Day, daily), snowshoe walks (Jan.–Mar.)

PLANNING YOUR VISIT

🏕 **Camping:** 8 campgrounds: no hookups, all open by July, some close in early Sept. (no reservations). Backcountry camping available (permit required, *see below*). Group campsites available (reservations required, tel. 530/595–4444 ext. 5155). Private campgrounds in Chester, Hat Creek, Mill Creek, Mineral, Old Station, Red Bluff, Redding, Shingletown. 🛏 **Lodging:** In the park: Drakesbad Guest Ranch (tel. 530/529–1512). Lodging also available outside the park in Chester, Hat Creek, Mill Creek, Mineral, Old Station, Red Bluff, Redding, Shingletown. ✕ **Food & Supplies:** In the park: camp store. Drakesbad Guest Ranch may have limited seats in summer for dinner (reservations required, tel. 530/529–1512). Food and supplies also available in Chester, Mill Creek, Mineral, Old Station, Red Bluff, Redding, Shingletown. ☞ **Tips & Hints:** Buy park road guide. Stay on boardwalks and watch children near thermal areas. Watch for lightning. Wear layers of clothing. Temperatures may vary from freezing to 90°F/32°C. Go between late July and mid-August for flowers, and between August and September for best hiking and car touring. Busiest in July and August, least crowded in December and January. 🎫 **Fees, Permits & Limitations:** Entrance fee: $5 per person on foot, bicycle, or by taxi, $10 per private vehicle. Backcountry permits (free) required for all backcountry camping. California state fishing license required. No hunting. Bikes on paved roads and campgrounds only. No motorized or mechanized equipment on trails. No pets beyond roads or campgrounds. Leashed pets only. Park open daily. Park road closes from late Oct. to mid-June because of snow. Park headquarters open weekdays 8–4:30, closed holidays. Southwest Information Station open mid-June–Memorial Day, daily 9–4; late May–mid June, weekends 9–4; Labor Day–late Sept., weekends 9–4. Loomis Museum open mid-June–late Sept., daily 9–5; late May–mid-June, weekends 9–5.

HOW TO GET THERE

52 mi/84 km east of Red Bluff via Hwy. 36 and 48 mi/77 km east of Redding via Hwy. 44. Closest airport: Redding (48 mi/77 km).

FOR MORE INFORMATION

Lassen Volcanic National Park (Box 100, Mineral, CA 96063-0100, tel. 530/595–4444, TDD 530/595–3480, fax 530/595–3262; Web site www.nps.gov/lavo). Shasta Cascade Wonderland Association (1699 Hwy. 273, Anderson, CA 96007, tel. 800/326–6944, fax 530/365–1258). Chester/Lake Almanor Chamber of Commerce (529 Main St., Box 1198, Chester, CA 96020, tel. 530/258–2426, fax 530/258–2760).

Plumas County Visitors Bureau (Box 4120, Quincy, CA 95971, tel. 800/326–2247, fax 530/283–5465). Red Bluff–Tehama County Chamber of Commerce (Box 850, Red Bluff, CA 96080, tel. 530/527–6220, fax 530/527–2908). Redding Convention and Visitors Bureau (777 Auditorium Dr., Redding CA 96001, tel. 800/874–7562, fax 530/225–4354).

Lava Beds National Monument

In the northern part of the state, near Tulelake

Lava Beds National Monument is on the north face of the Medicine Lake shield volcano, the largest in the Cascade Range. Numerous cinder cones, spatter cones, and lava flows cover the landscape, as well as over 450 lava-tube caves. The monument also contains sites associated with the Modoc War of 1872–73, including Captain Jack's Stronghold, a natural fortress used by Modoc Indians for four months to withstand a siege by the U.S. Army. A separate site—Petroglyph Point—contains an outstanding collection of Native American rock art. The site was proclaimed in 1925 and transferred from the Forest Service in 1933.

WHAT TO SEE & DO

Cave exploration, picnicking, walking. **Facilities:** Visitor center with interpretive exhibits (Indian Well), Mushpot Cave interpretive trail, caves, rock art. Book sale area, picnic area. **Programs & Events:** Fern Cave tour (Tues., June through Sept., and Sat., year-round, reservations required, tel. 530/667–2282). Guided walks, cave tours, evening programs, living-history programs (mid-May–mid-Sept.); Crystal Cave tours (Dec.–Mar., Sat. only; reservations required, tel. 530/667–2282 ext. 232). Modoc Reunion/Gathering (annually).

PLANNING YOUR VISIT

Camping: Campground: no hookups (no reservations). Backcountry camping available (register with ranger staff). Group camping available (reservation required, tel. 530/667–2282). Public and private campgrounds in Modoc National Forest, Tionesta, Tulelake. **Lodging:** Available in Tionesta and Tulelake, CA; Klamath Falls and Merrill, OR; none in park. **Food & Supplies:** Available in Tionesta and Tulelake, CA; Klamath Falls and Merrill, OR; none in park. **Tips & Hints:** Watch for low ceilings, steep trails and stairways, and uneven footing in lava-tube caves. Carry more than one light source (free at visitor center). Wear protective headgear (nominal charge at visitor center). Notify ranger if exploring caves not listed in park brochure or if using own lighting equipment. Watch for rattlesnakes. Busiest in July and August, least crowded in January and February. **Fees, Permits & Limitations:** Entrance fee: $3 pedestrians, bicycles, motorcycles, $5 per car. No hunting, gathering of specimens, or collecting souvenirs. No pets in caves or on trails. No trail bikes, motorized vehicles on trails. No backcountry fires. Park grounds open year-round. Visitor center open Labor

Day–Memorial Day, daily 8–5; Memorial Day–Labor Day, daily 8–6. Closed Dec. 25.

HOW TO GET THERE

The park visitor center is 24 mi/38 km from Tulelake and 58 mi/93 km from Klamath Falls, OR, off Rte. 139. Closest airport: Klamath Falls.

FOR MORE INFORMATION

Lava Beds National Monument (Box 867, Tulelake, CA 96134, tel. 530/667–2282, fax 530/667–2737; Web site www.nps.gov/labe).

Manzanar National Historic Site

In the eastern part of the state, near Independence

Manzanar War Relocation Center was one of 10 camps at which Japanese-American citizens and Japanese aliens were interned during World War II. Located at the foot of the imposing Sierra Nevada in eastern California's Owens Valley, Manzanar is the best preserved of these camps. The site was authorized on March 3, 1992.

WHAT TO SEE & DO

Touring former streets, orchards, and farming community site, including the pagoda-like police post and sentry post, ruins of the administrative complex, concrete foundations of many types, portions of the water systems, and the camp cemetery. **Facilities:** No Park Service facilities. No federal facilities on site. The Eastern California Museum in Independence has exhibits about Manzanar. **Programs & Events:** Manzanar Pilgrimage (last Sat. in Apr., tel. 323/662–5102).

PLANNING YOUR VISIT

⛺ **Camping:** Available in Inyo County and Inyo National Forest; none at site. 🛏 **Lodging:** Available in Big Pine, Bishop, Independence, Lone Pine, Olancha; none at site. ✕ **Food & Supplies:** Available in Independence, Lone Pine; none at site. ☞ **Tips & Hints:** Plan for a one- to two-hour walking tour of camp. Self-guided tour booklets available at Eastern Sierra Interagency Visitor Center in Lone Pine (tel. 760/876–6222), Eastern California Museum in Independence (tel. 760/878–0258), and at sentry post entrance. Be prepared for strong winds and blowing dust at any time of year. Wear sturdy walking shoes. 💲 **Fees, Permits & Limitations:** Free. Site open daily. No rest rooms.

HOW TO GET THERE

Manzanar is 12 mi/19 km north of Lone Pine, off U.S. 395 and 5 mi/8 km south of Independence. Closest airport: Bishop (40 mi/64 km).

FOR MORE INFORMATION

Manzanar National Historic Site (Box 426, Independence, CA 93526-0426, tel. 760/878–2932, fax 760/878–2949; Web site www.nps.gov/manz).

Mojave National Preserve

In the southeast part of the state, near Baker

Largely untouched by modern facilities, this 1.6-million-acre preserve offers outstanding sightseeing, hiking, camping, horseback riding, and four-wheel-drive travel. It is the third-largest unit of the park system outside of Alaska and the only unit where the Mojave, Great Basin, and Sonoran deserts meet. The vast area encompasses a variety of landscapes, geologic phenomena, historic sites, and recreation areas, as well as an immense diversity of plant and animal life. The preserve was established on October 1, 1994.

WHAT TO SEE & DO

Auto and four-wheel-drive touring (rentals, Barstow, CA, and Las Vegas, NV), hiking, hunting. **Facilities:** 3 information centers with interpretive exhibits—Baker, Hole-in-the-Wall, Needles. Zzyzx Desert Studies Consortium has trails, kiosks. Book and map sales areas. Hole-in-the-Wall: picnic area with fire grates, equestrian facilities (stalls, water, no horse rental). **Programs & Events:** Interpretive talks (on request). Campfire programs (Oct.–Apr.).

PLANNING YOUR VISIT

Camping: 2 campgrounds: no hookups (no reservations). Backcountry camping available. Group campsites at Black Canyon Equestrian and Group Campground across from Hole-in-the-Wall Information Center (reservations required, tel. 760/733–4040). Private campgrounds available in Barstow, Nipton, and Shoshone, CA, and Primm, NV. **Lodging:** Available in Amboy, Baker, Barstow, Ludlow, Needles, and Nipton, CA, and Laughlin and Primm, NV; none in preserve. ✕ **Food & Supplies:** In the preserve: small stores in Cima and Nipton, CA. Food, supplies, and restaurants at Baker, Barstow, and Needles, CA, and Primm, NV. ☞ **Tips & Hints:** Carry and drink plenty of water. In summer, one gallon per person per day is recommended. Fill gas tank and check fluids and tires before entering preserve. There are privately owned lands within the preserve; respect NO TRESPASSING signs. Be cautious of cattle in the road because of open-range grazing: approach slowly and pass quietly. Best times to visit are winter and spring, when temperatures are moderate. Go in spring for wildflower blooms. **Fees, Permits & Limitations:** Free. California state hunting license required. No target shooting. Confined or leashed pets only. Don't leave pets unattended or in closed vehicles or trailers in extreme heat. No bicycles or motorized vehicles allowed in wilderness areas. No collecting firewood. Preserve open daily. Baker Information Center open daily 9–5.

HOW TO GET THERE

The preserve is 60 mi/96 km southwest of Las Vegas, NV, and 60 mi/96 km northeast of Barstow, CA, between I–15 and I–40. Closest airports: Las Vegas, NV; Ontario, CA (150 mi/93 km).

FOR MORE INFORMATION

Headquarters, Mojave National Preserve (222 E. Main St., Suite 202, Barstow, CA 92311, tel. 760/255–8801, fax 760/255–8809; Web site www.nps.gov/moja). Baker Information Center (Box 241, Baker, CA 92309, tel. 760/733–4040, fax 760/733-4027). Baker Area Chamber of Commerce (Box 131, Baker, CA 92309, tel. 760/733–4469). Barstow Area Chamber of Commerce (222 E. Main St., Suite 216, Barstow, CA 92312, tel. 760/256–8617). Needles Area Chamber of Commerce (Box 705, Needles, CA 92363, tel. 760/326–2050).

Muir Woods National Monument

Near San Francisco

"This is the best tree-lovers monument that could possibly be found in all the forests of the world," declared conservationist John Muir when describing this grove of majestic coastal redwoods. The forest of towering trees and canyon ferns is a wonderfully tranquil place. Other park attractions are the redwood forest, Redwood Creek, wildflowers, and forest wildlife. The site was proclaimed on January 9, 1908.

WHAT TO SEE & DO

Hiking, viewing wildlife, walking. **Facilities:** Visitor center, trails. Cafe, sales area. **Programs & Events:** Ranger talks. Seasonal activities available. Earth Day (Jan.), Summer Solstice Celebration (June), Winter Solstice Celebration (Dec.).

PLANNING YOUR VISIT

🏕 **Camping:** Available in nearby Golden Gate National Recreation Area and Mt. Tamalpais State Park; none at monument. 🏨 **Lodging:** Available locally; none at monument. ✗ **Food & Supplies:** Cafe; food and supplies also available locally. ☞ **Tips & Hints:** Park is cool, shaded, and moist year-round. Busiest in June and August, least crowded in December and January. 🎟 **Fees, Permits & Limitations:** Entrance fee: $2 age 17 and older. No pets on trails. No bikes. No picnicking. No RV parking. No vehicles over 35 ft/10.6 m long on steep, winding road leading to monument. Park open daily 8–sunset.

HOW TO GET THERE

12 mi/19 km north of the Golden Gate Bridge via U.S. 101 and CA 1. Closest airport: San Francisco.

FOR MORE INFORMATION

Muir Woods National Monument (Mill Valley, CA 94941, tel. 415/388–2595, fax 415/389–6957; Web site www.nps.gov/muwo).

Pinnacles National Monument

In the central part of the state, entrances near Soledad and Hollister

The monument preserves the rock formations known as "The Pinnacles," talus caves, and wilderness areas. The spires and crags that inspired the park name are remnants of ancient volcanic activity that is part of the long geologic history of the San Andreas Rift Zone. Pinnacles is on the Pacific Plate. Its sister rock, the other part of the same volcanic activity, is on the North American Plate. Pinnacles has moved 195 mi/312 km northwest as the plates have shifted over millions of years. The monument was established on January 16, 1908.

WHAT TO SEE & DO

Bird-watching, caving, hiking, rock climbing, viewing wildflowers. **Facilities:** Visitor center with interpretive exhibits—Bear Gulch (east entrance on Hwy. 146 via CA 25); Chaparral Ranger Station (west entrance via Hwy. 146 from Soledad), wayside exhibits, trails. Book and map sale areas, picnic tables and grates, trails. **Programs & Events:** Guided hikes and interpretive talks (Mar.–May).

PLANNING YOUR VISIT

Camping: Private campground (Pinnacles) just outside east entrance; none at monument. **Lodging:** Available in Hollister, King City, Soledad; none at monument. **Food & Supplies:** Available in Hollister, King City, Pinnacles campground, and Soledad; none at monument. **Tips & Hints:** Prepare for temperatures of 110°F/ 43°C in summer. Carry plenty of water. Wear sturdy footwear. Trail elevations range from 800 ft/243 m to 3,300 ft/1,001 m. Bring flashlights to visit caves. Go between February and May for wildflower displays. Go during the week in spring because spring weekends are subject to limited parking because of crowds. Busiest March through May, least crowded in July and August. **Fees, Permits & Limitations:** Entrance fee: $5 per vehicle. No pets, bikes, or strollers on trails. No pets beyond parking and picnic areas. Leashed pets only. Charcoal fires only. No firewood gathering. No hunting. Park open daily sunrise–sunset. Visitor center open daily 9–5. Chaparral Ranger Station open weekends 9–5, intermittent weekdays.

HOW TO GET THERE

The monument's east entrance is 33 mi/53 km south of Hollister via CA 25 and Hwy. 146. The west entrance is 13 mi/21 km east of Soledad via Hwy. 146. No connecting road through the monument. Closest airport: San Jose (75 mi/120 km).

FOR MORE INFORMATION

Pinnacles National Monument (5000 Hwy. 146, Paicines, CA 95043, tel. 831/389–4485, fax 831/389–4489; Web site www.nps.gov/pinn). King City Chamber of Commerce (203 Broadway St., King City, CA 93930, tel. 831/385–3814). San Benito County Chamber of Commerce (tel. 831/637–5315).

Point Reyes
National Seashore

In the northern part of the state,
near Point Reyes Station

This peninsula north of San Francisco is noted for long beaches backed by tall cliffs, lagoons, and esteros; forested ridges; and offshore bird and sea lion colonies. The seashore was authorized in 1962, established in 1972, and designated a Biosphere Reserve in 1988.

WHAT TO SEE & DO

Beachcombing, bicycling (rentals, Olema), fishing, hiking, and horseback riding (rentals, Fivebrooks, tel. 415/663–1570). **Facilities:** 3 visitor centers with interpretive exhibits—Bear Valley (park headquarters near Olema), Lighthouse (23 mi/37 km from Bear Valley), and Ken Patrick (Drakes Beach); auditorium; radio information (1610 AM); 140 mi/224 km of hiking trails; 100 wayside exhibit panels. Sales area. **Programs & Events:** Programs on lighthouses and lifeboat stations, gray whales, seals and sea lions, wildflowers, birds, geology, Native Americans, tidepools (throughout the year). Native American Big Time Festival (4th Sat., July), Sand Sculpture Contest (Sun. of Labor Day weekend).

PLANNING YOUR VISIT

⚠ **Camping:** 4 hike-in and 20 boat-in backcountry campgrounds available (reservations available, tel. 415/663–8054; permit required, *see below*). Group campsites available (tel. 415/663–8054). Campgrounds also available in Olema and Samuel P. Taylor State Park. ⌂ **Lodging:** In the park: Point Reyes Hostel (tel. 415/663–8811). Lodging also available in Inverness, Olema, and Point Reyes Station. ✕ **Food & Supplies:** In the park: café at Drakes Beach. Delis and restaurants in Inverness, Olema, and Point Reyes Station. ☞ **Tips & Hints:** Go between February and May for flowers, December and April for migrating gray whales, November and April for breeding elephant seals, August and February for migrating birds. Busiest in August and December, least crowded in February and April. ▣ **Fees, Permits & Limitations:** Free. Shuttle fee for whale viewing ($4). Backcountry permits required ($10 per site per night). California fishing license required. No hunting. No pets or bikes in wilderness. Seashore open daily sunrise–sunset. Visitor center hours: Bear Valley—weekdays 9–5, weekends 8–5, closed Dec. 25; Lighthouse—Thurs.–Mon. 10–4:30; Ken Patrick—Labor Day–Memorial Day, Fri.–Tues. 10–5, closed Thanksgiving.

HOW TO GET THERE

The seashore is 45 mi/72 km north of San Francisco via U.S. 101 and Sir Francis Drake Blvd. or via U.S. 1 near Mill Valley. Closest airport: San Francisco.

FOR MORE INFORMATION

Bear Valley Visitor Center (Point Reyes National Seashore, Point Reyes, CA 94956, tel. 415/663–1092). Administrative office: Point Reyes National Seashore (Point Reyes Station, CA 94956, tel. 415/663-8522, fax 415/663–8132; Web site www.nps.gov/pore).

Redwood National Park

In the northwest part of the state, near Orick

The park, which runs for 40 mi/64 km along the Pacific Coast, is best known for its magnificent old-growth redwoods, some of the world's tallest trees. Less well known are the park's prairies, oak woodlands, and coastal and marine ecosystems. The park was established in 1968 and designated a World Heritage Site in 1980 and a Biosphere in 1983.

WHAT TO SEE & DO

Auto touring; backpacking; biking; bird-, elk-, and whale-watching; hiking; horseback riding and tours; picnicking. **Facilities:** 3 information centers—Crescent City, Redwood (Orick), and Hiouchi; scenic drives; hiking trails; wayside exhibits. Bookstores, picnic areas. **Programs & Events:** Ranger-led programs (mid-June–Labor Day), environmental education programs (Mar.–May, Oct., Nov.), children's program (mid-June–Labor Day). Wildflower walks (spring), Founders Day (Aug. 25).

PLANNING YOUR VISIT

⚠ **Camping:** 4 backcountry camps (permit required, *see below*). Camping also available in nearby state parks and national forests. 🏠 **Lodging:** In the park: Redwood Hostel (tel. 707/482–5785). Lodging also available locally. ✕ **Food & Supplies:** Available locally; none in park. ☞ **Tips & Hints:** Wear layers of clothing to handle varying temperatures between coastal and inland sections. Bring rain gear and good walking shoes. Borrow animal-proof food canisters at Redwood Information Center. Busiest in July and August, least crowded in December and January. 📧 **Fees, Permits & Limitations:** Free. Permit required for backcountry camping (tel. 707/464–6101). Tall Tree Outfitters offers guided day and overnight horseback rides (tel. 707/488–5785). Redwood Creek Trail is impassable during high water. Information center hours: Redwood and Crescent City—daily 9–5, Hiouchi—Memorial Day weekend–last weekend in Sept. Others closed Thanksgiving, Dec. 25, Jan. 1.

HOW TO GET THERE

The park runs along U.S. 101 from Hiouchi (Hwy. 199) to Crescent City (U.S. 101) and down to Orick. Park headquarters and information center is in Crescent City. Redwood information center is 397 mi/635 km north of San Francisco on U.S. 101 about 2 mi/3 km west of Orick. Closest airport: Eureka/Arcata.

FOR MORE INFORMATION

Redwood National Park (1111 2nd St., Crescent City, CA 95531, tel. 707/464–6101; Web site www.nps.gov/redw). Orick Chamber of Commerce (Box 234, Orick, CA 95555, tel. 707/488–2885). Crescent City

Chamber of Commerce (1001 Front St., Crescent City, CA 95531, tel. 707/464–3174 or 800/343–8300).

San Francisco Maritime National Historical Park

In San Francisco

Included in this park are a fleet of historic ships, a maritime museum, and a maritime library. The fleet includes the 1886 square-rigger *Balclutha;* the 1895 schooner *C.A. Thayer;* the 1891 scow schooner *Alma;* the 1890 ferryboat *Eureka;* the 1914 paddlewheel tug *Eppleton Hall;* and the 1907 steam tugboat *Hercules.* The *Hercules* and *Alma* have been restored and steam (and sail) to ports around the bay. The museum displays models, huge ships' parts, figureheads, and fine arts and includes the Steamship Room, which presents the history of West Coast steam. The Maritime Library houses books, periodicals, and oral histories and provides access to more than 250,000 photographs, 120,000 sheets of ships' plans, and other historic documents. The park's extensive artifact collections include oils and watercolors, scrimshaw, delicate fancywork, carvings, tools, and navigational instruments. The park was established in 1988.

WHAT TO SEE & DO

Attending boatbuilding classes, slide shows, readings, theater, videos, and other programs; doing library research; picnicking; touring historic vessels; viewing exhibits; visiting museum. **Facilities:** Museum, library, ships. Bookstore and gift shop. **Programs & Events:** Steam-engine and living-history demonstrations, boatbuilding and woodworking classes (year-round). Heritage month programs (Women's History, Asian/Pacific, Black History, etc.); Festival of the Sea (Sept.), Sea Music Concert Series (fall), Christmas at Sea (winter).

PLANNING YOUR VISIT

🏨 **Lodging:** Available in San Francisco; none in park. ✗ **Food & Supplies:** Available in San Francisco; none in park. ☞ **Tips & Hints:** Use public transportation to get to the park. The best time to visit is in the fall. Busiest in July and August, least crowded in December and January. 🎟 **Fees, Permits & Limitations:** Entrance fee: Hyde Street Pier (historic vessels): $5 per adult; $2 ages 12–17 and senior citizens; under 12 free. Museum and library free. No pets on Hyde Street Pier, in museum, or in library. No fires or stoves in picnic area. Hyde Street Pier open daily 9:30–5:30, closed Thanksgiving, Dec. 25, Jan. 1. Museum open daily 10–5, closed Thanksgiving, Dec. 25, Jan. 1. Library open Wed.–Fri. 1–5, Sat. 10–5.

HOW TO GET THERE

The park is on the west end of Fisherman's Wharf, at the Hyde Street cable-car terminus. Closest airport: San Francisco (15 mi/24 km).

FOR MORE INFORMATION
San Francisco Maritime National Historical Park (Bldg. E, Room 265, Fort Mason Center, San Francisco, CA 94123, tel. 415/556–1659, fax 415/556–1624; e-mail safr_administration@nps.gov; Web site www.nps. gov/safr). Visitor information (900 Beach St., San Francisco, CA 94109, tel. 415/556–3002, fax 415/556–6293).

Santa Monica Mountains National Recreation Area

Near Los Angeles

The Santa Monica Mountains rise above Los Angeles, widen to meet the curve of Santa Monica Bay, and reach their greatest height facing the ocean, forming a beautiful and multifaceted landscape. The recreation area is a cooperative effort that joins federal, state, and local park agencies with private preserves and landowners to protect the natural and cultural resources of this transverse mountain range and seashore. The area was established on November 10, 1978.

WHAT TO SEE & DO
Attending festivals, bird- and whale-watching, hiking, horseback riding (rentals), mountain biking, picnicking, surfing, swimming, walking. **Facilities:** Park visitor center—Thousand Oaks (401 W. Hillcrest Drive); Satwiwa Native American Indian Culture Center, Malibu Creek State Park Visitor Center, Malibu Lagoon Museum, Will Rogers State Historic Park, Topanga State Park Nature Center, Sooky Goldman Nature Center, Charmlee Nature Center, 580 mi/928 km of trails, 55-mi/88-km scenic drive. Bookstore. **Programs & Events:** Year-round programs available. Seasonal activities and special events available including nature walks, guided tours of Historic Paramount Ranch western movie set, Silent Films under the Stars.

PLANNING YOUR VISIT
⚠ **Camping:** Campground (no reservations). Group camping available at Circle X Ranch (reservations available, tel. 805/370–2311 ext. 1702). Individual and group campsites at Point Mugu, Leo Carrillo, and Malibu Creek state parks (reservations available, tel. 800/444–7275). Group campsites also available at Danielson and Sycamore group multiuse areas in Point Mugu State Park (reservations available, tel. 800/444–7275) and Decker Canyon (reservations available, tel. 213/485–4853). Private RV camping available at Malibu Beach RV Park (reservations available, tel. 310/456–6052). ▦ **Lodging:** Available locally; none in recreation area. ✕ **Food & Supplies:** Available locally; none in recreation area. ☞ **Tips & Hints:** Expect hot, dry summers (80°F/27°C–100°F/38°C) and relatively cool, wet winters (40°F/4°C–70°F/21°C). Plan for coastal side of the mountains to be 10–15 degrees cooler than inland side during summer (in winter this pattern is reversed). Busiest in May and June, least crowded in December and January. Contact

park for copy of "Outdoors" calendar of events. ✉ **Fees, Permits & Limitations:** Free. Parking fees charged at most state parks and some local parks within recreation area. Some special events charge fees. Horse rentals available at Dos Vientos Stables (tel. 805/498–9222) and Adventures on Horseback (tel. 818/706–0888). Permit required for group picnics (tel. 805/370–1854). Park open daily. Visitor center open daily 9–5. Closed Thanksgiving, Dec. 25, Jan. 1.

HOW TO GET THERE

The park is west of Griffith Park in Los Angeles County and east of Oxnard Plain in Ventura County. U.S. 101 (Ventura Freeway) borders the mountains on the north, and CA 1 (Pacific Coast Highway) and the Pacific Ocean form the southern boundary. Access is via many roads that cross the mountains between these two highways. Part of the park stretches into the Simi Hills north of U.S. 101. To reach the visitor center from U.S. 101, take Lynn Rd. exit, travel north on Lynn Rd, turn east (right) on Hillcrest Dr., turn left onto McCloud Ave. The driveway to the visitor center will be on the right-hand side. Closest airports: Burbank (20 mi/32 km), Los Angeles International (15 mi/24 km).

FOR MORE INFORMATION

Santa Monica Mountains National Recreation Area (National Park Service, 401 W. Hillcrest Dr., Thousand Oaks, CA 91360, tel. 805/370–2301; Web site www.nps.gov/samo).

Sequoia and Kings Canyon National Parks

In the east-central part of the state, near Three Rivers

Sequoia, the second-oldest national park in the United States, was established in 1890 to protect the Big Trees in Giant Forest, including the General Sherman Tree, the world's largest living tree. Sequoia also contains the Mineral King Valley and Mt. Whitney, the highest mountain in the lower 48 states. A small portion of what is now Kings Canyon was set aside in 1890 as General Grant National Park. In 1940, General Grant was absorbed into the new and larger Kings Canyon National Park, which eventually grew to include the South Fork of the Kings River and 456,552 acres of backcountry wilderness. Managed together, Sequoia and Kings Canyon have a total wilderness area of 736,980 acres.

WHAT TO SEE & DO

Auto touring, backpacking, cross-country skiing, fishing, hiking, horseback riding, snowshoeing, viewing sequoias. **Facilities:** 5 visitor centers—Ash Mountain, Grant Grove, Cedar Grove (bottom of Kings Canyon), Lodgepole, and Mineral King; nature center; roadside exhibits; 140 mi/224 km of scenic roads; 800 mi/1,280 km of trails. **Programs & Events:** Ranger-led walks, talks, and evening programs; field seminars (year-round). Horseback rides (June–Sept.), Crystal Cave tours (May–Sept.), snowshoe walks. Nation's Christmas Tree Ceremony (2nd Sun. of Dec., General Grant Tree in Kings Canyon).

PLANNING YOUR VISIT

⚠ **Camping:** Camping available: no hookups (reservations available Memorial Day–Sept. in Lodgepole, tel. 800/365–2267). Backcountry camping available (permit required; *see below*). Group campsites available at Grant Grove, Cedar Grove (Kings Canyon) (tel. 559/565-4335 Nov.–Apr., 559/565–3792 May–Oct. for information on mail or fax reservations for these two sites), and Dorst (Sequoia) (reservations available, tel. 800/365–2267). Camping also available in adjacent national forests. ⛺ **Lodging:** In the parks: Grant Grove Lodge (year-round, Kings Canyon) and Cedar Grove lodges (June–Sept.), tel. 559/335–5500 for both; Wuksachi Village (year-round, tel. 888/252–3757). ✗ **Food & Supplies:** In the parks: meals at Grant Grove, Lodgepole, Wuksachi Village (year-round); Stony Creek and Cedar Grove (summer); groceries at Grant Grove, Lodgepole (year-round); Wolverton (winter); Cedar Grove and Stony Creek (summer). ☞ **Tips & Hints:** Plan on a two-hour drive from Ash Mountain entrance on Hwy. 198 to Grant Grove at Hwy. 180 entrance. Add two–three hours for side trip from Grant Grove into Kings Canyon. First-time visitors should see General Sherman and General Grant trees. Bring rain gear and layered clothing for hiking. Parks busiest June through August, least crowded in January and February; Kings Canyon busiest in June and July, least crowded December through February. ▦ **Fees, Permits & Limitations:** Entrance fee: $10 per vehicle or $5 per cyclist or walk-in. Call park for commercial tour fees. Backcountry permit (free) required for all backcountry camping. California state fishing license required. No bikes on trails. Shuttle available in Sequoia between Wuksachi, Lodgepole, and the General Sherman Tree in Giant Forest (summer). Road to Mineral King in Sequoia National Park open Memorial Day–Oct., weather permitting. Vehicles longer than 22 ft/6.7 m not advised on Generals Hwy. between Potwisha Campground and Giant Forest in Sequoia. Hwy. 180 to Cedar Grove in Kings Canyon open mid-Apr.–mid-Nov. Park open daily. Foothills and Grant Grove visitor centers open daily. Walter Fry Nature Center in Lodgepole campground open July–Labor Day. Cedar Grove visitor center open late May–Sept. Lodgepole visitor center open daily Apr.–mid-Nov, Fri.–Mon. mid-Nov.–Mar. Mineral King visitor center open June–Labor Day. Giant Forest Museum opening summer 2001.

HOW TO GET THERE

There are no roads into the parks from the east. From the west, take Hwy. 180 from Fresno to enter Kings Canyon and Hwy. 198 from Visalia to enter Sequoia. Generals Hwy. connects the two roads, making loop trips possible. During the winter, the Generals Hwy. between Lodgepole and Grant Grove may be closed by snow. Closest airport: Fresno (53 mi/85 km).

FOR MORE INFORMATION

Sequoia and Kings Canyon National Parks (Visitor Information, 47050 Generals Hwy., Three Rivers, CA 93271, tel. 559/565–3341; Web site www.nps.gov/seki).

Whiskeytown-Shasta-Trinity National Recreation Area

In the northern part of the state, near Redding

Nestled in the rugged Klamath Mountains watershed, Whiskeytown preserves much of the colorful history of the California gold rush and has a wealth of water-oriented and backcountry opportunities. Although Whiskeytown Lake is smaller than Shasta or Trinity lakes, which are administered by the Forest Service, its clear, blue water and full pool level during the summer attract many recreationists to its shores. Activities range from camping, fishing, and swimming to waterskiing, sailing, and canoeing. The recreation area was authorized in 1965 and established in 1972.

WHAT TO SEE & DO

Backpacking (permit required, *see below*), boating (rentals, Oak Bottom Marina and in Redding), canoeing, fishing, hiking, horseback riding, hunting, jetskiing, mountain biking, picnicking, sailing, scuba diving, swimming, waterskiing. **Facilities:** Visitor information center with interpretive exhibits (junction of Hwy. 299 and Kennedy Memorial Dr., 8 mi/13 km west of Redding); amphitheater, beaches, boat-launch areas, 50 mi/80 km of backcountry roads and trails, wayside exhibits, interpretive signs. Picnic pavilions and areas, post office, sales outlet. **Programs & Events:** Guided walks, evening programs, demonstrations and talks pertaining to natural and cultural resources of the area, tours through the Tower House Historic District, Junior Ranger programs (all Memorial Day–Labor Day). National Park Week Celebration and Pick Up Lake Litter Volunteer Cleanup (both in Apr.).

PLANNING YOUR VISIT

⚲ **Camping:** 3 campgrounds: 2 with water and sewers (reservations available, tel. 800/365–2267). Primitive camping available (permit required, *see below*). Group campsites available at Dry Creek (reservations required, tel. 800/365–2267). Private campgrounds available in Redding. ▦ **Lodging:** Available in Redding; none at recreation area. ✕ **Food & Supplies:** In the recreation area: limited supplies and groceries at Oak Bottom Marina, snack bars (summer) at Oak Bottom and Brandy Creek beaches. Food and supplies also available in Redding. ☞ **Tips & Hints:** Keep all scented items (food, cosmetics, soap, toothpaste, and so forth) in airtight, bear-proof containers when available. Dispose of all trash in bear-proof garbage cans where available. Watch for western diamondback rattlesnakes. Beware of abandoned mine shafts. Go in spring for wildflowers and pleasant hiking, although trails may be too wet for mountain biking and horseback riding. Go in summer for all water activities, camping, and fishing; fall for foliage, pleasant hiking, mountain biking, and horseback riding before beginning of rainy season. Busiest in June and July, least crowded in December and January. ▣ **Fees, Permits & Limitations:** Entrance fee: $5 per vehicle, $20 annual pass available. Fee charged for Whiskey Creek Group Picnic Area (reservations required, tel. 800/365–2267). Permits required (free) for backpacking and backcountry camping. Permits for gold panning ($1) and wood collecting ($10 for 2 cords of wood) required. California hunting and fishing license required. No motorized vehicles on trails. Horses and mountain bikes restricted to certain trails. No dogs at Oak Bottom and Brandy Creek beaches. Leashed dogs elsewhere. No jetskiing after April 2002 at Whiskeytown Lake. Recreation area open daily. Certain areas (some rest rooms and several backcountry roads) close in winter. Visitor center generally open Memorial Day–Labor Day, daily 9–6; Labor Day–Memorial Day, daily 10–4. Closed Thanksgiving, Dec. 25, Jan. 1.

HOW TO GET THERE

8 mi/13 km west of Redding on Hwy 299. Closest airports: Redding Municipal, Sacramento (165 mi/264 km).

FOR MORE INFORMATION

Whiskeytown National Recreation Area (Box 188, Whiskeytown, CA 96095-0188, tel. 530/242–3400, fax 530/246–5154; Web site www.nps. gov/whis). Redding Chamber of Commerce (747 Auditorium Dr., Redding CA 96001, tel. 530/225–4433). Redding Convention and Visitors Bureau (777 Auditorium Dr., Redding, CA 96001, tel. 800/874–7562 or 530/225–4100, fax 530/225–4354).

Yosemite National Park

In the east-central part of the state, surrounding Yosemite Village

Yosemite Valley is the heart of the 1,200-square-mi/3108-km park that offers views of the 2,425-ft/736-m Yosemite Falls and the sheer granite faces of El Capitan and Half Dome. The park, which ranges from 2,000 ft/607 m to 13,000 ft/3,943 m above sea level, is also home to giant sequoias more than 2,000 years old and spectacular alpine lakes and wilderness. Yosemite Valley and Mariposa Big Tree Grove were granted to the State of California in 1864. The national park was established in 1890. The federal government accepted lands returned by the state in 1906. The El Portal site was authorized in 1958. The park was designated a World Heritage Site in 1984.

WHAT TO SEE & DO

Auto and bus touring, backpacking, bicycling (rentals), bird- and wildlife watching, cross-country skiing, driving to Glacier Point overlook and Mariposa Grove of Giant Sequoias, fishing, hiking, horseback riding, ice skating, rafting, rock climbing, skiing, swimming, viewing Yosemite Valley rock features and waterfalls. **Facilities:** 4 visitor centers—Valley (Yosemite Valley), Big Oak Flat, Wawona, and Tuolumne; Ansel Adams Gallery, 196 mi/314 km of scenic roads, 800 mi/1,280 km of trails, 9 mi/14 km of paved bikeways. Boarding kennels, bookstores, gas. **Programs & Events:** Ranger-led walks, talks, and evening programs; bus tours; horseback rides; tram tours (all year-round).

PLANNING YOUR VISIT

⚠ **Camping:** 13 campgrounds: no hookups. (Reservations available or required, tel. 800/436–7275 in U.S. or 301/722–1257 elsewhere). Backcountry camping available (permit required, *see below*). Group campsites at Wawona, Tuolumne Meadows, Hodgson Meadow, and Bridalveil Creek (reservations required, tel. 800/436–7275). 🏨 **Lodging:** In the park: Ahwahnee Hotel, Curry Village, Housekeeping Camp, and Yosemite Lodge in Yosemite Valley; Wawona Hotel; White Wolf Lodge and Tuolumne Meadows Lodge (tel. 559/252–4848 for all). Cabins in High Sierras camp (tel. 559/253–5674). Lodging also available in El Portal, Fish Camp, Groveland, Lee Vining, Mariposa, and Oakhurst. ✕ **Food & Supplies:** Meals, food, and supplies available in Yosemite Valley, Wawona, White Wolf, Glacier Point, and Tuolumne Meadows. Food and supplies also available in surrounding communities. ☞ **Tips & Hints:** Plan to spend at least four hours touring Yosemite Valley and two days to visit entire park. Dress in layers and bring rain gear to accommodate weather changes. Expect warm, dry summers; most moisture falls between January and March. Busiest in July and August, least crowded in November and January. ▨ **Fees, Permits & Limitations:** Entrance fee: $20 per vehicle or $10 per bus passenger, bicyclist, or walk-in. Free shuttle bus in east end of Yosemite Valley (year-round) and between Wawona and the Mariposa Grove of Giant Sequoias and from Tuolumne Meadows to Tenaya Lake (June–Sept.). California fishing license required. Wilderness permit (free in person, $5 for telephone reservations) required for any backcountry camping (tel. 209/372–0740). No pets on trails or beaches or in backcountry or public buildings. Leashed pets restricted to specific campgrounds. No hunting. No discharging weapons. Don't deface or remove natural historic features. The Tioga Pass entrance is closed Nov.–early June because of snow. Park open daily. Yosemite Valley visitor center open June 15–Sept. 15, daily 8–7, Sept. 16–June 14, daily 8–5.

HOW TO GET THERE

There are four entrances to the park: the south entrance on Hwy. 41N from Fresno, the Arch Rock entrance on Hwy. 140W from Merced, the Big Oak Flat entrance on Hwy. 120W from Modesto and Manteca, and the Tioga Pass entrance on Hwy. 120E from Lee Vining and U.S. 395. Closest airports: Merced (80 mi/128 km), Fresno (94 mi/150 km), San Francisco (200 mi/320 km).

FOR MORE INFORMATION

Public Information Office, Yosemite National Park (Box 577, Yosemite, CA 95389, tel. 209/372–0200; Web site www.nps.gov/yose). Mariposa Visitors Bureau (Box 425, Mariposa, CA 95338, tel. 209/966–2456 or 800/208–2434). Yosemite Sierra Visitors Bureau (41729 Hwy. 41, Oakhurst, CA 93644, tel. 209/683–4636; e-mail ysvb@sierranet.net). Lee Vining Chamber of Commerce (Box 130, Lee Vining, CA 93541, tel. 760/647–6629 or 760/647–6595).

See Also

....

AIDS Memorial Grove National Park, Affiliated Areas in Other National Parklands. *California National Historic Trail,* National Trails System in Other National Parklands. *Fort Chicago Naval Magazine National Memorial,* Affiliated Areas in Other National Parklands. *Juan Bautista de Anza National Historic Trail,* National Trails System in Other National Parklands. *Kern River,* Wild and Scenic Rivers System in Other National Parklands. *Kings River,* Wild and Scenic Rivers System in Other National Parklands. *Klamath River,* Wild and Scenic Rivers System in Other National Parklands. *Merced River,* Wild and Scenic Rivers System in Other National Parklands. *Pacific Crest National Scenic Trail,* National Trails System in Other National Parklands. *Pony Express National Historic Trail,* National Trails System in Other National Parklands. *Tuolumne River,* Wild and Scenic Rivers System in Other National Parklands.

COLORADO

Bent's Old Fort
National Historic Site

In the southeast part of the state,
between La Junta and Las Animas

Preserved here is a reconstructed adobe trading post on the old Santa
Fe Trail. In its heyday (1833–49), the fort was the largest American-
owned commercial center in the 700 mi/1,120 km between Independence, Missouri, and Santa Fe, New Mexico. The park was established
on June 3, 1960.

WHAT TO SEE & DO

Touring the fort, visiting the sales area in the Indian trade room and
bookstore. **Facilities:** Fort and fort furnishings. Audiovisual program,
bookstore, sales area with the Indian trade room. **Programs & Events:**
50-minute ranger guided tours (June–Aug., hourly; Sept.–May, by
reservation). 20-minute historic lifestyle demonstrations (June–Aug.).
Kid's Quarters (June), holiday celebration (2nd weekend Dec.).

PLANNING YOUR VISIT

⛺ **Camping:** Available nearby in La Junta and at John Martin Reservoir; none at site. 🏨 **Lodging:** Available nearby in La Junta, Las Animas, Rocky Ford; none at site. ✕ **Food & Supplies:** Available in La
Junta, Las Animas, and Rocky Ford; none at site. ☞ **Tips & Hints:** Go
from June to mid-October for best visit. ✉ **Fees, Permits & Limitations:**
Tour fee: $2 per person, ages 5 and under free. Permits required in ad-
vance for commercial filming. No pets in fort. Park open Memorial
Day–Labor Day, daily 8–5:30; Labor Day–Memorial Day, daily 9–4.
Closed Thanksgiving, Dec. 25, Jan. 1.

HOW TO GET THERE

6 mi/10 km east of La Junta and 13 mi/21 km west of Las Animas on
Hwy. 194; 75 mi/120 km east of Pueblo and 140 mi/224 km west of
Garden City, KS, via U.S. 50. Closest airport: Pueblo (75 mi/120 km).

FOR MORE INFORMATION

Bent's Old Fort National Historic Site (35110 Hwy. 194E, La Junta,
CO 81050-9523, tel. 719/383–5010, fax 719/383–5031; Web site
www.nps.gov/beol). La Junta Chamber of Commerce (110 Santa Fe
Ave., La Junta, CO 81050, tel 719/384–7411).

Black Canyon of the Gunnison National Park

In the southwest part of the state, east of Montrose

Carved by the Gunnison River, the walls of schist and gneiss in Black Canyon are some of the most imposing in North America. The canyon and its rims are home to black bear, mule deer, golden eagles, and peregrine falcon. The site was proclaimed a monument on March 2, 1933, and was redesignated a national park on October 21, 1999.

WHAT TO SEE & DO

Camping, cross-country skiing, fishing, hiking, kayaking, picnicking, rock climbing, snowshoeing, wildlife viewing. **Facilities:** Visitor center with interpretive exhibits (Gunnison Point, south rim), trails, amphitheater, auditorium, interpretive signs. Book sale area. **Programs & Events:** Ranger-guided and evening programs (daily, late May–late Sept); ranger-guided snowshoe walks (free snowshoes provided), full-moon ranger-guided cross-country ski programs along the rim (weekends only, mid-Jan.–early Mar., reservations required, tel. 970/641–2337).

PLANNING YOUR VISIT

⚠ **Camping:** 2 campgrounds: south rim campsite has electric hookups. Backcountry camping available (permit required, *see below*). Private campgrounds in Cimarron, Crawford, Gunnison, Hotchkiss, Montrose. 🛏 **Lodging:** Available nearby in Cimarron, Crawford, Delta, Gunnison, Hotchkiss, Montrose; none in park. ✗ **Food & Supplies:** Food and souvenirs at the Rim House (Pulpit Rock Overlook, south rim). Food and supplies also available in Delta, Gunnison, Hotchkiss, Montrose. ☞ **Tips & Hints:** Expect strenuous inner canyon hiking. Go in mid-May to mid-June for wildflowers, late September for fall foliage. Busiest in July and August, least crowded in December and January. 💲 **Fees, Permits & Limitations:** Entrance fee: $7 per vehicle in north rim and south rim. Backcountry permits (free) required. Colorado state fishing license required. No vehicles or bicycles off roads. No pets in wilderness, leashed pets elsewhere. Fires only in campground grates. Park south rim open year-round, north rim closed in winter. Gunnison Point Visitor Center open June–Aug., daily 8–6; Sept.–May, shorter hours. Closed Thanksgiving, Dec. 25, Jan. 1.

HOW TO GET THERE

South rim is 15 mi/24 km east of Montrose via Hwys. 50 and 347, north rim is 11 mi/18 km south of Crawford, off Hwy. 92 (6 mi/10 km unpaved). Closest airport: Montrose (15 mi/24 km).

FOR MORE INFORMATION

Black Canyon of the Gunnison National Park (102 Elk Creek, Gunnison, CO 81230, tel. 970/641–2337, fax 970/249–3127; Web site www.nps.gov/blca). Montrose Chamber of Commerce (1519 E. Main St., Montrose, CO 81401, tel. 970/249–5000, fax 970/249–2907).

Colorado National Monument

*In the west-central part of the state,
near Grand Junction*

The towering red monoliths, sheer-walled canyons, dinosaur fossils, and remains of prehistoric Indian culture here reflect the environment and history of this colorful sandstone country. Residents include bighorn sheep, golden eagles, mule deer, and mountain lions. The monument was proclaimed on May 24, 1911.

WHAT TO SEE & DO

Auto touring, biking, bird-watching, hiking, picnicking, rock climbing. **Facilities:** Visitor center with interpretive exhibits, scenic drive, overlooks, trails. Bookstore, picnic area. **Programs & Events:** Audiovisual program. Evening campfire and interpretive programs (mid-May–Labor Day, Fri. nights). Easter sunrise services.

PLANNING YOUR VISIT

Camping: Campground: no reservations. Backcountry camping available (permit required, *see below*). **Lodging:** Available in nearby communities; none at monument. **Food & Supplies:** Available in nearby communities; none at monument. **Tips & Hints:** Plan to spend two–five hours at the monument. Busiest in May and June, least crowded in December and January. **Fees, Permits & Limitations:** Entrance fee (Apr.–Sept.): $4 per car, $2 per person. Permit required (free) for backcountry camping. Leashed pets only. No pets in backcountry. Park open daily. Closed Dec. 25. Visitor center open Labor Day–Memorial Day, daily 9–5; Memorial Day–Labor Day, daily 8–6.

HOW TO GET THERE

From the east, exit I–70 at Horizon Dr. for east entrance. From the west, take Exit 19 to west entrance. Closest airport: Grand Junction (15 mi/24 km).

FOR MORE INFORMATION

Colorado National Monument (Fruita, CO 81521, tel. 970/858–3617, fax 970/858–0372; e-mail COLM_Superintendent@nps.gov; Web site www.nps.gov/colm).

Curecanti National Recreation Area

In the southwest part of the state, west of Gunnison

Three reservoirs, extending for almost 40 mi/64 km between the towns of Gunnison and Montrose, form the heart of Curecanti. Blue Mesa Reservoir, stocked with trout and salmon, is a mecca for anglers and water-sports enthusiasts. Bald eagles and sandhill and whooping cranes

migrate through the area in spring and fall. The area is named after
Curicata, a chief of the Ute Indians, who lived here when European
settlers arrived in the 1800s. The park is administered under a February 11, 1965, cooperative agreement with the Bureau of Reclamation.

WHAT TO SEE & DO

Boating (rentals, Elk Creek and Lake Fork marinas), camping, cross-
country skiing, fishing (rentals, Elk Creek and Lake Fork marinas), hiking, ice fishing, picnicking, snowmobiling, snowshoeing, swimming,
waterskiing, windsurfing. **Facilities:** 3 visitor centers with interpretive
exhibits—Elk Creek, Lake Fork and Cimarron. Bookstores, fire grates,
picnic tables. **Programs & Events:** Ranger-led afternoon and evening
programs, walks, talks, hikes (Memorial Day–Labor Day). Ranger-led
snowshoe walks, hikes, cross-country ski tours (Jan.–Mar., weekends).

PLANNING YOUR VISIT

⚠ **Camping:** 10 campgrounds (9 with no reservations): 2 for group
camping (Elk Creek, Red Creek, reservations required for both, tel.
970/641–2337). None has hookups. Backcountry camping available.
Private campgrounds in Cimarron, Gunnison, Montrose. 🏨 **Lodging:**
Available in Gunnison, Montrose; none in park. ✗ **Food & Supplies:** In
the park: Elk Creek Marina (tel. 970/641–0707), Lake Fork Marina (tel.
970/641–3048), Pappy's Restaurant (tel. 970/641–0403). All three open
summer only. Food and supplies also available in Gunnison and Montrose. ☞ **Tips & Hints:** Go between May and August for wildflowers,
May and September for bird migrations, all year for fishing. Busiest in
July and August, least crowded in December and March. 🎫 **Fees, Permits & Limitations:** Free. Boat permit required ($4 for 2 days, $10 per
14 days, $30 per year) on Blue Mesa Reservoir. Boat tours given 3 times
per day (Memorial Day–Labor Day), reservations available, tel. 970/
641–0707). Colorado fishing license required. Leashed pets only. No
bikes or motorized vehicles on trails. Park open daily. Elk Creek Visitor
Center open May–Sept., daily 8–6; Oct.–Apr., daily 8–4:30. Lake Fork
open Memorial Day–Labor Day, daily 9–4; Cimarron open May 15–
Sept. 15, daily 9–4.

HOW TO GET THERE

Park headquarters is 15 mi/24 km west of Gunnison on U.S. 50. Closest
airport: Gunnison.

FOR MORE INFORMATION

Curecanti National Recreation Area (102 Elk Creek, Gunnison, CO
81230, tel. 970/641–2337, fax 970/641–3127; Web site www.nps.gov/
cure). Gunnison County Chamber of Commerce (500 E. Tomichi Ave.,
Gunnison, CO 81230, tel. 970/641–1501). Montrose Chamber of Commerce (1519 E. Main St., Montrose, CO 81401, tel. 970/249–5515).

Dinosaur National Monument

In northwest Colorado and northeast Utah

The memorial is the only park that protects a dinosaur quarry: the Douglass Quarry is an internationally significant fossil site representing one of the best windows scientists have into the world of upper Jurassic (150-million-year-old) dinosaurs. Archaeological sites in the park represent one of the most complete records of human occupation and development in North America. The site's Green and Yampa river canyons are of great scenic and recreational value. The park was established on October 4, 1915.

WHAT TO SEE & DO

Auto touring, fishing, hiking, rafting, visiting Dinosaur Quarry, white-water boating. **Facilities:** 2 visitor centers with interpretive exhibits— Dinosaur Quarry (7 mi/11 km north of Jensen, UT) and Monument Headquarters (2 mi/1 km east of Dinosaur, CO); self-guided auto tours: Tour of the Tilted Rocks (22 mi/35 km, 2 hours, near Dinosaur Quarry), Journey Through Time (31 mi/50 km, 4 hours, Monument Headquarters); self-guided nature trails. Bookstores, picnic areas. **Programs & Events:** Quarry and nature talks, guided walks, evening campground talks (June–Aug., daily).

PLANNING YOUR VISIT

Camping: 6 campgrounds: no showers or hookups (no reservations). No trailers longer than 35 ft/11 m. Group camping available (reservations required, tel. 435/789–8277). All open Memorial Day–Labor Day, Split Mountain campground open in winter. Backcountry camping available (permit required, *see below*). Private campgrounds available in Blue Mountain, Craig, Dinosaur, Meeker, Rangely, CO; Jensen, Vernal, UT. **Lodging:** Available in Craig, Dinosaur, Rangely, CO; Vernal, UT; none in park. **Food & Supplies:** Available in Blue Mountain, Craig, Dinosaur, Meeker, Rangely, CO; Jensen, Vernal, UT; none in park. **Tips & Hints:** Plan to hike, auto tour, and see the Dinosaur Quarry. Go even in winter to see quarry and do Tour of the Tilted Rocks. Visit in fall for smallest crowds and nicest weather. Busiest in June and July, least crowded in December and January. **Fees, Permits & Limitations:** Entrance fee: $10 per vehicle, $5 for walk-in, bike, motorcycle. Utah or Colorado state fishing license required. White-water boating permit required (tel. 970/374–2468), backcountry camping permit required (free). Park open daily. Dinosaur Quarry Visitor Center open Labor Day–Memorial Day, daily 8–4:30; Memorial Day–Labor Day, daily 8–7. Monument Headquarters Visitor Center open Labor Day–Memorial Day, weekdays 8–4:30; Memorial Day–Labor Day, daily 8–6. Both visitor centers closed Thanksgiving, Dec. 25, Jan. 1. Headquarters also closed all federal holidays (fall–spring).

HOW TO GET THERE

The main access points to the park are Dinosaur Quarry, which is 7 mi/11 km north of Jensen, UT, on SR 149, and Monument Headquarters, which is 2 mi/3 km east of Dinosaur, CO, on U.S. 40.

FOR MORE INFORMATION

Dinosaur National Monument (4545 E. Hwy. 40, Dinosaur, CO 81610-9724, tel. 970/374–3000; Web site www.nps.gov/dino).

Florissant Fossil Beds National Monument

In the center of the state,
40 mi/64 km west of Colorado Springs

The 6,000-acre monument preserves one of the world's most comprehensive fossil sites of late Eocene life. Some 35 million years ago, a volcanic field erupted and buried a redwood forest at the site in volcanic mud. The ash and mudflows sealed the Florissant lake bottom sediments. Trapped within these sediment layers are thousands of insect species and 140 different plants, along with fish, birds, and mammals. The monument was established on August 25, 1969.

WHAT TO SEE & DO

Cross-country skiing (rentals, Colorado Springs, Woodland Park), hiking, picnicking, snowshoeing (free, park), taking interpretive walks, touring 1878 homestead and petrified redwood forest. **Facilities:** Visitor center with interpretive exhibits, 13 mi/19 km of trails, outdoor exhibits, trails, amphitheater, Hornbek Homestead. Book and map sales area, picnic areas. **Programs & Events:** Ranger-led interpretive programs (mid-June–Sept., daily 10–4 on the hour; guided walks follow most talks), guided walks (June–Sept.), wildflower walks (mid-June–mid-Aug., Fri. 10 AM); special programs mid-June–Oct., weekends (topics include fossils, elk watches, art in the park). Hornbek Homestead Open House (last weekend in July, 2nd weekend in Dec.).

PLANNING YOUR VISIT

⚠ **Camping:** Available in Mueller State Park, Pike National Forest, and locally; none at monument. 🛏 **Lodging:** Available in Colorado Springs, Cripple Creek, Divide, Florissant, Lake George, Woodland Park; none at monument. ✕ **Food & Supplies:** Available in Colorado Springs, Cripple Creek, Divide, Florissant, Lake George, Woodland Park; none at monument. ☞ **Tips & Hints:** Be prepared for high-altitude (8,400 ft/2,548 m) conditions, rapidly changing weather, and moderate physical activity. Go in June or July for wildflowers, September and October for fall colors, fewer people, and elk activity. Busiest in July and August, least crowded in December and January. 🎫 **Fees, Permits & Limitations:** Entrance fee: $2 per person, free under 17, or $4 per family. Reservations required (tel. 719/748–3253) for four-hour summer programs on wildlife, ecology, and history. No fossil collecting, hunting, off-road vehicle travel. No firearms. No pets in backcountry. No pets, horses, bicycles, or motorized vehicles on trails. Park and visitor center open Sept.–May, daily 8–4:30; June–Aug., daily 8–7. Closed Thanksgiving, Dec. 25, Jan. 1.

HOW TO GET THERE

Teller County Rd. 1½ mi/3 km south of Florissant, 35 mi/56 km west of Colorado Springs on U.S. 24. Closest airport: Colorado Springs.

FOR MORE INFORMATION

Florissant Fossil Beds National Monument (Box 185, Florissant, CO 80816, tel. 719/748–3253, fax 719/748–3164; Web site www.nps.gov/flfo). Woodland Park Chamber of Commerce (200 E. Midland, Woodland Park, CO 80863, tel. 719/687–9885).

Great Sand Dunes National Park and Preserve

In the south-central part of the state, near Alamosa

In a corner of the remote San Luis Valley in the Colorado Rockies, the Great Sand Dunes rise to heights of nearly 750 ft/228 m, forming the tallest sand dunes in North America. Covering 39 square mi/100 square km, the monument provides opportunities for hiking, wilderness camping, and exploring. The monument was proclaimed in 1932.

WHAT TO SEE & DO

Cross-country skiing, dune climbing, four-wheel-drive touring (tour reservations, tel. 719/378–2222), hiking, horseback riding (rentals, tel. 719/589–4186), picnicking, snowshoeing, walking. **Facilities:** Visitor center with interpretive exhibits and self-guided interpretive trails, outdoor amphitheater. Church service (Memorial Day–Labor Day, Sun.), grills, picnic tables. **Programs & Events:** Self-guided trails. Ranger-guided hikes, evening slide programs, interpretive talk (Memorial Day–Labor Day), summer concerts (Sun., July–Aug.). Sand Castle Building/Kite Flying Day (last Sat., June).

PLANNING YOUR VISIT

⚠ **Camping:** Campground: Pinyon Flats, no hookups (no reservations). Group camping available (reservations required, tel. 719/378–2312 ext. 221). Backcountry camping available (permit required, *see below*). Private campgrounds available nearby at Great Sand Dunes Oasis (Apr.–Oct., tel. 719/378–2222), San Luis Lakes State Park (year-round, tel. 719/378–2020). 🏨 **Lodging:** Available near the monument at Great Sand Dunes Lodge (Apr.–Oct., tel. 719/378–2900), Inn at Zapata (Mar.–Oct., tel 719/378–2356). Lodging also available in Alamosa, Blanca, Fort Garland, Mosca; none at monument. ✕ **Food & Supplies:** Restaurant, store at Great Sand Dunes Oasis (Apr.–Oct., tel. 719/378–2222); for nonguests, lunch Mon.–Sun., dinner Fri., Sat., Sun. only. Meals at The Inn at Zapata (Mar.–Oct., tel. 719/378–2356). Food and supplies also available in Alamosa. ☞ **Tips & Hints:** Hike dunes with shoes on early or late on summer days. Summer temperatures of 70°F/21°C–80°F/27°C cause the sand temperature to rise to 140°F/60°C. Go in spring or early summer to visit Medano Creek, which flows at the base of the dunes. Go in July for wildflowers, August and September for prairie sunflowers. Busiest in July and August, least crowded in December and January. **Fees, Permits & Limitations:** Entrance fee: $3 per person 17 years and older. Backcountry permits required (free). Colorado state fishing license required. Leashed pets only. Pets not recommended on hot dunes. Mountain bikes, motor vehicles on established roads only. No mechanical equipment on dunes. No all-terrain vehicles, hunting, firewood gathering. Monument open daily. Visitor center open Sept.–May, daily 8:30–4:30; extended hours June–Aug. Closed Thanksgiving, Dec. 25, Jan. 1.

HOW TO GET THERE

38 mi/61 km northeast of Alamosa on CO 150. Closest airport: Alamosa.

FOR MORE INFORMATION

Great Sand Dunes Monument and Preserve (11999 Hwy. 150, Mosca, CO 81146, tel. 719/378–2312, fax 719/378–2594; Web site www.nps. gov/grsa). Alamosa Chamber of Commerce (Cole Park, Alamosa, CO 81101, tel. 719/589–3681).

Hovenweep National Monument

In the southwest part of the state, near Cortez, and in southeast Utah

Hovenweep protects some of the finest examples of ancient stone architecture. The inhabitants of Hovenweep were part of the large farming culture that lived in the area from 500 BC until AD 1300, and their well-preserved stone towers and pueblo-style buildings perch on large boulders and slickrock canyon rims. The monument is noted for its solitude, clear skies, and undeveloped natural character and was proclaimed on March 2, 1923.

WHAT TO SEE & DO

Guided and self-guided tours of cliff dwellings, towers, and pueblos; picnicking. **Facilities:** Ranger station with interpretive exhibits, trails. Bookstore, picnic tables. **Programs & Events:** Ranger-led and self-guided tours. Evening programs (summer).

PLANNING YOUR VISIT

Camping: Campground: tent, limited RV. No hookups. Campgrounds available in Blanding and Bluff, UT, and Cortez, CO. No backcountry camping. **Lodging:** Available in Cortez, CO, or Blanding, UT; none at monument. **Food & Supplies:** Food and supplies available in Cortez, CO, Anath, UT, Blanding, UT, and Hatch, UT; none at monument. **Tips & Hints:** Plan one–two hours to visit Ranger Station and Square Tower Group area trails and archaeological sites. Go in spring and fall for best hiking. Bring insect repellent in late May when biting piñon gnats are out. Go before 10 AM in summer to avoid heat. Avoid late-afternoon winter visits because of remote location and possible storms. Gravel roads may become impassable during and after storms. Busiest in July and August, least crowded in December and January. ✉ **Fees, Permits & Limitations:** Free. No climbing on the ancient walls or collecting artifacts. Hiking on established trails only. Mountain bikes on roadways only. Ranger Station open 8–5. Trail open sunrise–sunset. Closed Dec. 25.

HOW TO GET THERE

From Cortez, CO, the monument can be reached via U.S. 666/160 south and County Rd. 6 (Airport Rd.) west. Follow Hovenweep signs. Route includes 12 mi/19 km of graded gravel road. From Blanding or Bluff, UT, turn east off U.S. 191 on UT 262 to the Hatch Trading Post. Follow Hovenweep signs. Closest airport: Cortez (20 mi/32 km).

FOR MORE INFORMATION

Superintendent, Hovenweep National Monument (McElmo Rte., Cortez, CO 81321, tel. 970/562–4282; fax 970/562–4284; Web site www.nps.gov/hove).

Mesa Verde National Park

In the southwest part of the state, near Cortez

Covered mostly by piñon and juniper forest, this 52,080-acre park preserves the cliff dwellings and surface sites of the Anasazi, or Ancestral Puebloan people, who lived in the area between 500 and 1300. Elevations range from 6,400 ft/1,941 m in the deep canyons to 8,500 ft/2,578 m at Park Point. The park was established in 1906 and designated a World Heritage Site in 1978.

WHAT TO SEE & DO

Hiking, touring cliff dwellings. **Facilities:** Visitor center with interpretive exhibits (Far View, Apr.–Oct.), Chapin Mesa Archeological Museum, Morefield Ranger Station (May–mid-Oct.), amphitheaters, kiosk. Gas station, gift shops (Morefield, Fairview, Chapin Mesa), laundry, picnic areas with grates, post office. **Programs & Events:** Tours of Spruce Tree House (guided Nov.–Mar., self-guided Apr.–Oct., schedules vary). Cultural demonstrations (Memorial Day–Labor Day). Pottery Firing (May), Luminaria Ceremony (Christmas).

PLANNING YOUR VISIT

⚠ **Camping:** Campground: limited electrical hookups (reservations for hookups available, tel. 970/533–7731). No backcountry camping. Group campsites available (reservations required, tel. 970/533–7731). Private campgrounds just outside park and in Cortez, Durango, and Mancos. ▦ **Lodging:** In the park: Far View Lodge (tel. 800/449–2288 or 970/533–7731). Lodging also available outside the park in Cortez, Durango, and Mancos. ✗ **Food & Supplies:** In the park: snack bar (summer), cafeterias, restaurant, and store (mid-Apr.–mid-Oct.). Food and supplies also available in Cortez, Durango, Mancos. ☞ **Tips & Hints:** Plan ahead for guided tours, which require advance tickets from Far View Visitor Center. Take it slow at 7,000 ft/2,123 m elevation. The park's best weather is in May, September, and October. Go in late May for flowers and late September for fall colors. Busiest in June, July, August, least crowded in January and February. ▧ **Fees, Permits & Limitations:** Entrance fee: $10 per private noncommercial vehicle or $5 per person. Call 970/529–4465 for tour information. No hunting. No pets in cliff dwellings or on trails. Leashed pets elsewhere. No mountain biking or trails for bicycles. Bicycling discouraged because of narrow roads. No motorized vehicles on trails. Entrance road open daily. Cliff dwelling loop drive open daily 7–sunset. Cliff Palace/Balcony House loop open only for cross-country skiing or walking in winter. Cliff Palace generally open Apr.–Oct. daily; Balcony House open mid-May–mid-Oct., daily. Wetherill Mesa Road open Memorial Day–Labor Day, daily 9–6. Visitor center open Apr.–Oct., daily 8–5. Museum open mid-Oct.–mid-Apr., daily 8–5; mid-Apr.–mid-Oct., daily 8–6:30.

HOW TO GET THERE

36 mi/58 km west of Durango and 8 mi/13 km east of Cortez via U.S. 160. Closest airports: Cortez (38 mi/61 km), Durango (65 mi/104 km).

FOR MORE INFORMATION

National Park Service (Box 8, Mesa Verde, CO 81330, tel. 970/529–4465, fax 970/529–4637; Web site www.nps.gov/meve). Cortez Chamber of Commerce (928 E. Main, Cortez, CO 81321, tel. 970/565–3414, fax 970/565–8373). Durango Chamber of Commerce (Box 2587, Durango, CO 81302, tel. 970/247–0312, fax 970/385–7884).

Rocky Mountain National Park

In the north-central part of the state, near Estes Park

Spectacular snow-mantled peaks overlooking verdant subalpine valleys and glistening lakes are the draw at this park. Tundra predominates in one-third of the park above the tree line and is a major reason why these peaks and valleys have been protected. More than one-quarter of the plants found here are also native to the Arctic. As elevation rises, ponderosa pine and juniper, Douglas fir, blue spruce, lodgepole pine, and aspen can be found. Wildflowers dot meadows and glades. Englemann spruce and subalpine fir take over in the subalpine ecosystem. Openings in these cool, dark forests produce wildflower gardens where the blue Colorado columbine reigns. At the upper edges of this zone, twisted, grotesque trees hug the ground. Then the trees disappear and you enter fragile alpine tundra. The park was established in 1915 and designated an International Biosphere Reserve in 1976.

WHAT TO SEE & DO

Auto touring, backpacking, cross-country skiing, fishing, hiking, horse-back riding, picnicking, snowshoeing, wildlife watching. **Facilities:** 5 visitor centers with interpretive exhibits—park headquarters (2.5 mi/4 km west of Estes Park on U.S. 36), Kawuneeche (north of Grand Lake on U.S. 34), Alpine (23 mi/37 km west of park headquarters), Fall River (U.S. 34, west of Estes Park, east of Fall River entrance station in Horseshoe Ranch), Lily Lake (7 mi/11 km south of Estes Park on CO 7); visitor station (Sheep Lakes, 2 mi/3 km west of Fall River entrance); Moraine Park Museum (Bear Lake Rd. near Beaver Meadows entrance on U.S. 36); Never Summer Ranch (7 mi/11 km north of Kawuneechee visitor center on U.S. 34); amphitheaters, auditoriums, roadside pull-outs with wayside interpretive exhibits, trails. Book and map sales areas, picnic areas. **Programs & Events:** Evening programs (year round, Sat., park headquarters and Kawuneeche). Evening programs (mid-June–mid-Aug., nightly in campgrounds), ranger-led walks, talks, snowshoe walks and cross-country skiing, campfire programs.

PLANNING YOUR VISIT

⚠ **Camping:** 5 campgrounds: Flush toilets and potable water in summer (reservations available, tel. 800/365–2267; summer only). No electrical or water hookups or showers, three with dump stations when water is on, three open year-round, two require reservations (Memorial Day–Labor Day, tel. 800/365–2267). Backcountry camping available (permit required, *see below*). Group camping available (reservations required June–Labor Day, tel. 800/365–2267). Private campgrounds available in Estes Park and Grand Lake. 🏨 **Lodging:** Available in Estes Park, Grand Lake; none in park. ✕ **Food & Supplies:** In the park: snack bar next to Alpine Visitor Center. Food and supplies also available in Estes Park and Grand Lake. ☞ **Tips & Hints:** Watch for signs of altitude sickness (nausea, dizziness, headache, insomnia, rapid heartbeat, and shortness of breath). Park roads are 7,500 ft/2,275 m–12,183 ft/3,696 m above sea level. Get below tree line by early afternoon to avoid lightning. Go in June or July to see bighorn sheep, July or August for wildflowers, mid-July–early September for nontechnical climb up Longs Peak, and September–early October for elk mating season. Busiest in July and August, least crowded in January and February. 📷 **Fees, Permits & Limitations:** Entrance fee: $10 per private vehicle, $5 per hiker, bicyclist, motorcyclist. Free under 17. Colorado state fishing license required. Backcountry permits (free Oct.–Apr., $15 May–Sept.) required (tel. 970/586–1242 or write Backcountry Office, Rocky Mountain National Park, Estes Park, CO 80517, no telephone reservations between May 15–Sept. 30). No hunting. No pets beyond roadsides, picnic areas, or campgrounds. Leashed pets only. Bicycles on roads only. No motorized vehicles permitted off-road. Park open daily. Trail Ridge Road (U.S. 34) usually closed mid-Oct.–Memorial Day weekend. Visitor center hours: Headquarters—Labor Day–mid-June, daily 8–5; mid-June–Labor Day, daily 8–9; Kawuneeche—Nov.–May, daily 8–4:30; Labor Day–Oct., daily 8–5; June–Labor Day, daily 7–7. Both closed Dec. 25. Alpine visitor center open late-May–mid-Oct.; Lily Lake open late June–Aug., daily; May and Sept., weekends only. Fall River (at press time) June–Aug., daily 8 AM–9 PM; Sept.–Oct., daily 8–8. Moraine Park Museum open May–mid-Oct.; Sheep Lakes Information Station open summer only; Never Summer Ranch open June–Aug.

HOW TO GET THERE

From the east via U.S. 34, U.S. 36, and CO 7; from the west via U.S. 40 and U.S. 34. Closest airports: Denver, CO (70 mi/112 km); Cheyenne, WY (91 mi/146 km).

FOR MORE INFORMATION

Rocky Mountain National Park (Estes Park, CO 80517, tel. 970/586–1206; Web site www.nps.gov/romo). Estes Park Chamber of Commerce (500 Big Thompson Ave., Estes Park, CO 80517, tel. 800/443–7837 or 970/586–4431; Web site www.rockymtntrav.com/estes). Grand Lake Chamber of Commerce (14700 Hwy. 34, Grand Lake, CO 80447, tel. 800/531–1019 or 970/627–3402; Web site www.grandlakechamber.com).

Yucca House National Monument

In the southwest part of the state, near Cortez

This large prehistoric Indian pueblo site west of Mesa Verde is as yet unexcavated. There are no public facilities or services. The monument was proclaimed on December 19, 1919.

WHAT TO SEE & DO

The site is currently undeveloped for visitors.

FOR MORE INFORMATION

Yucca House National Monument (c/o Box 8 Mesa Verde National Park, Mesa Verde National Park, CO 81330, tel. 970/529–4465; Web site www.nps.gov/yuho).

See Also

Cache la Poudre River, Wild and Scenic Rivers System in Other National Parklands. *Continental Divide National Scenic Trail,* National Trails System in Other National Parklands. *Pony Express National Historic Trail,* National Trails System in Other National Parklands. *Santa Fe National Historic Trail,* National Trails System in Other National Parklands.

CONNECTICUT

Weir Farm
National Historic Site

In the southwest part of the state, near Wilton

Weir Farm preserves and interprets the farm, summer home, and studio of J. Alden Weir (1852–1919), one of the founders of the Impressionist tradition in American art. The site also includes the studio of the sculptor Mahonri Young (1877–1957). The site was authorized on October 31, 1990.

WHAT TO SEE & DO

Fishing, painting, picnicking, touring art studios, walking trails. **Facilities:** Visitor center with interpretive exhibits, studio, trails. Gift shop. **Programs & Events:** Guided tours of historic art studios (year-round, Wed.–Sun. at 11, 1, and 3), self-guided walking tours. Artist-in-Residence and Visiting Artists Program available through Weir Farm Trust (tel. 203/761–9945). Children's art classes (July, tel. 203/761–9945). "Jazz in the Garden" (early Sept.), Holiday Open House (early Dec.).

PLANNING YOUR VISIT

⚠ **Camping:** State park campground information (tel. 860/424–3015); none in park. 🏨 **Lodging:** Available in Danbury, Norwalk, Ridgefield, Wilton; none in park. ✕ **Food & Supplies:** Available in Ridgefield, Wilton; none in park. ☞ **Tips & Hints:** Expect to see structures and landscapes that inspired artists to paint rather than an art gallery, which is planned for the future. Wear comfortable walking shoes for hikes. Visit in spring and fall. Busiest in August and October, least crowded in January and February. ▦ **Fees, Permits & Limitations:** Free. Group reservations required (tel. 203/834–1896). Connecticut state fishing license required. No buses, RVs, or large vehicles in parking lot. No hunting. Dogs on leashes permitted. No mountain or trail bikes, motorized or mechanized equipment on trails. Portable rest rooms only. Grounds open daily dawn–dusk. Visitor center open Wed.–Sun. 8:30–5. Closed Thanksgiving, Dec. 25, Jan. 1.

HOW TO GET THERE

From I–95 or I–84 via Rte. 7 and Rte. 102W make a left at Old Branchville Rd. and another left at Nod Hill Rd; go 0.7 mi/1.1 km to visitor center on right. Closest airport: Westchester/White Plains, NY (30 mi/48 km).

FOR MORE INFORMATION

Weir Farm National Historic Site (735 Nod Hill Rd., Wilton, CT 06897, tel. 203/834–1896, fax 203/834–2421; e-mail WEFA_Interpretation@nps.gov; Web site www.nps.gov/wefa). Ridgefield Chamber of Commerce (9 Bailey Ave., Box 191, Ridgefield, CT 06877, tel. 203/

438–5992 or 800/386–1708, fax 203/438–9175). Wilton Chamber of Commerce (73 Old Ridgefield Rd., Suite 2, Box 7094, Wilton, CT 06897, tel. 203/762–0567, fax 203/852–0583).

See Also

Appalachian National Scenic Trail, West Virginia. *Farmington River (west branch),* Wild and Scenic Rivers System in Other National Parklands. *Quinebaug and Shetucket Rivers Valley National Heritage Corridor,* Affiliated Areas in Other National Parklands.

DISTRICT OF COLUMBIA

Constitution Gardens

On the National Mall

The 50-acre garden, built during the U.S. Bicentennial in 1976, is a tribute to the founding of the nation with a memorial to the 56 signers of the Declaration of Independence. Included in the gardens are a 6½-acre lake and a 1-acre island. The site was authorized in 1974 and dedicated in 1978.

WHAT TO SEE & DO

Touring garden. **Facilities:** Trails, memorial. Bookstores at nearby Lincoln Memorial, Washington Monument, and Jefferson Memorial, benches. **Programs & Events:** Ranger-led interpretive programs and talks, walking tours (various sites around the Mall). Constitution Day Naturalization Ceremony (Sept. 17). Special events available.

PLANNING YOUR VISIT

🏨 **Lodging:** Available in Washington, DC, area; none in gardens. ✕ **Food & Supplies:** Five snack bars on the Mall. Food and supplies also available in Washington, DC, area. ☞ **Tips & Hints:** Plan to spend a day or more visiting the Mall. Busiest in April and May, least crowded in January and February. 🎫 **Fees, Permits & Limitations:** Free. Tourmobile (tel. 202/432–7328 or 800/551–7328) stops at 25 sites along the Mall and Arlington National Cemetery. Gardens open daily.

HOW TO GET THERE

Between the Washington Monument and the Lincoln Memorial, bordered by Constitution Ave., 17th St., and the Reflecting Pool; nearest Metro subway stations: the Foggy Bottom or Farragut West on the blue and orange lines. Closest airport: Reagan Washington National.

FOR MORE INFORMATION

National Capital Parks–Central (The National Mall, 900 Ohio Dr. SW, Washington, DC 20242, tel. 202/426–6841; Web site www.nps.gov/coga).

Ford's Theatre National Historic Site

In Washington, DC

On the night of April 14, 1865, President Abraham Lincoln was shot in Ford's Theatre by John Wilkes Booth. The president died in the early hours of April 15 in the small back bedroom of a boardinghouse across the street. An act of April 7, 1866, provided for purchase of Ford's Theatre by the Federal Government. It was redesignated as Lincoln Museum in 1932 and Ford's Theatre (Lincoln Museum) in 1965. The house where Lincoln died was authorized in 1896. Both were transferred to the Park Service in 1933 and combined as an historic site in 1970.

WHAT TO SEE & DO

Touring theater, museum, and boardinghouse. **Facilities:** Theater, museum, House Where Lincoln Died (Petersen's House). Bookstore. **Programs & Events:** 15-minute narratives (daily at 9:15, 10:15, 11:15, 2:15, 3:15, and 4:15). Theatrical productions (Sept.–June, Tue.–Sun, 7:30 PM; matinees Thurs. 1:30; Sun. 2:30).

PLANNING YOUR VISIT

🏨 **Lodging:** Available in Washington, DC, area; none at site. ✕ **Food & Supplies:** Available in Washington, DC, area; none at site. ☞ **Tips & Hints:** Take the subway (Metro) to Metro Center because parking is difficult. Plan to spend at least 45 minutes. 🎫 **Fees, Permits & Limitations:** Free. Site open daily 9–5. Closed Dec. 25. Theater closes during matinees (Thurs. and Sun. afternoons) and rehearsals; museum and Petersen House remain open.

HOW TO GET THERE

In downtown Washington, DC, at 511 10th St. NW, between E and F Sts.

FOR MORE INFORMATION

Ford's Theatre National Historic Site (511 10th St. NW, Washington, DC 20004, tel. 202/426–6924; e-mail Ford's_Theatre@nps.gov; Web site www.nps.gov/foth).

Franklin Delano Roosevelt Memorial

Along the Potomac River

The outdoor memorial to the nation's 32nd president is divided into four outdoor galleries, or rooms, one for each of FDR's terms in office. The red-granite memorial includes sculptures that depict the launching of the New Deal, a fireside chat, an urban breadline, FDR and his dog Fala, and Eleanor Roosevelt's role as First Lady and human-rights advocate. An FDR Memorial Commission was established in 1955, and the memorial was dedicated in 1997.

WHAT TO SEE & DO

Touring memorial. **Facilities:** Memorial, ranger office with interpretive panels. Bookstore. **Programs & Events:** Ranger-led interpretive programs.

PLANNING YOUR VISIT

🛏 **Lodging:** Available locally; none in park. ✕ **Food & Supplies:** Snack bars at nearby Lincoln and Jefferson memorials. Food and supplies also available locally. ☞ **Tips & Hints:** Take Metrorail or Tourmobile to avoid tough-to-find street parking. Go in early spring or fall for best weather, early to mid-April for cherry blossoms. ✉ **Fees, Permits & Limitations:** Free. Tourmobile fee: $16/adult; $7, ages 3–11 per day (tel. 202/554–7950), access points throughout National Mall or Arlington National Cemetery. Leashed pets only. No food or drink. No smoking, bicycling, skating, jogging, picnicking, or sports activity. Rangers on duty daily 8 AM–midnight. Closed Dec. 25. Parking access open daily 8 AM–1 AM. Bookstore open daily 8 AM–10 PM. Closed Dec. 25.

HOW TO GET THERE

At the junction of Ohio and W. Basin Drs., in W. Potomac Park, midway between the Lincoln and Jefferson memorials. Nearest Metrorail stations: Smithsonian Institution, Arlington National Cemetery, Foggy Bottom (all 1.25 mi/2 km). Closest airport: Reagan Washington National.

FOR MORE INFORMATION

Franklin Delano Roosevelt Memorial (Survey Lodge Ranger Station, National Capital Parks–Central, 900 Ohio Dr. SW, Washington, DC 20242, tel. 202/426–6841; www.nps.gov/fdrm). Washington Convention and Visitors Association (1212 New York Ave. NW, Suite 600, Washington, DC 20005-3992, tel. 202/789–7000).

Frederick Douglass National Historic Site

In the southeast part of the city

Frederick Douglass, the nation's leading 19th-century African-American spokesman, made his home here from 1877 to 1895. The site outlines Douglass's efforts to abolish slavery and his struggle for human rights, equal rights, and civil rights for all oppressed people. Among his achievements, Douglass was U.S. minister to Haiti in 1889. Cedar Hill, his 21-room mansion on 8.5 acres, has been preserved with 90% of its original furnishings. The site was authorized as the Frederick Douglass Home in 1962 and redesignated in 1988.

WHAT TO SEE & DO

Touring house, watching film. **Facilities:** Visitor center with interpretive exhibits, house. Bookstore. **Programs & Events:** Film (every ½ hour), interpretive talks, guided house tours (throughout day, reservations available, tel. 800/967–2283).

PLANNING YOUR VISIT

🛏 **Lodging:** Available in Washington, DC, area; none at site. ✕ **Food & Supplies:** Available in Washington, DC, area; none at site. ☞ **Tips & Hints:** Busiest January through June, least crowded July through September. ✉ **Fees, Permits & Limitations:** Home tours: $3 per adult, $1.50 62 and up, free under 6. Site open mid-Oct.–mid-Apr., daily 9–4; mid-Apr.–mid-Oct., daily 9–5. Closed Thanksgiving, Dec. 25, and Jan. 1.

HOW TO GET THERE

Take the 11th St. Bridge (toward Anacostia) to Martin Luther King Ave. Go 3 blocks, turn left on W St. Follow W St. for 4 blocks to the visitor center parking lot on right. Closest airport: Reagan Washington National.

FOR MORE INFORMATION

Frederick Douglass National Historic Site (1411 W St. SE, Washington, DC 20020-4813, tel. 202/426–5961; Web site www.nps.gov/frdo).

Korean War Veterans Memorial

On the National Mall

The garden memorial to the veterans of the Korean War (1950–54) includes a black granite wall with murals by Louis Nelson of New York City, a reflecting pool, and 19 statues of infantrymen by sculptor Frank C. Gaylord. The memorial was authorized in 1986 and dedicated in 1995.

WHAT TO SEE & DO

Viewing memorial. **Facilities:** Information kiosk with computer to look up and print out information on soldiers killed or missing in action during Korean War. Bookstore in Lincoln Memorial. **Programs & Events:** Ranger-led interpretive talks and programs. Special events available.

PLANNING YOUR VISIT

▥ **Lodging:** Available locally; none at memorial. ✗ **Food & Supplies:** Food and drinks at five locations around Mall; none at memorial. ☞ **Tips & Hints:** Plan to spend a day or more touring the National Mall. Take the Tourmobile, a narrated shuttle tour of 25 Mall sites and Arlington National Cemetery (tel. 202/432–7328 locally or 800/551–7328 outside DC, MD, and VA). ✉ **Fees, Permits & Limitations:** Free. No biking or in-line skating at memorial. Memorial open daily 8 AM–midnight. Closed Dec. 25. Bookstore located at the Lincoln Memorial open daily 8:30 AM–10 PM except Dec. 25.

HOW TO GET THERE

Off Independence Ave. and Daniel French Dr., across from the Lincoln Memorial. Nearest Metro subway station: Foggy Bottom, at 23rd and I Sts. NW, on the blue and orange lines. Limited parking available on Ohio Dr. SW, off Independence Ave. Closest airport: Reagan Washington National.

FOR MORE INFORMATION

National Capital Parks–Central (The National Mall, 900 Ohio Dr. SW, Washington, DC 20242, tel. 202/426–6841; Web site www.nps.gov/kwvm).

Lincoln Memorial

On the National Mall

Constructed as a tribute to the president who led the country through its greatest trial—the Civil War—the Lincoln Memorial houses the famous statue that is 19 ft/6 m tall, 19 ft/6 m wide, and carved from 28 blocks of white Georgia marble. The memorial was authorized in 1911, dedicated in 1922, and transferred to the Park Service in 1933.

WHAT TO SEE & DO

Viewing memorial. **Facilities:** Memorial. Bookstore. **Programs & Events:** Ranger-led talks and interpretive programs. Ranger-led walking tours (summer). Special events available.

PLANNING YOUR VISIT

Lodging: Available locally; none at memorial. **Food & Supplies:** Food and beverages available at five locations on Mall. **Tips & Hints:** Plan to spend a day or more visiting the Mall. Ride Tourmobile for narrated shuttle tour of 25 Mall sites and Arlington National Cemetery (tel. 202/432–7328 or 800/551–7328). Busiest in April and May, least crowded in January and February. **Fees, Permits & Limitations:** Free. No biking or in-line skating in memorial. Memorial open daily 8 AM-midnight. Closed Dec. 25. Bookstore hours 8:30 AM–10 PM daily except Dec. 25.

HOW TO GET THERE

Off Constitution Ave. and 23rd St. NW. Nearest Metro subway station: Foggy Bottom, 23rd St. and I St. NW, on the blue and orange lines. Closest airport: Reagan Washington National.

FOR MORE INFORMATION

National Capital Parks–Central (The National Mall, 900 Ohio Dr. SW, Washington, DC 20242, tel. 202/426–6841; Web site www.nps.gov/linc).

Lyndon Baines Johnson Memorial Grove on the Potomac

Along the Potomac River

This memorial to the nation's 36th president, in Lady Bird Johnson Park, consists of a serpentine pattern of walks and trails leading to a granite monolith. The trails are shaded by hundreds of white pine and dogwood trees and framed by azalea and rhododendron bushes. Thousands of yellow daffodils bloom in season. The focal point of the grove is a tall, rugged monolith of sunset-red granite that stands 19 ft/6 m high and weighs 43 tons. Spaced along the walkway surrounding the stone, four granite markers bear quotations from Lyndon B. Johnson's speeches. The site was authorized in 1973 and dedicated in 1976.

WHAT TO SEE & DO

Fishing, picnicking, strolling. **Facilities:** Grove and granite memorial. **Programs & Events:** Year-round programs available.

PLANNING YOUR VISIT

▥ **Lodging:** Available in Washington, DC, area; none at memorial. ✘ **Food & Supplies:** Available in Washington, DC, area; none at memorial. ☞ **Tips & Hints:** Busiest in June and July, least crowded in November and January. ▤ **Fees, Permits & Limitations:** Free. Washington, DC, fishing license required. Grove open daily during daylight hours.

HOW TO GET THERE

In Lady Bird Johnson Park, on the George Washington Memorial Pkwy. west of I–95 and the 14th St. Bridge. Parking at nearby Columbia Island Marina. Closest airport: Reagan Washington National.

FOR MORE INFORMATION

Lyndon Baines Johnson Memorial Grove on the Potomac (c/o George Washington Memorial Pkwy., Turkey Run Park, McLean, VA 22101-1717, tel. 703/289–2500; Web site www.nps.gov/gwmp).

Mary McLeod Bethune Council House National Historic Site

In Washington, DC

Commemorated here are the life of Mary McLeod Bethune (1875–1955) and the organization she founded, the National Council of Negro Women. The site includes her three-story Victorian home, which housed the council, and a two-story carriage house in which the National Archives for Black Women's History is located. Bethune founded Bethune-Cookman College in Daytona Beach, Florida, and served as an adviser on African-American affairs to four presidents. The site was authorized in 1991.

WHAT TO SEE & DO

Touring home. **Facilities:** Visitor center with interpretive exhibits, home, carriage house (by appointment only). Bookstore, research facility (by appointment only). **Programs & Events:** Ranger-guided tours for groups of 10 or more. Black History Month (Feb.), Women's History Month (Mar.), Annual Open House for Dupont-Kalorama Museum Walk Weekend (1st full weekend, June). Martin Luther King, Jr. Birthday Commenoration (Jan. 19), Bethune Birthday Celebration (July 10). Other special programs.

PLANNING YOUR VISIT

▥ **Lodging:** Available in Washington, DC, area; none at site. ✘ **Food & Supplies:** Available in Washington, DC, area; none at site. ☞ **Tips &**

Hints: Busiest in June and July, least crowded in October and November. ✉ **Fees, Permits & Limitations:** Free. Site and visitor center open Mon.–Sat. 10–4. Closed most federal holidays.

HOW TO GET THERE

In northwest Washington, DC, on Vermont Ave. Nearest metro stations: McPherson Sq. on the blue and orange lines; U St. Cardozo on the green line. Closest airport: Reagan Washington National.

FOR MORE INFORMATION

The National Park Service, Mary McLeod Bethune Council House National Historic Site (1318 Vermont Ave. NW, Washington, DC 20005, tel. 202/673–2402, fax 202/673–2414; Web site www.nps.gov/mamc).

National Capital Parks

In Washington, DC

The District of Columbia has more than 300 parks, parkways, and reservations, including Battleground National Cemetery, the President's Parks (Lafayette Park north of the White House and the Ellipse south of the White House), and a variety of military fortifications and green areas. The park was authorized in 1790 and transferred to the Park Service in 1933.

WHAT TO SEE & DO

Biking, fishing, golfing, ice skating, jogging, picnicking, playing team sports, paddleboating, sightseeing, swimming. **Facilities:** More than 300 parks, parkways, and reserved lands around the capital. **Programs & Events:** Year-round programs available.

PLANNING YOUR VISIT

🏨 **Lodging:** Available locally. ✕ **Food & Supplies:** Available locally. ☞ **Tips & Hints:** Busiest in July and October, least crowded in January and February. ✉ **Fees, Permits & Limitations:** Call park (tel. 202/619–7275).

HOW TO GET THERE

The 300 parks are located throughout the District of Columbia.

FOR MORE INFORMATION

National Capital Region (1100 Ohio Dr. SW, Washington, DC 20242-0001, tel. 202/619–7222; Web site www.nps.gov/nacc or www.nps.gov/nace). Washington Convention and Visitors Association (1212 New York Ave. NW, Suite 600, Washington, DC 20005-3992, tel. 202/789–7000).

National Mall

In Washington, DC

This tree-lined, 146-acre park stretches from the Capitol to the Washington Monument and is a principal axis in the plan developed by

French engineer Pierre L'Enfant in 1790. The Mall was authorized in 1790 and transferred to the Park Service in 1933.

WHAT TO SEE & DO

Attending outdoor events, jogging, picnicking, playing sports, strolling. **Facilities:** Mall. Bookstores. **Programs & Events:** Ranger-led interpretive programs and talks at surrounding monuments and memorials. Ranger-led walking tours (summer). Special events available.

PLANNING YOUR VISIT

🏨 **Lodging:** Available locally. ✕ **Food & Supplies:** Food and drinks available at five locations on Mall. ☞ **Tips & Hints:** Plan to spend a day or more to visit the Mall, monuments, memorials, and museums. Consider taking Tourmobile (tel. 202/432–7328 or 800/551–7328), a narrated shuttle tour to 25 sites on the Mall. Busiest in June and July, least crowded in January and February. ▦ **Fees, Permits & Limitations:** Free. Mall open daily. Memorials and monuments on Mall open daily 8 AM–midnight. Closed Dec. 25.

HOW TO GET THERE

The Mall is in downtown Washington, DC, between the Washington Monument and the U.S. Capitol, Constitution and Independence Aves. The Smithsonian Metro stop comes out on the National Mall. Closest airport: Reagan Washington National.

FOR MORE INFORMATION

National Capital Parks–Central, The National Mall (900 Ohio Dr. SW, Washington, DC 20242, tel. 202/426–6841; Web site www.nps.gov/nama).

Pennsylvania Avenue
National Historic Site

Between the White House and U.S. Capitol

The nation celebrates the election of a president every four years with a parade on the world-famous 1.25-mi/2-km stretch of Pennsylvania Avenue. Other national heroes and foreign leaders have been honored with parades and motorcades here as well. Known as "America's Main Street," the site also encompasses Ford's Theatre National Historic Site (*see separate entry*), several blocks of the Washington commercial district—including the Old Post Office—and a number of federal structures. The site was authorized on September 30, 1965.

WHAT TO SEE & DO

Attending theatrical performances; ice skating; shopping; sightseeing; touring National Archives, FBI, National Museum of American Art, and National Gallery. **Facilities:** Museums, theaters, and stores. **Programs & Events:** Year-round programs available.

PLANNING YOUR VISIT

▥ **Lodging:** Available locally. ✕ **Food & Supplies:** Available locally. ☞ **Tips & Hints:** Consider riding Tourmobile for narrated shuttle tour of 25 Mall sites and Arlington National Cemetery (tel. 202/432–7328 or 800/551–7328). Busiest in July and August, least crowded in January and February. ▧ **Fees, Permits & Limitations:** Free. Site open daily.

HOW TO GET THERE

The site is in downtown Washington, between the Capitol and the White House, and includes the architecturally and historically significant areas in the Pennsylvania Ave. area. There are Metro stations at Federal Triangle and Metro Center. Closest airport: Reagan Washington National.

FOR MORE INFORMATION

Pennsylvania Avenue National Historic Site (c/o National Capital Parks-Central, 900 Ohio Dr. SW, Washington, DC 20242, tel. 202/426–6841; Web site www.nps.gov/paav).

Potomac Heritage
National Scenic Trail

Along the Potomac River between Virginia and Maryland; Washington, DC; and south Pennsylvania

This 704-mi/1,126-km trail connects the tidewater regions along the Potomac River to the Laurel highlands of Pennsylvania. Areas currently open to the public are the 184-mi/294-km C&O Canal towpath, the 18-mi/29-km Mount Vernon Trail, and the 75-mi/120-km Laurel Highlands Trail in Pennsylvania. The trail is also part of the National Trails System. The trail was established on March 28, 1983.

WHAT TO SEE & DO

See separate entry for the Chesapeake and Ohio Canal National Historic Park.

FOR MORE INFORMATION

Potomac Heritage National Scenic Trail (c/o National Capital Region, 1100 Ohio Dr. SW, Washington, DC 20242, tel. 202/619–7222; Web site www.nps.gov/pohe). Potomac Heritage Trail Association (c/o Potomac Appalachian Trail Club, 118 Park St. SE, Vienna, VA, tel. 703/242–0693).

Rock Creek Park

In the northwest part of the city

One of the nation's oldest national parks, Rock Creek is home to more than 1,700 acres of hardwood forest, meadows, and streams that form a ribbon of green through the nation's capital. The park offers hiking, bicycling, horseback riding, picnicking, and boating. A nature center and planetarium, historic Pierce Mill, 18th-century Old Stone House, and the remains of Civil War forts round out the area's natural and cultural attractions. The park was authorized in 1890 and transferred to the Park Service in 1933.

WHAT TO SEE & DO

Attending concerts; bicycling (rentals, Thompson's Boat House and in city); bird-watching; boating (rentals, Thompson's Boat House); exercise trails and recreational fields; fishing; golfing (rentals, Rock Creek Golf Course); hiking; horseback riding (rentals, Rock Creek Horse Center); jogging; kite flying; painting and sketching; picnicking; playing tennis; touring the forts, Carter Barron Amphitheatre, Old Stone House, Pierce Mill, and Rock Creek Gallery; walking. **Facilities:** Nature Center and Planetarium with exhibits, children's nature discovery room, and auditorium (5200 Glover Rd. NW); Pierce Mill (Tilden St. and Beach Dr. NW); Old Stone House (3051 M St. NW, Georgetown); forts; trails; golf course; recreation fields; amphitheater; tennis courts. Book sales areas, picnic pavilions, tables, grills. **Programs & Events:** Ranger-guided nature walks and planetarium shows (Nature Center); ranger-guided tours (Pierce Mill and Old Stone House).

PLANNING YOUR VISIT

Lodging: Available in Washington, DC, area; none in park. ✕ **Food & Supplies:** Available in Washington, DC, area; none in park. ☞ **Tips & Hints:** The best seasons to visit are spring and fall. Busiest in July and August, least crowded in December and January. **Fees, Permits & Limitations:** Free. Washington, DC, fishing license required. Leashed pets only. Bikes on paved bike trails and roads only. No collecting rocks, firewood, animals, plants, natural or cultural objects. Park open daily during daylight hours. Traffic permitted all the time. No trucks or buses. Nature Center open Wed.–Sun. 9–5. Buildings closed Thanksgiving, Dec. 25, Jan. 1.

HOW TO GET THERE

In Washington, DC, at Military Rd. NW and Glover Rd. NW, about 1 mi/1.6 km east of Connecticut Ave. NW and 0.5 mi/0.8 km west of 16th St. NW. Closest airport: Reagan Washington National.

FOR MORE INFORMATION

Rock Creek Park (3545 Williamsburg La. NW, Washington, DC 20008-1207, tel. 202/282–1063, fax 202/282–7612; e-mail ROCR_Superintendentnps.gov; Web site www.nps.gov/rocr).

Theodore Roosevelt Island

On the Potomac River

This 89-acre wooded island is a memorial to the outdoorsman, naturalist, and visionary who was the 26th president. The outdoor memorial captures the spirit of this energetic president. Trails lead through the marsh, swamp, and forest on the island. The site was authorized in 1932 and transferred to the Park Service in 1933. The memorial was dedicated on October 27, 1967.

WHAT TO SEE & DO

Bird-watching, fishing, hiking, touring memorial. **Facilities:** Kiosk, memorial, wayside exhibits, trails, 2,800-ft/849-m boardwalk through swamp. **Programs & Events:** Group tours (reservations required). Ranger-led programs and tours (May–Sept., weekends). Roosevelt Birthday Celebration (late Oct.).

PLANNING YOUR VISIT

▥ **Lodging:** Available locally; none at memorial. ✕ **Food & Supplies:** Available locally; none at memorial. ☞ **Tips & Hints:** Busiest in July and August, least crowded in November and January. ▤ **Fees, Permits & Limitations:** Free. Washington, DC, fishing permit required. Island open during daylight hours.

HOW TO GET THERE

The parking area is reached via the northbound lane of the George Washington Memorial Pkwy. (*see separate entry*) on the Virginia side of the Potomac River in Rosslyn. A footbridge connects the island to the Virginia shore. Visitors may also exit the Metro at Rosslyn, take a 20-minute walk to the Key Bridge, and join the Mount Vernon Trail to the island. Closest airport: Reagan Washington National.

FOR MORE INFORMATION

Theodore Roosevelt Island (c/o George Washington Memorial Parkway, Turkey Run Park, McLean, VA 22101-1717, tel. 703/289–2500; Web site www.nps.gov/this).

Thomas Jefferson Memorial

Near the Potomac River

Thomas Jefferson, author of the Declaration of Independence and third U.S. president, is memorialized here. The interior walls present inscriptions from his writings. Rudolph Evans sculpted the statue. John Russell Pope and his associates Otto Eggers and Daniel Higgins designed the memorial. The memorial was authorized in 1934 and dedicated in 1943.

WHAT TO SEE & DO

Attending ranger interpretive programs and talks, viewing memorial. **Facilities:** Bookstore. **Programs & Events:** Ranger-led interpretive talks (daily). Ranger-led walking tours of National Mall (Memorial Day–Labor Day). Cherry Blossom Festival (early Apr.). Other special events also available.

PLANNING YOUR VISIT

⊞ **Lodging:** Available locally; none at memorial. ✕ **Food & Supplies:** Food and drink available at five locations on National Mall. Food and supplies also available locally. ☞ **Tips & Hints:** Consider taking Tourmobile (www.tourmobile.com), a daily narrated shuttle tour to 25 major sites on the National Mall and in Arlington National Cemetery (tel. 202/432–7328 or 800/551–7328 outside DC, MD, and VA). Busiest in April and July, least crowded in January and February. ▧ **Fees, Permits & Limitations:** Free. No in-line skating or bicycling in memorial. Memorial open daily 8 AM–midnight. Closed Dec. 25.

HOW TO GET THERE

The memorial is on the south bank of the Tidal Basin south of the National Mall (*see separate entry*). A parking lot at the memorial provides two-hour parking. The Smithsonian Metro stop comes out on the National Mall. Closest airports: Reagan Washington National.

FOR MORE INFORMATION

National Capital Parks–Central (The National Mall, 900 Ohio Dr. SW, Washington, DC 20242, tel. 202/426–6841; e-mail National_Mall@nps. gov; Web site www.nps.gov/thje).

Vietnam Veterans Memorial

On the National Mall

The names of more than 58,000 soldiers who were killed in the Vietnam War or are missing are engraved in the black granite walls of the memorial. The memorial's mirrorlike surface reflects the surrounding trees, lawns, monuments, and people, creating a quiet place to remember and honor all Vietnam veterans. The memorial also includes the Statue of Three Servicemen and the Vietnam Womens Memorial. The memorial was authorized in 1980 and dedicated in 1982.

WHAT TO SEE & DO

Viewing and finding names on memorial. **Facilities:** Memorials, statue. Bookstore in Lincoln Memorial. **Programs & Events:** Ranger-led talks and programs. Special events available.

PLANNING YOUR VISIT

⊞ **Lodging:** Available locally; none at memorial. ✕ **Food & Supplies:** Food and drink available at five Mall locations. Food and supplies also available locally. ☞ **Tips & Hints:** Plan to spend a day or more visiting all the sites on the National Mall. Consider taking Tourmobile (www.tourmobile.com), a daily narrated shuttle tour to 25 major sites on the National Mall and in Arlington National Cemetery (tel. 202/432–7328 or 800/551–7328 outside DC, MD, and VA). Busiest in April and May, least crowded in January and February. ▧ **Fees, Permits & Limitations:** Free. No bicycling or in-line skating at memorial. Memorial open daily 8 AM–midnight. Closed Dec. 25.

HOW TO GET THERE

Off Constitution Ave. and 23rd St. NW. Nearest Metro subway station: Foggy Bottom, 23rd and I St. NW, on the blue and orange lines. Closest airport: Reagan Washington National.

FOR MORE INFORMATION

National Capital Parks–Central (The National Mall, 900 Ohio Dr. SW, Washington, DC 20242, tel. 202/426–6841; e-mail National_Mall@ nps.gov; Web site www.nps.gov/vive).

Washington Monument

On the National Mall

The graceful, delicate obelisk rises 555 ft/169 m to dominate the capital skyline and serves as a memorial to the nation's first president and leader of the American Revolution, George Washington. The monument was authorized in 1848, dedicated in 1885, and transferred to the Park Service in 1933.

WHAT TO SEE & DO

Taking elevator to top of monument. **Facilities:** Monument and grounds. Bookstore. **Programs & Events:** Elevator rides to top of monument, ranger-led interpretive programs and talks (daily 8 AM–midnight, 8–5 in winter). Special events available.

PLANNING YOUR VISIT

⊞ **Lodging:** Available locally; none at monument. ✕ **Food & Supplies:** Food and drink available at five locations on Mall. Food and supplies also available locally. ☞ **Tips & Hints:** Plan to spend a day or more visiting sites on the Mall. Consider taking Tourmobile (www.tourmobile. com), a daily narrated shuttle tour to 25 major sites on the National Mall and in Arlington National Cemetery (tel. 202/432–7328 or 800/ 551–7328 outside DC, MD, and VA). Busiest in June and July, least crowded in January and March. ▨ **Fees, Permits & Limitations:** Free. Advance reservations for elevator ride available (tel. 800/505–5040 or pick up at ticket kiosk on 15th St., at base of monument). Monument open 1st Sun. in Apr.–Labor Day, daily 8 AM–midnight (last trip up 11:45); Labor Day–1st Sun in Apr., daily 9–5 (last trip up 4:45). Closed Dec. 25.

HOW TO GET THERE

In downtown Washington, DC, on the National Mall, midway between the U.S. Capitol and the Lincoln Memorial. The Metro stops at the Smithsonian on the Mall, and there is a parking lot at the monument. Closest airport: Reagan Washington National.

FOR MORE INFORMATION

Washington Monument (c/o National Capital Parks–Central, The National Mall, 900 Ohio Dr. SW, Washington, DC 20042, tel. 202/426– 6841; e-mail National_Mall@nps.gov; Web site www.nps.gov/wamo).

White House

North of the Washington Monument

Every president except George Washington has lived, entertained, and conducted the nation's business at the White House. The White House was transferred to the National Park Service on August 10, 1933.

WHAT TO SEE & DO

Touring White House. **Facilities:** Visitor center with interpretive exhibits, White House. **Programs & Events:** Self-guided and guided White House tours. Easter Egg Roll (Easter Mon.), Spring and Fall Garden Tours (Apr. and Oct.), Candlelight Tours (late Dec.).

PLANNING YOUR VISIT

Lodging: Available in Washington, DC, area. ✗ **Food & Supplies:** Available in Washington, DC, area. ☞ **Tips & Hints:** Go to White House Visitor Center before going on tour. Call information line (tel. 202/456–7041) the night before you plan to tour to make sure White House is open. Busiest in April and August, least crowded in January and February. **Fees, Permits & Limitations:** Free. Self-guided and guided tours available. Tickets required (free) for self-guided tours Tues.–Sat. Hours: 10–12:30, Mar. 15–Aug. 30; 10:00–noon, Sept. 1–Mar. 14. Tickets available at White House Visitor Center (southeast corner of 15th and E Sts. NW). Look for three American flags and blue awnings. Tickets issued on first-come, first-served basis starting at 7:30 AM on morning of tour. Go early to ensure receiving ticket. One person may obtain four tickets. Each person, including children, must have a ticket. Each ticket indicates when and where you join line. For guided tours, contact local or Washington office of your representative or senator at least 8–10 weeks before visit to request free, reserved tickets for guided tours. Guided tours begin between 8:15 and 8:45 AM. No photos or videotaping. No strollers (strollers stored at visitor center). No animals, oversize backpacks, balloons, food or beverages, chewing gum, electric stun guns, fireworks or firecrackers, guns or ammunition, knives with blades longer than 3 in/8 cm, mace, smoking, or suitcases. White House visitor center open daily 7:30–4. Closed Thanksgiving, Dec. 25, Jan. 1, and for all official functions. Tour delays may occur because of official functions.

HOW TO GET THERE

The White House is at 1600 Pennsylvania Ave. NW, in downtown Washington, DC. Visitors enter through the Visitor Entrance Building from East Executive Park for scheduled tours. Closest Metro station: Federal Triangle on blue and orange lines. Closest airport: Reagan Washington National.

FOR MORE INFORMATION

The White House (c/o National Capital Region, 1100 Ohio Dr., Room 344 SW, Washington, DC 20242, tel. 202/208–1631 or 202/456–7041; Web site www.nps.gov/whho or www.whitehouse.gov).

See Also

Sewall-Belmont House National Historic Site, Affiliated Areas in Other National Parklands.

FLORIDA

Big Cypress National Preserve

In the southern part of the state, near Ochopee

The preserve conserves and protects the natural scenic, floral and faunal, and recreational values of the Big Cypress Watershed. The importance of this watershed to the Everglades National Park (*see separate entry*) was a major consideration for its establishment. The name Big Cypress does not refer to the size of the trees, but to the vast number of cypress that cover about one-third of the 729,000-acre preserve. The preserve is also home to the endangered Florida panther and red-cockaded woodpecker. The preserve was authorized on October 11, 1974.

WHAT TO SEE & DO

Bicycling, bird-watching, fishing, hiking, hunting, off-road vehicle driving (permit required, *see below*), picnicking, scenic driving, wildlife viewing. **Facilities:** Visitor center with interpretive exhibit, scenic loop roads, trails. Bookstore, picnic areas. **Programs & Events:** Ranger-led wet walks, biking, canoeing excursions, campfire programs (Dec.–Mar.).

PLANNING YOUR VISIT

Camping: 5 primitive campgrounds, 1 with water. Backcountry camping available. **Lodging:** Available in Everglades City area; none in park. **Food & Supplies:** Available in Everglades City area; none in park. **Tips & Hints:** The preserve's climate is subtropical, with mild winters and hot, wet summers. Wear long sleeves, pants, sturdy shoes, and bug repellent when hiking. Allow at least two hours to drive the Loop Road, an hour for the Turner River–Birdon Road loop. Go to visitor center for information on closing of areas to ORVs, hunting, and road conditions. Go in winter (dry season) for best hiking conditions along Florida Trail. Busiest in February and December, least crowded in June and September. **Fees, Permits & Limitations:** Free. ORV permits: $50 a year, vehicle inspection required. Florida state fishing and hunting license required. Park open daily. Visitor center open daily 8:30–4:30.

HOW TO GET THERE

The visitor center is on Tamiami Trail (U.S. 41), halfway between Naples and Miami. Closest airports: Miami International (75 mi/120 km), Ft. Myers International (70 mi/112 km).

FOR MORE INFORMATION

Big Cypress National Preserve (HCR61, Box 110, Ochopee, FL 34141, tel. 941/695–4111; Web site www.nps.gov/bicy).

Biscayne National Park

In the southeast part of the state, near Homestead

The 180,000-acre park, 95% of which is water, is a wonderful place to boat, sail, fish, snorkel, dive, and camp. The park protects a deep green forest of mangroves, and its water provides habitat for the Florida spiny lobster, shrimp, fish, sea turtles, and manatees. Its stunning emerald islands, fringed with mangroves, harbor tropical hardwood forests, and its coral reefs support a kaleidoscope of fish, plants, and other animals. The park was established as a national monument in 1968 and redesignated a park in 1980.

WHAT TO SEE & DO

Boating (rentals, Miami and Key Largo), canoeing (Convoy Point), diving, fishing, sailing, snorkeling. **Facilities:** Visitor center with interpretive exhibits and 3 videos in English and Spanish (Convoy Point, 9 mi/14 km east of Homestead on S.W. 328th St.), nature trails on keys. Book sales area, grills, picnic tables. **Programs & Events:** Year-round glass-bottom boat trips to islands and reefs, snorkel trips, scuba diving.

PLANNING YOUR VISIT

Camping: 2 primitive campgrounds: Elliott Key, Boca Chita Key. No hookups. No reservations. Group campsites available on both keys (reservations required, tel. 305/230–7275). Private campgrounds available in the Homestead/Florida City area and nearby Everglades National Park (*see separate entry*). **Lodging:** Available in Florida City, Homestead; none in park. ✕ **Food & Supplies:** Available in Florida City, Homestead; none in park. ☞ **Tips & Hints:** To see the park, either bring your own boat, or make reservations (tel. 305/230–1100) with Biscayne National Underwater Park, Inc., to go on boat tours or snorkel or dive trips, or take water taxi service to the islands (campers). Bring your own water. Only Elliott Key has drinking water. Busiest in May and July, least crowded in October and November. **Fees, Permits & Limitations:** Free. Glass-bottom boat trips: $19.95 adults, $12.95 children 12 and under, $17.95 senior citizens. Snorkel trips: $29.95 per person. Reservations for all trips highly recommended (tel. 305/230–1100). Canoe rentals: $8 per hour. Kayak rentals: $16 per hour. For scuba trips and island shuttles, call Biscayne National Underwater Park, Inc. (tel. 305/230–1100). Overnight docking fee at Boca Chita and Elliot keys. Florida state fishing license required. Leashed pets only in the developed areas of Convoy Point and Elliott Key. No pets on all other islands or mainland, on boats moored to the islands, or in the shallow waters around the islands. No guns. No skateboards, roller skates, or in-line skates. Visitor center open daily 8:30–5. Closed Dec. 25. Adams Key open daily sunrise–sunset. Elliott Key, Boca Chita Key, and all park waters open daily.

HOW TO GET THERE

9 mi/14 km east of Homestead on S.W. 328th St. (N. Canal Dr.). Closest airport: Miami International Airport (35 mi/56 km).

FOR MORE INFORMATION

Biscayne National Park (9700 S.W. 328th St., Homestead, FL 33033, tel. 305/230–7275, fax 305/230–1190; Web site www.nps.gov/bisc). Tropical Everglades Visitor Association (160 U.S. 1, Florida City, FL 33034, tel. 800/388–9669). Greater Homestead/Florida City Chamber of Commerce (43 N. Krome Ave., Historic Old Town Hall, Homestead, FL 33030-6014, tel. 305/247–2332). The Greater Miami Convention and Visitors Bureau (701 Brickell Ave., Suite 2700, Miami, FL 33131, tel. 305/539–3000).

Canaveral National Seashore

In the east-central part of the state, near Titusville

The longest stretch of preserved coastline on the east coast of Florida is at this seashore. Besides its recreational appeal, the 24 mi/38 km seashore is situated on a barrier island and protects 57,662 acres of undeveloped beach and wetlands. The park offers sanctuary to 1,000 species of plants and 300 species of birds, including 14 threatened or endangered species. The seashore was established on January 3, 1975.

WHAT TO SEE & DO

Beachcombing, bird- and wildlife watching, boating, canoeing (rentals, outside North District), fishing, hiking, surfing, swimming, visiting Eldora State House, Turtle Mound and Seminole Rest Trail historical sites. **Facilities:** Information center with interpretive exhibits (North District New Smyrna Beach), Eldora State House. Bookstore. **Programs & Events:** Ranger-led walks, talks, canoe, and pontoon boat tours. Sea Turtle Watch programs (June–Sept.).

PLANNING YOUR VISIT

Camping: Backcountry beach and island camping available (permit required, *see below*). Camping also available locally. **Lodging:** Available locally; none at seashore. **Food & Supplies:** Available locally; none at seashore. **Tips & Hints:** Visit October through March for best island camping. Beaches busiest in April through August, least crowded in October and January. **Fees, Permits & Limitations:** Entrance fee: $5 per car or motorcycle, $1 per bicyclist or walk-in. Permit required ($10 per night/$15 per night for groups) for backcountry camping (tel. 904/428–3384 ext.10). Reservations required (tel. 904/428–3384) for ranger-led canoe trips, pontoon boat rides, and Turtle Watch programs. No beach camping in summer. Park closes when parking lots are full, which occurs during most summer weekends at the North District. Seashore open Nov.–Mar., daily 6–6; Apr.–Oct., daily 6 AM–8 PM. Information center open Nov.–Mar., daily 8–4:30; Apr.–Oct., daily 9–5; closed Dec. 25. South District (Titusville) closes three days prior to a shuttle launch at Kennedy Space Center and reopens the day following a successful launch.

HOW TO GET THERE

North District: Take I–95, Exit 84E on Hwy. 44 to A1A in New Smyrna Beach. South District: Take I–95 Exit 80E on Hwy. 406/402. Closest airport: Orlando (50 mi/80 km).

FOR MORE INFORMATION

Canaveral National Seashore (Park Headquarters, 308 Julia St., Titusville, FL 32796, tel. 321/267–1110; Web site www.nps.gov/cana).

Castillo de San Marcos
National Monument

In the northeast part of the state, in St. Augustine

Castillo de San Marcos was for many years the northernmost outpost of Spain's vast New World empire. Begun in 1672 and completed in 1695, it is the oldest masonry fort and the best-preserved example of a Spanish colonial fortification in the continental United States. The site was proclaimed a national monument on October 15, 1924.

WHAT TO SEE & DO

Attending ranger presentations, living-history reenactments, and cannon-firing demonstrations; self-guided tours. **Facilities:** Interpretive exhibits inside rooms within the fort. Bookstore, gift shop. **Programs & Events:** Ranger presentations (daily). Cannon-firing demonstrations (summer weekends at 11, 1:30, 2:30, 3:30). Confederate encampment (Jan.); Union encampment (Mar.); Spanish "Nightwatch" (June); Change of Flags ceremony (July); Siege of 1702 reenactment (Nov.); British "Nightwatch," Christmas open house (Dec.).

PLANNING YOUR VISIT

 Camping: Available in St. Augustine; none in park. **Lodging:** Available in St. Augustine; none in park. **Food & Supplies:** Available in St. Augustine; none in park. **Tips & Hints:** Busiest in April and July, least crowded in October and January. **Fees, Permits & Limitations:** Entrance fee: $4 adults, free 16 and under. Leashed dogs only on grounds. No pets in fort. No alcohol. Monument will be undergoing construction: some programs may change. Park is open 5:30–midnight; fort interior open 8:45–4:45. Closed Dec. 25.

HOW TO GET THERE

The monument is in the center of St. Augustine, on Matanzas Bay.

FOR MORE INFORMATION

Castillo de San Marcos National Monument (1 S. Castillo Dr., St. Augustine, FL 32084, tel. 904/829–6506, fax 904/823–9388; e-mail CASA_Administration@nps.gov; Web site www.nps.gov/casa). St. Augustine Chamber of Commerce (1 Riberia St., St. Augustine, FL 32084, tel. 904/829–5681, fax 904/829–6477). St. Augustine Visitor and Convention Bureau (88 Riberia St., Suite 400, St. Augustine, FL 32084, tel. 904/829–1711, fax 904/829–6149).

De Soto National Memorial

On Tampa Bay south shore, in Bradenton

The memorial pays tribute to the remarkable expedition led by Hernando de Soto, who reached Florida's Gulf Coast in May 1539. This was the first large-scale European expedition into what is now the interior southern United States. De Soto traveled 4,000 mi/6,400 km during his four-year mission and had a significant impact on the course of North American history. The memorial was authorized on March 11, 1948.

WHAT TO SEE & DO

Participating in living-history presentations, viewing movie, walking. **Facilities:** Visitor center with interpretive exhibits, 20-minute orientation film, self-guided trail through mangrove swamp, outdoor exhibit. Bookstore. **Programs & Events:** "Hernando de Soto in America" (hourly, 9–4). Costumed ranger-led living history programs (late Dec.–mid-Apr., daily), crossbow and musket firing (late Dec.–mid-Apr.). Other special programs and scheduled events.

PLANNING YOUR VISIT

⚠ **Camping:** Available in Bradenton, Sarasota; none in park. ⊞ **Lodging:** Available in Bradenton, St. Petersburg, Sarasota, Tampa; none in park. ✗ **Food & Supplies:** Available in Bradenton, Sarasota; none in park. ☞ **Tips & Hints:** High season is late-December–mid-April. Busiest in March, April, least crowded in September and August. ▨ **Fees, Permits & Limitations:** Free. Leashed pets only. No bikes on trail. Park grounds open daily sunrise–sunset. Visitor center open daily 9–5. Closed Thanksgiving, Dec. 25, Jan. 1.

HOW TO GET THERE

2.5 mi/4 km north of Manatee Ave. (SR 64) on 75th St. NW in Bradenton. Closest airports: Sarasota-Bradenton International (12 mi/19 km), Tampa International (55 mi/88 km).

FOR MORE INFORMATION

De Soto National Memorial (Box 15390, Bradenton, FL 34280, tel. 941/792–0458, fax 941/792–5094; e-mail DESO_Administration@nps.gov; Web site www.nps.gov/deso). Manatee County Chamber of Commerce (Box 321, Bradenton, FL 34206, tel. 941/748–3411). Tourist Information Center (5030 U.S. 301N, Ellenton, FL 34222, tel. 941/729–7040).

Dry Tortugas National Park

In the south, 70 nautical mi west of Key West, FL

Known for its famous marine and bird life and its legends of pirates and sunken treasure, the park includes a cluster of seven islands or "keys" amid 100 square mi/259 square km of shoals, water, and coral gardens. Fort Jefferson, its main cultural feature, is the largest 19th-century American coastal fort. The park was proclaimed as Fort Jefferson National Monument in 1935 and redesignated as Dry Tortugas National Park in 1992.

WHAT TO SEE & DO

Fishing, picnicking, sailing, scuba diving, snorkeling, touring historic structures. **Facilities:** Visitor center with interpretive exhibits (Ft. Jefferson). Book and chart sale areas, grates, picnic tables. **Programs & Events:** Occasional ranger-led tours, campfire talks, moat walks, living-history programs.

PLANNING YOUR VISIT

Camping: Campground: Garden Key, primitive camping, tent only (no reservations). No backcountry camping. Group camping available (reservations required, tel. 305/293–0152). **Lodging:** Available in Key West; none in park. **Food & Supplies:** Available in Key West or from concession boats and seaplanes; none in park. **Tips & Hints:** Go between mid-April and mid-May for migrating birds, between June and August for best weather. Busiest March through May, least crowded September through November. **Fees, Permits & Limitations:** Free. Florida saltwater fishing license required. Fort Jefferson open daily dawn–dusk. Grounds outside fort open daily. Bush Key closed to visitors from Feb. to Sept. to protect nesting sooty and noddy terns. Visitor center open daily 8–5.

HOW TO GET THERE

70 mi/112 km west of Key West, FL. Several boat and air-taxi services offer trips to the park. Closest airport: Key West International.

FOR MORE INFORMATION

Dry Tortugas National Park (Box 6208, Key West, FL 33041, tel. 305/242–7700, fax 305/242–7728; Web site www.nps.gov/drto). Key West Chamber of Commerce (Mallory Sq., Key West, FL 33041, tel. 305/294–2587).

Everglades National Park

In the southern part of the state, west of Homestead

The 1.5-million-acre park is the largest subtropical wilderness in the continental United States. It has extensive fresh, estuarine, and saltwater areas; open Everglades prairies; hardwood tree islands; cypress domes; pinelands; and mangrove forests. It is the only place in the world where alligators and crocodiles coexist. The park was authorized on May 30, 1934; dedicated on December 6, 1947; designated an International Biosphere Reserve on October 26, 1976; a World Heritage Site on October 26, 1979; and designated a Wetland of International Importance on June 4, 1987.

WHAT TO SEE & DO

Bicycling (rentals, Flamingo, Shark Valley), boating, boat touring (Flamingo, Gulf Coast), canoeing (rentals, Flamingo, Gulf Coast), fishing, hiking, kayaking (rentals, Flamingo, Gulf Coast), picnicking, tram touring (Shark Valley). **Facilities:** 5 visitor centers with interpretive exhibits—Ernest F. Coe (main entrance, west of Homestead/Florida City), Royal Palm (4 mi/6 km west of Coe), Flamingo (38 mi/61 km southwest of main entrance), Shark Valley (U.S. 41, north side of park), and Gulf Coast (Everglades City); interpretive displays, trails, roadside interpretive exhibits, amphitheaters, boat-launch areas. Book sale areas, gift shops, fire pits, gasoline (daytime only, Flamingo), picnic areas, religious services (winter only). **Programs & Events:** Guided walks, talks (Royal Palm), boat tours (Flamingo, Gulf Coast), tram tours (Shark Valley). Guided walks, talks, evening programs (Long Pine Key, Flamingo campgrounds), bicycle tours (Shark Valley), canoe tours (Flamingo, Gulf Coast), slough slogs (Shark Valley). All late Dec.–early Apr.

PLANNING YOUR VISIT

⚠ **Camping:** 2 campgrounds: Flamingo, Long Pine Key. No hookups. Both have dump stations. (Reservations suggested during winter season, tel. 800/365–2267.) Backcountry camping available (permit required, *see below*). Group campsites at Long Pine Key, Flamingo (reservations available, tel. 800/365–2267). Private campgrounds nearby in Chokoloskee, Everglades City, Florida City, Homestead, Ochopee. ⊞ **Lodging:** In the park: Flamingo Lodge (tel. 941/695–3101 or 800/ 600–3813). Lodging also available outside the park in Chokoloskee, Everglades City, Florida City, Homestead, Miami, and Naples areas. ✕ **Food & Supplies:** In the park: meals, groceries, and supplies at Flamingo. Food and supplies also available in Chokoloskee, Everglades City, Florida City, Homestead, Miami, and Naples areas. ☞ **Tips & Hints:** Go between December and April for best wildlife viewing. Busiest in December–April, least crowded May–November. ▨ **Fees, Permits & Limitations:** Entrance fee: $10 per family or $5 per person on foot or bicycle (main entrance); $8 per family or $4 per person on foot or bicycle (Shark Valley, Chekika). This rate may be applied toward the higher entrance fee at the main entrance. Backcountry camping permits ($10–$30 depending on group size, available at Flamingo, Gulf Coast visitor centers). Boat-launch fees are $5 ($3 for nonmotorized). Boat tours at Flamingo and Gulf Coast vary in price (Flamingo Lodge and Marina, tel. 941/695–3101; Everglades City Boat Tours, tel. 941/ 695–2591). Shark Valley tram tours: $9 per adult, $5.50 per child (tel. 305/221–8455). Reservations recommended for all tours Dec.–Apr. Florida state fishing license required. No hunting. No pets on trails or in backcountry. Leashed pets only in campgrounds. Bicycles on selected trails only. No motorized vehicles on trails. Motorized boat use restricted. No airboats. Main park entrance open all the time. Shark Valley open daily 8:30–6. Visitor center hours: Ernest Coe—daily 8–5; Royal Palm—daily 8–4:15; Flamingo—Dec.–Apr., daily 7:30–5, May–Nov. intermittently; Shark Valley—daily 8:30–5:15; Gulf Coast—Nov.–Apr., daily 7:30–5:30; May–Oct., daily 8:30–4:30.

HOW TO GET THERE

The park is in south Florida, southwest of Miami. Access points are Gulf Coast, in the northwest corner of the park, reached via U.S. 41 south of Naples and Fort Myers; Shark Valley, on the north side of the park, reached via U.S. 41 west of Miami or south of Naples/Fort Myers; Chekika, reached via S.W. 168th St. southwest of Miami; and the main park entrance, reached via SR 9336 west of Homestead and Florida City. Closest airports: Miami (45 mi/72 km northeast of main entrance), Fort Myers (70 mi/112 km northwest of Gulf Coast).

FOR MORE INFORMATION

Everglades National Park (40001 SR 9336, Homestead, FL 33034-6733, tel. 305/242–7700; Web site www.nps.gov/ever). Tropical Everglades Visitor Association (160 U.S. 1, Florida City, FL 33034, tel. 800/388–9669). Homestead and Florida City Chamber of Commerce (43 N. Krome Ave., Homestead, FL 33030, tel. 305/247–2332). Greater Miami Chamber of Commerce (1601 Biscayne Blvd., Omni International Complex, Miami, FL 33131, tel. 305/350–7700). Greater Miami Convention and Visitor Bureau (701 Brickell Ave., Suite 2700, Miami, FL 33131, tel. 305/539–3000 or 800/283–2707). Everglades Area Chamber of Commerce (Box 130, Everglades City, FL 34139, tel. 941/695–3941).

Fort Caroline National Memorial

In the northeast part of the state, near Jacksonville

The memorial pays tribute to the colony the French tried to establish near the mouth of the St. Johns River in 1564. The colony was plagued with hardship and conflicts with the Spanish, who were uneasy about a French settlement that was near the routes used by their treasure ships. The memorial was authorized on September 21, 1950.

WHAT TO SEE & DO

Hiking, picnicking, walking to Ft. Caroline exhibit. **Facilities:** Visitor center with interpretive exhibits, fort exhibit, trail, Spanish Pond area, Ribault Column. Bookstore, picnic area. **Programs & Events:** Year-round ranger programs (1 PM and 3 PM weekdays, 3 PM weekends). Special events and programs available.

PLANNING YOUR VISIT

⚑ **Camping:** Available at Little Talbot Island State Park and Huguenot Park (in Jacksonville); none in park. ▯ **Lodging:** Available locally; none in park. ✕ **Food & Supplies:** Available locally; none in park. ☞ **Tips & Hints:** Bring insect repellent. Visit in spring and fall. Busiest in January and February, least crowded in December and July. ▤ **Fees, Permits & Limitations:** Free. No hunting or fishing. Leashed pets only on trails. No bicycles on trails. Visitor center and memorial open daily 9–5. Closed Dec. 25.

HOW TO GET THERE

13 mi/21 km east of downtown Jacksonville. Closest airport: Jacksonville International (25 mi/40 km).

FOR MORE INFORMATION

Fort Caroline National Memorial (12713 Ft. Caroline Rd., Jacksonville, FL 32225, tel. 904/641–7155, fax 904/641–3798; Web site www.nps. gov/foca). Jacksonville and the Beaches Florida Convention and Visitors Bureau (201 E. Adam St., Jacksonville, FL 32202, tel. 904/798–9111, fax 904/798–9103).

Fort Matanzas National Monument

South of St. Augustine

Fort Matanzas ("slaughter" in English) marks the site where, on September 29 and October 12, 1565, almost 300 soldiers from the nearby French Fort Caroline were killed by the Spaniards in a battle for supremacy in the New World. The fort itself is a masonry fortification built by the Spanish between 1740 and 1742 to guard the "back door" to St. Augustine at the south end of Matanzas Inlet. The site was proclaimed a national monument in 1924.

WHAT TO SEE & DO

Riding ferry to fort, touring fort, walking on boardwalk trails. **Facilities:** Visitor center, fort, interpretive exhibits, boardwalk. **Bookstore/gift shop. Programs & Events:** Year- round ferry boat rides, ranger presentations (every hour on the half hour 9:30–4:30, group reservations requested), living-history reenactments.

PLANNING YOUR VISIT

Camping: Available between Fort Matanzas and St. Augustine; none in park. **Lodging:** Available in St. Augustine; none in park. **Food & Supplies:** Available in St. Augustine; none in park. **Tips & Hints:** Busiest April through August, least crowded in September and January. **Fees, Permits & Limitations:** Free. Leashed pets only. No alcohol. No driving or walking on sand dunes. Park open daily 8:30–5:30; visitor center open daily 9–4:30. Ferry runs 9:30–4:30, weather permitting. Park and ferry closed Dec. 25.

HOW TO GET THERE

The park is on Anastasia Island, 14 mi/22 km south of St. Augustine on Hwy. A1A. Closest airports: Jacksonville, Orlando.

FOR MORE INFORMATION

Fort Matanzas National Monument (8635 A1A S, St. Augustine, FL 32080, tel. 904/471–0116, fax 904/471–7605; e-mail FOMA_Site_Supervisor@nps.gov; Web site www.nps.gov/foma). St. Augustine/St. Johns County Chamber of Commerce (1 Riberia St., St. Augustine, FL

32084, tel. 904/829–5681, fax 904/829–6477). Visitor and Convention Bureau (88 Riberia St., Suite 400, St. Augustine, FL 32084, tel. 904/ 829–1711, fax 904/829–6149).

Gulf Islands National Seashore 🕶

In the northwest part of the state, near Pensacola, and in southeast Mississippi, near Ocean Springs

These offshore islands offer sparkling white-sand beaches, historic forts and structures, nature trails, and adjacent open waters. On the mainland are salt marshes and bayous in the Mississippi District; and there are a Naval Live Oak Reservation and military forts in the Florida District. Research, monitoring, and mitigation programs preserve, protect, and restore the natural and cultural resources within the park. The seashore was authorized on January 8, 1971.

WHAT TO SEE & DO

Bird-watching, bicycling (rentals, Gulf Breeze, Pensacola Beach), boating (rentals, Gulf Breeze, Pensacola Beach, Perdido Key), fishing, picnicking, swimming, touring forts, walking. **Facilities:** 4 visitor centers with interpretive exhibits—Naval Live Oaks (U.S. 98 east of Gulf Breeze, FL), Fort Pickens (Santa Rosa Island west of Pensacola Beach), Fort Barrancas (on Pensacola Naval Air Station), William M. Colmer (Ocean Springs, MS); beaches, forts, auditorium, nature trails, interpretive display boards. Ball field, boat launch, book and map sale areas, picnic areas and shelters. **Programs & Events:** Tours at Fort Pickens (daily at 2) and Fort Barrancas (weekends at 2), Advanced Redoubt (Sat. at 11). Guided tours of Fort Massachusetts on West Ship Island, MS (late Mar.–Oct., daily 10:30 and 1:30), candlelight tours. Beach cleanup (May and Sept., FL; Sept., MS), Davis Bayou Open House (Thanksgiving weekend), Earth Day (Apr. 22).

PLANNING YOUR VISIT

⚠ **Camping:** 2 campgrounds: both with water and electricity hookups (reservations available at Fort Pickens, tel. 800/365–2267). Primitive camping available on East Ship, Horn, and Petit Bois islands in MS and Perdido Key, FL (permit required, *see below*). Group campsites at Naval Live Oaks (tel. 850/934–2622) and Ft. Pickens (tel. 800/365–2267) in FL, Davis Bayou (tel. 601/875–9057) in MS. Private campgrounds in Gulf Breeze, Navarre, Pensacola, FL; Biloxi, Gulfport, and Ocean Springs, MS. 🏨 **Lodging:** Available in Fort Walton, Gulf Breeze, Navarre Beach, Pensacola, Pensacola Beach, FL; Biloxi, Ocean Springs, Pascagoula, MS. ✕ **Food & Supplies:** In the park: snack bars and stores. Food and supplies also available in Fort Walton Beach, Gulf Breeze, Navarre Beach, Pensacola, Pensacola Beach, FL; Biloxi, Gulfport, Ocean Springs, Pascagoula, MS. ☞ **Tips & Hints:** Don't swim alone in unguarded waters. Be cautious about rip currents, jellyfish, Portuguese men-of-war, and barnacle-covered rocks. Be alert for sudden storms and seek shelter during thunderstorms. Watch your step while exploring the forts and batteries. Go in April and October for good weather and blooms, late March–mid May and September–October for migrating birds. Busiest in May, June, and July, least crowded in January and February. ⌧ **Fees, Permits & Limitations:** Entrance fee: $6 per vehicle, $3 for walk-ins. Florida or Mississippi state fishing license required. Primitive camping permit required (free, must apply in person) for Perdido Key (tel. 850/492–7278). No glass containers on beaches. No motor vehicles off roads. No metal detectors. No pets on beaches in Florida, in swimming area of Ship Island, on tour boats, in historic structures or buildings. Leashed pets elsewhere. Don't feed or disturb wildlife. Seashore open daily 8–sunset. Visitor center hours: Fort Barrancas—Nov.–Feb., daily 8:30–3:45; Mar.–Oct., daily 9:30–4:45; Fort Pickens—Nov.–Mar., daily 8:30–4; Apr.–Oct., daily 8:30–4; Davis Bayou—Nov.–Feb. daily, 8–4:30; Mar.–Oct., daily 8:30–5. Closed Dec. 25.

HOW TO GET THERE

Mississippi District: the offshore access to Ship Island is provided by concession boats from Gulfport, MS (Mar.–Oct.). Private boats may dock near Ft. Massachusetts on West Ship Island during the day. NPS licensed or private boats provide access to Horn, Petit Bois, and East Ship islands. Follow the signs on U.S. 90 for the seashore to Davis Bayou, MS. Florida District, Johnson Beach (Perdido Key): take FL 292 southwest from Pensacola; for historic mainland forts and Naval Museum: use the main entrance of Pensacola Naval Air Station off Barrancas (FL 295); for Naval Live Oaks and the Fort Pickens and Santa Rosa Areas: take U.S. 98 from downtown Pensacola across the Pensacola Bay Bridge. Closest airports: Florida District—Pensacola (20 mi/32 km), Mississippi District—Gulfport (30 m/48 km).

FOR MORE INFORMATION

For the Mississippi District: Superintendent, Gulf Islands National Seashore (3500 Park Rd., Ocean Springs, MS 39564; tel. 228/875–0821, fax 228/872–2954). For the Florida District: Superintendent, Gulf Islands National Seashore (1801 Gulf Breeze Pkwy., Gulf Breeze, FL 32561, tel. 850/934–2600, fax 850/932–9654; e-mail for both GUIS_Interpretation@nps.gov; Web site for both www.nps.gov/guis). Pensacola Visitors Information Center (1401 E. Gregory St., Pensacola, FL 32501, tel. 800/874–1234). Pensacola Beach Visitors Information Center (735 Pensacola Beach Blvd., Pensacola Beach, FL 32561, tel. 800/635–4803). Emerald Coast Convention and Visitors Bureau (Box 609, Fort Walton Beach, FL 32549-0609, tel. 800/322–3319). Navarre Beach Area Chamber of Commerce (8543 Navarre Pkwy., Navarre, FL 32566, tel. 850/939–2691). Biloxi Visitors Center (710 Beach Blvd., Biloxi, MS 39530, tel. 228/374–3105). Ocean Springs Area Chamber of Commerce (1000 Washington Ave., Ocean Springs, MS 39564, tel. 228/875–4424).

Timucuan Ecological and Historic Preserve

In the northeast part of the state, in Jacksonville

Nestled between Northeast Florida's Lower St. Johns and Nassau rivers, the preserve protects 46,000 acres of estuarine natural resources and historic and prehistoric sites. The site includes four areas: Fort Caroline National Memorial (*see separate entry*), Kingsley Plantation, the Theodore Roosevelt Area, and Cedar Point. The Kingsley Plantation is the oldest remaining plantation house in Florida. The 18th- and 19th-century structures include the planter's home, kitchen house, barn, and 23 of the original 32 slave quarters. The Theodore Roosevelt Area preserves a maritime hammock forest and salt marsh and evidence of the Timucuan people who once inhabited Northeast Florida. The Cedar Point area is undeveloped but has informal hiking trails. The preserve was authorized on February 16, 1988.

WHAT TO SEE & DO

Bird- and wildlife watching, boating, hiking, picnicking, touring Kingsley Plantation and Fort Caroline. (*See Fort Caroline National Memorial entry for more information on fort.*) **Facilities:** Visitor centers with interpretive exhibits—Fort Caroline, Kingsley Plantation; plantation, fort, trails, marsh observation tower (Theodore Roosevelt Area). Bookstores, picnic areas. **Programs & Events:** Ranger talks at Kingsley Plantation, occasional ranger programs at Theodore Roosevelt Area and Fort Caroline. Kingsley Plantation special events (Feb. and Dec.).

PLANNING YOUR VISIT

Camping: Available at Hanna City Park, Huguenot Memorial Park, and Little Talbot Island State Park; none at preserve. **Lodging:** Available locally; none at preserve. **Food & Supplies:** Available locally; none at preserve. **Tips & Hints:** Busiest in February and March, least crowded in August and September. **Fees, Permits & Limitations:** Free. No hunting. Leashed pets only. No pets in buildings. No bicycles on trails. Fort Caroline National Memorial and visitor center open daily 9–5. Kingsley Plantation open daily 9–5. Theodore Roosevelt Area open Oct.–Apr., daily 6 AM–6 PM; Oct–Apr., daily 6 AM–8 PM. Closed Dec. 25.

HOW TO GET THERE

The preserve is in northeast Jacksonville. From I–95, exit on Heckscher Dr. (FL 105). Follow Heckscher east to FL 9A. For Kingsley Plantation, go 9 mi/14 km, turn left at the park sign onto Fort George Island, and follow signs to plantation; for Theodore Roosevelt area and Fort Caroline National Memorial, turn right onto 9AS, take the next exit, and at the traffic light, turn left and follow the signs to Fort Caroline National Memorial and Theodore Roosevelt; for Cedar Point, go 0.25 mi/0.4 km to the next light (New Berlin Rd.), turn left at the light and follow New Berlin to the intersection with Cedar Point Rd. (a triangle intersection), turn right on Cedar Point Rd. and follow it to the end.

The four sites are about 35 minutes driving time apart. Closest airport: Jacksonville International.

FOR MORE INFORMATION

Timucuan Ecological and Historic Preserve (12713 Ft. Caroline Rd., Jacksonville, FL 32225, tel. 904/641–7155, fax 904/641–3798; Web site www.nps.gov/timu).

See Also

Florida National Scenic Trail, National Trail System in Other National Parklands. *Wekiva River,* Wild and Scenic Rivers System in Other National Parklands.

GEORGIA

Andersonville National Historic Site

In the central part of the state, in Andersonville

Andersonville, or Camp Sumter, was the largest Confederate military prison established during the Civil War. More than 45,000 Union soldiers were confined in the camp during 14 months, during which almost 13,000 died from disease, poor sanitation, malnutrition, overcrowding, and exposure. The site is the only park that serves as a memorial to all Americans ever held as prisoners of war. The 495 acres include the national cemetery, with 18,000 interments, and the partially reconstructed prison site. The historic site was authorized on October 16, 1970.

WHAT TO SEE & DO

Auto touring, hiking, picnicking, researching, touring cemetery and prison, walking. **Facilities:** Visitor center with interpretive exhibits (National Prisoner of War Museum), cemetery, prison, monuments. Bookstore, picnic area. **Programs & Events:** Ranger-guided cemetery walks and prison-site talks (weekends). Andersonville Revisited (Feb., last weekend), Memorial Day ceremony (May, last Sun.), Andersonville Union Encampment Living History program (Oct., 1st weekend).

PLANNING YOUR VISIT

⛺ **Camping:** Available locally; none in park. ⌂ **Lodging:** Available locally; none in park. ✕ **Food & Supplies:** Available locally; none in park. ☞ **Tips & Hints:** Plan to stay at least two hours. Wear comfortable seasonal clothing and walking shoes. Summers are hot and humid, winters are mild and rainy. Busiest in March and July, least crowded in December and January. 🎫 **Fees, Permits & Limitations:** Free; donations accepted. Driving tour audio: $1 rental. Park grounds open daily 8–5. Visitor center/museum open daily 8:30–5; closed Dec. 25, Jan. 1.

HOW TO GET THERE

From I–75S, take Byron exit (Hwy. 49S), and travel 40 mi/64 km to park entrance on left. From I–75N, exit at Cordele, take GA 280W to Americus and Hwy. 49N for 10 mi/16 km to park entrance on right. Closest airports: Columbus (60 mi/96 km); Macon (60 mi/96 km); Atlanta (175 mi/280 km).

FOR MORE INFORMATION

Andersonville National Historic Site (496 Cemetery Rd., Andersonville, GA 31711, tel. 229/924–0343, fax 229/928–9640; Web site www.nps.gov/ande).

Chattahoochee River National Recreation Area

Near Atlanta

The recreation area has 14 units along a 48-mi/77-km stretch of the Chattahoochee River. In addition to fishing, hiking, picnicking, and boating, the park contains a wide variety of natural habitats, flora and fauna, 19th-century historic sites, and Native American archaeological sites. The site was established on August 15, 1978.

WHAT TO SEE & DO

Boating, canoeing (rentals, May–Labor Day; Johnson Ferry, Paces Mill, Powers Island), fishing, hiking, picnicking, rafting (rentals, May–Labor Day; Johnson Ferry, Paces Mill, Powers Island). **Facilities:** Visitor contact station (Island Ford), over 60 mi/96 km of hiking trails, stocked trout stream. Bookstores, picnic areas, and pavilion (reservations available, tel. 770/395–6851). **Programs & Events:** Special events available.

PLANNING YOUR VISIT

⚠ **Camping:** Available in Atlanta area; none in park. 🏠 **Lodging:** Available in Atlanta area; none in park. ✗ **Food & Supplies:** In the park: stores at Johnson Ferry, Paces Mill, Powers Island. Food and supplies also available in Atlanta area. ☞ **Tips & Hints:** Busiest in June and August, least crowded in November and January. 🎫 **Fees, Permits & Limitations:** Free. Shuttle bus (tel. 770/395–6851) runs among Johnson Ferry, Powers Island, and Paces Mill (May–Labor Day). Parking fee ($2 daily, $25 annual). Georgia fishing license and trout stamp required, age 16 and over. Park open dawn to dusk year-round. Visitor contact station open 10–5, extended hours in summer.

HOW TO GET THERE

The recreation area consists of 14 separate units along 48 mi/77 km of the Chattahoochee River extending into northwest Atlanta. Visitor contact station: From I–285, take GA 400N to Exit 6 (Northridge Rd.). Stay in right lane and follow signs. Closest airport: Atlanta (22 mi/35 km).

FOR MORE INFORMATION

Chattahoochee River National Recreation Area (1978 Island Ford Pkwy., Atlanta, GA 30350, tel. 770/399–8070, fax 770/399–8087; Web site www.nps.gov/chat).

Chickamauga and Chattanooga National Military Park

In the northwest part of Georgia, and in the southeast part of Tennessee, near Chattanooga

On the fields of what is now Chickamauga and Chattanooga National Military Park, about 60,000 Union troops and 43,000 Confederates clashed during the fall of 1863 in some of the hardest fighting of the Civil War. The battles ended in the fall of Chattanooga, the gateway to the deep South. The park was established on August 19, 1890, and transferred from the War Department on August 10, 1933.

WHAT TO SEE & DO

Auto touring, picnicking, walking, watching film. **Facilities:** 2 visitor centers with interpretive exhibits—Chickamauga Battlefield, (Ft. Oglethorpe, GA), Point Park (Lookout Mountain, TN); Cravens House and Ochs Museum (both at Lookout Mt.), trails. Bookstores, picnic areas. **Programs & Events:** Chickamauga Battlefield, a 26-minute multimedia presentation, shown hourly (9–4); Lookout Mt.: *The Walker Painting*, a short narrative on the Battle Above the Clouds, shown on request. Chickamauga: Car caravan tours (June–Sept., daily 10:30, 12:30, 2); living-history demonstrations (June–Sept., 10–4 hourly); Lookout Mt.: guided walks (June–Sept.); living-history demonstrations (June–Aug.); Cravens House tours (June–Aug.). Anniversary programs, living-history encampments, walks, tours, and talks (Chickamauga, Sept; Lookout Mt., Nov.); Christmas programs (Cravens House).

PLANNING YOUR VISIT

⚠ **Camping:** Available in Chattanooga, TN; Ft. Oglethorpe, GA; none in park. ▦ **Lodging:** Available in Chattanooga, TN; Ft. Oglethorpe, GA; none in park. ✕ **Food & Supplies:** Available in Chattanooga, TN; Ft. Oglethorpe, GA; none in park. ☞ **Tips & Hints:** Visit in spring and fall. Busiest in July and August, least crowded in January and February. ▨ **Fees, Permits & Limitations:** Entrance fee: Chickamauga Battlefield—free; Lookout Mt., Point Park—$2 per adult, $1 under 16 and over 62; Cravens House—$2 per person, summer only. Chickamauga Battlefield multimedia presentation: $3 per adult, $1.50 under 16 and over 62. No bicycles on trails. No hunting. No in-line skating, rollerskating, or skateboarding. No metal detecting. Park open daily 8–dark. Visitor centers open Sept.–May, daily 8–4:45; June–Aug., daily 8–5:45. Closed Dec. 25.

HOW TO GET THERE

The Chickamauga Battlefield Visitor Center is near Ft. Oglethorpe, on U.S. 27 off I–75 south of Chattanooga, TN. The Lookout Mt. Battlefield Visitor Center is at the entrance to Point Park, which may be reached from downtown Chattanooga via the Scenic or Ochs highways. Closest airport: Chattanooga (10 mi/16 km).

FOR MORE INFORMATION

Chickamauga and Chattanooga National Military Park (Box 2128, Ft. Oglethorpe, GA 30742, tel. 706/866–9241, fax 423/752–5215; Web site www.nps.gov/chch).

Cumberland Island
National Seashore

In the southeast part of the state, near St. Marys

The seashore offers outstanding opportunities for relaxation and solitude in an undisturbed island paradise. One of the largest undeveloped barrier islands in the world, the seashore contains federally designated wilderness and one of the largest maritime forests remaining in the United States. It also preserves a mansion built by Thomas Carnegie, the American industrialist who once owned most of the island. The seashore was established in 1972 and designated a Biosphere Reserve in 1986.

WHAT TO SEE & DO

Nature walking, swimming. **Facilities:** Visitor center with interpretive exhibits (park headquarters), Sea Camp Ranger Station (exhibits), Ice House at Dungeness Dock, Plum Orchard mansion, trails. Bookstore. **Programs & Events:** Ranger-guided tours (twice daily, Dungeness Dock), audiovisual slide program (Sea Camp Ranger Station), mansion tour (1st Sun. of month, Plum Orchard). Beach, marsh ecology program (intermittently), deer and hog hunts (Oct.–Feb., application required, *see below*).

PLANNING YOUR VISIT

 Camping: 5 campgrounds: no hookups (reservations required, tel. 912/882–4335). Backcountry camping available (permit required, *see below*). Group camping available (reservations required, tel. 912/882–4335). Private campgrounds available in Kingsland. **Lodging:** Available in Kingsland, St. Marys; none in park. ✗ **Food & Supplies:** Available in Kingsland, St. Marys; none in park. **Tips & Hints:** Access by boat and ferry only. Watch for ticks. Best time to visit: spring and fall. Busiest in April and May, least crowded in December and January.
Fees, Permits & Limitations: User fee: $4 per person. Deer and hog hunts by application only during July–Aug; selection is by lottery, $50 fee for those selected. Ferry fee (reservations required, tel. 912/882–4335): $10.17 per adult, $6.05 under 13, $8.03 over 64. Backcountry permits ($2 per person/night) available on island. No motorized vehicles allowed. No bicycles in wilderness area or trails. Park open daily 8:15–4:30. Ferry doesn't operate Oct.–Feb., Tues. and Wed.

HOW TO GET THERE

Seashore access at St. Marys, 10 mi/16 km east of I–95. Closest airport: Jacksonville (34 mi/54 km).

FOR MORE INFORMATION

Cumberland Island National Seashore (Box 806, St. Marys, GA 31558, tel. 912/882–4336, fax 912/882–6284; Web site www.nps.gov/cuis). St. Marys Tourism Council (Box 1191, 414 Osbourne St., St. Marys, GA 31558, tel. 800/868–8687). Kingsland Tourist and Convention Bureau (Box 1928, Kingsland, GA 31548, tel. 800/433–0225, fax 912/729–7618).

Fort Frederica
National Monument

On St. Simons Island

Fort Frederica's ruins are a reminder of the struggle for empire between Spain and Great Britain. James Edward Oglethorpe founded the Georgia colony and built the fort on St. Simons Island, where it flourished in the 1740s. The southernmost post of the British colonies in North America, the fort protected Georgia and South Carolina from the Spanish in Florida. The park is known for its exceptional beauty. Stately oaks, exceptionally large grapevines, and Spanish moss lend an air of antiquity that is unequaled on the coast. The park was authorized on May 26, 1936.

WHAT TO SEE & DO

Ranger-led or self-guided walking tour of town ruins, viewing film. **Facilities:** Visitor center with interpretive exhibits, 25-minute film *This is Frederica,* trail, wayside exhibits. Museum store. **Programs & Events:** Ranger-led tours. Costumed interpretive programs, woodworking, black powder demonstrations (summer, daily; weekends rest of year). Ft. Frederica Festival (1st Sat. in Mar.), National Park Day (Aug. 25), Holiday Open House (1st weekend after Christmas).

PLANNING YOUR VISIT

Camping: Available at Jekyll Island, Blythe Island Regional Park, and private campgrounds on the mainland; none at monument. **Lodging:** Available locally; none at monument. **Food & Supplies:** Available locally; none at monument. **Tips & Hints:** Plan to spend two hours at the monument. Sand gnats and mosquitoes are present year-round. Biting flies are worst in May and September. Busiest in February and March, least crowded in December and January. **Fees, Permits & Limitations:** Entrance fee: $4 per vehicle or $2 per bicyclist or walk-in. No vehicles or bikes allowed in town site. Monument open daily 8–5. Visitor center open 9–5. Closed Dec. 25.

HOW TO GET THERE

On St. Simons Island, 12 mi/19 km from Brunswick, accessible from I–95 and U.S. 17 via the F.J. Torras (Brunswick–St. Simons) Causeway. Directional signs to the park are located on all major roads to the island. The fort is on Frederica Rd. near Christ Church Episcopal Church.

FOR MORE INFORMATION

Superintendent, Fort Frederica National Monument (Rte. 9, Box 286-C, St. Simons Island, GA, 31522-9710, tel. 912/638–3639; e-mail fofr_superintendent@nps.gov; Web site www.nps.gov/fofr).

Fort Pulaski
National Monument

Near Savannah

On April 11, 1862, defense strategy changed forever when a Union-rifled cannon overcame a masonry fortification after only 30 hours of bombardment. Named for Revolutionary War hero Count Casimir Pulaski, the fort took 18 years to build. Constructing this fort was Robert E. Lee's first military assignment. This remarkably intact example of 19th-century military architecture, with its estimated 25 million bricks and 7.5-ft-/2.3-m-thick walls, is preserved for future generations as a reminder of the elusiveness of invincibility. The monument contains 5,365 acres, including some of the most pristine and scenic marshland on the Georgia coast. The monument was proclaimed in 1924 and transferred to the Park Service in 1933.

WHAT TO SEE & DO

Biking; bird-, wildlife-, and ship watching; boating; fishing; hiking; picnicking; self-guided touring of fort and nature trail. **Facilities:** Visitor center with interpretive exhibits, fort, nature trail, lighthouse. Bookstore, launching ramp, picnic areas. **Programs & Events:** Ranger-led talks and demonstrations (June–Aug., daily; Sept.–May, weekends); *The Battle for Fort Pulaski*, a 17-minute film (shown by request). Seasonal activities available. Troop encampments, special programs, and demonstrations (holiday weekends).

PLANNING YOUR VISIT

Camping: Available in Savannah, Tybee Island; none at monument. **Lodging:** Available in Savannah, Tybee Island; none at monument. **Food & Supplies:** Available on Tybee and Wilmington islands; none at monument. **Tips & Hints:** Plan to spend at least two hours. Busiest April through August, least crowded in December and January. **Fees, Permits & Limitations:** Entrance fee: $2 per person 17 and up, with maximum $4 per family. Permit required (free) for recreational, noncommercial shellfish harvesting in park waters. Cockspur Island Lighthouse (1857) accessible by private boat only. No bikes on trails leading to fort. Monument open daily, Memorial Day–Labor Day, 8–6:45; Labor Day–Memorial Day, 8–5:30. Visitor center open daily, Memorial Day–Labor Day, 9–6:30; Labor Day–Memorial Day, 9–5. Closed Dec. 25.

HOW TO GET THERE

15 mi/24 km east of Savannah on U.S. 80. Follow signs for Fort Pulaski, Tybee Island, and beaches. Closest airport: Savannah (30 mi/48 km).

FOR MORE INFORMATION

Fort Pulaski National Monument (Box 30757, U.S. 80E, Savannah, GA 31410-0757, tel. 912/786–5787; Web site www.nps.gov/fopu).

Jimmy Carter
National Historic Site

In the southwest part of the state, in Plains

The rural southern culture of Plains revolves around farming, church, and school and molded the character of the 39th U.S. president. The site includes President Carter's residence, boyhood home, school, and the railroad depot, which served as his campaign headquarters during the 1976 election. The area surrounding the residence is under the protection of the Secret Service and is not open to the public. The site was authorized on December 23, 1987.

WHAT TO SEE & DO

Touring Plains by car or bicycle, visiting boyhood farm and 1976 campaign headquarters, watching film. **Facilities:** Visitor center (Plains High School). Bookstore, picnic area in town park. **Programs & Events:** 27-minute film: historical piece about the Carters and their relationship to Plains. Plains Peanut Festival (last Sat., Sept.).

PLANNING YOUR VISIT

⚐ **Camping:** Available in Americus, Plains; none at site. ▣ **Lodging:** Available in Americus, Plains; none at site. ✗ **Food & Supplies:** Available in Americus, Plains; none at site. ☞ **Tips & Hints:** Plan to spend two–three hours visiting places associated with the Carters. Busiest in March and April, least crowded in December and January. ▧ **Fees, Permits & Limitations:** Free. Visitor center open daily 9–5. Closed Thanksgiving, Dec. 25, Jan. 1.

HOW TO GET THERE

From I–75, take Exit 33 (Cordele) and U.S. 280W to Plains. From Columbus, take U.S. 280S to Plains. Boyhood farm is 2 mi/3 km west of Plains on U.S. 280. Closest airport: Columbus (55 mi/88 km).

FOR MORE INFORMATION

Park Headquarters, Jimmy Carter National Historic Site (300 N. Bond St., Plains, GA 31780, tel. 229/824–4104; Web site www.nps.gov/jica).

Kennesaw Mountain
National Battlefield Park

Near Atlanta

Eleven miles (18 kilometers) of earthworks are preserved within the 2,884-acre park, which commemorates two Civil War battles where, during Sherman's 1864 Atlanta Campaign, Union General William T. Sherman met Confederate General Joseph E. Johnston. The site was authorized as a national battlefield in 1917, transferred to the Park Service in 1933, and redesignated in 1935.

WHAT TO SEE & DO

Auto touring to mountaintop or Cheatham Hill (main battlefield), hiking, picnicking, viewing exhibits and slides. **Facilities:** Visitor center, battlefield and earthworks, auto tour roads, 16 mi/26 km of trails. Bookstore, grills. **Programs & Events:** 19-minute film: *Kennesaw Mountains and the Atlanta Campaign.* Ranger program, living-history programs (June–Aug., weekends).

PLANNING YOUR VISIT

⚠ **Camping:** Available locally; none in park. 🏨 **Lodging:** Available locally; none in park. ✕ **Food & Supplies:** Available locally; none in park. ☞ **Tips & Hints:** Allow two hours for visit. Take shuttle bus to mountaintop on weekends. Stay on trails. Busiest in October and April, least crowded in November and January. Leashed pets only. No bicycles on trails. 💲 **Fees, Permits & Limitations:** Free. Exhibits are under construction, expected completion in summer 2001. Park open 7:30 AM–dusk year-round. Visitor center open 8:30–5 daily, weekends 8:30–6 (Mar.–Oct.). Closed Dec. 25.

HOW TO GET THERE

3 mi/5 km north of Marietta. From I–75, take Exit 269 and follow the brown-and-white park signs. Closest airport: Hartsfield Atlanta International (35 mi/56 km).

FOR MORE INFORMATION

Kennesaw Mountain National Battlefield Park (900 Kennesaw Mountain Dr., Kennesaw, GA 30152, tel. 770/427–4686, fax 770/528–8399; Web site www.nps.gov/kemo).

Martin Luther King Jr. National Historic Site

In Atlanta

In this two-block area, Atlanta honors the life, legacy, and teachings of Martin Luther King, Jr., the civil rights leader who was assassinated on April 4, 1968, at age 39. The site contains the home where King was born, Ebenezer Baptist Church, Martin Luther King Jr. Center for Nonviolent Social Change, King's gravesite, Fire Station #6 Museum, and the residential and commercial districts of the "Sweet Auburn" community. The site was established in 1980.

WHAT TO SEE & DO

Touring the site, watching films and puppet shows (for children). **Facilities:** Visitor center (450 Auburn Ave. NE) with interpretive exhibits and videos, Birth Home of Martin Luther King Jr., Ebenezer Baptist Church (407 Auburn Ave. NE), King Center Freedom Hall exhibits and King gravesite (449 Auburn Ave. NE), Fire Station #6 Museum, wayside exhibits in neighborhood. Bookstores and gift shops. **Programs & Events:** Year-round ranger-led tours of King's birth home, talks on historic role of black churches, puppet shows for children (tel. 404/331–

6922 ext. 3606 for reservations). Gospel concerts, arts programs (monthly). King Week Celebration (Jan.), Black History Month (Feb.), King Remembrance Day (Apr. 4), March on Washington Anniversary (Aug.), National Historic Site Birthday (Oct. 10), Candlelight Tour of Birth Home (Dec.).

PLANNING YOUR VISIT

⊞ **Lodging:** Available in Atlanta; none in park. ✕ **Food & Supplies:** Available in Atlanta; none in park. ☞ **Tips & Hints:** The best months to visit are October–December. Busiest in January, February, least crowded in March, December. ▦ **Fees, Permits & Limitations:** Free. Site and visitor center open daily Memorial Day–Labor Day 9–6; Labor Day–Memorial Day 9–5. Closed Dec. 25, Jan. 1.

HOW TO GET THERE

1.5 mi/2.5 km east of downtown Atlanta. Closest airport: Hartsfield-Atlanta International.

FOR MORE INFORMATION

Martin Luther King Jr. National Historic Site (450 Auburn Ave. NE, Atlanta, GA 30312, tel. 404/331–5190, fax 404/730–3112; e-mail MALU_Superintendent@nps.gov; Web site www.nps.gov/malu). Metro Atlanta Chamber of Commerce (235 International Blvd. NW, Atlanta, GA 30301, tel. 404/880–9000).

Ocmulgee National Monument

In the central part of the state, near Macon

Twelve thousand years of human habitation, from Ice Age "Paleo" hunters to the Muscogee (Creek) Confederacy of historic times, are on display at this monument. People of the Early Mississippian Period Macon Plateau culture 1,000 years ago built a large town that is now protected here. Huge earthen mounds and a unique ceremonial earth lodge, reconstructed over the original hand-molded clay floor, are reminders of this ancient agricultural society. One of two temple mounds at the Lamar site is the only remaining "spiral" mound. The British built a trading post at the site in the late 1600s. The Dunlap House and an earthen gun emplacement date from the Civil War battle that was fought here. The monument was authorized in 1936.

WHAT TO SEE & DO

Bird-watching, fishing, hiking, jogging, picnicking, touring the museum, viewing 17-minute movie, walking to earth lodge and mounds. **Facilities:** Visitor center with archaeological museum, theater, audio programs at two sites, 6-mi/10-km trail. Gift shop. **Programs & Events:** Ranger group programs and tours are available by reservation. Lantern Light Tours (Mar.); Field Trip to Lamar Mounds and Village, Artifact Identification Day (May, Nov.); "Ocmulgee University" Teachers'

Workshop (June); Children's Summer Workshops (July); Ocmulgee Indian Celebration (3rd weekend, Sept.).

PLANNING YOUR VISIT

Lodging: Available in Forsyth, Macon, Milledgeville, Warner Robins; none in park. ✕ **Food & Supplies:** Available in Forsyth, Macon, Milledgeville, Warner Robins; none in park. ☞ **Tips & Hints:** Visit in spring and fall. Busiest in September and November, least crowded in December and January. ▨ **Fees, Permits & Limitations:** Free. Permits required to visit Lamar Mounds unit. Georgia state fishing license required. Stay on trails. No bikes on trails. No climbing on mounds. No hunting. No kite flying. Leashed pets only. Park and visitor center open daily 9–5. Closed Dec. 25, Jan. 1.

HOW TO GET THERE

On the east edge of Macon, on U.S. 80E. From I–75, take I–16 Exit east, then U.S. 80E for 1 mi/1.6 km. Closest airport: Macon (12 mi/19 km).

FOR MORE INFORMATION

Ocmulgee National Monument (1207 Emery Hwy., Macon, GA 31201, tel. 912/752–8257, fax 912/752–8259; Web site www.nps.gov/ocmu). Macon-Bibb County Convention and Visitors Bureau (200 Cherry St., Macon, GA 31201, tel. 912/743–3401). Chamber of Commerce (Box 169, Macon, GA 31201-0169, tel. 912/741–8000), fax 912/741–8021.

See Also

Appalachian National Scenic Trail, West Virginia. *Augusta Canal National Heritage Area,* National Heritage Areas in Other National Parklands. *Overmountain Victory National Historic Trail,* National Trails System in Other National Parklands. *Trail of Tears National Historic Trail,* National Trails System in Other National Parklands.

HAWAII

Haleakala National Park

In east Maui

The park preserves the outstanding volcanic landscape of the upper slopes of Haleakala (10,023 ft/3,040 m) and protects the fragile ecosystems of Kipahulu Valley, the scenic pools along Oheò Gulch, and many rare and endangered species. Hike through rain forests or a cinder desert or picnic at the foot of a 400-ft/121-m waterfall in this park of extremes. Haleakala originally was one of two units of Hawaii National Park (along with Hawaii Volcanoes National Park, *see separate entry*). It was redesignated as a separate park in 1961 and designated a Biosphere Reserve in 1980.

WHAT TO SEE & DO

Bat- and bird-watching, bicycling, hiking, picnicking, stargazing, sunrise and sunset watching, swimming, walking, whale-watching. **Facilities:** 3 visitor centers with interpretive exhibits—Park Headquarters (Mile 11, Crater Rd.), Haleakala (Mile 21, Crater Rd.), Kipahulu (Mile 42, Rte. 31); trails, interpretive exhibits, pre-contact Hawaiian structures (prior to 1778), historic walls, Sugar Mill dam ruins. Bookstore. **Programs & Events:** Summit Area—guided walks and programs on geological, natural, and cultural history (daily at 9:30, 10:30, 11:30; Summit Bldg.), guided cinder desert hike (Tues. and Fri. at 9; Haleakala visitor center), guided cloud forest hike (Mon. and Thurs. at 9; Hosmer Grove, just inside park entrance), all-day crater hike (monthly); bamboo forest hike (Sun.–Fri. at 9:30; Kipahulu visitor center), hikes or orientation talks (daily at 12:30, 1:30, 2:30, 3:30; Kipahulu visitor center), Waikamoi Preserve hike (one Sun. every other month). Star programs (May–Aug.).

PLANNING YOUR VISIT

⚠ **Camping:** 4 campgrounds: primitive (no reservations). Backcountry camping available (permit required, *see below*). Group camping available (no reservations, restrictions apply, *see below*). Wilderness cabins available (obtained through advanced reservation lottery, *see below*; permit required, *see below*). State campgrounds at Polipoli and Waianapanapa. 🏨 **Lodging:** Available in Hana, Kahului, Pukalani; none in park. ✗ **Food & Supplies:** Available in Hana, Kahului, Pukalani; none in park. ☞ **Tips & Hints:** Wear study, comfortable shoes and lightweight, layered clothing that will keep you warm in wet weather at the summit. Temperatures range from 40°F/4°C to 65°F/18°C but can be below freezing with wind chill year-round. Watch for altitude sickness, flash flooding of pools and stream at Kipahulu, and mosquitoes. Rent binoculars at dive shops and stargaze. Go to Halemauu Trail and the Summit for sunsets. Busy year-round, but least crowded mid-January through February. ✉ **Fees, Permits & Limitations:** Entrance fee: $10 per vehicle, $5 for walk-ins and bicyclists. Backcountry permits (free) required for all backcountry camping. To enter wilderness cabin advanced reservation lottery, write the park, "Attention Cabins," at least 90 days before arrival. Include alternate dates and avoid weekends to increase chances of obtaining slot. Call park at 808/572–4400 ext. 0 daily between 1 and 3 to check on filling last-minute cancellations. Camping restrictions: Group camping maximum 12 people, paid group guides must have a commercial license, overnight stay lengths apply for groups and individuals. Fishing at Kipahulu must be done in accordance with state fishing regulations. Biking restricted to roads. No skateboarding, skating, or hang gliding. No pets on trails. Leashed pets allowed in campground only. Park open daily. Visitor center hours: park headquarters—daily 7:30–4; Haleakala—daily sunrise–3; Kipahulu—daily 9–5.

HOW TO GET THERE

The park's summit area is a 1½-hour drive from Kahului via Rtes. 37, 377, and 378. Kipahulu is a 3–4 hour drive from Kahului via Rtes. 36, 360, and 31. Closest airport: Kahului.

FOR MORE INFORMATION

Haleakala National Park (Box 369, Makawao, HI 96768, tel. 808/572–4400, fax 808/572–1304; Web site www.nps.gov/hale). Hawaii Visitor Bureau (Box 1738, Kahului, HI 96732, tel. 808/244–3530).

Hawaii Volcanoes National Park

On the south end of the island of Hawaii

The park preserves the natural setting of Mauna Loa (13,677 ft/4,149 m), the world's most massive volcano, and Kilauea (the world's most active). It contains lush rain forests, raw craters, acid deserts, and great areas covered by lava flows. The park was established in 1916 and designated a Biosphere Reserve in 1980 and a World Heritage Site in 1987.

WHAT TO SEE & DO

Hiking, scenic driving. **Facilities:** Visitor center with interpretive exhibits, museum, art center, 11-mi/18-km loop road, trails, overlook. Book and map sale areas, gift shop. **Programs & Events:** Year-round ranger talks and walks (daily); evening programs (2–3 times a month); evening slide presentations (Sun. nights, Volcano House). Kilauea Cultural Heritage (2nd weekend, July).

PLANNING YOUR VISIT

Camping: 2 campgrounds: no hookups (no reservations). Backcountry camping available (permit required, *see below*). Group camping available (no reservations). **Lodging:** In the park: Volcano House (tel. 808/967–7321), Kilauea Military Camp (active duty and retired military personnel and civilian employees of Defense Department only, tel. 808/967–7315). Lodging also available outside the park in Hilo, Naalehu, and Volcano Village. ✕ **Food & Supplies:** In the park: snack bar and restaurant (Volcano House, tel. 808/967–7321). Food and supplies also available in Hilo, Keaau, Naalehu, Pahala, and Volcano Village. ☞ **Tips & Hints:** Be prepared for anything from snow and high winds to heat exhaustion. Bring rain gear, light sweaters and windbreakers, sturdy shoes, hats, water bottles, sunglasses, and sunscreen with a high UV factor. Call 808/935–8555 for weather forecasts. Stay on trails and don't enter lava tubes (except Thurston Lava Tube). Avoid volcanic fumes. Busiest in July and August, least crowded in April and September. ✉ **Fees, Permits & Limitations:** Entrance fee: $10 per vehicle or $5 for walk-ins or bicyclists. Backcountry camping permit required for all backcountry (free). Park open daily. Visitor center open daily 7:45–5. Jagger Museum open daily 8:30–5.

HOW TO GET THERE

From Hilo, go 30 mi/48 km southwest on Hwy. 11; from Kailua-Kona, travel 96 mi/154 km southeast on Hwy. 11 or 125 mi/200 km through Waimea and Hilo via Hwys. 19 and 11. Closest airport: Hilo.

FOR MORE INFORMATION

Hawaii Volcanoes National Park (Box 52, Hawaii National Park, HI 96718-0052, tel. 808/985–6000 [ext. 1 for eruption information], fax 808/967–8186; e-mail HAVO_Interpretation@nps.gov; Web site www.nps.gov/havo). Big Island Visitors Bureau (250 Keawe St., Hilo, HI 96720, tel. 808/961–5797).

Kalaupapa National Historical Park

On north shore of Molokai

Kalaupapa and Kalawao, the historic Hansen's disease (leprosy) settlements, are preserved in this park. Kalaupapa is still home for many surviving patients. Although Hansen's disease is contagious, it is very unlikely visitors would contract the disease from anyone in Kalaupapa because all the patients have been cured by drug therapies introduced after World War II. In Kalawao are the churches of Siloama, established in 1866, and St. Philomena, associated with the work of Joseph De Veuster (Father Damien). Kalaupapa peninsula was inhabited by Hawaiian people prior to the establishment of the quarantine settlement at Kalawao in 1866. Evidence of this occupation in four *ahupuaa* (land divisions) is relatively undisturbed and represents one of the richest archaeological preserves in Hawaii. The 10,700-acre park contains spectacular sea cliffs, narrow valleys, a volcanic crater, a rain forest, lava tubes and caves, and offshore islands and waters. The park was authorized on December 22, 1980.

WHAT TO SEE & DO

Touring Kalaupapa and Kalawao settlements. **Facilities:** Wayside exhibits. Bookstore and sales shop. **Programs & Events:** Tours of Kalaupapa and Kalawao (Mon.–Sat.).

PLANNING YOUR VISIT

⚠ **Camping:** Available in Palaau State Park; none at site. 🏨 **Lodging:** Available in Kaunakakai; none in park. ✕ **Food & Supplies:** Visitors on tour must bring their own lunch; those on mule ride have lunch provided by mule ride operator. Food and supplies also available in Kaunakakai. ☞ **Tips & Hints:** Make reservations for commercial tours of the settlement, for mule rides on the Pali trail, and for flights to Kalaupapa from Oahu or Molokai (Molokai Shuttle, tel. 808/567–6847; Pacific Wings, tel. 888/575–4546). Go between November and March to see whales and migratory birds from Alaska. 🎟 **Fees, Permits & Limitations:** Free. Reservations and fees required for commercial tours, mule rides, and air flights. Contact Molokai Mule Rides, Inc. (tel. 808/567–6088 or 800/567–7550) for mule ride reservations, Damien Tours (tel. 808/567–6171) for tour reservations. Visitation limited to scheduled tour or personal guests of residents. No one under 16 allowed. No hunting or firearms. No pets. No photographs of patients without their written permission. Park open daily. Commercial tours operate Mon.–Sat. Closed Thanksgiving, Dec. 25, Jan. 1.

HOW TO GET THERE

The Kalaupapa Peninsula is located at the base of a 2,000 ft/609 m cliff. There is no road access from the rest of Molokai. Visitors must hike or ride a trail down the cliff or fly into the airport in the park. Visitors will be picked up by the tour bus at the trailhead or airport. Closest airport: Kalaupapa (2 mi/3 km).

FOR MORE INFORMATION

Kalaupapa National Historical Park (National Park Service, Box 2222, Kalaupapa, HI 96742, tel. 808/567–6802, fax 808/567–6729; e-mail KALA_Interpretation@nps.gov; Web site www.nps.gov/kala). Molokai Business Association (130 Kamehameha V-Hwy., Suite 210, Molokai, HI 96748, tel. 808/553–3034).

Kaloko-Honokohau National Historical Park

On west coast of island of Hawaii, near Kailua Kona

Kaloko-Honokohau preserves traditional native Hawaiian activities and culture. It is the site of an ancient Hawaiian settlement with four different *ahupuaa,* or traditional sea-to-mountain land divisions. Resources include fishponds, house-site platforms, petroglyphs, a stone slide, and a religious site. The park was established on November 10, 1978.

WHAT TO SEE & DO

Bird-watching, fishing, hiking, picnicking, snorkeling, surfing, swimming. **Facilities:** Contact station (Honokohau). **Programs & Events:** Interpretive programs (occasionally). Cultural Festival (Nov.).

PLANNING YOUR VISIT

Camping: Available in Hapuna State Park; none in park. **Lodging:** Available at Kailua-Kona; none at site. **Food & Supplies:** Supplies at park contact station; food and supplies available at Kailua-Kona. **Tips & Hints:** Busiest in June and July, least crowded in September and October. **Fees, Permits & Limitations:** Free. No collecting artifacts, plants, rocks, or coral. Kaloko road gate open daily 8–3:30. Visitors are welcome in the park after 3:30, but vehicles need to be out before gate closes. Headquarters open weekdays 8–4. Contact station open daily, 10–4.

HOW TO GET THERE

At the base of Hualalai Volcano along the Kona coast, 3 mi/5 km north of Kailua-Kona and south of the airport on Hwy. 19 (Queen Kaahumanu Hwy.). The Kaloko gate is across the highway from the Kaloko New Industrial Park across from Kona Trade Center building. The park can also be accessed from the south end, by way of the Honokohau small boat harbor. Park headquarters is in the Kaloko New Industrial Park on Hwy. 19. From the highway, turn toward the mountain on Hina Lani St. and make a right on Kanalani St. Turn right into the fourth driveway on your right. Headquarters is at the end. Closest airport: Keahole-Kona (3 mi/5 km).

FOR MORE INFORMATION

Kaloko-Honokohau National Historical Park (73-4786 Kanalani St., #14, Kailua-Kona, HI 96740, tel. 808/329–6881; Web site www.nps. gov/kaho). Big Island Visitors Bureau (250 Keawe, Hilo, HI, 96720, tel. 808/961–5797).

Pu'uhonua o Hōnaunau National Historical Park

In southwest Hawaii Island, near Ho'naunau

Until 1819, this park was a sanctuary for vanquished Hawaiian warriors, noncombatants, and kapu breakers. The park includes prehistoric house sites, royal fishponds, coconut groves, and spectacular shore scenery. The 182-acre park was authorized as City of Refuge National Historical Park in 1955 and renamed in 1978.

WHAT TO SEE & DO

Fishing, hiking, picnicking, self-guided tours, watching crafts demonstrations. **Facilities:** Visitor center with interpretive exhibits, restored temple, trail. Picnic area. **Programs & Events:** Year-round programs available. Cultural Festival (last weekend, June).

PLANNING YOUR VISIT

⊞ **Lodging:** Available in Captain Cook; none in park. ✗ **Food & Supplies:** Available in Captain Cook; none in park. ☞ **Tips & Hints:** Be alert for unexpected high waves. Watch for falling coconuts and coconut fronds off the trail. Busiest in February and July, least crowded in December and January. ▨ **Fees, Permits & Limitations:** Entrance fee: $2 per person. Park open daily, Mon.–Thurs., 6 AM–8 PM; Fri.–Sun. and holidays, 6 AM–11 PM. Visitor center open daily, 8–4:30.

HOW TO GET THERE

From the airport, take HI 19 to Kailua, then HI 11 to Honaunau, then HI 160 to the park. Closest airport: Kona (30 mi/48 km).

FOR MORE INFORMATION

Pu'uhonua o Ho'naunau National Historical Park (Box 129, Honaunau, HI 96726, tel. 808/328–2326; Web site www.nps.gov/puho). Kona-Kohala Chamber of Commerce (75–5737 Kuakini Hwy., Suite 208, Kailua-Kona, HI 96740, tel. 808/261–2727 or 808/329–1758).

Puukohola Heiau National Historic Site

In northwest Hawaii Island, near Kawaihae

High on a hill above the Pacific Ocean sits Puukohola Heiau, the last major religious structure of the ancient Hawaiian culture. Kamehameha I built the "Temple on the Hill of the Whale" between 1790 and 1791 during his rise to power and dedicated it to his family war god, Ku-kaili-moku. The 85-acre site was authorized on August 17, 1972.

WHAT TO SEE & DO

Bird-watching, guided and self-guided tours of historical sites, hiking, shark- and whale-watching. **Facilities:** Visitor center with interpretive exhibits, trails. **Programs & Events:** Interpretive talks, guided tours, Hawaiian programs. Arts-and-crafts demonstrations (once weekly, Jan.–Sept.). Pacific Islander Day (May). Hawaiian Cultural Festival (Aug.).

PLANNING YOUR VISIT

⚠ **Camping:** Available in Spencer Beach Park; none at site. ⊞ **Lodging:** Available in Kailua-Kona, Kohala Coast, Waimea; none at site. ✗ **Food & Supplies:** Available locally; none at site. ☞ **Tips & Hints:** Trail is long and rugged; hike only if you are in shape. Make guided-tour reservations two weeks in advance (tel. 808/882–7218). Busiest in May and August, least crowded in December and January. ▨ **Fees, Permits & Limitations:** Free. Group guided-tour fee: $1 per person (10 or more). Park gate closes at 4. Visitor center open daily 7:30–4.

HOW TO GET THERE

On the northwest shore of the island of Hawaii in the district of South Kohala. The visitor center is off Hwy. 270, 0.25 mi/0.4 km north of

Hwy. 270 and Hwy. 19 intersection. Closest airport: Kailua-Kona (32 mi/51 km).

FOR MORE INFORMATION

Puukohola Heiau National Historic Site (Box 44340, Kawaihae, HI 96743, tel. 808/882–7218, fax 808/882–1215; Web site www.nps.gov/ puhe). Kona-Kohala Chamber of Commerce (75–5737 Kuakini Hwy., Suite 208, Kailua-Kona, HI 96740, tel. 808/329–1758, fax 808/329–8564).

USS *Arizona* Memorial

In Hawaii, at Pearl Harbor

The USS *Arizona* Memorial grew out of a wartime desire to honor those who died in the December 7, 1941, attack. The memorial is the final resting place for many of the *Arizona's* 1,177 crewmen who lost their lives that day. Their names are inscribed on the memorial. The park was established on September 9, 1980.

WHAT TO SEE & DO

Taking shuttle boat to memorial, touring memorial and museum, watching 23-minute film. **Facilities:** Visitor center with interpretive exhibits, theaters, memorial. Bookstore. **Programs & Events:** Tours (June–Aug., daily 7:45–3; Sept.–May, daily 8–3). Local, military, and cultural history tours (Memorial Day, July 4, Veterans Day, Dec. 7).

PLANNING YOUR VISIT

Lodging: Available in Honolulu; none at memorial. **✕ Food & Supplies:** In the park: snack bar. Food and supplies also available in Aiea, Honolulu, and Pearl City. ☞ **Tips & Hints:** Plan for a two-hour visit. Secure all valuables in hotels or on person because the visitor center is in a high-theft area. Go early in day to avoid a long wait. Busiest June through August, least crowded December through February. **Fees, Permits & Limitations:** Free, but donations are encouraged. Small fee for program translations in Japanese and Mandarin Chinese. No baby strollers, carriages, or baby backpacks in the theaters or on the boats. No beach or swimwear. No pets. The memorial is open daily 7:30–5. Closed Thanksgiving, Dec. 25, and Jan. 1.

HOW TO GET THERE

The memorial is a half-hour drive from Waikiki. Take H-1 west, past the Honolulu International Airport, to the Arizona Memorial/Stadium Exit. Access is also available via a one-hour ride on Bus 20 or Bus 42 from Waikiki. Closest airport: Honolulu International (3 mi/5 km).

FOR MORE INFORMATION

Superintendent, USS *Arizona* Memorial (1 Arizona Memorial Pl., Honolulu, HI 96818-3145, tel. 808/422–2771; Web site www.nps.gov/usar). Hawaii Visitor and Convention Bureau (2270 Kalakaua Ave., Suite 801, Honolulu, HI 96815, tel. 808/923–1811).

IDAHO

City of Rocks
National Reserve

In the southern part of the state,
45 mi/72 km south of Burley

In this reserve are historic pioneer trails in the midst of geologic grandeur. The name "City of Rocks" refers to massive granite rock formations—up to 2.5 billion years old and 600 ft/182 m high—that reminded California-bound emigrants in the 1800s of city buildings. The park also has world-class rock climbing and a diversity of habitat, wildlife, and vegetation. City of Rocks, which is cooperatively managed by the National Park Service and the State of Idaho, was designated on November 18, 1988.

WHAT TO SEE & DO

Biking, cross-country skiing, hiking, horseback riding (rentals, Almo), hunting, picnicking, rock climbing, snowmobiling, snowshoeing. **Facilities:** Visitor center with interpretive exhibits (Almo), trails, wayside exhibits, kiosk. Gift shop, grills, picnic tables. **Programs & Events:** Interpretive talks, guided hikes, cultural demonstrations (Memorial Day–Labor Day, Fri. and Sat. nights). Stargazing (May–Oct.), City of Rocks Trail Ride (Sept.).

PLANNING YOUR VISIT

Camping: 78 campsites: no hookups (reservations available, tel. 208/824–5519). Backcountry camping available (permit required, *see below*). Group camping available (reservations available, tel. 208/824–5519). Private campground with hookups in Oakley. **Lodging:** Available in Albion, Almo; none in park. **Food & Supplies:** Available in Albion, Almo, Oakley; none in park. **Tips & Hints:** Go in late May to early June for wildflowers, May–June for birds, late September–early October for fall colors. Busiest in May and June, least crowded in January and February. **Fees, Permits & Limitations:** Free. Permit required (free) for backcountry camping and backpacking. Leashed dogs only. Hunting in designated areas only. Idaho state hunting license required. Bikes and horses on designated trails only. No motorized vehicles or equipment on trails. Reserve is open year-round but in winter (Dec.–Mar.) is accessible only by skis, snowmobile, snowshoes. Visitor center open Apr.–Oct., daily 8–4:30; Nov.–Mar., weekdays 8–4:30.

HOW TO GET THERE

In Almo, ID, on the Idaho–Utah border. From Boise and west, take I–84 to Declo exit 16/SR 77 to Almo. Closest airport: Twin Falls (85 mi/136 km).

FOR MORE INFORMATION

City of Rocks National Reserve (Box 169, Almo, ID 83312, tel. 208/824–5519, fax 208/824–5563; e-mail CIRO_Ranger_Activities@nps.gov; Web site www.nps.gov/ciro).

Craters of the Moon
National Monument

In the south-central part of the state,
southwest of Arco

The monument preserves 83 square mi/215 square km of the largest young basaltic lava field in the conterminous United States. There are more than 25 cones and 60 lava flows that range in age from 15,000 to just 2,000 years old. The park contains one of the largest basaltic cinder cones in the world (Big Cinder Butte) and some of the best examples of spatter cones in the world. The north end of the monument contains a portion of Goodale's Cutoff, which is part of the Oregon Trail. The monument was proclaimed on May 2, 1924.

WHAT TO SEE & DO

Bird-watching, bicycling, caving, driving loop drive, hiking, skiing, snowshoeing, telemarking. **Facilities:** Visitor center with interpretive exhibits, overlooks, trails, wayside exhibits, amphitheater. Bookstore, picnic tables. **Programs & Events:** Guided walks, evening programs (mid-June–Labor Day). Guided snowshoe hikes (Jan.–Feb., weekends, reservations required).

PLANNING YOUR VISIT

⚠ **Camping:** Campground: no hookups or showers (no reservations). Water available mid-May–Oct. 1. Backcountry camping available (permit required, *see below*). Group camping available (reservations required, tel. 208/527–3257 or write monument). Private campgrounds available in Arco. ⊡ **Lodging:** Available in Arco; none in park. ✗ **Food & Supplies:** In the monument: snacks (visitor center). Food and supplies also available in Arco. ☞ **Tips & Hints:** Bring sturdy ground cloth to protect tent bottoms. Go in mid-June for peak flower display, in late summer and fall for most ice-free caving. Busiest in July and August, least crowded in December and January. ▤ **Fees, Permits & Limitations:** Entrance fee: $4 per car, $2 per person on bicycle or on foot. Backcountry camping permit and permit to enter north section of monument required (free). No bikes except on Goodale's Cutoff. No hunting. No off-road vehicle travel. No pets on trails. Park road closed during winter months. Park open daily. Visitor center open Labor Day–mid-June, daily 8–4:30; mid-June–Labor Day, daily 8–6. Closed Veterans Day, Thanksgiving, Dec. 25, Jan. 1, Martin Luther King Jr. Day, Presidents Day.

HOW TO GET THERE

18 mi/29 km southwest of Arco on U.S. 20/26/93. Closest airport: Sun Valley (60 mi/96 km).

FOR MORE INFORMATION

Craters of the Moon National Monument (Box 29, Arco, ID 83213, tel. 208/527–3257, fax 208/527–3073; Web site www.nps.gov/crmo). Lost River Chamber of Commerce (Box 46, Arco, ID 82313, tel. 208/527–8977).

Hagerman Fossil Beds National Monument

In the south-central part of the state, in Hagerman

Here are the world's richest known deposits from the late Pliocene era, roughly 3.5 million years ago. The collection includes the largest concentration of fossil horses in North America and more than 100 other animal species. The monument provides a glimpse of life that existed before the Ice Age and the earliest appearance of modern flora and fauna. The site was authorized in 1988.

WHAT TO SEE & DO

Auto touring, hiking. **Facilities:** Temporary visitor center, self-guided driving tour, trails. Bookstore, overlooks. **Programs & Events:** Tours (Memorial Day–Aug., weekends). Hagerman Fossil Days Celebration (Memorial Day weekend).

PLANNING YOUR VISIT

⛺ **Camping:** Available in Hagerman and local communities; none at monument. 🛏 **Lodging:** Available in Bliss, Buhl, Gooding, Hagerman, Jerome, Twin Falls, Wendell; none at monument. ✕ **Food & Supplies:** Available in Bliss, Buhl, Gooding, Hagerman, Jerome, Twin Falls, Wendell; none at monument. ☞ **Tips & Hints:** Best time to visit is June–September. Go in December to see migratory waterfowl. ▦ **Fees, Permits & Limitations:** Free. Many areas closed to public. Monument open daily. Visitor center open Labor Day–Memorial Day, Thurs., Fri., Sat., Sun. 10–4; Memorial Day–Labor Day, daily 9–5.

HOW TO GET THERE

Visitor center is in Hagerman, on U.S. 30 across from the high school. Closest airport: Twin Falls (45 mi/72 km).

FOR MORE INFORMATION

Hagerman Fossil Beds National Monument (221 N. State St., Box 570, Hagerman, ID 83332, tel. 208/837–4793, fax 208/837–4857; Web site www.nps.gov/hafo). Hagerman Valley Chamber of Commerce (Box 599 Hagerman, ID 83332, tel. 208/837–9131). Hagerman Valley Historical Society (100 S. State St., Hagerman, ID 83332, tel. 208/837–6288).

Nez Perce
National Historical Park

*In the north-central part of Idaho, in Spalding;
and in Washington, Oregon, and Montana*

Nez Perce culture, traditions, and history are commemorated and celebrated in this park's 38 sites, which are located in four states. Sites range from small roadside pullouts to village sites and battlefields. The Nez Perce National Historic Trail, which is part of the park, runs from the Wallowa Valley of east Oregon to Bear Paw Battlefield in north-central Montana. The park was authorized on May 15, 1965.

WHAT TO SEE & DO

Fishing, picnicking, walking, watching film, wildlife viewing. **Facilities:** 2 visitor centers with interpretive exhibits—Spalding, ID, and at Big Hole National Battlefield, near Wisdom, MT; *see separate entry for Big Hole information*; trails, museums, interpretive display boards. Book and map sales areas, picnic tables. **Programs & Events:** Tours and walks (by reservation, tel. 208/843–2261 ext. 199). Guided hikes, interpretive talks, cultural demonstrations (mid-May–Sept., weekends). Commemorations of Nez Perce War of 1877 (White Bird, June 17; Big Hole, Aug. 6; Bear Paw, Oct. 5).

PLANNING YOUR VISIT

⚠ **Camping:** Available locally; none in park. ⛺ **Lodging:** Available in Lewiston, ID; none in park. ✗ **Food & Supplies:** Available in Lewiston and Lapwai, ID; none in park. ☞ **Tips & Hints:** Allow plenty of time to visit 38 sites that stretch 1,500 mi/2,400 km. Be prepared for extreme changes in climate and elevation. Busiest in May and August, least crowded in November and February. ▣ **Fees, Permits & Limitations:** Free. Idaho state fishing license required. Nez Perce Reservation permit required for steelhead. Leashed pets only. No hunting. Spalding unit open during daylight. Spalding visitor center open Oct.–May, daily 8–4:30; June–Sept., daily 8–5:30. Park closed Thanksgiving, Dec. 25, Jan. 1.

HOW TO GET THERE

Spalding visitor center is 10 mi/16 km east of Lewiston on ID 95. Closest airport: Lewiston.

FOR MORE INFORMATION

Nez Perce National Historical Park (Rte. 1, Box 100, Spalding, ID 83540, tel. 208/843–2261, fax 208/843–2001; Web site www.nps.gov/nepe). Lewiston Chamber of Commerce (111 Main St., Suite 120, Lewiston, ID 83501, tel. 208/743–3531).

See Also

California National Historic Trail, National Trails System in Other National Parklands. *Continental Divide National Scenic Trail,* National Trails System in Other National Parklands. *Lewis and Clark National Historic Trail,* National Trails System in Other National Parklands. *Nez Perce National Historic Trail,* National Trails System in Other National Parklands. *Oregon National Scenic Trail,* National Trails System in Other National Parklands. *Yellowstone National Park,* Wyoming.

ILLINOIS

Lincoln Home
National Historic Site

In Springfield

Abraham Lincoln bought this house in the spring of 1844 for his wife and son, and it was the only home the family ever owned. They lived in it for 17 years, during which time Lincoln built his law practice and began a political career that would lead him to the presidency in 1861. The house has been restored to its 1860s appearance. It stands in the midst of a four-block historic neighborhood that the National Park Service is restoring so the neighborhood, like the house, will appear much as Lincoln would have remembered it. The site was authorized in 1971 and established in 1972.

WHAT TO SEE & DO

Touring the home and neighborhood. **Facilities:** Visitor center (426 S. 7th St.) with exhibits, sculptures, film; home, neighborhood. Bookstore. **Programs & Events:** Guided home tours, interpretive programs, walks. Guided walks (June–Aug.). Lincoln's Birthday (Feb.), Lincoln Colloquium (Sept.), Christmas in Mr. Lincoln's Neighborhood (Dec.)

PLANNING YOUR VISIT

⚠ **Camping:** Available in Springfield area; none at site. ⌂ **Lodging:** Available in Springfield area; none at site. ✕ **Food & Supplies:** Available in Springfield area; none at site. ☞ **Tips & Hints:** Watch your footing on slippery boardwalks. Busiest in May and July, least crowded in December and January. ▧ **Fees, Permits & Limitations:** Free. Visitor parking lot fee ($2 per hour). No vehicles in the site's four city blocks. Leashed pets only. Park grounds open daily to pedestrians. Visitor center open Apr.–Oct., daily 8–6; Nov.–Mar., daily 8–5. Closed Thanksgiving, Dec. 25, Jan. 1.

HOW TO GET THERE

In downtown Springfield, at the intersection of 7th and Jackson Sts. Closest airport: Springfield (5 mi/8 km).

FOR MORE INFORMATION

Lincoln Home National Historic Site (413 S. 8th St., Springfield, IL 62704, tel. 217/492–4241 ext. 221, fax 217/492–4648; e-mail lincolnhome@nps.gov; Web site www.nps.gov/liho). Springfield Convention and Visitors Bureau (109 N. 7th St., Springfield, IL 62701, tel. 800/545–7300).

See Also

Lewis and Clark National Historic Trail, National Trails System in Other National Parklands. *Mormon Pioneer National Historic Trail,* National Trails System in Other National Parklands. *Trail of Tears National Historic Trail,* National Trails System in Other National Parklands.

INDIANA

George Rogers Clark National Historical Park

In the southwest part of the state, in Vincennes

The park, including a classic memorial building, is on the site of the Revolutionary War Battle of Fort Sackville. The memorial commemorates the capture of the fort from the British by Lieutenant Colonel George Rogers Clark and his men on February 25, 1779, and the subsequent settlement of the region north of the Ohio River. The site was authorized in 1966.

WHAT TO SEE & DO

Picnicking, touring Clark Memorial and surrounding 26 acres of landscaped lawns. **Facilities:** Visitor center with interpretive exhibits, memorial building, grounds. Book and gift shop sales area, picnic table area. **Programs & Events:** Reenactor Gathering (3rd Sun. of the month, Apr.–Nov.). Spirit of Vincennes Rendezvous (Memorial Day weekend), July 4th fireworks.

PLANNING YOUR VISIT

⛺ **Camping:** Available in Vincennes; none in park. 🏨 **Lodging:** Available in Vincennes; none in park. ✗ **Food & Supplies:** Available in Vincennes; none in park. ☞ **Tips & Hints:** Busiest in May and July, least crowded in January and February. 🎫 **Fees, Permits & Limitations:** Entrance fee: $2 (17 and older), $4 per family. Leashed pets only. Park and visitor center open daily 9–5. Closed Thanksgiving, Dec. 25, Jan. 1.

HOW TO GET THERE

In downtown Vincennes. Take Willow or 6th St. exit off U.S. 41 or 6th St. exit off U.S. 50. Closest airport: Evansville's Dress Regional Airport (60 mi/96 km).

FOR MORE INFORMATION

George Rogers Clark National Historic Park (401 S. 2nd St., Vincennes, IN 47591, tel. 812/882–1776, fax 812/882–7270; Web site www.nps.gov/gero). Vincennes/Knox County Convention and Visitors Bureau (Box 602, Vincennes, IN 47591, tel. 812/886–0400 or 800/886–6443). Knox County Chamber of Commerce (Box 553, Vincennes, IN 47591, tel. 812/882–6440; Web site accessknoxcounty.com).

Indiana Dunes National Lakeshore ▼▼

*Between Gary and Michigan City,
along Lake Michigan*

The 15,000-acre park preserves three main dune ridges that run parallel to Lake Michigan's shoreline. The younger dunes, which rise 180
ft/55 m, are still open and sandy but the 8,000- to 12,000-year-old dune
ridges are covered with oak and maple forests. Beaches, bogs, marshes,
swamps, prairie remnants, and a farm and homestead dating to 19th-
century fur-trading and pioneer agriculture are also open to the public.
The lakeshore was authorized on November 5, 1966.

WHAT TO SEE & DO

Bicycling (rentals, Chesterton), bird-watching, boating, cross-country
skiing, fishing, hiking, horseback riding, picnicking, swimming. **Facilities:** 2 visitor centers with interpretive exhibits—Dorothy Buell (Rte.
12 and Kemil Rd.), Bailly-Chellberg (Mineral Spring Rd. and Rte. 20,
Porter); Paul H. Douglas Center for Environmental Education,
beaches, biking and hiking trails, amphitheater. Bookstores, bathhouse,
picnic pavilions and shelters. **Programs & Events:** Ranger-guided hikes
and programs, farm feeding programs (weekends), musicals (3rd Fri.
of the month). Ranger-guided Pinhook Bog tours (May–Oct., weekends; reservations required, tel. 219/926–7561 ext. 225), day and night
hikes (May–Oct., daily), Chellberg Farm and Bailly Homestead house
tours and historic demonstrations (May–Oct., Sun. 1–4), sunset beach
and woodland hikes (frequent), campfire programs (May–Oct., weekend evening). Maple Sugar Time Festival (1st 2 weekends, Mar.),
Walpurgis Night (4th Sat., Apr.), Duneland Harvest Festival (3rd weekend, Sept.), Duneland Christmas (Dec.).

PLANNING YOUR VISIT

� **Camping:** Campground: no hookups (open Apr.–Oct.; no reservations). Public and private campgrounds nearby in Indiana Dunes State
Park, Michigan City, Portage, Valparaiso. 🏠 **Lodging:** Available in
Chesterton, Gary, Michigan City, Portage, Porter; none in park. ✗
Food & Supplies: Available in Chesterton, Gary, Miller, Michigan City,
Portage; none in park. ☞ **Tips & Hints:** Watch for rip currents. Don't
walk on shoreline shelf ice. Go in spring for migrating birds and wildflowers, summer for swimming and wildflowers, fall for fall colors and
prairie wildflowers. Busiest June through August, least crowded in December and January. 🎟 **Fees, Permits & Limitations:** Parking fee: $5 per
vehicle for day use at West Beach (Memorial Day–Labor Day). Indiana state fishing license required. Smelt fishing permit required. No
dune buggies or snowmobiles. No hunting. No open fires except in
campground. No pets on some beaches (May–Oct.). Park open daily
dawn–dusk. Visitor centers open Labor Day–Memorial Day, daily 8–5;
Memorial Day–Labor Day, daily 8–6. Closed Thanksgiving, Dec. 25,
Jan. 1.

HOW TO GET THERE

Take I–80, I–90, or I–94 to Rte. 49 in Chesterton or Rte. 249 in Portage at Burns Harbor. From Chesterton, take Rte. 49N and then either U.S. 20 or U.S. 12 to park. From Portage, take Rte. 249 to U.S. 12E to park. Closest airports: Chicago's Midway (45 mi/72 km), Gary Airport (10 mi/16 km).

FOR MORE INFORMATION

Indiana Dunes National Lakeshore (1100 N. Mineral Springs Rd., Porter, IN 46304, tel. 219/926–7561, fax 219/926–7561; e-mail INDU_ Superintendent@nps.gov; Web site www.nps.gov/indu). Duneland Chamber of Commerce (303 Broadway, Chestertown, IN 46304, tel. 219/926–5513, fax 219/926–7593). Porter County Tourism (800 Indian Boundary Rd., Chestertown, IN 46304, tel. 219/926–2255 or 800/283–8687, fax 219/929–5395).

Lincoln Boyhood National Memorial

In the southwest part of the state, in Lincoln City

On this Southern Indiana farm, Abraham Lincoln spent 14 years, from the ages of 7 to 21. He worked the land with his father, developed his love of reading and his curiosity for knowledge, and experienced the death of his mother, Nancy Hanks Lincoln, when he was nine years old. The memorial was authorized in 1962.

WHAT TO SEE & DO

Picnicking, touring living historical farm, visiting Nancy Hanks Lincoln's grave and Cabin Site Memorial. **Facilities:** Visitor center with 2 Memorial Halls, living historical farm, museum, auditorium, gravesite, cabin site, trail. Bookstore, picnic tables, post office. **Programs & Events:** Interpretive programs (June–Aug.). December Holidays (1st weekend, Dec.), Lincoln Day (Sun. preceding Feb. 12).

PLANNING YOUR VISIT

⚠ **Camping:** Available in adjoining Lincoln State Park and in Santa Claus; none at memorial. 🏨 **Lodging:** Available in Dale, Santa Claus; none at memorial. ✕ **Food & Supplies:** Available in Dale, Santa Claus; none at memorial. ☞ **Tips & Hints:** Visit between May and September, when living historical farm is open. Busiest in July and August, least crowded in January and February. ▦ **Fees, Permits & Limitations:** Entrance fee: $2 per person 17 and older, $4 per family. Leashed pets only. No bicycles or motorized equipment on trails. Visitor center open daily 8–5. Grounds open until dark. Living historical farm open May–Sept., daily 8–5 (8–6 Memorial Day–Labor Day). Closed Thanksgiving, Dec. 25, Jan. 1.

HOW TO GET THERE

In Lincoln City, 8 mi/13 km south of I–64 via U.S. 231 and Hwy. 162. Closest airports: Evansville, IN (40 mi/64 km); Louisville, KY (80 mi/128 km).

FOR MORE INFORMATION

Lincoln Boyhood National Memorial (Box 1816, Lincoln City, IN 47552, tel. 812/937–4541, fax 812/937–9929; e-mail LIBO_Superintendent@nps.gov; Web site www.nps.gov/libo). Spencer County Visitors Bureau (Box 202, Santa Claus, IN 47579, tel. 812/937–2848 ext. 209, or 888/444–9252; e-mail Info@LegendaryPlaces.org; Web site www.legendaryplaces.org).

IOWA

Effigy Mounds National Monument

In the northeast part of the state, near Marquette

One hundred ninety prehistoric burial and ceremonial mounds, some in the shapes of bears and birds, are preserved here. Woodland Native Americans built the mounds between 500 BC and AD 1300. The land was untouched by the glaciers of the Ice Age, so it provides a rugged terrain that includes bluffs towering 300 ft/91 m to 400 ft/121 m above the Mississippi River. Located where the eastern hardwood forest meets the midwestern prairie, the monument includes forests, prairies, rivers, and ponds. It was established on October 25, 1949.

WHAT TO SEE & DO

Hiking, skiing, viewing mounds. **Facilities:** Visitor center with interpretive exhibits, museum, and auditorium (3 mi/5 km north of Marquette), wayside exhibits, trails. Bookstore. **Programs & Events:** Ranger-guided walks (Memorial Day–Labor Day), moonlight hikes (June–Aug.), bird walks (June–Sept., once each month); film festival (Jan.–Mar., weekends). Iowa Archaeology Month (Sept.), Hawk Watch (last weekend of Sept.).

PLANNING YOUR VISIT

Camping: Private and public campgrounds available in McGregor, IA, and Prairie du Chien, WI; none in park. **Lodging:** Available in Marquette and McGregor, IA, and Prairie du Chien, WI; none in park. **Food & Supplies:** Available in Marquette and McGregor, IA, and Prairie du Chien, WI; none in park. **Tips & Hints:** Go in spring and late September for bird migrations, in winter to see bald eagles. Busiest in August and October, least crowded in December and January. **Fees, Permits & Limitations:** Entrance fee: $2 per adult with $4-per-car maximum, children ages 16 and under free. No bicycles or motorized vehicles on trails. Leashed pets only. Visitor center open Labor Day–Memorial Day, 8–4:30; Memorial Day–Labor Day, 8–7. Trails open daily 8–dark. Park closed for all federal holidays Nov.–Feb.

HOW TO GET THERE

3 mi/5 km north of Marquette, IA, on Hwy. 76. Closest airports: Prairie du Chien, WI (8 mi/13 km); La Crosse, WI (70 mi/113 km); Dubuque, IA (60 mi/96 km).

FOR MORE INFORMATION

Effigy Mounds National Monument (151 Hwy. 76, Harpers Ferry, IA 52146, tel. 319/873–3491, fax 319/873–3743; Web site www.nps.gov/efmo). McGregor/Marquette Chamber of Commerce (Box 105, McGregor, IA 52157, tel. 319/873–2186).

Herbert Hoover National Historic Site

In the east-central part of the state, in West Branch

In this 187-acre park are the birthplace, Friends Meetinghouse, and boyhood neighborhood of the 31st president, the gravesite of President and Mrs. Hoover, and the Hoover Presidential Library and Museum. A replica of a typical blacksmith shop, similar to the one operated by Herbert Hoover's father, is near the Birthplace Cottage and the first schoolhouse built in West Branch. Seventy-six acres of restored tallgrass prairie flank the south and west sides of the park. The Library-Museum is administered by the National Archives and Records Administration. The site was authorized on August 12, 1965.

WHAT TO SEE & DO

Cross-country skiing, hiking, picnicking, touring buildings and library-museum. **Facilities:** Visitor center with interpretive exhibits (Parkside Dr./Main St. intersection), library-museum, birthplace cottage and other buildings, gravesite, wayside exhibits. Fire grate, gift shop, picnic shelters, post office. **Programs & Events:** Ranger-guided tours for groups of 15 or more year-round, ranger-led tours for smaller groups (June–Aug.), prairie walks (with sufficient notice if ranger available, Apr.–Oct.). Hooverfest (1st weekend, Aug.), "Harvest Home" (1st weekend, Oct.), Christmas Past (1st weekend, Dec.), library-museum exhibits (occasionally, all year).

PLANNING YOUR VISIT

⚠ **Camping:** Available locally; none in park. 🏨 **Lodging:** Available in Iowa City, West Branch, West Liberty; none in park. ✕ **Food & Supplies:** Available in West Branch; none in park. ☞ **Tips & Hints:** Be careful on slippery boardwalks during frosty or wet weather. Busiest in July and August, least crowded in January and February. 🎫 **Fees, Permits & Limitations:** Entrance fee: $2 per adult 16–61, $1 62 or over, free under 16. Picnic shelter reservations available ($25, tel. 319/643–2541). Leashed pets only. No skateboarding. Bikes in designated areas only. Park and visitor center open daily 9–5. Closed Thanksgiving, Dec. 25, Jan. 1.

HOW TO GET THERE

The visitor center is at the intersection of Parkside Dr. and Main St., 0.4 mi/0.6 km north of Exit 254 off I–80. Closest airport: Cedar Rapids (28 mi/45 km).

FOR MORE INFORMATION

Superintendent, Herbert Hoover National Historic Site (Box 607, West Branch, IA 52358, tel. 319/643–2541; e-mail HEHO_Superintendent@nps.gov; Web site www.nps.gov/heho). West Branch Chamber of Commerce (Box 365, West Branch, IA 52358, tel. 319/643–2111).

See Also

California National Historic Trail, National Trails System in Other National Parklands. *Lewis and Clark National Historic Trail,* National Trails System in Other National Parklands. *Mormon Pioneer National Historic Trail,* National Trails System in Other National Parklands.

KANSAS

Brown v. Board of Education National Historic Site

In Topeka, 61 mi/98 km west of Kansas City

The site commemorates the landmark Supreme Court decision that made segregation in public schools illegal. On May 17, 1954, the U.S. Supreme Court unanimously declared that "separate but equal educational facilities are inherently unequal." Such facilities violate the 14th Amendment to the U.S. Constitution, which guarantees all citizens "equal protection of the laws," the court said. The site is located at the former Monroe Elementary School, which was the segregated school attended by the lead plaintiff's daughter when *Brown v. Board of Education of Topeka* was initially filed in 1951. The site was established on October 26, 1992 but is closed for renovation until May 2003.

WHAT TO SEE & DO

Visiting former courtroom, watching orientation video. **Facilities:** Visitor center with interpretive displays. Monroe School is closed for restoration until 2003. **Programs & Events:** Conference (2nd week May in some years).

PLANNING YOUR VISIT

Lodging: Available in Lawrence, Topeka; none at site. **Food & Supplies:** Available in Topeka; none at site. **Tips & Hints:** Conference may not be held in some years. **Fees, Permits & Limitations:** Free. Visitor center open weekdays 8–4. Closed federal holidays except Martin Luther King Jr. Day.

HOW TO GET THERE

The park office (424 S. Kansas Ave.) and Monroe School (1515 Monroe St.) are in downtown Topeka. Closest airport: Kansas City (70 mi/112 km).

FOR MORE INFORMATION

Brown v. Board of Education National Historic Site (424 S. Kansas Ave., Suite 220, Topeka, KS 66603-3441, tel 785/354–4273, fax 785/354–7213; Web site www.nps.gov/brvb). Greater Topeka Chamber of Commerce (120 S.E. 6th Ave., Suite 110, Topeka, KS 66603-3515, tel. 785/234–2644).

Fort Larned National Historic Site

In west-central Kansas, west of Larned

Fort Larned was built in 1859 to protect travelers on the Santa Fe Trail from conflicts with Native Americans. In the 1860s, the fort served as an agency of the Indian Bureau. Nine original buildings dating from 1866 still exist in a relatively undisturbed setting in a bend of the Pawnee River. The parade ground and most of the buildings have been fully restored, making Fort Larned one of the best surviving examples of an Indian Wars–era fort. A detached unit of the park contains a 44-acre plot of virgin prairie with visible Santa Fe Trail ruts and a prairie-dog town. The site was authorized in 1964 and established in 1966.

WHAT TO SEE & DO

Hiking, picnicking, touring buildings and grounds. **Facilities:** Visitor center with interpretive exhibits, auditorium, museum, 1.5-mi/2.4-km nature trail, wayside exhibits, viewing stand. Bookstore, grills, picnic areas. **Programs & Events:** Guided tours (by appointment). Living-history programs (June–Aug.). Fort Larned Old Guard Roll Call (3rd weekend, Apr.), Santa Fe Trail Days (Memorial Day weekend), Living History Days (July 4th and Labor Day weekends), Candlelight Tour (early Oct., reservations required), Santa Fe Trail Rendezvous (Sept.; the event takes place in even-numbered years).

PLANNING YOUR VISIT

Camping: Available at Jetmore City Lake, La Crosse, Larned; none at site. **Lodging:** Available in Dodge City, Great Bend, Hays, Larned; none at site. **Food & Supplies:** Available in Larned; none at site. **Tips & Hints:** Go on summer holidays for living-history programs. Busiest in June and July, least crowded in December and January. **Fees, Permits & Limitations:** Entrance fee: $2 per person (free under 17), $4 per family. Leashed pets only. No hunting or relic hunting. Park and visitor center open Sept.–May, daily 8:30–5; May–Sept., daily 8–6. Closed Thanksgiving, Dec. 25, Jan. 1.

HOW TO GET THERE

6 mi/10 km west of Larned, Kansas, Hwy. 156. Closest airports: Great Bend (28 mi/45 km), Wichita (136 mi/218 km).

FOR MORE INFORMATION

Fort Larned National Historic Site (Rte. 3, Larned, KS 67550-9733, tel. 316/285–6911, fax 316/285–3571; e-mail fols_superintendent@nps.gov; Web site www.nps.gov/fols). Larned Area Chamber of Commerce (502 Broadway, Larned, KS 67550, tel. 316/285–6916 or 800/747–6919).

Fort Scott
National Historic Site

In the southeast part of the state, in Fort Scott

Established in 1842, Fort Scott guarded the Permanent Indian Frontier and kept settlers and Native Americans out of each other's territory. As the frontier was pushed westward, Fort Scott became obsolete. It was abandoned in 1853. The fort then became a town and was drawn into the violence of "Bleeding Kansas" and the Civil War. Today, the site has been restored to its 1840s appearance. It contains 20 historic structures, a parade ground, and 5 acres of restored tallgrass prairie. The site was authorized in 1978.

WHAT TO SEE & DO

Touring buildings, walking trail. **Facilities:** Visitor center with interpretive exhibits, museum, 26 historic structures with 33 historically furnished rooms, exhibit areas, tallgrass prairie. Bookstore, picnic tables, RV and bus parking lot. **Programs & Events:** Self-guided tours. Civil War Encampment (Apr.), Frontier Garrison Life (Memorial Day and Labor Day weekends), Good Ol' Days (June), guided tours (daily, June–Aug.), Independence Day (1st weekend in July), American Indian Heritage Weekend (Sept.), Candlelight Tour (Dec.).

PLANNING YOUR VISIT

Camping: Available in town of Fort Scott; none in park. **Lodging:** Available in town of Fort Scott; none in park. **Food & Supplies:** Available in town of Fort Scott; none in park. **Tips & Hints:** Watch footing. Allow one–two hours to tour site. Busiest in May and June, least crowded in January and February. **Fees, Permits & Limitations:** Entrance fee: $2 per adult, free under 17, $4 per family. Leashed pets only. No bicycling, skating, skateboarding. No smoking in buildings or near prairie. No plant or artifact collecting. No metal detecting. Site and visitor center open Apr.–Oct., daily 8–5; Nov.–Mar., daily 9–5. Closed Thanksgiving, Dec. 25, Jan. 1.

HOW TO GET THERE

Near the intersection of U.S. 54 and U.S. 69, in downtown Fort Scott, 90 mi/144 km south of Kansas City via U.S. 69, 60 mi/96 km from Joplin via Hwy. 57 and U.S. 69. Closest airports: Fort Scott, Joplin, Kansas City.

FOR MORE INFORMATION

Fort Scott National Historic Site (Old Fort Blvd., Box 918, Fort Scott, KS 66701, tel. 316/223–0310, fax 316/223–0188; e-mail fosc_superintendent@nps.gov; Web site www.nps.gov/fosc). Fort Scott Chamber of Commerce (231 East Wall, Fort Scott, KS 66701, tel. 800/245–3678).

Nicodemus National Historic Site

In the northwest part of the state, in Nicodemus

Nicodemus was established in 1877 and settled by African-Americans during Reconstruction after the Civil War. It is the site of one of the oldest reported post offices supervised by blacks in the United States. Five historic buildings are located within the 161-acre Nicodemus National Historic Landmark: the First Baptist Church (1908); the African-Methodist-Episcopal Church (1885); Township Hall (1939); St. Francis Hotel (1878); and Nicodemus District No. 1 School (1918). The site was established on November 12, 1996.

WHAT TO SEE & DO

Auto or bike touring, walking. **Facilities:** Visitor center with interpretive exhibits, interpretive signs, Historical Society museum. Historic buildings currently closed to public. Nicodemus Historical Society bookstore, picnic area. **Programs & Events:** This is a new park unit. Ranger-led guided tours (Memorial Day–Labor Day). Emancipation Day/Homecoming (last weekend, July), Pioneer Days (2nd weekend, Oct.).

PLANNING YOUR VISIT

Camping: Available in Webster State Recreation Area; none in park. **Lodging:** Available in Hill City, Plainville, Stockton; none in park. **Food & Supplies:** Available in Bogue, Hill City, Plainville, Stockton; none in park. **Tips & Hints:** The park is currently under development and has very limited facilities. National Park Service staff are present occasionally. No public phones. **Fees, Permits & Limitations:** Free. Keep in mind that this is home for the residents. Respect their privacy and property rights. Remain on public roadways. Visitors welcome during daylight hours. Nicodemus Historical Society building is open irregularly. Groups may call 785/839–4280 for tour. Park open 8:30–5:00 daily mid-May–mid-August and also open again in October for Pioneer Days. Visitor center and bookstore open Memorial Day–Labor Day 8:30–5.

HOW TO GET THERE

Nicodemus is 11 mi/18 km east of Hill City via U.S. 24. Closest airports: Hill City (15 mi/24 km), Hays (50 mi/80 km).

FOR MORE INFORMATION

Nicodemus National Historic Site (c/o Fort Larned National Historic Site, Rte. 3, Larned, KS 67550, tel. 316/285–6911, fax 316/285–3571; e-mail: nico_superintendent@nps.gov; Web site www.nps.gov/nico). Hill City Chamber of Commerce (104 W. Main St., Hill City, KS 67642, tel. 785/421–5621, fax 785/421–6247).

Tallgrass Prairie National Preserve

In the east-central part of the state, near Strong City

Here is preserved a sample of the once vast tallgrass prairie ecosystem, historic buildings listed as National Historic Landmarks, and the cultural resources of the Spring Hill/Z Bar Ranch in the Flint Hills region of Kansas. The federal government will own up to 180 acres, and the National Park Trust—a nonprofit organization that bought the property in 1994—will retain ownership of the rest of the 10,894-acre preserve. The Park Service eventually will manage the entire preserve under a public-private agreement. The new site is under development and only a small portion is open to the public. The site was authorized on November 12, 1996.

WHAT TO SEE & DO

Hiking trail, touring historic buildings in groups, touring ranch by bus, touring ranch headquarters. **Facilities:** Information station (ranch headquarters), information kiosks, interpretive wayside exhibits, orientation video, self-guided brochures of ranch headquarters, 1.75 mi/2.8 km nature trail. Bookstore, gift shop. **Programs & Events:** Self-guided tours of ranch headquarters and nature trail (daily 9–4), group tours (reservation only, tel. 316/273–8494). Guided tours of ranch house, bus tours of tallgrass prairie (reservations available, tel. 316/273–8494; summer daily at 11, 1, 3).

PLANNING YOUR VISIT

Camping: Available in Chase County State Park near Cottonwood Falls, City Lake, Council Grove Reservoir, and Emporia; none in park. **Lodging:** Available in Cottonwood Falls, Council Grove, Elmdale, Emporia, Strong City; none in park. **Food & Supplies:** Available in Cottonwood Falls, Council Grove, Emporia, Strong City; none in park. **Tips & Hints:** Watch for poisonous snakes, biting insects, ticks, and uneven terrain. Go between mid-April and June or late August and September for wildflowers, early fall for tallgrass at peak height. **Fees, Permits & Limitations:** Call park for entrance fee information. Reservation suggested for bus tours and required for group tours (tel. 316/273–8494). Bus tours $5/adults. $3 children under 18. Leashed pets only. No horses or bicycles on nature trail. No visitors beyond ranch headquarters except by ranger-led bus tours. Preserve open daily 9–4. Closed Thanksgiving, Dec. 25, Jan. 1, and during bad weather.

HOW TO GET THERE

The ranch headquarters are 2 mi/3 km north of Strong City on Hwy. 177. Closest airports: Emporia (18 mi/29 km), Kansas City (100 mi/160 km), Wichita (80 mi/128 km).

FOR MORE INFORMATION

Tallgrass Prairie National Preserve (Attn: Park Rangers, Rte. 1, Box 14 Strong City, KS 66869, tel. 316/273–8494, fax 316/273–8247; Web site www.nps.gov/tapr). Tallgrass Prairie National Preserve (National Park

Service Office, Box 585, 226 Broadway, Cottonwood Falls, KS 66845, tel. 316/273–6034, fax 316/273–6099; Web site www.nps.gov/tapr; e-mail TAPR_Interpretation@nps.gov). Chase County Chamber of Commerce (318 Broadway, Cottonwood Falls, KS 66845, tel. 800/431–6344). Council Grove Chamber of Commerce (212 W. Main St., Council Grove, KS 66846, tel. 800/732–9211, fax 316/767–5553). Emporia Chamber of Commerce (719 Commercial St., Emporia, KS 66801, tel. 800/279–3730, fax 316/342–3223).

See Also

California National Historic Trail, National Trails System in Other National Parklands. *Lewis and Clark National Historic Trail,* National Trails System in Other National Parklands. *Oregon National Scenic Trail,* National Trails System in Other National Parklands. *Pony Express National Historic Trail,* National Trails System in Other National Parklands. *Santa Fe National Historic Trail,* National Trails System in Other National Parklands.

KENTUCKY

Abraham Lincoln Birthplace National Historic Site

65 mi/104 km south of Louisville

Abraham Lincoln, the 16th president of the United States, was born in a one-room log cabin on Sinking Spring Farm on February 12, 1809. One hundred acres of the original 348-acre farm are preserved at the Abraham Lincoln National Historic Site. In 1911, the Lincoln Farm Association erected a neoclassical structure on the land as a memorial and shrine for the symbolic birthplace cabin. The memorial overlooks Sinking Spring, the Lincoln family water source. The park unit was authorized July 17, 1916.

WHAT TO SEE & DO

Hiking, picnicking, self-guided touring, watching film. **Facilities:** Visitor center with exhibits, 18 minute film, and Memorial Building with symbolic birthplace cabin, trails. Book sale areas, grills, picnic pavilion, picnic tables. **Programs & Events:** Daily interpretive talks at the Memorial Building. Musical tribute to Dr. Martin Luther King Jr. (Jan.), wreath-laying ceremony at symbolic birthplace cabin (Feb. 12), founding of the National Park Service (Aug. 25), U.S. Constitution Week (Sept.).

PLANNING YOUR VISIT

Camping: Private campground in Elizabethtown; none in park. **Lodging:** Available nearby in Elizabethtown; none in park. **Food & Supplies:** Available in Hodgenville; none in park. **Tips & Hints:** Busiest in July and August, least crowded in December and January. **Fees, Permits & Limitations:** Free. Leashed pets only. No bikes, horses, or motorized equipment on trails. No hunting. Park and visitor center open Memorial Day–Labor Day, daily 8–6:45; Labor Day–Memorial Day, 8–4:45. Closed Thanksgiving, Dec. 25, Jan. 1.

HOW TO GET THERE

Near Hodgenville, where U.S. 31E and KY 61 meet. Closest airport: Louisville (55 mi/88 km).

FOR MORE INFORMATION

Abraham Lincoln Birthplace National Historic Site (2995 Lincoln Farm Rd., Hodgenville, KY 42748, tel. 270/358–3137, fax 270/358–3874; e-mail ABLI_Operations@nps.gov; Web site www.nps.gov/abli). LaRue Chamber of Commerce (72 Lincoln Sq., Box 176, Hodgenville, KY 42748-0176, tel. 270/358–3411).

Cumberland Gap National Historical Park

The junction of Kentucky, Virginia, and Tennessee

The opening of the West is commemorated at Cumberland Gap, a natural passageway across the Appalachian Mountains. From 1775 to 1810, as many as 300,000 settlers passed through here into what is now Kentucky. Prior to the western expansion, Native Americans learned of the gap by following the buffalo. It became a major route to the rich hunting grounds of Kentucky. The park was authorized in 1940.

WHAT TO SEE & DO

Auto touring, hiking, picnicking, watching film. **Facilities:** Visitor center with interpretive exhibits (U.S. 25E, south of Middlesboro, KY), wayside exhibits, trails, overlooks. Book and craft store, Iron Furnace remains, picnic areas with fire grates, tables. **Programs & Events:** Ranger-guided tours of abandoned log cabins of Hensley Settlement; Cudjo Cave tours (Memorial Day–Labor Day).

PLANNING YOUR VISIT

Camping: Campground: electrical hookups, dump stations (no reservations). Backcountry camping available (permit required, *see below*). Group camping available (reservation only, tel. 606/248–2817). Private campgrounds available in Morristown, Tazewell, TN, and Corbin, KY. **Lodging:** Available in Middlesboro, KY, and Cumberland Gap and Tazewell, TN; none in park. **Food & Supplies:** Available in Middlesboro, KY, and Harrogate and Tazewell, TN; none in park. **Tips & Hints:** Go between April and May for wildflowers, in September for great hiking, and in mid-October for peak foliage. Busiest in July and August, least crowded in November and December. **Fees, Permits & Limitations:** Free. Pinnacle Overlook shuttle fee (when operating): $1 per person. Hensley Settlement shuttle fee: $10 adults, $5 senior citizens with Golden Age Passport, $3 children 12 and under. Cudjo Cave fee: $7 adults, $3.50 senior citizens with Golden Age Passport and children 12 and under. Reservations suggested for Hensley Settlement and Cudjo Cave, tel. 606/248–2817 ext. 3. Backcountry permits required (free). No vehicles over 20 ft/6 m on Pinnacle Road. Leashed pets only. Bikes on paved roads and designated trails only. No in-line skates or skateboards. Park open daily. Visitor center open Memorial Day–Labor Day, daily 8–6; Labor Day–Memorial Day, daily 8–5. Closed Dec. 25.

HOW TO GET THERE

Via U.S. 25E in Tennessee and Kentucky, and U.S. 58 in Virginia. Closest airport: Knoxville (90 mi/144 km).

FOR MORE INFORMATION

Cumberland Gap National Historic Park (Box 1848, Middlesboro, KY 40965, tel. 606/248–2817, fax 606/248–7276; Web site www.nps. gov/cuga). Clairborne County Tourism Committee (3222-1, 25 E. Highway, Tazewell, TN 37879, tel. 423/626–4149 or 800/332–8164, fax 423/

626–1611). Bell County Tourism Commission (106 N. 20th St., Middlesboro, KY 40965, tel. 800/248–1075 or 800/988–1075, fax 606/248–8851). Town of Cumberland Gap (Box 78, Cumberland Gap, TN 37724, tel. 423/869–3860, fax 423/869–8534).

Mammoth Cave National Park

In the south-central part of the state, in Mammoth Cave

Extending for more than 350 mi/560 km, the Mammoth Cave system is the longest in the world. Below ground are giant vertical shafts, underground rivers, and many animals, including eyeless fish, crayfish, spiders, and beetles. Aboveground, the park offers 70 mi/112 km of backcountry trails for hiking and horseback riding and 31 mi/50 km of scenic riverway on the Green and Nolin rivers for canoeists and anglers. The site was established in 1941. It was designated a World Heritage Site in 1981 and an International Biosphere Reserve in 1990.

WHAT TO SEE & DO

Birding, canoeing (rentals, Brownsville, Bowling Green), cave touring, fishing, hiking, horseback riding (rentals, outside north park boundary). **Facilities:** Visitor center (center of park), caves, trails, wayside exhibits. Book and map sales, crafts shop, gas station, laundry, picnic tables and pavilions, post office, summer church services. **Programs & Events:** Ranger-guided cave tours (daily). Ranger-guided nature walks, evening programs (May–Oct.). Springfest (Apr.), Karstlands Music Series (monthly, Apr.–Oct.), Colorfall (Oct.).

PLANNING YOUR VISIT

⚠ **Camping:** 3 campgrounds: 2 primitive (no reservations), 1 for groups, campers, and horses (reservations available, tel. 800/967–2283). Backcountry camping available (permit required, *see below*). Private campgrounds nearby in Cave City, Horse Cave, Park City. 🏨 **Lodging:** In the park: Mammoth Cave Hotel (tel. 270/758–2225). Lodging also available outside the park in Bowling Green, Cave City, Horse Cave, Park City. ✕ **Food & Supplies:** In the park: camp store, meals at Mammoth Cave Hotel. Food and supplies also available in Brownsville, Cave City, Glasgow, Horse Cave, Park City. ☞ **Tips & Hints:** Wear comfortable walking shoes and a jacket in the cave. Go in spring for dogwood blooms, August for wildflower peak. Busiest in July and August, least crowded in December and January. ✉ **Fees, Permits & Limitations:** Free. Cave tour fees range from $3 to $35 (reservations available, tel. 800/967–2283). Group discounts available. Motorcoach tours can reserve tickets (tel. 800/967–2283). Backcountry permits (free) required for all backcountry camping. Picnic pavilion reservations available (tel. 800/967–2283). No hunting or firearms. No pets on cave tours (kennels are available). Leashed pets only elsewhere. Mountain bikes on designated roads only. No fireworks. No Jet Skis on river. No off-road motorized equipment. In-line skates in designated areas only. Park open daily. Cave tours offered daily except Dec. 25. Visitor center open Sept.–May, daily 8–5; June 24–Aug., daily 7:30–7:30. Closed Dec. 25.

HOW TO GET THERE

10 mi/16 km off I–65, via Cave City or Park City exits west. Closest airports: Louisville International (90 mi/144 km); Nashville, TN (100 mi/160 km).

FOR MORE INFORMATION

Mammoth Cave National Park (Box 7, Mammoth Cave, KY 42259, tel. 270/758–2328, fax 270/758–2349; e-mail MACA_PARK_INFORMATION@NPS.GOV; Web site www.nps.gov/maca). Cave City Convention Center (502 Mammoth Cave St., Cave City, KY 42127, tel. 270/773–3131, fax 270/773–8834). Edmonson County Tourist Commission (Box 628, Brownsville, KY 42210, tel. 800/624–8687 ; Web site www.cavesandlakes.com).

See Also

Big South Fork National River and Recreation Area, Tennessee. *Trail of Tears National Historic Trail,* National Trails System in Other National Parklands.

LOUISIANA

Cane River Creole National Historical Park

In the west-central part of the state, near Natchitoches

The park consists of two plantations—Magnolia and Oakland—that date to the 1820s. Both sites represent a continuum from 18th-century land grants to mid-20th-century occupation and use by the same families that owned the plantations and many of the families who worked for them, first as slaves and later as tenants and sharecroppers. The Oakland unit includes the 1820s "Big House" and most surviving out-buildings. The Magnolia unit has eight surviving brick cabins from the 1830s and wooden and steam cotton ginning and pressing equipment. The park was authorized on November 2, 1994.

WHAT TO SEE & DO

Touring plantations. **Facilities:** Visitor contact station (Oakland's Big House). **Programs & Events:** Guided tours (11 AM and 2 PM weekends at Oakland; weekdays at both units by arrangement with 24 hours' advance notice, tel. 318/352–0383).

PLANNING YOUR VISIT

Camping: Available in Natchitoches; none in park. **Lodging:** Available in Natchitoches; none in park. **Food & Supplies:** Available in Cloutierville, Natchez, Natchitoches; none in park. **Tips & Hints:** Expect to spend about one hour on the tour. **Fees, Permits & Limitations:** Free. Park is not officially open to the public but tours are available. Park office open weekdays 8–4:30.

HOW TO GET THERE

The Oakland plantation is 8 mi/13 km south of Natchitoches on LA 119. The Magnolia unit is 10 mi/16 km farther south on LA 119. Closest airports: Alexandria International (45mi/72 km); Shreveport (75 mi/120 km).

FOR MORE INFORMATION

Cane River Creole National Historical Park (4386 Hwy. 494, Natchez, LA 71456, tel. 318/352–0383, fax 318/352–4549; Web site www.nps.gov/cari). Natchitoches Chamber of Commerce (781 Front St., Natchitoches, LA 71457, tel. 318/352–4411).

Jean Lafitte National Historical Park and Preserve

In the southern part of the state, between Eunice and New Orleans

The park's many sites interpret the rich natural and cultural history of southern Louisiana. The Lafayette, Thibodaux, and Eunice sites have exhibits on Acadian and Native American cultures. Barataria Preserve near Crown Point interprets the natural and cultural history of the uplands, swamps, and marshlands. The 1815 Battle of New Orleans took place at Chalmette Battlefield. The park visitor center in New Orleans's French Quarter has displays on the history of the city and the Mississippi Delta. The Chalmette Monument and Grounds was established in 1907, transferred to the Park Service in 1933, renamed a national historic park in 1939, and incorporated into a new park in 1978.

WHAT TO SEE & DO

Attending cultural demonstrations; canoeing; hiking; participating in educational programs on train rides; taking walking tours; touring battlefield, cemetery, and historic house; watching films. **Facilities:** 6 visitor centers with exhibits—Acadian (501 Fisher Rd., Lafayette), Prairie Acadian (250 W. Park Ave., Eunice), Wetlands Acadian (313 St. Mary St., Thibodaux), Barataria (on West Bank from New Orleans near Crown Point on Hwy. 45), Chalmette (St. Bernard Hwy., Chalmette), French Quarter (419 Decatur, New Orleans); trails and boardwalks (Barataria); tour road, Malus–Beauregard House (circa 1833) and national cemetery (all in Chalmette). Bookstores at each site. **Programs & Events:** Acadian: film (9–4, hourly); Prairie Acadian: demonstrations, live radio performance (Sat. 6 PM–8 PM); Wetlands Acadian: ranger talks (weekends 11 and 2), music (Mon. 5:30 PM–7 PM), films (on request); Barataria: natural-history walks (daily at 2), group tours (reservation only), canoe trips (reservation only, Sun. at 8:30 AM), full-moon canoe trips (reservation only); Chalmette: battle talks (daily at 11:15 and 2:45), living-history demonstrations (Mar.–May and Sept.–Nov., Sat. 10–3), group tours (reservation only); French Quarter: walking tours (reservation only), interpretive programs (daily at 3). Trails and Rails program (educational program train trips, tel. 504/528–1630). Battle of New Orleans anniversary (2nd weekend, Jan.)

PLANNING YOUR VISIT

Camping: Available locally; none in park. **Lodging:** Available locally; none in park. **Food & Supplies:** Available locally; none in park. **Tips & Hints:** Busiest in April and October, least crowded in December and January. **Fees, Permits & Limitations:** Free. Unit hours: Acadian—daily 8–5; Prairie—daily 8–5, Sat. 8–6; Wetlands—Fri.–Sun. 9–5, Tues.–Thurs. 9–6, Mon. 9–7; Barataria—daily 9–5; Chalmette—

daily 9–5; French Quarter—daily 9–5; closed Mardi Gras. Closed Dec. 25.

HOW TO GET THERE

The units stretch 150 mi/240 km along the I–10 and U.S. 90 corridors between Eunice and New Orleans. Call individual sites for directions. Closest airports: Lafayette, New Orleans.

FOR MORE INFORMATION

Jean Lafitte National Historic Park and Preserve (365 Canal St., Suite 2400, New Orleans, LA 70130-1136, tel. 504/589–3882, ext. 100, fax 504/589–3851; Web site www.nps.gov/jela). Units: Acadian Culture Center (501 Fisher Rd., Lafayette, LA 70508-2033, tel. 318/232–0789); Barataria Preserve (6588 Barataria Blvd., Marrero, LA 700431, tel. 504/589–2330); Chalmette Battlefield (8606 St. Bernard Hwy., Chalmette, LA 70043, tel. 504/281–0510); French Quarter/New Orleans Visitor Center (365 Canal St., Suite 2400, New Orleans, LA 70130-1142, tel. 504/589–2133); Prairie Acadian Culture Center (250 W. Park Ave., Eunice, LA 70535, tel. 318/262–6862); Wetlands Acadian Culture Center (314 St. Mary St., Thibodaux, LA 70301, tel. 504/448–1375).

New Orleans Jazz National Historical Park

In the southeast part of the state, in New Orleans

The origins, early history, development, and progression of jazz are interpreted in this park. The site offers the sights, sounds, and places where jazz evolved and implements innovative ways to establish jazz educational partnerships. The park was authorized on October 31, 1994.

WHAT TO SEE & DO

Listening to youth bands, participating in interpretive music programs and parades, watching video. **Facilities:** Visitor center (916 N. Peters) with indoor and outdoor stages for live performances, interpretive exhibits. Sales area. This is a new national park area under development. **Programs & Events:** Jazz workshops, conferences, guest lectures, live musical performances and demonstrations, jazz walking tours of the French Quarter, special events and exhibits.

PLANNING YOUR VISIT

⛺ **Camping:** Available in Barataria, Chalmette, and east New Orleans; none in park. 🏨 **Lodging:** Available in New Orleans area; none in park. ✗ **Food & Supplies:** Available in New Orleans area; none in park. ☞ **Tips & Hints:** Prepare for high humidity. 🎫 **Fees, Permits & Limitations:** Free. Visitor center hours: Labor Day–Memorial Day, Wed.–Sun 9–5; Memorial Day–Labor Day, Wed.–Sun 9–6. Closed Thanksgiving, Dec. 25, Jan. 1.

HOW TO GET THERE

Visitor center in New Orleans at 916 N. Peters St. From the east, take I–10 to Exit 236 Esplanade, south to Decatur, west to N. Peters. From the west, take I–10 to Exit 235 Canal, south to Decatur, east to N. Peters.

FOR MORE INFORMATION

New Orleans Jazz National Historic Park (Attention: Superintendent, 365 Canal Pl., Suite 2400, New Orleans, LA 70130, tel. 877/529–9677 or 504/589–4806, fax 504/589–3865; Web site www.nps.gov/neor). French Quarter Visitor Center (916 N. Peters, New Orleans, LA 70116, tel. 504/589–4841). New Orleans and the River Regions Chamber of Commerce (601 Poydras St., New Orleans, LA 70130, tel. 504/527–6900, fax 504/527–6950; Web site www.gnofn.org/chamber).

Poverty Point National Monument/State Commemorative Area

In the northeast part of the state, near Epps

Owned and funded by the Louisiana Office of State Parks, this 402-acre park interprets the culture of the peoples who constructed the prehistoric earthworks between 1700 and 700 BC. The site was designated a national monument on October 31, 1988.

WHAT TO SEE & DO

Touring museum and site. **Facilities:** Visitor center, museum with audiovisual programs, observation tower, outdoor exhibits, interpretive trails. **Programs & Events:** Guided open-air tram tours (Easter–Labor Day).

PLANNING YOUR VISIT

Camping: Available in Chemin-A-Haut State Park (Bastrop), Lake D'Arbonne State Park (Farmerville), and in Monroe, Oak Grove, and Tallulah; none in park. **Lodging:** Available in Delhi, Monroe and Tallulah; none in park. **Food & Supplies:** Available in Delhi and Epps; none in park. **Tips & Hints:** Go early in day during summer to avoid heat. **Fees, Permits & Limitations:** Entrance fee: $2 per person 13–61. Park and visitor center open daily 9–5. Closed Thanksgiving, Dec. 25, Jan. 1.

HOW TO GET THERE

From I–20 in northeast Louisiana, take Exit 153 (Hwy. 17) north to Epps. Make a right on Hwy. 134. The monument is on the left. Closest airports: Monroe Municipal, LA (55 mi/88 km); Jackson, MS (75 mi/120 mi).

FOR MORE INFORMATION

Poverty Point National Monument (c/o Poverty Point State Commemorative Area, Box 276, Epps, LA 71237, tel. 318/926–5492 or 888/926–

5492; e-mail povertypoint@crt.state.la.us; Web site www.nps.gov/popo or www.crt.state.la.us and click on State Parks). Epps Town Hall (Box 253, Epps, LA 71237, tel. 318/926–5224).

See Also

Vicksburg National Military Park, Mississippi.

MAINE

Acadia National Park

On Mount Desert Island, southeast of Bangor

The park's glaciated coastal and island landscape includes mountains, lakes, and mixed evergreen and hardwood forests. Its rich cultural history, which included successive waves of indigenous, French, and English immigrants, can be traced back 5,000 years. The park was proclaimed as Sieur de Monts National Monument on July 8, 1916; established as Lafayette National Park on February 26, 1919, and changed to Acadia National Park on January 19, 1929.

WHAT TO SEE & DO

Bicycling and boating (rentals in Bar Harbor, Northeast Harbor, Southwest Harbor), camping, cross-country skiing (rentals in Bar Harbor), fishing, hiking, rock climbing, swimming. **Facilities:** Visitor center with interpretive exhibits—Hulls Cove (3 mi/5 km north of Bar Harbor, off Rte. 3), nature center (Sieur de Monts Spring, 1.5 mi/2.4 km south of Bar Harbor, off Rte. 3), and Islesford Historical Museum (Little Cranberry Island); trails, amphitheaters, beaches, 45 mi/72 km of carriage roads, wayside exhibits. Book and map sales areas, picnic areas, concessions, shuttle bus service around the island. **Programs & Events:** Ranger-guided walks, hikes, talks, demonstrations, amphitheater programs, boat cruises (all June–mid-Oct., daily).

PLANNING YOUR VISIT

Camping: 2 campgrounds on Mount Desert Island with dump stations but no hookups: Blackwoods (open year-round, reservations required June 15–Sept. 14, tel. 800/365–2267); Seawall (open Memorial Day–Sept. 30, no reservations). Five lean-tos on Isle de Haut, open May 15–Oct. 14, (permit required, *see below*; reservations available after Apr. 1, requests must be in writing). Group camping at Blackwoods (May 15–Oct. 15), Seawall (Memorial Day–Sept. 30), reservations available after Mar. 15, tel. 207/288–3338. Private campgrounds in Bar Harbor, Bass Harbor, Northeast Harbor, Southwest Harbor, Town Hill, Tremont. **Lodging:** Available nearby in Bar Harbor, Northeast Harbor, Southwest Harbor; none in park. **Food & Supplies:** In the park: meals at Jordan Pond House Restaurant (tel. 207/276–3316), snacks at Cadillac Mountain, Thunder Hole. Food and supplies also available at Bar Harbor, Bass Harbor, Northeast Harbor, Southwest Harbor. **Tips & Hints:** Avoid 10 AM–2 PM in July–August. Visit in late May–early June for wildflowers and migrating warblers or first half of October for fall foliage and raptor migration. Busiest in July and August, least crowded in January and February. **Fees, Permits & Limitations:** Entrance fee: $10 per vehicle. Permit required ($25) to camp at Isle de Haut. Write to the park for lean-to reservations. Maine fishing license required for freshwater fishing. Rock climbing permit required for groups of 6 or more. No hunting. No pets on beaches or ladder trails, leashed pets on the rest. No trail bikes. No bikes on hiking trails. No motorized vehicles on trails or carriage roads. No four-wheelers allowed in park. No swimming in lakes that serve as town water supplies. Park open daily but most scenic roads close in winter. Hulls Cove Visitor Center open mid-Apr.–Oct. 31, daily 8–4:30 (July–Aug., daily 8–6). Park headquarters serves as visitor center Nov. 1–mid-Apr. and is open daily 8–4:30. Closed Dec. 24–25, Jan. 1.

HOW TO GET THERE

Hulls Cove Visitor Center entrance is 3 mi/5 km north of Bar Harbor on Rte. 3. Closest airports: Trenton (12 mi/19 km from Bar Harbor), Bangor International Airport (45 mi/72 km from Bar Harbor).

FOR MORE INFORMATION

Acadia National Park (Box 177, Bar Harbor, ME 04609, tel. 207/288–3338, fax 207/288–5507; Web site www.nps.gov/acad). Bar Harbor Chamber of Commerce (Box 158, Bar Harbor, ME 04609-0158, tel. 800/288–5103). Southwest Harbor–Tremont Chamber of Commerce (Box 1143, Southwest Harbor, ME 04679, tel. 800/423–9264). Northeast Harbor Chamber of Commerce (Box 675, Northeast Harbor, ME 04662, tel. 207/276–5040). Acadia Information Center (Box 139, Mt. Desert, ME 04660, tel. 800/358–8550).

Saint Croix Island International Historic Site

In the northeast part of the state, near Calais

Pierre Dugua Sieur de Mons and his company of 78 men attempted to establish a French settlement on St. Croix Island in 1604–05. Preceding Jamestown (1607) and Plymouth (1620), Sieur de Mons' outpost was one of the earliest European settlements on the North Atlantic coast of North America. The settlement was short-lived. In the summer of 1605, the French moved to a more favorable location where they established the Port Royal Habitation on the shores of the present-day Annapolis Basin, Nova Scotia. The first international historic site in the National Park System was authorized as a national monument in 1949 and redesignated in 1984.

WHAT TO SEE & DO

Picnicking, walking to interpretive shelter with view of island. **Facilities:** Open shelter with interpretive panel on mainland. No facilities on island. Picnic tables, vault toilet. **Programs & Events:** 400th anniversary of settlement (summer, 2004).

PLANNING YOUR VISIT

⚠ **Camping:** Available in Calais; none at site. ⛺ **Lodging:** Available in Calais; none at site. ✕ **Food & Supplies:** Available in Calais; none at site. ☞ **Tips & Hints:** Plan to spend a half hour. Dress on the warm side of typical seasonal wear. Expect an onshore breeze and summer temperatures near 80°F/27°C. Bring drinking water. ⌨ **Fees, Permits & Limitations:** Free. No fires. Site open daily dawn–dusk.

HOW TO GET THERE

120 mi/192 km north of Bar Harbor via U.S. 1. From Bangor, take Rte. 9 to Calais and U.S. 1S for 6 mi/10 km to site. Access to the island by private boat only. Closest airport: Bangor (90 mi/144 km).

FOR MORE INFORMATION

Superintendent, Saint Croix Island International Historic Site (c/o Acadia National Park, Box 177, Bar Harbor, ME 04609, tel. 207/288–3338; Web site www.nps.gov/sacr).

See Also

Appalachian National Scenic Trail, West Virginia.

MARYLAND

Antietam
National Battlefield

In the northwest part of the state, near Sharpsburg

Antietam is one of the best-preserved battlefields in the nation. On these fields on September 17, 1862, the Union army stopped the northern advance of Confederate forces in the bloodiest single-day battle in U.S. history. Wayside exhibits and tablets describe the battle and cannons line the site's 8.5-mi/14-km auto tour. A stop along the route at a tower offers a view of the quarter-mile stretch known as "Bloody Lane," where 5,600 Union and Confederate soldiers were killed in three hours, more deaths than occurred during the entire eight years of the American Revolution. The site was established as a national battlefield in 1890 and transferred to the Park Service in 1933.

WHAT TO SEE & DO

Auto touring, cross-country skiing, hiking, horseback riding (permit required for groups, *see below*), picnicking, walking. **Facilities:** Visitor center with interpretive exhibits, wayside exhibits, trail. Bookstore, films. **Programs & Events:** 2 films: an hour-long documentary *Antietam,* shown at noon, and a short orientation film. Ranger programs (Memorial Day–Labor Day, daily; Apr., May, Sept., and Oct., weekends). Concert, fireworks (1st Sat., July), battle anniversary hikes, tours and programs (week closest to Sept. 17), Annual Memorial Illumination (1st Sat., Dec.).

PLANNING YOUR VISIT

Camping: Group camping available (Apr.–Nov., reservations required, tel. 301/432–2243). Private campgrounds available locally. **Lodging:** In the park: Piper House (bed-and-breakfast, tel. 301/797–1862). Lodging also available outside the park in Hagerstown and Sharpsburg, MD; Martinsburg and Shepherdstown, WV. **✕ Food & Supplies:** Available in Hagerstown, Sharpsburg; none in park. ☞ **Tips & Hints:** Weekdays in May and weekends in October are crowded. Busiest in July and August, least crowded in January and February. **Fees, Permits & Limitations:** Entrance fee: $2 per adult, $4 per family, free under 17. Permit required (tel. 301/432–2243) for horseback riding for groups of five or more. No firearms or edged weapons. No hunting, metal detecting, or relic hunting. Leashed pets only. Crop fields, pastures, reforested areas, barns, and other farm areas closed to public. No climbing on monuments or cannons. Bikes on roads only. No kite flying, ball games, sunbathing, model airplane or rocket flying, or throwing Frisbees. Park open daily dawn–dusk. Visitor center open Sept.–May, daily 8:30–5; June–Aug., daily 8:30–6. Closed Thanksgiving, Dec. 25, Jan. 1.

HOW TO GET THERE

1 mi/2 km north of Sharpsburg, MD, on Rte. 65.

FOR MORE INFORMATION

Antietam National Battlefield (Box 158, Sharpsburg, MD 21782-0158, tel. 301/432–5124, fax 301/432–4590; Web site www.nps.gov/anti). Hagerstown/Washington County Convention and Visitors Bureau (16 Public Sq., Hagerstown, MD 21740, tel. 301/791–3246, fax 240/420–5053).

Assateague Island National Seashore

In eastern Virginia, near Chincoteague; in southeastern Maryland, near Ocean City

The 37-mi/59 km-long seashore is one of the few protected and undeveloped barrier islands on the East Coast. This dynamic seashore environment provides refuge to wild horses and abundant and specialized flora, fauna, and marine life. It was authorized on September 21, 1965.

WHAT TO SEE & DO

Biking (rentals, Ocean City), canoeing (rentals, in park daily, June–Aug; weekends, Apr–May, Sept.–Oct.; and in Snow Hill, MD), clamming, crabbing, fishing, hiking, hunting, off-road driving (permit required, *see below*), swimming. **Facilities:** 2 visitor centers with interpretive exhibits, aquariums—Barrier Island (Maryland district), Tom's Cove (Virginia district); beaches, nature trails, bike paths. Bathhouses, bookstores, picnic areas. **Programs & Events:** Ranger-led shellfishing and surf fishing demonstrations, beach walks, marsh walks, bay exploring, canoe trips (reservations required, *see below*), campfire programs and night walks (mid-June–Labor Day). Pony penning (last Wed. and Thurs. of July) in nearby Chincoteague, VA.

PLANNING YOUR VISIT

⚠ **Camping:** Campgrounds at National Seashore: no hookups (reservations available, tel. 410/641–3030 or 800/365–2267). Campgrounds also available in Assateague State Park; Ocean City, MD: and Chincoteague Island, VA. Backcountry camping available (permit required, *see below*). Group camping available (reservations available, tel. 410/641–3030 or 800/365–2267). 🏨 **Lodging:** Available in Ocean City, MD, Chincoteague, VA; none available on seashore. ✗ **Food & Supplies:** Concession stand at Maryland State Park (summer). Food and supplies available outside the seashore in Ocean City, MD, Chincoteague, VA; none available on seashore. ☞ **Tips & Hints:** Bring insect repellent, screen tents, sunscreen, and sand stakes. Proper food storage strictly enforced. Busiest in July and August, least crowded in January and February. ✉ **Fees, Permits & Limitations:** Entrance fee: $5 per vehicle. Ranger-led canoe trips, $10 per canoe (reservations required in person, Barrier Island Visitor Center). Backcountry camping permits ($5) required. Off Road Vehicle Permit ($60 for 12 months, restrictions apply). Hunting permitted Sept.–Jan., Maryland state hunting license required. No stopping along park roads to view horses. Don't feed or touch wild horses. Leashed pets only at Assateague; no pets in Virginia areas. Seashore open year-round. Visitor centers open daily 9–5. Closed Thanksgiving, Dec. 25.

HOW TO GET THERE

The island is off the coast of Maryland and Virginia. The Maryland district entrance is at the south end of Rte. 611, 8 mi/13 km south of Ocean City. In Virginia, the park entrance is at Chincoteague, VA, which is east of U.S. 13 at the east end of Rte. 175. There is no road on Assateague Island connecting the north and south entrances. Closest airport: Salisbury, MD (40 mi/64 km west of Ocean City, MD, and 45 mi/72 km northwest of Chincoteague, VA).

FOR MORE INFORMATION

Assateague Island National Seashore (7206 National Seashore La., Berlin, MD 21811, tel. 410/641–1441, fax 410/641–1099; Web site www.nps.gov/asis). Ocean City Visitor's Bureau (4001 Coastal Hwy., Ocean City, MD 21842, tel. 800/626–2326). Chincoteague Chamber of Commerce (Box 258, Chincoteague, VA 23336, tel. 757/336–6161).

Catoctin Mountain Park

In the northern part of the state, near Thurmont

The eastern hardwood forest of Catoctin Mountain Park provides camping, picnicking, fishing, hiking, and scenic mountain vistas. Originally called the Catoctin Recreational Demonstration Area, it was built during the Great Depression by the Works Progress Administration and the Civilian Conservation Corps. It was planned to provide recreational camps for federal employees. One of the camps eventually became Camp David, which is not open to the public. Catoctin Recreation Demonstration Area was transferred to the Park Service in 1936 and renamed in 1954.

WHAT TO SEE & DO

Cross-country skiing, fishing, hiking, horseback riding, picnicking, rock climbing (permit required, *see below*), wildlife watching. **Facilities:** Visitor center with interpretive exhibits, trails, scenic overlooks. Bookstore. **Programs & Events:** Interpretive programs available year-round. Planned activities available seasonally.

PLANNING YOUR VISIT

⚠ **Camping:** 5 campgrounds: family campground (no reservations; open mid-Apr.–mid-Nov.); youth group campground (reservations required, tel. 301/663–9388); Adirondack Shelter (hike-in, permit required, *see below*); 2 large environmental education camps (reservations available, tel. 301/663–9330). Public campground also available in Cunningham Falls State Park. 🏠 **Lodging:** In the park: Camp Misty Mount (cabins, reservations required, tel. 301/271–3140; open mid-

Apr.–Oct.). Lodging also available outside the park in Thurmont. ✗ **Food & Supplies:** Available in Thurmont; none in park. ☞ **Tips & Hints:** Plan to spend 30 minutes in visitor center, 30 minutes–7 hours on hikes (average is 2–3 hours). Busiest in July and August, least crowded in January and February. ✉ **Fees, Permits & Limitations:** Free. Park Central Road and part of Manahan Rd. closed in winter for cross-country skiing. Permits required (free) for Adirondack Shelter campsite and rock climbing. Maryland state fishing license required. Park open daily sunrise–sunset. Visitor center open Mon.–Thurs. 10–4:30, Fri 10–5, weekends 8:30–5. Closed Thanksgiving, Dec. 25, Jan. 1, Martin Luther King Jr. Day, Presidents Day, Veterans Day.

HOW TO GET THERE

From I–270 or I–70, take U.S. 15N, exit on Rte. 77W for 3 mi/5 km. Closest airports: Dulles International (VA), Baltimore-Washington International.

FOR MORE INFORMATION

Superintendent, Catoctin Mountain Park (6602 Foxville Rd., Thurmont, MD 21788-1598, tel. 301/663–9330; Web site www.nps.gov/cato).

Chesapeake and Ohio Canal National Historical Park

The park runs 185 mi/296 km along the Potomac River from Georgetown in Washington, DC, to Cumberland, MD

The canal, built between 1828 and 1850 and used until 1924, preserves the history of the C&O Canal towpath and related structures. The canal system's 74 lift locks raise the canal from near sea level to an elevation of 605 ft/184 m and provide quiet waters for canoeists, boaters, and anglers. Its towpath offers a nearly level byway for hikers and bicyclists. The canal was established as a national historical park on January 8, 1971.

WHAT TO SEE & DO

Biking (rentals, Williamsport and Cumberland, MD), boating and canoeing (rentals Washington, DC; and Potomac, MD), hiking, picnicking, viewing falls. **Facilities:** 6 visitor centers with interpretive displays—Washington, DC; Brunswick, Great Falls, Williamsport, Hancock, and Cumberland, MD. Picnic pavilion, wayside exhibits, bookstores. **Programs & Events:** Replica canal boats operate at Great Falls, Georgetown (Apr.–Nov.), ranger walks and talks. Cumberland Heritage Days (Cumberland, MD; mid-June); C&O Canal Days (Williamsport, MD; last weekend Aug.); Canal–Apple Days (Hancock, MD; mid-Sept.); Brunswick Railroad Days (Brunswick, MD; early Oct.); Railfest (Cumberland, MD; early Oct.).

PLANNING YOUR VISIT

⚠ **Camping:** 5 drive-in campgrounds, 30 tent camps along towpath. Group camping at Marsden Tract (Mile 11; permit required, *see* *below*) and Fifteenmile Creek. Private campgrounds available at Harpers Ferry, WV; Hancock and Williamsport, MD. ⊞ **Lodging:** Available in Washington, DC; Harpers Ferry and Shepherdstown, WV; Leesburg, VA; Cumberland, Hancock, and Williamsport, MD; none in park. ✕ **Food & Supplies:** In the park: snack bar at Great Falls, MD. Outside the park: Washington, DC; Leesburg, VA; Harpers Ferry, Paw Paw, and Shepherdstown, WV; Hancock and Williamsport, MD. ☞ **Tips & Hints:** Avoid towpath after heavy rains. Go in April and October for best conditions. Busiest in June and August, least crowded in January and February. ▧ **Fees, Permits & Limitations:** Entrance fee: $4 per car (Great Falls only). Permit required for group camping (tel. 301/767–3714), Fee charged to ride canal boats (tel. 202/653–5190 Georgetown; 301/767–3714 Great Falls, MD). Reservations available (tel. 301/767–3714) for picnic pavilion. Maryland, Washington, DC, fishing license required. No gas-powered boats in park. Electric motors allowed in Big Pool, Little Pool. No motorized vehicles, mopeds, trail bikes on towpath. Bike riding on towpaths only. Leashed pets only. No hunting. Towpath open daily dawn–dusk. Visitor centers: Georgetown, Thur.–Sun, 9–4:30; Great Falls, daily 9–5; Brunswick, Thur.–Fri., 10–2, weekends, 10–4; Williamsport, Wed.–Sun. 9–4:30; Hancock, Fri.–Tues. 9–4:30; Cumberland, daily 9–5. Closed Thanksgiving, Dec. 25, Jan. 1.

HOW TO GET THERE

The park runs along the Potomac River from Washington, DC, to Cumberland, MD.

FOR MORE INFORMATION

Chesapeake and Ohio Canal National Historic Park (Box 4, Sharpsburg, MD 21782, tel. 301/739–4200, fax 301/739–5275; Web site www.nps.gov/choh).

Clara Barton
National Historic Site

Just outside Washington, DC

Clara Barton, humanitarian and founder of the American Red Cross, lived in Glen Echo the last 15 years of her life. Her 38-room house served as Red Cross headquarters from 1897 to 1904 and as a warehouse for disaster relief supplies. From this house, she organized and directed relief efforts for victims of natural disasters and war. The site was authorized on October 26, 1974.

WHAT TO SEE & DO

Picnicking, touring house. **Facilities:** House, exhibits, audiovisual programs. Bookstore, picnic area. **Programs & Events:** House shown by guided tour only (10–4, hourly). Lamplight Open House (late Apr. and late Sept.).

PLANNING YOUR VISIT

⛺ **Camping:** Available at Park Service sites in Greenbelt Park, MD; Prince William Forest Park, VA (*see separate entries for both*); and locally; none at site. 🏨 **Lodging:** Available in Montgomery County, MD, and Washington, DC, areas; none at site. ✕ **Food & Supplies:** Available in Montgomery County, MD, and Washington, DC, areas; none at site. ☞ **Tips & Hints:** Allow 30–45 minutes to tour the site. Busiest in December and June, least crowded in January and February. 🎟 **Fees, Permits & Limitations:** Free. Reservations required for groups of 10 or more, and a maximum of 40 are permitted. Audiovisual programs available by reservation only. Site open daily 10–5. Closed Thanksgiving, Dec. 25, Jan. 1.

HOW TO GET THERE

The house, adjacent to Glen Echo Park in Maryland and just outside northwest Washington, DC, is reached via MacArthur Blvd. Look for park directional signpostings on Clara Barton Pkwy. and MacArthur Blvd. From I–495/I–95 (Beltway), take Clara Barton Pkwy. to Glen Echo. Public transportation is available through Montgomery County Transit Authority Ride-on-Bus 29 from Bethesda and Friendship Heights Metro stations (red line) or by taxi. Closest airports: Reagan Washington National (11 mi/18 km), Dulles International (22 mi/35 km).

FOR MORE INFORMATION

Clara Barton National Historic Site (5801 Oxford Road, Glen Echo, MD 20812, tel. 301/492–6245; Web site www.nps.gov/clba).

Fort McHenry National Monument and Historic Shrine

In Baltimore

The American resistance of a British naval attack against Fort McHenry on September 13–14, 1814, prevented the capture of Baltimore during the War of 1812. A large flag was raised over the fort after the 25-hour battle, and the victory inspired Francis Scott Key to write "The Star-Spangled Banner." The fort was authorized as a national park under the War Department in 1925, transferred to the Park Service in 1933, and redesignated in 1939.

WHAT TO SEE & DO

Bicycling, jogging, picnicking, touring fort, watching film. **Facilities:** Visitor center with interpretive exhibits and film, fort, museum, seawall, restored barracks, wayside exhibits. Gift shop, picnic tables. **Programs & Events:** Ranger-guided interpretive programs (mid-June–Labor Day); living-history programs (mid-June–Aug., weekend afternoons); Tattoo Ceremonies (June–Aug., some Sun.). Civil War Encampment (last weekend in Apr.); Flag Day Program (June 14); Defenders Day Celebration (2nd weekend, Sept.).

PLANNING YOUR VISIT

⚑ **Camping:** Available in Millersville; none at monument. 🏨 **Lodging:** Available in Baltimore; none at monument. ✕ **Food & Supplies:** Available in Baltimore; none at monument. ☞ **Tips & Hints:** Visit in spring and fall. Busiest in May and June, least crowded in February and March. ✉ **Fees, Permits & Limitations:** Entrance fee: $5 per adult (17 and older). No pets in fort, leashed pets elsewhere. No climbing on cannons or earthworks. No skates or skateboards. No fishing off seawall. No public docking. No food or drink in visitor center. Park open Labor Day–mid–June, daily 8–5; mid-June–Labor Day, daily 8–8. Visitor center open fall–spring, daily 8–4:45; summer, daily 8–7:45. Closed Dec. 25, Jan. 1.

HOW TO GET THERE

3 mi/5 km southeast of the Baltimore Inner Harbor, just off I–95. Follow blue/green FORT MCHENRY signs. Closest airport: Baltimore-Washington International (10 mi/16 km).

FOR MORE INFORMATION

Fort McHenry National Monument and Historic Shrine (End of East Fort Ave., Baltimore, MD 21230-5393, tel. 410/962–4290, fax 410/962–2500; e-mail FOMC_Superintendent@nps.gov; Web site www.nps.gov/fomc).

Fort Washington Park

Outside Washington, DC

Fort Washington was built between 1814 and 1824 on the site of Fort Warburton, which was destroyed during the War of 1812. The fort was built to protect Washington, DC, housed Union forces during the Civil War, and was obsolete by 1872. It served various functions until the 1940s, when it became a park. The transfer to the Park Service was authorized in 1930 and became effective in 1940.

WHAT TO SEE & DO

Bird-watching, hiking, picnicking, touring fort and grounds. **Facilities:** Visitor center with interpretive exhibits, fort, trail. Bookstore, picnic areas. **Programs & Events:** Fort tours (weekends at 2 and 3; weekdays by request). Artillery firings (Apr.–Nov., one Sun. monthly), living-history programs (summer).

PLANNING YOUR VISIT

⚑ **Camping:** Available in Washington, DC, area; none in park. 🏨 **Lodging:** Available in Washington, DC, area; none in park. ✕ **Food & Supplies:** Available in Washington, DC, area; none in park. ☞ **Tips & Hints:** Allow one–two hours for a visit. Watch introductory film at visitor center to start. Busiest in June and July, least crowded in December and January. ✉ **Fees, Permits & Limitations:** Entrance fee: $4 per vehicle or $2 per walk-in, bicyclist, or bus passenger. Historic fort and visitor center open daily 9–5. Park grounds open daily 8–dark. Closed Thanksgiving, Dec. 25, Jan. 1.

HOW TO GET THERE

The park is at 13551 Fort Washington Rd., in Fort Washington, MD. From Washington, DC, take the Capital Beltway (I–495) to Exit 3A (Indian Head Hwy. or MD 210). Continue to Fort Washington Rd., turn right, and follow to park entrance. Closest airport: Reagan Washington National (15 mi/24 km).

FOR MORE INFORMATION

Superintendent, Fort Washington Park (13551 Fort Washington Rd., Fort Washington, MD 20744, tel. 301/763–4600; Web site www. nps.gov/fowa).

Greenbelt Park

Midstate, in Greenbelt

The park's 1,176 acres offer a green oasis between Washington, DC, and Baltimore, MD. It provides a refuge for native plants and animals and facilities for camping, hiking, and picnicking. The park was transferred from the Public Housing Authority on August 3, 1950.

WHAT TO SEE & DO

Bicycling, hiking, jogging, picnicking, walking. **Facilities:** Ranger station with information (campground entrance), 12 mi/19 km of trails. Picnic areas. **Programs & Events:** Natural and cultural resource programs available. National Trails Day events.

PLANNING YOUR VISIT

⚠ **Camping:** Campground: dump station, water hookup only. (Reservations available Apr.–Oct., tel. 800/365–2267). Six campers per site maximum. No backcountry camping. ⌂ **Lodging:** Available locally; none in park. ✕ **Food & Supplies:** Available locally; none in park. ☞ **Tips & Hints:** Busiest Memorial Day weekend, least crowded in January and February. 🎫 **Fees, Permits & Limitations:** Free. Reserve group picnics two weeks in advance (tel. 301/344–3944). Rangers on duty Sept.–Apr., Fri.–Sun. 7:30–4; Apr.–Sept., weekdays 7:30–7. Headquarters open weekdays 7:30–4. Self-registration campground daily.

HOW TO GET THERE

From I–95S, take Exit 23 (Kenilworth Ave. S). Turn left on Greenbelt Rd. E. Park is on right. From I–95N, take Exit 22A (Baltimore-Washington Pkwy. N), exit on Greenbelt Rd. (Rte. 193W). Park is on left. From Baltimore-Washington Pkwy., exit on Greenbelt Rd. (Rte. 193W). Park is on left. Metro buses stop at park entrance on Greenbelt Rd. Closest Metro subway stop is College Park/University of Maryland Station. Closest airport: Baltimore-Washington International (53 mi/85 km).

FOR MORE INFORMATION

Park Headquarters, Greenbelt Park (6565 Greenbelt Rd., Greenbelt, MD 20770, tel. 301/344–3948 or 301/344–3944 for ranger station; Web site www.nps.gov/gree).

Hampton
National Historic Site

In the central part of the state, in Towson

Hampton preserves and interprets what once was a vast agricultural and commercial estate owned by one family for over 150 years and supported by a large workforce including indentured servants and slaves. The mansion was the centerpiece of an estate of what was once an estate of 24,000 acres of land including an iron foundry, farm, formal grounds, and gardens. Some 20 buildings and 40,000 artifacts survive. The extant buildings include the mansion, slave quarters, family cemetery, farm, and outbuildings. The site was designated in 1948.

WHAT TO SEE & DO

Touring the mansion, outbuildings, grounds, and formal gardens. **Facilities:** Visitor center, mansion, outbuildings, cemetery. Gift shop. **Programs & Events:** Guided mansion tours (daily 9–4, on the hour). Guided grounds tours (Memorial Day–Labor Day). Special programs available.

PLANNING YOUR VISIT

Camping: Available in north Baltimore County; none at site. **Lodging:** Available in Baltimore, Towson; none at site. **Food & Supplies:** Food and supplies available outside the park in Baltimore, Cockeysville, Towson; none at site. **Tips & Hints:** Busiest in April and May, least crowded in January and February. **Fees, Permits & Limitations:** Free. Mansion interpretive tour fee: $5 per adult, $2 seniors age 62 and over, children 16 and under free. Park and visitor center open daily 9–5. Gift shop open mid-Mar.–mid-Dec. Closed Thanksgiving, Dec. 25, Jan. 1.

HOW TO GET THERE

The park is just outside the Baltimore Beltway (I–695) via Exit 27B. Closest airport: Baltimore-Washington International (40 mi/64 km).

FOR MORE INFORMATION

Hampton National Historic Site (535 Hampton La., Towson, MD 21286, tel. 410/823–1309, fax 410/823–8394; e-mail hamp_ superintendent@nps.gov; Web site www.nps.gov/hamp). Baltimore County Conference and Visitors Bureau (118 Shawan Rd., Hunt Valley, MD 21030, tel. 800/570–2836 or 410/329–1001).

Monocacy National Battlefield

Midstate, near Frederick

Known as the "Battle that Saved Washington," the Battle of Monocacy on July 9, 1864, was the last Confederate attempt to carry the Civil War into the north. Although Confederate General Jubal T. Early defeated Union forces commanded by Major Lew Wallace, Wallace's effort delayed Early long enough for Union forces to marshal a successful defense of nearby Washington, DC. The site was authorized as Monocacy National Military Park in 1934 and reauthorized and redesignated in 1976.

WHAT TO SEE & DO

Touring battlefield, viewing electric map orientation program. **Facilities:** Visitor center with interpretive exhibits, monuments, loop trail. Bookstore. **Programs & Events:** Ranger-led programs (Memorial Day–Labor Day), living-history programs, special events (monthly, Apr.–Aug.).

PLANNING YOUR VISIT

Camping: Available locally; none at battlefield. **Lodging:** Available locally; none at battlefield. **Food & Supplies:** Available locally; none at battlefield. **Tips & Hints:** Busiest in July and August, least crowded in December and January. **Fees, Permits & Limitations:** Free. Leashed pets only. No hunting or relic collecting. No bikes on trail. Visitor center open Apr.–Oct., daily 8–4:30; Nov.–Mar., Wed.–Sun. 8–4:30. Closed Thanksgiving, Dec. 25, Jan. 1.

HOW TO GET THERE

3 mi/5 km south of Frederick on MD 355. From I–270, take Exit 26 at Urbana. Follow Rte. 80E to stop light and turn left onto MD 355N. Proceed 3.7 mi/5.9 km to battlefield on right. From I–70, take Exit 54 (Market St., Rtes. 85 and 355). Follow MD 355S 3.7 mi/6 km to battlefield on right. Closest airports: Dulles International (45 mi/72 km), Reagan Washington National (50 mi/80 km).

FOR MORE INFORMATION

Monocacy National Battlefield (4801 Urbana Pike, Frederick, MD 21704, tel. 301/662–3515, fax 301/662–3420; Web site www.nps.gov/mono). Tourism Council of Frederick County (19 E. Church St., Frederick, MD 21701, tel. 301/663–8687).

Piscataway Park

In the southern part of the state, near Accokeek

The park stretches for 6 mi/10 km from Piscataway Creek to Marshall Hall on the Potomac River. It is part of a successful effort that began in 1952 to preserve the river view from Mount Vernon across the Potomac in Virginia as it was in George Washington's day. The park also offers opportunities to picnic, bird-watch, view Mount Vernon across the Potomac, and tour a working 18th-century farm. The park was authorized on October 4, 1961.

WHAT TO SEE & DO

Backcountry hiking, bird-watching, fishing, picnicking, touring farm. **Facilities:** National Colonial Farm. Picnic area. **Programs & Events:** Farm tours (weekends, 1 and 3).

PLANNING YOUR VISIT

⚠ **Camping:** Available locally; none in park. 🏠 **Lodging:** Available locally; none in park. ✕ **Food & Supplies:** Available locally; none in park. ☞ **Tips & Hints:** Busiest in July and October, least crowded in January and February. ✉ **Fees, Permits & Limitations:** Fee charged for National Colonial Farm tour (tel. 301/283–2113).

HOW TO GET THERE

From I–95 (Capital Beltway), take Exit 3A to Rte. 210S (Indian Head Hwy.) and drive 10 mi/16 km to the intersection in Accokeek. Turn right on Bryan's Point Rd. Park is 4 mi/6 km ahead on the Potomac River. Closest airport: Reagan Washington National (21 mi/34 km).

FOR MORE INFORMATION

Piscataway Park Superintendent (c/o Fort Washington Park, 13551 Fort Washington Rd., Fort Washington, MD 20744, tel. 301/763–4600; Web site www.nps.gov/pisc).

Thomas Stone
National Historic Site

In the southern part of the state, near Port Tobacco

Haberdeventure plantation was the home of Thomas Stone, one of Maryland's four signers of the Declaration of Independence. Stone was a delegate to the Continental Congress between 1775 and 1778 and again between 1783 and 1784. As a member of the Continental Congress, he served on the 13-member committee that drafted the country's first system of government under the Articles of Confederation. Today, the 322-acre site contains Thomas Stone's five-part tidewater plantation house and several outbuildings typical of an 18th- and 19th-century Maryland plantation. The site was authorized on November 10, 1978.

WHAT TO SEE & DO

Guided and self-guided tours, viewing exhibits. **Facilities:** Information center with interpretive exhibits, house. Bookstore and sales area. **Programs & Events:** Ranger-led tours, audiovisual programs. Seasonal activities and special events available; school and group tours available (reservations required, tel. 301/934–6027).

PLANNING YOUR VISIT

⚠ **Camping:** Available in Smallwood State Park; none at site. 🏠 **Lodging:** Available in La Plata and along U.S. 301; none at site. ✕ **Food & Supplies:** Available in La Plata, Port Tobacco; none at site. ☞ **Tips & Hints:** Plan to spend an hour visiting site. Busiest in June and July, least crowded in December and January. ✉ **Fees, Permits & Limitations:** Free. Site generally open Memorial Day–Labor Day, daily 9–5; Labor Day–Memorial Day, Wed.–Sun. 9–5. Closed Thanksgiving, Dec. 25, Jan. 1.

HOW TO GET THERE

30 mi/48 km south of Washington, DC, on Rose Hill Rd., between MD 6 and 225 near Port Tobacco. Closest airport: Reagan Washington National (30 mi/50 km).

FOR MORE INFORMATION

Thomas Stone National Historic Site (c/o George Washington Birthplace National Monument, RR 1, Box 717, Washington's Birthplace, VA 22443, tel. 301/934–6027, fax 301/934–8793; Web site www.nps.gov/thst). La Plata Chamber of Commerce (6360 Crane Hwy., La Plata, MD 20646, tel. 301/932–6500).

See Also

Appalachian National Scenic Trail, West Virginia. *George Washington Memorial Parkway,* Virginia. *Harpers Ferry National Historical Park,* West Virginia. *Potomac Heritage National Scenic Trail,* District of Columbia.

MASSACHUSETTS

Adams National Historical Park

In the eastern part of the state, in Quincy

This park houses the birthplace, home, and final resting place of presidents John Adams and John Quincy Adams, the nation's second and sixth presidents. A free trolley-bus service takes visitors to the early 18th-century homes where the Adamses were born. The tour also includes a visit to the "Old House," which was the family home for four generations of the Adams family, from 1788 to 1927. A visit to the United First Parish Church, final resting place of both presidents and first ladies, completes the tour. The site was designated on December 9, 1946, and redesignated by Congress in 1998.

WHAT TO SEE & DO

Touring the three homes, church, and grounds. **Facilities:** Visitor center with interpretive exhibits (1250 Hancock St., Presidents Place Galleria). Bookstore. **Programs & Events:** Interpretive tours (Apr. 19–Nov. 10, daily). Living-history and special programs, reenactments (Apr. 19–Nov. 10), lecture series (last full week in June).

PLANNING YOUR VISIT

Camping: Private campgrounds available in Wompatuck State Park and Boston Harbor Islands State Park (both in Hingham); none in park. **Lodging:** Available in Boston area; none in park. **Food & Supplies:** Available in the Boston area; none in park. **Tips & Hints:** Begin tour at visitor center. Park in Presidents Place Parking Garage. Go between April and August for garden blooms, September and November for fall foliage. Busiest in July and August, least crowded in January and February. **Fees, Permits & Limitations:** Entrance and tour fee: $2 per person, under 17 free. Church admission: $2 donation. Trolley tour tickets issued on first-come, first-served basis. Reservations required (tel. 617/770–1175) for groups of eight or more. No eating, drinking, or smoking in homes or on grounds. No backpacks, strollers, or video cameras allowed in homes. No pets. Park open Apr. 19–Nov. 10, daily. Visitor center open Apr. 19–Nov. 10, daily 9–5; Nov. 11–Apr. 18, Mon.–Fri 10–4. Closed Federal holidays in winter. Last full tour departs at 3:15; no tours Nov. 11–Apr. 18.

HOW TO GET THERE

The visitor center is in the Galleria in Presidents Place at 1250 Hancock St. in Quincy. Closest airport: Boston's Logan International (8 mi/13 km).

FOR MORE INFORMATION

Adams National Historical Park (135 Adams St., Quincy, MA 02169, tel. 617/770–1175, fax 617/472–7562; Web site www.nps.gov/adam).

Boston African American National Historic Site

In Boston

Located in the Beacon Hill neighborhood, the site is home to 15 pre–Civil War structures of note in the history of Boston's 19th-century African-American community, including the African Meeting House, the oldest standing African-American church in the United States. The sites are linked by the 1.6-mi/2.5-km Black Heritage Trail. Also on the trail is Augustus Saint-Gaudens's memorial to Robert Gould Shaw, the white officer who first led African-American troops during the Civil War. The site was authorized on October 10, 1980.

WHAT TO SEE & DO

Walking tour of the neighborhood. **Facilities:** African Meeting House (46 Joy St.), Black Heritage Trail. **Programs & Events:** Guided walking tours (Labor Day–Memorial Day, Tues.–Sat. at 10, noon, 2; Memorial Day–Labor Day, daily at 10, noon, 2). Groups are required to make reservations. Interested visitors meet at the Shaw monument. Living-history program (mid-July).

PLANNING YOUR VISIT

Camping: Available in Boston area; none at site. **Lodging:** Available in Boston area; none at site. **Food & Supplies:** Available in Boston area; none at site. **Tips & Hints:** Busiest in July and August, least crowded in December and January. **Fees, Permits & Limitations:** Free. Donations support the Museum of Afro-American History. Site open Memorial Day–Labor Day, daily 10–4; Labor Day–Memorial Day, Mon.–Sat. 10–4. Closed Thanksgiving, Dec. 25, Jan. 1.

HOW TO GET THERE

From the Massachusetts Turnpike (I–90), take Copley Square exit to Stuart St., then turn left on Rte. 28 (Charles St.) to Boston Common. From Rte. 93, take Storrow Dr. to the Copley Square exit, then turn left on Beacon St., right on Arlington St., left on Boylston St., and left on Charles St. (Rte. 28). There are several parking garages in the vicinity. Closest MBTA subway stops are Park St. on the red and green lines and the Bowdoin Square stop on the blue line. Closest airport: Boston's Logan International.

FOR MORE INFORMATION

Site Manager, Boston African American National Historic Site (14 Beacon St., Suite 503, Boston, MA 02108, tel. 617/742–5415; Web site www.nps.gov/boaf).

Boston Harbor Islands National Recreation Area

In Boston Harbor

One of the newest additions to the park system, the recreation area includes 30 islands that range in size from 1 to more than 200 acres. The islands are glacial drumlins and, as a system of islands, are unique in the United States. The area was authorized on November 12, 1996.

WHAT TO SEE & DO

Beachcombing, boat riding, fishing, hiking, kayaking, picnicking, sailing. **Facilities:** Information kiosk (Long Wharf, Boston), exhibit boards on islands. Landing dock, pavilions, picnic tables. **Programs & Events:** Nature walks, living-history programs, marine ecology programs (spring–Oct., daily). Civil War Encampment (mid-Aug.), Halloween program (Oct.).

PLANNING YOUR VISIT

Camping: Primitive camping on Bumpkin, Grape, Lovell, and Peddock islands. No water, electricity. Reservations required (for Bumpkin, Grape, call 877/422–6762; for Lovell, Peddock, call 617/727–7676). **Lodging:** Available locally; none in recreation area. ✕ **Food & Supplies:** Snacks at George's Island. Food and supplies also available in Boston and surrounding towns. ☞ **Tips & Hints:** Plan on 90-minute round-trip ferry ride to George's Island. Bring your own food and water. **Fees, Permits & Limitations:** Free. Ferry ride (10–5): $8 per adult (65 and older $7); $6 per child (children under 4 free). No bikes or motorized equipment. No pets. No alcohol. Information kiosk open Memorial Day–Labor Day, daily 9–4:30.

HOW TO GET THERE

The islands are in the "C" shape of the Greater Boston shoreline. There are five ferry departure points in downtown Boston. Closest airport: Boston's Logan International.

FOR MORE INFORMATION

Boston Harbor Islands National Recreation Area (408 Atlantic Ave., Suite 228, Boston, MA 02110-3350, tel. 617/223–8666; Web site www.nps.gov/boha). Boston Visitor Information Center (147 Tremont St., Boston, MA 02116, tel. 800/888–5515). Greater Boston Convention and Visitor Bureau (2 Copley Pl., Suite 105, Boston, MA 02116, tel. 617/536–4100, fax 617/424–7664). Transportation information Web site www.bostonislands.org

Boston National Historical Park

In Boston

The 2.5-mi/4-km Freedom Trail houses the relics of the revolutionary generation of Bostonians who blazed a trail from colonialism to independence. Included on the trail are the Old State House, Old South Meeting House, Faneuil Hall, Paul Revere House, Old North Church, Bunker Hill Monument, and Charlestown Navy Yard, where the USS *Constitution* ("Old Ironsides") is berthed. The park was authorized on October 1, 1974.

WHAT TO SEE & DO

Touring historic sites. **Facilities:** 2 visitor centers (downtown, 15 State St.; Charlestown Navy Yard), historic buildings, ships, tour trail. Bookstores, gift shops. **Programs & Events:** Ranger-led historical talks (Faneuil Hall and Bunker Hill Monument), U.S. Navy-led tours of USS *Constitution* (daily 9:30–3:50), and other programs. Ranger-led walking tours of downtown part of Freedom Trail (mid-Apr.–Nov., daily); ranger-led tours of the Charlestown Navy Yard, Commandant's House, and World War II destroyer USS *Cassin Young* (end of June–Labor Day, tours every hour, 10–4; fewer tours after Labor Day), and other programs. Boston's Harborfest (July 4 weekend), Charlestown Navy Yard international visiting ships program.

PLANNING YOUR VISIT

⚠ **Camping:** Available in Boston area; none in park. ☷ **Lodging:** Available in Boston area; none in park. ✕ **Food & Supplies:** Available in Boston area; none in park. ☞ **Tips & Hints:** Busiest in July and August, least crowded in January and February. ▨ **Fees, Permits & Limitations:** Federally owned sites, including the Bunker Hill Monument, USS *Constitution,* and Dorchester Heights Monument, free. Ranger-led programs on the Freedom Trail and at Faneuil Hall are also free. Fees are collected at the privately owned and operated sites, including the Old South Meeting House, Old State House, Paul Revere House, by self-supporting associations working cooperatively with the park. Visitor centers hours: Downtown (15 State St.)—daily 9–5; Charlestown Navy Yard—daily 9–5. Most historic sites open Monday closest to Patriot's Day (Apr. 19)–Labor Day, 9:30–5; Labor Day–Patriots Day, daily 10–4. USS *Constitution*—daily 9:30–3:50. All park sites (except USS *Constitution*) and visitor centers closed Thanksgiving, Dec. 25, Jan. 1.

HOW TO GET THERE

From Rte. 1S and Rte. 93 north or south, follow the signs to the Charlestown Navy Yard (berth of USS *Constitution*). Further directions to downtown Boston are available there. There are many parking garages in the downtown area. All sites are accessible by public transportation. Park-and-ride facilities at MBTA subway (T) stations are an alternative to driving into the downtown area. The downtown visitor center (15 State St.) is at the State St. stop of the blue and orange lines.

Water transportation runs frequently between downtown Boston (Long Wharf) and the Charlestown Navy Yard. Closest airport: Boston's Logan International.

FOR MORE INFORMATION

Superintendent, Boston National Historical Park (Charlestown Navy Yard, Boston, MA 02129-4543, tel. 617/242–5644, 617/242–5642 visitor center, 617/242–5601 Charlestown Navy Yard Visitor Information Center, 617/242–5641 Bunker Hill Monument; Web site www.nps.gov/bost).

Cape Cod National Seashore

On outer Cape Cod

Cape Cod National Seashore's 43,557 acres of shoreline and upland landscape include a 40-mi/64-km stretch of pristine sandy beach, dozens of clear, deep, freshwater kettle ponds, and upland scenes of past cultural influences on the land. A variety of historic structures are within the boundary of the seashore, including lighthouses, lifesaving stations, and Cape Cod–style houses. The park was authorized in 1961 and established in 1966.

WHAT TO SEE & DO

Biking; fishing; hiking; picnicking; swimming; touring historic houses, lighthouses, and Marconi Wireless Station. **Facilities:** 2 visitor centers with interpretive exhibits—Salt Pond (off Rte. 6 in Eastham), Province Lands (off Race Point Rd. in Provincetown); 6 swimming beaches, 10 self-guided nature trails, bike trails, Marconi Wireless Station, lighthouses, overlooks. Bookstores. **Programs & Events:** Year-round programs available. Interpretive ranger programs (mid-May–Thanksgiving weekend), guided hikes, canoe tours, beach walks, historic house tours campfire programs (summer, frequently).

PLANNING YOUR VISIT

⚠ **Camping:** Available in privately operated campgrounds within seashore and at Nickerson State Park in Brewster. ▦ **Lodging:** Available locally; none at seashore. ✗ **Food & Supplies:** Available locally; none at seashore. ☞ **Tips & Hints:** Plan on at least a half-day visit. Busiest in July and August, least crowded in January and February. ▧ **Fees, Permits & Limitations:** Entrance fee: $7 per vehicle or $1 per bicyclist or walk-in at lifeguard-protected swimming beaches (late June–Labor Day). Seasonal pass $20. Permits required for beach campfires and overnight fishing. Seasonal permit required ($65) for over-sand vehicle use; $40 for 7-day off-road vehicle permit. Parking lots open daily 6–midnight. Visitor center hours: Salt Pond—mid-Oct.–May, daily 9–4:30; June–mid-Oct., daily 9–5, closed Dec. 25; Province Lands—mid-May–late Nov., daily 9–5; Headquarters—weekdays 8–4:30, closed holidays.

HOW TO GET THERE

The seashore stretches from Chatham to Provincetown on the Outer Cape. From Boston, take Rte. 3S to the Sagamore Bridge in Bourne. Follow Rte. 6E to Eastham and Provincetown. From Providence, RI, take I–95N to I–195. Follow Rte. 6E as described above. Closest airports: Hyannis (35 mi/56 km), Boston's Logan International (120 mi/192 km).

FOR MORE INFORMATION

Cape Cod National Seashore (99 Marconi Site Rd., Wellfleet, MA 02667, tel. 508/349–3785; Web site www.nps.gov/caco). Salt Pond Visitor Center (Rte. 6, Eastham, MA 02642, tel. 508/255–1301). Cape Cod Chamber of Commerce (Box 790, Hyannis, MA 02601-0790, tel. 508/362–3225).

Frederick Law Olmsted National Historic Site

In the eastern part of the state, in Brookline

The site preserves the home and office of America's leading landscape architect and park maker. The Olmsted legacy—5,000 public and private landscapes, including Central Park and the United States Capitol grounds—is a vital part of our national heritage. In 1883, Olmsted opened the Brookline office that would continue into the next century under the direction of his sons, associates, and successors. More than 1 million landscape design documents were produced at the site. The grounds are a living exhibit of Olmsted's design ideals. The site was established in 1979.

WHAT TO SEE & DO

Touring historic Olmsted house, office, and grounds; watching film. **Facilities:** Visitor center with interpretive exhibits, home, office, grounds. Bookstore. **Programs & Events:** Interpretive tours (Fri.–Sun.). Ranger-led tours of Olmsted-designed landscapes in Boston area (weekends, May–Oct.). Holiday Open House (Dec.).

PLANNING YOUR VISIT.

⚠ **Camping:** Available locally; none at site. ▣ **Lodging:** Available locally; none at site. ✕ **Food and Supplies:** Available locally; none at site. ☞ **Tips & Hints:** Limited parking available. Best time to visit: spring and fall. Busiest in May and June, least crowded in November and January. ▦ **Fees, Permits & Limitations:** Free. No smoking or pets inside historic buildings. Site open Fri.–Sun. 10–4:30.

HOW TO GET THERE

The park is in Brookline, 3 mi/5 km from downtown Boston. Closest airport: Boston's Logan International (5 mi/8 km).

FOR MORE INFORMATION

Frederick Law Olmsted National Historic Site (99 Warren St., Brookline, MA 02445, tel. 617/566–1689, fax 617/232–3964; Web site www.nps.gov/frla). Brookline Chamber of Commerce (1330 Beacon St., Brookline, MA 02446, tel. 617/739–1330).

John Fitzgerald Kennedy National Historic Site

In the eastern part of the state, in Brookline

The site preserves the house where the 35th president of the United States was born in 1917. This was the first home shared by the president's father and mother, Joseph P. and Rose Fitzgerald Kennedy, and represents the social and political beginnings of one of the world's most prominent political families. The nine-room house was restored in the 1960s under the direction of Rose Kennedy as a memorial to her son. Included is a collection of household furnishings, photographs, and significant family mementos from the 1917 period that reflect the lifestyle and various pursuits and interests of the Kennedy family. The site was established in 1969.

WHAT TO SEE & DO

Touring the home. **Facilities:** Visitor center with interpretive exhibits. Bookstore. **Programs & Events:** Guided home tours (Apr.–early Nov.), walking tours of neighborhood (Sun., Apr.–early Nov.). Kennedy Birthday Weekend (last weekend in May).

PLANNING YOUR VISIT

Camping: Available in Greater Boston area; none at site. **Lodging:** Available locally; none at site. **Food & Supplies:** Available locally; none at site. **Tips & Hints:** Busiest in July and August, least crowded in April. **Fees, Permits & Limitations:** Guided home tour entrance fee: $2 per adult 17 and older. No smoking or pets in building. Park and visitor center open Apr.–early Nov., Wed.–Sun., 10–4.

HOW TO GET THERE

In Brookline, 3 mi/5 km from downtown Boston. Closest airport: Boston's Logan International (5 mi/8 km).

FOR MORE INFORMATION

John Fitzgerald Kennedy National Historic Site (83 Beals St., Brookline, MA 02446, tel. 617/566–7937, fax 617/730–9884; Web site www.nps.gov/jofi). Brookline Chamber of Commerce (1330 Beacon St., Brookline, MA 02446, tel. 617/739–1330).

Longfellow National Historic Site

Near Boston, in Cambridge

Henry Wadsworth Longfellow raised a family and wrote many of his most beloved poems here between 1837 and his death in 1882. The house, which was built in 1759, also served as George Washington's headquarters early in the American Revolution. On display in historically furnished rooms are an array of American and European decorative arts, paintings, and sculptures and Longfellow's library of 10,000 books. The house is an outstanding example of mid-Georgian architecture, and it is surrounded by formal gardens where the Longfellows entertained some of the world's famous writers and artists. The site was authorized in 1972.

WHAT TO SEE & DO

Touring the gardens. (The house is closed to the public for renovations; it is expected to reopen in 2002). **Facilities:** Gardens. **Programs & Events:** Self-guided tour of grounds and neighborhood. Guided tours of neighborhood available while site undergoes renovation (June–Oct.): "Longfellow's Cambridge", "George Washington in Cambridge." Summer Festival of Music and Poetry (July). Longfellow Birthday Weekend (Feb.), Longfellow Family Days (July).

PLANNING YOUR VISIT

⚠ **Camping:** Available locally; none at site. ☖ **Lodging:** Available locally; none at site. ✕ **Food & Supplies:** Available locally; none at site. ☞ **Tips & Hints:** There is no on-site parking. Busiest in August and October, least crowded in January and March. ▨ **Fees, Permits & Limitations:** Walking tours of "Longfellow's Cambridge" and "George Washington in Cambridge" are free. Closed on major holidays.

HOW TO GET THERE

In Cambridge, 3 mi/5 km from downtown Boston. Closest airport: Boston's Logan International (5 mi/8 km).

FOR MORE INFORMATION

Longfellow National Historic Site (105 Brattle St., Cambridge, MA 02138, tel. 617/876–4491, fax 617/497–8718; Web site www.nps.gov/long). Cambridge Chamber of Commerce (859 Massachusetts Ave., Cambridge, MA 02139, tel. 617/876–4100).

Lowell National Historical Park

In the northeast part of the state, in Lowell

America's Industrial Revolution is commemorated at this park. The park's Boott Cotton Mills Museum, which includes a weave room of 88 operating looms, "mill girl" boarding houses, the Suffolk Mill turbine, and guided tours, documents the Northeast's transition from farm to factory, the history of immigrant labor, and the technology of industrial trial labor technology. The site was authorized on June 5, 1978.

WHAT TO SEE & DO

Self-guided and guided tours. **Facilities:** Visitor center with interpretive exhibits (246 Market St.), Boott Cotton Mills Museum (400 Foot of John St.), "Working People Exhibit" at Mogan Cultural Center, Suffolk Mill turbine. **Programs & Events:** Self-guided tours, exhibits. Guided boat, trolley and walking tours (May–Oct., daily). Kids Week (Feb.,

Apr.), Lowell Women's Week, (1st week, Mar.), Lowell Folk Festival (last full weekend, July), Lowell Summer Music Festival (July–Aug.), National Park Day (Aug. 25), Banjo and Fiddle Contests (1st or 2nd Sat., Sept.).

PLANNING YOUR VISIT

⚠ **Camping:** Available locally; none at park. ⛺ **Lodging:** Available locally; none at park. ✕ **Food & Supplies:** Available locally; none at park. ☞ **Tips & Hints:** Tours go out rain or shine. Best time to visit is between March and November. Busiest in May and July, least crowded in December and February. ⛳ **Fees, Permits & Limitations:** Free. Boat tours: $6 per adult; $4 children 6–16; $2 per senior 62 and over. Reservations required for boat tours (tel. 978/970–5000). Trolley tours free. Boott Cotton Mills Museum fees: $4 per adult, $2 per child 6–16; $3 per senior 62 and over. No eating, drinking, or smoking. Park generally open daily 9–5. Closed Thanksgiving, Dec. 25, Jan. 1.

HOW TO GET THERE

Take the Lowell Connector from either I–495 or U.S. 3. Exit on Thorndike St. N, turn right on Dutton St. to marked parking lot. Closest airport: Boston's Logan International (25 mi/40 km).

FOR MORE INFORMATION

Lowell National Historical Park (67 Kirk St., Lowell, MA 01852-1029, tel. 978/970–5000, fax 978/275–1762; Web site www.nps.gov/lowe). Greater Lowell Chamber of Commerce (77 Merrimack St., Lowell, MA 01852, tel. 978/459–8154, fax 978/452–4145). Greater Merrimack Valley Convention and Visitors Bureau (9 Central St., Suite 201, Lowell, MA 01852, tel. 978/459–6150, fax 978/459–4595). Lowell Office of Cultural Affairs (66 Merrimack St., Lowell, MA 01852, tel. 978/441–3800.

Minute Man National Historical Park

In the eastern part of the state, in Concord, Lincoln, and Lexington

Preserved here are the historic sites, structures and landscapes associated with the events of April 19, 1775, and the beginning of the American Revolution. The North Bridge, Minute Man Statue, and Battle Road are global symbols of man's universal struggle for freedom and independence. The park also celebrates the 19th-century literary Renaissance, preserving and interpreting The Wayside, home of Nathaniel Hawthorne, Louisa May Alcott, and Margaret Sidney. The park was authorized on September 21, 1959.

WHAT TO SEE & DO

Biking, canoeing (rentals, Concord), hiking, picnicking, touring historic buildings and sites. **Facilities:** 2 visitor centers with interpretive exhibits (Minute Man, North Bridge), The Wayside, Hartwell Tavern, trails, interpretive display boards. Bookstores, brochure boxes, picnic tables, multimedia presentation shown at Minute Man Visitor Center. **Programs & Events:** Ranger programs year-round. Colonial living-history demonstrations, drills, musket firings, historic town meetings, fife-and-drum demonstrations and military encampments, concerts, colonial reenactments, historic military encampments (Apr.–Oct.). Patriots Day weekend celebrations (mid-Apr.). Winter lecture series (Feb.).

PLANNING YOUR VISIT

⛺ **Camping:** Available locally; none in park. ⌂ **Lodging:** Available locally; none in park. ✕ **Food & Supplies:** Available locally; none in park. ☞ **Tips & Hints:** Begin visit by watching multimedia presentation at Minute Man visitor center. Visit between late spring and fall. Busiest in July and October, least crowded in December and February. ▤ **Fees, Permits & Limitations:** Entrance fee for The Wayside only: $4 adults, free 16 and under. No campfires. No hunting. No horses or recreational vehicles on Battle Road Trail. Leashed dogs only. Visitor center hours: North Bridge—May–Oct, daily 9–5; Nov.–Apr., daily 9–4; closed Dec. 25, Jan. 1; Minute Man—May–Oct, daily 9–5; Nov.–Apr, daily 9–4. The Wayside—May–Oct., Thurs.–Tues. 10–5, closed Wed. Hartwell Tavern open May–Oct., daily 10–5. Battle Road Trail open daily sunrise–sunset.

HOW TO GET THERE

The Minute Man Visitor Center is on Rte. 2A in Lexington. From I–95, take Exit 30B. Closest airport: Boston's Logan International (22 mi/35 km).

FOR MORE INFORMATION

Minute Man National Historical Park (174 Liberty St., Concord, MA 01742, tel. 978/369–6993; Web site www.nps.gov/mima). Concord Chamber of Commerce (2 Lexington Rd., Concord, MA 01742, tel. 978/369–3120).

New Bedford Whaling National Historical Park

In the southeast part of the state, in New Bedford

This site—the only one of its kind in the National Park System—commemorates whaling and its impact on American history. The park includes a 13-block, 34-acre National Historic Landmark District, the schooner *Ernestina,* and the New Bedford Whaling Museum. The park was authorized on November 12, 1996.

WHAT TO SEE & DO

Touring historic district. **Facilities:** Park visitor center, orientation video, historic district, Waterfront Visitors Center and Working Waterfront.

The historic district includes the Rotch-Jones-Duff House and Garden Museum, New Bedford Whaling Museum, Seamen's Bethel, and the schooner *Ernestina*. **Programs & Events:** Walking tours of historic district (July–Aug., daily; Sept.–June, by reservation only).

PLANNING YOUR VISIT

⚠ **Camping:** Available in New Bedford area; none in park. 🏨 **Lodging:** Available in New Bedford area; none in park. ✕ **Food & Supplies:** Available in New Bedford area; none in park. ☞ **Tips & Hints:** Plan to spend a full day at the park. Start your visit at the visitor center, where a park ranger or volunteer can help plan your day. 🎫 **Fees, Permits & Limitations:** Free. Partner institutions within the park charge fees. Visitor center open daily 9–4. Closed Thanksgiving, Dec. 25, Jan. 1.

HOW TO GET THERE

New Bedford is on I–195, 30 mi/48 km east of Providence, RI; 20 mi/32 km west of Cape Cod; and 50 mi/80 km south of Boston via Hwys. 24 and 140. From I–195, take Exit 15 and proceed 1 mi to the downtown exit. Turn right on Elm St. The Elm St. garage is on the right, just beyond Bethel St. The visitor center is two blocks from the garage. The parking fee is $3.50 per day. There is also a limited amount of two-hour street parking available. Closest airports: New Bedford (4 mi/6 km), Boston (60 mi/96 km); Providence, RI (40 mi/64 km).

FOR MORE INFORMATION

Superintendent, New Bedford Whaling National Historical Park (33 William St., New Bedford, MA 02740, tel. 508/996–4095; e-mail NEBE_superintendent@nps.gov; Web site www.nps.gov/nebe). New Bedford Office of Tourism (Wharfinger Bldg., Pier #3, New Bedford, MA 02740, tel. 800/508–5353; Web site www.ci.new-bedford.ma.us). Rotch-Jones-Duff House and Garden Museum (396 County St., New Bedford, MA 02740, tel. 508/997–1401 or 508/996–4158); New Bedford Whaling Museum (Old Dartmouth Historical Society, 18 Johnny Cake Hill, New Bedford, MA 02740, tel. 508/997–0046; Web site www.whalingmuseum.org); Seamen's Bethel (New Bedford Port Society, 15 Johnny Cake Hill, New Bedford, MA 02740, tel. 508/992–3295); and the schooner *Ernestina* (New Bedford State Pier, Box 2010, New Bedford, MA 02741-2010, tel. 508/992–4900; Web site www.ernestina. org). New Bedford Chamber of Commerce (794 Purchase St., Box 8827, New Bedford, MA 02742, tel. 508/999–5231; Web site www.nbchamber.com).

Salem Maritime National Historic Site

In the northeast part of the state, in Salem

Salem was once a major trading port, and the site includes 18th- and 19th-century wharves, the Custom House, the Public Stores, the West Indies Goods Store, the 17th-century Narbonne-Hale house, and the home of 18th-century merchant E. H. Derby. The site was designated on March 17, 1938.

WHAT TO SEE & DO

Touring the wharves, historic buildings, neighborhoods, and 18th-century merchant sailing ship; viewing films; visiting 18th-century garden. **Facilities:** Visitor center with interpretive exhibits (2 New Liberty St., Salem); orientation center (waterfront); historic buildings; wharf; *Friendship,* an 18th-century merchant sailing ship. Bookstores. **Programs & Events:** Tours available year-round. Seasonal activities available. Salem Maritime Festival (July), visiting Tall Ships (occasionally).

PLANNING YOUR VISIT

⛺ **Camping:** Available locally; none at site. 🛏 **Lodging:** Available locally; none at site. ✕ **Food & Supplies:** Available locally; none at site. ☞ **Tips & Hints:** Allow a full day to see Salem, an extra day or two to see historic and cultural attractions in the rest of Essex County. Busiest in July and October, least crowded in January and February. 🎫 **Fees, Permits & Limitations:** Free. Program fees are charged for ranger-led tours of historic structures. Site open daily 9–5 (extended summer hours). Closed Thanksgiving, Dec. 25, Jan. 1.

HOW TO GET THERE

The visitor center (2 New Liberty St., Salem) is 15 mi/24 km north of Boston via Rte. 128N to Rte. 114E. By train, take the Rockport/Ipswich Commuter Line from Boston's North Station. By bus, take Bus 455 or 450 from Haymarket section of Boston to Salem rail depot. Haymarket is on Green and Orange lines of Boston subway system. Closest airport: Boston's Logan International.

FOR MORE INFORMATION

Superintendent, Salem Maritime National Historic Site (174 Derby St. Salem, MA 01970, tel. 978/740–1650, fax 978/740–1655; Web site www.nps.gov/sama).

Saugus Iron Works
National Historic Site

In the eastern part of the state, in Saugus

This is the site of the first integrated ironworks in North America. The site, which was in use from 1646 to 1668, includes the reconstructed blast furnace, forge, rolling mill, and a restored 17th-century house. It is on the Saugus River, has an open-air museum with working waterwheels, and was authorized on April 5, 1968.

WHAT TO SEE & DO

Touring museum, historic house, and site; viewing slide show; walking nature trail. **Facilities:** Visitor center with interpretive exhibits, ironworks, Iron Works House, nature trail. Book and map sale area. **Programs & Events:** Ranger-led tours of water wheels, machinery, and blacksmith shop (Apr.–Oct.). Evening concerts (July), Saugus Founder's Day (Sept.), Hammersmith Christmas Stroll (Dec.).

PLANNING YOUR VISIT

⚠ **Camping:** Available in Amesbury, Gloucester; none at site. 🏠 **Lodging:** Available in Saugus; none at site. ✕ **Food & Supplies:** Available in Saugus; none at site. ☞ **Tips & Hints:** Plan to spend two hours. Busiest June through August, least crowded in January and February. 🎫 **Fees, Permits & Limitations:** Free. Site open Nov.–Mar., daily 9–4; Apr.–Oct., daily 9–5. Closed Thanksgiving, Dec. 25, Jan. 1.

HOW TO GET THERE

20 minutes south of Salem and 20 minutes north of Boston. From I–95, take Exit 43 (Walnut St.). Drive east toward Lynn. Follow signs to park. From Rte. 1N, take Main St. Saugus exit. Follow park signs. From Rte. 1S, take the Walnut St. exit (east). Follow park signs. Closest airport: Boston's Logan International (10 mi/16 km).

FOR MORE INFORMATION

Saugus Iron Works National Historic Site (244 Central St., Saugus, MA 01906, tel. 781/233–0050, fax 978/740–1685; Web site www.nps.gov/sair).

Springfield Armory National Historic Site

In the western part of the state, in Springfield

The nation's first national armory, authorized by President George Washington, was created in 1794. The historic site encompasses 55 acres and original armory buildings. The main building houses a museum that maintains one of the most extensive and unique small firearms collections in the world. Also on exhibit are examples from the country's largest collection of experimental and standard military arms. Exhibits depict manufacturing processes and inventors and the women who worked there. The site was authorized in 1974 and established in 1978.

WHAT TO SEE & DO

Touring the museum and grounds, watching film and videos. **Facilities:** Museum with visitor information desk, auditorium, and interpretive exhibits; self-guided walking tour of grounds, wayside exhibits. Bookstore. **Programs & Events:** Exhibits on display year-round, ranger talks and blank firing demonstrations (Sat., 1:30 PM). National Park Week celebration (late Apr.), Military Encampment (June).

PLANNING YOUR VISIT

⚠ **Camping:** Available in Monson; none in park. 🏠 **Lodging:** Available in Springfield and surrounding towns; none in park. ✕ **Food & Supplies:** Available in Springfield and surrounding towns; none in park. ☞ **Tips & Hints:** Go in fall for foliage. Busiest June through August, least crowded in December and January. 🎫 **Fees, Permits & Limitations:**

Free. No firearms. Leashed pets only on grounds. Site open Wed.–Sun. 10–4:30. Closed Thanksgiving, Dec. 25, Jan. 1.

HOW TO GET THERE

On the Springfield Technical Community College campus, off Federal St. via the Broad St. exit of I–91. Closest airport: Bradley International (Windsor Locks, CT; 17 mi/27 km).

FOR MORE INFORMATION

Springfield Armory National Historic Site (1 Armory Sq., Springfield, MA 01105-1299, tel. 413/734–8551, fax 413/747–8062; e-mail SPAR_Interpretation@nps.gov; Web site www.nps.gov/spar). Greater Springfield Convention and Visitors Bureau (1500 Main St., Box 15589, Springfield, MA 01115, tel. 413/787–1548, fax 413/781–4607).

See Also

Appalachian National Scenic Trail, West Virginia. *Blackstone River Valley National Heritage Corridor,* Affiliated Areas in Other National Parklands. *Sudbury, Assabet and Concord,* Wild and Scenic Rivers System in Other National Parklands.

MICHIGAN

Isle Royale National Park

In Lake Superior

Isle Royale is an archipelago of more than 200 islands clustered around one large island that is 45 mi/72 km long and 9 mi/14 km wide. The forested wilderness island, the largest in Lake Superior, is home to moose, which may have swam here in the early 1900s, and wolves, which may have crossed a rare ice bridge from Canada in the late 1940s. The park was authorized in 1931 and designated a Biosphere Reserve in 1980.

WHAT TO SEE & DO

Backpacking, boat cruising, canoeing (rentals in park), diving, hiking, kayaking, powerboating (rentals in park), sailing. **Facilities:** 3 visitor centers with interpretive exhibits—Houghton, Rock Harbor, Windigo; Amygdaloid Ranger Station, Malone Bay Ranger Station, McCargoe Cove, Edisen Fishery, and Rock Harbor Lighthouse, trails, wayside exhibits, amphitheaters. Book and map sales areas, boat gas, fire pits, gift shops, laundry, picnic tables and shelters, religious services. **Programs & Events:** Evening programs (Rock Harbor and Windigo), interpretive program (twice weekly, Daisy Farm), guided walks and dockside talks (daily, Windigo), guided walks (daily, Rock Harbor), living-history fishing demonstration (four times weekly, Edisen Fishery): all available mid-June–Labor Day.

PLANNING YOUR VISIT

⚠ **Camping:** 36 campgrounds: no hookups (no reservations; permits required, *see below*). Rock Harbor Marina has electrical hookups and boat pump-out. Backcountry camping available (permit required, *see below*). Group campsites available (reservations required, tel. 906/487–7151; e-mail ISRO_GroupReserve@nps.gov, or write Group Camping, Isle Royale National Park, 800 E. Lakeshore Dr., Houghton, MI 49931). Private campgrounds available off-island in Copper Harbor and Houghton, MI, and Grand Portage, MN. 🛏 **Lodging:** In the park: Rock Harbor Lodge (tel. 906/337–4993 summer or 270/773–2191 winter). Lodging also available in Copper Harbor and Houghton, MI, and Grand Portage, MN. ✗ **Food & Supplies:** In the park: Rock Harbor Complex, Windigo Store. Food and supplies also available in Copper Harbor and Hancock and Houghton, MI, and Grand Portage, MN. ☞ **Tips & Hints:** Make arrangements well in advance. Come prepared for widely ranging weather. Weather is unpredictable but tends to be cool and wet April–early June and September–October. Go between June and August for flowers, September for migrating birds. Busiest in July and August, least crowded in May and October. 💲 **Fees, Permits & Limitations:** User fee: $4 per person per day, free under 11. Park access is summer only via ferry service, floatplane, or private boat. Private boats can access the island mid-Apr.–late Oct. Public transportation to island available mid-May–mid-Oct. Transportation is available from Grand Portage via the *Voyageur II* and *Wenonah* (tel. 715/392–2100); from Houghton, MI, via the *Ranger III* (tel. 906/482–0984 or e-mail ISRO_Ranger3Reserve @nps.gov for reservations); from Copper Harbor, MI, via the *Isle Royale Queen II* (tel. 906/289–4437). Seaplane service is available from Houghton (tel. 906/482–8850). Camping permits (free) required for all camping (available from Windigo and Rock Harbor visitor centers and *Ranger III* boat). Michigan state fishing license required when fishing in Lake Superior. Dive permits required (free) for all diving. No hunting, pets, bikes, motorized or mechanized equipment allowed. Wheelchairs allowed in developed areas only. Park open mid-Apr.–late Oct., daily. Houghton Visitor Center (off-island in Houghton, MI) open mid-June–end Aug., Mon.–Sat. 8–6; Sept.–mid-June, Mon.–Fri. 8–4:30. Rock Harbor Visitor Center open intermittently Apr.–May and Labor Day–Oct.; June–Labor Day, daily 8–8. Windigo Visitor Center open intermittently Apr.–May and Labor Day–Oct; June–Labor Day, daily 8–6.

HOW TO GET THERE

In Lake Superior, 22 mi/35 km east of Grand Portage, MN; 56 mi/90 km northwest of Copper Harbor, MI; and 73 mi/117 km north of Houghton, MI. Closest airport: Houghton/Hancock (10 mi/16 km).

FOR MORE INFORMATION

Headquarters, Isle Royale National Park (800 E. Lakeshore Dr., Houghton, MI 49931, tel. 906/ 482–0984, fax 906/482–8753; e-mail ISRO_ParkInfo@nps.gov; Web site www.nps.gov/isro).

Keweenaw National Historical Park

Upper Peninsula of Michigan, in Calumet

Copper mining, which has taken place on the Keweenaw Peninsula for 7,000 years, is commemorated in this park. Many of the processes developed here were fundamental to the success of mining in the United States. The park, which is under development, consists of 1,870 acres of private land in two units: Quincy, home of the world's largest steam hoist, and Calumet, home of one of the most productive copper mines in world history. There are no federal facilities at the park. The Keweenaw Tourism Council and cooperating sites provide information about the park. The park was established on October 27, 1992.

WHAT TO SEE & DO

Bicycling; cross-country skiing; hiking; mountain biking; snowmobiling; touring fort, mines, museums, and historic buildings. **Facilities:** No Park Service facilities. Keweenaw Tourism Council (Houghton, Calumet), scenic drives, trolley, hiking, ski and snowmobile trails, wayside exhibits, museum, self-guided brochures. **Programs & Events:** None by Park Service.

PLANNING YOUR VISIT

⚠ **Camping:** Cabin rentals at McLain and Porcupine Mountains Wilderness state parks. Reservations available for campgrounds at McLain, Porcupine, and Ft. Wilkins parks (tel. 800/447–2757). Backcountry camping available at Porcupine Mountains Wilderness State Park (permit required, *see below*). ⬚ **Lodging:** Available locally; none in park. ✕ **Food & Supplies:** Available locally; none in park. ☞ **Tips & Hints:** Go early in day during July and August to buy tickets for Quincy mine tour. Plan to spend three days to visit all cooperating sites. Expect summer high temperatures of 75°F/24°C. Go between late September and early October for fall foliage. Expect snow between Thanksgiving and Easter. Ride trackless trolley in Calumet unit and excursion boats in Keweenaw Waterway during summer. Busiest in July and August, least crowded in January and February. ▦ **Fees, Permits & Limitations:** Entrance fees to cooperating sites vary. Quincy mine and hoist tour: $12.50 per adult; $11.50 seniors; $7 children 6–12. Permit required for backcountry camping at Porcupine Mountains Wilderness State Park (tel. 906/885–5275). Daily or annual motor vehicle pass required for Ft. Wilkins, Porcupine Mountains Wilderness, and McLain state parks.

HOW TO GET THERE

The Quincy park unit is north of Hancock along U.S. 41. The Calumet unit is in the Calumet area, 8 mi/13 km farther north on U.S. 41. Directions to cooperating sites are available from the Keweenaw Tourism Council. Closest airport: Houghton County Memorial Airport (6 mi/10 km).

FOR MORE INFORMATION

Keweenaw National Historical Park (Box 471, Calumet, MI 49913, tel. 906/337–3168 or 800/338–7982; Web site www.nps.gov/kewe). Keweenaw Tourism Council, (Box 336, Houghton, MI 49931, tel. 800/ 338–7982 for general park information). Upper Peninsula Travel and Recreation Association (Box 400, Iron Mountain, MI 49801, tel. 800/ 562–7134).

Pictured Rocks
National Lakeshore

Upper Michigan, near Munising

This 73,236-acre park is 5 mi/8 km at its widest point and hugs the Superior shoreline for 40 mi/64 km. In the park are multicolored sandstone cliffs, beaches, sand dunes, waterfalls, inland lakes, wildlife, and northern hardwood forest. The lakeshore was authorized on October 15, 1966.

WHAT TO SEE & DO

Backpacking, boating, canoeing, cross-country skiing, fishing, ice fishing, kayaking, hiking, hunting, picnicking, snowmobiling, snowshoeing. **Facilities:** Visitor information center with interpretive exhibits—Pictured Rocks National Lakeshore (Hiawatha National Forest, 400 E. Munising Ave., junction of Hwy. M-28 and County Rd. H-58, Munising); Grand Sable Visitor Center with interpretive exhibits (E21090 County Rd. H-58, 1 mi/1.6 km west of Grand Marais); park headquarters (N8391 Sand Point Rd., Munising); Grand Marais Maritime Museum (Coast Guard Point, Grand Marais [E22030 Coast Guard Point Rd.]); Munising Falls Interpretive Center (1505 Sand Point Rd., Munising); Miners Castle Information Station (N9310 Miners Castle Rd., near Munising); self-guided nature trails; hiking trails; wayside and interpretive exhibits. Bookstores, picnic areas with tables and fire grills. **Programs & Events:** Guided day hikes and evening campfire programs (July–Labor Day), Au Sable Light Station tours (summer, daily). Artist-in-Residence public programs, and Fireside Chats interpretive programs (occasionally).

PLANNING YOUR VISIT

Camping: 3 campgrounds: no hookups (no reservations). Backcountry camping available (reservations available, permit required, *see below*). Group camping permitted in designated backcountry campgrounds. Private campgrounds available in Grand Marais and Munising. **Lodging:** Available in Grand Marais, Munising; none at lakeshore. **Food & Supplies:** Available in Grand Marais, Munising; none at lakeshore. **Tips & Hints:** Expect summer highs near 90°F/32°C with much cooler evenings and below-freezing temperatures in winter. Watch for Lake Superior storms year-round. Bring layered clothing and rain gear. Use caution when hiking cliff trails and while swimming, wading, or boating. Bring insect repellent in late spring or early summer when black flies and mosquitoes are out in force. Much of the main access road (H-58) is unpaved and uneven in sections. Busiest in July and August, least crowded in November and April. **Fees, Permits & Limitations:** Free. Backcountry permit ($15 for regular sites [1–6 people], $30 for group sites [7–20 people]) required for all backcountry camping. Reservations not accepted by phone; fax or write for reservations (Box 40, Munising, MI 49862-0040, fax 906/387–4457). Michigan state hunting and fishing license required. Private boat tours of park operate daily (late May–mid-Oct., tel. 906/387–2379) from Munising. Altran offers backpacker shuttle service (reservation required, tel. 906/387–4845) in summer. Only pedestrian and boat traffic permitted in backcountry. No motorized or wheeled vehicles, pets, or domestic pack animals. Leashed pets only in day-use areas and drive-in campgrounds. No hunting Apr. to Labor Day. No hunting in visitor-use areas. Park open daily. Visitor information center in Munising open mid-May–early June, daily 9–5; early-June–Labor Day, daily 8–6; Labor Day–mid-Oct., daily 9–5; mid-Oct.–mid-May, Mon.–Sat. 9–4:30. Grand Sable Visitor Center open July 1–Labor Day, daily. Miners Castle Information Station open Memorial Day–Labor Day, daily 9:30–5. Park headquarters open weekdays 8–4:30. Visitor information centers and park headquarters closed Thanksgiving, Dec. 25, Jan. 1, and some federal holidays.

HOW TO GET THERE

On the south shore of Lake Superior in Michigan's Upper Peninsula. Access is via County Rd. H-58 between Munising and Grand Marais.

Munising is on Hwy. M-28 and Grand Marais is on Hwy. M-77. Closest airports: Marquette (55 mi/88 km), Escanaba (65 mi/104 km).

FOR MORE INFORMATION

Pictured Rocks National Lakeshore (Box 40, N8391 Sand Point Rd., Munising, MI 49862-0040, tel. 906/387–3700 information or 906/387–2607 headquarters; e-mail piro_information@nps.gov; Web site www.nps.gov/piro). Alger Chamber of Commerce (Box 405, Munising, MI 49862, tel. 906/387–2138). Grand Marais Chamber of Commerce (Box 139, Grand Marais, MI 49839, tel. 906/494–2447).

Sleeping Bear Dunes National Lakeshore

Northwest lower Michigan, near Empire

The lakeshore protects 35 mi/56 km of Lake Michigan's coastline, which includes massive coastal sand dunes, 460-ft/140-m bluffs, beech-maple forests, clear lakes, quiet rivers, and two offshore wilderness islands. The park was authorized in 1970 and established in 1977.

WHAT TO SEE & DO

Apple and mushroom picking, auto touring, biking (rentals, Empire), bird-watching, canoeing (rentals in and near park), cross-country skiing (rentals, Traverse City), dune climbing, fishing, hang gliding (permit required, *see below*), hunting, picnicking, powered-model flying, scuba diving (rentals, Traverse City), snowshoeing (rentals, Traverse City), swimming, touring museum, tubing (rentals in and near park), walking beaches. **Facilities:** 2 visitor centers with interpretive exhibits—Empire, South Manitou Island; Maritime Museum (Glen Haven), Glen Haven Cannery, Boat Museum, scenic drive, wayside exhibits, hiking trails, amphitheaters. Picnic tables, shelters, and grills. **Programs & Events:** Guided walks (late June–Labor Day, usually twice daily), campfire programs (late June–Labor Day), snowshoe hikes. Coast Guard Day and cannon firing (Maritime Museum, Aug. 4).

PLANNING YOUR VISIT

⚠ **Camping:** 6 campgrounds: 1 with electrical hookups, 3 on islands (reservations accepted at Platte River, tel. 616/326–5134 or 800/365–2267). Backcountry camping available (permit required, *see below*). Group campsites at Platte River and D.H. Day (reservations available for both, tel. 616/326–5134 or 800/365–2267). State and private campgrounds available nearby. ⌂ **Lodging:** Available in Empire, Frankfort, Glen Arbor, Honor, Leland, Traverse City; none at lakeshore. ✕ **Food & Supplies:** Food and supplies available in Empire, Glen Arbor, and surrounding towns; none in park. ☞ **Tips & Hints:** Go in spring and fall for bird migrations, in spring for wildflowers and morel mushrooms, mid-October for fall colors. Watch for rapid weather changes on lake. Busiest in July and August, least crowded in December and January. ▧ **Fees, Permits & Limitations:** Park pass: $7 per car. Backcountry permits required ($5 per night) for all backcountry camping. Permit required for hang gliding and powered-model flying. Michigan state fishing and hunting licenses required. Stay on established trails, especially on dunes. No pets on Dune Climb, islands, swim beaches, or ski trails. Leashed pets elsewhere. No boat motors on most inland lakes. No glass on beaches. Some camping open year-round. Campgrounds and scenic drive open warm weather only. Park open daily. Empire visitor center open Memorial Day–Labor Day, daily 9–6; Labor Day–Memorial Day, daily 9–4. Closed on off-season holidays. Scenic drive open mid-Apr.–mid-Nov. Maritime Museum buildings open Memorial Day–Labor Day but grounds always open. Manitou Islands ferry runs from Leland May–Oct.

HOW TO GET THERE

Lakeshore headquarters is in Empire, 22 mi/35 km north of Frankfort via M-22 and 22 mi/35 km west of Traverse City via M-72. Closest airport: Traverse City.

FOR MORE INFORMATION

Sleeping Bear Dunes National Lakeshore (9922 Front St., Empire, MI 49630, tel. 231/326–5134, fax 231/326–5382; e-mail slbe@nps.gov; Web site www.nps.gov/slbe). Benzie County Chamber of Commerce (Box 204, Benzonia, MI 49616, tel. 231/882–5801, fax 231/882–9249). Glen Lake Chamber of Commerce (Box 217, Glen Harbor MI 49636, tel. 616/334–3238). Traverse City Area Chamber of Commerce (Box 387, Traverse City, MI 49685-0387, tel. 231/947–5075, fax 231/946–2565). Leelanau County Chamber of Commerce (Box 336, Lake Leelanau, MI 49653, tel. 231/256–9895, fax 231/256–2559).

See Also

Automobile National Heritage Area, National Heritage Areas in Other National Parklands. *North Country National Scenic Trail,* National Trails System in Other National Parklands.

MINNESOTA

Grand Portage National Monument

Near Grand Portage

The reconstructed stockade area appears as it did in the 1790s, when it was the North West Company's fur-trading headquarters on Lake Superior's western shore. The 8.5-mi/14-km portage was a vital link on one of the principal routes for Native Americans, explorers, missionaries, and fur trappers heading for the northwest. The site was designated a national historic site in 1951 and became a national monument in 1958.

WHAT TO SEE & DO

Hiking, picnicking, snowshoeing, touring post. **Facilities:** Reconstructed fur-trade post with interpretive exhibits, trails. Bookstore, dock, picnic area. **Programs & Events:** Interpretive talks, living-history demonstrations, cultural demonstrations (late May–mid-Oct.), daily boat service to Isle Royale National Park (June–Sept.). Grand Portage Rendezvous and Grand Portage Pow Wow (both 2nd weekend, Aug.).

PLANNING YOUR VISIT

Camping: Backcountry and group backcountry camping only (permit required, *see below*). Private campground available at Grand Portage Marina. **Lodging:** Available in Grand Marais, Grand Portage, and along North Shore; none in park. **Food & Supplies:** Available in Grand Marais, Grand Portage; none in park. **Tips & Hints:** Best time to visit: mid-June–mid-September. Busiest in July and August, least crowded in January and February. **Fees, Permits & Limitations:** Entrance fee: $3 per adult age 16 and over or $6 per family. Parking fee: $3.50 to leave car while taking Isle Royale boats. Backcountry permits required for all backcountry camping (free, Grand Portage ranger station, trailheads). No hunting. No motorized vehicles or bikes on trail. Leashed pets only on trail. No pets in buildings or within stockade. Park open mid-May–mid-Oct., daily 9–5.

HOW TO GET THERE

36 mi/58 km northeast of Grand Marais, off MN 61. Closest airports: Thunder Bay, Canada (45 mi/72 km); Duluth, MN (156 mi/250 km).

FOR MORE INFORMATION

Grand Portage National Monument (Box 668, Grand Marais, MN 55604, tel. 218/387–2788, fax 218/387–2790; e-mail GRPO_Superintendent@nps.gov; Web site www.nps.gov/grpo). Grand Marais Chamber of Commerce (Box 1048, Grand Marais, MN 55604, tel. 218/387–2524).

Mississippi National River and Recreation Area

In the southeast part of the state, from Anoka to Hastings

Museums, cultural centers, and natural and historical attractions along 72 mi/115 km of the Mississippi River corridor represent the dynamic history of the 2,500-mi/4,000-km river. Twenty-five communities are along this stretch of the river, each unique in its river attractions, ranging from quiet parks in rural areas to metropolitan riverfronts bustling with commerce. The area was established on November 18, 1988.

WHAT TO SEE & DO

Biking, boating, boat touring, canoeing, cross-country skiing, fishing, guided and self-guided tours, hiking, picnicking, swimming. **Facilities:** Park headquarters (St. Paul). **Programs & Events:** Numerous interpretive talks, museums and interpretive centers, stewardship programs, and special events, including "Stories of the Mississippi".

PLANNING YOUR VISIT

⚠ **Camping:** Available in the greater Minneapolis/St. Paul metro area. ⛺ **Lodging:** Available in the greater Minneapolis/St. Paul metro area. ✕ **Food & Supplies:** Available throughout the area. ☞ **Tips & Hints:** Go between late April and November for open water on the river. 🎫 **Fees, Permits & Limitations:** Free. Fees to enter some of the parks in the corridor. Minnesota fishing and watercraft license required. Area has no hours. Visitor center hours vary by site. Park headquarters open weekdays 8–4:30

HOW TO GET THERE

The area encompasses 54,000 acres alsong 72 mi/115 km of the Mississippi River, from Dayton and Ramsey, through the Minneapolis/St. Paul metro region, to south of Hastings. Closest airport: Minneapolis/St. Paul.

FOR MORE INFORMATION

Mississippi National River and Recreation Area (111 E. Kellogg Blvd., St. Paul, MN 55101-1256, tel. 651/290–4160, fax 651/290–3214; Web site www.nps.gov/miss). Minnesota Office of Tourism (100 Metro Sq., 121 7th Pl. E, St. Paul, MN, 55101, tel. 651/296–5029 or 800/657–3700).

Pipestone National Monument

In the southwest part of the state, near Pipestone

The 282-acre site preserves the noted Pipestone Quarries in their prairie setting. Native Americans obtained stone from these quarries for centuries to make pipes for ceremonial and social uses. About 160 acres of the area are bluestem prairie, an important remnant of the once-abundant prairies typical of the plains. The monument was established in 1937.

WHAT TO SEE & DO

Buying Native American crafts, hiking through prairie and quarries, picnicking, touring museum, watching pipe-making and crafts demonstrations. **Facilities:** Visitor center, cultural center, museum, trail, wayside exhibits. Native American crafts sales area, picnic area with tables and grills. **Programs & Events:** Cultural demonstrations of pipe-making and other crafts (Apr.–Oct.), ranger-guided trail walks (June–Aug.), videotape shows of craftwork and quarrying (Nov.–Mar.). Founders Day (Aug. 25).

PLANNING YOUR VISIT

⚠ **Camping:** Available in Pipestone and Slayton, MN, and Sioux Falls, SD; none at monument. ⛺ **Lodging:** Available in Luverne, Marshall, Pipestone, MN, and Brookings, Sioux Falls, SD; none at monument. ✕ **Food & Supplies:** Available in Jasper, Luverne, Marshall, Pipestone, MN, and Brookings, Sioux Falls, SD; none at monument. ☞ **Tips & Hints:** Busiest in July and August, least crowded in December and January. ▨ **Fees, Permits & Limitations:** Entrance fee: $2 per person or $4 per family. No hunting or fishing. Leashed pets on trail. No bikes, skateboards, or in-line skates on trail. Park is open daily. Trail open daily dawn–dusk. Visitor center open Labor Day–Memorial Day, daily 8–5; Memorial Day–Labor Day, Mon.–Thurs. 8–6, Fri.–Sun., 8–8. Closed Dec. 25, Jan. 1.

HOW TO GET THERE

The monument is just north of Pipestone. Follow signs from U.S. 75 or MN 23 or 30. Closest airport: Sioux Falls, SD (45 mi/72 km).

FOR MORE INFORMATION

Pipestone National Monument (36 Reservation Ave., Pipestone, MN 56164, tel. 507/825–5464, fax 507/825–5466; e-mail PIPE_Superintendent@nps.gov; Web site www.nps.gov/pipe). Pipestone Area Chamber of Commerce (Box 8, Pipestone, MN 56164, tel. 507/825–3316, 800/336–6125, fax 507/825–3317; e-mail pipecham@rconnect.com; Web site www.pipestone.mn.us).

Voyageurs National Park

In the northeast part of the state,
near International Falls

Water dominates the landscape of the park, which has more than 30 glacier-carved lakes. Lakes Rainy, Kabetogama, Namakan, and Sand Point offer boating, canoeing, kayaking, and sailing opportunities on more than 40% of this 218,000-acre park. Watch for bears and eagles, listen for loons and wolves, and smell the pines and wildflowers in a place preserved for its scenery and solitude. French Canadians traveled these waters in birch-bark canoes, creating the "voyageurs' highway" from the Great Lakes into the interior of northwestern North America. The park was authorized in 1971 and established in 1975.

WHAT TO SEE & DO

Canoeing, cross-country skiing, fishing, hiking, kayaking, motorboating, picnicking, sailing, snowmobiling. **Facilities:** 3 visitor centers with interpretive exhibits—Rainy Lake (11 mi/18 km east of International Falls), Kabetogama Lake, Ash River; Crane Lake ranger station, launch ramps, trails, beaches, interpretive display boards. Book and map sales areas, picnic areas with grills and tables. **Programs & Events:** Ranger-led walks, canoe trips, boat tours (mid-June–Labor Day, daily), Winter Wild Activities (Dec.–Mar.), Ice Box Days (International Falls, 3rd week in Jan.), Spring Birders' Rendezvous (Rainy Lake visitor center, Memorial Day weekend), Lady Slipper Festival (Kabetogama Lake visitor center, June), Autumn Celebration (Ash River visitor center, Labor Day weekend).

PLANNING YOUR VISIT

⚠ **Camping:** 220 sites (accessible by water only) scattered throughout the park for tent campers or houseboats (no reservations). Backcountry camping available. No group camping. Private campgrounds available in Ash River, Crane Lake, International Falls, and Kabetogama. ⊞ **Lodging:** In the park: Kettle Falls Hotel (tel. 888/534–6835). Lodging also available in Ash River, Crane Lake, International Falls, Kabetogama, and Orr. ✕ **Food & Supplies:** In the park: meals at Kettle Falls Hotel (tel. 888/534–6835). Food and supplies also available in International Falls and Orr. ☞ **Tips & Hints:** Visitor centers and tour boats accessible by vehicle. Primary access to the park, campsites, and the concession-run hotel/restaurant is by watercraft in the summer and snowmobile in the winter. Go in January or February for snowmobiling, year-round for fishing, in June for spring flowers, from June to September for eagles, and in mid-September for fall color. Busiest in July and August, least crowded in November and April. ▣ **Fees, Permits & Limitations:** Free. Concession tour boat fees: $12–$30 per adult, $8–$20 per child (reservations required, tel. 218/875–2111) for boat use on interior lakes. No personal watercraft use. Minnesota state fishing license required. No hunting or trapping. No mountain bikes, OHV, or ATV. No chain saws or guns. Leashed pets in front country only. No pets on trails. No snowmobiles off main lakes and designated safety portages. Park open daily. Main part of park not accessible mid-Nov.–Dec. because of thin ice, Apr.–early May because of thaws. Visitor center hours: Rainy Lake—mid-May–Sept., daily 9–5; Oct.–mid-May, Wed.–Sun. 9–4; Kabetogama Lake and Ash River—mid-May–Sept. daily 9–5.

HOW TO GET THERE

11 mi/18 km east of International Falls off Hwy. 53, 160 mi/256 km north of Duluth, and 300 mi/480 km north of Minneapolis via I–35 and U.S. 53. Closest airport: International Falls (15 mi/24 km).

FOR MORE INFORMATION

Voyageurs National Park (3131 Hwy. 53, International Falls, MN 56649, tel. 218/283–9821, fax 218/285–7407; Web site www.nps.gov/voya). International Falls Chamber of Commerce (International Falls, MN 56649, tel. 218/283–9400, fax 218/283–3572). Getaways Accommodations (tel. 888/749–5324).

See Also

North Country National Scenic Trail, National Trails System in Other National Parklands. *Saint Croix National Scenic Riverway,* Wisconsin.

MISSISSIPPI

Brices Cross Roads
National Battlefield Site

In the northeast part of the state, near Baldwyn

The 1-acre site commemorates a battle initiated by Union forces on June 10, 1864, to keep General Nathan Bedford Forrest's Confederate troops from disrupting General William Tecumseh Sherman's supply route. The site was established in 1929 and transferred to the Park Service in 1933.

WHAT TO SEE & DO

Reading interpretive granite markers, viewing battlefield. **Facilities:** Granite markers, view of battlefield, folder.

PLANNING YOUR VISIT

⛺ **Camping:** Available in Baldwyn, Booneville, Tupelo; none at site. 🏨 **Lodging:** Available in Baldwyn, Booneville, Tupelo; none at site. ✕ **Food & Supplies:** Available in Baldwyn, Booneville, Tupelo; none at site. ☞ **Tips & Hints:** Get battlefield folder at site or from Natchez Trace Parkway Visitor Center. Busiest in October and April, least crowded in December and January. 🎫 **Fees, Permits & Limitations:** Free.

HOW TO GET THERE

6 mi/10 km west of Baldwyn on MS 370. Closest airports: Memphis, Tupelo (25 mi/40 km).

FOR MORE INFORMATION

Superintendent, Natchez Trace Parkway (2680 Natchez Trace Pkwy., Tupelo, MS 38804, tel. 662/680–4025; Web site www.nps.gov/brcr).

Natchez National
Historical Park

In the southwest part of the state, in Natchez

Natchez has one of the largest numbers of significant antebellum properties in the United States. The park celebrates the city's history and role in the settlement of the old Southwest, the Cotton Kingdom, and the Antebellum South. The park has three units: Fort Rosalie is the location of an 18th-century fortification built by the French and occupied by the British, Spanish, and Americans; the William Johnson House was a house owned by William Johnson, a free black man, whose diary tells the story of everyday life in antebellum Natchez; Melrose was the estate of John T. McMurran, who rose from being a middle-class lawyer to a position of wealth and power in antebellum Natchez.

Melrose is the only unit currently open to the public. The park was authorized on October 7, 1988.

WHAT TO SEE & DO

Touring Melrose estate, if open. **Facilities:** Visitor information center (Melrose), Melrose estate, slavery exhibit, trails. Bookstore. **Programs & Events:** Guided tours of Melrose (year-round, hourly 9–4). Seasonal activities available. Spring and Fall Pilgrimages (Mar., Oct.), Natchez Literary Celebration (1st week, June), Christmas programs (2nd weekend in Dec.).

PLANNING YOUR VISIT

Camping: Available in Natchez; none in park. **Lodging:** Available in Natchez; none in park. **Food & Supplies:** Available in Natchez; none in park. **Tips & Hints:** Plan to spend about two hours touring Melrose, grounds, and outbuildings. Busiest in April and October, least crowded in January and February. **Fees, Permits & Limitations:** Melrose tour fee: $6 per adult, $3 per senior over 62; $3 per child 6–17; free under 6. No flash photography in mansion. Park open daily 8:30–5.

HOW TO GET THERE

From I–10 at Baton Rouge, take U.S. 61N to Natchez. From I–20 at Vicksburg, take U.S. 61S to Natchez. From I–20 at Jackson, follow the Natchez Trace Pkwy. to U.S. 61 to Natchez. To reach Melrose from U.S. 61, take Melrose Montebello Pkwy. Melrose is 0.5 mi/0.8 km on the right. Closest airport: Baton Rouge, LA (70 mi/112 km).

FOR MORE INFORMATION

Superintendent, Natchez National Historical Park (640 S. Canal St., Box E, Natchez, MS 39120, tel.601/442–7047 headquarters or 601/446–5790 Melrose; Web site www.nps.gov/natc). Natchez Convention and Visitors Bureau (640 S. Canal St., Box C, Natchez, MS 39120, tel. 601/446–6345).

Natchez Trace National Scenic Trail

From southwest Mississippi, in Natchez,
through northwest Alabama to north-central
Tennessee, in Nashville

Four segments of the proposed 694-mi/1,110-km trail have been constructed within the boundaries of the Natchez Trace Parkway (*see separate listing*), a 443-mi/709-km highway that commemorates the historic Natchez Trace. A 20-mi/32-km segment in Tennessee is south of Franklin, near the community of Leipers Fork. In Mississippi, a 6-mi/10-km segment near Tupelo, a 21-mi/34-km segment in Ridgeland near Jackson, and a 10-mi/16-km segment at the Rocky Springs camping area near Port Gibson, MS, are open to the public. The trail was established on March 28, 1983.

WHAT TO SEE & DO

Hiking, horseback riding. **Facilities:** Visitor center in Tupelo. Horse staging area at Hwy. 50, near Leipers Fork.

PLANNING YOUR VISIT

⚫ **Camping:** Campground at Rocky Springs. ⚫ **Lodging:** Available in surrounding communities. ✕ **Food & Supplies:** Available in surrounding communities. ⚫ **Fees, Permits & Limitations:** Free.

HOW TO GET THERE

The four trail segments are south of Franklin, TN, near Leipers Fork; and near Tupelo, Jackson, and Port Gibson, MS. Closest airports: Nashville, TN; Jackson, MS.

FOR MORE INFORMATION

Natchez Trace National Scenic Trail (c/o Natchez Trace Pkwy., 2680 Natchez Trace Pkwy., Tupelo, MS 38804, tel. 662/680–4025 or 800/305–7417, fax 662/680–4034; e-mail NATR_Interpretation@nps.gov; Web site www.nps.gov/natt). Natchez Trace Trail Conference (Box 1236, Jackson, MS 39215-1236, tel. 662/680-4016). Jackson Visitors Bureau (921 N. President St., Box 1450, Jackson, MS 39215-1450, tel. 800/354–7695). Tupelo Convention and Visitors Bureau (399 E. Main St., Tupelo, MS 38801, tel. 601/841–6521). Mississippi Tourism (tel. 800/927–6378). Tennessee Dept. of Tourism (320 6th Ave. N, Rachel Jackson Bldg., 5th floor, Nashville, TN 37243, tel. 615/741–2159). Williamson County Chamber of Commerce (Box 156, Franklin TN 37065-0156, or City Hall Bldg., 109 2nd Ave. S, Suite 137, Franklin, TN 37064, tel. 800/356–3445). Nashville Area Chamber of Commerce (211 Commerce St., Suite 100, Nashville, TN 37201, tel. 615/259-4700).

Natchez Trace Parkway

From southwest Mississippi, in Natchez,
to central Tennessee, in Nashville, through the
northwest corner of Alabama

The 443-mi/709-km parkway commemorates the historic Natchez Trace, a series of trails used by Natchez, Choctaw, Chickasaw, Creek, and Cherokee peoples. The Trace later served European explorers, boatmen, settlers, soldiers, outlaws, itinerant preachers, and missionaries as a trade and transportation route, helping to form the old Southwest. The unit was established as a parkway on May 18, 1938.

WHAT TO SEE & DO

Bicycling, driving, fishing, hiking, horseback riding. **Facilities:** Visitor center at Milepost 266 in Tupelo; interpreters staff Mount Locust (MP 15.5), the only remaining historic inn, open Feb.–Nov.; park personnel at Colbert Ferry (MP 327.3) Apr.–Nov.; non–Park Service information centers at Mississippi Crafts Center (MP 102.4) and Kosciusko Information Center (MP 160). Book sales outlet (visitor center, Mount Locust and Colbert Ferry seasonally), gas station/store at Jeff Busby (MP 193.1). **Programs & Events:** 12-minute film highlighting history and sites along the parkway (visitor center, upon request). Ranger-guided tours of Mount Locust (Feb.–Nov., daily); crafts demonstrations (May–Oct., weekends; Mississippi Crafts Center, tel. 662/856–7546). Meriwether Lewis Crafts Fair at the Meriwether Lewis Site, MP 385.9 (2nd weekend, Oct.); Pioneer and Indian Crafts Fair at Mississippi Crafts Center (Oct.).

PLANNING YOUR VISIT

⚠ **Camping:** 3 campgrounds at Meriwether Lewis (MP 385.9), Jeff Busby (MP 193.1), and Rocky Springs (MP 54.8). Rest rooms, no hookups, no dump stations, no showers. (No reservations.) Group camping available (reservations required, tel. 800/305–7417). Federal, state, and private campgrounds available along length of parkway. ▣ **Lodging:** Available in Columbia, Franklin, and Nashville, TN; Florence, AL; Jackson, Kosciusko, Natchez, and Tupelo, MS. ✕ **Food & Supplies:** Camp store at Jeff Busby (MP 193.1). Food and supplies available in adjacent communities; none in park. ☞ **Tips & Hints:** Get a map and guide to parkway. Go in March and April for wildflowers, October for fall colors. Busiest in April and October, least crowded in December and January. ▥ **Fees, Permits & Limitations:** Free. Mississippi, Alabama, or Tennessee state fishing license required. No hunting. Leashed pets only. No bicycling or motorized vehicles on trails. Speed limit is 50 miles per hour unless otherwise posted. No commercial vehicles. The parkway is open daily. The last 15 mi/24 km on north end closes during inclement weather. Visitor center open daily 8–5. Closed Dec. 25.

HOW TO GET THERE

Multiple towns are nearby. Memphis, TN, is two hours from Tupelo, MS, site of the visitor center and park headquarters. Closest airports: Nashville, TN (14 mi/22 km); Jackson, MS (96 mi/154 km).

FOR MORE INFORMATION

Natchez Trace Parkway (2680 Natchez Trace Pkwy., Tupelo, MS 38804, tel. 800/305–7417, fax 662/680–4034; e-mail NATR_Interpretation@ nps.gov; Web site www.nps.gov/natr). Natchez Tourism (640 S. Canal St., Natchez, MS 39120, tel. 800/647–6724). Vicksburg Convention Bureau (1221 Washington St., Vicksburg, MS 39181-0110, tel. 800/221–3536). Jackson Visitors Bureau (Box 1450, Jackson, MS 39215-1450, tel. 800/354–7695). Kosciusko Chamber of Commerce (Box 696, Kosciusko, MS 39090, tel. 662/289–2981). Tupelo Convention and Visitors Bureau (399 E. Main, Tupelo, MS 38801, tel. 601/841–6521). Mississippi Division of Tourism (Box 1705, Ocean Springs, MS 39566-1705, tel. 800/927–6378). The Shoals Chamber of Commerce (Box 1331, Florence, AL 35631, tel. 205/764–4661). Tennessee Department of Tourism (320 6th Ave. N, Rachel Jackson Bldg., 5th floor, Nashville, TN 37243, tel. 615/741–2159). Williamson County Chamber of Commerce (Box 156, Franklin, TN 37065-0156, tel. 800/356–3445). Nashville Area Convention and Visitors Bureau (211 Commerce St., Nashville, TN 37201, tel. 615/259–4700).

Tupelo National Battlefield

In the northeast part of the state, in Tupelo

The Battle of Tupelo, which was a part of a larger strategy by General William Tecumseh Sherman to protect his railroad supply line, occurred on July 13 and 14, 1864, when Federal troops under General A. J. Smith battled Confederates under General Nathan Bedford Forrest. Both sides also battled the heat that ultimately forced the Federal retreat. The 1-acre Tupelo National Battlefield Site was established in 1929, transferred to the Park Service in 1933, and redesignated in 1961.

WHAT TO SEE & DO

Visiting site and monument. **Facilities:** Monument, cannons, interpretive placards, brochure.

PLANNING YOUR VISIT

⚠ **Camping:** Available in Tupelo area; none at battlefield. ⊞ **Lodging:** Available in Tupelo area; none at battlefield. ✕ **Food & Supplies:** Available in Tupelo area; none at battlefield. ☞ **Tips & Hints:** Busiest in April and October, least crowded in December and January. ▦ **Fees, Permits & Limitations:** Free.

HOW TO GET THERE

The site is inside Tupelo city limits, on MS 6, about 1.3 mi/2 km west of its intersection with U.S. 45 and 1 mi/1.6 km east of the Natchez Trace Pkwy. Closest airports: Tupelo Municipal; Memphis (TN) International (100 mi/160 km).

FOR MORE INFORMATION

Tupelo National Battlefield (c/o Natchez Trace Parkway, 2680 Natchez Trace Pkwy., Tupelo, MS 38804, tel. 601/680–4025 or 800/305–7417; Web site www.nps.gov/tupe). Tupelo Convention and Visitors Bureau (399 E. Main, Tupelo, MS 38801, tel. 601/841–6521).

Vicksburg National Military Park

In the western part of the state, in Vicksburg

A key battle of the Civil War, the campaign, siege, and defense of Vicksburg from March 29 to July 4, 1863, is commemorated at this park. Sights in the park include more than 1,300 monuments and markers, reconstructed trenches and earthworks, one antebellum structure, more than 125 emplaced cannons, a restored Union gunboat (USS *Cairo*), and the Vicksburg National Cemetery. The Vicksburg campaign included battles at Port Gibson, Raymond, Jackson, Champion Hill, and Big Black River as well as the 47-day Union siege against the city of Vicksburg. Located high on the bluffs, Vicksburg was known as "The Gibraltar of the Confederacy" and guarded the Mississippi River. With the surrender at Vicksburg, the Union regained control of the lower

Mississippi River and split the Confederacy in two. The park was established in 1899 and transferred to the Park Service in 1933.

WHAT TO SEE & DO

Auto touring, bird-watching, hiking, touring museum and cemetery, viewing restored Union gunboat, walking. **Facilities:** Visitor center with interpretive exhibits (3201 Clay St.), USS *Cairo* Museum and Gunboat (Milepost 7.9, Vicksburg National Military Park), historic monuments, markers, and plaques. Bookstore, picnic tables. **Programs & Events:** Guided battlefield tours (upon request, reservations suggested), self-guided driving tours (audio tapes for sale). Ranger talks, black powder demonstration, living-history program (mid-June–mid-Aug.).

PLANNING YOUR VISIT

Camping: Available in Vicksburg area; none in park. **Lodging:** Available in Vicksburg area; none in park. **Food & Supplies:** Available in Vicksburg area; none in park. **Tips & Hints:** Wear comfortable sportswear and walking or hiking shoes. The best months to visit are March–May. Busiest in April and May, least crowded in November and December. **Fees, Permits & Limitations:** Entrance fee: $4 per vehicle. Guided battlefield tour fee: $25 per car, $35 per van, $50 per bus (reservations suggested, tel. 601/636–3827). No hunting. No metal detectors. No fires or cooking. Park is open daily and closes at dusk. Visitor center open daily 8–5. Closed Dec. 25. Cairo Museum open Nov.–Mar., daily 8:30–5; Apr.–Oct., daily, 9:30–6.

HOW TO GET THERE

The Clay St. visitor center can be reached from I–20/U.S. 61 via Exit 4B. Take Clay St. (U.S. 80) west for .25 mi/0.4 km to park entrance. Closest airport: Jackson (50 mi/80 km).

FOR MORE INFORMATION

Vicksburg National Military Park (3201 Clay St., Vicksburg, MS 39183, tel. 601/636–0583; Web site www.nps.gov/vick). Vicksburg Convention and Visitors Bureau (Box 110, Vicksburg, MS 39181, tel. 601/636–9421).

See Also

Gulf Islands National Seashore, Florida.

MISSOURI

George Washington Carver National Monument

In the southwest part of the state, near Diamond

The monument preserves the birthplace of George Washington Carver (1864–1943), who ascended from slavery to national prominence as a scientist, educator, and humanitarian. The monument was authorized in 1943 and established in 1953.

WHAT TO SEE & DO

Hiking, picnicking, touring 1881 home and cemetery, watching film. **Facilities:** Visitor center with interpretive exhibits, hands-on discovery center, trail, wayside exhibits. Book and gift sales area, picnic area, multipurpose training and classroom facility. **Programs & Events:** Ranger-guided tours; interpretive, living-history, cultural, and nature programs; Junior Ranger program; educational field trips. Black Heritage Month and 4th-grade Art & Essay Contest (Feb.), March for Parks (Apr.), Junior Ranger program (June–July), Carver Day Celebration (July); Prairie Day Program (Sept.); Holiday Open House (Dec.).

PLANNING YOUR VISIT

Camping: Available in Carthage; none at monument. **Lodging:** Available in Carthage, Joplin, Neosho; none at monument. **Food & Supplies:** Available in Carthage, Diamond, Joplin, Neosho; none at monument. **Tips & Hints:** Busiest in May and July, least crowded in December and January. **Fees, Permits & Limitations:** Free. No hunting or fishing. No motorized or mechanized equipment on trails. Leashed pets only. Monument and visitor center open daily 9–5. Closed Thanksgiving, Dec. 25, Jan. 1.

HOW TO GET THERE

Take Exit 11A off I–44 to U.S. 71. Take the Diamond exit 4 mi/6 km east and travel .5 m/.8 km south. Closest airport: Joplin (15 mi/24 km).

FOR MORE INFORMATION

George Washington Carver National Monument (5646 Carver Rd., Diamond, MO 64840, tel. 417/325–4151, fax 417/325–4231; e-mail gwca_interpretation@nps.gov; Web site www.nps.gov/gwca). Joplin Convention and Visitors Bureau (Box 1384, Joplin, MO 64802-1384, tel. 417/625–4789 or 800/657–2534). Carthage Chamber of Commerce (107 E. 3rd, Carthage, MO 64836, tel. 417/358–2373, fax 417/358–7479). Neosho Chamber of Commerce (Box 605, Neosho, MO 64850, tel. 417/451–1925, fax 417/451–8097).

Harry S Truman National Historic Site

*In the west-central part of the state,
near Independence*

A remarkably complete collection of structures and objects associated
with the life of Harry S Truman, 33rd president of the United States, is
preserved here. The park consists of five properties and associated
structures: the Truman Home (219 N. Delaware St.); Frank Wallace
House (601 W. Truman Rd.); George Wallace House (605 W. Truman
Rd.); Noland House (216 N. Delaware St.); and Truman Farm (Grandview, .5 mi/.8 km west of Hwy. 71 on Blue Ridge Blvd.). Truman lived
on the farm for 11 years before moving to the 219 North Delaware
house in 1919 after his marriage to Bess Wallace, whose family lived
there. He returned to the Delaware Street home after his term ended
in 1953. The Trumans lived there until his death in 1972 and her death
in 1982. The 219 North Delaware Street site was authorized in 1983.
The other three homes and the farm were acquired in 1991 and 1994.

WHAT TO SEE & DO

Touring the Truman home and farm and surrounding Harry S Truman
Historic District National Historic Landmark, watching slide program.
Facilities: Visitor center with interpretive exhibits (223 N. Main St., Independence), homes, farm, wayside display. Bookstore. **Programs &
Events:** Guided tours of the Truman home at 219 N. Delaware St. (tickets required, *see below*). Self-guided tours of Truman Farm grounds
(daily dawn–dusk). Landmark district walking tours (Memorial Day–
Labor Day, most days at 10, 2), Farm Home tours every half hour (tickets required, *see below*).

PLANNING YOUR VISIT

Camping: Available in Independence and Kansas City; none at site.
Lodging: Available locally in Grandview, Independence, and Kansas City;
none at site. **Food & Supplies:** Available locally in Grandview, Independence, and Kansas City; none at site. **Tips & Hints:** Arrive early to
get tickets for Truman Home tour (*see below*). Go in January and February to avoid crowds. Busiest in June and July, least crowded in January
and February. **Fees, Permits & Limitations:** Entrance fee at press time:
$2 per person above 16 for Truman Home tour, under 16 free but tickets
are required (tours every 15 mins Memorial Day–Labor Day, daily 9–
4:45; Labor Day–Memorial Day, Tues.–Sun.) Tour size limited to eight
people. Tickets issued on first-come, first-served basis at visitor center
(223 N. Main St., five blocks east of Truman Home). Tickets go on sale
for same-day tours at 8:30. No advance reservations. Truman Farm
Home tour (9:30–4 beginning May 8 and then every Fri.–Sun. until the
Sun. before Labor Day weekend) in Grandview is free. Tour size limited
to six people. All persons (including children) must have a ticket. Tickets
are issued on a first-come, first-served basis at the farm in Grandview.
Tickets available at 9:30 for same-day tours. No advance reservations accepted. No pets in buildings. Leashed pets allowed on grounds of farm

only. No smoking or picnicking. No vehicles off paved roads or parking lots. Visitor center open daily 8:30–5. Closed Thanksgiving, Dec. 25, Jan. 1. Truman Farm grounds open daily dawn–dusk.

HOW TO GET THERE

The visitor center is on the southeast corner of Truman Rd./Main St. in Independence. From I–70, take Noland Rd. north to Truman Rd. Turn left on Truman Rd. Go two blocks to corner of Truman and Main. From I–435, take Truman Rd. exit east to corner of Truman and Main. To reach Truman Farm in Grandview, take Hwy. 71 to Grandview. Exit west onto Blue Ridge Blvd. for .5 mi/.8 km. Closest airport: Kansas City (31 mi/50 km).

FOR MORE INFORMATION

Harry S. Truman National Historic Site (223 N. Main St., Independence, MO 64050, tel. 816/254–2720, fax 816/254–4491; Web site www.nps.gov/hstr). Independence Chamber of Commerce (210 W. Truman Rd., Independence, MO 64050, tel. 816/252–4745). Grandview Chamber of Commerce (12500 S. 71 Hwy., No. 100, Grandview, MO 64030, tel. 816/761–6505).

Jefferson National Expansion Memorial

In St. Louis, in the east-central part of the state

The memorial commemorates St. Louis's role between 1803 and 1890 in the westward growth of the United States. The memorial includes St. Louis' Old Courthouse, built between 1839 and 1862; the Gateway Arch, an internationally renowned work of architecture designed by Eero Saarinen and completed in 1965; and the Museum of Westward Expansion, which chronicles the Western experience during the 19th century. The memorial was established on December 21, 1935.

WHAT TO SEE & DO

Riding to the top of the arch, touring museum and courthouse, viewing films. **Facilities:** Visitor center, arch, courthouse, museum, kiosks. Museum stores. **Programs & Events:** Ranger-guided tours (when staffing permits). African-American Heritage Month (Feb.), St. Louis Storytelling Festival (1st weekend, May), Victorian 4th of July, Victorian Christmas (Dec.).

PLANNING YOUR VISIT

Camping: Available in St. Louis area; none at memorial. **Lodging:** Available in St. Louis area; none at memorial. **Food & Supplies:** Available in St. Louis area; none at memorial. **Tips & Hints:** Park in garage at north end of grounds on Washington Ave. South-end lot handles oversize vehicles (higher than 7 ft/2.1 m). Gateway Arch requires hiking up at least 96 nonstandard steps. Inform ranger beforehand about fear of heights or confined spaces. Spring and autumn are the best times to visit. Busiest in July and August, least crowded in January and February. **Fees, Permits & Limitations:** Entrance fee: $2 per adult or $4 per family. Separate charge for arch ride and films. Old Courthouse free. Leashed pets only on grounds. No in-line skating, skateboarding, and other recreational activities, except walking and jogging. The Gateway Arch and visitor center open Labor Day–Memorial Day, daily 9–6; Memorial Day–Labor Day, daily 8 AM–10 PM. The Old Courthouse open daily 8–4:30. Closed Thanksgiving, Dec. 25, Jan. 1.

HOW TO GET THERE

The visitor center, at the base of Gateway Arch, is in downtown St. Louis along the Mississippi River. Closest airport: Lambert Field (8 mi/13 km).

FOR MORE INFORMATION

Superintendent, Jefferson National Expansion Memorial (11 N. 4th St., St. Louis, MO 63102, tel. 314/665–1700, fax 314/655–1642; Web site www.nps.gov/jeff). St. Louis Convention and Visitors Commission (1 Metropolitan Sq., Suite 1100, St. Louis, MO 63102, tel. 314/992–0653 or 800/325–7962, fax 314/421–0394).

Ozark National Scenic Riverways

In the southeast part of the state, near Van Buren

The park's 134 mi/214 km of water along the Current and Jacks Ford rivers provide canoeing, tubing, fishing, and swimming opportunities. Over 300 springs pour thousands of gallons of clear, cold water into the streams. Ozark culture also is preserved throughout the 80,790-acre park. The park was authorized in 1964 and established in 1972.

WHAT TO SEE & DO

Boating, canoeing (rentals at campgrounds and in Eminence, Salem, Van Buren), fishing, hunting, swimming, tubing. **Facilities:** 2 visitor contact stations—Alley Mill (Alley Spring near Eminence), park headquarters (Van Buren); wayside exhibits, amphitheaters. Picnic pavilions. **Programs & Events:** Evening programs (Memorial Day–Labor Day, weekends), Round Spring Cave tours (June–Aug., daily at 10 and 2), concerts (summer).

PLANNING YOUR VISIT

Camping: 5 campgrounds: no hookups (no reservations). Semideveloped and gravel-bar camping available. Group campsites available (reservations required, tel. 573/323–4236). Private campgrounds available in Eminence, Mountain View, Salem, and Van Buren. **Lodging:** In the park: Big Spring Lodge (tel. 573/323–4332). Lodging also available in Eminence, Mountain View, Salem, and Van Buren. **Food & Supplies:** In the park: meals at Big Spring Lodge (tel. 573/323–4423). Camp stores at Akers Ferry, Alley Spring, Round Spring, Two Rivers. Food and supplies also available in Eminence, Mountain View, Salem, and Van Buren. **Tips & Hints:** Wear personal flotation devices on river. Go any time of year for canoeing. Busiest in July and August, least crowded in January and February. ✉ **Fees, Permits & Limitations:** Free. Missouri state fishing license required. No inboard motors. No jetskiing. Horsepower limits apply. Leashed pets only. Park open daily. Visitor contact station hours: Alley Mill—June–Aug., daily 9–4; park headquarters—daily 8–4:30.

HOW TO GET THERE

The Riverways is 175 mi/280 km south of St. Louis and 250 mi/400 km southeast of Kansas City. Developed areas are off MO 19 at Akers Ferry, Pulltite, and Round Spring. Alley Spring and Two Rivers can be reached via Hwy. 106 out of Eminence. Big Spring is on Hwy. 103, 4 mi/6 km from Van Buren. Closest airports: St. Louis, Springfield (200 mi/320 km).

FOR MORE INFORMATION

Ozark National Scenic Riverways (Box 490, Van Buren, MO 63965, tel. 573/323–4236, fax 573/323–4140; Web site www.nps.gov/ozar).

Ulysses S. Grant National Historic Site

In St. Louis, in the east-central part of the state

The 9.6-acre heart of the former 1,000-acre plantation owned by Ulysses and Julia Grant is preserved at this site, which also includes the main house, summer kitchen, chicken house, ice house, and barn. A National Historic Landmark, the property is significant for its association with the apparently "average" man who led the army that saved the Union, served two terms as president, and wrote the most important military commentary of modern times. The site was authorized on October 3, 1989.

WHAT TO SEE & DO

Ranger-led and self-guided tours of buildings and grounds. **Facilities:** Visitor center with interpretive exhibits (barn), historic buildings and grounds. Museum shop. **Programs & Events:** Ranger-led tours (daily). Special lectures, living history, children's programs (monthly). Night Walk into the Past living-history program (Aug.), Holidays at White Haven (Dec.).

PLANNING YOUR VISIT

⛺ **Camping:** Available in the St. Louis area; none at site. 🛏 **Lodging:** Available in the St. Louis area; none at site. ✕ **Food & Supplies:** Available in the St. Louis area; none at site. ☞ **Tips & Hints:** The site is being restored to its 1875 appearance; avoid construction areas. Be careful on narrow roads. Watch for uneven ground and slippery surfaces. Busiest in July and August, least crowded in January and February. ✉ **Fees, Permits & Limitations:** Free. Reservations suggested for Sat. events (tel. 314/842–3298). Leashed pets only. Site is open daily 9–5. Closed Thanksgiving, Dec. 25, Jan. 1.

HOW TO GET THERE

The site is in south St. Louis County at 7400 Grant Rd., between Gravois Rd. (Hwy. 30) and Watson Rd.(Hwy. 366). Closest airport: Lambert International (20 mi/32 km).

FOR MORE INFORMATION

Ulysses S. Grant National Historic Site (7400 Grant Rd., St. Louis, MO 63123, tel. 314/842–3298, fax 314/842–1659; e-mail ULSG_Interpretation@nps.gov; Web site www.nps.gov/ulsg). Convention and Visitors Bureau (1 Metropolitan Sq., Suite 1100, St. Louis, MO 63102, tel. 314/421–1023). St. Louis Visitors Center (308 Washington Ave., St. Louis, MO 63102-2117, tel. 314/241–1764). Missouri Tourism Information Center (Box 38182, St. Louis, MO 63138, tel. 314/869–7100).

Wilson's Creek National Battlefield

In the southwest, near Springfield

On August 10, 1861, the first major Civil War engagement west of the Mississippi River, involving about 5,000 Union troops and 10,000 Confederates, was fought here. It was a Confederate victory, though not a decisive one. It was also here that the first Union General, General Nathaniel Lyon, met his death. With the exception of the vegetation, the 1,750-acre battlefield has changed little from its historic setting. Major features include a 5-mi/8-km tour road, the restored 1852 Ray House, and "Bloody Hill," the scene of the major battle. The site was authorized as a national battlefield park in 1960 and redesignated in 1970.

WHAT TO SEE & DO

Hiking, self-guided auto tour of battlefield, touring Ray House. **Facilities:** Visitor center with interpretive exhibits, tour road, wayside exhibits, trails. Bookstore, picnic pavilion. **Programs & Events:** Self-guided auto tour, self-guided tours of Bloody Hill. Living-history programs (Memorial Day–Labor Day, Sun.), Ray House tours as staffing permits (Memorial Day–Labor Day, weekends). Battle anniversary (Aug. 10).

PLANNING YOUR VISIT

⛺ **Camping:** Available in Springfield area; none at battlefield. 🛏 **Lodging:** Available in Springfield area; none at battlefield. ✗ **Food & Supplies:** Available in Republic and Springfield area; none at battlefield. ☞ **Tips & Hints:** Plan to spend at least two hours. Busiest June through August, least crowded in November and January. ✉ **Fees, Permits & Limitations:** Entrance fee: $4 per vehicle or $2 per person 17 and up. Park open daily 8–5; extended hours in summer. Closed Dec. 25, Jan. 1. Visitor center open daily 8–5.

HOW TO GET THERE

The battlefield is at the intersection of Rte. ZZ and Farm Rd. 182. From I–44, take Exit 70 (Rte. MM) south to Rte. ZZS to intersection with Farm Rd. 182. From U.S. 60/65, drive west on MO 14 to Rte. ZZ, then north to the intersection with Farm Rd. 182. Closest airport: Springfield (10 mi/16 km).

FOR MORE INFORMATION

Wilson's Creek National Battlefield (6424 W. Farm Rd. 182, Republic, MO 65738, tel. 417/732–2662; Web site www.nps.gov/wicr).

See Also

California National Historic Trail, National Trails System in Other National Parklands. *Lewis and Clark National Historic Trail,* National Trails System in Other National Parklands. *Oregon National Scenic Trail,* National Trails System in Other National Parklands. *Pony Express National Historic Trail,* National Trails System in Other National Parklands. *Santa Fe National Historic Trail,* National Trails System in Other National Parklands. *Trail of Tears National Historic Trail,* National Trails System in Other National Parklands.

MONTANA

Big Hole
National Battlefield

In the southwest part of the state, near Wisdom

In the summer of 1877, five groups of Nez Perce fleeing from United States Army troops fought at the site of the battlefield. The overwhelming loss of life was a tragic turning point in the Nez Perce War of 1877. The site was established as a national monument in 1910, transferred to the Park Service in 1933, and changed to a battlefield in 1963.

WHAT TO SEE & DO

Fishing, picnicking, touring battlefield, watching slide show. **Facilities:** Visitor centers with interpretive exhibits, trails, museum. Book and map sales areas, picnic tables. **Programs & Events:** Guided hikes, interpretive talks. Big Hole Battle Annual Commemoration (Aug. 9).

PLANNING YOUR VISIT

Camping: Available locally; none at battlefield. **Lodging:** Available in Wisdom, MT; none at battlefield. **Food & Supplies:** Available in Jackson and Wisdom, MT; none at battlefield. **Tips & Hints:** Busiest in July and August, least crowded in December and January. **Fees, Permits & Limitations:** Entrance fee: $2 per person or $4 per car (May–Sept.). Montana state fishing license required. Leashed pets only. No hunting. Trails open until dusk. Visitor center open daily 9–5. Park closed Thanksgiving, Dec. 25, Jan. 1.

HOW TO GET THERE

Visitor center is 10 mi/16 km west of Wisdom on MT 43. Closest airport: Missoula (100 mi/160 km).

FOR MORE INFORMATION

Big Hole National Battlefield (Box 237, Wisdom, MT 59761, tel. 406/689–3155, fax 406/689–3151; Web site www.nps.gov/biho).

Bighorn Canyon
National Recreation Area

From the south-central part of Montana, near Hardin, to north-central Wyoming, near Lovell

The recreation area's most compelling attraction is the geology of the canyon, which is several thousand feet deep in places. Bighorn also features bighorn sheep, the nation's first wild horse range, the Bad Pass Trail, and several historic ranches. The area was established in 1966.

WHAT TO SEE & DO

Boating (rentals, lake marinas), fishing, hiking, hunting, ice fishing, swimming, touring. **Facilities:** 2 visitor centers with interpretive exhibits (Yellowtail Dam, Fort Smith, MT; Lovell, WY), 4 historic ranches, amphitheaters, beach, wayside exhibits. Book and map sales areas, fire pits and grates, gasoline, picnic tables. **Programs & Events:** Tours of Yellowtail Dam (May–late Sept., daily 10:30 and 2:30). Guided hikes, horseback rides, canoe trips, interpretive talks, campfire programs (June–Aug.). Mustang Days fireworks (last Sun. in June, Horseshoe Bend), July 4 fireworks (Afterbay Dam, MT).

PLANNING YOUR VISIT

Camping: 5 campgrounds: 3 drive in, 2 boat-in only, no hookups, dump stations at Afterbay and Horseshoe Bend campgrounds. (No reservations.) Private campgrounds available in Fort Smith, MT, and Lovell, WY. **Lodging:** Available in Fort Smith, MT, and Lovell, WY; none in recreation area. **Food & Supplies:** In the park: grill and staples at Ok-A-Beh and Horseshoe Bend marinas. Food and supplies also available in Fort Smith, MT, and Lovell, WY. **Tips & Hints:** Watch for rattlesnakes and fragile edges near drop-offs. Be aware of and respect the Crow Indian Reservation boundaries. Bighorn Canyon is an undiscovered treasure, and there are usually few visitors at any time. Busiest in July and August, least crowded in December and January. **Fees, Permits & Limitations:** Entrance fee: $5 per vehicle. Montana or Wyoming state fishing license required. No hunting in restricted areas. Leashed pets only. No motorized or mechanical vehicles off paved or dirt roads. Park open daily. Yellowtail Dam Visitor Center open Memorial Day–Labor Day, daily 8–5:30; Labor Day–Memorial Day, some weekends. Lovell Visitor Center open daily, Memorial Day–Labor Day, 8–6; Labor Day–Memorial Day, 8:30–5. Closed Thanksgiving, Dec. 25, Jan. 1.

HOW TO GET THERE

North District (Montana side) is 1 mi/2 km from Fort Smith. Closest airport: Billings (90 mi/144 km). South Unit (Wyoming side) is 11 mi/18 km from Lovell. Closest airport: Cody (50 mi/80 km).

FOR MORE INFORMATION

Bighorn Canyon National Recreation Area, North District (Box 7458, Fort Smith, MT 59035, tel. 406/666–2412, fax 406/666–2415; Web site www.nps.gov/bica). Big Canyon National Recreation Area, South District Unit (20 Hwy. 14A E, Lovell, WY 82431, tel. 307/548–2251, fax 307/548–7826). Hardin Area Chamber of Commerce (21 E. 4th St., Hardin, MT 59034, tel. 406/665–1672). Lovell Area Chamber of Commerce (287 E. Main St., Box 295, Lovell, WY 82431, tel. 307/548–7552).

Glacier National Park

In the northwest part of the state, near West Glacier

This ruggedly beautiful park includes nearly 50 glaciers, precipitous peaks more than 10,000 ft/3,033 m tall, many lakes and streams, an expansive variety of wildflowers, and wildlife that includes grizzly bears and gray wolves. It is considered one of the most ecologically intact areas remaining in the temperate regions of the world. The 1-million-acre park offers spectacular scenery and increasingly rare primitive wilderness experiences. The park was established in 1910, authorized as part of the Waterton-Glacier International Peace Park in 1932, designated a Biosphere Reserve in 1976 and a World Heritage Site in 1995.

WHAT TO SEE & DO

Auto touring, backpacking (rentals, Columbia Falls and West Glacier), bicycling (rentals, East Glacier), boating (Apgar, Lake McDonald, Many Glacier, Two Medicine), canoeing (rentals, Apgar, Lake McDonald, Many Glacier, Two Medicine), cross-country skiing (rentals, Essex), fishing, golfing (East Glacier, Columbia Falls), hiking, horseback riding, kayaking (rentals, Apgar, Lake McDonald, Many Glacier, Two Medicine), picnicking, rafting (trips, West Glacier), snowshoeing, wildlife watching. **Facilities:** 3 visitor centers—Apgar (west side of park), Logan Pass (Going-to-the-Sun Rd.), St. Mary (east side of park); Many Glacier, Polebridge, and Two Medicine ranger stations, wayside exhibits, 700 mi/1,120 km of trails. Book and map sale areas, gift stores, laundry, picnic areas, post offices, religious services. **Programs & Events:** Ranger evening talks, slide shows, boat tours, guided walks and day-long hikes, Native America Speaks series by Blackfeet, Salish and Kooterai tribal members (Jul.–Aug.). Show Me Day (snow removal, Apr. or May).

PLANNING YOUR VISIT

Camping: 13 campgrounds, 8 with dump stations (reservations available for St. Mary and Fish Creek, tel. 800/365–2267). No electrical or water hookups. Backcountry camping available (permit required, *see below*). Group campsites at Apgar, Many Glacier, St. Mary, and Two Medicine (reservations available for St. Mary, tel. 800/365–2267). Private campgrounds in Babb, Browning, Coram, East Glacier, Essex, Hungry Horse, Martin City, St. Mary, West Glacier. **Lodging:** In the park: Apgar Village Lodge (tel. 406/888–5484); Granite Park Chalet (tel. 800/521–7238); Lake McDonald Lodge, Many Glacier Hotel, Rising Sun Motor Inn, Swiftcurrent Motor Inn, Village Inn (all tel. 406/756–2444); Sperry Chalet (tel. 888/345–2649). Lodging also available outside the park in Babb, Browning, Coram, East Glacier, Essex, Martin City, Polebridge, St. Mary, West Glacier. **Food & Supplies:** In the park: late May–Sept., meals only at Cedar Tree Deli (tel. 406/888–5232), Charlie's Pizzeria (tel. 406/888–5160), Eddie's Restaurant (tel. 406/888–5361), Italian Gardens Restaurant (tel. 406/732–5531), Ptarmigan Dining Room (tel. 406/732–4411), Two Dog Flats Mesquite Grill (tel. 406/732–5523); snack bar at Two Medicine Campstore. Food and supplies also available in Babb, Browning, Coram, East Glacier,

Essex, Hungry Horse, Martin City, Polebridge, St. Mary, West Glacier. ☞ **Tips & Hints:** Watch for water and snow hazards, altitude sickness, hypothermia, ticks, and wild animals. Go in September to avoid crowds. Busiest in July and August, least crowded in November and December. ☒ **Fees, Permits & Limitations:** Entrance fee: $10 per vehicle or $5 per pedestrian, bicyclist, or motorcyclist. Glacier Park, Inc., sightseeing buses (tel. 406/756–2444). Backpacking permits ($4 per person per night, $20 additional fee for advance reservation). Backcountry Camping Permits, Glacier National Park, West Glacier, MT 59936) required for all backcountry camping. No vehicles wider than 8 ft/2.4 m or longer than 21 ft/6.4 m allowed on Logan Pass between Avalanche and Sun Point. No hunting. No pets or bikes on trails. No personal watercraft or snowmobiles. Park open daily. The highest portion of Going-to-the-Sun Rd. open over Logan Pass mid-June–mid-Oct. Visitor centers open daily in summer, 8 AM–8 PM. Apgar open Nov.–Apr., weekends 9–4.

HOW TO GET THERE

The west entrance to the park near West Glacier is 19 mi/30 km east of Columbia Falls via U.S. 2; the east entrance in St. Mary is 32 mi/51 km northwest of Browning via U.S. 89. Closest airport: Kalispell (35 mi/56 km).

FOR MORE INFORMATION

Glacier National Park (West Glacier, MT 59936, tel. 406/888–7800, fax 406/888–7808; Web site www.nps.gov/glac). Flathead Convention and Visitor Bureau (15 Depot Park, Kalispell, MT 59901, tel. 800/543–3105). Cut Bank Area Chamber of Commerce (715 E. Main St., Box 1243, Cut Bank, MT 59427, tel. 406/873–4041). Glacier Country (836 Holt Dr., Suite 320, Box 1035, Bigfork, MT 59911-1035, tel. 406/837–6211 or 800/956–6537). Waterton Townsite Chamber of Commerce (Superintendent, Waterton Lakes National Park, Waterton Park, Alberta, Canada T0K 2M0, tel. 403/859–2204). Columbia Falls Chamber of Commerce (Box 312, Columbia Falls, MT 59912, tel. 406/892–2072). Kalispell Chamber of Commerce (15 Depot Park, Kalispell, MT 59901, tel. 406/758–2800).

Grant-Kohrs Ranch National Historic Site

In the southwest part of the state, in Deer Lodge

Established by Canadian fur trader John Grant and expanded by cattle baron Conrad Kohrs, the site was the headquarters of one of the largest 19th-century range ranches in the country. The 1,500-acre site is maintained today as a working ranch, and the 89 historic structures serve as a living museum of the frontier cattle industry of the 1860s–1930s. The site was authorized in 1972.

WHAT TO SEE & DO

Bird-watching; observing cattle, poultry, and horses; touring ranch and outbuildings; walking nature trail. **Facilities:** Visitor center with interpretive exhibits, ranch house and buildings, trails. Bookstore. **Programs & Events:** Ranger-led ranch house tours, self-guided walks of ranch outbuildings. Living-history programs on blacksmithing, chuck-wagon cooking, 1890s cowboy life (May–Sept.). Western Heritage Days (2nd full weekend in July).

PLANNING YOUR VISIT

⛺ **Camping:** Available in Deer Lodge; none at site. 🛏 **Lodging:** Available in Deer Lodge; none at site. ✗ **Food & Supplies:** Available in Deer Lodge; none at site. ☞ **Tips & Hints:** Plan two hours for visit. Busiest in July and August, least crowded in January and February. 🎟 **Fees, Permits & Limitations:** Free. No smoking or pets beyond parking lot or visitor center areas. Site open summer, daily 8–5:30; fall–spring, daily 9–4:30. Closed Thanksgiving, Dec. 25, Jan. 1.

HOW TO GET THERE

From I–90, take either Deer Lodge exit and follow signs. Park is at north end of town. Closest airports: Butte (36 mi/58 km), Helena (60 mi/96 km), and Missoula (80 m/128 km).

FOR MORE INFORMATION

Superintendent, Grant-Kohrs Ranch National Historic Site (Box 790, Deer Lodge, MT 59722. tel. 406/846–3388 or 406/846–2070; Web site www.nps.gov/grko).

Little Bighorn Battlefield National Monument

In the southeast part of the state, near Hardin

One of the last armed efforts of the Northern Plains people to preserve their way of life is memorialized here. On June 25 and 26, 1876, in the valley of the Little Bighorn River, more than 260 soldiers and attached personnel of the U.S. Army met defeat and death at the hands of several thousand Lakota and Cheyenne warriors. Among the dead was Lieutenant Colonel George Armstrong Custer and every member of his immediate command. Although the Native Americans won the battle, they subsequently lost the war against the expansion of Euro-Americans into the Northern Plains. The monument was designated a national cemetery in 1879 and a national monument in 1946.

WHAT TO SEE & DO

Touring battlefield by car (cassettes can be purchased for $12.95). **Facilities:** Visitor center with interpretive exhibits, interpretive wayside exhibits, tour road, trails. Bookstore. **Programs & Events:** Ranger talks (Memorial Day–Labor Day). Battle Anniversary (June 25).

PLANNING YOUR VISIT

⛺ **Camping:** Available in Hardin; none in park. 🏨 **Lodging:** Available in Hardin; none in park. ✕ **Food & Supplies:** Available along U.S. 212 and Hardin; none in park. ☞ **Tips & Hints:** Visit between late spring and early fall. Busiest June through August, least crowded in December and January. 🎫 **Fees, Permits & Limitations:** Entrance fee: $3 per person or $6 per vehicle. No pets. Park and visitor center open Oct.–Apr. 29, daily 8–4:30; Apr. 30–Memorial Day and Labor Day–Oct., daily 8–6; Memorial Day–Labor Day, daily 8 AM–9 PM (visitor center closes at 7:30). Closed Thanksgiving, Dec. 25, Jan. 1.

HOW TO GET THERE

The park is near the junction of I–90 and U.S. 212. Closest airport: Billings (60 mi/96 km).

FOR MORE INFORMATION

Little Bighorn Battlefield National Monument (Box 39, Crow Agency, MT 59022, tel. 406/638–2621, fax 406/638–2623; e-mail libi_administration@nps.gov; Web site www.nps.gov/libi). Custer Country, County Museum Complex (Rte. 1, Box 1206A, Room 22, Hardin, MT 59034, tel. 406/665–1671). Hardin Area Chamber of Commerce (21 E. 4th St., Hardin, MT 59034, tel. 406/665–1672, fax 406/665–2917).

See Also

Continental Divide National Scenic Trail, National Trails System in Other National Parklands. *Flathead River,* Wild and Scenic Rivers System in Other National Parklands. *Fort Union Trading Post National Historic Site,* North Dakota. *Lewis and Clark National Historic Trail,* National Trails System in Other National Parklands. *Nez Perce National Historical Site,* Idaho. *Nez Perce National Historic Trail,* National Trails System in Other National Parklands. *Yellowstone National Park,* Wyoming.

NEBRASKA

Agate Fossil Beds National Monument

In the northwest part of the state,
50 mi/80 km north of Scottsbluff

Animal fossils in beds of sedimentary rock, formed about 19 million years ago by the compression of mud, clay, and eroded materials deposited by water and wind, are concentrated under the grass-covered hills at this monument along the Niobrara River. Native American artifacts document the visits of Lakota Chief Red Cloud and others to pioneer rancher James Cook from 1890 to 1940. The monument was authorized on June 5, 1965.

WHAT TO SEE & DO

Attending ranger talks, fishing, hiking, picnicking, touring historic quarry sites, viewing exhibits, watching film. **Facilities:** Visitor center, museum, trails, wayside exhibits. Book sale area. **Programs & Events:** Ranger-guided tours (on request). Guided walks, talks, cultural demonstrations (summer, weekends).

PLANNING YOUR VISIT

Camping: Available in Crawford, Harrison; none at monument. **Lodging:** Available in Crawford, Harrison, Scottsbluff, NE; and Lusk, WY; none at monument. ✕ **Food & Supplies:** Available in Crawford, Harrison, Mitchell, Morrill, Scottsbluff, NE; and Lusk, Torrington, WY; none at monument. ☞ **Tips & Hints:** Go in late May–September for wildflowers. Busiest in June and July, least crowded in December and February. **Fees, Permits & Limitations:** Entrance fee: $2 per adult 17 and over or $5 per vehicle. Nebraska state fishing license required. No hunting. Leashed pets only. No motorized or mechanized equipment except wheelchairs on trails or off roads. Monument open daily dawn–dusk. Visitor center open Labor Day–Memorial Day, daily 8–5; Memorial Day–Labor Day, daily 8–6. Closed Thanksgiving, Dec. 25.

HOW TO GET THERE

On Hwy. 29, between Harrison and Mitchell. Closest airport: Scottsbluff (50 mi/80 km).

FOR MORE INFORMATION

Agate Fossil Beds National Monument (301 River Rd., Harrison, NE 69346-2734, tel. 308/668–2211, fax 308/668–2318; e-mail agfo_ranger_activities@nps.gov; Web site www.nps.gov/agfo). Scottsbluff-Gering United Chamber of Commerce (1517 Broadway, Scottsbluff, NE 69361, tel. 308/632–2133 or 800/788–9475, fax 308/632–7128; Web site www.visitnebraska.com).

Homestead National Monument of America

In the southeast part of the state, near Beatrice

The monument memorializes the Homestead Act of 1862 and those who helped settle the West under the Act's provisions. It encompasses the site of the Daniel Freeman homestead, one of the very first claimed on January 1, 1863, the first day the Act took effect. The Homestead Act was in effect until 1976 (1986 in Alaska). The monument includes 100 acres of restored tallgrass prairie and the Freeman School, an original one-room prairie schoolhouse. The site was established in 1936.

WHAT TO SEE & DO

Cross-country skiing, hiking, picnicking, touring facilities, watching videos. **Facilities:** Visitor center, museum, hiking trails, Freeman School, Palmer-Epard Cabin. Bookstore, picnic tables. **Programs & Events:** Ranger-led interpretive talks and walks. Homestead Days (last full weekend, June), Winter Festival of Prairie Cultures (Thanksgiving–Jan. 1). Special events year-round.

PLANNING YOUR VISIT

Camping: Available in Beatrice and locally; none at monument. **Lodging:** Available in Beatrice, Lincoln, Wilber, Wymore; none at monument. **Food & Supplies:** Available in Beatrice, Wilber, Wymore; none at monument. **Tips & Hints:** Go in August and September to see tallgrass prairie at full height; between May and September for wildflowers; and in March, May, September, and October for migrating birds. Busiest in May and June, least crowded in January and February. **Fees, Permits & Limitations:** Free. No hunting or fishing. No mountain or trail bikes or motorized vehicles on trails. Leashed pets in picnic area only. Trails open daily sunrise–sunset. Visitor center hours: Memorial Day–Labor Day, daily 8:30–5; Labor Day–Memorial Day, weekdays 8:30–5, weekends 9–5. Closed Thanksgiving, Dec. 25, Jan. 1.

HOW TO GET THERE

4 mi/6 km west of Beatrice on NE 4. Closest airport: Lincoln (49 mi/78 km).

FOR MORE INFORMATION

Homestead National Monument of America (8523 W. State Hwy. 4, Beatrice, NE 68310, tel 402/223–3514, fax 402/228–4231; e-mail Home_Superintendent@nps.gov; Web site www.nps.gov/home). Beatrice Chamber of Commerce (226 S. 6th, Beatrice, NE 68310, tel. 402/223–2338).

Missouri National Recreational River

Southeast South Dakota, near Yankton, to northeast Nebraska, near Ponca

The recreational river includes two sections of the Missouri, west and east of Lewis and Clark Lake along the Nebraska–South Dakota border, as well as 20 mi/32 km of the lower Niobrara River and 8 mi/13 km of its tributary, Verdigree Creek. The rivers represent the environment that existed when Lewis and Clark made their journey nearly 200 years ago. High chalk bluffs, stands of cottonwood, marshy areas, and plains dominate the area. Farming is practiced by landowners, and descendants of Czech, German, and Finnish immigrants maintain a rich cultural heritage. The recreational river was authorized in 1978 and expanded in 1991.

WHAT TO SEE & DO

Bird-watching, boating, fishing, hiking, horseback riding, hunting, swimming at state parks. **Facilities:** No Park Service facilities. Army Corps of Engineers visitor centers at Fort Randall and Gavins Point dams, Nebraska state visitor centers at Niobrara and Ponca state parks. **Programs & Events:** None by Park Service. Army Corps of Engineers, state parks, and local communities sponsor activities during summer.

PLANNING YOUR VISIT

⚠ **Camping:** Cabins and campgrounds available in Ponca and Niobrara state parks. Group campsites available (Niobrara State Park, tel. 402/857–3373; Ponca State Park, tel. 402/755–2284). 🛏 **Lodging:** Available in Crofton, Niobrara, Ponca, NE; and Pickstown, Wagner, Yankton, SD. ✗ **Food & Supplies:** Available in Crofton, Niobrara, Ponca, NE; and Pickstown, Wagner, Yankton, SD. ☞ **Tips & Hints:** Most surrounding land is privately owned; respect landowners' property rights. Visit May–October, although high summer can be hot and windy. Busiest in July and August, least crowded in December and January. 🎫 **Fees, Permits & Limitations:** State parks entry fee: $2.50. Nebraska or South Dakota state hunting and fishing licenses required. Landowner permission needed for hunting. No trespassing on private land. No rest rooms. Army Corps of Engineers Lewis and Clark Lake visitor center hours: Memorial Day–Labor Day, weekdays 8–6, weekends 10–6; Labor Day–Memorial Day, weekdays 8–4:30, weekends 10–5. Closed Dec., Jan.

HOW TO GET THERE

The recreational rivers are along the Missouri River east and west of Yankton, SD. Closest airport: Yankton, SD.

FOR MORE INFORMATION

Missouri National Recreational River (Box 591, O'Neill, NE 68763, tel. 402/336–3970, fax 402/336–3981; Web site www.nps.gov/mnrr). U.S. Army Corps of Engineers (Box 710, Yankton, SD 57078, tel. 402/667–7873). Yankton Area Chamber of Commerce (218 W. 4th St., Box 588, Yankton, SD 57078, tel. 605/665–3636).

Niobrara National Scenic River

In the north-central part of the state, near Valentine

Eastern deciduous, western pine, and northern boreal ecosystems merge with short and mixed-grass prairie in the Niobrara River valley. Free-grazing cattle, windmills, abandoned historic barns and homes offset the natural landscape. The upper portion of the 76-mi/122-km stretch of scenic river provides excellent canoeing. The scenic river was authorized on May 24, 1991.

WHAT TO SEE & DO

Canoeing and tubing (rentals, Valentine and along river). **Facilities:** No Park Service facilities. Fort Niobrara National Wildlife Refuge (NWR) visitor center at primary canoe access area (3 mi/5 km east of Valentine off Hwy. 12), Smith Falls State Park. **Programs & Events:** Canoe Outfitters River Clean-up (usually Sept.), Ft. Niobrara NWR buffalo roundup and auction (Oct.).

PLANNING YOUR VISIT

Camping: 8 private campgrounds along river, Smith Falls State Park. Group campsites at state park (tel. 402/376–1306) and private campgrounds. **Lodging:** Available in Ainsworth, Bassett, Valentine. **Food & Lodging:** Some outfitters sell drinks, snacks, and camping supplies. Food and supplies also available in Ainsworth, Bassett, Springview, and Valentine. **Tips & Hints:** Go on weekdays to avoid crowds; between May and October to run river; between May and June and October for migrating birds; in June for flowers; or in mid-October for fall colors. Much of river frontage is privately owned; respect landowners' property rights. Busiest in July and August, least crowded in December and January. **Fees, Permits & Limitations:** Free. River access fee at wildlife refuge: $2. Parking fee at Smith Falls State Park: $2.50. River open daily, but it freezes in winter. Wildlife refuge visitor center open Memorial Day–Labor Day, daily 8–4:30; Labor Day–Memorial Day, weekdays 8–4:30.

HOW TO GET THERE

The scenic river runs from 3 mi/5 km east of Valentine near NE 12 to Hwy. 137 bridge. The most commonly canoed section begins just east of Valentine and runs for 30 mi/50 km. Closest airport: O'Neill Municipal (3 mi/5 km).

FOR MORE INFORMATION

Niobrara National Scenic River (Box 591, O'Neill, NE 68763, tel. 402/336–3970, fax 402/336–3981; Web site www.nps.gov/ninr). Valentine Chamber of Commerce (239 S. Main St., Valentine, NE 69201, tel. 402/376–2969).

Scotts Bluff National Monument

In the western part of the state, near Gering

A prominent natural landmark for emigrants on the Oregon Trail, Scotts Bluff (800 ft/243 m), Mitchell Pass, and the adjacent prairie lands are set aside in a 3,000-acre national monument. This site preserves the memory of the historic Oregon, California, and Mormon trails, remnants of which still can be seen. The monument museum contains exhibits about the human and natural history of the area and also houses a unique collection of watercolor paintings by the frontier photographer and artist William Henry Jackson. The site was proclaimed on December 12, 1919.

WHAT TO SEE & DO

Driving or hiking to bluff summit, hiking to remnants of Oregon/California Trail, touring museum. **Facilities:** Oregon Trail Museum (visitor center), trailside interpretive panels, amphitheater. Book and gift shop. **Programs & Events:** Summit shuttle, living-history programs, interpretive walks and talks (Memorial Day–Labor Day); amphitheater program (mid-June–mid Aug., Tues.). Local art show, Spring Up the Bluff relay race (end of Apr.), Christmas on the Prairie (first Sat. in Dec.).

PLANNING YOUR VISIT

⚠ **Camping:** Available in Gering, Scottsbluff; none at monument. 🏠 **Lodging:** Available in Bayard, Gering, Morrill, Scottsbluff; none at monument. ✕ **Food & Supplies:** Available in Gering, Mitchell, Scottsbluff; none at monument. ☞ **Tips & Hints:** Carry plenty of water when hiking in summer. Watch for rattlesnakes. Go in spring for prairie flowers, fall for cooler temperatures and fewer people. Busiest in July and August, least crowded in December and January. 🎫 **Fees, Permits & Limitations:** Entrance fee: $5 per car. Groups should make reservations (tel. 308/436–4340). Stay on trails. Leashed pets only. No hunting. No rock, plant, or animal gathering. No off-road usage. No vehicles longer than 25 ft/7.6 m or taller than 11 ft 7 in/3.5 m on summit road. Monument open daily dawn–dusk. Visitor center open daily 8–5, extended hours in summer; closed Dec. 25, Jan. 1.

HOW TO GET THERE

3 mi/5 km west of Gering on NE 92 Closest airport: Scottsbluff (10 mi/16 km).

FOR MORE INFORMATION

Scotts Bluff National Monument (Box 27, Gering, NE 69341-0027, tel. 308/436–4340, fax 308/436–7611; e-mail scbl_superintendent@nps.gov; Web site www.nps.gov/scbl).

See Also

California National Historic Trail, National Trails System in Other National Parklands. *Chimney Rock National Historic Site,* Affiliated Areas in Other National Parklands. *Lewis and Clark National Historic Trail,* National Trails System in Other National Parklands. *Mormon Pioneer National Historic Trail,* National Trails System in Other National Parklands. *Oregon National Scenic Trail,* National Trails System in Other National Parklands. *Pony Express National Historic Trail,* National Trails System in Other National Parklands.

NEVADA

Great Basin National Park

In the east-central part of the state, near Baker

Attractions in this park are an ice field on 13,063-ft/3,962-m Wheeler Peak; an ancient bristlecone-pine forest; the 75-ft/23-m Lexington Arch; and the Lehman Caves. Lehman Caves National Monument was proclaimed in 1922, transferred to the Park Service in 1933, and incorporated into Great Basin National Park in 1986.

WHAT TO SEE & DO

Auto touring, cave touring, caving, fishing, hiking, picnicking. **Facilities:** Visitor center with interpretive exhibits (Lehman Cave entrance), scenic drive, wayside exhibit, nature trail, amphitheaters. Bookstore, gift shop, mail drop, picnic area. **Programs & Events:** Cave tours, slide show and movie. Ranger-led hikes, walks, talks, and evening programs; scenic drive to Wheeler Peak (Memorial Day–Labor Day).

PLANNING YOUR VISIT

Camping: 4 campgrounds: dump station, some accommodate large trailers/motor homes (no reservations). Backcountry camping available (registration requested, *see below*). Group camping available (reservations strongly recommended, tel. 775/234–7331). Private campgrounds available in Baker and Ely. **Lodging:** Available in Baker and Ely, NV; and Delta, UT; none in park. ✕ **Food & Supplies:** In the park: café (mid-Apr.–mid-Oct., tel. 775/234–7221). Food and supplies also available in Baker. ☞ **Tips & Hints:** Watch for altitude sickness. Wear good walking shoes or boots in cave. Leave pets at home. Visit year-round for caves, April–mid-October to explore landscape and bristlecone pines. Busiest in May and July, least crowded in December and January. **Fees, Permits & Limitations:** Free. Cave tour fees at press time: $4 per adult, $2 children 11 and under. Advanced tickets available in summer (tel. 775/234–7331). Backcountry registration strongly recommended. Wild caving permits required two weeks in advance. Nevada state fishing license required. No bikes on trails. No fireworks. No guns. No pets on trails or in caves. Leashed pets elsewhere. No vehicles over 24 ft/7.3 m long on Scenic Drive to Wheeler Peak. No watercraft on lakes. Park open daily. No cave walks on Thanksgiving, Dec. 25, Jan. 1. Visitor center open Memorial Day–Labor Day, daily 7–6; Labor Day–Memorial Day, daily 8:30–5. Closed Thanksgiving, Dec. 25, Jan. 1.

HOW TO GET THERE

5 mi/8 km west of Baker on Hwy. 488 and 68 mi/109 km east of Ely via U.S. 6/50. Closest airports: Ely (68 mi/109 km), Salt Lake City (234 mi/374 km), Las Vegas (286 mi/458 km).

FOR MORE INFORMATION

Great Basin National Park, Baker, NV 89311, tel. 775/234–7331, fax 775/234–7269; Web site www.nps.gov/grba). White Pine County Chamber of Commerce (636 Aultman St., Ely, NV 89301, tel. 775/289–8877).

Lake Mead National Recreation Area 👓

Near Las Vegas in southern Nevada and northwest Arizona

The 1.5-million-acre recreation area, the nation's first, draws nearly 10 million visitors a year. Boating, fishing, and swimming are available on the two huge lakes formed by the Hoover and Davis dams. Three of America's four desert ecosystems—the Mojave, Great Basin, and Sonoran deserts—meet at Lake Mead. Bighorn sheep, mule deer, coyotes, kit foxes, bobcats, ringtail cats, desert tortoise, numerous lizards, and snakes all can be found in the recreation area. The area is administered under agreements with the Bureau of Reclamation signed in 1936 and 1947. It was redesignated in 1947 and established in 1964.

WHAT TO SEE & DO

Auto touring, boating (rentals), canoeing, diving, fishing, hiking, kayaking, picnicking, sailing, sunbathing, swimming, waterskiing. **Facilities:** Visitor center with interpretive exhibits (4 mi/6 km northeast of Boulder City, NV, on U.S. 93), 8 contact stations (Lake Mead: Callville Bay, Echo Bay, Las Vegas Bay, and Overton Beach in NV; Temple Bar in AZ. Lake Mohave: Cottonwood Cove in NV, Katherine and Willow Beach in AZ), marinas, beaches, trails. Bookstore, fuel. **Programs & Events:** Ranger-led programs and hikes, paddle-wheel tour boats to Hoover Dam (tel. 702/293–6180), rafting tours (tel. 702/293–3776). Lecture series (Jan.–Apr.).

PLANNING YOUR VISIT

⚠ **Camping:** 7 campgrounds (no reservations): All have dump stations. No hookups. Backcountry camping available. Group campsites available (reservations required, tel. 702/294–0331). Private campgrounds with hookups also available. 🏨 **Lodging:** In the recreation area: 5 motels—Cottonwood (tel. 702/297–1464); Echo Bay (tel. 702/394–4000); Lake Mead Lodge (tel. 702/293–2074); Lake Mohave (at Katherine Landing, tel. 520/754–3245); and Temple Bar (tel. 520/767–3211). Lodging also available in Boulder City, Henderson, Las Vegas, Laughlin, Overton, and Searchlight, NV; Bullhead City and Kingman, AZ; and Needles, CA. ✕ **Food & Supplies:** Stores and snack bars or restaurants at all marinas. Food and supplies also available in Boulder City, Henderson, Las Vegas, Laughlin, Overton, and Searchlight, NV; Bullhead City and Kingman, AZ; and Needles, CA. ☞ **Tips & Hints:** Summer temperatures reach 120°F/49°C in the shade. Go between October and May for best hiking weather. Busiest in June and July, least crowded in November and December. 🎫 **Fees, Permits & Limitations:** Entrance fee (1–5 days): $5 per vehicle; $10 per vessel lake use fee. Recreation area open daily. Visitor center open daily 8:30–4:30.

HOW TO GET THERE

The visitor center is 27 mi/43 km east of Las Vegas via U.S. 93. Other lake access available via I–15 north of Las Vegas, U.S. 95 south of Las Vegas, and U.S. 93 in Arizona. Closest airports: McCarren International in Las Vegas, Bullhead City, AZ.

FOR MORE INFORMATION

Superintendent, Lake Mead National Recreation Area (601 Nevada Hwy., Boulder City, NV 89005, tel. 702/293–8907, fax 702/293–8936; Web site www.nps.gov/lame).

See Also

California National Historic Trail, National Trails System in Other National Parklands. *Death Valley National Monument,* California. *Pony Express National Historic Trail,* National Trails System in Other National Parklands.

NEW HAMPSHIRE

Saint-Gaudens National Historic Site

In the western part of the state, near Cornish

Augustus Saint-Gaudens (1848–1907), one of America's most popular and talented sculptors, spent his most productive years at "Aspet," an 18th-century Federal style house. Saint-Gaudens transformed the bare New Hampshire hillside into an artist's retreat with studios, gardens, and his artwork. The site was authorized in 1964 and established in 1977.

WHAT TO SEE & DO

Hiking nature trails, picnicking, touring house and gallery. **Facilities:** House, gallery, gardens, grounds, visitor kiosk, trails. Picnic areas. **Programs & Events:** Interpretive tours of house, art exhibits. Sunday concert series (June–mid-Aug.).

PLANNING YOUR VISIT

Camping: Available locally; none at site. **Lodging:** Available locally; none at site. **Food & Supplies:** Available in Hanover and West Lebanon, NH; and White River Junction and Windsor, VT; none at site. **Tips & Hints:** Busiest in July and August, least crowded in January and February. **Fees, Permits & Limitations:** Entrance fee: $4 per person, free 16 and under. Difficult turn-around for large RVs towing vehicles. No snowmobiles or off-road vehicles allowed. Site open Memorial Day–Oct., daily 9–4:30.

HOW TO GET THERE

Off NH 12A in Cornish, 9 mi/14 km north of Claremont and 2 mi/3 km from Windsor, VT. From I–91, take Exit 8 or 9. From I–89, take Exit 20 12 mi south. Closest airport: Lebanon (11 mi/18 km).

FOR MORE INFORMATION

Superintendent, Saint-Gaudens National Historic Site (RR 3, Box 73, Cornish, NH 03745, tel. 603/675–2175; Web site www.nps.gov/saga).

See Also

Appalachian National Scenic Trail, West Virginia. *Lamprey Wild and Scenic River,* Wild and Scenic Rivers System in Other National Parklands.

NEW JERSEY

Edison National Historic Site

In the northeast part of the state, in West Orange

Thomas Edison's lab and 29-room estate, Glenmont, were home to the inventor from 1887 until his death in 1931. At his "Invention Factory," he developed the phonograph, invented the movie camera and the nickel-iron-alkaline battery, and was awarded over half of his 1,093 patents. The complex includes his chemistry lab, machine shop, library, and a replica of the world's first picture studio. The graves of Thomas and Mina Edison are on the Glenmont grounds. Edison Home National Historic Site was designated in 1955. Edison Laboratory National Monument was proclaimed in 1956, and the sites were combined as Edison National Historic Site in 1962.

WHAT TO SEE & DO

Touring lab complex and 16-acre Glenmont estate. **Facilities:** Visitor center with interpretive exhibits, theater, lab complex, Glenmont estate. Bookstore. **Programs & Events:** Guided tours of lab and Glenmont. Seasonal activities and special events available.

PLANNING YOUR VISIT

⛕ **Camping:** Available locally; none at site. 🛏 **Lodging:** Available locally; none at site. ✗ **Food & Supplies:** Available locally; none at site. ☞ **Tips & Hints:** Allow three hours to tour the lab, Glenmont, and visitor center. Allow 15 minutes travel time between Glenmont and lab. There is no air-conditioning and tours are partly outdoors. Busiest in July and August, least crowded in January. 🎫 **Fees, Permits & Limitations:** Entrance fee: $2 per adult 17 and up. No access beyond visitor center except by guided tour. Glenmont tickets are required and limited. No strollers or video cameras on tours. No late admission to tours. Reservations required for groups (tel. 973/736–0550). Site open daily. Closed Thanksgiving, Dec. 25, Jan. 1. Call 973/736–0550 ext. 42 for visitor center hours and tour information. No rest rooms at Glenmont.

HOW TO GET THERE

The site is in West Orange, about 15 mi/24 km west of New York City. The lab is on the corner of Main St. and Lakeside Ave. The visitor center is on Lakeside Ave. with parking on Main St. across from lab. From the Garden State Pkwy., take Exit 145 to I–280W. From the New Jersey Tpk., take Exit 15W to I–280W. Follow I–280 to Exit 10 and take the first right from the ramp. Go to end of street and make a left onto Main St. Follow Main St. for 0.75 mi/1.2 km. Parking on left. From the west, take I–280E to Exit 9. Make a left at end of ramp. Make left on Main St. at second light. Park is 0.5 mi/.8 km on left. Call 800/772–2222 for information on public transportation to site. Closest airport: Newark (20 mi/32 km).

FOR MORE INFORMATION

Edison National Historic Site (Main St. and Lakeside Ave., West Orange, NJ 07052, tel. 973/736–0550, fax 973/736–8496; e-mail EDIS_Superintendent@nps.gov; Web site www.nps.gov/edis).

Great Egg Harbor Scenic and Recreational River

In the southern part of the state, near Atlantic City

The 129 mi/206 km of the Great Egg Harbor River and its 17 tributaries, which Congress designated as scenic and recreational river, drains 304 mi/486 km of pristine wetlands in the heart of New Jersey's Pinelands Reserve. Fallen leaves and cedar roots tint the river the color of tea. The river's freshwater and tidal wetlands draw waterfowl throughout the year. The cooperatively managed river (the National Park Service owns no land here) was designated in 1992.

WHAT TO SEE & DO

Bicycling, bird-watching, boating, canoeing, fishing, hiking. **Facilities:** Boat-launch facilities. **Programs & Events:** Environmental education programs, hikes, orienteering courses.

PLANNING YOUR VISIT

⚠ **Camping:** Available along the river corridor. 🏨 **Lodging:** Available in Mays Landing, Ocean City, Somers Point, other shore towns. ✕ **Food & Supplies:** Available locally. ☞ **Tips & Hints:** River runs primarily through private property, obtain brochure for entry points. 🎫 **Fees, Permits & Limitations:** Free.

HOW TO GET THERE

The river corridor runs from Camden County, NJ, to the Great Egg Harbor Bay near Somers Point.

FOR MORE INFORMATION

Great Egg Harbor National Scenic and Recreational River (National Park Service, Philadelphia Support Office, Custom House, 3rd floor, 200 Chestnut St., Philadelphia, PA 19106, tel. 215/597–9175, fax 215/597–5747; Web site www.nps.gov/greg). Atlantic County Parks (Estell Manor Park, Rte. 50, Mays Landing, NJ 08330, tel. 609/645–5960).

Morristown National Historical Park

In the northern part of the state, near Morristown

During two winters, Morristown sheltered the main encampment of the Continental Army. General George Washington held his troops together and rebuilt his forces through the winter of 1777 and encountered one of the greatest tests of his leadership during the winter of 1779–80, when starvation and cold drove his men to mutiny. The site was authorized in 1933.

WHAT TO SEE & DO

Attending programs, hiking, picnicking, touring museum and buildings. **Facilities:** Visitor center with interpretive exhibits (Jockey Hollow), Washington's Headquarters and Museum, historic buildings, wayside exhibits. Book and map sales, picnic tables. **Programs & Events:** Guided tours (Ford Mansion), interpretive talks, soldier-life demonstrations, living-history demonstrations (Wick Farm House). National Trails Day (1st Sat., June), reading of the Declaration of Independence (July 4), Holly Walk (1st week, Dec.).

PLANNING YOUR VISIT

⚠ **Camping:** Available locally; none in park. ▦ **Lodging:** Available in Florham Park, Madison, Morristown; none in park. ✗ **Food & Supplies:** Available in Bernardsville, Mendham, Morristown; none in park. ☞ **Tips & Hints:** Busiest in April and June, least crowded in December and January. ▨ **Fees, Permits & Limitations:** Entrance fee: $4 per adult 17 and older. Leashed pets only. No bikes on trails. No motorized or mechanized equipment on trails. Visitor center and museum open daily 9–5. Wick House open daily 9:30–4:30 (when staff is available). Closed Thanksgiving, Dec. 25, Jan. 1.

HOW TO GET THERE

Take I–287 to Exits 30 (Jockey Hollow) and 36 (Washington Headquarters and Museum). Closest airport: Newark International (18 mi/29 km).

FOR MORE INFORMATION

Morristown National Historical Park (30 Washington Pl., Morristown, NJ 07960, tel. 973/539–2016, fax 973/539–8361; Web site www.nps.gov/morr). Chamber of Commerce of Morris County (25 Lindsley Dr., Suite 105, Morristown, NJ 07960, tel. 973/539–3882, fax 973/539–3960). Historic Morris Visitor Center (6 Court St., Morristown, NJ 07960, tel. 973/631–5151).

See Also

Appalachian National Scenic Trail, West Virginia. *Delaware Water Gap National Recreation Area,* Pennsylvania. *Gateway National Recreation Area,* New York. *Maurice Scenic and Recreational River,* Wild and Scenic Rivers System in Other National Parklands. *Middle Delaware National Scenic River,* Pennsylvania. *Pinelands National Reserve,* Affiliated Areas in Other National Parklands. *Statue of Liberty National Monument,* New York.

NEW MEXICO

Aztec Ruins National Monument

In the northwest part of the state, near Aztec

The monument preserves structures and artifacts of ancestral Pueblo people, known as Anasazi, from the 12th and 13th centuries. People associated with Chaco Canyon to the south built and used the structures, which were later inhabited by people related to the Mesa Verde region to the north. The West Ruin, a pueblo of 400 rooms, is open to the public through a 0.25-mi/0.4-km self-guided trail. The reconstructed Great Kiva is a highlight of the trail. The site was proclaimed a national monument January 24, 1923, and designated a World Heritage Site in 1986.

WHAT TO SEE & DO

Hiking, watching video program. **Facilities:** Visitor center with museum and interpretive exhibits. Picnic area. **Programs & Events:** Interpretive talks (Memorial Day–Labor Day, daily; May and Sept.–Oct., less frequently).

PLANNING YOUR VISIT

🏕 **Camping:** Available nearby in Aztec, Bloomfield, Navajo Lake State Park; none at monument. 🛏 **Lodging:** Available nearby in Aztec, Farmington; none at monument. ✕ **Food & Supplies:** Available in Aztec, Farmington; none at monument. ☞ **Tips & Hints:** Busiest in July and August, least crowded in December and January. Visit in May for wildflowers and October for fall colors. 🎫 **Fees, Permits & Limitations:** Entrance fee: $4 per person (17 and older). Leashed pets in picnic area, no pets on trail. Monument and visitor center open Memorial Day–Labor Day, daily 8–6; Labor Day–Memorial Day, daily 8–5. Closed Thanksgiving, Dec. 25, Jan. 1.

HOW TO GET THERE

¼ mi/½ km north of Hwy 516, on Hwy. 550 near Aztec, 10 mi/16 km east of Farmington, 35 mi/56 km south of Durango, CO. Closest airport: Albuquerque (180 mi/288 km).

FOR MORE INFORMATION

Aztec Ruins National Monument (Box 640, Aztec, NM 87410-0640, tel. 505/334–6174, fax 505/334–6372; e-mail azru_front_desk@nps.gov; Web site www.nps.gov/azru). Aztec Chamber of Commerce (110 N. Ash, Aztec, NM 87410, tel. 505/334–9551, fax 505/334–7648).

Bandelier
National Monument

In the north-central part of the state, near Los Alamos

Pajarito Plateau is rich with archeological sites which were the homes of ancestral Pueblo people from the twelfth through sixteenth centuries. Trails afford access to tan cliffs, forested mesas, and deep gorges in a dramatic lanscape formed by a huge volcanic eruption more than a million years ago. Two-thirds of the 32,737-acre park is wilderness. The park was proclaimed on February 11, 1916, and transferred from the Forest Service on February 25, 1932.

WHAT TO SEE & DO

Camping, cross-country skiing, fishing, hiking, picnicking, taking guided and self-guided walks, viewing evening slide programs. **Facilities:** Visitor center with interpretive exhibits at park headquarters in Frijoles Canyon (3 mi/5 km from entrance station), trails, museum. Book and map sale areas, gift shop, mail drop, picnic area. **Programs & Events:** Guided walks, interpretive talks, evening programs, cultural demonstrations (all June–Sept.).

PLANNING YOUR VISIT

Camping: 2 campgrounds: one public and one group. (Reservations required for group campground, tel. 505/672–3861 ext. 534). Dump station and water tank filler available. Backcountry camping available, permit required (*see below*). Camping also available in Santa Fe and in national forests. **Lodging:** Available in Española, Los Alamos, Santa Fe, and White Rock; none at monument. **Food & Supplies:** In the park: snack bar and firewood. Food and supplies also available in Los Alamos and White Rock. **Tips & Hints:** Visit in April, May, September, and October. Busiest in July and August, least crowded in December and January. **Fees, Permits & Limitations:** Entrance fee: $10 per vehicle for 7-day permit. Commercial fees vary. Permit required (free) for backcountry camping. New Mexico state fishing license required. No bikes or motorized or mechanized equipment on trails. No hunting. No pets on trails or backcountry. Leashed pets allowed in campground, picnic area. Park open dawn–dusk. Visitor center open beginning of daylight saving time–Memorial Day, daily 9–5:30; Memorial Day–Labor Day, daily 8–6; Labor Day–end of daylight saving time, daily 9–5:30; end of daylight saving time to beginning of daylight saving time, daily 8–4:30. Park and visitor center closed Dec. 25, Jan. 1.

HOW TO GET THERE

From Los Alamos, take Hwy. 501S to Rte. 4, turn left onto Rte. 4 for 8 mi/13 km to entrance. From White Rock, take Rte. 4 southwest 12 mi/19 km to entrance. From Santa Fe, take Hwy. 84/285 N to Hwy. 502; west on 502 to Rte. 4; south on Rte. 4 to park entrance (47 mi/75 km). Closest airport: Santa Fe.

FOR MORE INFORMATION

Bandelier National Monument (HCR 1, Box 1, Suite 15, Los Alamos, NM 87544, tel. 505/672–3861 ext. 517, fax 505/672–0343; Web site www.nps.gov/band). Los Alamos County Chamber of Commerce (Box 460, Los Alamos, NM 87544, tel. 505/662–8105).

Capulin Volcano National Monument

In the northeast part of the state, 30 mi/48 km east of Raton

Capulin Volcano is a cinder cone formed by a volcanic eruption that occurred between 56,000 and 62,000 years ago. The 1,082 ft/330 m mountain consists mostly of loose cinders and ash. The volcano is an outstanding example of a young cinder cone and is one of the most accessible cinder cones in the United States. The pinyon-juniper woodland and brush-covered slopes in the High Plains ecosystem of the Raton-Clayton Volcanic Field provide habitat for a number of animal species. "Capulin" is Spanish for chokecherry. The monument was proclaimed August 9, 1916, as Capulin Mountain National Monument. The park name was changed to Capulin Volcano National Monument on December 31, 1987.

WHAT TO SEE & DO

Driving, hiking, picnicking, watching movie. **Facilities:** Visitor center with interpretive exhibits, theater, trails. Book sale area, fire grates, picnic area with tables. **Programs & Events:** Ranger-led volcano talks (June–Aug., daily).

PLANNING YOUR VISIT

⚠ **Camping:** Available in Capulin, Clayton Lake State Park, Sugarite Canyon State Park; none at monument. 🛏 **Lodging:** Available in Clayton, Des Moines, Raton; none at monument. ✕ **Food & Supplies:** Available in Capulin, Clayton, Des Moines, Raton; none at monument. ☞ **Tips & Hints:** Avoid rim trail during threatening weather. Go in June and July for wildflower bloom peaks and ladybug swarming on rim trail. Visit in May, late August, and September to avoid crowds. Busiest in June and July, least crowded in January and February. 🏷 **Fees, Permits & Limitations:** Entrance fee: $4 per vehicle or $2 per person on motorcycle. No hunting. No off-trail hiking. No pets or strollers on trails. No trailers, towed vehicles, pedestrians, or bikes on volcano road. Park and visitor center open Memorial Day–Labor Day, daily 7:30–6:30; Labor Day–Memorial Day, daily 8–4. Closed Thanksgiving, Dec. 25, Jan. 1.

HOW TO GET THERE

3 mi/5 km north of Capulin on NM 325. Capulin is 30 mi/50 km east of Raton and 58 mi/93 km west of Clayton on U.S. 64/87. Closest airport: Raton, NM (30 mi/50 km west).

FOR MORE INFORMATION

Capulin Volcano National Monument (Box 40, Capulin, NM 88414, tel. 505/278–2201, fax 505/278–2211; e-mail cavo_interpretation@nps.gov; Web site www.nps.gov/cavo). Raton Visitor Center (100 Clayton Rd., Raton, NM 87740, tel. 505/445–2761). Raton Chamber of Commerce (100 Clayton Rd., Raton, NM 87740, tel. 505/445–3689). Clayton Chamber of Commerce (Box 476, Clayton, NM 88415, tel. 505/374–9253).

Carlsbad Caverns National Park

In the southeast part of the state, near Carlsbad

Carlsbad Cavern contains one of the world's largest underground chambers and is an incomparable realm of gigantic subterranean chambers, beautiful cave formations, and surprising cave residents, including the famous Mexican free-tail bat. The park's more than 70 caves include the nation's deepest limestone cave (1,597 ft/487 m). The park was proclaimed Carlsbad Cave National Monument on October 25, 1923, and established as Carlsbad Caverns National Park on May 14, 1930. It became a World Heritage Site on December 6, 1995.

WHAT TO SEE & DO

Attending bat-flight programs, hiking, picnicking, touring caves. **Facilities:** Visitor center with interpretive exhibits, caves, trails. Bookstore, gift shop, pet kennel. **Programs & Events:** Ranger-guided tours (daily; reservations recommended, tel. 800/967–2283), evening bat programs (May–Oct.). Bat Flight Breakfast Program (3rd Thurs. in Aug.), Founders Day (Aug. 25).

PLANNING YOUR VISIT

Camping: Available in Carlsbad, White's City; none in park. **Lodging:** Available in Carlsbad, White's City; none in park. **Food & Supplies:** In the park: restaurant in visitor center (tel. 505/785–2281), lunchroom in cave. Food and supplies also available in Carlsbad, White's City. **Tips & Hints:** Go between March and late October to see bats. Wear rubber-soled shoes and a light jacket or sweater on cave tours. Be prepared for 75-story descent on Natural Entrance Route. Busiest in June and July, least crowded in November and January. **Fees, Permits & Limitations:** Cave entry fee: $6 per adult, $3 children 6–15, free under 6 for two self-guided cave tours (Natural Entrance and Big Room routes, both 1 mi/1.6 km each). Audio guide rental: $3. Ranger-guided King's Palace tour (reservations recommended, tel. 505/785–2232 ext. 429, or 800/967–2283) an additional $8 for adults, $4 children 6–15. Minimum age: 4. Ranger-guided Slaughter Canyon Cave tour (reservations recommended, tel 505/785–2232 ext. 429, or 800/967–2283) $15 adults, $7.50 children 6–15. Children under 6 not permitted. Guided wild cave tours $7–$20 (tel. 505/785–2232 ext. 429). Park open daily except Dec. 25. Visitor center open Memorial Day–

mid-Aug., daily 8–7; mid-Aug.–Memorial Day, daily 8–5:30. Self-guided tours Memorial Day–mid-Aug., daily 8:30–5; rest of year, daily 8:30–3:30.

HOW TO GET THERE

Just off U.S. 62-180, 20 mi/32 km from Carlsbad and 150 mi/240 km from El Paso, TX. The visitor center, near the Carlsbad Cavern entrance, is 7 mi/11 km from White's City, NM. Closest airports: Carlsbad, El Paso, TX.

FOR MORE INFORMATION

Superintendent, Carlsbad Caverns National Park (3225 National Parks Hwy., Carlsbad, NM 88220, tel. 505/785–2232; e-mail cave_interpretation@nps.gov; Web site www.nps.gov/cave).

Chaco Culture
National Historical Park

In the northwest part of the state,
between Grants and Bloomfield

The park preserves the extraordinary architecture and cultural legacy of the Chaco Anasazi, the ancestral Pueblo people whose culture flourished in Chaco Canyon from the mid-9th century to the early 12th century. This area was the cultural hub of an integrated region-wide system of communities linked by communications and an elaborate road network located throughout the present Four Corners area of the Southwest. The site was proclaimed Chaco Canyon National Monument on March 11, 1907, redesignated and renamed in 1980, and designated a World Heritage Site on December 8, 1987.

WHAT TO SEE & DO

Attending video presentations and evening interpretive programs, biking and hiking to backcountry archaeological sites, camping, picnicking, taking self-guided and ranger-led tours, touring visitor center museum. **Facilities:** Visitor center with interpretive displays, videos, and museum; 8-mi/13-km loop road; wayside exhibits; backcountry trails; interpretive display boards. Book and map sale areas, campground with fire pits/fire grates, picnic tables. **Programs & Events:** Video programs (daily). Ranger-guided tours, evening astronomy programs (both Apr.–Oct.); guided hikes and campfire programs (both May–Sept.).

PLANNING YOUR VISIT

⚠ **Camping:** Campground and 2 group campsites: no hookups. (Reservations required for group camping, tel. 505/786–7014). Private campgrounds in Farmington, Gallup, Grants. 🏠 **Lodging:** Available in Farmington, Gallup, Grants, Nageezi Trading Post; none in park. ✗ **Food & Supplies:** Available in Crownpoint, and along Hwy. 44/550; none in park. ☞ **Tips & Hints:** Call ahead for road conditions in inclement weather (tel. 505/786–7014). North access to park from Highway 44/550 requires driving 16 mi/27 km on graded dirt road. South access requires 21 mi/35 km driving on dirt road. No food or gas in park. Bring firewood and charcoal. Visit between May and September for wildflowers. Busiest in May and June, least crowded in December and January. ▨ **Fees, Permits & Limitations:** Entrance fee: $8 per vehicle or $4 per person. Backcountry hiking permit required (free, visitor center). No collecting, disturbing, or removing pottery or artifacts. No firearms. No hunting. No motorized or mechanized equipment on trails. No touching, defacing, or chalking petroglyphs or rock paintings. Leashed pets permitted on backcountry trails. Mountain bikes on two designated trails only. Northern and southern routes to the park contain long dirt stretches. Roads from the south can be very rough to impassable. Park open daily. Visitor center open Labor Day–Memorial Day, daily 8–5; Memorial Day–Labor Day, daily 8–6. Closed Dec. 25, Martin Luther King Jr. Day, Presidents Day. Loop drive closes at sunset.

HOW TO GET THERE

From the north, turn off Hwy. 44/550 at County Rd. 7900, 3 mi/5 km southeast of Nageezi and follow signs 21 mi/34 km to park boundary.

FOR MORE INFORMATION

Chaco Culture National Historical Park (Box 220, Nageezi, NM 87037, tel. 505/786–7014, fax 505/786–7061; e-mail CHCU_Interpretation@NPS.GOV; Web site www.nps.gov/chcu). Farmington Convention and Visitors Bureau (3041 E. Main, Farmington, NM 87402, tel. 505/326–7602 or 800/448–1240).

El Malpais
National Monument

In the west-central part of the state, near Grants

El Malpais means "the badlands" in Spanish. Volcanic lava flows, cinder cones, pressure ridges, and complex lava tube systems dominate the landscape. Sandstone bluffs and mesas border the eastern side of the monument, providing access to vast wilderness. Historic and archaeological sites provide reminders of the 10,000 years of human habitation in the area. Cultural resources are kept alive by the spiritual and physical presence of contemporary Native Americans, including the Puebloan peoples of Acoma, Lagunan, and Zuni, and the Ramah Navajo. These tribes continue their ancestral uses of El Malpais including gathering herbs and medicines, paying respect, and renewing ties. El Malpais is managed jointly by the National Park Service and the Bureau of Land Management. The site was established on December 31, 1987.

WHAT TO SEE & DO

Backpacking, bird- and wildlife watching, caving, four-wheel-drive touring, hiking, horseback riding, mountain biking, picnicking. **Facilities:** Information center with interpretive exhibits (23 mi/37 km south of Grants on NM 53), overlooks, trails. Bookstore, picnic tables. **Programs & Events:** Ranger-led hikes, programs, cave explorations (June–Aug.).

PLANNING YOUR VISIT

⛺ **Camping:** Backcountry camping available (permit required, *see below*). Campgrounds available in Grants and near El Morro National Monument (*see separate entry*). 🏨 **Lodging:** Available in Grants; none at monument. ✘ **Food & Supplies:** Available in Grants; none at monument. ☞ **Tips & Hints:** Be prepared for unpredictable weather. Bring warm clothing, protective headgear, three sources of light, and leather gloves when exploring lava tube caves. Don't hike or cave alone. Use extreme caution and bring sturdy hiking boots when hiking on lava terrain. Carry a day pack with water, snacks, rain gear, first-aid kit, and sunscreen. Bring topographical maps and compass or global-positioning devices for backcountry exploration. Busiest in July and August, least crowded in December and January. 💲 **Fees, Permits & Limitations:** Free. Backcountry camping permit (free) required for all backcountry camping. Permit required for some cave exploring. High-clearance and four-wheel-drive vehicles only on backcountry dirt roads. No mechanized vehicles in wilderness areas. Monument open daily. Sandstone Bluffs Overlook closes at dusk. Information center open daily 8:30–4:30. Closed Thanksgiving, Dec. 25, Jan. 1.

HOW TO GET THERE

El Malpais is south of Grants and is accessible via Hwy. 117 (exit 89) and Hwy. 53 (exit 81). El Malpais Information Center is 23 mi/37 km south of Grants on Hwy. 53. Closest airport: Albuquerque (72 mi/115 km).

FOR MORE INFORMATION

Superintendent, El Malpais National Monument (123 E. Roosevelt, Grants, NM 87020-0939, tel. 505/783–4774, fax 505/285–5661; Web site www.nps .gov/elma). Northwest New Mexico Visitor Center (1900 E. Santa Fe Ave., Grants, NM 87020, tel. 505/876–2783).

El Morro
National Monument

In the western part of the state, near Grants

Rising some 200 ft/61 m above the valley floor, El Morro is a massive sandstone mesa. A natural basin at the bottom of the mesa held the area's only water for Native Americans, explorers, and travelers. Petroglyphs carved by the prehistoric Anasazi people are the oldest inscriptions on El Morro, probably dating from AD 1000 to AD 1400. The earliest known European inscription is that of Don Juan de Onate, in 1605. The monument's two most significant prehistoric pueblo sites, on top of El Morro, are Atsinna and North Ruin. They were built in the 13th century and abandoned in the late 14th century. Atsinna also is part of the Zuni Indian tradition and folklore. The monument was proclaimed on December 8, 1906.

WHAT TO SEE & DO

Hiking to the inscriptions and ruins, picnicking. **Facilities:** Visitor center with interpretive exhibits, inscriptions, prehistoric pueblo, trail. Book, map, and pottery sale area; fire grate; group picnic site. **Programs & Events:** Cultural fair (summer months, once monthly).

PLANNING YOUR VISIT

⚠ **Camping:** Primitive campground (no reservations, open mid-May–mid-Oct.). No backcountry or group camping. Private full-service campground available 2 mi/3 km from park. ☷ **Lodging:** Available in Gallup, Grants; none at monument. ✕ **Food & Supplies:** Available in Gallup, Grants; none at monument. ☞ **Tips & Hints:** Busiest in July and August, least crowded in December and January. ▣ **Fees, Permits & Limitations:** Entrance fee: $4 per car or $2 per person, free under 16 (with adult). Leashed pets only. No mountain bikes, trail bikes, motorized equipment on trails. Group picnic site available (reservations requested). Park trails open Labor Day–Memorial Day, daily 9–4; Memorial Day–Labor Day, daily 8–6. Closed Dec. 25, Jan. 1. Visitor center open Labor Day–Memorial Day, daily 9–5; Memorial Day–Labor Day, daily 8–7.

HOW TO GET THERE

From Gallup (56 mi/90 km), take Hwy. 603S and Hwy. 53E through Ramah to the monument. Closest airport: Albuquerque.

FOR MORE INFORMATION

El Morro National Monument (Rte. 2, Box 43, Ramah, NM 87321-9603, tel. 505/783–4226, fax 505/783–4689). Gallup Chamber of Commerce (103 W. Hwy. 66, Gallup, NM 87301, tel. 505/722–2228). Grants Chamber of Commerce (Box 297, Grants, NM 87020, tel. 505/287–4802).

Fort Union National Monument

In the northeast part of the state, near Watrous

Three forts, the first of which was constructed in 1851 on this site near the Santa Fe Trail, served as headquarters and supply depot for the Military Department of New Mexico. A 1.5-mi/2.5-km trail leads visitors past the ruins of the last two forts. Wagon ruts along the Santa Fe Trail are visible here. The monument was established on April 5, 1956.

WHAT TO SEE & DO

Picnicking, touring the ruins. **Facilities:** Visitor center with interpretive exhibits, ruins, trails. Book, map, and audiovisual sales; picnic tables. **Programs & Events:** Self-guided tours. Guided walks, talks (spring and fall, weekends; June–Aug., daily). First Fort Site Tour (June), Cultural Encounters on the Santa Fe Trail (July), An Evening at Fort Union (Aug.). Living-history demonstrations (during special events).

PLANNING YOUR VISIT

⛺ **Camping:** Available in Las Vegas, NM; none at monument. 🏠 **Lodging:** Available in Las Vegas, NM; none at monument. ✗ **Food & Supplies:** Available in Las Vegas, NM; none at monument. ☞ **Tips & Hints:** Plan to spend two hours. Self-guided walking tour (1.5 mi/2.4 km) takes 1½ hours. Busiest in July and August, least crowded in December and January. 🎟 **Fees, Permits & Limitations:** Entrance fee: $2 per adult 17 and over or $4 per vehicle. Group reservations recommended (tel. 505/425–8025). Don't climb on walls or foundations of ruins. Stay on trail to avoid rattlesnakes in the tall grass. The first fort arsenal site is closed to the public. No pets in buildings, leashed pets permitted on trails only. Monument open Labor Day–Memorial Day, daily 8–5; Memorial Day–Labor Day, daily 8–6. Closed Dec. 25, Jan. 1.

HOW TO GET THERE

8 mi/13 km north of I–25 (Exit 366), at the end of NM 161. Closest airport: Albuquerque (153 mi/245 km).

FOR MORE INFORMATION

Fort Union National Monument (Box 127, Watrous, NM 87753, tel. 505/425–8025; e-mail FOUN_Administration@nps.gov; Web site www.nps.gov/foun). Chamber of Commerce (Box 128 Las Vegas, NM 87701, tel. 505/425–8631 or 800/832–5947, fax 505/425–3057; e-mail www.lasvegasnewmexico.com).

Gila Cliff Dwellings National Monument

In the southwest part of the state, near Silver City

Well-preserved cliff dwellings offer a glimpse of the lives of the Native Americans who built the structures in the 1280s through the early 1300s. The surroundings probably look today very much as they did when the cliff dwellings were inhabited. The monument was proclaimed in 1907, transferred to the Park Service in 1933, and administered by the Forest Service beginning in 1975.

WHAT TO SEE & DO

Touring cliff dwellings, watching video. Bird-watching, camping, fishing, hiking, and horseback riding available in the Gila Wilderness that surrounds the monument. **Facilities:** Visitor center with interpretive exhibits, contact station, trail, cliff dwellings. Bookstore. **Programs & Events:** Guided tours (daily).

PLANNING YOUR VISIT

⛺ **Camping:** Available in surrounding Gila National Forest and Gila Hot Springs; none at monument. 🏠 **Lodging:** Available in Gila Hot Springs, Mimbres, Pinos Altos, Silver City; none at monument. ✗ **Food & Supplies:** Available in Gila Hot Springs, Mimbres, Pinos Altos, Silver City; none at monument. ☞ **Tips & Hints:** Call ahead for winter road conditions and hours of operation. Busiest in March and July, least crowded in December and January. ✉ **Fees, Permits & Limitations:**. User fee: $3 per person 12 and older. Trailers over 20 ft/6 m must take Hwy. 35 to reach monument (*see below*). Monument open Memorial Day–Labor Day, daily 8–6; Labor Day–Memorial Day, daily 9–4. Visitor center open Memorial Day–Labor Day, daily 8–5; Labor Day–Memorial Day, daily 8–4:30.

HOW TO GET THERE

44 mi/70 km north of Silver City on Hwy. 15, a two-hour, narrow, winding drive. An alternative route is U.S. 180E from Silver City, then Hwy. 152 and Hwy. 35 to Hwy. 15. Route is 25 mi/40 km longer but takes the same time. Closest airport: Silver City–Grant County Airport (64 mi/102 km).

FOR MORE INFORMATION

Gila Cliff Dwellings National Monument (HC 68, Box 100, Silver City, NM 88061, tel. 505/536–9461; Web site www.nps.gov/gicl).

Pecos National Historical Park

In the northeast part of the state, near Pecos

Preserved in this park are the ruins of the 15th-century Pueblo of Pecos, the remains of two Spanish colonial missions built in the 17th and 18th centuries, sections of the Santa Fe Trail, the site of the Civil War Battle of Glorieta Pass, and a former cattle ranch. The park consists of the Pecos and Glorieta units. Pecos National Monument was authorized in 1965 and redesignated in 1990.

WHAT TO SEE & DO

Picnicking; touring Forked Lightning Ranch, ruins of pueblo and missions, Glorieta battlefield, and Kowlowski's Trading Post. **Facilities:** Visitor center with interpretive exhibits (off NM 63), 1.25-mi/2-km self-guided trail, ruins of Pecos Pueblo and Spanish missions, Forked Lightning Ranch, Kowlowski's Trading Post. Bookstore, picnic area. **Programs & Events:** Ruin tours, battlefield tours (if arranged in advance). Cultural demonstrations (Memorial Day–Labor Day, weekends), full-moon tours (Memorial Day–Labor Day), ranch tours (Memorial Day–Labor Day; and other times if arranged in advance). Feast Day Mass (1st Sun. in Aug.).

PLANNING YOUR VISIT

⛰ **Camping:** Available in Pecos District of Santa Fe National Forest; none in park. 🏠 **Lodging:** Available in Glorieta, Pecos, Las Vegas, Santa Fe; none in park. ✕ **Food & Supplies:** Available in Pecos, Santa Fe; none in park. ☞ **Tips & Hints:** Plan a one- to two-hour visit. Busiest in July and August, least crowded in January and February. ✉ **Fees, Permits & Limitations:** Entrance fee: $2 per person or $4 per vehicle. Park open Labor Day–Memorial Day, daily 8–5; Memorial Day–Labor Day, daily 8–6. Visitor center open daily 8–5, closed Dec. 25, Jan. 1.

HOW TO GET THERE

2 mi/3 km south of the village of Pecos on NM 63 and 28 mi/45 km southeast of Santa Fe via I–25. From I–25, take Exit 299 (if traveling north) or Exit 307 (if traveling south) to reach park. Closest airports: Santa Fe (28 mi/45 km), or Albuquerque (87 mi/138 km).

FOR MORE INFORMATION

Pecos National Historical Park (Box 418, Pecos, NM 87552, tel. 505/757–6414 ext. 2, fax 505/757–8460; Web site www.nps.gov/peco).

Petroglyph National Monument

On the west side of Albuquerque

Nearly 20,000 petroglyphs carved by ancestral Puebloans, Hispanic sheepherders, and early settlers stretch 17 mi/27 km along the volcanic escarpment on the west side of Albuquerque. The petroglyphs and associated archaeological sites relate a 12,000-year story of human habitation on Albuquerque's West Mesa. The park was authorized on June 27, 1990.

WHAT TO SEE & DO

Hiking, picnicking, self-guided trails. **Facilities:** Visitor center with interpretive exhibits (Unser Blvd., 3 mi/5 km north of I–40), self-guided trails at Boca Negra Canyon. Book sales area, picnic areas. **Programs & Events:** Ranger-guided tours (Memorial Day–mid-Oct., weekends; mid-Oct.–Memorial Day, by reservation), cultural demonstrations (Memorial Day–Labor Day, weekends). Founders Day (around Aug. 25).

PLANNING YOUR VISIT

🏕 **Camping:** Available in Albuquerque; none at monument. 🏨 **Lodging:** Available in Albuquerque, Bernalillo, Santa Fe; none at monument. ✘ **Food & Supplies:** Available in Albuquerque; none at monument. ☞ **Tips & Hints:** Spring is the best time for cactus and wildflower blooms but is very windy; September and October have the best weather. Busiest in May and October, least crowded in December and January. 🎟 **Fees, Permits & Limitations:** Entrance fee: $1 per car on weekdays, $2 per car on weekends. No hunting. No motorized equipment. No pets. Stay on trails. Park and visitor center open daily 8–5. Closed Thanksgiving, Dec. 25, Jan. 1.

HOW TO GET THERE

On Albuquerque's west mesa, 3 mi/5 km north of I–40 on Unser Blvd. Closest airport: Albuquerque (12 mi/ 19 km).

FOR MORE INFORMATION

Petroglyph National Monument (6001 Unser Blvd. NW, Albuquerque, NM 87120, tel. 505/899–0205, fax 505/839–4594; Web site www.nps.gov/petr).

Salinas Pueblo Missions National Monument

Midstate, near Mountainair

Three separate sites of stone ruins—Abo, Quarai, and Gran Quivira—make up the monument in the Salinas Valley, an area that was a major trade center and one of the most populous parts of the Pueblo world during the 17th century. Built between 1622 and 1660 by the Tompiros and Tiwa people, the pueblos were abandoned in the 1670s after drought, famine, and attacks by hostile tribes. Gran Quivira was proclaimed a national monument in 1909. Abo and Quarai became monuments in 1981, when Salinas was established.

WHAT TO SEE & DO

Picnicking, touring ruins and museum, watching video. **Facilities:** Visitor center with interpretive exhibits (1 block west of U.S. 60/NM 55 intersection), three ruin sites. Picnic area. **Programs & Events:** Ranger-led tours by request, self-guided tours.

PLANNING YOUR VISIT

⛺ **Camping:** Available in Cibola National Forest, Manzano Mountains State Park; none at monument. 🏨 **Lodging:** Available in Mountainair; none at monument. ✕ **Food & Supplies:** Available in Mountainair; none at monument. ☞ **Tips & Hints:** Busiest July through September, least crowded in December and January. Call ahead for ranger-guide tours. 🎫 **Fees, Permits & Limitations:** Free. Monument open Memorial Day–Labor Day, daily 9–7; Labor Day–Memorial Day, daily 9–5. Visitor center open daily, 9–5. Closed Thanksgiving, Dec. 25, Jan. 1.

HOW TO GET THERE

Visitor center is one block west of intersection of U.S. 60 and NM 55. From intersection, Abo Ruins are 9 mi/14 km west on U.S. 60 and 0.5 mi/1 km north on NM 513; Quarai Ruins are 8 mi/13 km north on NM 55 and 1 mi/1.6 km west; and Gran Quivira Ruins are 25 mi/40 km south on NM 55. Closest airport: Albuquerque (70 mi/112 km).

FOR MORE INFORMATION

Salinas Pueblo Missions National Monument (Box 517, Mountainair, NM 87036, tel. 505/847–2585, fax 505/847–2441).

White Sands National Monument

In the southern part of the state, near Alamogordo

The monument protects part of the world's largest gypsum dunefield. The glistening white sands rise 60 ft/18 m in places and cover 176,000 acres. Through extremes of adaptation and natural selection, the White

Sands flora and fauna survive in one of nature's toughest proving grounds. The monument was proclaimed on January 18, 1933.

WHAT TO SEE & DO

Auto touring, hiking, picnicking, watching video. **Facilities:** Visitor center with interpretive exhibits, Heart of the Sands Nature Center, 8-mi/13-km scenic drive, roadside exhibits, trails, amphitheater. Bookstore, gift shop, picnic areas with grills. **Programs & Events:** Sunset nature walks (daily), Lake Lucero tours (monthly). Evening campfire programs (Memorial Day–Labor Day). Full-moon programs (May–Sept.).

PLANNING YOUR VISIT

⚠ **Camping:** Backcountry camping available (no reservations, permit required, *see below*). Group campsite available (reservations available, tel. 505/679–2599). Public and private campgrounds also available in Alamogordo, nearby state parks, national forests, and Bureau of Land Management lands. ⛺ **Lodging:** Available in Alamogordo; none in park. ✕ **Food & Supplies:** In the park: snacks. Food and supplies also available outside the park in Alamogordo. ☞ **Tips & Hints:** Bring water if hiking, and a compass and map if hiking off trails. Call ahead to see if park is closed for White Sands Missile Range testing. Go in fall and winter for best weather, spring for whitest dunes and dune movement because of winds, mid-April for wildflowers, mid-May–early June for yucca blooms. Busiest in July and August, least crowded in November and January. 📧 **Fees, Permits & Limitations:** Entrance fee: $3 per person over 16. Backcountry permits ($3 per night) required for all backcountry camping. No backcountry camping on nights of White Sands Missile Range testing. No hunting. No vehicles or bikes on trails or off roads. Leashed pets on trails. Dunes Dr. open Labor Day–Memorial Day, daily 7–sunset; Memorial Day–Labor Day, daily 7–9. Closed during testing. Visitor center open Labor Day–Memorial Day, daily 8–5; Memorial Day–Labor Day, daily 8–7. Closed Dec. 25.

HOW TO GET THERE

15 mi/24 km southwest of Alamogordo and 52 mi/83 km northeast of Las Cruces via U.S. 70. Closest airport: El Paso, TX (90 mi/144 km).

FOR MORE INFORMATION

White Sands National Monument (Box 1086, Holloman AFB, NM 88330-1086, tel. 505/679–2599, fax 505/479–4333; Web site www.nps.gov/whsa). Alamogordo Chamber of Commerce (1301 N. White Sands Blvd., Alamogordo, NM 88310, tel. 800/437–6120 or 800/826–0294; Web site www.alamogordo.com).

See Also

Continental Divide National Scenic Trail, National Trails System in Other National Parklands. *Santa Fe National Historic Trail,* National Trails System in Other National Parklands. *Trail of Tears National Historic Trail,* National Trails System in Other National Parklands.

NEW YORK

Castle Clinton
National Monument

In New York City

The site preserves the fort built between 1808 and 1811 to defend New York City during the War of 1812. In 1817, the Southwest Battery, constructed on the rocks off the tip of Manhattan, was renamed Castle Clinton in honor of DeWitt Clinton, mayor of New York City. The site later became a restaurant and entertainment center, opera house and theater, an immigrant landing depot where 8 million people entered the United States, and finally the New York City Aquarium. It closed in 1941. The site was authorized on August 12, 1946.

WHAT TO SEE & DO

Self- and ranger-guided tours of the site. **Facilities:** Museum with interpretive exhibits, building. Bookstore. **Programs & Events:** Ranger-led programs and tours (daily). Seasonal activities and special events available.

PLANNING YOUR VISIT

Camping: Available in New York City area; none at monument. **Lodging:** Available in New York City area; none at monument. **Food & Supplies:** Available in New York City area; none at monument. **Tips & Hints:** Use mass transit. Plan on 25 minutes to tour site. Busiest in July and August, least crowded in January and February. **Fees, Permits & Limitations:** Free. Monument open Sept.–Apr., daily 8:30–5; May–Aug., daily 8–5. Closed Dec. 25.

HOW TO GET THERE

The monument is in Battery Park at the southern tip of Manhattan. Public transportation is recommended. The west-side 1 and 9 subway trains stop at South Ferry station in Battery Park. The east-side 4 and 5 subway trains stop at Bowling Green station adjacent to Battery Park. The crosstown N and R subway trains stop at Whitehall Street station adjacent to Battery Park. Frequent bus service to South Ferry is provided by route M-6, which operates daily on Broadway; route M-1, which operates weekdays on 5th Ave., Park Ave., and Broadway; and by route M-15, which operates daily on 2nd Ave. Closest airports: JFK and LaGuardia (New York); Newark (New Jersey).

FOR MORE INFORMATION

Superintendent, Castle Clinton National Monument (26 Wall St., New York, NY 10005, tel. 212/344–7220; Web site www.nps.gov/cacl).

Eleanor Roosevelt
National Historic Site

Near Hyde Park

Eleanor Roosevelt used Val-Kill Cottage as a retreat in her younger years and as her home in her later years where she entertained heads of state and had time to relax. It was built as a factory building for Val-Kill Industries before being converted to a home in 1937. The site was authorized on May 27, 1977.

WHAT TO SEE & DO

Touring home and grounds. **Facilities:** Playhouse with introductory film, furnished home of Eleanor Roosevelt (Val-Kill Cottage), Rose Garden, Cutting Garden, The Stone Cottage conference center, walkways and trails. **Programs & Events:** Guided tours, ranger talks.

PLANNING YOUR VISIT

⚲ **Camping:** Available in Hyde Park area; none at site. 🏠 **Lodging:** Available in Hyde Park area; none at site. ✕ **Food & Supplies:** Available in Hyde Park area; none at site. ☞ **Tips & Hints:** Allow one hour for film and tour, more for viewing landscaped grounds and walking trail. Busiest in August and October, least crowded in January and February. 🎫 **Fees, Permits & Limitations:** Entrance fee: $5 per adult 17 and up. Combination pass for Eleanor Roosevelt site and nearby home of FDR and Vanderbilt Mansion sites: $18. Reservations required for groups of 10 or more, recommended for individuals (tel. 800/967–2283). Pedestrian traffic only after arrival. Site open May–Oct., daily 9–5; Nov.–Apr., weekends 9–5; closed Thanksgiving, Dec. 25, Jan. 1. Grounds open daily until sunset.

HOW TO GET THERE

Two hours north of New York City on Rte. 9G, near Hyde Park. From Rte. 9, make a right on St. Andrews Rd. (County Route 40A). Turn left on Rte. 9G. Home is on the right. Closest airport: Newburgh (45 mi/72 km).

FOR MORE INFORMATION

Eleanor Roosevelt National Historic Site (4097 Albany Post Rd., Hyde Park, NY 12538, tel. 845/229–9115; Web site www.nps.gov/elro). Dutchess County Tourism (3 Neptune Rd., Suite M-17, Poughkeepsie, NY 12601, tel. 800/445–3131).

Federal Hall
National Memorial

In New York City

This graceful building occupies the site of the original Federal Hall, where the trial of John Peter Zenger, involving freedom of the press, was held in 1735. The Stamp Act Congress convened here in 1765 and the Second Continental Congress met here in 1785. George Washington took the oath as first U.S. president and the Bill of Rights was adopted here in 1789. The present building was completed in 1842. The statue of Washington is by John Quincy Adams Ward. The site was designated as Federal Hall Memorial National Historic Site in 1939 and redesignated in 1955.

WHAT TO SEE & DO

Attending ranger program, self-guided tours of museum, viewing video. **Facilities:** Museum with interpretive exhibits. Museum shop. **Programs & Events:** Self-guided tours, ranger-led programs and tours, orientation video (daily). Seasonal activities and special events available.

PLANNING YOUR VISIT

 Lodging: Available locally; none at memorial. ✕ **Food & Supplies:** Available locally; none at memorial. ☞ **Tips & Hints:** Use mass transit to get to memorial. Busiest in July and August, least crowded in January and February. 💷 **Fees, Permits & Limitations:** Free. Memorial open weekdays 9–5. Closed Federal holidays.

HOW TO GET THERE

The 7th Ave. 2 and 3 subway trains stop at Wall and William Sts., one block east of Federal Hall. The Lexington Ave. 4 and 5 subway trains stop at Wall St. and Broadway, one block west of Federal Hall. On weekdays, the J, M, and Z subway trains stop at Wall and Broad Sts. Frequent bus service is provided by route M-6 on Broadway, one block to the west, and by route M-15 on Water St., three blocks to the east. Closest airports: JFK and LaGuardia (New York); Newark (New Jersey).

FOR MORE INFORMATION

Federal Hall National Memorial (26 Wall St., New York, NY 10005, tel. 212/825–6888; Web site www.nps.gov/feha).

Fire Island National Seashore

In southeast New York, on Long Island's south shore

The seashore's 32-mi-/51-km-long barrier island contains extensive salt marshes, a 300-year-old American holly forest, and the only federally protected wilderness in New York State. It includes the Fire Island Light Station; Sailors Haven; Watch Hill; the Wilderness Visitor Center at Smith Point; and the 612-acre estate of William Floyd, a signer of the Declaration of Independence, in Mastic Beach, Long Island. The seashore was authorized in 1964.

WHAT TO SEE & DO

Boating, canoeing, fishing, hiking, house and tower touring, kayaking, picnicking, swimming. **Facilities:** 3 visitor centers—Watch Hill, Sailors

Haven, Fire Island Wilderness Visitor Center; Fire Island Light Station Keepers' Quarters (all on Fire Island); William Floyd Estate (Mastic Beach); beaches, marinas, trails. Book sale areas, gift shops, grills, picnic tables. **Programs & Events:** Guided nature walks (Sailors Haven and Watch Hill, July–Aug.), canoe program (Watch Hill, July–Aug.), tower tours (Fire Island Light Station, Apr.–Oct.), house tours (William Floyd Estate, Memorial Day–Oct.). Cultural programs Fire Island Light Station, William Floyd Estate (occasional).

PLANNING YOUR VISIT

⚠ **Camping:** Campground: Watch Hill, tent camping only (reservations required, tel. 631/597–6633). Backcountry camping available (permit required, *see below*). Group camping (reservations available, tel. 631/289–4810). ▣ **Lodging:** Available on Fire Island, Long Island; none at seashore. ✕ **Food & Supplies:** At the seashore: meals, snack bar, and store at Watch Hill (tel. 631/597–6655), snack bar at Sailors Haven (tel. 631/597–6171). Food and supplies also available outside the seashore at Bayshore, Cherry Grove, Davis Park, Mastic, Patchogue, Sayville. ☞ **Tips & Hints:** Island has no roads and is accessible by boat or passenger ferry only. Bring adequate food, water, and supplies for day trips. Go in late April, May, September, or October for songbird migration; between September and October for hawk migration; between June and August for wildflower blooms. Busiest in July and August, least crowded in January and February. ▤ **Fees, Permits & Limitations:** Free. Ferry fees vary: Watch Hill (tel. 631/475–1665), Sailors Haven (tel. 631/589–8980). Backcountry permits required (free, tel. 631/281–3010). Leashed pets only. No skating, bicycling, or skateboarding. No mechanical equipment or metal detectors. Visitor center hours: Sailors Haven and Watch Hill—July and Aug., Wed.–Sun. 9:30–5:30; William Floyd estate—Memorial Day–Labor Day, Fri.–Sun. 11–5.

HOW TO GET THERE

The seashore is accessible by ferry or boat off the south shore of Long Island in Bayshore, Patchogue, Sayville. Closest airport: MacArthur (Islip).

FOR MORE INFORMATION

Fire Island National Seashore (120 Laurel St., Patchogue, NY 11772, tel. 631/289–4810, fax 631/289–4898; Web site www.nps.gov/fiis). Fire Island Tourism Bureau (Box 626, Sayville, NY 11782, tel. 631/563–8448).

Fort Stanwix
National Monument

In central New York, in Rome

The British built a fort at the site in 1758 to protect the Oneida Carry portage that linked the waterway between the Atlantic Ocean and Great Lakes. Fort Stanwix was rebuilt by Americans in 1776 and then, in 1777, attacked by the British from August 3 to 23 until British troops retreated to Canada. The fort has been almost entirely reconstructed to its 1777 appearance. The site was authorized in 1935. It became a National Historic Landmark in 1963 and was listed on the National Register of Historic Places in 1984.

WHAT TO SEE & DO

Touring the fort. **Facilities:** Visitor center with interpretive exhibits, fort, museum, living-history quarters, trail. Bookstore. **Programs & Events:** Ranger-guided tours, interpretive programs, living-history demonstrations (Apr.–Dec.). Syracuse Symphony Orchestra (last Sat., July), occasional reenactments.

PLANNING YOUR VISIT

⚠ **Camping:** Available in Delta Lake State Park and locally; none at monument. 🏠 **Lodging:** Available in Rome; none at monument. ✕ **Food & Supplies:** Available in Rome; none at monument. ☞ **Tips & Hints:** Busiest in July and August, least crowded in November and April. 🎫 **Fees, Permits & Limitations:** Free. Reservations required for ranger-guided group tours (tel. 315/336–2090). No pets in fort buildings. Leashed pets elsewhere. Fort open Apr.–Dec., daily 9–5; closed Thanksgiving, Dec. 25. Monument grounds open year-round.

HOW TO GET THERE

The monument is in downtown Rome. Closest airports: Oneida County (6 mi/10 km), Syracuse (50 mi/80 km).

FOR MORE INFORMATION

Fort Stanwix National Monument (112 E. Park St., Rome, NY 13440, tel. 315/336–2090, fax 315/339–3966; e-mail fost_interpretation@nps. gov; Web site www.nps.gov/fost). Rome Area Chamber of Commerce (139 W. Dominick St., Rome, NY 13440, tel. 315/337–1700). Oneida County Convention and Visitors Bureau (Box 551, Utica, NY 13502, tel. 315/724–7221).

Gateway National Recreation Area

In New York City; and in northeast New Jersey, on Sandy Hook peninsula

Gateway, one of two major urban national parks in the country, offers residents of New York, New Jersey, and Connecticut a national-park experience with diverse cultural, historical, and recreational opportunities. It is the nation's fifth most visited national park site, with more than 7 million visitors each year. The recreation area includes Jamaica Bay in Queens and Brooklyn; Staten Island; and Sandy Hook in New Jersey. The park was authorized on October 17, 1972.

WHAT TO SEE & DO

Attending ethnic and special events, beach-going, bicycling, bird-watching, boating, fishing, hiking, jogging, participating in organized athletics, sunbathing, swimming, touring forts and lighthouses, walking. **Facilities:** 5 visitor centers with interpretive exhibits (Floyd Bennett Field; Jamaica Bay Wildlife Refuge; Fort Tilden; Fort Wadsworth; Sandy Hook), Ecology Village (Jamaica Bay), Canarsie Pier, Great Kills Park Beach Center, Fort Hancock Museum, History House (Ft. Hancock), Sandy Hook Lighthouse, Battery Potter, beaches, trails, waysides, boardwalk, theater. At Jamaica Bay Unit: picnic areas (Fort Tilden, Riis Park, and Floyd Bennett Field), bookshop (Jamaica Bay Wildlife Refuge), marina (Jamaica Bay), nonmotorized, car-top boating ramp (Floyd Bennett Field), post office (Fort Tilden); at Staten Island Unit: picnic areas (Miller Field and Great Kills Park), bookshop (Fort Wadsworth Visitor Center), changing rooms (Great Kills Beach House), marina (Great Kills Park), boat-launching ramp (Great Kills Park); at Sandy Hook Unit: picnic areas (Fort Hancock and beach areas), bookshop and map sales area (visitor center and Fort Hancock Museum), beach concessions and ferry service (summer), post office (Fort Hancock). **Programs & Events:** Ranger-led programs and walks (several times weekly, weekends). Outdoor programs (May–Oct.). At Jamaica Bay Unit: Canarsie Pier Concert Series (June–Aug.), Fort Tilden Concert Series (June–Aug.); at Staten Island Unit: New York City Five Borough Bike Tour (May), Metropolitan Opera Concert (June), New York Philharmonic Orchestra Concert (July), New York City Half Marathon (Oct.), New York City Marathon (Nov.); at Sandy Hook Unit: Clearwater Festival (Aug.), Beach Concert Series (June–Aug.).

PLANNING YOUR VISIT

Camping: 2 campgrounds: Floyd Bennett Field (for organized groups with nonprofit status only, reservations and permit required, tel. 718/338–4306), no hookups; Sandy Hook (primitive, for organized youth groups only, Apr.–Nov., reservations required, tel. 732/872–5970). Private campgrounds available only near Sandy Hook unit at Cheesequake State Park, Matawan, NJ. **Lodging:** In the Staten Island Unit: Navy Lodge (military, retired military, and government workers only, tel. 718/442–0413 or 800/628–9466). Lodging also available in New York City area. **Food & Supplies:** Jamaica Bay: restaurant at Canarsie Pier; snack bar at Riis Park Boardwalk (Memorial Day–Labor Day). Staten Island: snack bar and evening bar at Carriage House at Fort Wadsworth; seasonal snack bar and roving meal mobiles at Miller Field and Great Kills. Sandy Hook: Meals at Seagull's Nest Restaurant (tel. 732/872–0025), seasonal snack bars at beach houses. Food and supplies also available in New York City area. **Tips & Hints:** Watch for deer ticks. Get to Sandy Hook beach early on summer weekends. Access can be limited or closed between 10 and 3. Best weather: April–October. Go in spring and fall to see migrating bird species and in September and October to see monarch butterflies. Busiest in July and August, least crowded in January and February. **Fees, Permits & Limitations:** Free. Sandy Hook parking fee Memorial Day–Labor Day: $8 weekdays, $10 weekends. $25 annual fee for anglers to use designated parking lots. Permits for group picnics ($25 and up plus possible parking fee; Jamaica Bay, tel. 718/338–3799; Staten Island, tel. 718/354–4500; Sandy Hook, tel. 732/872–5970) and special events. Leashed dogs only. No dogs on swimming beach

Mar. 15–Labor Day at Sandy Hook or at Great Kills Park. Permit required to drive on beach at Breezy Point. No off-road cycling in park. No horse trails. Park open daily sunrise–sunset except in designated fishing/beach areas that are covered under a permit. Visitor center hours: At Jamaica Bay, Fort Tilden Visitor Center open daily 8:30–5; Ryan Visitor Center at Floyd Bennett Field open daily 8:30–5; Canarsie Pier open Memorial Day–Labor Day, daily 8:30–5; Jamaica Bay Wildlife Refuge open daily 8:30–5. Closed Thanksgiving, Dec. 25, Jan. 1. At Staten Island Unit, Fort Wadsworth open Wed.–Sun. 10–5; call 718/354–4500 for current hours. Sandy Hook visitor center open daily 10–5. Closed Thanksgiving, Dec. 25, Jan. 1.

HOW TO GET THERE

Breezy Point District is on Rockaway Peninsula in Queens. Take Flatbush Ave. (Exit 11S) off Belt Pkwy. over the Marine Park Bridge. The Jamaica Bay District is in Brooklyn. Take Flatbush Ave. (Exit 11S) off Belt Pkwy. The Jamaica Bay Wildlife Refuge is in Queens. Take Cross Bay Blvd. (Exit 17S) off Belt Pkwy. Closest airports: JFK and LaGuardia Airports. Staten Island Unit: Fort Wadsworth is on Staten Island. Take Verrazano Narrows Bridge/Staten Island Expressway to Bay St. exit and follow signs. Miller Field is on Staten Island. Take New Dorp La. off Hylan Blvd. Great Kills Park is on Staten Island off Hylan Blvd. south of New Dorp La. Closest airport: Newark, NJ (10 mi/16 km). The Sandy Hook Unit is on Sandy Hook Peninsula in New Jersey. Take the Garden State Pkwy. to Exit 117, then Rte. 36E past Highlands, NJ. Closest airport: Newark, NJ (25 mi/40 km).

FOR MORE INFORMATION

Gateway National Recreation Area (Public Affairs Office, 210 New York Ave., Staten Island, NY 10305, tel. 718/338–3687, fax 718/338–6284; Web site www.nps.gov/gate). Jamaica Bay Unit Visitor Center (Floyd Bennett Field, Bldg. 69, Brooklyn, NY 11234, tel. 718/338–3799). Staten Island Unit, Fort Wadsworth Visitor Center (210 New York Ave., Staten Island, NY 10305, tel. 718/354–4500). Sandy Hook Unit Visitor Center (Box 530, Highland, NJ 07732, tel. 732/872–5970). New York State Dept. of Economic Development, Division of Tourism (Box 2603, Albany, NY 12220-0603, tel. 800/225–5697). New Jersey Department of Tourism and Travel (Box 826, 20 W. State St., Trenton, NJ 08625, tel. 800/537–7397).

General Grant National Memorial

In New York City

The memorial, popularly known as Grant's Tomb, is the final resting place of Ulysses S. Grant and his wife, Julia Dent Grant. After serving as Union commander during the Civil War, Grant served two terms as president before entering business on Wall Street. As president, Grant signed an act on March 1, 1872, establishing Yellowstone as the nation's first national park. His tomb, designed by architect John Duncan, is constructed of 8,000 tons of granite and marble. The 150-ft-/46-m-tall memorial is the largest mausoleum in North America. It was dedicated in 1897 and authorized to be transferred to federal ownership and Park Service administration in 1958.

WHAT TO SEE & DO

Touring memorial and museum. **Facilities:** Memorial, museum. Museum shop. **Programs & Events:** Ranger-led programs and tours, costumed interpretations.

PLANNING YOUR VISIT

⊞ **Lodging:** Available locally; none at memorial. ✕ **Food & Supplies:** Available locally; none at memorial. ☞ **Tips & Hints:** Plan on 20–30 minutes for tours and programs. Busiest in July and August, least crowded in January and February. ▦ **Fees, Permits & Limitations:** Free. Memorial open daily 9–5. Closed Thanksgiving, Dec. 25, Jan. 1.

HOW TO GET THERE

The memorial is at Riverside Dr. and 122nd St. in Manhattan in New York City. Subway trains 1 or 9, which run along 7th Ave. and Broadway, stop at the West 116th St. Station at Broadway, two blocks east and six blocks south of Grant's Tomb. Bus service is provided on Riverside Dr. up to 120th St. by route M-5. Closest airports: JFK and LaGuardia (New York); Newark (New Jersey).

FOR MORE INFORMATION

Superintendent, General Grant National Memorial (26 Wall St., New York, NY 10005, tel. 212/666–1640; Web site www.nps.gov/gegr).

Hamilton Grange National Memorial

In New York City

Alexander Hamilton, American patriot, co-author of the "Federalist Papers," and first U.S. Treasury Secretary, built the Grange on Manhattan's Upper West Side in 1802. The Grange, named after the Hamilton family's ancestral home in Scotland, served as his home for two years. On July 11, 1804, Hamilton was fatally wounded in a duel with his political rival, Aaron Burr. The memorial was authorized on April 27, 1962.

WHAT TO SEE & DO

Touring renovated parts of house, viewing exterior of building. **Facilities:** Partially renovated house. **Programs & Events:** Ranger-led costumed guided tours, period music. Hamilton's Birthday (Sun. nearest Jan. 11).

PLANNING YOUR VISIT

⊞ **Lodging:** Available locally; none at memorial. ✕ **Food & Supplies:** Available locally; none at memorial. ☞ **Tips & Hints:** Busiest in June and July, least crowded in January and February. ▦ **Fees, Permits &**

Limitations: Free. Part of the house is open Fri.–Sun. 9–5. Closed Thanksgiving, Dec. 25, Jan. 1. Rangers lead guided tours of the parts of the house that have been renovated. The rest of the house is closed pending relocation and restoration.

HOW TO GET THERE

The house is at 287 Convent Ave., between W. 141st and W. 142nd Sts., in New York City. From I–87 (Major Deegan Expressway), take Exit 4 (E. 149th St). Go west on 149th St. across bridge onto W. 145th St.; west on 145th St. six blocks to Convent Ave.; south four blocks to house. The 1 or 9 subway trains, which run along Seventh Ave.–Broadway, stop at the W. 137th St. station on Broadway, two blocks west and five blocks south of Hamilton Grange. The A, B, C, and D subway trains stop at the W. 145th St. station on St. Nicholas Ave., four blocks north and two blocks east of Hamilton Grange. Frequent bus service is provided on Broadway two blocks to the west by routes M-4 and M-5, on Amsterdam Ave. one block to the west by routes M-100 and M-101, and by route BX-19 operating crosstown on 145th St. Half-hourly bus service on Convent Avenue is provided by route M-18. Closest airports: JFK and LaGuardia (New York); Newark (New Jersey).

FOR MORE INFORMATION

Superintendent, Hamilton Grange National Memorial (26 Wall St., New York, NY 10005, tel. 212/666–1640; Web site www.nps.gov/hagr).

Home of Franklin D. Roosevelt National Historic Site

In southeast New York, in Hyde Park

Springwood was the birthplace and lifetime residence of the 32nd president. The gravesites of Franklin Delano Roosevelt and Eleanor Roosevelt are in the Rose Garden. Also on site is the FDR Library and Museum. The site was designated on January 15, 1944.

WHAT TO SEE & DO

Touring home and adjacent library and museum. **Facilities:** Furnished home of FDR, memorial Rose Garden, ice house, stables, grounds, trails. Bookstore, tourist information center. **Programs & Events:** Ranger-led or self-guided tours, ranger talks.

PLANNING YOUR VISIT

⚠ **Camping:** Available in Hyde Park area; none at site. 🏨 **Lodging:** Available in Hyde Park area; none at site. ✕ **Food & Supplies:** Available in Hyde Park area; none at site. ☞ **Tips & Hints:** Allow one to two hours to see house and grounds. Allow one to two more hours to see adjoining FDR Library and Museum. Busiest in August and October, least crowded in January and February. 🎫 **Fees, Permits & Limitations:** Entrance fee: $10 per adult 17 and up, which includes admission to FDR

Library and Museum, or $18 for combination pass to FDR site and nearby Eleanor Roosevelt and Vanderbilt Mansion national historic sites (*see separate listings for both*). Reservations required for groups of 10 or more, recommended for individuals (tel. 800/967–2283). Site open daily 9–5. Grounds open daily 7–sunset. Closed Thanksgiving, Dec. 25, Jan. 1.

HOW TO GET THERE

The site is on Rte. 9 in Hyde Park, just north of Poughkeepsie and two hours north of New York City. Closest airport: Newburgh (45 mi/72 km).

FOR MORE INFORMATION

Home of Franklin D. Roosevelt National Historic Site (4097 Albany Post Rd., Hyde Park, NY 12538, tel. 845/229–9115; Web site www. nps.gov/hofr). Dutchess County Tourism (3 Neptune, Suite M17, Poughkeepsie, NY 12601, tel. 800/445–3131).

Martin Van Buren National Historic Site

In east-central New York, in Kinderhook

The 36-room mansion and retirement home of Martin Van Buren, the nation's eighth president, is located at this 40-acre site. Van Buren bought the Federalist home in 1839. He hired architect Richard Upjohn to remodel "Lindenwald" and build an Italianate addition. The mansion has been restored to the Van Buren period. The site was authorized on October 26, 1974.

WHAT TO SEE & DO

Touring home and grounds, watching video. **Facilities:** Visitor center, orientation video, home, grounds, wayside exhibits. Bookstore. **Programs & Events:** Ranger-led tours of home. Interpretive talks, bike tours, hikes, living-history programs, crafts demonstrations. Special events available.

PLANNING YOUR VISIT

⚑ **Camping:** Available locally; none at site. ☷ **Lodging:** Available locally; none at site. ✕ **Food & Supplies:** Available locally; none at site. ☞ **Tips & Hints:** Plan to spend 1½ hours touring home and grounds. House isn't air-conditioned and some activities are outdoors. Busiest in July and August, least crowded in September and October. ☷ **Fees, Permits & Limitations:** Entrance fee: $3 per adult 17 and up. Reservations required for groups of 11 or more (tel. 518/758–9689). No strollers or video cameras. Still photography with no flash only. Visitor center open Memorial Day–Oct., Thurs.–Mon. 9–4:30; Nov.–1st weekend Dec., weekends 9–4:30. House open by guided tour only with signup at ranger station.

HOW TO GET THERE

Site is on NY 9H in Kinderhook. From I–90E, take Exit B1 to U.S. 9S. Bear right on NY 9H to site 5 mi/8 km on right. From I–90W, take Exit 12 onto U.S. 9S and follow directions above. From I–87S (New York State Thruway), take Exit 21 to NY 23E. Cross Rip Van Winkle Bridge (toll), turn left on NY 9H north. Site is 15 mi/24 km north on left. Be careful not to confuse Rtes. 9, 9J, 9G, and 9W, all of which are near site, with Rte. 9H, which is the location of the site.

FOR MORE INFORMATION

Superintendent, Martin Van Buren National Historic Site (1013 Old Post Rd., Kinderhook, NY 12106, tel. 518/758–9689, fax 518/758–6986; e-mail MAVA_Info@nps.gov; Web site www.nps.gov/mava).

Sagamore Hill
National Historical Site

On Long Island, NY, near Oyster Bay

Sagamore Hill was the home of Theodore Roosevelt (1887–1919), 26th president of the United States from 1901 to 1909. The rambling 23-room, Queen Anne–style house reflects the many roles this man played: cowboy, conservationist, big-game hunter, scientist, politician, naval strategist, orator, soldier, family man, and Nobel Peace Prize winner. Also on the 83-acre site are the outbuildings of the Sagamore Hill Farm and Old Orchard Museum, the former home of Roosevelt's son, Congressional Medal of Honor winner Brigadeer General Theodore Roosevelt Jr. The site was authorized in 1962.

WHAT TO SEE & DO

Touring home, grounds, and museum; watching film. **Facilities:** Visitor center, Theodore Roosevelt home, Old Orchard Museum. Bookstore. **Programs & Events:** Ranger-guided tours of home. Nature walks, grounds tours (Memorial Day–Labor Day, weekends). Navy Day (spring), Fourth of July Celebration, Neighborhood Night (summer).

PLANNING YOUR VISIT

⛺ **Camping:** Camping on Long Island is extremely limited and availability varies widely throughout the year; none at site. 🏨 **Lodging:** Available in Cold Spring Harbor, East Norwich, Syosset, Woodbury (check Web site www.island-metro.com/lodging for more); none at site. ✗ **Food & Supplies:** Available in Huntington, Oyster Bay, Syosset; none at site. ☞ **Tips & Hints:** Go early to pick up house tour tickets for later in the day. House tours sell out by early afternoon on the weekends and in summer. The best times to visit are early summer weekdays or weekday afternoons in the spring and fall. Go between mid-October and mid-November for fall foliage. Busiest in July and August, least crowded in January and February. ▨ **Fees, Permits & Limitations:** Free. Home tour fee: $5 per adult 17 and older. Admission to home by guided tour only. No hunting. Leashed pets only. Bicycles and vehicles on entry road and parking area only. Grounds open daily dawn–dusk. Visitor center open daily 9–4:30. Theodore Roosevelt home open May–Oct., daily 9:30–4; Nov.–Apr., Wed.–Sun. 9:30–4; closed for tours Memorial Day–Labor Day, Mon. and Tues. Old Orchard Museum open daily 10–4:30. Park closed Thanksgiving, Dec. 25, Jan. 1.

HOW TO GET THERE

3 mi/5 km east of Oyster Bay via Cove Rd. and Cove Neck Rd. The Long Island Railroad connects with Amtrak from New York City's Pennsylvania Station at 7th Ave. and 33rd St. Get off at Oyster Bay Station (on the Oyster Bay Line) or Syosset Station (on the Port Jefferson Line). Take taxi to site. By car, take either Exit 41N from I–495/Long Island Expressway or Exit 35N from the Northern State Pkwy. to Rte. 106N. Follow Sagamore Hill signs. Closest airports: JFK (28 mi/45 km), LaGuardia (27 mi/43 km), MacArthur (30 mi/48 km).

FOR MORE INFORMATION

Sagamore Hill National Historic Site (20 Sagamore Hill Rd., Oyster Bay NY 11771-1899, tel. 516/922–4788; e-mail sahi_information@nps.gov; Web site www.nps.gov/sahi). Long Island Convention and Visitors Bureau (350 Vanderbilt Motor Pkwy., Suite 103, Hauppauge NY 11788, tel. 800/441–4601, fax 516/951–3439; Web site www.licvb.com). Oyster Bay Chamber of Commerce (8 Cove Plaza, Oyster Bay, NY 11771, tel. 516/922–6464).

Saint Paul's Church National Historic Site

In southeast New York, in Mount Vernon

Located on the former village green of Eastchester, the park contains a 5-acre burial ground dating to 1665, an 18th-century church associated with the American Revolution, and a site museum. The site was designated in 1943 and transferred to the Park Service in 1980.

WHAT TO SEE & DO

Touring church, burial ground, and museum. **Facilities:** Visitor center with interpretive exhibits, church, burial ground, museum, 1833 organ, 1758 church bell. **Programs & Events:** Site tours (weekdays), burial-ground tours (occasional weekends). Tower walks (Apr.–Oct., Fri. 3 PM), living history programs, costumed interpretation programs with special activities for children (July, Aug., Wed. at 12:15 PM), Black History Month (Feb.), Women's History Month (Mar.). Military encampment and reenactment commemorating 1776 Battle of Pell's Point (3rd Sat., Oct.).

PLANNING YOUR VISIT

🏨 **Lodging:** Available in New Rochelle, White Plains, Yonkers; none at site. ✗ **Food & Supplies:** Available in the Bronx, Mount Vernon, New Rochelle; none at site. ☞ **Tips & Hints:** Visit between April and October. Busiest in June and July, least crowded in January and February. ⬚

Fees, Permits & Limitations: Free. Site and visitor center open week-days 9–5.

HOW TO GET THERE

From the Hutchinson River Pkwy. Exit 7, turn left onto Boston Post Rd., take Boston Post Rd. to Pelham Pkwy., and make a right; 4 stop-lights later make left on to South Columbus Ave. Closest airport: La-Guardia (10 mi/16 km).

FOR MORE INFORMATION

Saint Paul's Church National Historic Site (897 S. Columbus Ave., Mount Vernon, NY 10550, tel. 914/667–4116, fax 914/667–3024; Web site www.nps.gov/sapa). Mount Vernon Chamber of Commerce (53 Valentine Ave., Mount Vernon, NY 10550, tel. 914/667–7500).

Saratoga National Historical Park

In east-central New York, near Stillwater

The Battles of Saratoga, the first significant American military victory during the American Revolution, rank among the 15 most decisive battles in world history. Here in 1777, American forces met, defeated, and forced a major British army to surrender, an event that led France to rec-ognize the independence of the United States and enter the war as a de-cisive military ally of the struggling Americans. The park comprises three units—the Battlefield in Stillwater, the General Philip Schuyler House in Schuylerville, and the Saratoga Monument, a 155-ft-/47-m-tall obelisk in the village of Victory. The park was authorized on June 1, 1938.

WHAT TO SEE & DO

Auto or bike touring of battlefield, cross-country skiing, guided tour-ing of Schuyler House, hiking, picnicking, viewing orientation film, vis-iting monument, walking. **Facilities:** Battlefield visitor center with interpretive exhibits, tour road (taped tour rentals), 4.5-mi/7-km Wilkinson National Historic Trail, 6 mi/10 km of road trace trails, way-side exhibits, Neilson House (1777). Bookstore and sales area, picnic areas. **Programs & Events:** Guided tours of Schuyler House (June–Labor Day, Wed.–Sun. 10–4), costumed interpretation (May–Sept.), military encampments and demonstrations. Frost Faire, March for Parks, July 4 Celebration, Battle Anniversary Commemoration (Sept.), Schuyler House Candlelight Tour (mid-Oct.).

PLANNING YOUR VISIT

⛺ **Camping:** Available in Saratoga Springs, Schuylerville, and Stillwater; none in park. 🛏 **Lodging:** Available in Saratoga Springs, Schuylerville, and Stillwater; none in park. ✕ **Food & Supplies:** Available in Saratoga Springs, Schuylerville, and Stillwater; none in park. ☞ **Tips & Hints:** Plan to stay overnight in area to visit battlefield and other sites. Some land is privately owned; respect rights of landowners. Make lodging and dining reservations early if you plan to visit during Saratoga horse racing season (end of July–Aug.). Busiest in July and August, least crowded in December and February. ✉ **Fees, Permits & Limitations:** Entrance fee: $4 per vehicle or $2 per bicyclist or walk-in for touring battlefield (May–Nov. 1). General Philip Schuyler House or Saratoga Monument free. Visitor center open daily 9–5. Closed Thanksgiving, Dec. 25, Jan. 1. Tour road usually open Apr.–mid-Nov. Schuyler House open for guided tours June–Labor Day, Fri.–Sun. Saratoga Monument grounds are open but interior is closed for renovations until summer 2001.

HOW TO GET THERE

40 mi/64 km north of Albany and 15 mi/24 km southeast of Saratoga Springs on U.S. 4/NY 32. From I–87 (Northway), take Exit 12 (if heading north) right to NY 67, left onto US 9, right onto NY 9P, right onto NY 423, left on NY 32, right to battlefield; or Exit 14 (if headed south). Head east on Rte. 29 and south on U.S. 4/NY 32 to park. Closest airport: Albany.

FOR MORE INFORMATION

Saratoga National Historical Park (648 Rte. 32, Stillwater, NY 12170-1604, tel. 518/664–9821, fax 518/664–9830; e-mail sara_info@nps.gov; Web site www.nps.gov/sara). Saratoga County Tourism Department (28 Clinton St., Saratoga Springs, NY 12866, tel. 800/526–8970).

Statue of Liberty National Monument

In New York Harbor and off Jersey City shoreline

The 152-ft/46-m copper statue bearing the torch of freedom was a gift from the French people to the United States in 1886 to commemorate the alliance of the two nations during the American Revolution. Designed by Frederic Bartholdi, the statue symbolized freedom for the nearly 12 million immigrants who arrived at nearby Ellis Island between 1892 and 1954. Reopened in 1990 after a massive restoration, the main building on Ellis Island is now a museum dedicated to the history of immigration. The statue was proclaimed a national monument in 1924, transferred to the Park Service in 1933, and designated a World Heritage Site in 1984. Ellis Island was incorporated into the national monument in 1965.

WHAT TO SEE & DO

Taking elevator to top of statue pedestal, taking ferry to Liberty and Ellis islands, touring museums, walking up to statue crown, watching Ellis Island documentary. **Facilities:** Statue, Ellis Island Main Building, museums, Ellis Island library and oral-history collection. **Programs & Events:** Ranger-led tours (when staffing permits at Ellis and Liberty Islands).

PLANNING YOUR VISIT

🛏 **Lodging:** Available in New York metropolitan area; none at monument. ✕ **Food & Supplies:** Cafeterias on both islands. Food and supplies also available in New York metropolitan area. ☞ **Tips & Hints:** In summer only passengers on first boat will gain access to crown. The wait to enter monument may exceed three hours. Drink plenty of fluids in summer. Dress warmly in winter. Visitors taking the elevator to statue pedestal can't then climb to crown from pedestal. Don't climb up statue if you have health problems: climb is 354 steps (22 stories) and the statue interior can get very hot in summer. Busiest in July and August, least crowded in January and February. ▦ **Fees, Permits & Limitations:** Free. Round-trip ferry fee (includes both islands): $7 adults, $6 senior citizens, $3 children under 18. Monument open Sept.–May, daily 9–5:30; June–Aug., Mon.–Fri. 8:30–5:30, weekends 8:30–8:30. Closed Dec. 25.

HOW TO GET THERE

Islands accessible by ferry only. Ferries (tel. 212/269–5755) leave Battery Park in lower Manhattan and Liberty State Park in Jersey City, NJ. Closest airports: Newark, NJ; JFK and LaGuardia, NY.

FOR MORE INFORMATION

Statue of Liberty National Monument (Liberty Island, New York, NY 10004, tel. 212/363–3200, fax 212/363–8347; Web site www.nps.gov/stli).

Theodore Roosevelt Birthplace National Historic Site

In New York City

Theodore Roosevelt, apostle of the strenuous life, larger-than-life hero to millions of Americans, and 26th president of the United States, was born in a brownstone house on this site on October 27, 1858. His family lived here until he was 13. The house was demolished in 1916, reconstructed in 1923, and furnished by the Women's Roosevelt Memorial Association with the assistance of the president's widow and sisters. The site was authorized on July 25, 1962.

WHAT TO SEE & DO

Touring house, viewing video and museum exhibits. **Facilities:** Five rooms furnished and decorated as they were during Roosevelt's occupancy, museum. Museum shop. **Programs & Events:** Ranger-led programs and tours (throughout the day). Weekend concerts (Sept.–early June at 2, tel. 212/260–1616).

PLANNING YOUR VISIT

🛏 **Lodging:** Available locally; none at site. ✕ **Food & Supplies:** Available locally; none at site. ☞ **Tips & Hints:** Use mass transit to get to house. Plan to spend 60 minutes at ranger-led programs, tours, and exhibits. 30 min house tours start on the hour, last tour at 4. Busiest in March and April, least crowded in July and January. ▦ **Fees, Permits & Limitations:** Entrance fee: $2 per person 18 and older, free 17 and under. House open Wed.–Sun. 9–5. Closed federal holidays.

HOW TO GET THERE

The reconstructed house is in Manhattan at 28 E. 20th St., between Broadway and Park Ave. Use mass transit to get to house because parking is scarce. The 6 subway, which runs along Lexington Ave., stops at the E. 23rd St. station on Park Ave. S. The N and R subway trains stop at the E. 23rd St. station on Broadway. Frequent bus service is provided by routes M-6 and M-7 on Broadway, by route M-1 on Park Ave. S, and by route M-23 operating crosstown on 23rd St. Closest airports: JFK and LaGuardia, NY; Newark, NJ.

FOR MORE INFORMATION

Theodore Roosevelt Birthplace National Historic Site (28 E. 20th St., New York, NY 10003, tel. 212/260–1616, fax 212/677–3587; Web site www.nps.gov/thrb).

Theodore Roosevelt Inaugural National Historic Site

In Buffalo

Theodore Roosevelt was sworn in here on September 14, 1901, to become the 26th president of the United States after William McKinley was assassinated. The house, which was built in the 1830s as officers' quarters for the Buffalo Barracks, is an outstanding example of Greek Revival architecture. The site was designated in 1966 and opened in 1971.

WHAT TO SEE & DO

Touring house, gardens, and neighborhood (audiocassette rentals); watching audiovisual program. **Facilities:** Visitor center, house, grounds. Gift shop, research library. **Programs & Events:** Guided house tours, self-guided architectural walking tours. Sunday Lecture Series (Jan.–Mar.), Victorian Days Children's Program (July–Aug.), guided architectural and historical walking tours (May–Sept.). Mother-Daughter Tea (Apr.), Teddy Bear Picnic (Aug.), Inaugural Anniversary Commemoration (Sept.), Victorian Christmas (Dec.).

PLANNING YOUR VISIT

Camping: Available in Grand Island; none at site. Lodging: Available in Buffalo area; none at site. Food & Supplies: Available in Allentown Historic District, Buffalo area; none at site. Tips & Hints: Park in lot behind site on Franklin St. Visit between May and September for garden blooms, in December for Victorian holiday decorations. Busiest in May and December, least crowded in September and January. Fees, Permits & Limitations: Entrance fee: $3 adults, $2 senior citizens, $1 children 6–14, or $6.50 per family. Self-guided walking tour: $5 adults, $2.50 children. No smoking. Site and visitor center open weekdays 9–5, weekends noon–5. Closed Thanksgiving, Dec. 24–25 and 31, Jan. 1, Easter Sunday, Memorial Day, July 4, Labor Day.

HOW TO GET THERE

1 mi/1.6 km north of downtown Buffalo at 641 Delaware Ave. Closest airport: Greater Buffalo International (5 mi/8 km).

FOR MORE INFORMATION

Theodore Roosevelt Inaugural National Historic Site (641 Delaware Ave., Buffalo, NY 14202, tel. 716/884–0095, fax 716/884–0330; Web site www.nps.gov/thri). Greater Buffalo Convention and Visitors Bureau (617 Main St. Suite 400, Buffalo, NY 14203, tel. 716/852–0511, fax 716/852–0131).

Vanderbilt Mansion National Historic Site

Near Hyde Park

Once the country home of Frederick W. Vanderbilt, a grandson of Cornelius Vanderbilt who amassed the family fortune, the Vanderbilt Mansion is a magnificent example of the great estates built by wealthy financial and industrial leaders between 1880 and 1900. The site was designated on December 18, 1940.

WHAT TO SEE & DO

Guided and self-guided tours of home, formal garden, and grounds. **Facilities:** Visitor center with interpretive exhibits, furnished home of Frederick Vanderbilt, grounds and gardens, trails. Bookstore. **Programs & Events:** Ranger-led mansion tours, talks on lifestyle of the Vanderbilts and their contemporaries, industrial expansion, turn-of-the-20th-century technology, and landscape architecture.

PLANNING YOUR VISIT

⚠ **Camping:** Available in Hyde Park area; none at site. ▦ **Lodging:** Available in Hyde Park area; none at site. ✕ **Food & Supplies:** Available in Hyde Park area; none at site. ☞ **Tips & Hints:** Allow one or two hours to see house and grounds and four to eight hours to fully explore the house, grounds, and trails. Busiest in June and August, least crowded in January and February. ▣ **Fees, Permits & Limitations:** Entrance fee: $8 per adult 17 and up or $18 for combination pass to Vanderbilt Mansion; Home of Franklin D. Roosevelt National Historic Site, FDR Library and Museum; and Eleanor Roosevelt National Historic Site (reservations required for groups of 10 or more, recommended for individuals, tel. 800/967–2283). Site open daily 9–5; closed Thanksgiving, Dec. 25, Jan. 1. Grounds open daily 7 AM–sunset.

HOW TO GET THERE

Two hours north of New York City on the east bank of the Hudson River on U.S. 9, 8 mi/13 km north of Poughkeepsie. Closest airport: Newburgh (45 mi/72 km).

FOR MORE INFORMATION

Vanderbilt Mansion National Historic Site (4097 Albany Post Rd., Hyde Park, NY 12538, tel. 845/229–9115; Web site www.nps.gov/vama). Dutchess County Tourism (3 Neptune Rd., Suite M17, Poughkeepsie, NY 12601, tel. 800/445–3131).

Women's Rights National Historical Park

In central New York, in Seneca Falls

Seneca Falls is the birthplace of the women's rights movement in the United States. Park sites include the Wesleyan Methodist Chapel, the site of the first Women's Rights Convention in 1848; the Elizabeth Cady Stanton house, home of one of the founders of the women's rights movement; the Hunt House, where the convention organizers first met; the M'Clintock House, where the "Declaration of Rights and Sentiments" was written; and other sites related to notable early women's rights activists. The park was authorized on December 28, 1980.

WHAT TO SEE & DO

Touring museum, historic buildings, district, and homes; watching *Dreams of Equality* movie. **Facilities:** Visitor center with interpretive exhibits (136 Fall St.), Elizabeth Cady Stanton home, Women's Education and Cultural Center (116 Fall St.). Bookstore. **Programs & Events:** Wesleyan Chapel talks and Stanton House programs (daily). Ranger-guided programs at Wesleyan Chapel, Stanton House, M'Clintock House, and Suffrage Press Workshop (May–Sept., twice daily). Women's History Month (Mar.), Canalfest (June), Convention Days (3rd weekend, July), Elizabeth Cady Stanton's Birthday (Nov. 12).

PLANNING YOUR VISIT

⚠ **Camping:** Available in Seneca County; none in park. 🏨 **Lodging:** Available in Auburn, Geneva, Ithaca, Rochester, Seneca Falls, Syracuse, Waterloo; none in park. ✕ **Food & Supplies:** Available in Seneca Falls, Waterloo; none in park. ☞ **Tips & Hints:** Visit May through October. Busiest in July and August, least crowded in January and February. 🎫 **Fees, Permits & Limitations:** Entrance fee: $2 per person for visitor center and movie, $1 for historic home (over 15). Reservation required ($25; tel. 315/568–2991) for groups of 10 or more touring historic homes. No pets in visitor center. Park open daily 9–5. Closed Thanksgiving, Dec. 25, Jan. 1, Martin Luther King Jr. Day, Presidents Day, Veterans Day.

HOW TO GET THERE

Park visitor center is at 136 Fall St. (Rte. 5/20), which is reached via Exit 41 off New York State Thruway (I–90), then NY 414 for 4 mi/6 km and Rte. 5/20E for 2 mi/3 km. Closest airports: Syracuse (48 mi/77 km), Rochester (55 mi/88 km).

FOR MORE INFORMATION

Women's Rights National Historical Park (136 Fall St., Seneca Falls, NY 13148, tel. 315/568–2991, fax 315/568–2141, TDD 315/568–9039; Web site www.nps.gov/wori). Seneca County Chamber of Commerce (Box 70, 2020 Rtes. 5/20 W., Seneca Falls, NY 13148, tel. 800/732–1848; Web site www.senecachamber.org).

See Also

Appalachian National Scenic Trail, West Virginia. *Hudson River Valley National Heritage Area,* National Heritage Areas in Other National Parklands. *North Country National Scenic Trail,* National Trails System in Other National Parklands. *Upper Delaware Scenic and Recreational River,* Pennsylvania.

NORTH CAROLINA

Blue Ridge Parkway

The parkway follows the Blue Ridge and Southern Appalachian mountains for 469 mi/750 km through western Virginia and North Carolina

The parkway provides recreational opportunities and scenic overlooks and preserves remnants of Appalachian culture from the late 19th and early 20th centuries. With elevations ranging from 600 ft/182 m to 6,000 ft/1,820 m, the parkway protects a wide variety of plant and animal life. Within the park are 1,200 identified types of vascular plants and more than two dozen rare or endangered plants and animals. Parkway construction began on September 11, 1935, with funding from the National Industrial Recovery Act. The parkway was established on June 30, 1936.

WHAT TO SEE & DO

Bicycling, boating (rentals Julian Price Park, Milepost 295), camping, driving, fishing, hiking, picnicking. **Facilities:** 469-mi-/750-km-long parkway and 11 visitor centers (listed by milepost beginning at the Virginia end)—Humpback Rocks (Milepost 6); James River (Milepost 63); Peaks of Otter (Milepost 86); Rocky Knob (Milepost 169); Cumberland Knob (Milepost 217); Moses H. Cone Memorial Park (Milepost 294); Linn Cove (Milepost 304); Linville Falls (Milepost 316); Museum of North Carolina Minerals (Milepost 331); Craggy Gardens (Milepost 364); and Waterrock Knob (Milepost 451). The Northwest Trading Post (Milepost 258) sells crafts and foods produced in the northwest North Carolina mountains, and the Folk Art Center (Milepost 382, open daily) sells products from the Southern Highlands Craft Guild. Trails, wayside exhibits, bulletin boards. Gift shops, picnic facilities, sales outlets. **Programs & Events:** Ranger-led crafts demonstrations and/or interpretive talks at all major parkway locations (May–Oct.). Brinegar Days (Aug.) at Brinegar Cabin (Milepost 238), Mountain Music (May–Oct., Sun.) at Mabry Mill (MP 276) and Roanoke Mountain Campground (MP 120).

PLANNING YOUR VISIT

Camping: 9 campgrounds: Otter Creek (Milepost 60); Peaks of Otter (Milepost 86); Roanoke Mountain (Milepost 120); Rocky Knob (Milepost 167); Doughton Park (Milepost 241); Price Park (Milepost 297); Linville Falls (Milepost 316); Crabtree Meadows (Milepost 339); and Mount Pisgah (Milepost 408). No hookups. (No reservations.) Backcountry camping available at Rocky Knob area at Rockcastle Gorge and Doughton Park area at Basin Cove (permit required, *see below*). All open May–Oct. One primitive campground (location varies) open year-round in each state. Group camping in certain areas (contact ranger stations or visitor centers). Private campgrounds in towns adjacent to parkway. ⊡ **Lodging:** In the park: Peaks of Otter (Milepost 86, tel. 540/586–1081); Rocky Knob Cabins (Milepost 169, tel. 540/593–3503); Bluffs Lodge (Milepost 241, tel. 336/372–4499); and Pisgah Inn (Milepost 409, tel. 828/235–8228). Lodging also available outside the parkway along its 469-mi/750-km length. ✕ **Food & Supplies:** Restaurants at Whetstone Ridge (Milepost 29, tel. 540/377–6397); Otter Creek (Milepost 61, tel. 804/299–5862); Peaks of Otter (Milepost 86, tel. 540/586–1081); Mabry Mill (Milepost 176, tel. 540/952–2947); Bluffs Lodge and Coffee Shop (Milepost 241, tel. 336/372–4499); Crabtree Meadows (Milepost 339, tel. 828/675–4236); Pisgah Inn (Milepost 409, tel. 828/235–8228). Snacks at Northwest Trading Post (Milepost 259, tel. 336/982–2543). Food and supplies also available in towns adjacent to the parkway. ☞ **Tips & Hints:** Don't be in a hurry (speed limit is 45 mi/72 km per hour). Go during the week to avoid traffic, in April and May for wildflowers, or mid-October for fall leaf color. Winter weather can close sections for long periods. Get gas at Peaks of Otter (MP 86), Doughton Park (MP 241), Mount Pisgah (MP 408). Busiest in July and October, least crowded in January and February. ▨ **Fees, Permits & Limitations:** Free. Shuttle bus to Sharp Top Mountain at the Peaks of Otter (Milepost 86), $3.75 round-trip, children 12 and under $1.75 round-trip. Backcountry permits required (free; available from Rockcastle Gorge, tel. 540/745–9664, or Basin Cove, tel. 336/372–8568). Virginia or North Carolina state fishing license required. No hunting. Pets on leash or under physical control only. Trails for foot travel only, except designated horse trails. Park open daily except for weather closure. All visitor centers are open generally May–Oct., except Peaks of Otter, which is open year-round. Visitor centers open at least 9–5 daily.

HOW TO GET THERE

Major cities along the Blue Ridge Parkway are Waynesboro (U.S. 250 and I–64) and Roanoke (U.S. 220, 460, and I–81) in Virginia and Boone (U.S. 321, 221), Asheville (I–40, 26, and U.S. 70 and 74), and Waynesville (U.S. 19-23 and I–40) in North Carolina. Closest regional airports: Roanoke, VA; Asheville, NC.

FOR MORE INFORMATION

Blue Ridge Parkway (199 Hemphill Knob Rd., Asheville, NC 28803, tel. 828/298–0398 for recorded information or 828/271–4779 for headquarters; Web site www.nps.gov/blri). Waynesboro Augusta County Chamber of Commerce (301 W. Main St., Waynesboro, VA 22980, tel. 540/949–8203). Roanoke Valley Convention and Visitors Bureau, VA (114 Market St., Roanoke, VA 24011, tel. 540/342–6025). Boone, NC, Convention and Visitors Bureau (208 Howard St., Boone, NC 28607, tel. 800/852–9506).

Cape Hatteras National Seashore

On Outer Banks

The nation's first national seashore, Cape Hatteras preserves significant portions of North Carolina's famed barrier islands—Bodie, Hatteras, and Ocracoke. Cape Hatteras Light, the tallest brick lighthouse in the world, harks back to the days when this area of the surrounding Atlantic Ocean was known as the "Graveyard of the Atlantic" because of its treacherous currents and offshore shoals. The seashore was authorized in 1937.

WHAT TO SEE & DO

Beach-going, bird-watching, boardsailing, fishing, hiking, hunting, surfing, swimming, touring lighthouses. **Facilities:** 3 visitor centers with interpretive exhibits—Bodie Island (8 mi/13 km south of U.S. 158/U.S. 64 intersection); Hatteras Island (Buxton, 45 mi/72 km south of U.S. 158/U.S. 64 intersection); and Ocracoke Island (Ocracoke); contact station at Whalebone Junction (U.S. 158/U.S. 64 intersection, Nags Head); lighthouses and restored keepers' homes, nature trails, wayside exhibits. Book sale areas, changing and shower facilities, picnic areas. **Programs & Events:** Guided beach walks, nature trail hikes, ecology demonstrations, ranger-led recreational demonstrations, campfire programs (Apr.–mid-Oct.).

PLANNING YOUR VISIT

Camping: 4 campgrounds. (Reservations available for Ocracoke, tel. 800/365–2267). Group camping available (permit required, *see below*). Private campgrounds nearby in Buxton, Frisco, Ocracoke, Rodanthe, Salvo, Waves. **Lodging:** Available in Avon, Buxton, Hatteras, Ocracoke; none at park. **Food & Supplies:** Available in Avon, Buxton, Frisco, Hatteras, Ocracoke, Rodanthe, Salvo, Waves; none at park. **Tips & Hints:** Call ahead for lighthouse hours. Plan for a wait in summer for free 40-minute ferry from Hatteras to Ocracoke Island. Go in March–April and October–November for bird migrations. Busiest in July and August, least crowded in January and February. **Fees, Permits & Limitations:** Free. North Carolina state and U.S federal migratory bird-hunting licenses required. North Carolina salt water fishing license required. Group camping permit required (tel. 919/473–2111 ext. 118). Leashed pets only. No all-terrain vehicles. Access to some areas barred because of habitat/nesting and endangered species. Seashore open daily. Visitor centers open Sept.–May, daily 9–5; extended hours in summer. Closed Dec. 25.

HOW TO GET THERE

Via U.S. 168/158 from the north, U.S. 64 from the west, and U.S. 70 and Cedar Island ferry from the south. Closest airport: Norfolk (85 mi/136 km).

FOR MORE INFORMATION

Cape Hatteras National Seashore (1401 National Park Dr., Manteo, NC 27954, tel. 252/473–2111, fax 252/473–2595; Web site www.nps.gov/

caha). Outer Banks Chamber of Commerce (Box 1757, Kill Devil Hills, NC 27948, tel. 252/441–8144). Outer Banks Tourist Bureau (704 Hwy. 64/264, Manteo, NC 27954, tel. 252/473–2138). Hyde County Chamber of Commerce (Box 178, Swan Quarter, NC 27885, tel. 252/925–5201).

Cape Lookout
National Seashore

In the eastern part of the state, near Morehead City

The 56-mi-/90-km-long barrier islands of Cape Lookout National Seashore run from Ocracoke Inlet to Beaufort Inlet. They consist mostly of wide, bare beaches with low dunes, flat grasslands, and large expanses of salt marsh along the Core Sound. Attractions include the Cape Lookout lighthouse and two lifesaving stations. The seashore was authorized in 1966.

WHAT TO SEE & DO

Beachcombing, boating, fishing, shelling, swimming. **Facilities:** 3 visitor centers with interpretive exhibits—Cape Lookout (Harkers Island), Keepers Quarters, Portsmouth. Bookstores. **Programs & Events:** Lighthouse talks, walks (summer).

PLANNING YOUR VISIT

Camping: Backcountry camping available. Private campgrounds nearby in Beaufort, Morehead City. **Lodging:** At the seashore: Morris Marina (tel. 252/225–4261), Willis Marina (tel. 252/729–2791). Lodging also available outside the seashore in Beaufort, Morehead City. **Food & Supplies:** Available in Beaufort, Morehead City; none at seashore. **Tips & Hints:** Bring everything you'll need with you. Visit in spring and fall. Busiest in August and November, least crowded in February and March. **Fees, Permits & Limitations:** Free. No pets on public ferries. Park open daily. Cape Lookout Visitor Center open daily 8–4:30. Keepers Quarters, Portsmouth visitor centers open Apr.–Nov. 8–4:30. Closed Dec. 25, Jan. 1.

HOW TO GET THERE

21 mi/34 km from Beaufort, NC. From Hwy. 70E, take right on State Rd. 1333 to Harkers Island. Ferry service and visitor center on Harkers Island. Closest airport: New Bern (45 mi/72 km).

FOR MORE INFORMATION

Cape Lookout National Seashore (131 Charles St., Harkers Island, NC 28531, tel. 252/728–2250; e-mail calo_information@nps.gov; Web site www.nps.gov/calo). Carteret County Tourism Development Bureau (3409 Avendale St., Morehead City, NC 28557, tel. 252/726–8148).

Carl Sandburg Home
National Historic Site

In the western part of the state, in Flat Rock

The site preserves Connemara, the 245-acre farm where Pulitzer Prize–winning author Carl Sandburg (1878–1967) and his family lived the last 22 years of his life. The farm consists of a 22-room house, barns, sheds, rolling pastures, mountainside woods, trails, two small lakes, a trout pond, flower and vegetable gardens, and an orchard. The site was authorized on October 17, 1968.

WHAT TO SEE & DO

Bird-watching, hiking, picnicking, touring house and grounds. **Facilities:** Visitor information station, house, trails, amphitheater. Bookstore. **Programs & Events:** Guided house tours, self-guided walking tours of grounds, barn, and Chikaming goat herd. Ranger-led programs and walks (June–Aug. and Oct.), plays (late June–mid-Aug.), Poetry Celebration (Apr.), Sandburg Folk Music Festival (Memorial Day), Christmas at Connemara (Dec., Sat. before Christmas). Book signings, special presentations by noted authors and historians (consult park for schedule).

PLANNING YOUR VISIT

⚠ **Camping:** Available in Flat Rock and Hendersonville area; none at site. ⊞ **Lodging:** Available in Flat Rock and Hendersonville area; none at site. ✕ **Food & Supplies:** Available in Flat Rock and Hendersonville area; none at site. ☞ **Tips & Hints:** Plan to spend at least two hours. Be prepared for rain. Temperatures are moderate. Weather is unpredictable in spring and fall. Busiest in July and October, least crowded in January and February. ⊠ **Fees, Permits & Limitations:** Guided house tour: $3 adults 17 and up. Reservations available for groups of 17 or more (Mar.–Nov.). Site open daily 9–5. Closed Dec. 25.

HOW TO GET THERE

Take U.S. 25 south for 5 mi/8 km from Hendersonville, turn on Little River Rd. at the Flat Rock Playhouse. From Asheville, take I–26 south for 26 mi/42 km to Upward Rd. exit and follow park signs. Closest airport: between Asheville and Hendersonville.

FOR MORE INFORMATION

Carl Sandburg Home National Historic Site (1928 Little River Rd., Flat Rock, NC 28731, tel. 828/693–4178; Web site www.nps.gov/carl).

Fort Raleigh
National Historic Site

In the northeast part of the state, near Manteo

The first British attempts to colonize the New World in 1585–87 are commemorated here. These efforts, sponsored by Sir Walter Raleigh, ended with the disappearance of 116 men, women, and children. The fate of this colony remains a mystery. The park includes a reconstruction of an earthen fort built by the British. The site also is home to the outdoor symphonic drama, *The Lost Colony,* performed since 1937. The site was designated on April 5, 1941.

WHAT TO SEE & DO

Attending outdoor drama, touring restored earthen fort, walking trails, watching video. **Facilities:** Visitor center with interpretive exhibits, restored earthen fort, Waterside Theater, trails. Gift shop. **Programs & Events:** Video. *The Lost Colony* drama (mid-June–Aug., Mon.–Sat. nights; tel. 252/473–3414 or 800/488–5012). Virginia Dare birthday commemoration (Aug. 18): she was the first child born to English parents (1587) in the New World.

PLANNING YOUR VISIT

⛺ **Camping:** Available in Manteo and Outer Bank communities; none at site. ⊞ **Lodging:** Available in Manteo and Outer Bank communities; none at site. ✕ **Food & Supplies:** Available in Manteo and Outer Bank communities; none at site. ☞ **Tips & Hints:** Plan to spend two hours to view the exhibits and video and tour the grounds. Evening productions of *The Lost Colony* drama run 2½ hours. Bring insect repellent if you plan to attend outdoor drama. Busiest in June and July, least crowded in December and January. ▦ **Fees, Permits & Limitations:** Free. Separate fee for *The Lost Colony* drama. Site open June–Aug., Mon.–Sat. 9–8, Sun. 9–6; Sept.–May, daily 9–5. Closed Dec. 25.

HOW TO GET THERE

On Roanoke Island, off U.S. 64-264 and about 3 mi/5 km north of Manteo, 92 mi/147 km southeast of Norfolk, VA, and 197 mi/315 km east of Raleigh. Closest airport: Dare County Municipal Airport (3 mi/5 km).

FOR MORE INFORMATION

Fort Raleigh National Historic Site (c/o Cape Hatteras National Seashore, Rte. 1, Box 675, Manteo, NC 27954, tel. 252/473–5772; Web site www.nps.gov/fora).

Guilford Courthouse
National Military Park

Midstate, in Greensboro

The battle fought here on March 15, 1781, was the largest, most hotly contested action of the Revolutionary War's climactic Southern Campaign. The loss of British soldiers at Guilford Courthouse foreshadowed the final American victory at Yorktown seven months later. The park was established in 1917 and transferred to the Park Service in 1933.

WHAT TO SEE & DO

Auto touring, bicycling, hiking, watching film. **Facilities:** Visitor center with interpretive exhibits, tour roads, bike and foot trails, roadside interpretive stations and displays, monuments. Bookstore. **Programs & Events:** Self-guided audio tours, conducted programs. Battle Anniversary (Mar. 15).

PLANNING YOUR VISIT

⚠ **Camping:** Available in Greensboro; none in park. ⊞ **Lodging:** Available in Greensboro; none in park. ✗ **Food & Supplies:** Available in Greensboro; none in park. ☞ **Tips & Hints:** Busiest in May and July, least crowded in December and January. ▦ **Fees, Permits & Limitations:** Free. Leashed pets only. Bicycling only in bike lanes. No motorized or mechanized equipment or bicycles on walking trails. No climbing on cannons or monuments. Park and visitor center open daily 8:30–5. Closed Thanksgiving, Dec. 25, Jan. 1.

HOW TO GET THERE

In northwest Greensboro. From U.S. 220 (Battleground Ave.), turn east on New Garden Rd. to reach entrance. Closest airport: Piedmont Triad International (6 mi/10 km).

FOR MORE INFORMATION

Guilford Courthouse National Military Park (2332 New Garden Rd., Greensboro, NC 27410-2355, tel. 336/288–1776, fax 336/282–2296; E-mail GUCO_Administration@nps.gov; Web site www.nps.gov/guco). Greensboro Visitor Center (317 S. Greene St., Greensboro, NC 27401, tel. 336/274–2202 or 800/344–2282).

Moores Creek National Battlefield

In the southeast part of the state, near Currie

The 87-acre park commemorates the decisive American Revolution victory by 1,000 Patriots over 1,600 Loyalists at the Battle of Moores Creek Bridge on February 27, 1776. The battle ended British Royal Governor Josiah Martin's hopes of regaining control of the colony. This first decisive Patriot victory of the war raised morale for Patriots throughout the colonies. The Loyalist defeat ended British plans for an invasionary force to land in Brunswick, North Carolina. The colony of North Carolina voted to declare independence from the British on April 12, 1776. The site was established as a national military park in 1926, transferred to the Park Service in 1933, and redesignated in 1980.

WHAT TO SEE & DO

Bird- and wildlife watching, picnicking, touring battlefield by walking trails. **Facilities:** Visitor center with interpretive exhibits, video, trails. Bookstore, grills, picnic areas, shelter, tables. **Programs & Events:** Talks, walks, and demonstrations (summer, weekends). Battle anniversary commemoration (last full weekend, Feb.), Colonial Day with living-history programs (early May), Scots Heritage Day (early June), "Celebrating the Constitution" (Sept.), "In Defense of Liberty" (early Nov.).

PLANNING YOUR VISIT

🏕 **Camping:** Available in Wilmington area; none at battlefield. 🏨 **Lodging:** Available in Wilmington area; none at battlefield. ✕ **Food & Supplies:** Limited food and supplies available locally. Food and supplies also available in Burgaw and Wilmington. ☞ **Tips & Hints:** Plan to spend an hour touring visitor center, exhibits, and trails and watching video. Busiest in May and June, least crowded in December and January. 🎫 **Fees, Permits & Limitations:** Free. Site open daily 9–5. Closed Dec. 25, Jan. 1.

HOW TO GET THERE

20 mi/32 km northwest of Wilmington via U.S. 421 and NC 210. From I–40, take NC 210 west for 15 mi/24 km to park. Closest airport: New Hanover International (25 mi/40 km).

FOR MORE INFORMATION

Moores Creek National Battlefield (400 Patriots Mall Dr., Currie, NC 28435, tel. 910/283–5591, fax 910/283–5351; Web site www.nps.gov/mocr).

Wright Brothers National Memorial

In Kill Devil Hills on Outer Banks

The first successful, sustained, controlled, powered flights in a heavier-than-air machine were made here by Wilbur and Orville Wright on December 17, 1903. A 60-ft/197 m granite monument perched atop 90-ft-tall/295 m Kill Devil Hill commemorates the achievements of the two visionaries from Dayton, Ohio. The site was authorized in 1927, transferred to the Park Service in 1933, and renamed in 1953.

WHAT TO SEE & DO

Air touring, touring visitor center and reconstructed living quarters and hangar building, viewing reproduction of Wright flyer and glider, walking first-flight grounds to monument. **Facilities:** Visitor center with interpretive exhibits, wayside exhibits, monument. Bookstore. **Programs & Events:** Ranger talks (daily at 10, 11, noon, 2, 3, and 4). Ranger-led interpretive children's programs on kite building, flying objects, plane takeoffs, paper airplanes, and first-flight tours (mid-June–Aug.). First Flight Anniversary Celebration (Dec. 17), National Aviation Day and Orville Wright's Birthday (Aug. 19).

PLANNING YOUR VISIT

🏕 **Camping:** Available near Kill Devil Hills; none at memorial. 🏨 **Lodging:** Available in Kill Devil Hills, Kitty Hawk, Nags Head; none at memorial. ✕ **Food & Supplies:** Available in Kill Devil Hills and nearby towns; none at memorial. ☞ **Tips & Hints:** Watch for cacti and sandspurs. Stay on walkway. Visit in fall. Busiest in July and August, least crowded in January and February. 🎫 **Fees, Permits & Limitations:** Entrance fee: $2 per person or $4 per vehicle, free under 17. Leashed pets only. No motorized vehicles or skateboards on trails. Airstrip daylight use only. 24-hour parking limit for planes. Park and visitor center open Labor Day–mid-June, daily 9–5; mid-June–Labor Day; daily 9–6. Closed Dec. 25.

HOW TO GET THERE

At Milepost 7.5 on U.S. 158. Closest airports: at Memorial; Dare County in Manteo (18 mi/29 km); Norfolk, VA International (77 mi/123 km).

FOR MORE INFORMATION

Superintendent, Wright Brothers National Memorial (800 Colington Rd., Kill Devil Hills, NC 27948, tel. 252/441–7430, fax 252/441–7730; Web site www.nps.gov/wrbr). Dare County Tourist Bureau (704 Hwy. 64/264, Manteo, NC 27954, tel. 252/473–2138). Kill Devil Hills Chamber of Commerce (Box 1757, Kill Devil Hills, NC 27948, tel. 252/441–8144).

See Also

Appalachian National Scenic Trail, West Virginia. *Great Smoky Mountains National Park*, Tennessee. *Overmountain Victory National Historic Trail*, National Trails System in Other National Parklands. *Trail of Tears National Historic Trail*, National Trails System in Other National Parklands.

NORTH DAKOTA

Fort Union Trading Post National Historic Site

In the northwest part of the state, near Williston

The park is a reconstruction of the most significant fur-trading post on the upper Missouri River. John Jacob Astor's American Fur Company built Fort Union in 1828. In its heyday, the post employed 100 people to trade beaver furs and buffalo robes. In the 1860s, the fort was dismantled by the Army for materials to complete nearby Fort Buford. The site was authorized in 1966.

WHAT TO SEE & DO

Picnicking, touring the fort. **Facilities:** Visitor center with interpretive exhibits, fort, wayside exhibits. Book sales area, picnic area. **Programs & Events:** Ranger-guided tours (mid-May–mid-Sept.). Rendezvous (3rd weekend, June), Indian Arts Showcase (mid-Aug.), Living History Weekend (Labor Day), Winter Camp (Dec.).

PLANNING YOUR VISIT

Camping: Available in Fort Buford State Park and in Williston area; none in site. **Lodging:** Available in Williston, ND, and Sidney, MT; none in site. **Food & Supplies:** Available in Williston, ND, and Fairview and Sidney, MT; none in site. **Tips & Hints:** Visit between May and October. Busiest in June and July, least crowded in December and January. **Fees, Permits & Limitations:** Free. No hunting. Leashed pets only. Park and visitor center open Memorial Day–Labor Day, daily 8–8; Labor Day–Memorial Day, daily 9–5:30. Closed Thanksgiving, Dec. 25, Jan. 1.

HOW TO GET THERE

On ND 1804, 25 mi/40 km southwest of Williston via ND 1804. Closest airport: Williston (25 mi/40 km).

FOR MORE INFORMATION

Fort Union Trading Post National Historic Site (15550 ND Hwy. 1804, Williston, ND 58801, tel. 701/572–9083, fax 701/572–7321; e-mail fous_administration@nps.gov; Web site www.nps.gov/fous). Williston Chamber of Commerce (Box G, Williston, ND 58802, tel. 701/572–3768, fax 701/572–8591).

Knife River Indian Villages National Historic Site

Midstate, near Stanton

Remnants of historic and prehistoric Native American villages are preserved at this 1,759-acre site, which was last occupied in 1845 by the Hidatsa and Mandan. An array of artifacts of the Plains Native American culture and a full-scale furnished earth lodge are on exhibit. The area also was the home of Sacagawea, who accompanied Lewis and Clark on their expedition to the Northwest. The site was authorized in 1974.

WHAT TO SEE & DO

Boating, cross-country skiing, fishing, hiking, picnicking, touring the site. **Facilities:** Visitor center, museum, trails, interpretive waysides. Bookstore, picnic tables. **Programs & Events:** Guided tours of earth lodge (Memorial Day–Labor Day). Northern Plains Indian Culture Fest (last weekend, July).

PLANNING YOUR VISIT

⚠ **Camping:** Available in Beulah, Hazen, Pick City, Sanger, Stanton; none in site. 🏨 **Lodging:** Available locally; none in site. ✕ **Food & Supplies:** Available locally; none in site. ☞ **Tips & Hints:** Visit June through August. Busiest June through August, least crowded in November and December. 🎫 **Fees, Permits & Limitations:** Free. North Dakota fishing license required. Leashed pets only on trails. No hunting. No mountain bikes, trail bikes, motorized or mechanized equipment on trails. Earth lodge closed Nov.–Mar. Park and visitor center open Labor Day–Memorial Day, daily 8–4:30; Memorial Day weekend–Labor Day, daily 7:30–6. Closed Thanksgiving, Dec. 25, Jan. 1.

HOW TO GET THERE

0.5 mi/1 km north of Stanton on County Road 37. Closest airport: Bismarck (50 mi/80 km).

FOR MORE INFORMATION

Knife River Indian Villages National Historic Site (Box 9, Stanton, ND 58571-0009, tel. 701/745–3309, fax 701/745–3708; e-mail knri_ranger_activities@nps.gov; Web site www.nps.gov/knri). Hazen Chamber of Commerce (146 E. Main, Hazen, ND 58545, tel. 701/748–6848).

Theodore Roosevelt National Park

In the western part of the state, near Medora (South Unit) and Watford City (North Unit)

Theodore Roosevelt first came to Dakota Territory in September 1883 to hunt bison. Before returning home to New York, he became interested in the cattle business and established the Maltese Cross Ranch partnership. The next year he returned to the badlands and started a second open-range ranch, the Elkhorn. Roosevelt witnessed the decline in wildlife and saw the grasslands destroyed because of overgrazing. Today the colorful North Dakota badlands provide the scenic backdrop to the park that memorializes the 26th president for his enduring contributions to the conservation of our nation's resources. The Little Missouri River shapes this 70,448-acre park, which is home to a variety of plants and animals. The area was established as a memorial park in 1947 and became a national park in 1978.

WHAT TO SEE & DO

Auto touring, bird-watching, canoeing (rentals, Medora), fishing, hiking, horseback riding (rentals, Peaceful Valley and North Unit), picnicking, skiing, touring Maltese Cross Cabin, viewing wildlife. **Facilities:** 3 visitor centers—Medora (South Unit entrance), Painted Canyon (7 mi/11 km east of Medora on I–94), and North Unit (near entrance); Maltese Cross Cabin, amphitheaters, wayside exhibits, trails, scenic drives. Book and map sale areas, picnic sites with fire grates. **Programs & Events:** Orientation films. Talks, evening campfire programs, nature walks and hikes, cultural demonstrations (June–mid-Sept.); tours of Maltese Cross Cabin (mid-June–early Sept., guided tours daily; self-guided tours during rest of year). Guided ski tours, winter walks (occasionally).

PLANNING YOUR VISIT

Camping: 2 campgrounds: no hookups. (No reservations.) Backcountry camping available (permit required, *see below*). Group campsites at Roundup Horse Camp and Cottonwood Campground in South Unit and Juniper Campground in North Unit (reservations only beginning early Mar.; tel. 701/623–4466 for Roundup and Cottonwood, 701/842–2333 for North Unit). Private campgrounds in Beach, Belfield, Dickinson, Medora, and Watford City. **Lodging:** Available in Beach, Belfield, Dickinson, Medora, Watford City; none in park. **Food & Supplies:** Available in Beach, Belfield, Dickinson, Medora, Watford City; none in park. **Tips & Hints:** Be prepared for variable weather in summer. Go between May and September for the best weather. Busiest in July and August, least crowded in December and January. **Fees, Permits & Limitations:** Entrance fee: $5 per person or $10 per vehicle. Backcountry permits (free) required for all backcountry camping. North Dakota state fishing license required. No hunting. No pets on trails or in backcountry. Leashed pets elsewhere. No mountain or trail bikes on trails. No horses in campground or on nature trails. Weed-free horse feed required. Park open daily. Scenic drives sometimes closed in winter. Visitor center hours: Medora—Labor Day–mid-June, daily 8–4:30; mid-June–Labor Day, daily 8–8; Painted Canyon—Apr.–mid-June and Sept.–mid-Nov., daily 8:30–4:30; mid-June–Labor Day, daily 8–6; North Unit—Memorial Day–Sept., daily 9–5:30; Oct.–Memorial Day, 9–5:30 weekends and most weekdays. Closed Thanksgiving, Dec. 25, Jan. 1.

HOW TO GET THERE

South Unit: near Medora via I–94. North Unit: 15 mi/24 km south of Watford City via U.S. 85. Closest airports: Dickinson (35 mi/56 km from Medora); Williston (60 mi/96 km from North Unit); Bismarck (167 mi/267 km from North Unit, 133 mi/212 km from South Unit).

FOR MORE INFORMATION

Theodore Roosevelt National Park (Box 7, Medora, ND 58645, tel. 701/623–4466, fax 701/623–4840; e-mail thro_administration@nps.gov; Web site www.nps.gov/thro). Medora Chamber of Commerce (Box 186, Medora, ND 58645, tel. 701/483–4988 or 800/279–7391). Dickinson Convention and Visitors Bureau (72 Museum Dr., Dickinson, ND 58601, tel. 701/225–4988). McKenzie County Tourism Bureau (Box 699, Watford City, ND 58854, tel. 701/842–2804 or 800/701–2804).

See Also

International Peace Garden, Affiliated Areas in Other National Parklands. *Lewis and Clark National Historic Trail,* National Trails System in Other National Parklands. *North Country National Scenic Trail,* National Trails System in Other National Parklands.

OHIO

Cuyahoga Valley National Park

In the northeast part of the state, between Cleveland and Akron

The area preserves 33,000 acres of pastoral valley along 22 mi/35 km of the Cuyahoga River. It includes the river and its floodplain, steep and gentle valley walls forested by deciduous and evergreen woods, and numerous tributaries and their ravines. The area was authorized as a national recreation area on December 27, 1974, established on June 26, 1975, and redesignated as a national park on October 11, 2000.

WHAT TO SEE & DO

Attending performing arts and cultural and natural-history programs, biking (rentals, Peninsula), cross-country skiing, hiking, snowshoeing (rentals). **Facilities:** 5 visitor centers with interpretive exhibits—Canal (Valley View), Happy Days (S.R. 303), Hunt Farm (Bolanz Rd. near Towpath Trail), Boston Store with museum on canal boatbuilding (Boston), Frazee House with early settlement exhibits (Canal Rd.); trails. Book and sales area, meeting rooms, picnic shelters. **Programs & Events:** Interpretive programs year-round. Lecture series (Jan.–Mar., Fri. evenings); costumed Lock 38 demonstrations (Canal Visitor Center, Memorial Day–Labor Day, weekends 1–4).

PLANNING YOUR VISIT

⚠ **Camping:** Available in Peninsula; none in recreation area. 🛏 **Lodging:** In the recreation area: The Inn at Brandywine Falls (tel. 330/467–1812), Stanford Youth Hostel (tel. 330/467–8711). Lodging also available outside the park in the Cleveland/Akron area. ✗ **Food & Supplies:** Available locally; none in recreation area. ☞ **Tips & Hints:** Busiest in June and August, least crowded in November and December. 🎫 **Fees, Permits & Limitations:** Free. Some interpretive programs, picnic shelters, and meeting rooms have fees. Leashed pets only. No hunting. Bikes on designated trails only. Park open daily. Canal Visitor Center open daily 8–5. Happy Days Visitor Center open May–Oct., daily 8–5; Nov.–Apr., Tues.–Sun. 8–5. Hunt Farm Visitor Center hours vary seasonally. Frazee House open Apr.–Oct., weekends. Boston Store hours vary seasonally. All closed Thanksgiving, Dec. 25, Jan. 1.

HOW TO GET THERE

The recreation area is east of I–77, between Cleveland and Akron. Closest airports: Cleveland (10 mi/16km), Akron (25 mi/40 km).

FOR MORE INFORMATION

Cuyahoga Valley National Park (15610 Vaughn Rd., Brecksville, OH 44141, tel. 216/524–1497; Web site www.nps.gov/cuva).

Dayton Aviation Heritage National Historical Park

In the western part of the state, in Dayton

The park preserves sites associated with Wilbur and Orville Wright and the early development of aviation. It also honors the life and work of African American poet Paul Laurence Dunbar. The park, a cooperative effort between the National Park Service and three partners, includes four sites: The Wright Cycle Company building and the Wright brothers' print shop building, Huffman Prairie Flying Field, the *1905 Wright Flyer III*, and the Paul Laurence Dunbar House State Memorial. The park was authorized on October 16, 1992.

WHAT TO SEE & DO

Touring four sites. **Facilities:** Restored museum with interpretive exhibits (The Wright Cycle Company building), exhibits at Paul Laurence Dunbar State Memorial and Carillon Historical Park, self-guided facilities at Huffman Prairie Flying Field. Bookstores. **Programs & Events:** Year-round: programs on aviation, early transportation history, African-American lifestyles, and accomplishments of Paul Laurence Dunbar and Wilbur and Orville Wright. Seasonal activities and special events available. Centennial events in 2002–2003 to be announced.

PLANNING YOUR VISIT

⚠ **Camping:** Available in Dayton area; none in park. 🛏 **Lodging:** Available in Dayton area; none in park. ✕ **Food & Supplies:** Available in Dayton area; none in park. ☞ **Tips & Hints:** Plan to spend 45 minutes touring The Wright Cycle Company building, an hour at the Paul Laurence Dunbar State Memorial, 30 minutes each at the Wright Hall at Carillon Historical Park and Huffman Prairie Flying Field. Exploring Carillon Historical Park takes two–four hours. Travel time between park units can take up to 45 minutes. 🎫 **Fees, Permits & Limitations:** Entrance fees: The Wright Cycle Company building and Huffman Prairie Flying Field are free; Paul Laurence Dunbar State Memorial is $3 per person, $1.25 for ages 5–12, members are free, groups are 75¢ per person; Wright Hall—Carillon Historical Park is $2 per adult, $1 for ages 3–17, members are free. Reservations required for group visits to Paul Laurence Dunbar State Memorial and Carillon Historical Park. The Wright Cycle Company building open Memorial Day–Labor Day, Mon.–Sat. 8:30–4:30, Sun. 11–4:30; Labor Day–Memorial Day, Wed.–Sat. 8:30–4:30, Sun. 11–4:30. Closed Thanksgiving, Dec. 25, Jan. 1, Veterans Day. Paul Laurence Dunbar State Memorial open Memorial Day–Labor Day, Wed.–Sat. 9:30–4:30, Sun. and holidays 12–4:30; Labor Day–Oct., Sat. 9:30–4:30, Sun. 12:30–4:30; Nov.–Memorial Day, weekdays 9:30–4:30. Huffman Prairie Flying Field open daylight hours when the Wright-Patterson Air Force Base is open. Wright Hall–Carillon Historical Park open Apr. 1–Oct. 31, Tues.–Sat. 9:30–5, Sun. and holidays 12–5. Closed Mon.

HOW TO GET THERE

To reach The Wright Cycle Company building, exit I–75 at 3rd St. in downtown Dayton. Cross the Miami River and turn left at the third stoplight on west side of river on Williams St. The building is on the left. From I–70 or U.S. 35, exit onto I–75 and follow above directions. Closest airport: Dayton (10 mi/16 km).

FOR MORE INFORMATION

Superintendent, Dayton Aviation Heritage National Historical Park (22 S. Williams St., Box 9280, Wright Brothers Station, Dayton, OH 45409, tel. 937/225–7705, fax 937/225–7706; e-mail DAAV_Interpretation@ nps.gov; Web site www.nps.gov/daav). Paul Laurence Dunbar State Memorial (tel. 937/224–7061). Carillon Historical Park (tel. 937/293–2841). Huffman Prairie Flying Field (tel. 937/257–5535 ext. 254). Greene County Convention and Visitors Bureau (1221 Meadowbridge Dr., Suite A, Beaver Creek, OH 45434, tel. 937/429–9100). Dayton-Montgomery County Convention and Visitors Bureau (1 Chamber Plaza, Suite A, Dayton, OH 45402-2400, tel. 937/226–8211 or 800/221–8235). Dayton Area Chamber of Commerce (1 Chamber Plaza, Dayton, OH 45402, tel. 937/226–1444).

Hopewell Culture National Historical Park

In the south-central part of the state, near Chillicothe

Archaeological remnants of earthwork and mound complexes built by the Hopewell, who inhabited the Ohio River valley between 200 BC and AD 500, are preserved in this park. The Mound City Group, a 13-acre rectangular earth enclosure with at least 23 mounds, provides insight into the social, ceremonial, political and economic life of the Hopewell people. The site was proclaimed the Mound City Group National Monument in 1923 and renamed in 1992.

WHAT TO SEE & DO

Picnicking, self-guided tours of earthworks, watching video. **Facilities:** Visitor center with interpretive exhibits, museum, interpretive trails. Book sales area, picnic area. **Programs & Events:** Year-round: illustrated programs, crafts demonstrations, nature and archaeology walks, ranger-guided group tours (reservation required, tel. 740/774–1125). National Parks week (3rd week in May), Ohio Archaeology week (3rd. week in June).

PLANNING YOUR VISIT

Camping: Available locally; none in park. **Lodging:** Available in Chillicothe; none in park. **Food & Supplies:** Available in Chillicothe; none in park. **Tips & Hints:** Busiest in July and August, least crowded in December and January. **Fees, Permits & Limitations:** Entrance fee: $2 per adult or $4 per vehicle. Leashed pets only. Park open daily sunrise–sunset. Visitor center open Mar.–Nov., daily 8:30–5; Dec.–

Feb., Wed.–Sun., 8:30–5; extended hours in summer. Closed Thanksgiving, Dec. 25, Jan. 1.

HOW TO GET THERE

3 mi/5 km north of Chillicothe on SR 104. Closest airport: Columbus (50 mi/80 km).

FOR MORE INFORMATION

Hopewell Culture National Historic Park (16062 SR 104, Chillicothe, OH 45601, tel. 740/774–1125, fax 740/774–1140; Web site www.nps.gov/hocu). Ross/Chillicothe Convention and Visitors Bureau (Box 353, Chillicothe, OH 45601, tel. 740/702–7677 or 800/413–4118).

James A. Garfield National Historic Site

In the northeast part of the state, in Mentor

The site preserves Lawnfield, the family's farm, and other property associated with the 20th president of the United States, who was assassinated shortly after becoming president in 1881. The site was authorized in 1980.

WHAT TO SEE & DO

Touring visitor center (a restored carriage barn), home, and grounds of Lawnfield; viewing interpretive displays and artifacts; watching video. **Facilities:** Visitor center with interpretive exhibits, family home, grounds, wayside exhibits. Gift shop. **Programs & Events:** Year-round: interpretive talks, lectures, and home tours. Special events available.

PLANNING YOUR VISIT

Camping: Available in Chardon, Mantua, Newbury; none at site. **Lodging:** Available in Mentor; none at site. **Food & Supplies:** Available in Mentor; none at site. **Tips & Hints:** Busiest in July and August, least crowded in January and February. **Fees, Permits & Limitations:** Free. Guided tours of home: Adults 13 and up $6; 60 and older $5; children 6–12 $4; 5 and under free. Golden Passports and National Park pass holders $3. AAA members receive $1 discount off list price for tours. Park and visitor center open Mon.–Sat. 10–5, Sun. noon–5. Last tour of home at 4:15 PM. Closed Memorial Day, Labor Day, Thanksgiving, Dec. 24–25, Jan. 1.

HOW TO GET THERE

25 mi/40 km east of Cleveland, off I–90 on Mentor Ave. (OH 20). Closest airport: Cleveland–Hopkins International (35 mi/56 km).

FOR MORE INFORMATION

James A. Garfield National Historic Site (8095 Mentor Ave., Mentor, OH 44060, tel. 440/255–8722, fax 440/255–8545; Web site www.nps.gov/jaga). Lake County Visitors Bureau (1610 Mentor Ave., Suite 2, Painesville, OH 44077, tel. 800/368–5253, fax 440/354–3213). Mentor

Area Chamber of Commerce (7547 Mentor Ave., Suite 302, Mentor OH 44060, tel. 440/946–2625).

Perry's Victory and International Peace Memorial

On South Bass Island in Lake Erie

The monument that rises 352 ft/107 m above Lake Erie commemorates war and peace. Oliver Hazard Perry's victory over a British fleet in the Battle of Lake Erie served as the turning point in the War of 1812. It helped the United States retain its territory in the Treaty of Ghent. Later events led to more than 180 years of peace between Canada and the United States. The Perry's Victory Memorial Commission built and operated the monument for its first 21 years; it was established as a national monument in 1936 and redesignated in 1972.

WHAT TO SEE & DO

Fishing; kite flying; sunbathing; touring memorial, rotunda, and observation deck. **Facilities:** Information station with interpretive exhibits, monument. Bookstore. **Programs & Events:** Ranger talks (mid-June–Aug.), costumed presentations and musket firings (mid-June–Aug.). Battle Anniversary (weekend after Labor Day), concerts, and ceremonies.

PLANNING YOUR VISIT

⚠ **Camping:** Available in Put-in-Bay, South Bass Island; none at memorial. 🛏 **Lodging:** Available in Put-in-Bay, South Bass Island; none at memorial. ✗ **Food & Supplies:** Available in Put-in-Bay, South Bass Island; none at memorial. ☞ **Tips & Hints:** Plan to spend two hours visiting memorial. In summer, expect a wait to ride elevator to observation deck. Spring in Lake Erie is cool and windy into June. Busiest in July and August, least crowded in December and March. ✉ **Fees, Permits & Limitations:** Entrance fee: $3 per adult 17 and up. Memorial open late Apr.–Memorial Day and late Sept.–mid-Oct., daily 10–5; Memorial Day–mid-June and Labor Day–late Sept., daily 10–6; mid-June–Labor Day, daily 10–7; mid-Oct.–late Apr., by appointment.

HOW TO GET THERE

On South Bass Island in the village of Put-in-Bay. Access to the island by public ferry or plane only. Facilities available on the island for private planes and boats. Griffing Island Airlines/Flying Service provides year-round flights (reservation required, tel. 800/368–3743) to Put-in-Bay from Sandusky; Port Clinton Island Airways (reservation required, tel. 419/734–4700) from Port Clinton. Miller Boat Line (no reservations, tel. 800/500–2421) provides auto and passenger ferry service Apr.–Nov. from Catawba Point, near Port Clinton, to island. Leave your car on the mainland and walk on the ferry because of vehicle transportation restrictions. Put-in-Bay Boat Lines–Jet Express (tel. 800/245–

1538) provides passenger-only ferry service seasonally from Port Clinton to Put-in-Bay. Closest airports: Cleveland (85 mi/136 km), Toledo, OH (50 mi/80km); and Detroit, MI (75 mi/120 km).

FOR MORE INFORMATION

Perry's Victory and International Peace Memorial (93 Delaware Ave., Box 549, Put-in-Bay, OH 43456, tel. 419/285–2184, fax 419/285–2516; e-mail pevi_superintendent@nps.gov; Web site www.nps.gov/pevi). Put-in-Bay Chamber of Commerce (Box 250, Put-in-Bay, OH 43456, tel. 419/285–2832).

William Howard Taft National Historic Site

In Cincinnati

William Howard Taft is the only person in U.S. history to have served as both president (1909–13) and Chief Justice of the United States (1921–30). He was born and raised in this 1840s Greek Revival–style home. Four furnished rooms have been restored to depict the lifestyle of Taft and his family during the 1860s. The site was authorized on December 2, 1969.

WHAT TO SEE & DO

Taking ranger-guided and self-guided tours of home. **Facilities:** Home, Taft Education Center with interactive displays, orientation film. Bookstore, gift shop. **Programs & Events:** Year-round: ranger-guided and self-guided tours. New Year's Open House (Jan.), Constitution Day and Taft's Birthday (Sept.), Father Christmas (Dec.), Christmas Decoration Workshop (Dec.).

PLANNING YOUR VISIT

Camping: Available in Hamilton County Park District; none at site. **Lodging:** Available in Cincinnati, OH, and Covington, KY; none at site. **Food & Supplies:** Available in Cincinnati; none at site. **Tips & Hints:** Home is kept at 70°F/21°C, so wear a light jacket or sweater in summer. Busiest in April and May, least crowded in November and January. **Fees, Permits & Limitations:** Free. No smoking, pets, food, or drink in house. House open daily 8–4. Closed Thanksgiving, Dec. 25. Jan. 1.

HOW TO GET THERE

The Taft House is at 2038 Auburn Ave., in the Mount Auburn section of Cincinnati. From I–71N, take Exit 2 (Reading Rd.). Make a left onto Dorchester St. Turn right on Auburn and drive 1½ blocks to the home. From I–71S, take Exit 3 (Taft Rd.) to Auburn Ave. Turn left to home. Closest airport: Greater Cincinnati International (10 mi/16 km).

FOR MORE INFORMATION

William Howard Taft National Historic Site (2038 Auburn Ave., Cincinnati, OH 45219-3025, tel. 513/ 684–3262, fax 513/684–3627; e-mail wiho_superintendent@nps.gov; Web site www.nps.gov/wiho). Cincinnati Convention and Visitors Bureau (300 W. 6th St., Cincinnati, OH 45202, tel. 513/621–2142). Ohio Travel Information Center (77 S. High St., Box 1001, Columbus, OH 43216, tel. 800/282–5393).

See Also

David Berger National Memorial, Affiliated Areas in Other National Parklands. *North Country National Scenic Trail,* National Trails System in Other National Parklands. *Ohio & Erie Canal National Heritage Corridors,* National Heritage Areas in Other National Parklands.

OKLAHOMA

Chickasaw National Recreation Area

In the south-central part of the state, near Sulphur

Camping, boating, fishing, swimming, hiking, hunting, and enjoying nature are all available at the recreation area's springs, streams, and lakes. The recreation area was named in honor of the Chickasaw, the land's longtime inhabitants. Sulphur Springs Reservation was authorized in 1902, renamed and redesignated Platt National Park in 1906, combined with Arbuckle National Recreation Area, and renamed and redesignated in 1976.

WHAT TO SEE & DO

Auto touring, boating, fishing, hiking, hunting, picnicking, swimming, watching film, waterskiing. **Facilities:** Information and nature center, 18 mi/29 km of trails, scenic roads. Bookstore. **Programs & Events:** Year-round: ranger-led nature walks, creek walks, campfire programs (weekends). Sulphur Days, Art in the Park, the Hills of Oklahoma Bicycle Tour, Bald Eagle Watch, and the "1906 Historic Candlelight Tour."

PLANNING YOUR VISIT

Camping: 6 campgrounds: utility hookups in Buckhorn and the Point. Group campsites in Rock Creek, Central, Cold Springs (reservations available, tel. 580/622–6677). **Lodging:** Available in Davis, Sulphur; none in recreation area. **Food & Supplies:** Available in Davis, Sulphur; none in recreation area. **Tips & Hints:** Busiest in June and July, least crowded in December and January. **Fees, Permits & Limitations:** Free. Boat launching and picnic pavilion reservation fees. Park open daily. Travertine Information and Nature Center closed Dec. 25, Jan. 1.

HOW TO GET THERE

On OK 177, south of Sulphur, 90 mi/144 km south of Oklahoma City, and 120 mi/192 km north of Dallas, TX. From U.S. I–35S, take Exit 55 to OK 7. From I–35N, take Exit 51 to OK 7. After Sulphur (10 mi/16 km), turn south on OK 177. Park headquarters is on the right. Closest airports: Oklahoma City, Dallas.

FOR MORE INFORMATION

Chickasaw National Recreation Area (Box 201, Sulphur, OK 73086, tel. 580/622–3165, fax 580/622–2296; Web site www.nps.gov/chic). Sulphur Chamber of Commerce (717 W. Broadway, Sulphur, OK 73086, tel. 580/622–2824). Davis Chamber of Commerce (300 E. Main, Davis, OK 73030, tel. 580/369–2402).

Oklahoma City
National Memorial

In Oklahoma City

The memorial is on the former site of the Alfred P. Murrah Federal Building, which was bombed April 19, 1995, killing 168 people in the most deadly terrorist attack ever on American soil. The memorial is composed of 168 bronze and glass chairs arranged in nine rows, representing the number of victims on each floor of the Murrah Building when the explosion occurred. The site, which opened partially in 2000, will include a memorial, museum, visitor center, and a terrorism institute. The memorial was authorized on October 9, 1997 and dedicated on April 19, 2000.

WHAT TO SEE & DO

Facilities: Memorial, picnic areas. Museum slated to open in Feb. 2001.

PLANNING YOUR VISIT

 Lodging: In Oklahoma City; none at site. ✕ **Food & Supplies:** In Oklahoma City; none at site. ☞ **Tips & Hints:** Group tour reservations encouraged (tel. 405/235–3313). **Fees, Permits & Limitations:** Free. Outdoor Symbolic Memorial open daily. Fees will be charged upon completion for Memorial Center.

HOW TO GET THERE

Take the downtown Oklahoma City exit off I–40 or I–235. The site is on 5th St. between Robinson and Harvey. Closest airport: Oklahoma City.

FOR MORE INFORMATION

Oklahoma City National Memorial Trust (Box 323, Oklahoma City, OK 73101, tel. 405/235–3313, fax 405/235–3315; Web site www.oklahoman.net/connections/memorial).

Washita Battlefield
National Historic Site

In the western part of the state, near Cheyenne

The park preserves the site of the Battle of the Washita (November 27, 1868), one of the largest engagements between Plains tribes and the U.S. Army on the southern Great Plains. Lieutenant Colonel George A. Custer attacked the sleeping Cheyenne village of Peace Chief Black Kettle and killed about 50 men, women, and children. The events symbolize the struggle of the southern Great Plains tribes to maintain their traditional way of life and not to submit to reservation confinement. The park was authorized on November 12, 1996.

WHAT TO SEE & DO

Viewing battlefield from overlook, walking on trails. This new park is under development. **Facilities:** Overlook with historical plaque, commemorative monument, and a panel indicating approximate route, approach, and attack of Custer and approximate location of the Indian village, 1.5 mi/2.5 km trail system. Black Kettle Museum in Cheyenne, operated by the Oklahoma Historical Society, contains battle exhibits and information. Bookstore in Black Kettle Museum, picnic tables at overlook. **Programs & Events:** Ranger-led guided walks and talks (May–Aug.). Battle anniversary symposium (Nov., in even-numbered years).

PLANNING YOUR VISIT

⛺ **Camping:** Available in Cheyenne; none at site. 🏨 **Lodging:** Available in Cheyenne, Elk City, Sayre; none at site. ✕ **Food & Supplies:** Available in Cheyenne, Elk City, Sayre; none at site. ☞ **Tips & Hints:** This is a new site, and facilities are limited. Visit in spring and fall, summers are very hot. 🎫 **Fees, Permits & Limitations:** Free. No hunting. No pets. Site open daily dawn–dusk. Black Kettle Museum in Cheyenne open summer, June–Aug., daily 8–6; Sept.–May, weekdays 9–5; Sun. 1–5.

HOW TO GET THERE

2 mi/3.2 km west of Cheyenne on Hwy. 47A and 30 mi/48 km north of I–40 via Exit 20 (U.S. 283N). Closest airports: Oklahoma City, OK, or Amarillo, TX (both 140 mi/224 km).

FOR MORE INFORMATION

Washita Battlefield National Historic Site (Box 890, Cheyenne, OK 73628, tel. 580/497–2742, fax 580/497–2712; e-mail WABA_Ranger_Activities@nps.gov; Web site www.nps.gov/waba). Cheyenne Chamber of Commerce (Box 57, Cheyenne, OK 73628, tel. 580/497–3318).

See Also

Fort Smith National Historic Site, AR. *Santa Fe National Historic Trail*, National Trails System in Other National Parklands. *Trail of Tears National Historic Trail*, National Trails System in Other National Parklands.

OREGON

Crater Lake National Park

In the southern part of the state,
60 mi/96 km northwest of Klamath Falls

Crater Lake is one of the most famous lakes on Earth, principally because of its unusual blue color and its mountain setting. At a depth of 1,958 ft/597 m, Crater Lake is the deepest lake in the United States and the seventh deepest in the world, and it holds the world record for natural water clarity. The mature forests that surround Crater Lake are largely untouched. The park was established on May 22, 1902.

WHAT TO SEE & DO

Auto and boat touring, cross-country skiing (rentals, Klamath Falls, Medford), hiking. **Facilities:** Information center with interpretive exhibits (Steel, at park headquarters) and visitor center (Rim Village, summer only), wayside exhibits. Map sale areas, picnic areas, post office. **Programs & Events:** Ranger-led boat tours, campfire programs, geology and natural and cultural history walks (July–Labor Day, daily), snowshoe walks (late. Nov.–Mar.).

PLANNING YOUR VISIT

Camping: 2 campgrounds: one with dump station (late June–early Oct.), one tents only (mid-July–late Sept.). (No reservations.) Backcountry camping available (permit required, *see below*). No group camping. Private campgrounds in Chiloquin, Diamond Lake, Fort Klamath, Prospect, Shady Cove, Union Creek. **Lodging:** In the park: Crater Lake Lodge (mid-May–mid-Oct.), Mazama Village (early June–Sept.). Call 541/830–8700 for information. Lodging also available outside the park in Chiloquin, Diamond Lake, Fort Klamath, Prospect, Union Creek. **Food & Supplies:** In the park: meals at Crater Lake Lodge, cafeteria at Rim Village, food and snacks at Mazama Village. Food and supplies also available in Chiloquin, Diamond Lake, Fort Klamath, Prospect. **Tips & Hints:** Go between early July and late September to avoid snow, between mid-July and early August for wildflowers. Busiest in July and August, least crowded in December and February. **Fees, Permits & Limitations:** Entrance fee: $10 per car, $5 for cyclists and walk-ins. Backcountry permits required (free). No bicycles, off-road vehicles allowed off paved roads. Leashed pets allowed in front country only. No private boats. No wildlife feeding or hunting. No climbing or hiking inner caldera walls except on Cleetwood Cove Trail. Park open daily. Steel Information Center open daily 9–5. Closed Dec. 25. Rim Village Visitor Center open June–Sept., daily 9:30–5; July 1–Labor Day, extended hours.

HOW TO GET THERE

In south Oregon on SR 62, 60 mi/96 km northwest of Klamath Falls and 80 mi/128 km northeast of Medford. Closest airports: Medford, Klamath.

FOR MORE INFORMATION

Crater Lake National Park (Box 7, Crater Lake, OR 97604-0007, tel. 541/594–2211, fax 541/594–2299; Web site ww.nps.gov/crla).

Fort Clatsop
National Memorial

In the northwest part of the state, near Astoria

After their epic journey across the West, the 33-member Lewis and Clark Expedition spent the winter of 1805–06 at Fort Clatsop. In 1955, local citizens built a replica of the explorers' fort in a lush spruce and hemlock forest that is the focal point of the memorial. The Salt Works site in nearby Seaside commemorates where the explorers set up a camp to boil seawater to produce salt for use at the fort and on the return trip. The memorial was authorized on May 29, 1958.

WHAT TO SEE & DO

Picnicking, touring fort replica and saltworks, walking trails. **Facilities:** Visitor center with interpretive exhibits, audiovisual programs, trails, trailside interpretive panels, replica of stone oven (Seaside). Bookstore, picnic area. **Programs & Events:** Slide shows and movies year-round. Costumed ranger-led talks and demonstrations (fort replica, mid-June–Labor Day). Newfoundland Dog Day (July), National Park Service Founders Day (Aug. 25), Explorers' Christmas at Ft. Clatsop (Dec. 25–Jan. 1), occasional special themes and guest speakers.

PLANNING YOUR VISIT

⛺ **Camping:** Available in Gearhart, Seaside, Warrenton; none at memorial. 🛏 **Lodging:** Available in Astoria, Cannon Beach, Gearhart, Seaside, and Warrenton, OR; and Ilwaco and Long Beach, WA; none at memorial. ✕ **Food & Supplies:** Available in Astoria, Cannon Beach, Gearhart, Seaside, and Warrenton, OR; and Ilwaco and Long Beach, WA; none at memorial. ☞ **Tips & Hints:** Fort replica floors are slippery and uneven. Go in winter for more authentic expedition weather. Busiest in July and August, least crowded in January and February. 🏕 **Fees, Permits & Limitations:** Entrance fee: $2 per person (free under 17) or $4 per car. No hunting or fishing. No bikes on trails. No skateboards. No pets in fort or visitor center. Leashed pets elsewhere. Park and visitor center open Labor Day–mid-June, daily 8–5; mid-June–Labor Day, daily 8–6. Closed Dec. 25.

HOW TO GET THERE

6 mi/10 km southwest of Astoria, off U.S. 101. Closest airport: Portland (100 mi/160 km).

FOR MORE INFORMATION

Fort Clatsop National Memorial (92343 Ft. Clatsop Rd., Astoria, OR 97103, tel. 503/861–2471, fax 503/861–2585; e-mail FOCL_Administration@NPS.GOV; Web site www.nps.gov/focl). Astoria/Warrenton Chamber of Commerce (111 W. Marine Dr., Astoria, OR 97103, tel. 503/325–6311). Warrenton Visitor Center (143 S. Hwy. 101, Warrenton, OR 97146, tel. 503/861–1031). Seaside Chamber of Commerce (7 N. Roosevelt, Seaside, OR 97138, tel. 503/738–6391).

John Day Fossil Beds National Monument

In the north-central part of the state, near Dayville, Mitchell, and Clarno

The heavily eroded volcanic deposits of the scenic John Day River basin house a well-preserved fossil record of plants and animals that spans more than 40 of the 65 million years of the Cenozoic Era, or Age of Mammals. The monument is composed of three widely separated units: Sheep Rock, Painted Hills, and Clarno. The monument was authorized in 1974 and established in 1975.

WHAT TO SEE & DO

Auto touring, self-guided trail tours, visiting fossil museum at Sheep Rock. **Facilities:** Visitor center with fossil museum (Cant Ranch house and grounds, Sheep Rock), theater, indoor and outdoor exhibits, exhibits at Painted Hills and Clarno, scenic roads, overlooks, trails, trailside exhibits. Bookstore. **Programs & Events:** Year-round: self-guided tours, ranger-led fossil museum talks, trail hikes, off-site presentations. Campfire programs (monthly, Apr.–Oct., nearby state campgrounds). Fossil Identification Days, National Park Service Birthday Celebration (Aug.).

PLANNING YOUR VISIT

⚠ **Camping:** Available locally; none at monument. 🏠 **Lodging:** Available locally; none at monument. ✕ **Food & Supplies:** Available locally; none at monument. ☞ **Tips & Hints:** Go to Claro in morning, Sheep Rock in early afternoon, and Painted Hills in late afternoon for best light for scenic views and photography. Go between mid-April and mid-May for wildflowers at Painted Hills. Busiest in July and August, least crowded in January and February. 🎫 **Fees, Permits & Limitations:** Free. No collecting or disturbing fossils or geologic or biological resources. Park trails, overlooks, and grounds open during daylight. Museum/visitor center open Mar.–Memorial Day and Labor Day–Thanksgiving, daily 9–5; Memorial Day–Labor Day, daily 9–6; Thanksgiving–Feb., weekdays 9–5. Closed Thanksgiving, Dec. 25, Jan. 1, Presidents' Day, Martin Luther King Jr. Day.

HOW TO GET THERE

Visitor center and fossil museum at Sheep Rock are 9 mi/14 km west of Dayville, near intersection of U.S. 26 and OR 19. Painted Hills is 10 mi/16 km west of Mitchell off U.S. 26. Clarno is 18 mi/29 km west of Fossil on OR 218. Closest airports: Redmond (80 mi/128 km), Portland, OR (250 mi/400 km), and Boise, ID (240 mi/384 km).

FOR MORE INFORMATION

John Day Fossil Beds National Monument (HCR 82, Box 126, Kimberly, OR 97848-9701, tel. 541/987–2333, fax 541/987–2336; Web site www.nps.gov/joda). Grant County Chamber of Commerce (281 W. Main St., John Day, OR 97845, tel. 541/575–0547). Wheeler County Chamber of Commerce (Box 467, Fossil, OR 97830, tel. 541/763–2698). Crook County Chamber of Commerce (390 N.E. Fairview, Prineville, OR 97754, tel. 541/447–6304). Eastern Oregon Visitors Association (490 Campbell St., Baker City, OR 97814, tel. 800/523–1235). Central Oregon Recreation Association (63085 N. Hwy. 97, Suite 107, Bend, OR 97701, tel. 800/800–8334). Oregon Tourism Division (775 Summer St. NE, Salem, OR 97310, tel. 800/547–7842). U.S. Bureau of Land Management (Prineville office, Box 550, Prineville, OR 97754, or 3050 N.E. 3rd St., Prineville, OR 97754, tel. 541/416–6700). Forest Service (Hines office) (HC 74, Box 12870, Hines, OR 97738, tel. 541/573–4383). Oregon State Parks & Recreation (Salem office, 555 Liberty St., Room 300, Salem, OR 97301, tel. 503/588–6261).

Oregon Caves National Monument

In the southwest part of the state, near Cave Junction

Below ground at this monument is a marble cave created by natural forces over hundreds of thousands of years in one of the world's most diverse geologic realms. Above ground, the 480-acre monument's three trails pass through a remnant of old-growth coniferous forest, a fantastic array of plants, and a Douglas-fir tree with the widest known girth in Oregon. In addition to its unique geologic setting, Oregon Caves has Pleistocene mammal fossils and one of the largest assortments of endemic cave life in the country. The monument was proclaimed in 1909 and transferred to the Park Service in 1933.

WHAT TO SEE & DO

Cave touring, hiking. **Facilities:** Visitor center with interpretive displays (Cave Junction, Hwy. 46, one block from Hwy. 199), trails. Book sales area. **Programs & Events:** Ranger-guided walks, day programs (Memorial Day–Labor Day).

PLANNING YOUR VISIT

⚠ **Camping:** Available in surrounding Siskiyou National Forest and along Hwys. 46 and 199; none at monument. ▦ **Lodging:** In the park: Oregon Caves Chateau (May–Oct., tel. 541/592–3400). Lodging also available outside the park in Cave Junction, Grants Pass, Kerby, O'Brien. ✕ **Food & Supplies:** In the park: meals at Oregon Caves Chateau (Mar.–Nov., tel. 541/592–3400). Food and supplies also available in Cave Junction. ☞ **Tips & Hints:** Wear tennis shoes or boots and a jacket for cave tours. Temperature is 41°F/5°C in cave. Don't take tour if you have breathing or heart problems. Tour is 1.5 mi/2.4 km and climbs 250 ft/76 m. Go in late April or May for wildflowers in valleys, June for meadow flowers. Busiest in July and August, least crowded in December and January. ▨ **Fees, Permits & Limitations:** Free. Cave tour fees: $7.50 adults 12 and up, $5 children, $6.50 senior citizens holding Golden Age Passports. Cave restrictions: children must be at least 42 inches/1.06 m tall and able to climb a set of test stairs unassisted. No infants or young children allowed in caves. No child care available. Canes allowed in first cave room only. First room (only) wheelchair accessible. No pets on trails, leashed pets elsewhere. Mountain bikes on existing roads only. No motorized equipment on trails. Cave tours Oct.–Nov. and Mar.–Apr., daily 10–4; May–Memorial Day, daily 9–5; Memorial Day–Labor Day, daily 9–7; Sept., daily 9–5. Closed Dec.–Mar.

HOW TO GET THERE

20 mi/32 km southeast of Cave Junction via Hwy 46. Closest airport: Medford (80 mi/128 km).

FOR MORE INFORMATION

Oregon Caves National Monument (19000 Caves Hwy., Cave Junction, OR 97523, tel. 541/592–2100, fax 541/592–3981; Web site www.nps. gov/orca). Illinois Valley Visitor Center (201 Caves Hwy., Cave Junction, OR 97523, tel. 541/592–2631). Illinois Valley Forest Service (Illinois Valley Ranger District, 26568 Redwood Hwy., Cave Junction, OR 97523, tel. 541/592–2166). Illinois Valley Chamber of Commerce (Box 312, Cave Junction, OR 97523, tel. 541/592–3326).

See Also

California National Historic Trail, National Trails System in Other National Parklands. *Lewis and Clark National Historic Trail,* National Trails System in Other National Parklands. *McLoughlin House National Historic Site,* Affiliated Areas in Other National Parklands. *Nez Perce National Historical Park,* Idaho. *Nez Perce National Historic Trail,* National Trails System in Other National Parklands. *Oregon National Scenic Trail,* National Trails System in Other National Parklands. *Pacific Crest National Scenic Trail,* National Trails System in Other National Parklands.

PENNSYLVANIA

Allegheny Portage Railroad National Historic Site

Midstate, 10 mi/16 km west of Altoona

Preserved here are the remains of the first railroad to cross the Allegheny Mountains. The 36-mi-/58-km-long Portage Railroad, completed in 1834, used a series of 10 inclined planes to lift canal boats loaded on railroad-type flatcars across the mountains between Hollidaysburg and Johnstown. The railroad, in conjunction with the Pennsylvania Main Line Canal, reduced the time to travel the 390 mi/624 km between Philadelphia and Pittsburgh to four or five days from three weeks. The site was authorized on August 31, 1964.

WHAT TO SEE & DO

Cross-country skiing (rentals, Altoona), hiking, picnicking, viewing the historic area of the park, walking. **Facilities:** Visitor center with interpretive exhibits and 20-minute film; interpretive displays at Engine House #6, Historic Lemon House Tavern, wayside exhibits. Book sale area, picnic pavilion with grills, tables. **Programs & Events:** Year-round interpretive tours of Lemon House. Costumed ranger presentations including log hewing, stonecutting, and lifestyles of the past (summer, daily). Evening on the Summit concert and guest lectures (summer, Sat. nights), guided Heritage Hikes and bus tours to lesser-known areas of the railroad (June–Aug., Sun.; reservations required, tel. 814/886–6150).

PLANNING YOUR VISIT

⛺ **Camping:** Private campgrounds nearby in Cresson and Ebensburg; none at site. 🏨 **Lodging:** Available nearby in Altoona and Ebensburg; none at site. ✕ **Food & Supplies:** Available nearby in Altoona, Cresson, Ebensburg, Gallitzin; none at site. ☞ **Tips & Hints:** Go in April and May for wildflowers, October for fall colors. Busiest in July and August, least crowded in December and January. 🎫 **Fees, Permits & Limitations:** Entrance fee: $2 per person. Bikes restricted to hard-surface roads. No hunting. Leashed pets only. Visitor center open daily 9–5, extended hours in summer. Closed Thanksgiving, Dec. 25, Jan. 1.

HOW TO GET THERE

10 mi/16 km west of Altoona, 15 mi/24 km east of Ebensburg on U.S. 22 (Gallitzin exit).

FOR MORE INFORMATION

Allegheny Portage Railroad National Historic Site (110 Federal Park Rd., Gallitzin, PA 16641, tel. 814/886–6150, fax 814/884–0206; e-mail alpo_visitor_center@nps.gov; Web site www.nps.gov/alpo). Allegheny Mountains Convention and Visitors Bureau (tel. 814/943–4183 or 800/842–5866, fax 814/943–8094; Web site www.alleghenymountains.com).

Greater Johnstown/Cambria Convention and Visitors Bureau (111 Market St., Johnstown, PA 15901, tel. 814/536–7993 or 800/237–8590; Web site www.visitjohnstownpa.com).

Delaware Water Gap National Recreation Area 🕶

The Delaware River on the Pennsylvania–New Jersey border, from East Stroudsburg to Milford, Pennsylvania

The recreation area contains 70,000 acres of forest along a 40-mi/64-km stretch of the Delaware River; the geologically significant "water gap," a mile-wide cut in the Kittatinny Ridge created by the Delaware River; and thousands of acres of woodland open to hiking and other recreational activities. One of the last free-flowing rivers on the East Coast, the river is home to threatened and endangered plants and animals. Significant prehistoric and historic sites are located throughout the park. The park was authorized on September 1, 1965.

WHAT TO SEE & DO

Boating, canoeing (rentals), cross-country skiing, fishing, hiking, hunting, picnicking, snowshoeing, swimming. **Facilities:** 3 visitor centers with interpretive exhibits—Kittatinny Point (off Exit 1, I–80 in New Jersey), Bushkill (Rte. 209), Dingman's Falls (Rte. 209; closed until further notice); Millbrook Village (Old Mine Rd., New Jersey side); beaches, trails, roadside radio interpretation, bulletin boards. Picnic areas with tables but no fire rings or pits. **Programs & Events:** Year-round: nature study programs (weekends, Pocono Environmental Education Center, 5 mi/8 km south of Dingman's Visitor Center). Guided hikes, children's programs, waterfall walks, campfire programs (June–Sept., weekends); cultural history demonstrations (May–Oct., weekends; Millbrook Village). Delaware River Sojourn (mid- to late June); Peter's Valley Craft Fair (last weekend in Sept.); Millbrook Days Folk Life Festival (1st weekend in Oct.); Van Campen Day (3rd weekend in Oct.). Special programs available for groups.

PLANNING YOUR VISIT

🏕 **Camping:** 2 campgrounds: 1 with electric and water but no sewage hookup. (Reservations required, tel. 570/828–2266.) Worthington State Forest (reservations available, tel. 908/841–9575). Backcountry camping available to Appalachian Trail users only. 1 group campsite available (permit required, *see below*). 26 private campgrounds available within 40 mi/64 km of park. 🏨 **Lodging:** Available in Delaware Water Gap, Milford, Stroudsburg, PA; none in recreation area. ✕ **Food & Supplies:** In the park: meals at Walpack Inn (NJ, tel. 973/948–9849). Food and supplies also available outside the park in Delaware Water Gap, Marshall's Creek, Milford, Stroudsburg, PA; Blairstown, Columbia, NJ. ☞ **Tips & Hints:** Bring your own cookstove. Go in fall for hawk-watching, winter for eagles. Busiest in July and August, least crowded in

January and February. ⌧ **Fees, Permits & Limitations:** Free. Smithfield and Milford beaches: $7 weekends, $5 weekdays per vehicle. Group camping permit required (tel. 570/588–2440). No pets in Worthington State Forest Campground, leashed pets only elsewhere. Bicycling in designated areas only. Pedestrian traffic only on trails. No ground fires. Kittatinny Point Visitor Center open May–Oct., daily 9–5; Nov.–Apr., weekends 9–4:30. Dingman's Falls Visitor Center closed until further notice. Bushkill Visitor Center open May–Oct., daily 9–5. Millbrook Village open May–Oct., Fri.–Sun. 9–5.

HOW TO GET THERE

The recreation area is on the Pennsylvania–New Jersey border from I–80 (Delaware Water Gap, PA) to I–84 (just north of Milford, PA). Closest airport: Lehigh Valley International Airport near Allentown, PA.

FOR MORE INFORMATION

Delaware Water Gap National Recreation Area (River Rd., Bushkill, PA 18324, tel. 570/588–2451, fax 570/588–2780; Web site www.nps.gov/dewa). Kittatinny Point Visitor Center (tel. 908/496–4458). Dingman's Falls Visitor Center (tel. 570/828–7802). Bushkill Visitor Center (tel. 570/588–7044).

Edgar Allan Poe National Historic Site

In Philadelphia

The life and work of Edgar Allan Poe, one of America's most gifted authors, are explored in a three-building complex at 532 N. Seventh Street, where he lived from 1843 to 1844. The site was authorized on November 10, 1978.

WHAT TO SEE & DO

Touring unfurnished home, viewing exhibits, watching slide presentation. **Facilities:** Sales area. **Programs & Events:** Ranger-guided and self-guided home tours year-round. Edgar Allan Poe's literary legacy tours: Poetry Month (Apr.), Mystery Month (July), Science Fiction Month (Aug.), "In the Master's Ghastly Grip" (Oct.).

PLANNING YOUR VISIT

⌂ **Lodging:** Available locally; none at site. ✕ **Food & Supplies:** Available locally; none at site. ☞ **Tips & Hints:** Busiest in August and October, least crowded in January and February. ⌧ **Fees, Permits & Limitations:** Free. Reservations suggested for tour groups and school groups (tel. 215/597–8780). Site open June–Oct., daily 9–5; Nov.–May, Wed.–Sun. 9–5.

HOW TO GET THERE

At 532 N. 7th St., 2 mi/3 km from the visitor center at the Independence National Historical Park (*see separate entry*), 1 mi/1.6 km from the Liberty Bell. Closest airport: Philadelphia.

FOR MORE INFORMATION

Edgar Allan Poe National Historic Site (532 N. 7th St., Philadelphia, PA 19123, tel. 215/597–8780, fax 215/597–1901; Web site www.nps.gov/edal). Philadelphia Convention and Visitors Bureau (1515 Market St., Philadelphia, PA 19102, tel. 215/636–1666, fax 215/636–1649).

Eisenhower National Historic Site

In Gettysburg

The 230-acre site preserves the former home and farm of President and Mrs. Dwight D. Eisenhower. The farm served as a weekend retreat, a refuge in time of illness, and a gathering place for political groups and the Eisenhower family. Premier Khrushchev, Chancellor Adenauer, President de Gaulle, and other VIPs trooped over its fields and toured the cattle barns during Eisenhower's terms as president, when he used the farm for his personal style of diplomacy. From 1961 to 1969, the farm served as the couple's retirement home. The site was designated on November 27, 1967.

WHAT TO SEE & DO

Touring home, farm, and cattle barns. **Facilities:** Visitor center with exhibits, home, barns, farm. Bookstore. **Programs & Events:** Tours of grounds and home, Junior Secret Service Program (daily, year-round). Tours and interpretive talks, living history programs (Apr.–Oct.), cattle show barn (Apr.–Oct.). "Fabulous Fifties Weekend" (June), World War II Weekend (Sept.), Eisenhower Seminar (Oct.), Christmas with the Eisenhowers (Dec.).

PLANNING YOUR VISIT

Camping: Youth group camping available in Gettysburg National Military Park (reservations required, tel. 717/334–1124 ext. 423, *see separate entry*). Other campgrounds available in Gettysburg area. None at site. **Lodging:** Available in Gettysburg; none at site. **Food & Supplies:** Available in Gettysburg; none at site. **Tips & Hints:** Go between April and October, when all facilities are open and tours and programs scheduled. Busiest in July and October, least crowded in January and February. **Fees, Permits & Limitations:** Entrance fee: $5.25 adults, $3.25 children 13–16, $2.25 children 6–12. All visits by shuttle bus. No on-site parking. No pets. Park and visitor center open Apr.–Oct., daily 9–4; Nov.–Mar., Wed.–Sun. 9–4. Closed Thanksgiving, Dec. 25, Jan. 1.

HOW TO GET THERE

Via shuttle bus from Gettysburg National Park Visitor Center, 1 mi/1.6 km south of Gettysburg, PA, off U.S. 15 Business. Closest airport: Harrisburg (60 mi/96 km).

FOR MORE INFORMATION

Eisenhower National Historic Site (97 Eisenhower Farm La., Gettysburg, PA 17325, tel. 717/338–9114, fax 717/338–0821; e-mail eise_site_ manager@nps.gov; Web site www.nps.gov/eise). Gettysburg Convention and Visitors Bureau (35 Carlisle St., Gettysburg, PA 17325, tel. 717/334–6274, fax 717/334–1166).

Fort Necessity National Battlefield

In the southwest part of the state, southeast of Uniontown

On July 3, 1754, the opening battle of the French and Indian War took place at a palisade fort built here by a 22-year-old George Washington. He was forced to surrender to an enemy for the first and only time in his military career. The fort has been reconstructed on the site. The site was established as a national battlefield in 1931, transferred to the Park Service in 1933, and redesignated in 1961.

WHAT TO SEE & DO

Cross-country skiing; hiking; picnicking; touring fort, historic tavern, grave site, and glen. **Facilities:** Visitor center with interpretive exhibits, historic tavern, trails, wayside exhibits, grave. Bookstore, grills, pavilions, picnic area. **Programs & Events:** Ranger-guided walks, soldier-life programs (mid-June–mid-Aug.). National Road Festival (3rd weekend in May), Battle Anniversary Memorial Program (July 3).

PLANNING YOUR VISIT

Camping: Available in Farmington, Ohiopyle; none at battlefield. **Lodging:** Available in Chalk Hill, Farmington, Ohiopyle; none at battlefield. **Food & Supplies:** Available in Chalk Hill, Hopwood, Ohiopyle, Uniontown; none at battlefield. **Tips & Hints:** Go in summer for interpretive programs, fall for foliage. Busiest in July and August, least crowded in December and January. **Fees, Permits & Limitations:** Entrance fee: $2 per adult, free under 17. No hunting. Leashed pets only. No motorized or mechanized equipment on trails. Visitor center open daily 9–5; extended hours in summer. Closed Thanksgiving, Dec. 25, Jan. 1, Martin Luther King Jr. Birthday, Presidents Day. Fort open daily 8–sunset. Mount Washington Tavern open for guided tours only, daily. Jumonville Glen open mid-Apr.–Oct., daily. Braddock Grave site open daily.

HOW TO GET THERE

On U.S. 40, 11 mi/18 km east of Uniontown. Closest airports: Connellsville, PA (16 mi/26 km); Morgantown, WV (37 mi/59 km); Pittsburgh, PA (75 mi/120 km).

FOR MORE INFORMATION

Fort Necessity National Battlefield (1 Washington Pkwy., Farmington, PA 15437, tel. 724/329–5512, fax 724/329–8682; Web site www.nps.gov/fone). Fayette County Chamber of Commerce (Box 2124, Uniontown, PA 15401, tel. 724/437–4571). Laurel Highland Convention & Visitors Bureau (120 E. Main St., Ligonier, PA 15658, tel. 724/238–5661).

Friendship Hill
National Historic Site

In the southwest part of the state, near Point Marion

This site, on the Monongahela River, preserves the brick, frame, and stone home that belonged to Albert Gallatin, Secretary of the Treasury from 1801 to 1814 under presidents Jefferson and Madison. It was authorized in 1978.

WHAT TO SEE & DO

Cross-country skiing, hiking, picnicking, touring the mansion. **Facilities:** Visitor center with interpretive exhibits, mansion, trail, wayside exhibits. Bookstore, picnic area and pavilion. **Programs & Events:** Self-guided audio tour of mansion year-round. Ranger-guided tours, special talks (Memorial Day–Labor Day). FestiFall (last Sun., Sept.).

PLANNING YOUR VISIT

Lodging: Available in Uniontown, PA, and Morgantown, WV; none at site. ✕ **Food & Supplies:** Available in Masontown, Point Marion, Smithfield; none at site. ☞ **Tips & Hints:** Busiest in May and September, least crowded in January and February. **Fees, Permits & Limitations:** Free. No hunting. Leashed pets only. No cars or bikes on trails. No off-trail hiking. Park and visitor center open daily 9–5. Closed Thanksgiving, Dec. 25, Jan. 1, Martin Luther King Jr. Birthday, Presidents Day.

HOW TO GET THERE

On PA 166, 3 mi/5 km north of Point Marion. Closest airports: Morgantown, WV (10 mi/16 km); Pittsburgh, PA (60 mi/96 km).

FOR MORE INFORMATION

Friendship Hill National Historic Site (1 Washington Pkwy., Farmington, PA 15437, tel. 724/725–9190, fax 724/725–1999; Web site www.nps.gov/frhi). Fayette County Chamber of Commerce (Box 2124, Uniontown, PA 15401–2124, tel. 724/437–4571). Laurel Highland Convention & Visitors Bureau (120 E. Main St., Ligonier, PA 15658, tel. 724/238–5661).

Gettysburg National
Military Park

Near Gettysburg

The Civil War battle fought here on July 1–3, 1863, resulted in a Union victory that repelled the second Confederate invasion of the North, a major turning point in the war. More than 51,000 soldiers were killed, wounded, or captured in this battle, making it the bloodiest of the war. The Soldiers' National Cemetery at Gettysburg contains more than 7,000 interments, of which 3,500 are from the Civil War. President Abraham Lincoln delivered his immortal Gettysburg Address here on

November 19, 1863. The park was established in 1895 and transferred to the Park Service in 1933.

WHAT TO SEE & DO

Auto touring; biking; horseback riding; viewing electric map, cyclorama, museum, battlefield, cemetery, and monuments. **Facilities:** Visitor center with interpretive exhibits (between Taneytown Rd. [PA 134] and Steinwehr Ave. [U.S. 15 Business] 1 mi/1.6 km south of Gettysburg), electric battlefield map, Cyclorama Center, auditorium, film, battlefield, cemetery, tour roads, hiking trails, horse trail, and 1,600 monuments, markers, and memorials. Bookstores. **Programs & Events:** Interpretive programs on battle, national cemetery, and Gettysburg Address (Apr.–Oct.); walking tours (mid-June–mid-Aug, several times daily; as staffing permits at other times), campfire programs (mid-June–mid-Aug.), living-history demonstrations (Apr–Oct., weekends). Memorial Day Ceremony, Battle Anniversary (July 1–3), Gettysburg Address Anniversary (Nov. 19), Remembrance Day (closest Sat. to Nov. 19).

PLANNING YOUR VISIT

⛺ **Camping:** 1 group campground for organized youth groups only (reservations required, tel. 717/334–1124 ext. 423. Reservations accepted beginning first business day after Jan. 1). Camping also available in Gettysburg area. 🏨 **Lodging:** Available in Gettysburg area; none in park. ✕ **Food & Supplies:** Available in Gettysburg area; none in park. ☞ **Tips & Hints:** Plan to spend at least four hours. Busiest in July and August, least crowded in January and February. 🎫 **Fees, Permits & Limitations:** Free. Electric Map and Cyclorama fees: $3 per adult, $2.50 62 and up, $1.50 6–15. Reservations recommended for larger groups and organizations for the Electric Map, Cyclorama, and licensed battlefield guides (tel. 717/334–4474 or 877/438–8929). Park grounds and roads open daily 6 AM–10 PM. Visitor center open mid-Aug.–mid-June, daily 8–5; mid-June–mid-Aug., daily 8–6. Cyclorama Center open daily 9–5. Closed Thanksgiving, Dec. 25, Jan. 1.

HOW TO GET THERE

From U.S. 15, follow signs to park. For visitors traveling west on PA 30, exit onto U.S. 15S and follow park signs. From PA 30E, proceed into town, turn right on Washington St. Go 1 mi/1.6 km to visitor center on right. Closest airport: Harrisburg (60 mi/96 km).

FOR MORE INFORMATION

Gettysburg National Military Park (97 Taneytown Rd., Gettysburg, PA 17325, tel. 717/334–1124; Web site www.nps.gov/gett). Gettysburg Convention and Visitors Bureau (35 Carlisle St., Gettysburg, PA 17325, tel. 717/334–6274; Web site www.gettysburg.com).

Hopewell Furnace
National Historic Site

In the southeast part of the state, near Elverson

This rural American 19th-century iron plantation is home to a blast furnace, the ironmaster's mansion, and auxiliary structures. Hopewell Furnace was founded in 1771 by Ironmaster Mark Bird and operated until 1883. The site was designated in 1938 and renamed in 1985.

WHAT TO SEE & DO

Touring site. **Facilities:** Visitor center with interpretive exhibits, furnace complex and buildings, charcoal hearth, tour trail, wayside exhibits, audio stations. Bookstore. **Programs & Events:** Self-guided tours year-round. Living-history programs, molding and casting demonstrations (June–Labor Day), apple sales (Sept.–Oct.). Sheep shearing (May), Establishment Day (1st weekend, Aug.), Apple Harvest Day (Sept.), "Women's Work" (Oct.), Iron Plantation Christmas (Dec.).

PLANNING YOUR VISIT

⚲ **Camping:** Available in adjacent French Creek State Park (tel. 610/582–9680); none at site. 🏨 **Lodging:** Available locally; none at site. ✕ **Food & Supplies:** Available locally; none at site. ☞ **Tips & Hints:** Plan to stay two–four hours for a visit. Busiest in August and September, least crowded in January and February. 🎫 **Fees, Permits & Limitations:** Entrance fee: $4 per adult 17 and up. Fees also charged for interpretive programs. Site open daily 9–5. Closed Jan. 1, Martin Luther King Jr.'s Birthday, President's Day, Veterans Day, Thanksgiving Day, Dec. 25.

HOW TO GET THERE

5 mi/8 km south of Birdsboro on PA 345 and 10 mi/16 km from the Morgantown interchange on the PA Tpk. (I–76) via PA 23E and 345N. Closest airports: Reading (21 mi/34 km); Allentown (41 mi/66 km); Philadelphia (53 mi/85 km); Harrisburg (79 mi/126 km).

FOR MORE INFORMATION

Park Superintendent, Hopewell Furnace National Historic Site (2 Mark Bird La., Elverson, PA 19520, tel 610/582–8773, fax 610/582–2768; e-mail HOFU_superintendent@nps.gov; Web site www.nps.gov/hofu).

Independence National
Historical Park

In Philadelphia

Here are the Liberty Bell, an international symbol of freedom, and Independence Hall, where the nation's founders drafted both the Declaration of Independence and the U.S. Constitution. The park, which spans 45 acres in downtown Philadelphia, includes Carpenter's Hall, Christ Church, and 17 other buildings open to the public. The park was authorized in 1948. Independence Hall was designated a World Heritage Site in 1979.

WHAT TO SEE & DO

Touring historic buildings; using interactive exhibits; viewing films, 18th-century artifacts, paintings, and furnishings. **Facilities:** Visitor center with interpretive exhibits (3rd and Chestnut Sts.), buildings. Museum shops. **Programs & Events:** Year-round: guided tours of Independence Hall (every 15 mins), tours of Todd House and Bishop White House, ranger programs at other sites. Seasonal activities available.

PLANNING YOUR VISIT

Lodging: In the park: Thomas Bond House (bed-and-breakfast, tel. 215/923–8523). Lodging also available in Philadelphia area. ✕ **Food & Supplies:** In the park: meals at City Tavern (2nd and Walnut Sts., tel. 215/413–1443). Food and supplies also available in Philadelphia area. ☞ **Tips & Hints:** Visit between December and early March to avoid crowds. Busiest in June and July, least crowded in January and February. **Fees, Permits & Limitations:** Entrance fee: $2 per person 17 or over for tours of Bishop White and Todd houses and entrance to Second Bank of the United States Portrait Gallery. All other buildings are free. Buildings generally are open daily 9–5 with extended hours in some buildings late June–late Aug. Some buildings closed Thanksgiving, Dec. 25, Jan. 1. Visitor center open daily 9–5. Closed some holidays. Contact park for details.

HOW TO GET THERE

The visitor center is at 3rd and Chestnut Sts., in Philadelphia's downtown. From I–95, follow signs for CENTRAL PHILA./I–676. Exit on 6th St. Turn left on Market St. Turn right on 2nd St., cross Chestnut St., and park in midblock on left. New visitor center to open Spring 2002, on 6th St. between Archer and Market St. This will replace 3rd and Chestnut St. visitor center. Closest airport: Philadelphia.

FOR MORE INFORMATION

Visitor Information, Independence National Historic Park (313 Walnut St., Philadelphia, PA 19106, tel. 215/597–8974; Web site www.nps.gov/inde). Philadelphia Convention and Visitors Bureau (1515 Market St., Suite 2020, Philadelphia, PA 19102, tel. 215/636–1666).

Johnstown Flood National Memorial

In the southwest part of the state, in St. Michael

Johnstown, a steel company town with a population of 30,000 in 1889, was built on a floodplain at the fork of the Little Conemaugh and Stony Creek rivers. When an old dam broke on May 31, 1889, after a night of heavy rains, 20 million tons of water devastated the town and killed more than 2,200 people. The memorial was authorized on August 31, 1964.

WHAT TO SEE & DO

Hiking, touring house and visitor center, watching film. **Facilities:** Visitor center with interpretive exhibits (Lake Rd.), Historic Unger House, trails. Bookstore, picnic area. **Programs & Events:** Film (hourly year-round). Memorial program, luminaria commemorating flood victims (May 31), ranger presentations (summer).

PLANNING YOUR VISIT

⚠ **Camping:** Available locally; none at memorial. 🏠 **Lodging:** Available locally; none at memorial. ✕ **Food & Supplies:** Available locally; none at memorial. ☞ **Tips & Hints:** Busiest in July and August, least crowded in January and February. 🎟 **Fees, Permits & Limitations:** Entrance fee: $2 per person 17 and up. Visitor center open Sept.–May, daily 9–5; June–Aug., daily 9–6. Closed Thanksgiving, Dec. 25, Jan. 1.

HOW TO GET THERE

10 mi/16 km northeast of Johnstown. Take U.S. 219 to the Saint Michael/Sidman exit. Head east on PA 869 for 1.5 mi/2.4 km. Turn left on Lake Rd. at the memorial sign. Follow Lake Rd. 1.5 mi/2.4 km to visitor center on the right. Closest airport: Johnstown.

FOR MORE INFORMATION

Superintendent, Johnstown Flood National Memorial (733 Lake Rd., South Fork, PA 15956, tel. 814/495–4643; Web site www.nps.gov/jofl).

Middle Delaware
National Scenic River

In northeast Pennsylvania and northwest New Jersey

The river flows 40 mi/64 km through the Delaware Water Gap National Recreation Area (*see separate listing*). The scenic river was established Nov. 10, 1978.

WHAT TO SEE & DO

Boating, fishing, swimming. (*For details, see entry for Delaware Water Gap National Recreation Area.*)

FOR MORE INFORMATION

Middle Delaware National Scenic River (c/o Delaware Water Gap National Recreation Area, River Rd., Bushkill, PA 18324, tel. 570/588–2451; Web site www.nps.gov/dewa).

Steamtown National
Historic Site

In the northeast part of the state, in Scranton

In the former Scranton Yards of the Delaware, Lackawanna & Western Railroad, this site interprets the story of main-line steam railroading and its effect on the country. Included are an operating roundhouse, locomotive shop, museum, train tours, and excursions. The park was authorized in 1986.

WHAT TO SEE & DO

Picnicking; riding steam railroad train; touring museum, train, and locomotive shop; watching film. **Facilities:** Visitor center, trains, museum, locomotive shop, roundhouse, theater. Museum store, picnic tables. **Programs & Events:** Ranger tours, walking tours year-round. Two-hour steam train excursion to Moscow, PA (Memorial Day–1st weekend in Nov., weekends; reservations recommended, tel. 570/340–5203, 570/340–5204, or 888/693–9391), train tours on site (late Apr.–Dec. when excursions aren't running). National Park Week (3rd week in Apr.); Memorial Day Celebration; Rail Expo (Labor Day weekend); Toys for Tots (Fri. and Sat. after Thanksgiving); Polar Express (mid-Dec.); Festival of Trees (3rd week in Dec.–1st week in Jan.).

PLANNING YOUR VISIT

⚠ **Camping:** Available locally (call 800/229–3526 for details); none at site. ⊞ **Lodging:** Available locally (call 800/229–3526 for details); none at site. ✕ **Food & Supplies:** Available locally (call 800/229–3526 for details); none at site. ☞ **Tips & Hints:** Visitor center and museums are climate controlled. The rest of the site is outdoors. Trains have heat but no air-conditioning. Busiest in July and August, least crowded in January and February. ▦ **Fees, Permits & Limitations:** Free. Museum interpretive fee: $8 adult, $7 senior citizens 62 and older, $3 children 6–12, free for children 5 and under. Golden Age, Golden Eagle, Golden Access passports not honored. Excursion fee: $12 per adult, $10 62 and older, $6 children 12 and under. Discount on combination museum/excursion fee. No pets, food, drink, or tobacco in any building. Food and drink allowed on excursion, but no pets or tobacco. Leashed pets only elsewhere. No alcohol. Bicycles on park roads only. Site open daily 9–5, extended hours in summer. Closed Thanksgiving, Dec. 25, Jan. 1.

HOW TO GET THERE

In downtown Scranton via Exit 53 (Central Scranton Expressway) off I–81.

FOR MORE INFORMATION

Steamtown National Historic Site (150 S. Washington Ave., Scranton, PA 18503, tel. 570/340–5200 or 888/693–9391, fax 570/340–5235; Web site www.nps.gov/stea). Northeast Pennsylvania Convention & Visitors Bureau (99 Glenmaura National Blvd., Moosic, PA 18507, tel. 800/229–3526).

Thaddeus Kosciuszko
National Memorial

In Philadelphia

Thaddeus Kosciuszko, Polish-born patriot and hero of the American Revolution, is commemorated at 301 Pine Street, Philadelphia. His efforts on behalf of the American fight for independence are remembered at the small town house where he rented a room during the winter of 1797–98. The memorial was authorized on October 21, 1972.

WHAT TO SEE & DO

Viewing exhibits and slide program (in English and Polish). **Facilities:** House with interpretive exhibits. Sales area. **Programs & Events:** Exhibits and slide program (June–Oct., daily; Nov.–May, Wed.–Sun.). Thaddeus Kosciuszko Birthday (Feb. 4).

PLANNING YOUR VISIT

Lodging: Available in Philadelphia; none at memorial. **Food & Supplies:** Available in Philadelphia; none at memorial. **Tips & Hints:** Busiest in July and August, least crowded in December and January. **Fees, Permits & Limitations:** Free. Memorial open June–Oct., daily 10–5; Nov.–May, Wed.–Sun. 10–5.

HOW TO GET THERE

At 301 Pine St., five blocks from the Independence National Historical Park Visitor Center (*see separate entry*). Closest airport: Philadelphia (10 mi/16 km).

FOR MORE INFORMATION

Superintendent, Thaddeus Kosciuszko National Memorial (313 Walnut St., Philadelphia, PA 19106, tel. 215/597–9618, fax 215/597–1416; Web site www.nps.gov/thko). Philadelphia Convention and Visitors Bureau (1515 Market St., Philadelphia, PA 19102, tel. 215/636–1666, fax 215/636–3327).

Upper Delaware Scenic
and Recreational River

In southeast New York and northeast Pennsylania, along the states' border

The 73-mi/117-km stretch of free-flowing river between Hancock and Port Jervis, New York, includes the Roebling Bridge, believed to be the oldest existing wire-cable suspension bridge, and the Zane Grey home and museum. The park was authorized on November 10, 1978.

WHAT TO SEE & DO

Boating, eagle watching, fishing, kayaking. **Facilities:** Narrowsburg Information Center (NY), park headquarters (near Narrowsburg), Zane

Grey Museum (Lackawaxen, PA), Roebling's Delaware Aqueduct and Tollhouse (Minisink Ford, NY), Barryville Office (Barryville, NY), Milanville Office (Milanville, PA), bulletin boards at river accesses; traveler's information radio station (1610 AM) at Sparrowbush, NY. **Programs & Events:** Seasonal activities available. River festivals (July–Aug.). Shad fests (May), Delaware River Sojourn (June), Annual River Clean-up (July), Fall Foliage Train Tours, Oktoberfests (Oct.).

PLANNING YOUR VISIT

⚠ **Camping:** Backcountry camping available in Pennsylvania State Forest along the Upper Delaware River at Stairway Rapids (for river use only; permit required, *see below*). Private campgrounds along or near the river. 🛏 **Lodging:** Available in towns along river in New York and Pennsylvania. ✗ **Food & Supplies:** Available in towns along river in New York and Pennsylvania. ☞ **Tips & Hints:** Respect rights of private property owners who own most of the land along the river. Busiest in July and August, least crowded in December and January. 🏷 **Fees, Permits & Limitations:** Free. Zane Grey Museum tour fee: $2 per adult, $1 per child 10–15. New York or Pennsylvania state hunting and fishing license required. Permit required (free) for backcountry camping at Stairway Rapids (tel. 845/557–0222). River open all the time. Public river access open daily 5 AM–10 PM. Visitor contact facilities open Memorial Day–Labor Day.

HOW TO GET THERE

From New York, take I–84 to Port Jervis (Exit 1), then U.S. 6W to NY 97N, which parallels most of the river. Northern sections may be reached off NY 17. From Pennsylvania, take I–84E to U.S. 6W (Exit 10), then follow signs to Lackawaxen, Zane Grey Museum, and Roebling Bridge. Closest airports: Stewart International, Newburgh, NY (85 mi/136 km); Wilkes-Barre/Scranton International, PA (45 mi/72 km).

FOR MORE INFORMATION

Upper Delaware Scenic and Recreational River (RR 2, Box 2428, Beach Lake, PA 18405-9737, tel. 570/685–4871, fax 570/685–4874; e-mail upde_interpretation@nps.gov; Web site www.nps.gov/upde).

Valley Forge National Historical Park

In the southeast part of the state, in Valley Forge

Protected here is the site of the third winter encampment of George Washington's Continental Army. The army lived here from December 19, 1777, to June 19, 1778, during the American Revolution, and 2,000 soldiers died here from disease caused by shortages of food, blankets, and clothing needed to protect them from the bitter cold. Local residents now use the park for recreation and visitors tour the park for its history. On display are part of Washington's tent and one of the largest collections of 18th-century military equipment in the nation. The park was authorized on July 4, 1976.

WHAT TO SEE & DO

Auto touring, bicycling, cross-country skiing, fishing, hiking, horseback riding, jogging, picnicking, watching 18-minute film. **Facilities:** Visitor center with interpretive exhibits, museum, historic buildings, 10-mi/16-km driving tour, 6-mi/10-km trail, interpretive waysides. Bookstore, picnic areas. **Programs & Events:** Interpretive programs (year-round, monthly). Walking tours (Memorial Day–Labor Day, daily), Commander-in-Chief talks, "Baking Bread for Washington's Soldiers" (Memorial Day–Labor Day). George Washington Birthday (Feb.), French Alliance (about May 4), March-Out of the Continental Army (mid-June), March-In of Washington's Army (mid-Dec.).

PLANNING YOUR VISIT

⚠ **Camping:** Available in French Creek State Park (Morgantown) and West Chester; none in park. 🏨 **Lodging:** Available in Exton, King of Prussia, Norristown, Philadelphia, Pottstown, Reading; none in park. ✕ **Food & Supplies:** In the park: meals at Kennedy-Supplee Mansion (tel. 610/337–3537), snack bar at Washington Memorial Chapel. Food and supplies also available in Devon, King of Prussia, Phoenixville, and Wayne. ☞ **Tips & Hints:** Visit Valley Forge Historical Society's museum and Washington Memorial Chapel, privately owned facilities within the park. Be careful during driving tours when crossing three busy state roads. Go in April or May for dogwood blooms, late September or October for fall foliage. Busiest in July and August, least crowded in December and January. 🔲 **Fees, Permits & Limitations:** Entrance fee: $2 per person over 16 to visit Washington's Headquarters. Summer bus tour fees (tel. 610/783–5788). Pennsylvania state fishing license required. No hunting. Leashed pets only. Bikes and horseback riding on designated paths and areas only. No motorized vehicles off tour road. No in-line skating or skateboarding. Park open daily dawn–dusk (some areas remain open until 10 PM). Visitor center and Washington Headquarters open daily 9–5; closed Dec. 25. Varnum's Quarters open May, weekends 11–4; June–Apr., Mon.–Sat. 11–4. Dewee's House open daily 11–4.

HOW TO GET THERE

20 mi/32 km west of Philadelphia, at the intersection of Rte. 23 and N. Gulph Rd. Closest airport: Philadelphia.

FOR MORE INFORMATION

Valley Forge National Historical Park (Box 953, Valley Forge, PA 19482, tel. 610/783–1077, fax 610/783–1053; Web site www.nps.gov/vafo). Valley Forge Convention and Visitors Bureau (600 W. Germantown Pike, Plymouth Meeting, PA 19462, tel. 610/834–1550 or 800/441–3549, fax 610/834–0202).

See Also

Appalachian National Scenic Trail, West Virginia. *Benjamin Franklin National Memorial,* Affiliated Areas in Other National Parklands.

Delaware and Lehigh Navigation Canal National Heritage Corridor, Affiliated Areas in Other National Parklands. *Gloria Dei (Old Swedes') Church National Historic Site,* Affiliated Areas in Other National Parklands. *North Country National Scenic Trail,* National Trails System in Other National Parklands. *Potomac Heritage National Scenic Trail,* District of Columbia. *Southwestern Pennsylvania Industrial Heritage Route,* National Heritage Areas in Other National Parklands. *Steel Industry American Heritage Area,* National Heritage Areas in Other National Parklands. *White Clay Creek,* Wild and Scenic Rivers System in Other National Parklands.

RHODE ISLAND

Roger Williams National Memorial

In northeastern Rhode Island, in Providence

The memorial commemorates the life of Roger Williams, the founder of Rhode Island. A champion of religious freedom, Williams was banished from Massachusetts and founded Providence in 1636. This colony served as a refuge where all could come to worship freely. The memorial is located on a common lot of the original settlement and includes 4.5 acres of landscaped park. The memorial was designated on October 22, 1965.

WHAT TO SEE & DO

Picnicking, viewing exhibits and video, walking. **Facilities:** Visitor center with interpretive exhibits (N. Main and Smith Sts.), wayside exhibits. Bookstore. **Programs & Events:** Junior Ranger program. Seasonal activities and special events available.

PLANNING YOUR VISIT

⚙ **Camping:** Available in Coventry, Glocester; none at memorial. 🛏 **Lodging:** Available in Providence; none at memorial. ✕ **Food & Supplies:** Available in Providence; none at memorial. ☞ **Tips & Hints:** Combine visit with trips to Rhode Island State House, Historic Benefit St., and other sites along Providence Banner Trail. Go in June and September for the best weather, in September or October for fall foliage. Busiest in May and October, least crowded in January and February. 🎫 **Fees, Permits & Limitations:** Free. Leashed pets only. Memorial and visitor center open daily 9–4:30. Closed Thanksgiving, Dec. 25, Jan. 1.

HOW TO GET THERE

From I–95 N or S take the downtown Providence exit. Turn left onto Francis St., right at Gaspee St, right onto Smith St, right onto Canal St. Entrance to parking lot is on the left. Closest airport: T. F. Green (10 mi/16 km).

FOR MORE INFORMATION

Roger Williams National Memorial (282 N. Main St., Providence, RI 02903, tel. 401/521–7266, fax 401/521–7239; e-mail rowi_interpretation@nps.gov; Web site www.nps.gov/rowi). Rhode Island Economic Development Corporation Tourism (1 W. Exchange St., Providence, RI 02903, tel. 800/556–2484, fax 401/273–8270; Web site www.visitrhodeisland.com). Providence and Warwick Convention and Visitors Bureau (1 W. Exchange St., 3rd floor, Providence, RI 02903, tel. 800/233–1636).

See Also

....

Blackstone River Valley National Heritage Corridor, Affiliated Areas in Other National Parklands. *Touro Synagogue National Historic Site,* Affiliated Areas in Other National Parklands.

SOUTH CAROLINA

Charles Pinckney National Historic Site

In the southeast part of the state, north of Charleston

Charles Pinckney (1754–1824) was a statesman, officer in the American Revolution, and a principal framer of the U.S. Constitution. He served four terms as governor of South Carolina and in the State Assembly. He also served in the U.S. Senate, House of Representatives, and as President Jefferson's minister to Spain. His ancestral home, Snee Farm, once consisted of 715 acres, 28 of which are today preserved at this site. Archaeological remains of brick foundations from the Pinckney era and an 1820s tidewater cottage also are maintained. The site was authorized on September 8, 1988.

WHAT TO SEE & DO

Touring facility and grounds. **Facilities:** Visitor center with interpretive exhibits, wayside exhibits. Bookstore. **Programs & Events:** Self-guided walking tours through the house and grounds year-round. Constitution Week (3rd week, Sept.), Archaeology Week (last week, Sept).

PLANNING YOUR VISIT

Camping: Available in the Charleston area; none at site. **Lodging:** Available in Charleston, Mt. Pleasant, N. Charleston; none at site. **Food & Supplies:** Available in Charleston, Mt. Pleasant; none at site. **Tips & Hints:** Go in late March or mid-April for azalea and camellia blooms. **Fees, Permits & Limitations:** Free. No hunting. No mountain or trail bikes. Leashed pets only. Park and visitor center open daily 9–5. Closed Dec. 25.

HOW TO GET THERE

The park is at 1254 Longpoint Rd., off Hwy. 17 in Mt. Pleasant, north of Charleston. Closest airport: Charleston (10 mi/16 km).

FOR MORE INFORMATION

Charles Pinckney National Historic Site (c/o Fort Sumter National Monument, 1214 Middle St., Sullivan's Island, SC 29482, tel. 843/881–5516, fax 843/881–7070; Web site www.nps.gov/chpi). Mt. Pleasant Visitors Information Center (291 Johnnie Dodds Blvd., Mt. Pleasant, SC 29464, tel. 843/849–6154). Chamber of Commerce (81 Mary St., Charleston, SC 29403, tel. 843/577–2510, fax 843/723–4853). Charleston Convention and Visitors Bureau (81 Mary St., Charleston, SC 29403, tel. 843/853–8000).

Congaree Swamp National Monument

Midstate, near Hopkins

The 22,200-acre monument contains the last significant tract of old-growth bottomland hardwood forest in the United States. The swamp, most of which is managed as wilderness, is home to over 75 tree species, including state and national champion trees, and abundant wildlife that includes the endangered red-cockaded woodpecker. The monument was authorized in 1976 and designated an International Biosphere Reserve in 1983.

WHAT TO SEE & DO

Bird-watching, camping, canoeing, fishing, hiking, kayaking, picnicking. **Facilities:** Visitor center with interpretive exhibits, 25 mi/40 km of hiking trails, 2.5-mi/4-km boardwalk. Bookstore, picnic tables. **Programs & Events:** Year-round ranger-led guided walks, self-guided walks, guided canoe trips. Owl prowls (Mar.–May and Sept.–Nov., every other Fri. evening). Naturefest (one week in Apr.), American Rivers Month Programs (June), Public Lands Day, River Sweep (both in Sept.), Harry Hampton Memorial Walk (Nov.).

PLANNING YOUR VISIT

⚠ **Camping:** Backcountry camping available (permit required, *see below*). Group primitive camping available (permit required, *see below*). ▦ **Lodging:** Available in Columbia area; none at monument. ✕ **Food & Supplies:** Groceries in Columbia; none at monument. ☞ **Tips & Hints:** Plan to stay at least two–four hours. Longer trails can take eight hours to explore. Canoe trips vary from four hours to overnight. Busiest in March and April, least crowded in December and January. ▤ **Fees, Permits & Limitations:** Free, donations accepted. Reservations for guided programs should be made two weeks in advance, six weeks in advance during spring and fall. Permits required (free) for all camping. South Carolina state fishing license required. Monument open daily dawn–dusk. Visitor center open daily 8:30–5. Closed Dec. 25.

HOW TO GET THERE

From I–77, take exit 5 onto SC 48 (Bluff Rd.), and follow signs. Closest airport: Columbia Metropolitan (25 mi/40 km).

FOR MORE INFORMATION

Superintendent, Congaree Swamp National Monument (100 National Park Rd., Hopkins, SC 29061, tel. 803/776–4396, fax 803/783–4241; Web site www.nps.gov/cosw). Columbia Visitors Center (tel. 803/254–0479).

Cowpens National Battlefield

In the northwest part of the state, near Chesnee

The battlefield commemorates a decisive Revolutionary War battle that helped turn the tide of war in the South. On this field on January 17, 1781, Daniel Morgan led his army of tough Continentals, militia, and cavalry to a brilliant victory over Banastre Tarleton's larger force of British regulars. Walking trails, auto tour road, monuments, and an 1828 log cabin are available. Cowpens was established as a national battlefield site in 1929, transferred to the Park Service in 1933, and redesignated in 1972.

WHAT TO SEE & DO

Auto touring, biking, bird- and wildlife watching, hiking, jogging, picnicking, walking. **Facilities:** Visitor center with interpretive exhibits, fiber-optic battle program, tour roads and trails, wayside exhibits, overlooks, circa 1828 log cabin, monuments. Bookstore, picnic area. **Programs & Events:** "Daybreak at the Cowpens" presentation (year-round 9–4, hourly). Battle anniversary (weekend nearest Jan. 17). Seasonal activities available.

PLANNING YOUR VISIT

Lodging: Available in Gaffney, Greenville, and Spartanburg, SC; and Asheville and Charlotte, NC; none at battlefield. **✕ Food & Supplies:** Available in Chesnee, Gaffney, and Spartanburg; none at battlefield. **☞ Tips & Hints:** Plan to stay at least two hours. Busiest in June and July, least crowded in November and December. **Fees, Permits & Limitations:** Free. "Daybreak at the Cowpens" fee: $1 per adult, 50¢ for ages 6–12, Battlefield open daily 9–5. Closed Thanksgiving, Dec. 25, and Jan. 1.

HOW TO GET THERE

At the intersection of Hwys. 11 and 110, 2 mi/3 km east of Chesnee and 10 mi/16 km west of Gaffney and I–85 via Exit 92 and 17 mi/27 km northeast of Spartanburg via Hwy. 221. From I–26, take Exit 5 to eastbound Hwy. 11. Closest airports: Greenville/Spartanburg (45 mi/72 km); Charlotte, NC (60 mi/96 km).

FOR MORE INFORMATION

Cowpens National Battlefield (Box 308, Chesnee, SC 29323, tel. 864/461–2828, fax 864/461–7077 or 864/461–7795; Web site www.nps.gov/cowp).

Fort Sumter
National Monument

In the southeast part of the state,
in Charleston Harbor (and Sullivan's Island)

Fort Sumter was one of many coastal fortifications built by the United States after the War of 1812. The first shots of the Civil War were fired here on April 12, 1861, during a Confederate two-day bombardment that ended with the Union troops' withdrawal. Fort Moultrie, administered with Fort Sumter, is the site of the first Patriot victory over the British Navy in the American Revolution, a victory that contributed to British reluctance to invade the South. The fort served as the Charleston operational headquarters of the Confederate Army during the opening battle of the Civil War and the siege of Charleston. The monument was authorized in 1948. Fort Moultrie was transferred to the Park Service in 1961.

WHAT TO SEE & DO

Touring the forts. **Facilities:** Fort Sumter: fort museum with interpretive exhibits, wayside exhibits in fort; Fort Moultrie: visitor center with interpretive exhibits, wayside exhibits. A tour boat facility with interpretive exhibits (downtown Charleston) is under development. Bookstores. **Programs & Events:** Year-round: Fort Sumter: ranger orientation and history talks; Fort Moultrie: self-guided walking tours. Fort Moultrie: interpretive talks (June–Aug.). Battle anniversary and living-history programs: Fort Sumter (Apr. 12), Fort Moultrie (June 28).

PLANNING YOUR VISIT

Camping: Available in the Charleston area; none at monument. **Lodging:** Available in Charleston, Mt. Pleasant, N. Charleston; none at monument. **Food & Supplies:** Fort Sumter: snack bar on tour boats. Food and supplies also available in Charleston, Mt. Pleasant, N. Charleston. Fort Moultrie: Food and supplies available in Mt. Pleasant, Isle of Palms, Sullivan's Island; none at fort. **Tips & Hints:** Fort Sumter: Get to boat departure area at least 15 minutes early. Go in September or October for best weather and smaller crowds. Fort Moultrie: Allow two hours for tour. Busiest in April and July, least crowded in December and January. **Fees, Permits & Limitations:** Fort Sumter: free; some activities require special use permits (fee). Tour boat fees apply, reservations required for larger groups (tel. 843/722–2628). No pets. Fort open Mar. and Sept.–Nov., daily 10–4; Apr.–Labor Day, daily 10–5:30; variable hours rest of year. Closed Dec. 25, Jan. 1. Fort Moultrie—User fee: $2 per person, $1 under 16, $5 per family. No pets. Fort open daily 9–5. Closed Dec. 25, Jan. 1.

HOW TO GET THERE

Fort Sumter is in Charleston Harbor and accessible only by boat. Departures at City Marina (Lockwood Dr., downtown Charleston) and Patriots Point (Patriots Point Naval and Maritime Museum, Mt. Pleasant).

Fort Moultrie is on Sullivan's Island. From Mt. Pleasant, take SR 703 to Middle St. Closest airport: Charleston (20 mi/32 km).

FOR MORE INFORMATION

Fort Sumter National Monument (1214 Middle St., Sullivan's Island, SC 29482, tel. 843/883–3123, fax 843/883–3910; Web site www.nps.gov/fosu). Chamber of Commerce (81 Mary St., Charleston, SC 29402, tel. 843/577–2510, fax 843/723–4853). Charleston Convention and Visitors Bureau (Box 975, Charleston SC 29402, tel. 843/853–8000). Fort Moultrie (1214 Middle St., Sullivan's Island, SC 29482, tel. 843/883–3123, fax 843/883–3910; Web site www.nps.gov/fomo).

Kings Mountain National Military Park

In the north-central part of the state, near Gaffney

Preserved in this park is the site of a pivotal American Revolution battle, which was fought here on October 7, 1780. After a series of British victories, patriots from Virginia, the Carolinas, and Georgia defeated British Major Patrick Ferguson at Kings Mountain. The U.S. victory forced British General Charles Cornwallis to retreat back into South Carolina for the winter and helped turn the tide of the war against the British. The park was established in 1931.

WHAT TO SEE & DO

Hiking, touring battlefield, viewing film. **Facilities:** Visitor center with interpretive exhibits, trail, wayside exhibits, amphitheater. Bookstore. **Programs & Events:** Occasional living-history encampments year-round. Evening programs and concerts (May–Oct.), musket and rifle demonstrations (May–Oct., weekends). Battle anniversary (Oct. 7).

PLANNING YOUR VISIT

Camping: Backcountry camping available (check-in required). Camping available in adjoining Kings Mountain State Park. **Lodging:** Available in Gaffney, SC, and Kings Mountain, NC; none in park. ✗ **Food & Supplies:** Available in Gaffney, SC, and Kings Mountain, NC; none in park. ☞ **Tips & Hints:** Best times to visit are spring and fall. Go in spring and summer for wildflowers. Busiest in May and June, least crowded in December and January. **Fees, Permits & Limitations:** Free. No hunting, mountain biking, or ATV use. No metal detecting. Leashed pets only. Park open daily 9–5. Closed Thanksgiving, Dec. 25, Jan. 1.

HOW TO GET THERE

On Hwy. 216, 4 mi/6 km from I–85 via Exit 2. Closest airports: Greenville, SC (70 mi/112 km); Charlotte, NC (40 mi/64 km).

FOR MORE INFORMATION

Kings Mountain National Military Park (2625 Park Rd., Blacksburg, SC 29702, tel. 864/936–7921, fax 864/936–9897; e-mail KIMO_Ranger Activities@nps.gov.; Web site www.nps.gov/kimo).

Ninety Six National Historic Site

In the southern part of the state, near Greenwood

Ninety Six was named by traders who thought the stopping place was 96 mi/154 km from the Cherokee village of Keowee. The park commemorates the role the settlement played during British settlement of the frontier and the southern campaign of the American Revolution. It also offers historic roads and paths, the earthen British-built Star Fort (circa 1781), and the partially reconstructed Stockade Fort. Archaeological complexes abound, including the underground remains of two villages, plantations, houses, and forts. The site was authorized on August 16, 1976.

WHAT TO SEE & DO

Fishing, hiking interpretive trail, picnicking, viewing museum exhibits, watching video. **Facilities:** Visitor center with interpretive exhibits, auditorium, trail, wayside exhibits. Book sales area, picnic tables. **Programs & Events:** "Lifeways of the Cherokee Indians and Colonial Settlers" (2002, 2004), Revolutionary War Days Encampment (Apr., 2001, 2003). Annual Autumn Candlelight Tour (2nd Sat., Oct.).

PLANNING YOUR VISIT

⚠ **Camping:** Camping available nearby in Greenwood State Park; none at site. 🏨 **Lodging:** Available in Greenwood; none at site. ✕ **Food & Supplies:** Available in town of Ninety Six; none at site. ☞ **Tips & Hints:** Visit in spring and fall when temperatures are cooler. Busiest in May and October, least crowded in January and February. 🎟 **Fees, Permits & Limitations:** Free. South Carolina state fishing license required. Leashed pets only. No hunting. No mechanized equipment on trails. No bicycles on walking trail. Park is open daily dawn–dusk. Visitor center open daily 8–5. Closed Thanksgiving, Dec. 25, Jan. 1.

HOW TO GET THERE

2 mi/3.2 km south of the town of Ninety Six, which is on SC 34, 10 mi/16 km east of Greenwood. Closest airport: Greenville (65 mi/104 km).

FOR MORE INFORMATION

Ninety Six National Historic Site (Box 496, Ninety Six, SC 29666, tel. 864/543–4068, fax 864/543–2058; Web site www.nps.gov/nisi). Ninety Six Chamber of Commerce (Box 8, Ninety Six, SC 29666, tel. 864/543–2200).

See Also

....

Historic Camden, Affiliated Areas in Other National Parklands. *Overmountain Victory National Historic Trail,* National Trails System in Other National Parklands. *South Carolina National Heritage Corridor,* National Heritage Areas in Other National Parklands.

SOUTH DAKOTA

Badlands National Park

In the southwest part of the state, near Interior

The 244,000-acre park is well known for its outstanding geological features—steep canyons, sharp ridges, gullies, spires, and knobs—and its rich paleontological resources, especially Oligocene-era mammal fossils. But it also contains the largest protected mixed-grass prairie in the National Park Service, 64,000 acres of wilderness, and the site of the reintroduction of the black-footed ferret, one of the most endangered land mammals in North America. The Stronghold Unit, which is managed under an agreement with the Oglala Sioux Tribe, includes the sites of the 1890s Ghost Dances. The site was authorized as a national monument in 1939 and redesignated a national park in 1978.

WHAT TO SEE & DO

Auto touring, hiking, horseback riding. **Facilities:** 2 visitor centers with interpretive exhibits—Ben Reifel (Cedar Pass, State Hwy. 240 northeast of Interior) and White River (Stronghold Unit); loop roads, trails. Book and map sale areas, gift shop, picnic tables. **Programs & Events:** Guided walks, talks, and slide programs (mid-June–Labor Day).

PLANNING YOUR VISIT

Camping: Campground with running water and flush toilets (May–Sept., primitive rest of year): no hookups (no reservations). Backcountry camping available. Group camping available (reservations required, tel. 605/433–5235). Private camping (primitive) available within park boundaries at Sage Creek. **Lodging:** In the park: Cedar Pass Lodge (tel. 605/433–5460; mid-Apr.–mid-Oct.). Lodging also available outside the park in Interior, Kadoka, Rapid City, Wall. **Food & Supplies:** In the park: meals at Cedar Pass Lodge (mid-Apr.–mid-Oct.). Food and supplies also available in Interior, Kadoka, Rapid City, Wall. **Tips & Hints:** Bring hats and sunglasses to protect against high winds. Watch for cactus. Give bison plenty of room. Busiest in July and August, least crowded in December and January. **Fees, Permits & Limitations:** Entrance fee: $5 per person or $10 per vehicle. No hunting, collecting, open campfires, off-road travel. Bicycling on established roads only. No pets in wilderness or on trails. Leashed pets only elsewhere. Park is open daily. Ben Reifel Visitor Center open daily 9–4, extended hours in summer; closed Thanksgiving, Dec. 25, Jan. 1. White River Visitor Center open early June–late Aug., daily 9–4.

HOW TO GET THERE

The park loop road (240) can be accessed from I–90 via Exits 110 or 131. Follow signs to visitor center. Closest airport: Rapid City (80 mi/128 km).

FOR MORE INFORMATION

Badlands National Park (Box 6, Interior, SD 57750, tel. 605/433–5361, fax 605/433–5404; e-mail badl_seasonal_interpreters@nps.gov; Web site www.nps.gov/badl). South Dakota Tourism (711 E. Wells Ave., Pierre, SD 57501, tel. 800/732–5682).

Jewel Cave
National Monument

In the southwest part of the state, near Custer

With more than 122 mi/197 km surveyed, Jewel Cave is recognized as the third-longest cave in the world. Air flow inside the cave's passages indicates a vast area yet to be explored. Cave tours provide opportunities for viewing this pristine cave system and its wide variety of speleothems, including stalactites, stalagmites, draperies, flowstone, frostwork, boxwork, and hydromagnesite balloons. The cave is an important hibernaculum for several species of bats. Above ground the monument protects Hell and Lithograph canyons, a ranger cabin listed on the National Register of Historic Structures, and some of the last unlogged ponderosa pine forest in the Black Hills. The monument was established in 1908 and transferred to the Park Service in 1933.

WHAT TO SEE & DO

Hiking surface trails, picnicking, touring caves. **Facilities:** Visitor center with interpretive exhibits and video, Historic Area Ranger Station, trails. Book sales areas, picnic tables. **Programs & Events:** Ranger-led scenic cave tours (year-round, daily). Ranger-led Candlelight Tours (mid-June–Labor Day, 6 to 9 times daily), Spelunking cave tours (mid-June–mid-Aug., daily 12:30).

PLANNING YOUR VISIT

⚠ **Camping:** Campgrounds available in surrounding Black Hills National Forest, Custer, SD, and Newcastle, WY; none at monument. 🏨 **Lodging:** Available in Custer, SD, and Newcastle, WY; none at monument. ✕ **Food & Supplies:** Available in Custer, SD, and Newcastle, WY; none at monument. ☞ **Tips & Hints:** Arrive early in the day, especially in July and August, to avoid a wait for cave tours. Cave is 49°F/10°C year-round. Busiest in July and August, least crowded in December and January. 🎫 **Fees, Permits & Limitations:** Free. Cave tour fees: Scenic Tour (1½ hours) $8 adults, $4 children 6–16, free under 5; Candlelight Tour (1¾ hours) $8 adults, $4 children 6–16, no children under 6; Spelunking Tour (3–4 hours) $20 ages 16 and up, no children under 16. Reservations available (tel. 800/967–2283) two or more hours in advance for Scenic and Candlelight Cave tours. Reservations required (tel. 800/967–2283) for Spelunking Tours. No pets, tripods, or walking sticks in cave. Leashed pets only on trails. No mountain or trail bikes, motorized or mechanized equipment on trails. No hunting or open fires. Monument open Labor Day–Memorial Day, daily 8–4; Memorial Day–Labor Day, daily 8–7:30.

HOW TO GET THERE

13 mi/21 km west of Custer, SD, and 24 mi/38 km east of Newcastle, WY, via U.S. 16. Closest airport: Rapid City (53 mi/85 km).

FOR MORE INFORMATION

Jewel Cave National Monument (RR 1, Box 60AA, Custer, SD 57730, tel. 605/673–2288, fax 605/673–3294; Web site www.nps.gov/jeca). Custer County Chamber of Commerce (615 Washington St., Custer, SD 57730, tel. 605/673–2244, fax 605/673–3726). Newcastle Chamber of Commerce (6 W. Warwick, Newcastle, WY 82701, tel. 307/746–2739).

Minuteman Missile National Historic Site

In southwestern South Dakota, in Interior

The site consists of a Launch Control Center (an aboveground facility attached to a subterranean capsule which contained two Air Force officers, awaiting the command to launch nuclear warfare), a Launch Facility (also known as a missile silo), and will include interpretation of Cold War era issues. The site was established on December 2, 1999.

WHAT TO SEE & DO

This is a new site under development. *See Badlands National Park (separate entry)* for information on nearby facilities.

FOR MORE INFORMATION

Minuteman Missile National Historic Site (c/o Badlands National Park, Box 6, Interior, SD 57750, tel. 605/433–5240, fax 605/433–5248; Web site www.nps.gov/mimi).

Mount Rushmore National Memorial

In the southwest part of the state, near Keystone

The faces of four U.S. presidents—George Washington, Thomas Jefferson, Abraham Lincoln, and Theodore Roosevelt—are carved into the southeast side of the granite mountain. Sculptor Gutzon Borglum and 400 workers spent 14 years (1927–41) carving the images that collectively represent the birth, growth, development, and expansion of the first 150 years of the United States. The memorial was authorized in 1925.

WHAT TO SEE & DO

Climbing, hiking, viewing the memorial. **Facilities:** Information center, Lincoln Borglum Museum, Sculptors Studio, amphitheater, theaters, trails. Bookstore, religious services (summer). **Programs & Events:**

Guided talks, guided walks to Sculptors Studio, evening lighting ceremony (all mid-May–Sept.). July 4 Celebration.

PLANNING YOUR VISIT

⚑ **Camping:** Available in Black Hills National Forest, Custer State Park, and private campgrounds in Custer, Hill City, Keystone, and Rapid City; none at memorial. ☗ **Lodging:** Available in Custer, Hill City, Keystone, and Rapid City; none at memorial. ✕ **Food & Supplies:** In the park: meals available (tel. 605/574–2515). Food and supplies also available in Custer, Hill City, Keystone, and Rapid City. ☞ **Tips & Hints:** Visit in the early morning for the best light. Busiest in July and August, least crowded in December and January. ▨ **Fees, Permits & Limitations:** Free. Parking fees: $8 for one-year pass. Leashed pets only. Trails for walking only. No off-road travel. Park open daily. Information center and Museum open Labor Day–Memorial Day, daily 8–5; Memorial Day–Labor Day, daily 8 AM–10 PM. Closed Dec. 25.

HOW TO GET THERE

The memorial, which is surrounded by the Black Hills National Forest, is 25 mi/40 km southwest of Rapid City via U.S. 16 and 3 mi/5 km from Keystone via U.S. 16A and SD 244. Closest airport: Rapid City.

FOR MORE INFORMATION

Superintendent, Mount Rushmore National Memorial (Box 268, Keystone, SD 57751, tel. 605/574–2523, fax 605/574–2307; Web site www.nps.gov/moru). Keystone Chamber of Commerce (Box 653, Keystone, SD 57751, tel. 605/666–4896). Rapid City Chamber of Commerce (Box 747, Rapid City, SD 57709, tel. 605/343–1744). South Dakota Department of Tourism (711 E. Wells Ave., Pierre, SD 57501, tel. 605/773–3301).

Wind Cave National Park

In the southwest part of the state, near Hot Springs

Wind Cave, in the scenic Black Hills, is one of the longest and most complex caves in the world. It contains beautiful boxwork—a rare cave formation—in greater variety and profusion than any other cave in the world. The 28,295-acre park's rolling mixed-grass prairie, pine-covered hills, and woodland ravines also are home to a diverse mix of eastern and western plant and wildlife species, including bison, elk, pronghorn, mule deer, coyotes, and prairie dogs. The park was established on January 9, 1903.

WHAT TO SEE & DO

Cave touring, fishing, hiking, picnicking, wildlife watching. **Facilities:** Visitor center with interpretive exhibits, Cave Elevator Building with exhibits, amphitheater, self-guided nature trails, wayside exhibits, fire lookout tower (summer only). Bookstore, fire grates, picnic tables. **Programs & Events:** Cave tours (year-round). Guided prairie hikes, interpretive talks, campfire programs (all June–Aug.).

PLANNING YOUR VISIT

△ **Camping:** Campground: no hookups, water available mid-May–mid-Sept. (no reservations). Backcountry camping available (permit required, *see below*). Group campsites available (reservations available, tel. 605/745–4600). Private and public campgrounds in Custer and Hot Springs, Angostura State Recreation Area, Black Hills National Forest, Cold Brook Recreation Area, and Custer State Park. ⊞ **Lodging:** Available in Custer, Hot Springs; none in park. ✕ **Food & Supplies:** Available in Custer, Hot Springs, Pringle; none in park. ☞ **Tips & Hints:** Wear low-heeled walking shoes and sweater or jacket in cave. Cave temperature is 53°F/12°C. Stay away from bison and prairie dogs and their burrows, which harbor rattlesnakes. Go in spring or fall to avoid crowds. Busiest in July and August, least crowded in December and January. ▦ **Fees, Permits & Limitations:** Free. Cave tour fees: $6–$20 per adult, reduced fee for children 6–16, free under 6. Reservations available (tel. 605/745–4600) for cave tours. South Dakota state fishing license required. Backcountry permits (free, visitor center or Centennial Trail trailheads) required for all backcountry camping. No hunting. No pets on trails or in backcountry. Leashed pets elsewhere. No bikes off road. Fires in campground fire grates and picnic area only. No food, drink, or camera tripods in caves. Park open daily. Visitor center open mid-Oct.–mid-Mar., daily 8–4:30; mid-Mar.–early May and late Sept.–mid-Oct., daily 8–5; May and mid-Aug.–late Sept., daily 8–6; June–mid-Aug., daily 8– 7:30. Closed Thanksgiving and Dec. 25.

HOW TO GET THERE

7 mi/11 km north of Hot Springs and 20 mi/32 km south of Custer via U.S. 385. Closest airport: Rapid City (60 mi/96 km).

FOR MORE INFORMATION

Wind Cave National Park (RR 1, Box 190 WCNP, Hot Springs, SD 57747, tel. 605/745–4600, fax 605/745–4207; e-mail wica_interpretation@nps.gov; Web site www.nps.gov/wica). Hot Springs Area Chamber of Commerce (801 S. 6th St., Hot Springs, SD 57747, tel. 800/325–6991). Custer County Chamber of Commerce (615 Washington St., Custer, SD 57730, tel. 800/992–9818).

See Also

Lewis and Clark National Historic Trail, National Trails System in Other National Parklands. *Missouri National Recreational River,* Nebraska. *Niobrara National Scenic Riverway,* Nebraska.

TENNESSEE

Andrew Johnson
National Historic Site

In the northeast part of the state, in Greeneville

At this site are two homes, the tailor shop, and the burial site of Andrew Johnson, who became president in 1865 after Abraham Lincoln was assassinated. Guided tours explore the presidential homestead, which belonged to Johnson from 1851 until his death in 1875. The site was authorized as a national monument August 29, 1935; established April 27, 1942; and redesignated a national historic site December 11, 1963.

WHAT TO SEE & DO

Touring the facilities. **Facilities:** Visitor center with museum and tailor shop, early Johnson home with museum, president's homestead, national cemetery where Johnson is buried. Book sales area. **Programs & Events:** Ranger-guided tours (year-round, daily at 9:30, 10:30, 11:30, 1:30, 2:30, 3:30, and 4:30). Memorial Day program (May 30), Christmas Tour of Homestead (2nd weekend, Dec.).

PLANNING YOUR VISIT

⚠ **Camping:** Available nearby in U.S. Forest Service and Tennessee State parks; none at site. 🏨 **Lodging:** Available in Greeneville; none at site. ✗ **Food & Supplies:** Available in Greeneville; none at site. ☞ **Tips & Hints:** Busiest in May and October, least crowded in January and February. 💲 **Fees, Permits & Limitations:** Free. Homestead tour fee: $2 per adult, under 17 free (tel. 423/638–3551). Leashed pets only. Site open daily 9–5. Closed Thanksgiving, Dec. 25, Jan. 1.

HOW TO GET THERE

In downtown Greeneville, at the corner of College and Depot Sts. Closest airport: Tri-Cities Tennessee Airport (40 mi/64 km).

FOR MORE INFORMATION

Andrew Johnson National Historic Site (Box 1088, Greeneville, TN 37744-1088, tel. 423/639–3711, fax 423/798–0754; Web site www.nps.gov/anjo). Greene County Partnership/Chamber of Commerce (115 Academy St., Greenville, TN 37743, tel. 423/638–4111, fax 423/638–5345).

Big South Fork National River and Recreation Area

In northeast Tennessee and south-central Kentucky

The free-flowing Big South Fork of the Cumberland River and its tributaries pass through 90 mi/144 km of scenic gorges and valleys containing a range of natural and historic features. Recreational opportunities abound. Planning and development by the U.S. Army Corps of Engineers was authorized in 1974, Park Service management was authorized in 1976, and transfer to Park Service was settled in 1991.

WHAT TO SEE & DO

Biking, canoeing (rentals), fishing, hiking, horseback riding (rentals), hunting, kayaking, rafting (rentals), swimming. **Facilities:** 2 visitor centers with interpretive exhibits—Bandy Creek (15 mi/24 km west of Oneida, TN, off TN 297); Kentucky center (KY 92 in Stearns), outdoor museum (Blue Heron Mining Community, KY), hiking and horse trails, overlooks, pool. Bookstores. **Programs & Events:** Year-round programs available including astronomy programs, dulcimer concerts. Evening programs (Memorial Day–Sept., Sat.)., Storytelling and Craft Festival (Sept.), Pioneer Encampments (Oct.).

PLANNING YOUR VISIT

⚠ **Camping:** 3 campgrounds: 2 with water and electrical hookups, dump station (reservations available Apr.–Oct., tel. 800/365–2267); 2 horse camps (tel. 423/569–3321). Backcountry camping available (permit required, *see below*). Group campsites available (reservations required, tel. 931/879–4869 or 800/365–2267). ▦ **Lodging:** In the park: Charit Creek Lodge (backcountry lodge accessible on foot or horseback, no electricity or phones, tel. 865/429–5704). Lodging also available locally. ✖ **Food & Supplies:** Available in local towns; none at recreation area. ☞ **Tips & Hints:** Use caution when crossing rivers on foot or horseback. Be careful when swimming in rivers, approaching overlooks, and in weather when hypothermia is risk. Busiest in September and October, least crowded in January and February. ▧ **Fees, Permits & Limitations:** Free. Guided horseback rides available (tel. 931/879–4013). Big South Fork Scenic Railway offers train excursions from Stearns, KY, to the Blue Heron Mining Community (tel. 800/462–5664). Permit required ($5 to $25, depending on group size) for backcountry camping. Hunting allowed in recreation area only. Tennessee or Kentucky state hunting and fishing licenses required. Park open daily. Bandy Creek Visitor Center (TN) open Nov.–May, daily 8–4:30; June–Oct., daily 8–6. Kentucky Visitor Center open Apr.–Nov., daily 9–5:30; Dec.–Mar., weekends 9–5:30. Closed Dec. 25.

HOW TO GET THERE

The Tennessee visitor center is 15 mi/24 km west of Oneida, off TN 297. The Kentucky visitor center is on KY 92 in Stearns. Park headquarters is 9 mi/14 km west of Oneida on TN 297. Closest airports: Knoxville (80 mi/128 km) and Nashville, TN (150 mi/240 km); and Lexington, KY (261 mi/416 km).

FOR MORE INFORMATION

Big South Fork National River and Recreation Area (Park Headquarters, 4564 Leatherwood Rd., Oneida, TN 37841, tel. 931/879–3625 or 606/376–5073 in KY; Web site www.nps.gov/biso).

Fort Donelson National Battlefield

In the northwest part of the state, near Dover

Fort Donelson was created to preserve and interpret the remains of the Battle of Fort Donelson, the 1862 Civil War conflict. The park includes the fort, river batteries, outer defense earthworks, Surrender House (Dover Hotel), and a national cemetery. The historical significance of the park centers on three major themes: Union commander Ulysses S. Grant ("Unconditional Surrender" Grant) and his capture of the fort and 13,000 Confederate prisoners; the use of ironclad gunboats on inland rivers; and the beginning of the Union Army's control of the north-to-south inland waters of the Tennessee and Cumberland rivers. The park was established as a national military park on March 26, 1928, transferred to the Park Service in 1933, and redesignated in 1985.

WHAT TO SEE & DO

Auto touring, hiking, picnicking, visiting museum, watching slide program. **Facilities:** Visitor center with interpretive exhibits, Surrender House (Dover Hotel), museum, wayside exhibits, trails, interpretive tour tapes. Book and map sale area, picnic tables. **Programs & Events:** Slide program (year-round). Surrender House (Dover Hotel) open June–Sept., daily noon–4. Costume interpretive programs (occasionally, Feb.–Oct.).

PLANNING YOUR VISIT

Camping: Available in Dover; none at battlefield. **Lodging:** Available in Clarksville, Dover; none at battlefield. **Food & Supplies:** Available in Dover; none at battlefield. **Tips & Hints:** Go between April and June for flowers, September and March for smaller crowds. Busiest in June and July, least crowded in January and February. **Fees, Permits & Limitations:** Free. Leashed pets only. No metal detectors, skating, skateboards, vehicles on trails, hunting. Park open daily sunrise–sunset. Visitor center open daily 8–4:30; closed Dec. 25.

HOW TO GET THERE

1 mi/1.6 km west of Dover, TN, off U.S. 79. Closest airport: Nashville (90 mi/144 km).

FOR MORE INFORMATION

Fort Donelson National Battlefield (Box 434, Dover, TN 37058, tel. 931/232–5706, fax 931/232–6331; Web site www.nps.gov/fodo). Dover/Stuart County Chamber of Commerce (Box 147, Dover, TN 37058, tel. 931/232–8290).

Great Smoky Mountains National Park

In east Tennessee, near Gatlinburg; and west North Carolina, near Cherokee

The 521,621-acre forested park is world renowned for the diversity of its plants and animals, the beauty of its ancient mountains, the quality of its remnants of American pioneer culture, and the depth and integrity of the wilderness sanctuary within its boundaries. It is one of the largest protected areas in the East. The park was authorized in 1926 and designated a Biosphere Reserve in 1976 and a World Heritage Site in 1983.

WHAT TO SEE & DO

Auto touring, bicycling (rentals, Cades Cove), fishing, hiking, horseback riding (rentals), picnicking, swimming, tubing. **Facilities:** 3 visitor centers with interpretive exhibits—Sugarlands (2 mi/3 km south of Gatlinburg, TN, on U.S. 441), Oconaluftee (1 mi/1.6 km north of Cherokee, NC), and Cades Cove (near Townsend, TN); Mountain Farm Museum, 850 mi/1,360 km of trails, 170 mi/272 km of paved roads, 100 mi/160 km of gravel roads. Bookstores, picnic areas, orientation film at Sugarlands. **Programs & Events:** Ranger-led interpretive walks and talks, slide presentations, and campfire programs (June–Sept.). Old Timers' Day, Storytelling, Quilt Show, Women's Work, Mountain Life Festival, Sorghum Molasses and Apple Butter Making, and living-history programs (all May–Oct.).

PLANNING YOUR VISIT

⛺ **Camping:** 10 campgrounds: no hookups, (reservations available, tel. 800/365–2267). Backcountry camping (reservations available, tel. 865/436–1231; permit required, *see below*). ⌂ **Lodging:** In the park: LeConte Lodge (accessible only on foot or horseback) sits atop 6,593-ft/2,000-m Mt. LeConte (reservations required, tel. 865/429–5704; open Mar.–mid-Nov.). Lodging also available in surrounding communities. ✗ **Food & Supplies:** Available in surrounding communities; none in park. ☞ **Tips & Hints:** Expect temperatures to be 10–20 degrees cooler on mountaintops (up to 6,643 ft/2,015 m). Summers are hot and humid at lower elevations; frost begins in late September; the driest weather is in the fall; and winters are moderate. Busiest in July and August, least crowded in January and February. ▧ **Fees, Permits & Limitations:** Free. Fees charged at developed campgrounds. Permit required (free) for backcountry camping. Great Smoky Mountains Institute at Tremont offers workshop (tel. 865/448–6709). Smoky Mountain Field School offers weekend workshops (tel. 800/284–8885). Reservations available for 5 horse camps (tel. 800/365–2267). Call park for private stables within park. Tennessee or North Carolina fishing license required. No pets on most trails. Leashed pets elsewhere. Park, Sugarlands, and Oconaluftee open daily 9–4, longer hours in summer; closed Dec. 25. Cades Cove open daily.

HOW TO GET THERE

The park has three main entrances. From I–40 east of Knoxville, take Exit 407 (Sevierville) to TN 66S, continue to U.S. 441S, follow U.S. 441 to park. From I–40 in Knoxville, take Exit 386B on U.S. 129S to Alcoa/Maryville. At Maryville proceed on U.S. 321N through Townsend. Continue straight on TN 73 into park. From I–40 in North Carolina, take U.S. 19W through Maggie Valley. Proceed to U.S. 441N at Cherokee into the park. From Atlanta and points south, follow U.S. 441 and 23N. U.S. 441 leads to the park. Closest airports: Knoxville, TN (50 mi/80 km); Asheville, NC (60 mi/96 km).

FOR MORE INFORMATION

Great Smoky Mountains National Park (107 Park Headquarters Rd., Gatlinburg, TN 37738, tel. 865/436–1200, fax 865/436–1220; Web site www.nps.gov/grsm).

Obed Wild and Scenic River

In the east-central part of the state, near Wartburg

Clear and Daddy's creeks, about 45 mi/72 km of free-flowing streams on the Obed and Emory rivers, are protected in this park. The river provides some of the most rugged scenery in the Southeast and has spectacular gorges 500 ft/152 m deep. The river was authorized on October 12, 1976.

WHAT TO SEE & DO

Fishing, hiking, hunting, picnicking, rock climbing, swimming, whitewater boating. **Facilities:** Visitor center with interpretive exhibits (Wartburg), trails. Bookstore. **Programs & Events:** Slide presentations (year-round, on request). Ranger-led talks and walks (most weekends, Memorial Day–Labor Day). Seasonal activities and special events available.

PLANNING YOUR VISIT

Camping: Primitive camping available at Rock Creek Campground near Nemo Bridge (no reservations). Camping available in Cumberland Mountain State Park and Frozen Head State Park. Private campgrounds available along I–40 and in Crossville area. **Lodging:** Available locally. **Food & Supplies:** Available in Crossville, Wartburg. **Tips & Hints:** Be aware of changing weather conditions if boating or climbing. Expect white-water conditions suitable for experienced boaters only. Go between January and April for best white-water boating. Call park for water levels and float information. **Fees, Permits & Limitations:** Free. No glass bottles at river access points. No alcohol. Tennessee hunting and fishing licenses required. Visitor center open daily 8–4:30. Closed Dec. 25.

HOW TO GET THERE

From I–40, follow Hwy. 27N. From the south, follow I–75 and I–40W to Hwy. 27N. From the north, exit I–75 on Hwy. 63W and take U.S. 27S. Closest airport: Knoxville (50 mi/80 km).

FOR MORE INFORMATION

Obed Wild and Scenic River (Box 429, Wartburg, TN 37887, tel. 423/346–6294; Web site www.nps.gov/obed).

Shiloh National Military Park

In the southwest part of the state, near Savannah

The largest battle of the 1862 Civil War campaign for possession of the railroads of the western Confederacy and military control of the lower Mississippi River occurred on this site. The park includes 4,000 acres of preserved battlefield, with more than 150 monuments; 217 cannons; 450 iron interpretive tablets; and the historic Peach Orchard, Hornets Nest, and Bloody Pond. Shiloh also protects an extensive Native American mound complex. The park was established in 1894 and transferred to the Park Service in 1933.

WHAT TO SEE & DO

Auto or bike tours, genealogy and military research, hiking, touring museum, walking, watching film. **Facilities:** Visitor center with interpretive exhibits (Pittsburg Landing), museum and film, 450 tablets, 151 monuments, 14 wayside panels, and 5 audio boxes. Bookstore, fire pits and grates, pavilion, picnic tables. **Programs & Events:** Film, *Shiloh: Portrait of a Battle* (daily, every half hour), ranger-guided tours and talks (occasionally). Guided hikes, interpretive talks, cultural demonstrations (May–Aug.). Shiloh anniversary (closest weekend to Apr. 6–7), Memorial Day Service (May), living-history demonstrations (occasionally).

PLANNING YOUR VISIT

⚠ **Camping:** Available in Counce, Savannah, community of Shiloh; none in park. 🏨 **Lodging:** Available in Counce, Savannah, and Selmer, TN, and Corinth, MS; none in park. ✕ **Food & Supplies:** Available in Adamsville, Counce, Crump, Savannah, Selmer, and Shiloh, TN, and Corinth, MS; none in park. ☞ **Tips & Hints:** Observe 25-mph speed limit. Watch for pedestrians, bicyclists, and wildlife. Face traffic when hiking on road. Watch for snakes. Go in early spring when crowds are smaller and historic Peach Orchard is blooming, fall for foliage. Busiest in April and May, least crowded in December and January. 🖼 **Fees, Permits & Limitations:** Entrance fee: $2 per person or $4 per family. No hunting, metal detecting, or removing archaeological resources. Leashed pets only. Bicycles on pavement only. No in-line skating or skateboarding. Visitor center open daily 8–5. Grounds open until sunset. Closed Dec. 25.

HOW TO GET THERE

12 mi/19 km south of Savannah via U.S. 64 and Hwy. 22 and 22 mi/35 km north of Corinth, MS, via U.S. 45 and Hwy. 22. Closest airport: Hardin County (15 mi/24 km).

FOR MORE INFORMATION

Superintendent, Shiloh National Military Park (1055 Pittsburgh-Landing Rd., Shiloh, TN 38376, tel. 901/689–5696, fax 901/689–5450; e-mail SHIL_interpretation@NPS.GOV; Web site www.nps.gov/shil). Team Hardin County, Department of Tourism (507 Main St., Savannah, TN 38372, tel. 901/925–2364 or 800/552–3866).

Stones River National Battlefield

Midstate, in Murfreesboro

Between December 31, 1862, and January 2, 1863, the Union Army of the Cumberland and the Confederate Army of the Tennessee fought here in a battle that cost each side nearly 30% in casualties. The battle was a key Union victory that marked the start of the campaign to take Chattanooga and Atlanta. Stones River National Cemetery, with 6,831 interments and 2,562 unidentified, adjoins the battlefield. The cemetery was established in 1865 and the park was established in 1927.

WHAT TO SEE & DO

Self-guided or audiotape-guided auto touring; self-guided bicycle or walking tours of the battlefield. **Facilities:** Visitor center with interpretive exhibits (3501 Old Nashville Hwy., Murfreesboro), interpretive waysides and exhibits along tour route and trail, Fortress Rosecrans (Old Fort Park, off TN 96), trails. Bookstore, connections to Stones River Greenway, picnic tables. **Programs & Events:** 18-minute slide program (year-round). Interpretive walks and talks (June–Sept.), living-history demonstrations (mid-June–Aug.), "Hallowed Ground" cemetery tour by lantern (mid-June–Aug.). Battle Anniversary (Dec. 31–Jan. 2).

PLANNING YOUR VISIT

⚠ **Camping:** Available in Lavergne, Lebanon, Manchester, Smyrna; none at battlefield. ▥ **Lodging:** Available in Murfreesboro; none at battlefield. ✕ **Food & Supplies:** Available in Murfreesboro; none at battlefield. ☞ **Tips & Hints:** Go to visitor center first. Go in early to mid-spring and most of fall for best weather. Busiest in July and October, least crowded in December and January. ▨ **Fees, Permits & Limitations:** Free. Stay on trails. No hunting. Leashed pets only. No metal detectors. No removing artifacts. No in-line skating, rollerblading, or skateboarding. Bikes on park roads only. Battlefield open daily 8–5, grounds open until dark for visitors on foot. Closed Dec. 25.

HOW TO GET THERE

On Old Nashville Hwy. (US 40/70S) in Murfreesboro, 27 mi/43 km south of Nashville. Closest airport: Nashville (27 mi/43 km).

FOR MORE INFORMATION

Stones River National Battlefield (3501 Old Nashville Hwy., Murfreesboro, TN 37129, tel. 615/893–9501, fax 615/893–9508; e-mail stri_administration@nps.gov; Web site www.nps.gov/stri). Rutherford County

Chamber of Commerce (501 Memorial Blvd., Murfreesboro, TN 37129, tel. 615/893–6565 or 800/716–7650, fax 615/890–7600).

See Also

Appalachian National Scenic Trail, West Virginia. *Chickamauga and Chattanooga National Military Park*, Georgia. *Cumberland Gap National Historical Park*, Kentucky. *Natchez Trace National Scenic Trail*, Mississippi. *Natchez Trace Parkway*, Mississippi. *Overmountain Victory National Historic Trail*, National Trails System in Other National Parklands. *Tennessee Civil War Heritage Area*, National Heritage Areas in Other National Parklands. *Trail of Tears National Historic Trail*, National Trails System in Other National Parklands.

TEXAS

Alibates Flint Quarries National Monument

Texas Panhandle north of Amarillo

Few prehistoric Native American archaeological sites in the Canadian River region of the Texas Panhandle are as dramatic as Alibates Flint Quarries. People quarried flint for tools here for 12,000 years, since the time of the Ice Age Clovis culture, when Native Americans used Alibates flint for spear points to hunt the Imperial Mammoth. The monument was authorized as Alibates Flint Quarries and Texas Panhandle Pueblo Culture National Monument on August 21, 1965, and redesignated on November 10, 1978.

WHAT TO SEE & DO

Flint-chipping demonstrations, guided tours. **Facilities:** Contact station. Picnic tables. **Programs & Events:** Guided tours (Labor Day–Memorial Day, reservations required; Memorial Day–Labor Day, daily 10 and 2). Flint-chipping demonstrations, school tours.

PLANNING YOUR VISIT

Camping: Available nearby in Fritch, Lake Meredith National Recreation Area (*see separate entry*); none at monument. **Lodging:** Available nearby in Amarillo, Borger, Dumas, Fritch, Pampa; none at monument. **Food & Supplies:** Available nearby in Amarillo, Borger, Dumas, Fritch, Pampa; none at monument. **Tips & Hints:** Call several days in advance between Labor Day and Memorial Day for tour reservations. Busiest in May and June, least crowded in December and January. **Fees, Permits & Limitations:** Free. No entrance to monument except with ranger. Entrance to monument by guided tour only. Reservations required Labor Day–Memorial Day (tel. 806/857–3151). Reservations for tours not required Memorial Day–Labor Day. Contact station open Memorial Day–Labor Day, daily 9:30–4:30. Park Headquarters at 419 E. Broadway open weekdays 8–4:30. Closed winter holidays.

HOW TO GET THERE

12 mi/19 km southwest of Fritch. Closest airport: Amarillo (40 mi/64 km).

FOR MORE INFORMATION

Alibates Flint Quarries National Monument (Box 1460, Fritch, TX 79036, tel. 806/857–3151; Web site www.nps.gov/alfl).

Amistad National Recreation Area

*140 mi/224 km west of San Antonio,
60 mi/96 km east of Langtry*

Amistad—the name means "friendship"—is a 58,000-acre international recreation area on the United States–Mexico border. The Amistad Reservoir offers outstanding water sports and was created by the 6-mi-/10-km-long Amistad Dam on the Rio Grande, a joint U.S.–Mexico project. Archaeological research shows that Native Americans lived in this area continuously for 10,000 years before the arrival of Europeans. The rock paintings they left are considered to be as significant as sites in Europe, Australia, and Baja California. The region also contains some of the oldest and best-preserved archaeological deposits in North America. The park is administered under a November 11, 1965, cooperative agreement with the International Boundary and Water Commission as Amistad Recreation Area and was authorized as Amistad National Recreation Area on November 28, 1990.

WHAT TO SEE & DO

Boating (rentals), camping, fishing, hunting, picnicking, scuba diving, swimming, visiting rock art sites, waterskiing. **Facilities:** Headquarters (Hwy. 90, west of Del Rio) with visitor information and bookstore, 2 unstaffed visitor centers with exhibits (Amistad Dam, Rough Canyon); nature trails, beaches, fishing docks, boat ramps, amphitheater, interpretive panels, park information on radio (1540 AM). Book and map sales, picnic areas with grills, tables and shade shelters, group picnicking (reservations required, tel. 830/775–7491). **Programs & Events:** 25-minute video on rock art (on request) at park headquarters (year-round). Evening interpretive programs (Nov.–Mar.), ranger-led guided bird walks (Sept.–June, 3rd Sat. of the month), other interpretive programs (periodically Dec.–Apr.). Seminars on rock art, archaeology, and other natural history topics several times a year.

PLANNING YOUR VISIT

⚠ Camping: 4 primitive campgrounds (no reservations). Backcountry camping accessible by boat only. Group camping (reservations required, tel. 830/775–7491) Private campgrounds in Del Rio and along Hwy. 90. Dump stations at Diablo East and Del Rio. **⌂ Lodging:** Available nearby in Del Rio; none at recreation area. **✗ Food & Supplies:** In the park: snacks, drinks, fuel, bait, and ice at Diablo East and Rough Canyon. Food and supplies also available in Comstock and Del Rio. **☞ Tips & Hints:** Get drinking water at Diablo East and Park Headquarters. Watch for strong lake winds. Go in spring for wildflower blooms. Busiest in April and May, least crowded in November and December. **▦ Fees, Permits & Limitations:** Free. Lake-use permits required on U.S. side of Lake Amistad ($4/day or $40/year; Golden Age and Access Passport holders get 50% discount. Permits available from automated fee machines at Diablo East and Rough Canyon or at Park Headquarters.) Texas state and Mexico fishing license required in respective waters. Texas state hunting license and free park hunting license required. Hunting allowed in designated areas in certain seasons only. Leashed pets only. No off-road travel. Vehicle access to reservoir and boat launch sites restricted. Park open daily. Park Headquarters open daily 8–5. Closed Thanksgiving, Dec. 25, Jan. 1.

HOW TO GET THERE

Closest lake access: 8 mi/13 km west of Del Rio on Hwy. 90 or 277. Closest airport: Del Rio.

FOR MORE INFORMATION

Amistad National Recreation Area (HCR 3, Box 5 J, Del Rio, TX 78840, tel. 830/775–7491, fax 830/775–7299; e-mail Amis_interpretation@nps.gov; Web site www.nps.gov/amis). Del Rio Chamber of Commerce (1915 Ave. F, Del Rio, TX 78840, tel. 830/775–3551).

Big Bend National Park

In the southwest part of the state, near Marathon

The 801,163-acre park is a land of borders. Situated on the U.S.–Mexico border on the Rio Grande, it is a place where countries and cultures meet. It is also a place that merges natural environments from desert to mountains while offering a great diversity of plants and animals. The park was authorized in 1935, established in 1944, and designated an International Biosphere Reserve in 1976.

WHAT TO SEE & DO

Auto touring, biking (rentals, Study Butte/Terlingua), bird- and wildlife watching, hiking, rafting (rentals, Study Butte/Terlingua). **Facilities:** 4 visitor centers with interpretive exhibits—Persimmon Gap, Panther Junction, Chisos Basin, and Rio Grande Village; 1 visitor contact station (Castolon); trails; paved and primitive roads. Bookstore, gas station, laundry. **Programs & Events:** Nature walks, workshops, and evening slide programs (year-round). Seasonal activities available. International Good Neighbor Day Fiesta and Dia del Rio Celebration (3rd Sat., Oct.).

PLANNING YOUR VISIT

⚠ **Camping:** 4 campgrounds: 1 with hookups (no reservations). Backcountry camping available (permit required, *see below*). ⊞ **Lodging:** In the park: Chisos Mountain Lodge (tel. 915/477–2291). Lodging also available in Lajitas, Marathon, and Terlingua. ✕ **Food & Supplies:** In the park: meals at Chisos Basin, limited groceries at campgrounds. Food and supplies also available in Alpine and Study Butte. ☞ **Tips & Hints:** The park is very large and remote. Remember that you will be at least 100 mi/160 km from a bank, hospital, pharmacy, or supermarket. Plan to spend two days to see most of the park from the main roads or a week if hiking. Carry drinking water. Park gets crowded during spring break (Mar., Apr.), Easter, Thanksgiving, and Dec. 25–Jan. 1 but is otherwise uncrowded. Busiest in March and April, least crowded in December and January. ⊠ **Fees, Permits & Limitations:** Entrance fee:

$10 per vehicle, $5 per cyclist, bus passenger, or walk-in. Permit required (free) for backcountry camping. Trailers over 20 ft/6 m or RVs over 24 ft/7.3 m not recommended on Ross Maxwell Scenic Drive to Castolon and the road to the Chisos Mountains Basin. High-clearance vehicles only on dirt roads. No pets in backcountry or on trails. Leashed pets only on roads and in drive-in campground. Park open daily. Visitor center hours: Panther Junction—daily 8–6, shorter hours on Dec. 25; Chisos—daily, 9–4:30; Persimmon Gap—Oct.–May, daily 9–5 (staff permitting); Rio Grande Village—Nov.–Apr, daily 8:30–4:30.

HOW TO GET THERE

Park headquarters is 70 mi/112 km south of Marathon via U.S. 385 and 108 mi/73 km from Alpine via Hwy. 118. Closest airports: Midland (230 mi/368 km), El Paso (325 mi/520 km).

FOR MORE INFORMATION

Big Bend National Park (Box 129, Big Bend National Park, TX 79834, tel. 915/477–2251; Web site www.nps.gov/bibe).

Big Thicket National Preserve

In the southeast part of the state, near Beaumont

The preserve protects an area of rich biological diversity where the eastern hardwood forests, the southern coastal wetlands, the western prairies, and the arid southwest converge. It consists of eight land units and four water corridors encompassing 86,000 acres. The preserve was authorized in 1974 and designated a Biosphere Reserve in 1981.

WHAT TO SEE & DO

Bicycling, bird-watching, boating, canoeing, fishing, hiking, horseback riding, hunting, picnicking, powerboating. **Facilities:** Information station with interpretive exhibits, trails. Bookstore, picnic sites. **Programs & Events:** Guided walks, tours, off-site talks, and environmental education programs (reservation only, tel. 409/246–2337).

PLANNING YOUR VISIT

Camping: Backcountry camping available (permit required, *see below*); none in preserve. **Lodging:** Available in nearby communities; none in preserve. **Food & Supplies:** Available in nearby communities; none in preserve. **Tips & Hints:** Allow two hours for visiting the information station and hiking the inside loop of the Kirby Nature Trail and 1-mph hiking time on other trails. Watch for flooded trails after rains and heavy releases from Steinhagen Reservoir that can flood popular campsites along the Neches River. Go in spring and fall for best weather. Wear comfortable sportswear and walking shoes and carry rain gear. Rain, heat, and humidity are typical. Summer temperatures typically reach 85°F/30°C–95°F/35°C, winter is 55°F/13°C. Go between September and May for best hiking; March and October for wildflower identification; mid-April and mid-May for bird-watching; April and October for boating, fishing, and canoeing; October and mid-January for hunting. Busiest in April and October, least crowded in January and February. ⊠ **Fees, Permits & Limitations:** Free. Backcountry camping permit (free) required for all backcountry camping. Texas state fishing, hunting, and trapping licenses required. Hunting and trapping by permit (free) only. No vehicles on trails. Leashed pets on trails. All-terrain bicycles and horses on Big Sandy Trail only. Information station open daily 9–5. Closed Dec. 25, Jan. 1.

HOW TO GET THERE

The information station is 7 mi/11 km north of Kountze on FM 420. Major north–south access is via U.S. 69/287; major east–west access is via U.S. 190, U.S. 90, or I–10. Closest airports: Beaumont/Port Arthur (10 mi/16 km), Houston (90 mi/144 km).

FOR MORE INFORMATION

Superintendent, Big Thicket National Preserve (3785 Milam, Beaumont, TX 77701, tel. 409/839–2689; Web site www.nps.gov/bith).

Chamizal National Memorial

In the western part of the state, in El Paso

Chamizal National Memorial commemorates the peaceful settlement of a century-old boundary dispute between Mexico and the United States. The Chamizal Treaty of 1963 was a milestone in the diplomatic relations between the two countries and is celebrated in parks across the river from each other. The memorial focuses on the arts and provides an avenue for cross-cultural understanding and enrichment that transcends barriers of race, ethnicity, and language. The park was authorized in 1966 and established in 1974.

WHAT TO SEE & DO

Attending indoor theater and outdoor amphitheater events, bicycling, jogging, picnicking, touring facility. **Facilities:** Visitor center (800 S. San Marcial, between Paisano St. and Delta Dr.), indoor theater, trail. Art gallery, bookstore, grills, outdoor amphitheater, picnic tables. **Programs & Events:** Plays, musicals, recitals, ballet (year-round, weekly). Siglo de Oro Spanish Drama Festival (first week in Mar.), Music Under the Stars (June–Aug., Sunday eve.). Fourth of July evening concert, Mexican Independence Day Celebration (Sept. 15), Chamizal Festival (1st weekend, Oct.).

PLANNING YOUR VISIT

⚠ **Camping:** Available in El Paso; none at memorial. 🛏 **Lodging:** Available in El Paso; none at memorial. ✗ **Food & Supplies:** Available in El Paso; none at memorial. ☞ **Tips & Hints:** Go between May and September for best weather. Busiest in June and July, least crowded in January and February. ⊠ **Fees, Permits & Limitations:** Free. Leashed pets only. No motorized vehicles on trail. Park grounds open daily 5 AM–10 PM. Visitor center open daily 8–5. Park closed Thanksgiving, Dec. 25, Jan. 1.

HOW TO GET THERE

In downtown El Paso at 800 S. San Marcial, between Paisano and Delta Sts. Closest airport: El Paso International.

FOR MORE INFORMATION

Chamizal National Memorial (800 S. San Marcial, El Paso, TX 79905, tel. 915/532–7273, fax 915/532–7240; Web site www.nps.gov/cham). El Paso Convention and Visitor Bureau (1 Civic Center Plaza, El Paso, TX 79901, tel. 915/534–0653, fax 915/532–2963). El Paso Hispanic Chamber of Commerce (2829 Montana, Suite B-100, El Paso, TX 79903, tel. 915/566–4066). The Greater El Paso Chamber of Commerce (10 Civic Center Plaza, El Paso, TX 79901, tel. 915/534–0500).

Fort Davis National Historic Site

In the western part of the state, in Fort Davis

Soldiers from Fort Davis helped open the area to settlement and protected travelers and mail carriers from Comanches and Apaches along the San Antonio–El Paso Road from 1854 to 1891. Today the fort is regarded as one of the best-preserved in the Southwest. The site, which contains 474 acres, was authorized in 1961 and established in 1963.

WHAT TO SEE & DO

Hiking, picnicking, self-guided tours of 5 restored fort buildings and ruins. **Facilities:** Visitor center with museum, fort buildings, ruins, and trails. Bookstore, picnic area. **Programs & Events:** Interpretive programs (Memorial Day–Labor Day). Friends of Fort Davis Festival (Sat. of Columbus Day weekend), special evening tours (Nov., Sat. closest to the full moon).

PLANNING YOUR VISIT

⚠ **Camping:** Available in Fort Davis and Davis Mountains State Park; none at site. 🛏 **Lodging:** Available in town of Fort Davis; none at site. ✕ **Food & Supplies:** Available in town of Fort Davis; none at site. ☞ **Tips & Hints:** Plan to stay at least two to three hours. Busiest in March and July, least crowded in December and January. 🎫 **Fees, Permits & Limitations:** Entrance fee: $2 per person 17 and up. Large groups should contact park two weeks before visit (tel. 915/426–3224 ext. 23). Fort open Labor Day–Memorial Day, daily 8–5; Memorial Day–Labor Day, daily 8–6. Closed Dec. 25.

HOW TO GET THERE

On the north edge of the town of Fort Davis on Hwys. 17/118. The site can be reached from the north on I–10, from the south on U.S. 90, from the west on TX 17 and 118 and U.S. 90, and on TX 505, 166, and 17. The town of Marfa is 21 mi/34 km to the south. Closest airport: Midland-Odessa (150 mi/240 km).

FOR MORE INFORMATION

Fort Davis National Historic Site (Box 1456, Ft. Davis, TX 79734, tel. 915/426–3224, fax 915/426–3122; Web site www.nps.gov/foda).

Guadalupe Mountains National Park

In the western part of the state, near Pine Springs

The 86,416-acre park includes part of the Capitan Reef, one of the most extensive and significant noncoral Permian-period fossil reefs in the world. Guadalupe contains over 1,000 identified plant species, 296 bird species, 58 mammal species, 56 reptile and amphibian species, and numerous archaeological sites. The park is also home to Guadalupe Peak, the highest point in Texas (8,749 ft/2,654 m), and McKittrick Canyon, which contains the park's only perennial stream. Also on view are relic forest and riparian areas, spectacular scenery, historic structures such as the Pinery, a remnant of the Butterfield overland mail route, and various cultural resources from prehistoric to pioneer ranching. The park was authorized in 1966 and established in 1972.

WHAT TO SEE & DO

Backpacking, bird-watching, hiking, observing wildlife, picnicking. **Facilities:** Visitor center with interpretive exhibits (Pine Springs), 3 visitor contact stations with exhibits (McKittrick Canyon, Frijole Ranch, Dog Canyon), trails, amphitheater. Bookstore, picnic tables. **Programs & Events:** Slide show (year-round). Interpretive programs (Memorial Day–Labor Day).

PLANNING YOUR VISIT

Camping: 2 campgrounds: no hookups or showers (no reservations). Backcountry camping available (permit required; *see below*). Group camping available (reservations available, tel. 915/828–3251 ext. 0). Private campgrounds in White's City, NM. **Lodging:** Available in El Paso and Van Horn, TX, and Carlsbad and White's City, NM; none in park. **Food & Supplies:** Available in Carlsbad and White's City, NM, and Van Horn, TX; none in park. **Tips & Hints:** Watch for high winds and rapid weather changes. Prepare for steep, rocky trails. Carry plenty of water. Go in spring for birds, May and September for wildflowers, October for fall colors. Busiest in March and October, least crowded in January and February. **Fees, Permits & Limitations:** Free. Backcountry permits (free) required for all backcountry camping. No fishing or hunting. No fires in park (including charcoal). No pets outside campgrounds, leashed pets only in campgrounds. No mountain bikes or trail bikes except on Williams Ranch Rd. No motorized or wheeled vehicles on trails. No pack and riding stock except on designated trails. No overnight use of stock in backcountry. No swimming, bathing, or wading. Park open daily. Closed Dec. 25. Visitor center open Labor Day–Memorial Day, daily 8–4:30; Memorial Day–Labor Day, daily 8–6. Closed Dec. 25. Highway gate to McKittrick Canyon open 8–4:30, until 6 during daylight saving time.

HOW TO GET THERE

110 mi/176 km east of El Paso via U.S. 62/180, 65 mi/104 km north of Van Horn via Hwy. 54, and 55 mi/88 km southwest of Carlsbad, NM, via U.S. 62/180. Closest airports Carlsbad, NM; El Paso, TX.

FOR MORE INFORMATION

Guadalupe Mountains National Park (HC 60 Box 400, Salt Flat, TX 79847, tel. 915/828–3251, fax 915/828–3269; e-mail gumo_ superintendent@nps.gov; Web site www.nps.gov/gumo). Carlsbad Chamber of Commerce (Box 910, Carlsbad, NM 88220, tel. 505/887–6516).

Lake Meredith National Recreation Area

Near Amarillo, in the Panhandle

Each year more than 1.5 million visitors come to this lake, which is the prime recreation area in the Texas Panhandle and was created by the Sanford Dam on the Canadian River. The 12-mi-/19-km-long lake is bordered by the redbeds of the Permian formations and the white dolomite of the Alibates formation. The lake has been administered in cooperation with the Bureau of Reclamation since 1965.

WHAT TO SEE & DO

Bird-watching, boating, fishing, horseback riding, hunting, motorcycle and off-road vehicle riding, parasailing, picnicking, scuba diving, swimming. **Facilities:** Park headquarters, Alibates contact station, lake. Picnic areas, sales areas.

PLANNING YOUR VISIT

⚠ **Camping:** In the park: 15 designated campgrounds (tel. 806/857–3151), two accessible by boat only. Backcountry camping available. Group campsites available (tel. 806/857–3151). Private camping available in Fritch. 🏠 **Lodging:** Available in Amarillo, Borger, Dumas, Fritch, Pampa; none in recreation area. ✗ **Food & Supplies:** In the park: food and supplies at the marina. Food and supplies also available in Fritch, Sanford. ☞ **Tips & Hints:** Go between February and spring, in fall, or in December for bird migrations. Busiest in July and August, least crowded in January and February. ▨ **Fees, Permits & Limitations:** Free. Boating fee: $4 per day. Texas state hunting and fishing licenses required. Permits required for parasailing. Leashed pets only. Horses restricted to Plum Creek, McBride Creek, and while hunting. Park open daily. Park headquarters open weekdays 8–4:30. Closed Columbus Day, Thanksgiving, Veterans Day, Dec. 25, Jan. 1, Martin Luther King Jr. Birthday, Presidents Day.

HOW TO GET THERE

Park headquarters is on Hwy. 136 in Fritch. Closest airports: Borger (20 mi/32 km), Amarillo (35 mi/56 km).

FOR MORE INFORMATION

Lake Meredith National Recreation Area (Box 1460, 419 E. Broadway, Fritch, TX 79036, tel. 806/857–3151, fax 806/857–2319; e-mail lamr@nps.gov; Web site www.nps.gov/lamr). Amarillo Chamber of Commerce (Box 9480, Amarillo, TX 79105, tel. 806/373–7800). Texas Travel Information Center (9400 E. I–40, Amarillo, TX 79118, tel. 806/ 335–1441).

Lyndon B. Johnson National Historical Park

In the south-central part of the state, in Johnson City and Stonewall

Historically significant properties associated with Lyndon B. Johnson, the 36th president of the United States, are preserved here. In the Johnson City District are the President's Boyhood Home and the Johnson Settlement, a complex of restored historic structures that traces the evolution of the Texas Hill Country from the open-range cattle kingdom of President Johnson's grandfather, Sam E. Johnson Sr., to the local ranching and farming of more recent times. At the LBJ Ranch, visitors can view the one-room schoolhouse attended by Johnson, his Reconstructed Birthplace, the Johnson Family Cemetery, where the president is buried, the Texas White House, and the ranching operation that continues today. The park was authorized in 1969 as a national historic site and enlarged and redesignated as a national historical park in 1980.

WHAT TO SEE & DO

Touring LBJ Ranch, Boyhood Home, Johnson Settlement; viewing exhibits and films. **Facilities:** 2 visitor centers with interpretive exhibits (100 Ladybird La., Johnson City; LBJ State Historical Park, Hwy. 290, near Stonewall), ranch, home, settlement. Bookstores (both sites), education center (at National Historical Park), amphitheater, fishing, picnic tables with grills, pool, softball field, tennis courts (all at LBJ State Historical Park). **Programs & Events:** Year-round: guided bus tour of LBJ Ranch (daily from LBJ State Historical Park, except Thanksgiving, Dec. 25, Jan. 1), ranger-guided tours of Boyhood Home (daily except Thanksgiving, Dec. 25, Jan. 1). Guided tours begin at 9 AM and are offered every half hour, last tour at 4:30. Costumed interpretive programs (Mar.–June and Oct.–Dec., daily, Johnson Settlement). Night Skies (spring and fall). LBJ Ranch Roundup (Mar.), Cowboy Songs and Poetry (May), Birthday Party for President Johnson (Aug.), Wreath laying at Johnson Family Cemetery (Aug. 27), Heritage Crafts Day (Oct.), Christmas Tour of the Boyhood Home and Johnson Settlement, Tree Lighting and Tour of LBJ Ranch (Dec.).

PLANNING YOUR VISIT

⚠ **Camping:** Available in Blanco, Fredericksburg, Johnson City; none in park. ☎ **Lodging:** Available in Fredericksburg, Johnson City,

Stonewall; none in park. ✗ **Food & Supplies:** Available in Fredericksburg, Johnson City, Stonewall; none in park. ☞ **Tips & Hints:** Dress casually. Summers can be very hot. Don't approach longhorn cattle or wildlife. Go in March, April, or October for best weather. Go in March or April for migratory birds and wildflowers. Busiest in March and April, least crowded in December and January. ▨ **Fees, Permits & Limitations:** Free. Bus tours of the LBJ Ranch: $3 per person 7 and up. Reservation suggested (tel. 830/868–7128 ext. 231) for groups over 15. No pets allowed on LBJ Ranch Bus Tour, inside park buildings, or at the Johnson Settlement. Leashed pets elsewhere. Access to the LBJ Ranch is by tour bus only. Johnson Settlement open daily sunrise–sunset. LBJ Ranch Bus Tours available 10–4. Private vehicles allowed on part of LBJ Ranch 5 PM–sunset. LBJ State Historical Park open daily until 10 PM. Johnson City visitor center open daily 8:45–5. LBJ State Historical Park visitor center open daily 8–5. Closed Thanksgiving, Dec. 25, Jan. 1.

HOW TO GET THERE

The Johnson City District is at 100 Ladybird La., in Johnson City, 48 mi/77 km west of Austin on Hwy. 290 and 65 mi/104 km north of San Antonio on Hwy. 281. The LBJ Ranch and LBJ State Historical Park are on Hwy. 290, 14 mi/22 km west of Johnson City and 16 mi/26 km east of Fredericksburg. Closest airports: Austin, San Antonio.

FOR MORE INFORMATION

Lyndon B. Johnson National Historical Park (Box 329, Johnson City, TX 78636, tel. 830/868–7128 ext. 244, fax 830/868–0810; e-mail LYJO_Ranger_Activities@nps.gov; Web site www.nps.gov/lyjo). Johnson City Chamber of Commerce (Box 485, Johnson City, TX 78636, tel. 830/868–7684, fax 830/868–7830). Stonewall Chamber of Commerce (Box 1, Stonewall, TX 78671, tel. 830/644–2735). Lyndon B. Johnson State Historical Park (Box 238, Stonewall, TX 78671, tel. 830/ 644–2252, fax 830/644–2430). Fredericksburg Convention and Visitor Bureau (106 N. Adams, Fredericksburg, TX 78624, tel. 830/997–6523, fax 830/997–8588).

Padre Island
National Seashore

In the southeast part of the state, near Corpus Christi

The seashore provides a rare opportunity for primitive beach recreation on 80 mi/128 km of the longest barrier island in the world. Padre Island is well known for its wide sandy beaches, excellent fishing, and abundant bird and marine life. The seashore was authorized in 1962 and established in 1968.

WHAT TO SEE & DO

Beachcombing, bird-watching, boating, fishing, picnicking, swimming, windsurfing (rentals, Bird Island Basin). **Facilities:** Visitor center with interpretive exhibits (Malaquite, Park Rd. 22), orientation video, swim beach, boat launch ramp, nature trail. Book and map sale areas, gift shop. **Programs & Events:** Year-round programs available. Ranger-led campfire programs, beach walks, deck talks, and Junior Ranger programs (mostly Memorial Day–Labor Day). Sea-turtle hatchling releases (June and Aug.), Adopt-A-Beach Cleanup (Apr. and Sept.), Center for Marine Conservation Cleanup (Apr. and Sept.).

PLANNING YOUR VISIT

⚠ **Camping:** Campground: no hookups (no reservations). Private campgrounds available locally. 🏠 **Lodging:** Available locally; none at seashore. ✕ **Food & Supplies:** In the park: store at Malaquite visitor center. Food and supplies also available locally. ☞ **Tips & Hints:** Go in spring for wildflowers, spring and fall for neotropical migratory birds. Go to Bird Island Basin in spring for windsurfing. Go between May and August to view nesting sea turtles. Go in winter to see winter waterfowl and fish for black drum and bull redfish. Watch for rattlesnakes. Busiest in July and August, least crowded in September and October. 🎫 **Fees, Permits & Limitations:** Entrance fee: $10 per vehicle. Bird Island day use fee: $5. Texas state fishing license and saltwater stamp required. No hunting, loaded firearms, large boat launching into gulf, vehicles in dunes. Leashed pets only. Park open daily. Visitor center open Labor Day–Memorial Day, daily 8:30–4:30; Memorial Day–Labor Day, daily 8:30–6. Closed Dec. 25, Jan. 1.

HOW TO GET THERE

On North Padre Island, 10 mi/16 km southeast of Corpus Christi via South Padre Island Dr., which turns into Park Rd. 22. Closest airport: Corpus Christi.

FOR MORE INFORMATION

National Park Service, Padre Island National Seashore (Box 181300, Corpus Christi, TX 78480, tel. 361/949–8068, fax 361/949–9951; Web site www.nps.gov/pais). Corpus Christi Chamber of Commerce (1201 N. Shoreline, Corpus Christi, TX 78401, tel. 800/766–2322).

Palo Alto Battlefield National Historic Site

In the southern part of the state, near Brownsville

On May 8, 1846, the Battle of Palo Alto took place—the first major battle of the Mexican-American War (1846–48). General Zachary Taylor's 2,300-man U.S. Army of Occupation used its superior cannon and innovative artillery methods to outduel General Mariano Arista's 3,600-man force. At war's end, Mexico ceded claims to what is now Texas, New Mexico, Arizona, Utah, Nevada, and California to the United States. The site was authorized in 1978 and dedicated in 1993.

WHAT TO SEE & DO

Viewing exhibits, watching video. **Facilities:** Interim visitor contact area with exhibits (1623 Central Blvd., Brownsville), walking trail with wayside exhibits. Book sales area. **Programs & Events:** Under development.

PLANNING YOUR VISIT

⚠ **Camping:** Available in Brownsville, Harlingen, McAllen, Mercedes, Port Isabel, San Benito, South Padre Island, Weslaco; none at site. 🏨 **Lodging:** Available in Brownsville, Harlingen, and South Padre Island, TX, and Matamoros, Mexico; none at site. ✗ **Food & Supplies:** Available in Brownsville, Harlingen, Los Fresnos, Port Isabel, San Benito, South Padre Island; none at site. ☞ **Tips & Hints:** An expanded trail is under construction. ▤ **Fees, Permits & Limitations:** Free. Visitor contact area open weekdays 8–4:30. New contact station at entrance to park will open in early 2001, open daily, 8–5. Closed federal holidays.

HOW TO GET THERE

In Brownsville on FM 1847, .2 mi/.3 km north of the intersection with FM 511. Interim visitor center is at 1623 Central Blvd, Brownsville. Closest airport: Brownsville.

FOR MORE INFORMATION

Palo Alto Battlefield National Historic Site (1623 Central Blvd., Suite 213, Brownsville, TX 78520, tel. 956/541–2785, fax 956/541–6356; e-mail paal_interpretation@nps.gov; Web site www.nps.gov/paal). Brownsville Convention and Visitors Bureau (Box 4697, Brownsville TX 78523, tel. 956/546–3721, fax 956/546–3972).

Rio Grande Wild and Scenic River

In the south, along the Rio Grande

This remote, undeveloped 191-mi/306-km strip on the American shore of the Rio Grande in the Chihuahuan Desert protects the river. It begins in Big Bend National Park and continues downstream to the Terrell–Val Verde county line. There are no Park Service facilities outside of Big Bend National Park (*see separate entry*). The wild and scenic river was authorized on November 10, 1978.

WHAT TO SEE & DO

See entry for Big Bend National Park.

PLANNING YOUR VISIT

☞ **Tips & Hints:** Busiest in March and April, least crowded in January and February.

FOR MORE INFORMATION

Rio Grande Wild and Scenic River (c/o Big Bend National Park, Box 129, Big Bend National Park, TX 79834, tel. 915/477–2251; Web site www.nps.gov/rigr).

San Antonio Missions National Historical Park

In the south-central part of the state, in San Antonio

Preserved here are four 18th-century Spanish missions—Concepcion, San Jose, San Juan, and Espada—that were built along the San Antonio River to introduce Coahuiltecan Native Americans to Spanish society and Catholicism. These missions, along with their presidio and settlement, were the foundation of the city of San Antonio. The missions still serve as active parishes and represent a virtually unbroken link with the past. The park was authorized in 1978 and established in 1983.

WHAT TO SEE & DO

Picnicking, touring missions, viewing museum exhibits, watching film. **Facilities:** Visitor center with interpretive exhibits (San Jose), 3 park contact stations (Concepcion, San Juan, Espada), trail. Picnic tables, sales outlets. **Programs & Events:** Ranger-guided walks and talks (year-round, daily), ranger-guided walk of Rancho de Las Cabras (year-round, first Sat. of each month).

PLANNING YOUR VISIT

⚠ **Camping:** Available in San Antonio; none in park. ▦ **Lodging:** Available in San Antonio; none in park. ✕ **Food & Supplies:** Available in San Antonio; none in park. ☞ **Tips & Hints:** Prepare for summer heat. Watch for fire ants. Busiest in July and October, least crowded in January and February. ▦ **Fees, Permits & Limitations:** Free. No hunting. Leashed pets only. No bicycles in mission compounds. No motorized equipment on trails. Park and visitor center open daily 9–5. Closed Thanksgiving, Dec. 25, Jan. 1.

HOW TO GET THERE

From I–37, exit on West Southcross, then turn left on Roosevelt to Mission San Jose. From I–10, exit on Probandt and follow Park Service signs to Concepcion. Closest airport: San Antonio International (15 mi/24 km).

FOR MORE INFORMATION

San Antonio Missions National Historical Park (2202 Roosevelt Ave., San Antonio, TX 78210-4919, tel. 210/534–8833, fax 210/534–1106; Web site www.nps.gov/saan). South San Antonio Chamber of Commerce (908 McCreless Mall, San Antonio, TX 78223, tel. 210/533–5867, fax 210/532–7788). Greater San Antonio Visitor Information Center (317 Alamo Plaza, San Antonio, TX 78205, tel. 210/270–8748 or 800/447–3372, fax 210/207–6842).

UTAH

Arches National Park

In the east-central part of the state, near Moab

The 76,519-acre park contains one of the largest concentrations of natural sandstone arches in the world. The arches and numerous other extraordinary geologic features, including spires, pinnacles, pedestals, and balanced rocks, are highlighted in striking foreground and background views created by contrasting colors, land forms, and textures. The site was proclaimed a national monument in 1929 and redesignated in 1971.

WHAT TO SEE & DO

Auto touring, biking, hiking, picnicking. **Facilities:** Visitor center with interpretive exhibits, scenic road, overlooks, trails. Book and map sale area, picnic areas. **Programs & Events:** Ranger-led walks, guided hikes, evening campfire programs (mid-Mar.–Oct.). Easter Sunrise Service.

PLANNING YOUR VISIT

⚠ **Camping:** Campground: preregistration required. Group campsites available (reservations available, tel. 435/259–4351). Camping also available in Moab and vicinity. ⛏ **Lodging:** Available in Moab; none in park. ✕ **Food & Supplies:** Available in Moab; none in park. ☞ **Tips & Hints:** Plan on a half-day visit for basic road tour and stops at overlooks. Conditions are hot and dry in summer. Carry drinking water. Go early in day to register for campsite. Register up to seven days ahead for popular Fiery Furnace guided hike. Hikes fill up quickly. Busiest in July and August, least crowded in December and January. ▣ **Fees, Permits & Limitations:** Entrance fee: $10 per vehicle. Fees also charged for Fiery Furnace permits and guided walks. Walks are limited to 25 people each and usually fill a day ahead. Concessioner offers four-wheel drive tours. Park open daily. Visitor center open Nov.–Mar., daily 8–4:30; Apr.–Oct., extended hours daily. Closed Dec. 25.

HOW TO GET THERE

5 mi/8 km north of Moab on UT 191. Closest airports: Canyonlands (15 mi/24 km) and Salt Lake City (250 mi/400 km), UT; Grand Junction, CO (120 mi/192 km).

FOR MORE INFORMATION

Arches National Park (Box 907, Moab, UT 84532, tel. 435/719–2299, fax 435/719–2305; Web site www.nps.gov/arch). Grand County Travel Council (Box 550, Moab, UT 84532 or 40 N. 100 E, Moab, UT 84532, tel. 800/635–6622).

Bryce Canyon National Park

In the south-central part of the state, near Tropic

The park is named for one of a series of horseshoe-shape amphitheaters carved from the eastern edge of the Paunsaugunt Plateau. Erosion has shaped colorful Claron limestones, sandstones, and mudstones into thousands of spires, fins, pinnacles, and mazes. These unique formations, called "hoodoos," are whimsically arranged and tinted with many colors. Ponderosa pines, high-elevation meadows, and spruce-fir forests border the rim of the plateau, and panoramic views of three states spread beyond the park's boundaries. The park was proclaimed a national monument on June 8, 1923; provisionally authorized as Utah National Park on June 7, 1924; renamed on February 25, 1928; and established in September 1928.

WHAT TO SEE & DO

Camping, cross-country skiing (rentals, Ruby's Inn), guided trail rides (tel. 435/679–8665), hiking, picnicking, snowshoeing, stargazing, van touring. **Facilities:** Visitor center with interpretive exhibits, amphitheater, slide program, overlooks, trails, picnic areas. Gift shop, publication sales. **Programs & Events:** Hikes, walks, geology talks, evening slide programs, night sky programs, star parties, moonlight walks (all late May–Sept.).

PLANNING YOUR VISIT

⚠ **Camping:** 2 campgrounds: no hookups. Backcountry camping available (permit required, *see below*). Group camping available (reservations required, tel. 435/834–4801). Private campgrounds nearby in Hatch, Panguitch, Tropic. 🏨 **Lodging:** In the park: Bryce Canyon Lodge (Apr.–Oct., tel. 303/297–2757). Lodging also available outside the park at Cannonville, Hatch, Henrieville, Panguitch, Ruby's Inn, Tropic. ✕ **Food & Supplies:** In the park: meals at Bryce Canyon Lodge (Apr.–Oct, tel. 435/834–5361). Food and supplies available at Sunrise Point General Store (Apr.–Oct.) in the park and outside the park in Cannonville, Hatch, Henrieville, Panguitch, Ruby's Inn, Tropic. ☞ **Tips & Hints:** Use caution if unaccustomed to altitude. Busiest in August and September, least crowded in January and February. 🔲 **Fees, Permits & Limitations:** Entrance fee: $20 per vehicle. Camping permits $10, backcountry permits required ($5; visitor center), group camping permits ($30 per season) required. Shuttle bus service (free) available along roads in park. No bikes on trails. No trailers beyond Sunset Campground. No hunting. No pets on trails, leashed pets only otherwise. Park open daily. Visitor center open May–Sept., daily 8–8; Oct.–Apr., daily 8–4:30. Closed Thanksgiving, Dec. 25.

HOW TO GET THERE

From north or south on U.S. 89, turn east on Rte. 12 (7 mi/11 km south of Panguitch, Utah). Turn south on Rte. 63 and travel 3 mi/5 km to reach the park entrance. From the east, travel west on Rte. 12. Turn south on Rte. 63 to reach the park entrance. Closest airport: Bryce Canyon Airport.

FOR MORE INFORMATION

Bryce Canyon National Park (Box 170001, Bryce Canyon, UT 84717-0001, tel. 435/834–5322, fax 435/834–4102; e-mail brca_interpretation@ nps.gov; Web site www.nps.gov/brca). Garfield County Travel Council (Box 200, Panguitch, UT 84759, tel. 800/444–6689).

Canyonlands National Park

In the east-central part of the state, near Moab

Located at the intersection of the Green River and the Colorado River, this park preserves 527 square mi (848 square km) of colorful canyons, mesas, buttes, fins, arches, and spires. Prehistoric American Indian rock art and ruins dot the red-rock landscape. The mighty river canyons divide the park into three districts, each offering spectacular sightseeing and exploration opportunities. The park was established on September 12, 1964.

WHAT TO SEE & DO

Four-wheel-drive touring, hiking, mountain biking, river running, rock climbing. **Facilities:** 2 visitor centers with interpretive exhibits—Island in the Sky (Hwy. 313 off U.S. 191) and Needles (Hwy. 211 off U.S. 191); information center (Maze, Hans Flat Ranger Station, dirt road off Hwy. 24), trails, backcountry roads. Bookstores. **Programs & Events:** Year-round Junior Ranger program (ages 6–12). Evening programs, overlook talks and other programs (Mar.–Sept.)

PLANNING YOUR VISIT

⚠️ **Camping:** 2 campgrounds (no reservations). Backcountry camping available (permit required, reservation recommended, *see below*). Group campsites available (reservation recommended, tel. 435/259–4351). Camping also available locally. 🛏 **Lodging:** Available in Green River, Moab, Monticello; none in park. ✗ **Food & Supplies:** Available in Green River, Moab, Monticello; none in park. ☞ **Tips & Hints:** Canyonlands is primarily a backcountry destination. Plan on very hot summers, cold winters, and pleasant temperatures in between. Busiest in April and October, least crowded in December and January. 🏷 **Fees, Permits & Limitations:** Entrance fee (Mar.–Oct.): $10 per vehicle, $5 per person, free rest of the year. Permit required (fee varies) and reservations recommended for backcountry camping (tel. 435/259–4351). No pets on trails or in backcountry, even in vehicles. No ATVs. No mountain bikes on hiking trails or off designated roads. Park open daily. Visitor center hours: Needles District: Mar.–May, daily 8–6; June–Oct., daily 8–5; Nov.–Feb., daily 8–4:30; Island in the Sky District—Mar.–Oct., daily 8–6; Nov.–Feb., daily 8–4:30. Closed on some federal holidays.

HOW TO GET THERE

Canyonlands is divided into three districts that are two to six hours apart by car. To reach Needles District from Moab, take U.S. 191S and UT 211W. To reach Island in the Sky District from Moab, take U.S. 191N and UT 313W. To reach the Maze District from Moab, take U.S. 191N to I–70W. Take Exit 147 off I–70 to UT 24S, and then a graded dirt road east to the Hans Flat Ranger Station. Closest airports: Canyonlands (18 mi/29 km) and Salt Lake City, UT; Grand Junction, CO.

FOR MORE INFORMATION

Canyonlands National Park (2282 S.W. Resource Blvd., Moab, UT 84532, tel. 435/719–2313; Web site www.nps.gov/cany). San Juan Visitor's Center (117 S. Main St., or Box 490, Monticello, UT 84535, tel. 800/574–4386).

Capitol Reef National Park

In the south-central part of the state, near Torrey

The park's Waterpocket Fold, a giant, sinuous wrinkle in the Earth's crust created 65 million years ago, stretches for 100 mi/160 km with colorful cliffs, massive domes, soaring spires, and stark monoliths. The park also protects a section of the free-flowing Fremont River, the site of the prehistoric Fremont culture, remains of a Mormon pioneer settlement, and orchards of Fruita. The site was proclaimed a national monument in 1937 and redesignated in 1971.

WHAT TO SEE & DO

Bicycling (rentals), fishing, hiking, horseback riding (rentals), Jeep touring (rentals), picking fruit (in season), picnicking. **Facilities:** Visitor center with interpretive exhibits, pioneer buildings and homes, trails, wayside panels, amphitheater, remains of uranium mine. Bookstore, sales outlet. **Programs & Events:** Geology talks, ranger presentations, evening programs (June–Sept., daily as staffing allows).

PLANNING YOUR VISIT

⚠ **Camping:** 3 campgrounds: 1 with dump station (closed; to re-open in 2001), 2 primitive (no reservations). Backcountry camping available (permit required, *see below*). Group campsites at Fruita (reservations required, tel. 435/425–3791). Private campgrounds in Bicknell, Boulder, Caineville, Hanksville, Loa, Teasdale, Torrey. 🛏 **Lodging:** Available in Bicknell, Boulder, Caineville, Hanksville, Loa, Teasdale, Torrey; none in park. ✘ **Food & Supplies:** In the park: pioneer-style snacks. Food and supplies also available in Bicknell, Boulder, Caineville, Hanksville, Loa, Teasdale, Torrey. ☞ **Tips & Hints:** Go in spring or fall for best hiking weather and wildflowers, summer and fall for fruit harvest. Watch for thunderstorms and flash floods July–September. Busiest in July and September, least crowded in December and January. 🎫 **Fees, Permits & Limitations:** Entrance fee: $4 for Scenic Drive. Backcountry permits (free) required for all backcountry camping. Utah state fishing license required. No hunting. No pets on trails, in buildings, or off roads; leashed pets elsewhere. Carry water on hikes. No rock, plant, animal, or artifact collecting. No mountain bikes off roads. Park open daily. Visitor center open Labor Day–Memorial Day, daily 8–4:30; Memorial Day–Labor Day, daily 8–6. Closed Dec. 25.

HOW TO GET THERE

37 mi/59 km west of Hanksville and 10 mi/16 km east on Torrey on Hwy. 24. Closest airports: Hanksville, Bicknell (18 mi/29 km), Salt Lake City (195 mi/312 km), UT; Grand Junction, CO (180 mi/288 km).

FOR MORE INFORMATION

Capitol Reef National Park (HC 70, Box 15, Torrey, UT 84775, tel. 435/425–3791, fax 435/425–3026; e-mail CARE_interpretation@nps.gov; Web site www.nps.gov/care). Wayne County Travel Council (Box 7, Teasdale, UT 84773, tel. 435/425–3365 or 800/858–7951; e-mail info@capitolreef.org; Web site www.capitolreef.org).

Cedar Breaks National Monument

In the southwest part of the state, near Cedar City

The monument preserves a large, multicolored geologic amphitheater that is 2,500 ft/758 m deep and 3 mi/5 km across. The rim of the amphitheater sits at 10,500 ft/3,185 m above sea level and is lined with forests of spruce and fir and subalpine meadows full of wildflowers that are brilliant with color in the summer. The monument was proclaimed on August 22, 1933.

WHAT TO SEE & DO

Camping, car touring, cross-country skiing, hiking, picnicking, snowmobiling, snowshoeing. **Facilities:** Visitor center with interpretive exhibits (Cedar Breaks Visitor Center at Point Supreme Overlook), amphitheater (Point Supreme Campground), 6-mi/10-km scenic drive, scenic overlooks, trails. Book sale area, fire grates, picnic tables. **Programs & Events:** Interpretive programs (Memorial Day–Columbus Day, daily 10–5, hourly), evening campfire programs (June 15–Sept. 1, nightly 9 PM), guided hikes (June 15–Sept. 1, weekends 10 AM).

PLANNING YOUR VISIT

⚠ **Camping:** Campground: no hookups. Private campgrounds available in Cedar City, Panguitch Lake. ⊞ **Lodging:** Available in Brian Head, Cedar City, Duck Creek, Panguitch, Parowan; none at monument. ✗ **Food & Supplies:** Available in Brian Head, Cedar City, Duck Creek, Panguitch, Parowan; none at monument. ☞ **Tips & Hints:** Come prepared for cool weather and high elevation (summertime high: 60°F/15°C, rim elevation: 10,000 ft/3,033 m). Visit in late June–late September. Busiest in July and August, least crowded in January and February. ▤ **Fees, Permits & Limitations:** Entrance fee: $5 per vehicle or $3 per person. Utah state fishing license required. No hunting. Leashed pets only on roadsides, paved walkways, campground. No mountain bikes on trails. No motorized vehicles off paved roads. Park open daily. Visitor center open Memorial Day–Columbus Day, daily 8–6. Scenic drive open mid-May–mid-Nov. Park may be closed by snow in winter (mid-Nov.–mid-May).

HOW TO GET THERE

Cedar Breaks National Monument is located along State Rd. 148, between State Rds. 143 and 14. The visitor center is 23 mi/37 km from Cedar City via State Rds. 148 and 14, 8 mi/13 km from Brian Head via State Rds. 148 and 143, and 25 mi/40 km from Parowan via State Rds. 148 and 143. Closest airport: Cedar City.

FOR MORE INFORMATION

Cedar Breaks National Monument (2390 W. Hwy. 56, Suite 11, Cedar City, UT 84720, tel. 435/586–9451, fax 435/586–3813; Web site www.nps.gov/cebr). Cedar City Chamber of Commerce (581 N. Main St., Cedar City, UT 84720, tel. 435/586–4484).

Golden Spike
National Historic Site

In the northwest part of the state, in Promontory

The site commemorates the completion of the first transcontinental railroad on May 10, 1869, at Promontory Summit. On that day, a golden spike was symbolically tapped into a polished laurel-wood tie and then a final iron spike was driven to complete the railroad, thus linking East and West for the first time. The site was established in 1965.

WHAT TO SEE & DO

Auto touring, hiking, viewing golden spike reenactment ceremony and last spike site. **Facilities:** Visitor center with interpretive exhibits, 1869 steam locomotive replica, museum, auto tours. Bookstore. **Programs & Events:** Ranger talks (Memorial Day–Labor Day, daily; Labor Day–Memorial Day, weekends). Engine house tours (Columbus Day–Apr.) golden spike reenactment (mid-May–Columbus Day, Sat.). Golden Spike Anniversary Celebration (May 10), Railroader's Festival (2nd Sat., Aug.), Winter Film Festival and Steam Demonstration (last weekend, Dec.).

PLANNING YOUR VISIT

⚠ **Camping:** Available in Brigham City; none at site. ☷ **Lodging:** Available in Brigham City, Ogden, Tremonton; none at site. ✕ **Food & Supplies:** In the park: snacks from vending machines. Food and supplies also available outside the park in Brigham City, Tremonton. ☞ **Tips & Hints:** Plan to spend two–three hours. Go anytime to see locomotives, but go from May–early October to see them operate. Steam locomotive runs May–Columbus Day, daily 9:30–4; Memorial Day–Labor Day, daily 10:30–5. Busiest in May and July through August, least crowded in December and January. ▦ **Fees, Permits & Limitations:** Entrance fee: May–Columbus Day, $3.50 per adult or $7 per vehicle; rest of the year, $2 per person or $4 per vehicle. No hunting. Leashed pets only. No mechanized recreational vehicles on trails. Park and visitor center open Labor Day–Memorial Day, daily 8–4:30; Memorial Day–Labor Day, daily 8–6. Closed Thanksgiving, Dec. 25, Jan. 1.

HOW TO GET THERE

In Promontory, 32 mi/51 km west of Brigham City via UT 13 and 83. Closest airport: Salt Lake City (95 mi/152 km).

FOR MORE INFORMATION

Golden Spike National Historic Site (Box 897, Brigham City, UT 84302, tel. 435/471–2209, fax 435/471–2341; Web site www.nps.gov/gosp). Brigham City Chamber of Commerce (06 N. Main St., Brigham City, UT 84302, tel. 435/723–3931). Bear River Chamber of Commerce (718 E. Main St., Tremonton, UT 84337, tel. 435/257–5968). Box Elder County Economic Development, Tourism Council (102 W. Forest St., Brigham City, UT 84302, tel. 435/734–2634).

Natural Bridges
National Monument

In the southeast part of the state, near Blanding

Owachomo Bridge, Sipapu Bridge, and Kachina Bridge depict the three phases in a natural bridge's history, as running water forms and then ultimately destroys these perforated rock walls. Utah's first national monument also offers outstanding examples of geological and erosional processes and preserves numerous ancestral Puebloan archaeological sites. The site was proclaimed on April 16, 1908.

WHAT TO SEE & DO

Auto and bike touring, hiking. **Facilities:** Visitor center with interpretive exhibits (Hwy. 275, off UT 95), 9-mi/14-km drive, solar photovoltaic array, trails, overlooks. Book and map sales area. **Programs & Events:** Guided walks and campfire programs (May–mid-Oct.).

PLANNING YOUR VISIT

⚠ **Camping:** Campground: 26-ft/8-m combined-length vehicle limit (no reservations). No backcountry or group camping. Private campgrounds available in Blanding, Hanksville, Lake Powell, Mexican Hat, Moab, Monticello, Monument Valley. 🏠 **Lodging:** Available in Blanding, Fry Canyon, Mexican Hat; none at monument. ✗ **Food & Supplies:** Available in Blanding, Fry Canyon, Mexican Hat; none at monument. ☞ **Tips & Hints:** Get drinking water at visitor center and carry plenty of water on hikes. Watch for flash floods and severe lightning between July and September. Avoid midget prairie rattlesnakes. Respect cultural sites. Visit between late April and October. Busiest in May and September, least crowded in December and January. 🎟 **Fees, Permits & Limitations:** Entrance fee: $6 per vehicle or $3 per person traveling by bicycle or motorcycle. No climbing on bridges. No pets on trails or in canyons. Leashed pets elsewhere. Bikes on paved roads only. No hunting or gathering of flora or fauna. Bridge View Dr. open daily 7–1 hour before sunset. Visitor center open Mar.–Apr. and Oct., daily 8–5; May–Sept., daily 8–6; Nov.–Feb., daily 8–4:30. Closed Thanksgiving, Dec. 25, Jan. 1.

HOW TO GET THERE

The visitor center is 38.5 mi/62 km west of Blanding via UT 95 and Hwy. 275; 44 mi/70 km north of Mexican Hat via Rte. 261; and 50 mi/80 km east of Hite Marina on Lake Powell via UT 95. Closest airports: Salt Lake City (353 mi/565 km), UT; Cortez (120 mi/192 km) and Denver (480 mi/768 km), CO; Phoenix, AZ (389 mi/622 km).

FOR MORE INFORMATION

Natural Bridges National Monument (HC 60 Box 1, Lake Powell, UT 84533, tel. 435/692–1234, fax 435/692–1111; Web site www.nps.gov/nabr). Blanding Chamber of Commerce (50 W. 100 St., Blanding, UT 84511, tel. 435/678–2539). Monticello Chamber of Commerce (Box 490, Monticello, UT 84535, tel. 435/587–2992).

Rainbow Bridge
National Monument

In south-central Utah, near Lake Powell

Rainbow Bridge is the world's largest natural bridge. The 275-ft-/83-m-wide, 290-ft-/88-m-tall bridge has inspired people throughout time—from the neighboring Native American tribes, who consider Rainbow Bridge sacred, to the 300,000 people from around the world who visit it each year. The monument was proclaimed on May 30, 1910.

WHAT TO SEE & DO

Boating (rentals), boat touring, hiking. **Facilities:** Ranger station with bulletin board (Dangling Rope Marina, 10 mi/16 km from bridge), outdoor exhibits, 0.5-mi/0.8-km trail. **Programs & Events:** Boat tours (May–Sept., daily; Oct.–Apr., intermittently). Ranger-led natural- and cultural-history programs (mostly Memorial Day–Sept.). Special events available.

PLANNING YOUR VISIT

⚠ **Camping:** Lakeshore camping from boats available in Glen Canyon National Recreation Area (*see separate entry*); none at monument. 🏕 **Lodging:** Available in some marinas at Glen Canyon National Recreation Area (*see separate entry*); none at monument. ✗ **Food & Supplies:** Boat gas, limited groceries, and water at Dangling Rope Marina (10 mi/16 km from Rainbow Bridge on Lake Powell); none at monument. ☞ **Tips & Hints:** Plan on at least a four-hour round trip to travel by boat to bridge (six hours from Hite). Wear lightweight, light-color clothing and a hat in summer, layers of clothing rest of year. Be prepared for summer temperatures up to 110°F/44°C with little, if any, shade; winter temperatures to 0°F/-18°C; and windy springs. Respect the religious significance of Rainbow Bridge to neighboring tribes. Consider viewing Rainbow Bridge from the viewing area rather than walking up to or under the bridge. Busiest in June and September, least crowded in January and February. 🎟 **Fees, Permits & Limitations:** Free. Fee is charged at Glen Canyon National Recreation Area (*see separate entry*).

ARAMARK (tel. 800/528–6154) provides boat tours to Rainbow Bridge May–Sept., daily, and intermittently rest of year. Half-day and full-day tours available at Wahweap. Full-day tours only available from Bullfrog and Halls Crossing. Hiking permit required (tel. 520/871–6647 or 520/698–2808) from Navajo Nation to backpack around Navajo Mountain to Rainbow Bridge. No water-based recreation activities (swimming, fishing, waterskiing, and so forth) allowed within monument. Ranger station at Dangling Rope Marina staffed intermittently year-round.

HOW TO GET THERE

The bridge is in San Juan County, UT, immediately adjacent to Navajo Mountain and the Navajo Reservation. Public access is by boat across Lake Powell. Trips to the bridge may be made in private, rental, or tour boats. Courtesy dock available for short-term docking while people make the 0.5-mi/0.8-km walk to the bridge. By boat, it is 50 mi/80 km from Wahweap, Bullfrog, or Halls Crossing to Rainbow Bridge. Closest airport: Page, AZ (7 mi/11 km from Wahweap Marina).

FOR MORE INFORMATION

Rainbow Bridge National Monument (Box 1507, Page, AZ 86040, tel. 520/608–6404; Web site www.nps.gov/rabr). Glen Canyon National Recreation Area (Box 1507, Page, AZ 86040, tel. 520/608–6404; Web site www.nps.gov/glca).

Timpanogos Cave National Monument

In the north-central part of the state, near American Fork

Hansen Cave, Middle Cave, and Timpanogos Cave, three small but wonderfully decorated limestone caves, are the attractions at this monument. These exquisitely beautiful caverns are decorated with a dazzling display of helictites and anthodites in a variety of fantastic shapes. The monument was proclaimed in 1922 and transferred to the Park Service in 1933.

WHAT TO SEE & DO

Fishing, hiking, picnicking, touring caves, watching video. **Facilities:** Visitor center with interpretive exhibits, video of cave tour, ¼-mi/½-km nature trail. Bookstore, fire grills, gift shop, picnic area. **Programs & Events:** Cave tours (mid-May–Oct., daily), weekend evening programs.

PLANNING YOUR VISIT

Camping: Available in surrounding Uinta National Forest, Lehi, Provo; none at monument. **Lodging:** Available in American Fork, Lehi, Orem, Provo, Salt Lake City; none at monument. **Food & Supplies:** In the park: snack bar (tel. 801/756–5702). Food and supplies also available in American Fork, Lehi, Orem, Pleasant Grove, Provo, and Salt Lake City. **Tips & Hints:** Buy cave tour tickets in advance or arrive early in the day. Ticket reservations can be made with a credit card (tel. 801/756–1679 or 801/756–5238). Bring a jacket or sweater. Cave temperature is 45°F/7°C. Bring water on three-hour cave hike. The 1.5-mi/2.4-km trail rises 1,065 ft/323 m. Visit early in the morning or on weekdays. Busiest in July and August, least crowded in December and January. ▨ **Fees, Permits & Limitations:** Entrance fee: $3 per vehicle. Cave tour tickets: $6 adults 16 and older, $5 children 6–15, $3 children 3–5, free 2 and under, $3 senior citizens 62 and older with Golden Age Passport. Utah state fishing license required. No cave tours in winter. No pets, strollers, or other wheeled vehicles on cave trail. Tours run 8:30–6:30. Picnic areas open dawn–dusk. Visitor center open May–Sept., daily 7–5:30; Sept.–Oct., daily 8–5.

HOW TO GET THERE

24 mi/38 km south of Salt Lake City via Exit 287 (Alpine Highland) off I–15. Turn east on Hwy. 92 for 10 mi/16 km to monument. Closest airport: Salt Lake City.

FOR MORE INFORMATION

Timpanogos Cave National Monument (RR 3, Box 200, American Fork, UT 84003, tel. 801/756–5238, fax 801/756–5661; Web site www.nps.gov/tica). Uinta National Forest (88 W. 100 N, Provo, UT 84601, tel. 801/377–5780). Utah Tourism and Recreation Information Center (300 N. State, Salt Lake City, UT 84114, tel. 801/538–1030 or 800/200–1160). Provo/Orem Chamber of Commerce (51 S. University Ave., Suite 215, Provo, UT 84601, tel. 801/379–2555). Utah County Visitors Center (51 S. University Ave., Suite 111, Provo, UT 84601, tel. 801/370–8393).

Zion National Park

In the southwest part of the state, near Springdale

Protected within Zion's 229 square mi/593 square km are a spectacular landscape of cliffs and canyons and a wilderness full of the unexpected. Colorful canyon and mesa scenery includes erosion and rock-fault patterns that create phenomenal shapes and landscapes. The park is home to Kolob Arch, the world's largest arch, with a span that measures 310 ft/94 m. Mule deer, golden eagles, and mountain lions also call Zion home. Mukuntuweap National Monument was proclaimed in 1909 and established as Zion National Park in 1919.

WHAT TO SEE & DO

Auto touring, biking, bird- and wildlife watching, hiking, horseback riding, picnicking, wading. **Facilities:** 2 visitor centers with interpretive exhibits—Kolob Canyons (off I–15) and Zion Canyon (east of Springdale off Hwy. 9); nature center, trails. Fire grates, picnic sites and tables, religious services (May–Sept.). **Programs & Events:** Guided walks, evening programs, talks, and horseback rides (late Mar.–early Nov.); Nature Center for kids (Memorial Day–Labor Day).

PLANNING YOUR VISIT

⚲ **Camping:** 3 campgrounds: dump stations, hookups (reservations available, tel. 800/365–2267). Backcountry camping available (permit required, *see below*). Group campsites available (reservations required, tel. 800/365–2267). Private campgrounds in Springdale and surrounding towns. ⊞ **Lodging:** In the park: Zion Lodge (tel. 303/297–2757). Lodging also available in Cedar City, Hurricane, Kanab, Mt. Carmel, Springdale, St. George. ✕ **Food & Supplies:** In the park: meals at Zion Lodge. Food and supplies also available in Springdale. ☞ **Tips & Hints:** Don't hike alone. Stay on trails and stay out of drainage areas during thunderstorms. Watch for rockfalls and landslides. Shuttle system (Apr.–Oct., free) operates along the 6 mi/10 km Zion Scenic Drive; access to this part of the park by shuttle only. All other park roads are open to private vehicles. Parking lot at visitor center is often full 10–3: park in Springdale and ride the town loop bus to the park. Busiest in July and August, least crowded in December and January. ▨ **Fees, Permits & Limitations:** Entrance fee: $20 per vehicle or $10 per walk-in, bicyclist, or motorcyclist with $20 maximum per family. No vehicles over 11 ft, 4 inches/3.4 m in Zion–Mt. Carmel Highway Tunnel. Permit required for hikes through Virgin River Narrows. Backcountry permits required ($5 per permit).

HOW TO GET THERE

The Kolob Canyons visitor center can be reached via Exit 40 off I–15. The Zion Canyon visitor center is east of Springdale off Hwy. 9. Closest airport: St. George (46 mi/74 km).

FOR MORE INFORMATION

Superintendent, Zion National Park (Springdale, UT 84767-1099, tel. 435/772–3256; Web site www.nps.gov/zion).

See Also

California National Historic Trail, National Trails System in Other National Parklands. *Dinosaur National Monument,* Colorado. *Glen Canyon National Recreation Area,* Arizona. *Hovenweep National Monument,* Colorado. *Mormon Pioneer National Historic Trail,* National Trails System in Other National Parklands. *Oregon National Historic Trail,* National Trails System in Other National Parklands. *Pony Express National Historic Trail,* National Trails System in Other National Parklands.

VERMONT

Marsh-Billings-Rockefeller National Historical Park

In the east-central part of the state, in Woodstock

The park, the first in the system to focus on conservation history, protects the home of some of America's most distinguished conservationists. George Perkins Marsh, who grew up here, wrote *Man and Nature,* which was published in 1864. Frederick Billings created a progressive dairy farm and forest on the estate here in the late 1800s. His granddaughter, Mary French Rockefeller and her husband Laurance, who have made enormous contributions to the national parks, lived here and recently donated the site to the National Park Service. The park contains one of the oldest professionally managed woodlands in the United States, and the mansion includes hundreds of artworks from influential 19th-century landscape painters. The site, which opened to the public in June 1998, is managed as a partnership between the National Park Service and the Woodstock Foundation, which operates the Billings Farm and Museum located on private land within the park. The adjoining museum manages the farm as both a historic site and a working dairy farm. The park was established on August 26, 1992.

WHAT TO SEE & DO

Touring mansion, grounds, farm, and museum. **Facilities:** Visitor center with interpretive exhibits (Billings Farm and Museum), mansion and grounds, 1890 farmhouse, museum, carriage roads, trails. **Programs & Events:** Guided tours of mansion, gardens, and grounds; conservation stewardship programs.

PLANNING YOUR VISIT

⛺ **Camping:** Available in Woodstock area; none in park. 🏨 **Lodging:** Available in Woodstock area; none in park. ✖ **Food & Supplies:** Available in Woodstock area; none in park. ☞ **Tips & Hints:** Expect to spend up to a full day at park. 🎟 **Fees, Permits & Limitations:** Free. Guided tour of Billings/Rockefeller Mansion and gardens: $6 adults, $3 children 5–15, $3 seniors 62 and older. Billings Farm and Museum fee: $8 adults, $7 senior citizens 65 and up, $6 students 13–17, $4 children 5–12, $1 children 3–4. Park open May–Oct., daily 10–4. Farm and museum open May–Oct., daily 10–5.

HOW TO GET THERE

Off Rte. 12 in Woodstock, next to the Billings Farm and Museum. Closest airports: Lebanon, NH (17 mi/27 km); Burlington, VT (85 mi/136 km).

FOR MORE INFORMATION

Marsh-Billings-Rockefeller National Historical Park (Box 178, Woodstock, VT 05091, tel. 802/457–3368, fax 802/457–3405; Web site www.nps.gov/mabi). Billings Farm and Museum (Box 489, Woodstock, VT 05091, tel. 802/457–2355, fax 802/457–4663). Tourist Information (Box 486, Woodstock, VT 05091, tel. 802/457–3555 or 888/496–6378).

See Also

Appalachian National Scenic Trail, West Virginia.

VIRGINIA

Appomattox Court House National Historical Park

In the south-central part of the state,
25 mi/40 km east of Lynchburg

General Robert E. Lee surrendered the Confederate Army of Northern Virginia to Lieutenant General Ulysses S. Grant at this historic village and battleground, bringing an end to the Civil War, which killed 365,000 Americans. The site was authorized as a national historic monument on August 13, 1935, and designated a national historic park on April 15, 1954.

WHAT TO SEE & DO

Touring historic village, walking tours of the battlefield. **Facilities:** Visitor center and museum in reconstructed courthouse building, furnished room exhibits throughout the historic village, wayside exhibits in battlefield areas. Bookstore. **Programs & Events:** Audiovisual programs every half hour in visitor center (year-round). Ranger-guided tours, living-history and other programs (Memorial Day–Labor Day).

PLANNING YOUR VISIT

⚠ **Camping:** Private campgrounds available nearby in Appomattox; none in park. 🛏 **Lodging:** Available nearby in Appomattox, Lynchburg; none in park. ✕ **Food & Supplies:** Available nearby in Appomattox, Lynchburg; none in park. ☞ **Tips & Hints:** Plan a two-hour stay to see the park. Spend another six hours driving the associated Lee's Retreat Route, which covers 100 mi/160 km and has 26 wayside stops with radio messages. Go in mid-April–mid-May and September–October. Busiest in June and July, least crowded in January and February. 🖃
Fees, Permits & Limitations: Entrance fee: $4 per person or $10 per car (Memorial Day–Labor Day), $2 per person or $5 per car (Labor Day–Memorial Day), under 17 free. No pets in buildings, leashed pets otherwise. No vehicles, bikes, or horses on trails or historic roads. Park and visitor center open Memorial Day–Labor Day, daily 9–5:30; Labor Day–Memorial Day, daily 8:30–5. Closed Thanksgiving, Dec. 25, Jan. 1.

HOW TO GET THERE

25 mi/40 km east of Lynchburg, VA; 2 mi/3 km north of Appomattox on Rte. 24. Closest airport: Lynchburg.

FOR MORE INFORMATION

Appomattox Court House National Historical Park (Box 218, Hwy. 24, Appomattox, VA 24522-0218, tel. 804/352–8987, fax 804/352–8330; Web site www.nps.gov/apco). Appomattox County Chamber of Commerce (Box 704, Appomattox, VA 24522, tel 804/352–2621).

Arlington House, the Robert E. Lee Memorial

In the northern part of the state, in Arlington

The house that Robert E. Lee lived in for 30 years today is a memorial to Lee, who gained the respect of northerners and southerners through his service in the Civil War. The antebellum home overlooks the Potomac River and Washington, DC. The memorial was authorized in 1925, transferred to the Park Service in 1933, designated the Custis-Lee Mansion in 1955, and renamed in 1972.

WHAT TO SEE & DO

Touring the house. **Facilities:** House and museum. **Programs & Events:** Self-guided tours (year-round). Guided tours (groups only by reservation, Sept.–May). Lee's Birthday (Jan.), Lee's wedding anniversary (June 30).

PLANNING YOUR VISIT

Lodging: Available in Washington, DC, area; none at memorial. **Food & Supplies:** Available in Washington, DC, area; none at memorial. **Tips & Hints:** Busiest in April and July, least crowded in January and February. **Fees, Permits & Limitations:** Free. Access by ticket only. Free tickets distributed at site beginning at 9:15. Arrive early to reserve tickets. Tickets are stamped with entry time. Ticket system in place Memorial Day to Labor Day only. Memorial open daily 9:30–4:30. Closed Dec. 25. Jan. 1.

HOW TO GET THERE

The memorial is accessible by shuttle bus or by a 10-minute walk from the Arlington National Cemetery Visitor Center/parking area. Access from Washington, DC, is via the Memorial Bridge. Access from Virginia is from the George Washington Memorial Pkwy. The memorial is also accessible by the blue line of the Metro subway system. Closest airport: Reagan Washington National.

FOR MORE INFORMATION

Arlington House, the Robert E. Lee Memorial (c/o National Park Service, George Washington Memorial Pkwy., Turkey Run Park, McLean, VA 22101, tel. 703/557–0613; Web site www.nps.gov/arho).

Booker T. Washington National Monument

In the southwest part of the state,
22 mi/35 km southeast of Roanoke

Booker T. Washington, educator, orator, and presidential advisor, was born into slavery, reared, and emancipated at this former plantation site. The park is one of the few places where visitors can see how slavery and the plantation system worked on a smaller scale. It provides a focal point for discussions about one of the most powerful African-Americans in history and the evolving context of race in American society. It was authorized on April 2, 1956.

WHAT TO SEE & DO

Attending interpretive tours, viewing exhibits and audiovisual programs, walking historic and nature trails. **Facilities:** Visitor center with interpretive exhibits (VA 122), wayside exhibits. Bookstore, picnic area. **Programs & Events:** Ranger-guided tours (year-round, daily). Living-history program and demonstrations (periodically). Christmas program and open house (1st weekend of Dec.).

PLANNING YOUR VISIT

⛺ **Camping:** Available nearby in Blue Ridge Parkway (*see separate entry*), Fairystone and Smith Mountain state parks; none at monument. 🏠 **Lodging:** Available nearby in Bedford, Roanoke, Rocky Mount; none at monument. ✗ **Food & Supplies:** Available nearby; none at monument. ☞ **Tips & Hints:** Busiest in July and August, least crowded in December and January. ▩ **Fees, Permits & Limitations:** Free. Group tours and education programs (reservations required, tel. 540/721–2094). No hunting or bike riding. Leashed pets only. Park open daily 9–5. Closed Thanksgiving, Dec. 25, Jan. 1.

HOW TO GET THERE

On VA 122, 16 mi/26 km northwest of Rocky Mount, 22 mi/35 km southeast of Roanoke via VA 116S and VA 122N, and 21 mi/34 km south of Bedford via VA 122S. Closest airport: Roanoke.

FOR MORE INFORMATION

Booker T. Washington National Monument (12130 Booker T. Washington Hwy., Hardy, VA 24101, tel. 540/721–2094, fax 540/721–8311; Web site www.nps.gov/bowa). Smith Mountain Lake Chamber of Commerce (16430 Booker T. Washington Hwy., #2, Moneta, VA 24121, tel. 800/676–8203).

Colonial National Historical Park

In the southeast part of the state, near Williamsburg

The park includes most of Jamestown Island, the site of the first permanent British settlement in North America; Yorktown, the site of the last major battle of the American Revolution; and the 23-mi-/37-km-long scenic Colonial Parkway that connects the two. Also included is the Cape Henry Memorial, which marks the approximate site of the first landing of Jamestown's colonists in 1607. The park was authorized as Colonial National Monument on July 3, 1930; proclaimed on December 30, 1930; and redesignated Colonial National Historical Park on June 5, 1936.

WHAT TO SEE & DO

Auto touring, biking, learning area history, walking. **Facilities:** 2 visitor centers with interpretive exhibits—Jamestown, Yorktown; wayside exhibits. At Jamestown: Glasshouse, Jamestown Archaeology Lab, Memorial Church. At Yorktown: Gov. Thomas Nelson House; Moore House, site of surrender negotiations; Surrender Field, interpretive pavilion at actual surrender site. Bookstore. **Programs & Events:** Ranger-guided tours. Living-history tours (Jamestown: Sept.–May, weekends; June–Aug., daily), historical drama (Nelson House: mid-June–mid-Aug., daily). Lamb's Artillery Firing Program (Yorktown: periodically Mar.–Sept.); Jamestown Weekend (mid-May); Memorial Day Weekend/Civil War Weekend (Yorktown: end of May); Independence Day Celebration (Yorktown: July 4); First Assembly Day Commemoration (Jamestown: late July); Yorktown Victory Celebration (Yorktown: Oct. 19).

PLANNING YOUR VISIT

⚠ **Camping:** Available near Jamestown, Newport News, Williamsburg; none in park. 🏨 **Lodging:** Available in Newport News, Williamsburg, Yorktown; none in park. ✕ **Food & Supplies:** Available in Jamestown, Newport News, Williamsburg, Yorktown; none in park. ☞ **Tips & Hints:** Allow two–three hours to visit each site. Go in winter to avoid crowds. Busiest in July and August, least crowded in January and February. 🖼 **Fees, Permits & Limitations:** Entrance fees: Jamestown, $5 adults 17 and over; Yorktown, $4 adults 17 and over; combination ticket, $7 adults 17 and over. Jamestown open daily 8:30–dusk. Jamestown Visitor Center open daily 9–4:30. Closed Dec. 25. Grounds open daily dawn–dusk, but last entry to site is at 4:30. Yorktown Visitor Center open Apr.–May and Aug.–Sept., daily 8:30–5; June–July, daily 8:30–5:30; Oct.–Mar., daily 9–5. Closed Dec. 25.

HOW TO GET THERE

Off I–64, near Williamsburg, with sections in Jamestown and Yorktown and a parkway connecting the two. Closest airports: Newport News/Williamsburg 11 mi/18 km, Richmond International (56 mi/90 km), Norfolk (37 mi/59 km).

FOR MORE INFORMATION

Colonial National Historical Park (Box 210, Yorktown, VA 23690, tel. 757/898–2410, fax 757/898–6346; Web site www.nps.gov/colo). Williamsburg Area Convention and Visitors Bureau (421 N. Boundary St., Williamsburg, VA 23187, tel. 757/253–0192, fax 757/229–2047).

Fredericksburg and Spotsylvania County Battlefields Memorial National Military Park

In the eastern part of the state, in Fredericksburg area

One hundred thousand men became Civil War casualties in the four major battles fought in the vicinity of Fredericksburg—Fredericksburg, Chancellorsville, Wilderness, and Spotsylvania Court House. The park also includes the historic structures of Chatham, Salem Church, and the "Stonewall" Jackson Shrine and encompasses 9,000 acres, making it the largest military park in the world. The Fredericksburg National Cemetery, with 15,333 interments, 12,746 unidentified, is within the park. The park was established in 1927 and transferred to the Park Service in 1933.

WHAT TO SEE & DO

Touring battlefields by car and on foot. **Facilities:** 2 visitor centers with interpretive exhibits—Fredericksburg, Chancellorsville; 2 exhibit centers (Wilderness, Spotsylvania Court House), Chatman, Salem Church, "Stonewall" Jackson Shrine, tour roads, trails. Bookstores. **Programs & Events:** Guided tours. National Cemetery Luminaria (Memorial Day weekend), Battle of Fredericksburg Commemoration Ceremony (Dec.).

PLANNING YOUR VISIT

⛺ **Camping:** Available in Fredericksburg area; none in park. 🏨 **Lodging:** Available in Fredericksburg area; none in park. ✕ **Food & Supplies:** Available in Fredericksburg area; none in park. ☞ **Tips & Hints:** Allow two days to tour all four battlefields. Busiest in June and July, least crowded in January and February. 🎫 **Fees, Permits & Limitations:** Entrance fee: $3 adults over 16, children under 16 free. Visitor centers open daily 9–5, extended hours in spring and summer. Park open daily. Closed Dec. 25, Jan. 1.

HOW TO GET THERE

Fredericksburg is 50 mi/80 km south of Washington, DC; 50 mi/80 km north of Richmond; and 3 mi/5 km east of I–95. Fredericksburg Battlefield Visitor Center is at 1013 Lafayette Blvd. in Fredericksburg. Chancellorsville Battlefield Visitor Center is on Rte. 3, 8 mi/13 km west of I–95. Closest airport: Reagan Washington National (55 mi/88 km), Richmond International (55 mi/88 km).

FOR MORE INFORMATION

Fredericksburg and Spotsylvania County Battlefields Memorial National Military Park (120 Chatham La., Fredericksburg, VA 22405, tel. 540/371–0802; Web site www.nps.gov/frsp).

George Washington Birthplace National Monument

In the northeast part of the state, near Colonial Beach

The park evokes the spirit of the 18th-century tobacco farm where Washington was born and includes a memorial mansion and gardens and the tombs of several generations of Washingtons. The historic buildings, groves of trees, livestock, gardens, rivers, and creeks were the earliest scenes of Washington's childhood. The site was established on January 23, 1930.

WHAT TO SEE & DO

Hiking, picnicking, touring site, viewing film and exhibits, watching wildlife. **Facilities:** Visitor center with interpretive exhibits, home site, Colonial farm area, burial grounds, trails, beach. Bookstore. **Programs & Events:** Guided tours with costumed interpreters. Seasonal activities available. George Washington's Birthday (Presidents Day and Feb. 22), Christmas at Pope's Creek.

PLANNING YOUR VISIT

⚠ **Camping:** Available at Westmoreland State Park; none at monument. ⬚ **Lodging:** Available in nearby towns; none at monument. ✕ **Food & Supplies:** Available in nearby towns; none at monument. ☞ **Tips & Hints:** Plan one–two hours for the visit. Busiest in June and July, least crowded in December and January. ▧ **Fees, Permits & Limitations:** Entrance fee: $2 per person 17 and up. Visitor center and monument open daily 9–5. Closed Dec. 25, Jan. 1.

HOW TO GET THERE

On the Potomac River, 38 mi/61 km east of Fredericksburg, and accessible via Rtes. 3 and 204. Closest airport: Richmond (75 mi/120 m).

FOR MORE INFORMATION

George Washington Birthplace National Monument (1732 Popes Creek Rd., Washington's Birthplace, VA 22443, tel. 804/224–1732; Web site www.nps.gov/gewa).

George Washington Memorial Parkway

In the northeast part of the state, near McLean

Natural scenery along the Potomac River, across the water from Washington, DC, is preserved along this parkway. It connects the historic sites from Mount Vernon, where Washington lived, past the nation's capital, which he founded, to the Great Falls of the Potomac, where the president demonstrated his skill as an engineer. The parkway was authorized in 1930 and transferred to the Park Service in 1933.

WHAT TO SEE & DO

Biking, hiking, scenic driving, touring sites. **Facilities:** The 7,200-acre parkway includes 15 sites—Arlington House; Clara Barton National Historic Site; Lyndon Baines Johnson Memorial Grove on the Potomac, and Theodore Roosevelt Island (*see separate entries for all four*); the Arlington Memorial Bridge; Claude Moore Farm; Dyke Marsh; Fort Hunt Park; Fort Marcy; Glen Echo Park; Great Falls Park; Netherlands Carillon; Turkey Run Park; U.S. Marine Corps Memorial (Iwo Jima); and the Women in Military Service to America Memorial—and trails. Boat ramps, marinas, picnic areas. **Programs & Events:** Year-round: interpretive programs (daily at Great Falls and Glen Echo parks). Other programs available by reservation at Turkey Run Park, Ft. Marcy, Theodore Roosevelt Island, Lyndon Baines Johnson Memorial Grove, Dyke Marsh, and Fort Hunt Park. Park also sponsors guided walks, children's camps, marathons among other activities. Seasonal activities available. Concerts (Netherlands Carillon, May–Sept., Sat.); Sunset Parade (U.S. Marine Corps War Memorial, Memorial Day–Aug., Tues. evenings).

PLANNING YOUR VISIT

🏨 **Lodging:** Available in Washington, DC, area. ✕ **Food & Supplies:** Available in Washington, DC, area. ☞ **Tips & Hints:** Busiest in June and July, least crowded in January and February. 🎫 **Fees, Permits & Limitations:** Free. Reservations required for many interpretive programs offered at sites that are not regularly staffed. Permit required for group picnicking at Fort Hunt Park Thurs.–Sun. and holidays Apr.–Oct. Permit required to consume alcohol. No weapons.

HOW TO GET THERE

The parkway runs parallel to the Potomac River north and south of Washington, DC, and is accessible from all major travel routes from the south and west, including I–495, I–95, and I–66. Closest airport: Reagan Washington National.

FOR MORE INFORMATION

Superintendent, George Washington Memorial Parkway (700 George Washington Memorial Pkwy., McLean, VA 22101, tel. 703/289–2500, fax 703/289–2598; e-mail gwmp_superintendent@nps.gov; Web site www.nps.gov/gwmp).

Maggie L. Walker National Historic Site

In the southeast part of the state, in Richmond

This rowhouse, at 110½ E. Leigh Street, was the home of Maggie Lena Walker (1867–1934), a prominent African-American civic and fraternal leader who rose to prominence in post–Civil War Richmond. She is best known as the first woman bank president in the United States. The site was authorized in 1978.

WHAT TO SEE & DO

Touring house, watching film. **Facilities:** Visitor center with interpretive exhibits, home. Bookstore. **Programs & Events:** Ranger-guided tours (year-round, Mon.–Sat.). Second Street Festival (1st weekend, Oct.).

PLANNING YOUR VISIT

⚠ **Camping:** Available in Richmond area; none at site. ⊞ **Lodging:** Available in Richmond area; none at site. ✕ **Food & Supplies:** Available in Richmond area; none at site. ☞ **Tips & Hints:** Busiest in February and July, least crowded in September and January. ▨ **Fees, Permits & Limitations:** Free. No pets. Site and visitor center open Mon.–Sat. 9–5. Closed Thanksgiving, Dec. 25, Jan. 1.

HOW TO GET THERE

In Richmond, at 110½ E. Leigh St. via Exits 76A or B off I–95/I–64. Closest airport: Richmond International (5 mi/8 km).

FOR MORE INFORMATION

Maggie L. Walker National Historic Site (c/o 3215 E. Broad St., Richmond, VA 23223, tel. 804/771–2017, fax 804/771–2226; Web site www.nps.gov/malw). Metro Richmond Convention and Visitors Bureau (5550 E. Marshall, Richmond, VA 23219, tel. 804/782–2777).

Manassas National Battlefield Park

In the northeast part of the state, in Manassas

Two battles between Union and Confederate troops during the Civil War are commemorated here. Nearly 900 men lost their lives in July 1861, and another 3,300 died during a three-day battle in August 1862, which brought the Confederacy to the height of its power. The park was designated on May 10, 1940.

WHAT TO SEE & DO

Auto touring, hiking, picnicking. **Facilities:** Visitor center with interpretive exhibits (Henry Hill, VA 234); contact station (Stuart's Hill, U.S. 29), interpretive trails, auto tours. Bookstore, picnic area. **Programs & Events:** Ranger-guided tours and programs, living-history demonstrations (mid-June–Aug.). Battlefield Hike (Apr. and Oct.).

PLANNING YOUR VISIT

⚠ **Camping:** Available in Centreville, Gainsville, Manassas; none in park. ⊞ **Lodging:** Available in Manassas; none in park. ✕ **Food & Supplies:** Available in Manassas; none in park. ☞ **Tips & Hints:** Use caution while driving heavily traveled roads that divide the park. Visit between June and October. Busiest in June and July, least crowded in December and February. ▨ **Fees, Permits & Limitations:** Entrance fee: $2 adults over 16. No hunting. No bikes, motorized or mechanized equipment on trails. Leashed pets only. Park open daily dawn–dusk. Closed Thanksgiving, Dec. 25. Visitor center open Labor Day–mid-June, daily 8–5; mid-June–Labor day, daily 8:30–6. Closed Thanksgiving, Dec. 25. Contact station open daily, mid-June–Labor Day.

HOW TO GET THERE

The park is 26 mi/42 km west of Washington, DC. Henry Hill Visitor Center is 1 mi/1.6 km north of I–66, via Exit 47B and VA 234. Closest airports: Dulles International (25 mi/40 km), Reagan Washington National (30 mi/48 km).

FOR MORE INFORMATION

Manassas National Battlefield Park (6511 Sudley Rd., Manassas, VA 20109, tel. 703/361–1339, fax 703/361–7106; Web site www.nps.gov/mana). Manassas City Visitor Center (9431 West St., Manassas, VA 20110, tel. 703/361–6599).

Petersburg National Battlefield

In the southeast part of the state, near Petersburg

Preserved in this park are three tracts associated with General Ulysses S. Grant's attack and siege of Petersburg during the Civil War. In the spring of 1864, after failing to defeat General Robert E. Lee's army and capture Richmond, the Confederate capital, Grant moved his army across the James River and attacked Petersburg. A 10-month siege resulted, ending when the last supply lines to Lee's army and Richmond were cut. The site was established as a national military park in 1926, transferred to the Park Service in 1933, and changed to a national battlefield in 1962.

WHAT TO SEE & DO

Auto touring, biking, hiking, horseback riding, picnicking, watching 17-minute map show. **Facilities:** 3 visitor centers with interpretive exhibits—Eastern Front (State Rte. 36 east of Petersburg); Five Forks (Courthouse Rd. [SR 627], Dinwiddie County); Grant's Headquarters (Cedar La., Hopewell); interpretive signs, waysides. Gift shops, picnic area (Eastern Front). **Programs & Events:** 17-minute map show (year-round). Musket firings and ranger-guided walks (mid-June–mid-Aug., daily); cannon and mortar firings (mid-June–mid-Aug.).

PLANNING YOUR VISIT

🛏 **Lodging:** Available in Hopewell, Petersburg, Prince George; none in battlefield. ✗ **Food & Supplies:** Available in Hopewell, Petersburg, Prince George; none in battlefield. ☞ **Tips & Hints:** Visit in spring and fall. Go in April for dogwood blooms, late October for fall foliage. Busiest in June and July, least crowded in January and February. ▨ **Fees, Permits & Limitations:** Entrance fee: $3 per person Sept.–May, maximum $5 per vehicle; $5 per person June–Aug., maximum $10 per vehicle. Stay off earthworks and on trails. No metal detectors or artifact hunting. No hunting. Leashed pets only. No mechanized equipment on trails. No horseback riding on paved trails. Park open daily sunrise–half hour before sunset. Visitor center hours: Eastern Front open Sept.–May, daily 8–5; June–Aug., daily 8–5:30; Grant's Headquarters open daily 8:30–4:30; Five Forks open daily 9–5.

HOW TO GET THERE

Eastern Front visitor center is 2.5 mi/4 km east of central Petersburg on SR 36. Grant's Headquarters is in Appomattox Manor on Cedar La. in Hopewell. From I–95 or I–295, take Rte. 10, then make a left on Appomattox St., and a left on Cedar La. Five Forks is on Courthouse Rd., off I–85 in Dindiddie County. Closest airport: Richmond International (30 mi/48 km).

FOR MORE INFORMATION

Superintendent, Petersburg National Battlefield (1539 Hickory Hill Rd., Petersburg, VA 23803, tel. 804/732–3531, fax 804/732–0835; Web site www.nps.gov/pete).

Prince William Forest Park

In the northeast part of the state, near Triangle

The 18,572-acre park contains the largest example of an eastern piedmont forest in the National Park System and is a sanctuary for native plants and animals in a rapidly developing region. The park encompasses the Quantico Creek watershed and a heritage of land usage that includes Colonial tobacco production, subsistence farming, iron pyrite mining, the Civilian Conservation Corps, and a World War II U.S. Army spy-training base. Congress created the Chopawamsic Recreational Demonstration Area in 1933. It was transferred to the Park Service in 1936 and renamed in 1948.

WHAT TO SEE & DO

Bird- and wildlife watching, fishing, hiking, on- and off-road biking, picnicking. **Facilities:** Visitor center, 11-mi/18-km scenic drive, 3-mi/5-km paved bike trail, 18 mi/29 km of fire roads for mountain biking, 35 mi/56 km of hiking trails. Map sale area. **Programs & Events:** Ranger-led tours and talks (year-round, weekends). Seasonal activities and special events available.

PLANNING YOUR VISIT

⚑ **Camping:** 4 campgrounds. RV camping available (reservations available at Travel Trailer Village, tel. 703/221–2474). Group campsites available at Turkey Run Ridge (reservations required, tel. 703/221–7181). Backcountry camping available mid-Apr.–Oct. (permit required, *see below*). ⊞ **Lodging:** In the park: 5 cabin camps (capacity 120–200) available for clubs, groups, and reunions (reservations required, tel. 703/221–5843). Individual cabins available seasonally (reservations available, tel. 703/221–5843). Lodging also available in Dumfries and

Triangle. ✕ **Food & Supplies:** Available in Dumfries, Triangle; none in park. ☞ **Tips & Hints:** Busiest in May and June, least crowded in November and January. ▨ **Fees, Permits & Limitations:** Entrance fee: $4 per vehicle or $2 per bicyclist or walk-in. Backcountry permit (free) required for all backcountry camping. Park open daily dawn–dusk. Registered campers and cabin campers have access 24 hours. Visitor center open daily 8:30–5.

HOW TO GET THERE

32 mi/51 km south of Washington, DC, and 20 mi/32 km north of Fredericksburg, VA, via I–95 and Exit 150 (VA 619) west. Closest airports: Reagan Washington National, Dulles International.

FOR MORE INFORMATION

Prince William Forest Park (18100 Park Headquarters Rd., Triangle, VA 22172, tel. 703/221–7181; Web site www.nps.gov/prwi).

Richmond National Battlefield Park

In the southeast part of the state, in Richmond

Between 1861 and 1865, Union armies repeatedly tried to capture Richmond, capital of the Confederacy, to end the Civil War. Three of those campaigns came within a few miles of the city. The 763-acre park commemorates 11 different sites associated with those campaigns, including the battlefields at Gaines' Mill, Malvern Hill, and Cold Harbor. The park was authorized on March 2, 1936.

WHAT TO SEE & DO

Picnicking at Ft. Harrison, touring battlefield sites. **Facilities:** Visitor center with interpretive exhibits, audiovisual programs and film (5th and Tredegar Sts.); 4 contact stations—Chimborazo Park, Cold Harbor, Glendale Cemetery, and Fort Harrison; interpretive walking trails at Gaines Mill, Cold Harbor, Malvern Hill, Fort Harrison, and Drewry's Bluff; tour roads at Cold Harbor and Fort Harrison; audio stations. Bookstores. **Programs & Events:** Self-guided driving tours (cassette tape available). Ranger-led walking tours, talks, living history (June–Aug.); youth programs (June–Aug. daily, reservation and fee required). Battle anniversary commemorations: Drewry's Bluff (May 15), Memorial Day, Cold Harbor (June 3), Seven Days' Battle (June 26–July 1), and Fort Harrison (Sept. 29).

PLANNING YOUR VISIT

⛺ **Camping:** Available in Richmond area; none in park. ▥ **Lodging:** Available in Richmond area; none in park. ✕ **Food & Supplies:** Available in Richmond area; none in park. ☞ **Tips & Hints:** Plan to spend at least a day visiting all 11 sites. Busiest in June and July, least crowded in January and February. ▨ **Fees, Permits & Limitations:** Free. Parking fee at Tredegar St. visitor center: $2 for 1st hour, $1 per subsequent hour. Battlefield sites open daily dawn–dusk. Visitor center, Chimborazo Park and Cold Harbor contact stations open daily 9–5. Glendale and Fort Harrison contact stations open seasonally. Closed Thanksgiving, Dec. 25, Jan. 1.

HOW TO GET THERE

The visitor center (5th and Tredegar Sts.) is accessed via I–95. Southbound use exit 75, northbound use exit 74C W and then follow signs. From I–64 westbound, exit 5th St. Closest airport: Richmond (7mi/11 km).

FOR MORE INFORMATION

Park Headquarters, Richmond National Battlefield Park (3215 E. Broad St., Richmond, VA 23223, tel. 804/226–1981, fax 804/771–8522; Web site www.nps.gov/rich).

Shenandoah National Park

In the northwest part of the state, near Luray

Skyline Drive, which winds along the crest of the Blue Ridge Mountains between Front Royal and Waynesboro, is the central feature of the park. Along the 105-mi/168-km drive are 75 pullouts that overlook mountain peaks, gorges, and hollows. The heavily forested park also includes 500 mi/800 km of trails, including a section of the Appalachian Trail, along which are streams, waterfalls, black bear, and deer. The 196,466-acre park was authorized in 1926 and established in 1935.

WHAT TO SEE & DO

Auto touring, bird-watching, fishing, hiking, horseback riding (guided rides, Skyland), picnicking, taking field study seminars. **Facilities:** 3 visitor centers with interpretive exhibits—Dickey Ridge (Mile 4.6), Harry F. Byrd (Milepost 51), and Loft Mountain (Mile 79.5)—overlooks, wayside exhibits, amphitheaters, 500 mi/800 km of hiking trails. Book and map sales areas, fire pits and grates, gas, gift shops, laundries, picnic tables, showers. **Programs & Events:** Ranger-led nature and night walks, talks, evening programs (mostly late May–Aug.). Wildflower Weekend (mid-May), Butterfly Count (early July), Civilian Conservation Corps Reunion (late Sept.), Christmas Bird Count (late Dec.).

PLANNING YOUR VISIT

⚠ **Camping:** 5 campgrounds: no hookups (reservations available, tel. 800/365–2267). Backcountry camping available (permit required, *see below*). Group campsites available at Dundo Group Campground (Mile 83.7, tel. 540/298–9625). Camping also available outside the park in surrounding communities (tel. 540/740–3132, 540/347–4414 for brochures). 🏨 **Lodging:** In the park: Skyland (Mile 41.7), Big Meadows Lodge (Mile 51.3), and Lewis Mountain (Mile 57.5) cabins (tel. 800/999–4714); 6 backcountry cabins (tel. 703/242–0693). Lodging also available in Charlottesville, Culpeper, Front Royal, Harrisonburg, Luray, Madison, New Market, Warrenton, and Waynesboro. ✕

Food & Supplies: In the park: meals at Panorama (Mile 31.5), Skyland (Mile 41.7), and Big Meadows (Mile 51.3); grill service at Elkwallow (Mile 24.1) and Loft Mountain (Mile 79.5); camping supplies and limited groceries at Elkwallow (Mile 24.1), Big Meadows (Mile 51.3), Lewis Mountain (Mile 57.5), and Loft Mountain (Mile 79.5). Call 800/999–4714 for information. Food and supplies also available in Charlottesville, Culpeper, Front Royal, Harrisonburg, Luray, Madison, New Market, Warrenton, and Waynesboro. ☞ **Tips & Hints:** Plan to spend one–two days for visit. Go in spring for wildflowers, migratory birds, and full streams leading to waterfalls; summer for more deer and bear sightings; fall for foliage; and winter for clearest views. Stay off rocks above waterfalls. Avoid fall weekends when the park is crowded with leaf-peepers. Park is usually 10 degrees cooler than valley below. Busiest in July and October, least crowded in January and February. **Fees, Permits & Limitations:** Entrance fee: $10 per vehicle or $5 per individual. Backcountry permit (free) required for all backcountry camping (tel. 540/999–3500). Virginia fishing (or five-day nonresident) license required. Reservation required for horseback rides (tel. 540/999–2210). Reservation required for one- to two-day field-study seminars (June–Sept., tel. 540/999–3489). No hunting or feeding wild animals. Leashed pets only. No pets on some trails. No bicycles or motorized vehicles on trails. No open fires except in campgrounds and picnic areas. Park open daily. Park headquarters (on U.S. 211 east of Luray) open weekdays 8–4:30. Visitor centers, lodges, restaurants, campgrounds, and gift shops open generally Apr.–Nov., daily 9–5. Skyline Dr. closes during bad weather and at night during hunting season.

HOW TO GET THERE

The park is between Front Royal and Waynesboro. The north entrance is on U.S. 340 in Front Royal. The south entrance is just east of Waynesboro on U.S. 250 and I–64. Closest airports: Charlottesville-Albemarle (45 mi/72 km), Shenandoah Valley Airport (20 mi/32 km), Dulles International (80 mi/128 km).

FOR MORE INFORMATION

Shenandoah National Park (3655 U.S. 211E, Luray, VA 22835-9036, tel. 540/999–3500, fax 540/999–3601; Web site www.nps.gov/shen). Front Royal Chamber of Commerce (414 E. Main St., Front Royal, VA 22630, tel. 540/635–3185 or 800/338–2576). Harrisonburg Chamber of Commerce (10 E. Gay St., Harrisonburg, VA 22802, tel. 540/434–2319). Madison County Chamber of Commerce (RR 8 Box 40, Madison VA 22727, tel. 540/948–4455). Waynesboro Chamber of Commerce (301 W. Main St., Waynesboro, VA 22980, tel. 540/949–8203). Shenandoah Valley Travel Association (Box 1040, New Market, VA 22844, tel. 540/740–3132).

Wolf Trap Farm Park for the Performing Arts

In the northeast part of the state, near Vienna

Wolf Trap is the only national park dedicated to the performing arts. Within the boundaries of the park are 130 acres of rolling hills and woods. The Filene Center is an open-air performing arts pavilion that accommodates 7,000 people, including 3,100 on the lawn, from May to September. Along with the Barns of Wolf Trap, a 352-seat indoor theater in a rebuilt 18th-century barn just outside the park boundary, it hosts performances ranging from opera to dance to rock. The park was authorized on October 15, 1966.

WHAT TO SEE & DO

Attending performances, picnicking. **Facilities:** Performing arts pavilion, indoor theater, lawn, restaurant. Picnic area. **Programs & Events:** Performances (the Barns, year-round). Filene Center performances (May–Sept.), Theatre-in-the Woods performances for children (summer, tel. 703/255–1893), Backstage tour of the Filene Center (winter, tel. 703/255–1890).

PLANNING YOUR VISIT

Camping: Available locally; none at park. **Lodging:** Available locally; none at park. **Food & Supplies:** In the park: meals before performances during Filene Center season (reservations recommended, tel. 703/255–4017). Prepared picnics also available (tel. 703/519–3505). Snacks and bar at the Barns (tel. 703/938–2404). Food and supplies also available locally. **Tips & Hints:** Arrive early for best lawn seats. Filene Center gates open about 1½ hours before performance. Bring a picnic. Busiest in July and August, least crowded in January. **Fees, Permits & Limitations:** Entrance free, performance fees vary. Tickets available by phone (tel. 703/218–6500 or 800/955–5566), on line (www.wolftrap.org or www.tickets.com), or in person at The Barns (weekdays 10–6, weekends noon–5, performance nights until 9).

HOW TO GET THERE

Take Exit 67 off I–66W and Exit 12 off Capital Beltway to reach Rte. 267W (Dulles Toll Rd.). Follow signs to local exits, pay a 50¢ toll, and exit at the Wolf Trap ramp. The Filene Center is on the right. From Rte. 7W, turn left on Towlston Rd., go 1 mi/1.6 km to Filene Center on left. From West Falls Church Metrorail station (orange line), take Wolf Trap Shuttle (tel. 202/637–7000). Closest airports: Dulles International (14 mi/22 km), Reagan Washington National (14 mi/22 km).

FOR MORE INFORMATION

Wolf Trap Farm Park for the Performing Arts (1551 Trap Rd., Vienna, VA 22182, tel. 703/255–1800; Web site www.nps.gov/wotr). Wolf Trap Foundation (1624 Trap Rd., Vienna, VA 22182, tel. 703/255–1900).

See Also

....

Appalachian National Scenic Trail, West Virginia. *Assateague Island National Seashore*, Maryland. *Blue Ridge Parkway*, North Carolina. *Cumberland Gap National Historical Park*, Kentucky. *Green Springs National Historic Landmark District*, Affiliated Areas in Other National Parklands. *Harpers Ferry National Historical Park*, West Virginia. *Jamestown National Historic Site*, Affiliated Areas in Other National Parklands. *Potomac Heritage National Scenic Trail*, District of Columbia. *Red Hill Patrick Henry National Memorial*, Affiliated Areas in Other National Parklands. *Shenandoah Valley Battlefields*, National Heritage Areas in Other National Parklands.

WASHINGTON

Ebey's Landing National Historical Reserve

On Whidbey Island

This rural historic district preserves an unbroken historical record of Puget Sound exploration and settlement from the 19th century to the present. Historic farms, still under cultivation in the prairies of Whidbey Island, reveal land-use patterns unchanged since settlers claimed the land in the 1850s under the Donation Land Claim Act. The Victorian seaport community of Coupeville is also in the reserve. The prairies, seaport, and dramatic coastal beaches and cliffs create a cultural landscape of national significance. The 19,000-acre reserve was authorized on November 10, 1978.

WHAT TO SEE & DO

Bird-watching, boating, hiking, picnicking, scuba diving, self-guided touring of Coupeville and surroundings on foot or by bike or car. **Facilities:** Island County Historical Museum (downtown Coupeville), scenic vistas and pullouts, wayside exhibits, historic homes and farmsteads, trails. Boat launch area. **Programs & Events:** Self-guided tours year-round. Seasonal activities and special events available. Contact museum (tel. 360/678–3310) for details.

PLANNING YOUR VISIT

⚠ **Camping:** Available in Fort Casey (tel. 360/678–4519) and Fort Ebey (tel. 360/678–4636) state parks; none at reserve. ⌂ **Lodging:** Available in Coupeville, Oak Harbor; none at reserve. ✕ **Food & Supplies:** Available in Coupeville, Oak Harbor; none at reserve. ☞ **Tips & Hints:** Stop at museum (tel. 360/678–3310) to pick up brochure for self-guided tours of Coupeville and surrounding reserve. Use caution on beach to avoid being caught on headlands during high tides. Busiest in July and August, least crowded in December and January. ▨ **Fees, Permits & Limitations:** Free. No beach fires. Respect property rights of landowners. Hike on designated trails only. Leashed pets only. No collecting driftwood, plants, rocks, or other natural features.

HOW TO GET THERE

The reserve, on central Whidbey Island, can be reached by car via WA 20 or by the Washington State Ferry system (tel. 206/464–6400 or 888/808–7977 in Washington), which provides year-round car and passenger service from Port Townsend and Mukilteo. Closest airport: Oak Harbor (8 mi/13 km).

FOR MORE INFORMATION

Ebey's Landing National Historical Reserve (Box 774, Coupeville, WA 98239, tel. 360/678–6084; Web site www.nps.gov/ebla). Oak Harbor

Chamber of Commerce (32630 SR 20, Oak Harbor, WA 98277, tel. 360/675–3535).

Fort Vancouver National Historic Site

In the southwest part of the state, in Vancouver

This Columbia River site displays rebuilt structures from the 19th-century fort that was a key fur-trading post in North America. More than 20 Hudson's Bay Company posts in the Northwest shipped their furs here between 1825 and 1860 for shipment overseas. The fort attracted American emigrants newly arrived in the Oregon country and played a significant role in the settlement of the Northwest. The fort was established as a Park Service unit in 1947.

WHAT TO SEE & DO

Picnicking, touring fort and blacksmith shop. **Facilities:** Visitor center with interpretive exhibits (Evergreen Blvd.), reconstructed fort, blacksmith shop, carpenter shop. Gift shop, picnic shelter and tables. **Programs & Events:** Guided tours or costumed interpreters in buildings (year-round). Special presentations (summer, weekends). Queen Victoria's Birthday (late May); Brigade Encampment (late July); "Founder's Day" (Aug. 25); Candlelight Tour (Sept.); Christmas (early Dec.).

PLANNING YOUR VISIT

Lodging: Available in Portland, Vancouver; none at site. ✕ **Food & Supplies:** Available in Portland, Vancouver; none at site. ☞ **Tips & Hints:** Go during special events to see the fort at its most vibrant. Go between May and October for best weather. Winter is rainy season, spring is school-group season. Busiest in May and July, least crowded in December and January. **Fees, Permits & Limitations:** Entrance fee: $2 per person or $4 per family (summer); free (winter). No dogs. No smoking. No food or drink inside fort. Park and visitor center open Oct.–Mar., daily 9–4; Apr.–Sept., daily 9–5. Closed Thanksgiving, Dec. 24, Dec. 25.

HOW TO GET THERE

From I–5, exit on Mill Plain Blvd. Go east. Turn right on Ft. Vancouver Way and left on Evergreen Blvd. to reach visitor center. Closest airport: Portland International (6 mi/10 km).

FOR MORE INFORMATION

Fort Vancouver National Historic Site (612 E. Reserve St., Vancouver, WA 98661, tel. 360/696–7655 or 800/832–3599; Web site www.nps.gov/fova).

Lake Chelan National Recreation Area

In the north-central part of the state, near Stehekin

Lake Chelan rests in a trough carved by glaciers in the Cascades Range. With a depth of 1,500 ft/455 m, it is one of the nation's deepest lakes. Although the lake's average width is less than 2 mi/3.2 km, it extends almost 55 mi/88 km into the Cascade Mountains. At its deepest point, Lake Chelan drops to 400 ft/121 m below sea level. The Stehekin River drainage area and the upper 4 mi/6 km of the lake are protected by the recreation area. The area was established on October 2, 1968.

WHAT TO SEE & DO

Boating (rentals), biking (rentals), cross-country skiing, fishing, hiking, horseback riding and pack trips (rentals), hunting, mountain climbing, picnicking, river rafting, snowshoeing (rentals). **Facilities:** Visitor center with interpretive exhibits (Golden West, Stehekin Landing), wayside exhibits, self-guided interpretive trails. Book and map sale areas, post office. **Programs & Events:** Seasonal activities available. Earth Week (mid-Apr.).

PLANNING YOUR VISIT

Camping: Camping available along Stehekin Valley road (permit required, *see below*) and along lake (boat-in only). (No reservations.) Backcountry camping available (permit required, *see below*). Group campsites available (reservations required, tel. 360/856–5700 ext. 340). **Lodging:** In the recreation area: lodge rooms and housekeeping facilities available year-round (tel. 509/682–4494). Cabins available (Stehekin Valley Ranch, tel. 509/682–4677; Silver Bay Inn and Cabins, tel. 509/682–2212). Lodging also available in Chelan. **Food & Supplies:** In the recreation area: meals at North Cascades Stehekin Lodge (tel. 509/682–4494). Small stores at Stehekin Landing. Food and supplies also available in Chelan. **Tips & Hints:** See separate listings for other two units of the North Cascades Complex: North Cascades National Park and Ross Lake National Recreation Area. Be prepared for rapid weather changes. The North Cascades Complex is primarily a wilderness park with few frontcountry activities. Hang all food out of the reach of bears in backcountry. Beware of hazardous stream crossings. Check conditions before starting trips. Crossing snowfields may require special equipment. Busiest in July and August, least crowded in December and January. **Fees, Permits & Limitations:** Free. Shuttle bus fee: $5 per zone each way on bus in the Stehekin Valley. Reservations recommended (tel. 360/856–5700 ext. 340, then ext. 14). The bus operates May 15–Oct. 15. No dogs on shuttle. Backcountry permit (free) required for all backcountry camping (tel. 360/873–4590 ext. 39). Permits issued in person only. Permits required for Stehekin Valley road campsites. Use of federal docks on lake requires Forest Service dock permit ($5/ day or $40/season). Washington state fishing and hunting licenses required. Hunting permitted in recreation area only. Leashed pets only. Recreation area open daily. Heavy winter snows restrict travel and close roads. Golden West visitor center open Mar. 15–May 15, daily 12:30–2; May 16–Sept. 30, daily 8:30–5; Oct. 1–15, daily 10:30–2. Closed mid-Oct.–mid-Mar.

HOW TO GET THERE

The main access to Stehekin is by boat (tel. 509/682–2224) or float-plane (509/682–5555) from the town of Chelan on Hwy. 97. Area can be reached by hiking trail in summer. Closest airport: Seattle/Tacoma (177 mi/283 km).

FOR MORE INFORMATION

North Cascades National Park Service Complex (2105 State Rte. 20, Sedro-Woolley, WA 98284, tel. 360/856–5700, fax 360/856–1934; e-mail NOCA_Interpretation@nps.gov; Web site www.nps/gov/noca). Lake Chelan Tourist Information (102 E. Johnson St., Lake Chelan, WA 98816, tel. 800/424–3526).

Lake Roosevelt National Recreation Area

In the northeast part of the state, near Grand Coulee

The 1941 damming of the Columbia River, which was part of the Columbia River Basin project, created a 130-mi/208-km lake. Named for President Franklin D. Roosevelt, the lake is the largest recreation feature in the recreation area. Boating, fishing, swimming, camping, and hiking are all available, as are tours of Fort Spokane and the dam. Coulee Dam Recreation Area was administered under a cooperative agreement signed in 1946 with the Bureau of Reclamation, Bureau of Indian Affairs, and the U.S. Department of Interior; revised and renegotiated in 1990 by the Bureau of Reclamation, Bureau of Indian Affairs, National Park Service, Colville Confederated Tribes, and the Spokane Tribe of Indians; renamed in 1997.

WHAT TO SEE & DO

Bird-watching, boating (rentals; Keller Ferr, Fort Spokane, and Kettle Falls), fishing, hiking, hunting, picnicking, swimming, touring Fort Spokane and Grand Coulee Dam, waterskiing. **Facilities:** Visitor center, bathhouse. Boat dump stations, boat ramps, picnic areas. **Programs & Events:** Year-round programs available. Interpretive talks.

PLANNING YOUR VISIT

🔥 **Camping:** 9 campgrounds (no reservations). Dump stations. Camping also available locally. ⛺ **Lodging:** Available locally; none in park. ✕ **Food & Supplies:** In the park: meals (Memorial Day–Labor Day) at Spring Canyon Campground and Seven Bays Marina (tel.509/725–1676), food and supplies at marinas. Food and supplies also available outside the park in Colville, Coulee Dam, Grand Coulee, Kettle Falls, Northport. ☞ **Tips & Hints:** Busiest in July and August, least crowded in December and January. ▩ **Fees, Permits & Limitations:** Free. Boat launch fee. Fishing and hunting permits required. No off-road vehicle use. Recreation area open daily. Recreation season is May–Oct. Visitor center open Memorial Day–Labor Day, daily; Labor Day–Memorial Day, intermittently. Closed Thanksgiving, Dec. 25, Jan. 1.

HOW TO GET THERE

From I–90, the recreation area headquarters in Coulee Dam can be reached via Exit 179, then north on Rte. 17E, and Rte. 155N to Coulee Dam. From Spokane, take U.S. 2W to Rte. 174 to Coulee Dam. Closest airport: Spokane (80 mi/128 km).

FOR MORE INFORMATION

Lake Roosevelt National Recreation Area (1008 Crest Dr., Coulee Dam, WA 99116, tel. 509/633–9441; Web site www.nps.gov/laro). Chamber of Commerce (319 Midway Ave., Grand Coulee, WA 99133, tel. 509/633–0361).

Mount Rainier National Park

In the west-central part of the state, near Ashford

This majestic 14,410-ft/4,392-m volcanic mountain, now glacier capped, sports rain forests with 1,000-year-old trees at its base, waterfalls, and subalpine flowering meadows. Native Americans called it "Tahoma," the snowy mountain. The 235,613-acre park is nearly all wilderness. The park was established on March 2, 1899.

WHAT TO SEE & DO

Auto touring, backpacking, bird-watching, cross-country skiing (rentals, Longmire), fishing, hiking, horseback riding, mountain climbing, picnicking, snowshoeing, wildflower and wildlife viewing. **Facilities:** 4 visitor centers with interpretive exhibits—Paradise, Ohanapecosh, Sunrise, Longmire; White River information center, Longmire museum, trails, tour roads. Gift shops, picnic areas. **Programs & Events:** Ranger-led interpretive programs and walks, campfire programs, movies and slide programs (June–early Sept.), guided snowshoe walks (weekends, Paradise).

PLANNING YOUR VISIT

⚠ **Camping:** 5 campgrounds: no hookups (reservations available, tel. 800/365–2267). Backcountry camping available (permit required, *see below*). Group campsites available (reservations available, tel. 800/365–2267). Campgrounds also available on surrounding federal, state, and private lands. ▦ **Lodging:** In the park: National Park Inn at Longmire (year-round) and Paradise Inn (mid-May–early Oct.). Call 360/569–2275 for both. Lodging also available in Alder, Ashford, and Elbe. ✗ **Food & Supplies:** In the park: meals at National Park Inn at Longmire and Paradise Inn, snack bars at Paradise and Sunrise visitor centers. Limited groceries at National Park Inn, Paradise Inn, and Sunrise Lodge (early June–early Sept.). Food and supplies also available in Ashford, Elbe, Eatonville, Enumclaw, Fairfax, and Packwood. ☞ **Tips & Hints:** Bring rain gear. Get gas before entering park. Go on weekdays September–early October to avoid crowds, late June–early September for wildflowers in subalpine meadows, September–early October for elk-mating season, December–April for cross-country ski season. Busiest in July and August, least crowded in December and February. **▣ Fees, Permits & Limitations:** Entrance fee: $10 per vehicle or $5 per bicyclist, motorcyclist, pedestrian, or bus passenger. Backcountry permit (free) required for all backcountry camping. Climbers must register with park and pay fee ($15/climb or $25/year). No bikes on trails. Visitor center hours: Longmire—daily 9–4, with extended summer hours; Jackson Memorial (Paradise)—May and Sept.–early Oct., daily 10–6; June–Aug., daily 10–7; mid-Oct.–May, weekends and holidays 10–5; Ohanapecosh—late May–Oct., daily 9–6; Sunrise—July–late Sept., daily 9–6.

HOW TO GET THERE

The park can be reached from I–5, U.S. 12, and State Rtes. 7, 706, 123, 410, and 165. The park's southwest Nisqually entrance, on State Rte. 706, is open daily. Closest airport: Seattle/Tacoma (70 mi/112 km).

FOR MORE INFORMATION

Mount Rainier National Park (Tahoma Woods, Star Route, Ashford, WA 98304-9751, tel. 360/569–2211; Web site www.nps.gov/mora).

North Cascades National Park

In the northwest part of the state, near Marblemount

Nearly all wilderness, the 505,000-acre North Cascades National Park contains some of America's most breathtakingly beautiful scenery. Attractions include more than 300 glaciers, waterfalls, rivers, lakes; lush forests; and diverse flora and fauna. The park was established on October 2, 1968.

WHAT TO SEE & DO

Bird- and wildlife watching, boating, fishing, hiking, horseback riding (rentals), mountain climbing (rentals), river running (rentals). **Facilities:** Visitor center with interpretive exhibits (North Cascades, Milepost 120 on WA 20 in Newhalem), Wilderness Information Center (Marblemount, Milepost 105 on WA 20), Glacier Public Service Center (Glacier, Hwy. 542), trails, wayside exhibits. Bookstore. **Programs & Events:** Art exhibits and workshops (summer); talks, demonstrations, guided hikes, children's programs, evening presentations (mostly July–Sept, and winter holidays). Earth Day and Week (Apr.).

PLANNING YOUR VISIT

⚠ **Camping:** Backcountry camping available (permit required, *see below*). ⊟ **Lodging:** Call 360/856–5700 and *see* separate listings for Lake Chelan and Ross Lake National Recreation Areas for lodging information; none in park. ✗ **Food & Supplies:** Available in Chelan, Concrete, Marblemount, Newhalem, Stehekin; none in park. ☞ **Tips &**

Hints: Visit from mid-June to late September for best weather. Heavy snow and rain, depending on elevation, characterize the North Cascades from fall into spring. Snow is usually off all but the highest trails by July. Summer storms are common. Be prepared for rain and wind. Take good, light rain gear and tent if you are going into high and remote areas. Warm, waterproof clothing and a tent are virtually mandatory for spring, fall, and winter trips into the backcountry. Hang food and other items with fragrance at least 10 ft/3 m up and 4 ft/1.2 m out from tree trunk, away from animals, in backcountry. Be cautious crossing streams. Crossing snowfields and glaciers may require special equipment. Fragile vegetation, such as heather, particularly in subalpine areas, is easily damaged by foot traffic. Practice "Leave No Trace" hiking and camping techniques to minimize your impact on wilderness. Busiest in July and August, least crowded in November and January. ⌦ **Fees, Permits & Limitations:** Free. Northwest Forest Pass ($5/day or $30 annual) required for parking along the Cascade River and at some trailheads within Ross Lake. Permit required (free) for backcountry camping (Wilderness Information Center, tel. 360/873–4500, ext. 39, May–Oct. in Marblemount for any backcountry area; National Park Headquarters, tel. 360/856–5700 ext. 515, winter). Permits issued in person only, up to one day before trip. Reservations required (tel. 360/856–5700 ext. 340, then ext. 14, after May 14) for park shuttle buses in Stehekin Valley that serve the south end of the park. No pets on shuttle. Leashed dogs only on Pacific Crest Trail. No pets in any other backcountry. No wood fires except in forested, low-elevation areas with iron fire grates. No grazing of horses; bring feed. Washington state fishing license required. No hunting. No mountain or trail bikes or mechanized or motorized equipment on trails. Park open daily. Access limited by snow in winter.

HOW TO GET THERE

The park is divided by WA 20, which runs from Burlington (I–5) on the east to Okanogan on the west, with branch routes to Baker Lake (at Concrete) and the Cascade River (at Marblemount). Hiking access and roadside views of the northwest corner of the park are available from WA 542, east from Bellingham. Two gravel roads enter the park: the Cascade River Rd. from Marblemount and the Stehekin Valley Rd. The latter does not connect to any roads outside the Stehekin Valley. Closest airport: Seattle/Tacoma (140 mi/224 km).

FOR MORE INFORMATION

North Cascades NPS Complex (2105 State Rte. 20, Sedro-Woolley, WA 98284, tel. 360/856–5700, fax 360/856–1934; Web site www.nps.gov/noca). Mt. Vernon Chamber of Commerce (Box 1007, Mt. Vernon, WA 98273, tel. 360/428–8547). Sedro-Woolley Chamber of Commerce (714 B Metcalf St., Sedro-Woolley, WA 98284, tel. 360/855–1841). Concrete Chamber of Commerce (Box 743, Concrete, WA 98237, tel. 360/853–7042). Winthrop Chamber of Commerce (202 Riverside, Winthrop, WA 98862, tel. 509/996–2125). Methow Valley Central Reservations (Box 505, Winthrop, WA 98862, tel. 509/996–2148 or 800/422–3048). Chelan Chamber of Commerce (Box 216, Chelan, WA 98816, tel. 509/682–2022 or 800/424–3526). Wenatchee Chamber of

Commerce (116 N. Wenatchee Ave., Wenatchee, WA 98801, tel. 509/663–3723 or 800/572–7753).

Olympic National Park

In the northwest part of the state, near Port Angeles

Olympic encompasses three distinctly different ecosystems—rugged glacier-capped mountains, more than 60 mi/96 km of wild Pacific coast, and magnificent stands of old-growth and temperate rain forest. About 95% of the park is designated wilderness, so these diverse ecosystems are largely pristine in character. Isolated for eons by glacial ice, the waters of Puget Sound, and the Strait of Juan de Fuca, the Olympic Peninsula has developed its own distinct array of plants and animals. Eight kinds of plants and fifteen kinds of animals are found on the peninsula and live nowhere else in the world. Mount Olympus National Monument was proclaimed in 1909, transferred to the Park Service in 1933, renamed and redesignated in 1938, and designated a Biosphere Reserve in 1976 and a World Heritage Site in 1981.

WHAT TO SEE & DO

Auto touring, backpacking, bird- and wildlife watching, fishing, hiking, mountain climbing, picnicking, skiing, snowshoeing, swimming. **Facilities:** 3 visitor centers with interpretive exhibits—Port Angeles, Hurricane Ridge, and Hoh Rain Forest; 11 ranger stations including 4 with exhibits—Staircase, Storm King (at Lake Crescent), Quinault, and Kalaloch; 168 mi/269 km of roads; 600 mi/960 km of trails. **Programs & Events:** Ranger-led programs and activities (July and Aug.); ranger-led snowshoe walks (Dec.–Mar., weekends); Olympic Park Institute 1- to 3-day field seminars on natural history; nature photography; and kayak, canoe, and backpacking outings (Apr.–Oct., tel. 360/928–3720 or www.yni.org/opi).

PLANNING YOUR VISIT

Camping: 16 campgrounds (no reservations, tel. 360/452–0330 for information). RV campsites with hookups at Log Cabin Resort and Sol Duc Hot Springs Resort. Permit required (*see below*) for all backcountry camping (reservation required in some areas Memorial Day–Labor Day). Camping also available in Olympic National Forest and locally. **Lodging:** In the park: Kalaloch Lodge (open year-round, tel. 360/962–2271 or www.visitkalaloch.com); Lake Crescent Lodge (late Apr.–Oct., tel. 360/928–3211); Log Cabin Resort (Apr.–Oct. 1, tel. 360/928–3325); Sol Duc Hot Springs Resort (Apr.–mid-May, weekends; mid-May–Sept., daily; tel. 360/327–3583 or www.northolympic.com/solduc/). Lodging also available in surrounding communities. **Food & Supplies:** In the park: meals at Kalaloch Lodge (open year-round, tel. 360/962–2271); Lake Crescent Lodge (late Apr.–Oct., tel. 360/928–3211); Log Cabin Resort (Apr.–Oct. 1, tel. 360/928–3325); Sol Duc Hot Springs Resort (Apr.–mid-May, weekends; mid-May–Sept., daily; tel. 360/327–3583); grocery and camper supply stores at Fairholm General Store, Log Cabin Resort, Sol Duc Hot Springs Resort, and Kalaloch

Lodge. Food and supplies also available in surrounding communities. ☞ **Tips & Hints:** Drive to Hurricane Ridge for high country and mountain vistas, Hoh Rain Forest where 12 ft/3.6 km of rain a year creates huge trees and greenery, and Rialto or Ruby Beach for view of Pacific beaches. Come prepared for a variety of weather. Bring rain gear and layered clothing. Buy topographic maps for most hikes (tel. 360/452–0339). Busiest in August and September, least crowded in January and February. ▦ **Fees, Permits & Limitations:** Entrance fee: $10 per vehicle or $5 per bicyclist or bus passenger. Hurricane Ridge entrance fee: $10 (winter weekends). RV sewage dump station fee: $3 per use. Ozette parking fee: $1 per day. Backcountry permit ($5, tel. 360/452–0330) required for all backcountry camping. Stay on trails and use existing wilderness campsites. Park open daily. Main visitor center open Sept.–May, daily 9–4; June–Aug., daily 9–5 (approximately). Smaller, seasonal visitor sites keep varied and flexible hours.

HOW TO GET THERE

The park, which occupies the center of the Olympic Peninsula and a 63-mi/101-km strip along the Pacific Coast, can be reached from the Seattle–Tacoma area via U.S. 101 or by ferry (www.wsdot.wa.gov/ferries/). For car and passenger ferry service between Victoria, British Columbia, and Port Angeles, call 360/457–4491. For passenger ferry service in summer between Victoria and Port Angeles, call 360/452–8088. Closest airport: Fairchild International in Port Angeles (20 mi/32 km).

FOR MORE INFORMATION

Olympic National Park (600 E. Park Ave., Port Angeles, WA 98362-6798, tel. 360/452–0330; Web site www.nps.gov/olym). North Olympic Peninsula Visitor and Convention Bureau (Box 670, Port Angeles, WA 98362, tel. 360/452–8552 or 800/942–4042; Web site www.olympicpeninsula.org).

Ross Lake National Recreation Area

In the northwest part of the state, near Diablo

The 118,000-acre recreation area provides the corridor for the popular North Cascades Highway (WA 20). Its three lakes—12,000-acre Ross Lake, 910-acre Diablo Lake, and 210-acre Gorge Lake—afford water access to the more remote areas in the North Cascades National Park and Mount Baker–Snoqualmie National Forest. The area was established on October 2, 1968.

WHAT TO SEE & DO

Auto touring, bird- and wildlife watching, boating (rentals, Ross Lake Resort), canoeing, fishing, hiking, hunting, picnicking, river rafting, rock climbing. **Facilities:** Visitor center with interpretive exhibits (North Cascades, WA 20 in Newhalem), amphitheaters, trails, wayside exhibits.

Book and map sales area, boat-launching ramps. **Programs & Events:** Interpretive programs, guided and self-guided walks (mostly July–Sept.). Earth Day (mid-Apr.).

PLANNING YOUR VISIT

🏕 **Camping:** 4 campgrounds (no reservations). Backcountry camping available (permit required, *see below*). Group campsites available at Goodell Creek (reservations required, tel. 360/873–4590 ext. 16) and Newhalem Creek (reservations required, tel. 206/386–4495 ext. 16). Private campgrounds available in Concrete, Marblemount, Rockport, Sedro-Woolley. 🏨 **Lodging:** In the Ross Lake NRA: Ross Lake Resort (tel. 206/386–4437). The resort offers cabin rentals, water taxi, boat rentals, and boat portage service. There is no road access to the resort. No restaurant or phones; no pets allowed. Lodging also available in Concrete and Marblemount. ✗ **Food & Supplies:** Available in Concrete, Marblemount, Rockport, Sedro-Woolley; none in recreation area. ☞ **Tips & Hints:** See separate listings for adjacent Lake Chelan National Recreation Area and North Cascades National Park. Be prepared for rapid changes in weather. North Cascades is primarily a wilderness park with few frontcountry activities. Hang all food out of the reach of bears in backcountry. Check stream conditions before starting trips. Crossing snowfields may require special equipment. Go between Memorial Day and September for best weather. Busiest in July and August, least crowded in December and January. 🎫 **Fees, Permits & Limitations:** Free. Northwest Forest Pass ($5/day or $30 annual) required for parking along the Cascade River and at some trailheads within Ross Lake. Permits required (free) for all backcountry and boat-in camping (Wilderness Information Center, tel. 360/873–4500 ext. 39, May–Oct. in Marblemount; National Park Headquarters, tel. 360/856–5700 ext. 515, winter). Permits issued in person only, up to one day before trip. Washington state fishing and hunting licenses required. Leashed pets only on trails. Recreation area open daily. Visitor center (Newhalem) open mid-Apr.–early Nov., daily; early Nov.–mid-Apr., weekends. Part of WA 20 closes during winter. Exact opening and closing dates of highway depend on snow and avalanche conditions.

HOW TO GET THERE

Access to the area is via WA 20 from Burlington to the west and Winthrop to the east. The north end of Ross Lake is reached by a 39-mi/62-km gravel road exiting from Trans-Canada Hwy. 1 near Hope, BC. There is no road access from WA 20 to the south end of Ross Lake. Closest airport: Seattle-Tacoma (140 mi/224 km).

FOR MORE INFORMATION

North Cascades National Park Service Complex (2105 State Rte. 20, Sedro Woolley, WA 98284, tel. 360/856-5700, fax 360/856–1934; e-mail NOCA_Interpretation@nps.gov; Web site www.nps.gov/rola). Sedro-Woolley Chamber of Commerce (714 B Metcalf St., Sedro-Woolley, WA 98284, tel. 360/855–1841). Concrete Chamber of Commerce (Box 743, Concrete, WA 98237, tel. 360/853–7042).

San Juan Island National Historical Park

On San Juan Island

Commemorated in this park are the 1853–72 events relating to the settlement of the Oregon boundary dispute between the United States and Great Britain. In 1859, military forces from both countries confronted each other in a crisis precipitated by the nations' dual claims to the island and the death of a Hudson's Bay Company pig at the hands of an American farmer. On view are remains of American and British camps. The island is also home to glacial landscapes with grasslands, forests, beaches, tidepools, and lagoons. The park was authorized in 1966.

WHAT TO SEE & DO

Beachcombing, hiking, picnicking, walking. **Facilities:** Information center with interpretive exhibits (125 Spring St., Friday Harbor), 2 contact stations with interpretive exhibits (American Camp, 6 mi/10 km from Friday Harbor; and English Camp, 9 mi/14 km from Friday Harbor), beaches, trails. Picnic areas with tables and fire pits/grates, sales outlets. **Programs & Events:** Guided walks (June–Aug.), historical reenactments (June–Aug., Sat.), cultural and natural-history programs (June–Aug., Fri.–Sun.).

PLANNING YOUR VISIT

⚠ **Camping:** Private campgrounds and county park available on island; none in park. 🏨 **Lodging:** Available in Friday Harbor and on the island; none in park. ✕ **Food & Supplies:** Available in Friday Harbor and Roche Harbor; none in park. ☞ **Tips & Hints:** Go in late spring for wildflowers, summer for whale-watching and good weather, winter for migrating birds. Busiest in July and August, least crowded in November and December. 🎫 **Fees, Permits & Limitations:** Free. Permits required (free) for horseback riding. Washington state fishing license required. Shellfish/seaweed license required for clamming. No hunting or collecting. Leashed pets only. Bikes and motorized vehicles restricted to roads and parking areas. Park grounds open daily dawn–11 PM. Friday Harbor information center open Memorial Day–Labor Day, daily 8:30–5; Labor Day–Memorial Day, weekdays 8:30–4:30; closed federal holidays in winter. American Camp contact station open Memorial Day–Labor Day, daily 8:30–5; Labor Day–Memorial Day, Thurs.–Sun. 8:30–4:30; closed federal holidays in winter. English Camp contact station open Memorial Day–Labor Day, daily 8:30–5; closed in winter.

HOW TO GET THERE

The island is accessible by Washington State Ferries from Anacortes (83 mi/133 km north of Seattle) or from Sidney, BC (15 mi/24 km north of Victoria). Closest airport: Friday Harbor.

FOR MORE INFORMATION

San Juan Island National Historical Park (Box 429, Friday Harbor, WA 98250, tel. 360/378–2240; e-mail SAJH_Administration@nps.gov; Web site www.nps.gov/sajh). San Juan Island Chamber of Commerce (Box 98, Friday Harbor, WA 98250–0098, tel. 360/378–5240).

Whitman Mission
National Historic Site

In the southeast part of the state, near Walla Walla

Marcus and Narcissa Whitman founded a Protestant mission here in 1836 to convert the Cayuse people to Christianity and provide a way station for Oregon Trail pioneers. In 1847, a measles epidemic killed half the Cayuse. The survivors blamed Marcus Whitman for his inability to cure the measles and killed him, his wife, and 11 others on November 29, 1847. Another 50 hostages were ransomed a month later by agents from the Hudson's Bay Company. The site was authorized in 1936 and renamed in 1963.

WHAT TO SEE & DO

Fishing; picnicking; touring original building sites, a section of the Oregon Trail, and a mass grave of Whitman and others. Book sales area, picnic area with tables. **Facilities:** Visitor center with interpretive exhibits, trails, wayside exhibits. **Programs & Events:** Slide program (year-round). Cultural demonstrations (June–Aug., weekends).

PLANNING YOUR VISIT

⚠ **Camping:** Available in Walla Walla; none at site. 🏨 **Lodging:** Available in Walla Walla; none at site. ✕ **Food & Supplies:** Available in Walla Walla; none at site. ☞ **Tips & Hints:** Wear walking shoes. The best times to visit are early summer and fall. Busiest in May and June, least crowded in December and January. 🎟 **Fees, Permits & Limitations:** Entrance fee: $2 per adult or $4 per family. Washington state fishing license required. No hunting. Leashed pets only. Walk bicycles on trails. Park open daily dawn–dusk. Visitor center open Memorial Day–Labor Day, daily 8–6; Labor Day–Memorial Day, daily 8–4:30. Closed Thanksgiving, Dec. 25, Jan. 1.

HOW TO GET THERE

7 mi/11 km west of Walla Walla, off U.S. 12. Closest airport: Walla Walla.

FOR MORE INFORMATION

Whitman Mission National Historic Site (328 Whitman Mission Rd., Walla Walla, WA 99362, tel. 509/522–6360, fax 509/522–6355; Web site www.nps.gov/whmi). Walla Walla Area Chamber of Commerce (Box 644, Walla Walla, WA 99362, tel. 509/525–0850).

See Also

Klondike Gold Rush National Historical Park, Alaska. *Lewis and Clark National Historic Trail*, National Trails System in Other National Parklands. *Nez Perce National Historical Park*, Idaho. *Oregon National Scenic Trail*, National Trails System in Other National Parklands. *Pacific Crest National Scenic Trail*, National Trails System in Other National Parklands.

WEST VIRGINIA

Appalachian National Scenic Trail 👓

In the Appalachian Mountains,
from Katahdin, ME, to Springer Mountain, GA

The 2,167-mi/3,467-km trail was the nation's first designated national scenic trail. The federally protected trail corridor protects the habitats of hundreds of rare, threatened, and endangered species and preserves some of the East Coast's finest remaining wildlands. Topography along the trail ranges from the rugged White Mountains in New Hampshire to the rolling farmlands of Pennsylvania's Cumberland Valley to the high-elevation grassy balds of Roan Mountain, Tennessee. The trail was built by volunteers and completed in 1937. It is maintained and managed primarily by volunteers, whose efforts are coordinated by the non-profit Appalachian Trail Conference. It became a national scenic trail in 1968.

WHAT TO SEE & DO

Backpacking, hiking. **Facilities:** Visitor center—the Appalachian Trail Conference's national office in Harpers Ferry, WV; trail, shelters, huts. Map and guidebook sales area (Harpers Ferry, WV).

PLANNING YOUR VISIT

⚠ **Camping:** No developed campgrounds. Backcountry camping and rustic shelters available (no reservations). Private campgrounds available in towns near the trail. 🏨 **Lodging:** On the trail: rustic shelters are available a day's hike apart along the trail (no running water, electricity); 8 "full-service" huts in the White Mountains in New Hampshire (reservations suggested, tel. 603/466–2727). Off the trail: lodging available in nearby towns. ✗ **Food & Supplies:** On the trail: meals available in White Mountain huts (spring–early fall; reservations suggested, tel. 603/466–2727). Off the trail: available in nearby towns. ☞ **Tips & Hints:** Carry map, compass, whistle (3 blasts are an international call for help), flashlight (with extra batteries), sharp knife, fire starter (a candle, for instance), waterproof matches, first-aid kit, extra food, water (and some means to treat naturally occurring water), warm clothing and rain gear, and a heavy-duty garbage bag (to serve as an emergency shelter). 🏕 **Fees, Permits & Limitations:** Free. Overnight camping permits or user registration required at Great Smoky Mountains and Shenandoah National parks (*see separate entries*) and parts of the White Mountain National Forest in New Hampshire and Baxter State Park in Maine. No motor vehicles, bicycles, or mountain bikes on off-road sections. No horses or pack animals except in part of Great Smoky Mountains National Park. Leashed dogs only. Hunting is allowed on many of the lands through which the trail passes. No groups larger than 10 in some areas. No rest rooms available. Trail open year-round. Visitor center open weekdays 9–5 and weekends 9–4 during peak hiking months.

HOW TO GET THERE

The trail has 500 access points along its 2,167-mi/3,467-km length from Katahdin, ME, to Springer Mountain, GA. It passes through Maine, New Hampshire, Vermont, Massachusetts, Connecticut, New York, New Jersey, Pennsylvania, Maryland, West Virginia, Virginia, Tennessee, North Carolina, and Georgia.

FOR MORE INFORMATION

Appalachian Trail Conference (Box 807, Harpers Ferry, WV 25425, tel. 304/535–6331, fax 304/535–2667; e-mail info@appalachiantrail.org; Web site www.appalachiantrail.org).

Bluestone National Scenic River

In the southern part of the state, between Hinton and Princeton

This scenic river preserves relatively unspoiled land in southern West Virginia, contains natural and historic features of the Appalachian plateau, and offers excellent warm-water fishing, hiking, boating, and scenery in its lower 11 mi/18 km. The river was authorized on October 26, 1988.

WHAT TO SEE & DO

Canoeing, fishing, hiking, hunting, white-water boating. **Facilities:** Bluestone Trail, 8 mi. hiking, bicycling, horseback riding trail. **Programs & Events:** Guided hikes, interpretive programs (seasonal).

PLANNING YOUR VISIT

⚠ **Camping:** Available in Pipestem Resort and Bluestone state parks. 🏨 **Lodging:** Available at Pipestem Resort and Bluestone state parks and in Athens, Hinton, Princeton. ✕ **Food & Supplies:** Available in Pipestem Resort and Bluestone state parks and Athens, Hinton, Princeton. ☞ **Tips & Hints:** Intermediate skill required for Class I and II white water. Busiest in July and August, least crowded in January and February. 🎫 **Fees, Permits & Limitations:** Free. No hunting or trapping on upper river. Open daily.

HOW TO GET THERE

The scenic river is south of Hinton and northeast of Princeton. Access is through the Bluestone and Pipestem Resort state parks on Rte. 20. A tram that can transport boats provides access to the river from Pipestem Resort State Park. Closest airport: Charleston.

FOR MORE INFORMATION

Bluestone National Scenic River (Box 246, Glen Jean, WV 25846, tel. 304/465–0508; Web site www.nps.gov/blue).

Gauley River National Recreation Area

In the southern part of the state, near Summersville

Twenty-five miles/40 kilometers of free-flowing Gauley River and 6 mi/10 km of the Meadow River have Class V + rapids and are some of the most challenging white-water boating sites in the East. The area was authorized on October 26, 1988.

WHAT TO SEE & DO

Fishing, hunting, kayaking, trapping, white-water rafting. **Programs & Events:** Ranger-led hikes (seasonal). Civil War battle reenactments (Sept., at Carnifex Ferry Battlefield State Park).

PLANNING YOUR VISIT

Camping: Available at Tailwaters area and private campgrounds; none in recreation area. **Lodging:** Available at Hawk's Nest and Babcock state parks and in Ansted, Fayetteville, Glen Ferris, Hico, Lookout, Summersville; none in recreation area. **Food & Supplies:** Available seasonally at Summersville Lake and in Gauley Bridge, Mount Nebo, and Summersville; none in recreation area. **Tips & Hints:** Most land along the Gauley River is privately owned. Go to Carnifex Ferry Battlefield State Park for scenic overlook and to access hiking trails. Go on weekends between mid-September and mid-October for rafting season, which depends on releases from Summerville Dam. Be skilled enough to handle Class V+ rapids. Busiest in September and October, least crowded in December and January. **Fees, Permits & Limitations:** Free.

HOW TO GET THERE

The recreation area is between Summersville Dam and the town of Swiss, WV. Access is via Rte. 129 at the Summersville Dam, off U.S. 19. Other access points include Carnifex Ferry Battlefield State Park, off Rte. 129, and Swiss Rd., off Rte. 39. Closest airport: Charleston (75 mi/120 km).

FOR MORE INFORMATION

Gauley River National Recreation Area (Box 246, Glen Jean, WV 25846, tel. 304/465–0508; Web site www.nps.gov/gari).

Harpers Ferry National Historical Park

In the eastern part of the state, in Harpers Ferry

John Brown's raid on Harpers Ferry in 1859 thrust this small West Virginia town into national prominence. Located at the scenic confluence of the Shenandoah and Potomac rivers, the park includes 2,500 acres in the states of West Virginia, Virginia, and Maryland. A variety of museums, exhibits, and trails illustrate the six nationally significant themes interpreted here—natural environment, industry, the Brown raid, the Civil War, African-American history, and transportation—and how they are connected. Harpers Ferry was designated as a national monument in 1944 and changed to a national historical park in 1968.

WHAT TO SEE & DO

Fishing, hiking, picnicking, rock climbing, visiting museums and exhibits. **Facilities:** Visitor center (Cavalier Heights District) and visitor information center (Lower Town District); museums, exhibits, trails with wayside exhibits. Bookstore, picnic area. **Programs & Events:** Ranger-guided tours (Memorial Day–Labor Day), concerts (June–Sept.), living-history programs (June–Oct.). Independence Celebration, Christmas Celebration.

PLANNING YOUR VISIT

Camping: Available in town of Harpers Ferry and across river in Maryland; none in park. **Lodging:** Available in Charles Town, Harpers Ferry, Shepherdstown; none in park. **✕ Food & Supplies:** Restaurants available in merchants district across the street from the park's Lower Town District. Food and supplies also available outside the park in Charles Town and the town of Harpers Ferry. **☞ Tips & Hints:** Stay on trails. Go in fall for foliage. Busiest in July and August, least crowded in January and February. **Fees, Permits & Limitations:** Entrance fee: $3 per person for walk-ins and cyclists, $5 per vehicle. Rock-climbing registration required at ranger station. West Virginia, Maryland, or Virginia state fishing license required. No hunting. No bikes or motorized or mechanized equipment on trails. Leashed pets only. Park open daily. Visitor center open daily 8–5. Closed Thanksgiving, Dec. 25, Jan. 1.

HOW TO GET THERE

In the eastern panhandle of West Virginia, 65 mi/104 km northwest of Washington, DC, and 20 mi/32 km southwest of Frederick, MD, via U.S. 340. Closest airport: Washington-Dulles (50 mi/80 km).

FOR MORE INFORMATION

Harpers Ferry National Historical Park (Box 65, Harpers Ferry, WV 25425, tel. 304/535–6223, fax 304/535–6244; Web site www.nps.gov/hafe). Jefferson County Chamber of Commerce (Box 426, Charles Town, WV 25414–0426, tel. 304/725–2055).

New River Gorge National River

In the southern part of the state, from Hinton to Fayetteville

New River protects 53 mi/85 km of free-flowing waterway. The 71,000-acre park and surroundings are rich in cultural and natural history and contain an abundance of scenic and recreational opportunities. The

New River is one of the most renowned fishing streams in the state and offers premier white-water boating. The 65-million-year-old river, one of the oldest on the continent, has cut a deep gorge that exposes rocks 330 million years old and harbors rare plants. The site was authorized on November 10, 1978.

WHAT TO SEE & DO

Fishing, hiking, horseback riding, hunting, mountain biking (rentals, Fayetteville), picnicking, recreational climbing, white-water canoeing (rentals, Hinton). **Facilities:** 4 visitor centers with interpretive exhibits— Canyon Rim (U.S. 19, 2 mi/3 km north of Fayetteville), Thurmond Depot (WV 25, 7 mi/11 km from the Glen Jean exit of U.S. 19), Grand-view (WV 9, 6 mi/10 km north of Exit 129B on I–64), Hinton (west of Hinton on Rte. 20); amphitheater, boardwalk, hiking trails. Bookstores, picnic shelters, tables, and fire grates. **Programs & Events:** Ranger-led walks, hikes, bike rides, slide shows, and programs (year-round). Guided walks and hikes; mountain bike rides; and evening programs (May–Oct.). New River Train (Oct., tel. 304/453–1641), New River Gorge Bridge Pedestrian Day (3rd Sat., Oct.),

PLANNING YOUR VISIT

Camping: 5 primitive camping areas. Backcountry camping available. Group campsites available at Burnwood and Dunglen (reservations required, tel. 304/465–6517 for both). Private campgrounds available in Beaver, Beckley, Clifftop, Fayetteville, Hico, Hinton, Minden, Mossy, Oak Hill, Pipestem, and Summersville. **Lodging:** Available in Beaver, Beckley, Fayetteville, Hinton, Oak Hill, and Summersville. **Food & Supplies:** Available in Beaver, Beckley, Fayetteville, Hinton, Mount Hope, Oak Hill, and Summersville. **Tips & Hints:** Allow extra time, because the park is very long and narrow, with several access points into the gorge, rather than one main entrance. Book white-water rafting trips on Sundays or weekdays to get discounts and avoid Saturday crowds. Narrow, winding, one-lane roads require driving with passenger-side wheels on the shoulder when meeting on-coming traffic. Some park roads are unsuitable for large recreational vehicles. Stay off CSX railroad property that runs through park. Go in April, May, September, or October for cool, crisp weather; mid-May for Grandview rhododendron blooms; late June–early July for wild rhododendron blooms; April and September for peak bird migrations; mid-October for peak fall foliage. Busiest in July and August, least crowded in January and February. **Fees, Permits & Limitations:** Free. Picnic shelter reservation and fees (tel. 304/465–6517 Burnwood and Dunglen, 304/465–8064 Grandview). West Virginia state fishing license required. Hunting on federally owned lands within the park only, except at Grandview and Burnwood. No trapping. No recreational climbing at Grandview. Leashed pets only. Horses or pack animals on designated trails only. Swimming and wading not recommended because of strong currents and undercut rocks. No alcohol at park headquarters, Dunglen, Grandview, and Stonecliff. Bikes on designated trails only. Park open daily. Visitor center hours: Canyon Rim—daily 9–5, extended hours in summer; closed Thanksgiving, Dec. 25, and Jan. 1; Thurmond Depot—Memorial Day–Labor Day, daily 9–5; intermittent weekend hours spring and fall; Grandview—Labor Day–Memorial Day, weekends 9–5; Memorial Day–Labor Day, daily with extended hours; Hinton—Memorial Day–Labor Day, daily 9–5; Labor Day–Memorial Day, intermittent weekend hours.

HOW TO GET THERE

The river is one hour east of Charleston and 20 minutes from Beckley. It is accessible from the West Virginia Tpke., I–64 and 77, and U.S. 19 and 60. Closest airports: Beckley (30 mi/48 km) and Charleston (65 mi/104 km).

FOR MORE INFORMATION

New River Gorge National River (Box 246, Glen Jean, WV 25846, tel. 304/465–0508, fax 304/465–0591; e-mail neri_interpretation@nps.gov; Web site www.nps.gov/neri). West Virginia Convention and Visitor Center (511 Ewart Ave., Beckley, WV 25801, tel. 800/847–4898, fax 304/252–2252; Web site www.visitwv.com or www.visitwv.org). Fayette County Chamber of Commerce (310 Oyler Ave., Oak Hill, WV 25901, tel. 800/927–0263). West Virginia Travel Council (Box 50312, 2101 Washington St. E, Charleston, WV 25305-0317, tel. 800/225–5982).

See Also

Chesapeake and Ohio Canal National Historical Park, Maryland. *National Coal Heritage Area,* National Heritage Areas in Other National Parklands.

WISCONSIN

Apostle Islands National Lakeshore ◥◣

On the south shore of Lake Superior,
90 mi/144 km east of Duluth, MN

These sheltered islands on the world's largest freshwater lake offer pristine beaches, sandstone cliffs, sea caves, dense forests, and a variety of wetlands. Native Americans, voyageurs, loggers, quarrymen, farmers, and commercial fishermen have left their marks on the islands. Six historic light stations provide glimpses into the region's maritime history. The national lakeshore encompasses 21 of the 22 Apostle Islands and a 12-mi/19-km stretch of mainland shoreline. The park was established on September 26, 1970.

WHAT TO SEE & DO

Beachcombing, boating, camping, cross-country skiing, fishing, hiking, hunting, kayaking (rentals, Bayfield), picnicking, riding excursion boats, sailing (rentals, Bayfield), scuba diving, swimming, touring lighthouses. **Facilities:** 2 visitor centers with interpretive exhibits—Bayfield Visitor Center (Washington Ave., Bayfield) and Little Sand Bay Visitor Center (13 mi/21 km north of Bayfield), contact station with interpretive exhibits—Presque Isle Point (Stockton Island, open June–Sept.), trails. Book and map sale areas, docks, theater. **Programs & Events:** Daily lighthouse lens talks (on request) at Bayfield Visitor Center (year-round). Guest lectures (mid-June–Aug., weekly); guided hikes, campfire programs (mid-June–Labor Day); guided lighthouse tours (mid-June–Sept.),.

PLANNING YOUR VISIT

⚠ **Camping:** Backcountry campsites on 14 islands (permit required, *see below*; reservations available, tel. 715/779–3397). Group backcountry camping available (permit required, *see below*; reservations available, tel. 715/779–3397). Private and public campgrounds in Ashland, Bayfield, Little Sand Bay, Red Cliff, Washburn, on Madeline Island, and in the Chequamegon/Nicolet National Forest. 🛏 **Lodging:** Available nearby in Ashland, Bayfield, Cornucopia, La Pointe, Washburn; none at lakeshore. ✕ **Food & Supplies:** Food and supplies are available in Ashland, Bayfield, Cornucopia, La Pointe, Red Cliff, Washburn; none at lakeshore. ☞ **Tips & Hints:** Monitor near-shore marine weather forecasts; weather can change dramatically on short notice. Get drinking water from wells on seven islands. Go in May and June for best flowers, July and August for moderate waves, May and September for bird migrations, February and March for over-ice travel to islands. Take insect repellent, especially in June and July. Busiest in July and August, least crowded in December and January. 🗓 **Fees, Permits & Limita-**

tions: Free. Camping permits ($15, $30 for groups; tel. 715/779–3397))
required. Wisconsin state hunting license and fishing license with Great
Lakes trout stamp required. Scuba permit (free) required. Leashed
pets only. No bikes on trails. No motorized vehicles on islands. No
metal detectors. No personal watercraft or floatplanes. No snowmobiles. No hunting May 15–Sept. 30 except for bear hunting on Stockton, Sand, and Oak Islands. Park open daily. Bayfield Visitor Center
open Nov.–Apr., weekdays 8–4:30; May 1–Memorial Day, daily 8–4:30;
Memorial Day–Labor Day, daily 8–6; Labor Day–Oct., daily 8–5.
Closed Thanksgiving, Dec. 25, Jan. 1. Little Sand Bay Visitor Center
open early June–Sept., daily 9–5.

HOW TO GET THERE
Bayfield Visitor Center is one block off Hwy. 13 in Bayfield, WI, 23
mi/37 km north of Ashland, WI, and 90 mi/145 km east of Duluth, MN.
Islands scattered across 700 square mi/1,813 square km of Lake Superior. Closest airport: Duluth.

FOR MORE INFORMATION
Apostle Islands National Lakeshore (Rte. 1, Box 4, Old County Courthouse Bldg., Bayfield, WI 54814, tel. 715/779–3397, fax 715/779–3049;
e-mail apis_superintendent @nps.gov; Web site www.nps.gov/apis).
Bayfield Chamber of Commerce (42 S. Broad, Bayfield, WI 54814, tel.
800/447–4094, fax 715/779–5080).

Saint Croix National
Scenic Riverway

*On the Minnesota–Wisconsin border
and in northwest Wisconsin*

Free-flowing and unpolluted, beautiful St. Croix River and its Namekagon tributary flow through some of the most scenic and least developed country in the upper Midwest. The 252-mi/403-km stretch of
protected river offers canoeing, a variety of fishing opportunities, hiking, bird-watching, and picnicking. The park was authorized on October 2, 1968.

WHAT TO SEE & DO
Bird- and wildlife watching, boating, canoeing (rentals near park),
cross-country skiing, fishing, hiking, hunting, snowshoeing. **Facilities:** 4
visitor centers with interpretive exhibits—Headquarters (St. Croix
Falls, WI); Namekagon (Trego, WI); Marshland (Hwy. 5 mi/8 km west
of Grantsburg, WI); Lower River (Stillwater, MN); hiking and cross-
country ski trails, adjacent state parks. Bookstores, picnic shelters. **Programs & Events:** Campfire programs at state parks, ranger-guided
tour-boat cruises (both June–Aug.).

PLANNING YOUR VISIT
⚠ **Camping:** Backcountry camping available along river. Group campsites available (no reservations). State park and private campgrounds

also available. ⊞ **Lodging:** Available in Cable, Grantsburg, Hayward, Osceola, St. Croix Falls, Spooner, and Trego, WI, and Pine City, Stillwater, and Taylor Falls, MN. ✗ **Food & Supplies:** Available locally. ☞ **Tips & Hints:** Watch for deer ticks. Wear life preservers. Bring extra paddle, insect repellent, small gas stove, and drinking water if canoeing. Expect challenging canoeing for beginners. Go between April and October for ice-free river, in May for migrating birds, between May and June for wildflowers, between late September and early October for fall colors, in October for waterfowl. Busiest in July and August, least crowded in January and February. ▨ **Fees, Permits & Limitations:** Free. Make picnic shelter reservations at Osceola Landing. Minnesota or Wisconsin state fishing license required. Leashed pets only. No bicycles or motorized vehicles on trails. Obey slow speed and no-wake zones on river. No trapping. Park open daily. Visitor center hours: Headquarters—Memorial Day–Labor Day, Mon.–Thurs. 8:30–5, Fri.–Sun. 8:30–6; May and Sept., daily 8:30–4:30; Oct.–Apr., weekends 8:30–4:30; Namekagon—May and Sept., weekends 8–4:30; Memorial Day–Labor Day, daily 8–4:30; Marshland—May and Sept., weekends 8:30–5; Memorial Day–Labor Day, Thurs.–Mon. 8:30–5; Lower River—Memorial Day–Labor Day, Mon.–Thurs. 9–5, Fri.–Sun. 9–6; Labor Day–Memorial Day, Fri.–Sun. 9–5.

HOW TO GET THERE

Park headquarters and visitor center is at the corner of Massachusetts and Hamilton Sts. in St. Croix Falls, WI. Closest airport: Minneapolis-St. Paul International (55 mi/88 km).

FOR MORE INFORMATION

Saint Croix National Scenic Riverway (Box 708, St. Croix Falls, WI 54024, tel. 715/483–3284, fax 715/483–3288; Web site www.nps.gov/sacn). Polk County Information Center (710 Hwy. 35S, St. Croix Falls, WI 54024, tel. 715/483–1410). Minnesota Office of Tourism (121 7th Pl. E, 100 Metro Sq., St. Paul 55101-2112, tel. 800/657–3700). Wisconsin Division of Tourism (201 W. Washington Ave., Madison, WI 53703, tel. 800/372–2737). State park information: Minnesota Department of Natural Resources Information Center (500 Lafayette Rd., St. Paul, MN 55101, tel. 651/296–6157). Wisconsin Department of Natural Resources Bureau of Parks and Recreation (Dept. of Natural Resources, Box 7921 Madison, WI 53707-7921, tel. 608/266–2181).

See Also

Ice Age National Scenic Trail, National Trails System in Other National Parklands. *Ice Age National Scientific Reserve,* Affiliated Areas in Other National Parklands. *Lewis and Clark National Historic Trail,* National Trails System in Other National Parklands. *North Country National Scenic Trail,* National Trails System in Other National Parklands.

WYOMING

Devils Tower
National Monument

In the northeast part of the state, near Devils Tower

Devils Tower was the nation's first national monument. An igneous intrusion exposed by erosion, Devils Tower rises 867 ft/263 m from its base and is a magnet for rock climbers. Today, it is surrounded by pine forests of the Black Hills and the grasslands of the rolling plains. Visitors can see a healthy prairie dog town as well as numerous flora and fauna. The tower remains sacred to numerous Plains Indian tribes. The monument was proclaimed in 1906.

WHAT TO SEE & DO

Fishing, hiking, picnicking, rock climbing. **Facilities:** Visitor center with interpretive exhibits, wayside exhibits, trails. Bookstore, picnic area with pavilion and fire grates. **Programs & Events:** Guided walking tours, special cultural programs and evening campfire programs (Memorial Day–Labor Day). Cowboy Poetry Festival (Labor Day weekend).

PLANNING YOUR VISIT

⚠ **Camping:** Campground: no hookups (no reservations). No backcountry camping. Group camping available (no reservations). Private campground just outside park entrance. ▦ **Lodging:** Available in Hulett, Moorcroft, Sundance; none at monument. ✕ **Food & Supplies:** Available in Hulett, Moorcroft, Sundance; none at monument. ☞ **Tips & Hints:** Plan to spend at least two hours visiting the monument. Prepare for summer heat of 95°F/35°C or higher. Voluntary climbing closure during June. Busiest in July and August, least crowded in December and February. ▦ **Fees, Permits & Limitations:** Entrance fee: $3 per person (walk-ins, bicycles, or motorcycles) or $8 per vehicle. Wyoming state fishing license required. Climbers must register with park. No hunting or collecting park resource materials. No pets on tower or on trails. Leashed pets elsewhere. No vehicles, including bicycles, off maintained roadways. Park open daily. Closed Thanksgiving, Dec. 25, Jan. 1. Visitor center open Memorial Day–Labor Day, daily 8 AM–8 PM; Mar.–Memorial Day and Labor Day–Oct., daily 8:30–5; shorter hours possible depending on staffing.

HOW TO GET THERE

From I–90, the monument can be reached via U.S. 14N and WY 24. Closest airport: Gillette (60 mi/96 km).

FOR MORE INFORMATION

Devils Tower National Monument (Box 10, Devils Tower, WY 82714, tel. 307/467–5283, fax 307/467–5350; Web site www.nps.gov/deto).

Sundance Chamber of Commerce (Box 1004, Sundance, WY 82729, tel. 307/283–1000).

Fort Laramie
National Historic Site

In the southeast part of the state, near Fort Laramie

The 12 restored historic buildings on the site interpret life at this "Queen Outpost of the Frontier Army." During the 1800s, the Wyoming wilderness fort on the Laramie River, near the river's confluence with the Platte, played a crucial role in the West's transformation. First serving as a fur-trading center, the fort later became a military garrison along the Oregon Trail. The military post played an essential role in western Army operations during the Indian wars. After 41 years of service, the post closed in 1890. The site was proclaimed a national monument in 1938 and redesignated a national historic site in 1960.

WHAT TO SEE & DO

Touring the fort, watching audiovisual program. **Facilities:** Visitor center with interpretive exhibits, fort. Bookstore. **Programs & Events:** Self-guided and audio tours year-round. Interpretive programs, guided tours, living-history demonstrations (June–Aug.).

PLANNING YOUR VISIT

⚠ **Camping:** Available in Fort Laramie, Guernsey, Lingle, Torrington; none at site. ⊞ **Lodging:** Available in Fort Laramie, Guernsey, Lingle, Torrington; none at site. ✕ **Food & Supplies:** Available in Fort Laramie, Guernsey, Lingle, Torrington; none at site. ☞ **Tips & Hints:** Busiest in July and August, least crowded in December and January. ▩ **Fees, Permits & Limitations:** Entrance fee: $2 per person 17 and older, 16 and under, free.

HOW TO GET THERE

3 mi/5 km southwest of the town of Fort Laramie, on SR 160. Closest airport: Torrington (20 mi/32 km).

FOR MORE INFORMATION

Fort Laramie National Historic Site (HC 72, Box 389, Fort Laramie, WY 82212, tel. 307/837–2221, fax 307/837B-2120; Web site www.nps.gov/fola).

Fossil Butte
National Monument

In the southwest part of the state, near Kemmerer

The 8,198-acre site contains one of the best-preserved and most complete paleoecosystems of fossilized plants, fish, insects, mammals, birds, and reptiles. The fossilized remnants of this freshwater lake date to a period of warmer climate that existed 50 million years ago. The monument was established in 1972.

WHAT TO SEE & DO

Hiking, picnicking, road touring. **Facilities:** Visitor center with interpretive exhibits, trails. Bookstore, picnic area. **Programs & Events:** Porch programs and guided nature hikes (June–Sept.).

PLANNING YOUR VISIT

⚠ **Camping:** Available in Kemmerer; none at monument. 🛏 **Lodging:** Available in Kemmerer; none at monument. ✕ **Food & Supplies:** Available in Kemmerer; none at monument. ☞ **Tips & Hints:** Hiking trails are 7,000–8,000 ft/2,123–2,427 m above sea level and considered moderately strenuous. Go in late summer for best weather. Busiest in July and August, least crowded in December and January. 🎫 **Fees, Permits & Limitations:** Free. No hunting. Leashed pets only. Park open daily. Visitor center open Labor Day–Memorial Day, daily 8–4:30; Memorial Day–Labor Day, daily 8–7. Closed federal holidays in winter.

HOW TO GET THERE

13 mi/21 km west of Kemmerer, on U.S. 30. Closest airports: Salt Lake City, UT (145 mi/232 km); Rock Springs, WY (100 mi/160 km).

FOR MORE INFORMATION

Fossil Butte National Monument (Box 592, Kemmerer, WY 83101, tel. 307/877–4455, fax 307/877–4457; Web site www.nps.gov/fobu). Kemmerer Chamber of Commerce (800 Pine Ave., Kemmerer, WY 83101-2907, tel. 307/877–9761).

Grand Teton National Park

In the northwest part of the state, near Jackson

Towering more than a mile above the valley known as Jackson Hole, the Grand Teton rises 13,770 ft/4,177 m above sea level. Twelve Teton peaks reach above 12,000 ft/3,640 m, high enough to support a dozen mountain glaciers. The park offers ribbons of green riparian plants bordering the Snake River and other streams, sagebrush flats, lodgepole pine and spruce forests, subalpine meadows, and alpine stone fields. Also included in the park is part of Jackson Hole, winter feeding ground of the largest American elk herd. Moose, buffalo, pronghorn antelope, bears, eagles, and trumpeter swans also inhabit the park. The park was initially established on February 26, 1929. Through the 1930s, John D. Rockefeller, Jr. purchased 33,000 acres of valley land from local ranchers and donated it to the National Park Service in 1943. In 1950, the current boundaries of the park were established with the inclusion of the valley land.

WHAT TO SEE & DO

Auto touring, backpacking, bicycling (rentals, Dornan's and in Jackson), boating, canoeing, fishing (rentals, in park and in Jackson), floating (rentals, in park and in Jackson), hiking, horseback riding (rentals, Colter Bay and Jackson Lake Lodge), mountaineering (rentals), skiing, snowmobiling (rentals, Flagg Ranch), snowshoeing, swimming, wildlife viewing. **Facilities:** 3 visitor centers—Moose (12 mi/19 km north of Jackson on Hwys. 89/191/26); Jenny Lake (20 mi/32 km north of Jackson); and Colter Bay (42 mi/67 km north of Jackson); Flagg Ranch Information Station (16 mi/26 km north of Colter Bay); auditorium, Indian Arts Museum, amphitheater at Colter Bay; 100 mi/160 km of scenic roads; 200 mi/320 km of trails. Bookstores, gas, gift shops, marina. **Programs & Events:** Ranger-led walks, talks, museum tours, evening slide presentations, and campfire programs (early June–late Sept.).

PLANNING YOUR VISIT

Camping: 5 campgrounds: dump stations (no reservations); trailer village (reservations available, tel. 307/543–2811). Backcountry camping available (permit required; *see below*). Group campsites available (reservations available in writing only, Jan.–May 15 at park address or fax). Private campgrounds in Jackson, east and south of park. **Lodging:** In the park: Dornan's Spur Ranch Cabins (tel. 307/733–2522), Flagg Ranch (tel. 800/443–2311), Grand Teton Lodge Company (tel. 800/628–9988), Signal Mountain Lodge (tel. 800/672–6012), Triangle X Ranch (tel. 307/733-B2183). Lodging also available in Jackson and Teton Village. **Food & Supplies:** Meals at Dornan's, Jenny Lake Lodge, Signal Mountain Lodge, Jackson Lake Lodge, and Flagg Ranch. Buffet and snack bar service at Signal Mountain Lodge, Jackson Lake Lodge, Colter Bay, and Flagg Ranch. Camp stores at Dornan's, South Jenny Lake, Signal Mountain, Colter Bay, and Flagg Ranch. Food and supplies also available in Jackson. **Tips & Hints:** Plan ahead or make reservations in summer for lodging, camping, and dining. Summer highs are near 75°F/24°C, lows near 45°F/7°C; winters are long and cold, with heavy snows from December through February. Bring rain gear spring–fall. Busiest in July and August, least crowded October–November, January, and April. **Fees, Permits & Limitations:** Entrance fee: $20 per car, good for Yellowstone and Grand Teton national parks. Backcountry permit (free) required for all backcountry camping (reservations available Jan.–May 15 and up to 24 hrs before first night's stay). Permit required (fee, varies depending on boat type) for motorized and nonmotorized watercraft. Wyoming state fishing license required. Park open daily. Visitor center hours: Moose—Labor Day–Memorial Day, daily 8–5; Memorial Day–Labor Day, daily 8–7; Jenny Lake—June–Labor Day, daily 8–7; Colter Bay—mid-May–June and Labor Day–Sept. 30, daily 8–5; June–Labor Day, daily 8–8; Flagg Ranch Information Station—June–Labor Day, daily 9–6. Visitor centers closed Dec. 25.

HOW TO GET THERE

The Moose Visitor Center is 13 mi/21 km north of Jackson on U.S. 26, 89, and 191. Closest airport: Jackson Hole (8 mi/13 km).

FOR MORE INFORMATION

Grand Teton National Park (Drawer 170, Moose, WY 83012, tel. 307/739–3300, fax 307/739–3438; Web site www.nps.gov/grte).

John D. Rockefeller Jr. Memorial Parkway

In the northwest part of the state, near Jackson

This scenic 82-mi/131-km corridor commemorates Rockefeller's role in aiding the establishment of many parks, including Grand Teton. The parkway connects West Thumb in Yellowstone with the south entrance of Grand Teton National Park. The 23,777-acre parkway was authorized on August 25, 1972.

WHAT TO SEE & DO

See Grand Teton National Park. ☞ **Tips & Hints:** Busiest in July and August, least crowded in December and January.

FOR MORE INFORMATION

John D. Rockefeller Jr. Memorial Parkway (c/o Grand Teton National Park, Drawer 170, Moose, WY 83012, tel. 307/733-2880; Web site www.nps.gov/jodr).

Yellowstone National Park

In northwest Wyoming, southeast Montana, and northeast Idaho

Yellowstone, the world's oldest national park, is a true wilderness, one of the few large natural areas (2.2 million acres) remaining in the lower 48 states. Led by the fabled Old Faithful, the park has approximately 10,000 geysers and hot springs, the greatest number on the planet. Human history in the park is evidenced by cultural sites dating back at least 10,000 years. The park's 1,000 mi/1,600 km of trails allow visitors to see bison, bighorn sheep, elk, grizzly bears, moose, pronghorn, and trumpeter swans. The park was established in 1872 and designated a Biosphere Reserve in 1976 and a World Heritage Site in 1978.

WHAT TO SEE & DO

Backpacking, bicycling, bird- and wildlife watching, boating, bus touring, canoeing, cross-country skiing, fishing, hiking, horseback riding, photography touring, picnicking, snow-coach touring, snowmobiling, wildlife and nature touring. **Facilities:** 5 visitor centers—Albright (Mammoth Hot Springs), Old Faithful, Canyon, Fishing Bridge, and Grant Village; Norris Geyser Basin Museum and Bookstore; Museum of the National Park Ranger (Norris); Madison and West Thumb information stations; scenic roads; overlooks; 8 self-guided nature trails; 1,000 mi/1,600 km of trails. Bookstores, gasoline, gift shops, marina, religious services. **Programs & Events:** Exhibits at Albright Visitor Center at Mammoth Hot Springs year-round. Ranger-led talks, demonstrations, walks, and hikes (mostly June–Aug.).

PLANNING YOUR VISIT

🏕 **Camping:** 12 campgrounds: hookups available at one RV park (reservations available, tel. 307/344–7311). Backcountry camping available (permit required, *see below*). Group camping available at Madison, Grant, and Bridge Bay (reservations required, tel. 307/344–7311). Camping also available in surrounding area. 🛏 **Lodging:** In the park: Canyon Lodge, Grant Village, Lake Lodge, Lake Yellowstone Hotel, Mammoth Hot Springs Hotel, Old Faithful Inn, Old Faithful Lodge, Old Faithful Snow Lodge, and Roosevelt Lodge (reservations for all, tel. 307/344–7311). Lodging also available in surrounding area. ✗ **Food & Supplies:** In the park: meals at Canyon Lodge Cafeteria, Canyon Lodge Dining Room, Grant Village Lakehouse Restaurant, Grant Village Restaurant, Lake Lodge Cafeteria, Lake Yellowstone Hotel Dining Room, Mammoth Hot Springs Hotel Dining Room, Old Faithful Inn Dining Room, Old Faithful Lodge Cafeteria, Old Faithful Snow Lodge Restaurant, Roosevelt Lodge Dining Room (reservations, tel. 307/344–7311). Light meals and fast food at Mammoth Hot Springs, Canyon, Tower Fall Store, Lake, Grant Village, Fishing Bridge, Bridge Bay, and Old Faithful; stores at Mammoth Hot Springs, Canyon, Tower Fall, Lake, Grant Village, Fishing Bridge, Bridge Bay, and Old Faithful. Food and supplies also available in surrounding area. ☞ **Tips & Hints:** Make lodging and camping reservations as early as possible. Limit your travels to one or two areas if you have one day or less to spend in the park. Allow two days or more to see major park attractions. Expect slow traveling in July and August because of crowds. Busiest in July and August, least crowded in November and December. 🎫 **Fees, Permits & Limitations:** Entrance fee: $20 per vehicle, $15 per snowmobile or motorcycle, $10 per bicyclist, walk-in, or skier 16 and up. Fee valid for Yellowstone and adjacent Grand Teton National Park (*see separate entry*). Bus (summer) and snow-coach tour fees (tel. 307/344–7311). Permit required ($15) for all backcountry camping (reservations available, Backcountry Office, Box 168, Yellowstone National Park, WY 82190). No commercial hauling/travel through park. Permit required for fishing and boating. Summer season is mid-Apr.–late Oct. All park roads close at 8 AM after first Sun. in Nov. except North Entrance road to Northeast entrance. Only over-snow vehicles are allowed on other park roads. Winter season begins mid-Dec. and runs through mid-Mar. Only the road from the north entrance at Gardiner, MT, to northeast entrance at Cooke City, MT, is open to cars year-round. Oversnow vehicles only on other park roads. Winter season is mid-Dec.–mid-Mar. Visitor center seasons: Albright—daily; Old Faithful—mid-Apr.–late Oct. and mid-Dec.–mid-Mar.; Canyon, Fishing Bridge, Grant Village, Museum of the National Park Ranger, and Norris Geyser Basin Museum and Bookstore—mid-May–Sept.; Madison Information Station—early June–Oct.; West Thumb Information Station—early June–Labor Day.

HOW TO GET THERE

There are five park entrances. To reach the north entrance, take U.S. 89 from I–90 at Livingston, MT; northeast entrance, take U.S. 212 from I–90 at Billings, MT., or Hwy. 296 from Cody, WY; west entrance, take U.S. 191 from Bozeman, MT, or U.S. 20 from Idaho Falls, ID; east entrance, take U.S. 16 from Cody, WY; south entrance, take U.S. 89 from Jackson, WY. Closest airports: Cody (90 mi/144 km) and Jackson, WY (115 mi/184 km); Bozeman (105 mi/168 km), Billings (195 mi/312 km), and West Yellowstone (June–early Sept.; 5 mi/8 km), MT; and Idaho Falls, ID (135 mi/216 km).

FOR MORE INFORMATION

Yellowstone National Park (Box 168, Yellowstone National Park, WY 82190-0168, tel. 307/344–7381; Web site www.nps.gov/yell). Big Sky Chamber of Commerce (Box 160100, Big Sky, MT 59716, tel. 800/943–4111), Billings Chamber of Commerce (Box 31177 or 815 S. 27th St., Billings, MT 59107, tel. 406/245–4111). Bozeman Chamber of Commerce (Box B, Bozeman, MT 59771 or 2000 Commerce Way, Bozeman, MT 59715, tel. 406/586–5421). Cooke City/Silver Gate Chamber of Commerce (Box 1071, Cooke City, MT 59020, tel. 406/838B-2495). Gardiner Chamber of Commerce (Box 81 or 3rd St. Gardiner, MT 59030, tel. 406/848–7971). Livingston Chamber of Commerce (303 E. Park, Livingston, MT 59047, 406/222–0850). Red Lodge Chamber of Commerce (Box 988, Red Lodge, MT 59068, tel. 406/446–1718). West Yellowstone Chamber of Commerce (Box 458, West Yellowstone, WY 59758, tel. 406/646–7701). Cody Chamber of Commerce (836 Sheridan Ave., Cody, WY 82414, tel. 307/587–2297). Dubois Chamber of Commerce (Box 632, Dubois, WY 82513, tel. 307/455–2556). Jackson Chamber of Commerce (Box 550 or 990 W. Broadway, Jackson, WY 83001, tel. 307/733–3316). Idaho Falls Chamber of Commerce and Eastern Idaho Visitor Information Center (Box 50498 or 505 Lindsay Blvd., Idaho Falls, ID 83405-0498, tel. 208/523–1010 or 800/634–3246).

See Also

Bighorn Canyon National Recreation Area, Montana. *California National Historic Trail,* National Trails System in Other National Parklands. *Continental Divide National Scenic Trail,* National Trails System in Other National Parklands. *Mormon Pioneer National Historic Trail,* National Trails System in Other National Parklands. *Nez Perce National Historic Trail,* National Trails System in Other National Parklands. *Oregon National Scenic Trail,* National Trails System in Other National Parklands. *Pony Express National Historic Trail,* National Trails System in Other National Parklands.

AMERICAN SAMOA

National Park of American Samoa

In the South Pacific

An old-world rain forest, the Indo-Pacific Coral Reef, and 3,000-year-old Samoan culture are protected in this park. It is located on three tropical volcanic islands—the main island of Tutuila and the Manua Islands of Ofu and Tau—separated by 60 mi/96 km of water. The park, which also protects the habitat of two species of flying fox (fruit bats), was authorized in 1988 and established in 1993.

WHAT TO SEE & DO

Auto touring on Tutuila (rentals on all three islands), bat and bird-watching, hiking on shore, hiking to the summit of Mount Alava (1610 ft/488 m) on Tutuila, snorkeling on Ofu. **Facilities:** Visitor center with interpretive displays—Pago Plaza (Pago Pago).

PLANNING YOUR VISIT

Lodging: Available locally; none in park. ✗ **Food & Supplies:** Available locally; none in park. ☞ **Tips & Hints:** This is a new park. The visitor center is the only park facility. Come prepared to experience Samoa on Samoan terms. Be open to new cultural experiences, and don't expect the same standards for visitor services that can be found on the mainland. The weather is hot and humid all year. Bring your own binoculars and snorkel gear. Always hike and snorkel with a partner: the rain forest can be an unforgiving place if you venture into it and become hurt with no one to help. Stay away from breaking waves and steep areas. Don't touch corals, especially fire coral, which produces a nasty sting. Don't swim near an "ava"—a crevice in the reef face where water drains out as the tide goes out. Carry plenty of water. Visit between May and September (winter in the Southern Hemisphere), when the temperature is about 80°F/27°C with southeast trade winds and less rain, but expect rain almost every day. **Fees, Permits & Limitations:** Free. No fishing. No rest rooms in park. Park open daily. Visitor center open weekdays 8–4:30, Sat. 8–noon.

HOW TO GET THERE

Park headquarters is in Pago Pago, American Samoa. Closest airport: Pago Pago International (10 mi/16 km).

FOR MORE INFORMATION

National Park of American Samoa (Pago Pago, American Samoa 96799, tel. 011/684/633–7082, 011/684/633–7083, or 011/684/633–7084, fax 011/684/633–7085; e-mail NPSA_Administration@nps.gov; Web site www.nps.gov/npsa). Tourism Office (Dept. of Commerce, American Samoa Government, Pago Pago, American Samoa 96799, tel. 684/633–1092).

GUAM

War in the Pacific
National Historical Park

In the Pacific Ocean, on Guam

In 1944, during World War II, American troops recaptured Guam. This park has seven sites, including the summit of Mt. Tenjo (1,033 ft/313 m), underwater relics on the offshore coral reefs (132 ft/40 m deep), and aging gun emplacements and other military equipment relics. The park was authorized on August 18, 1978.

WHAT TO SEE & DO

Hiking, picnicking, scuba diving, touring historic battle sites. **Facilities:** Visitor center with interpretive exhibits (beach side of Marine Dr. in Asan), beaches, trails. Picnic areas. **Programs & Events:** Ranger-led walks and talks (as staffing permits).

PLANNING YOUR VISIT

⊞ **Lodging:** Available on the island; none in park. ✕ **Food & Supplies:** Available on the island; none in park. ☞ **Tips & Hints:** Live ordnance still may be found in the park. Report any ammunition or military explosives you find on- or offshore. Some open caves still may contain booby traps. Some areas of the park are privately owned; observe NO TRESPASSING signs. Busiest in February and March, least crowded in August and October. ▦ **Fees, Permits & Limitations:** Free. Visitor center open weekdays 9–4:30, weekends and federal holidays 10–noon and 1–4:30. Closed Thanksgiving, Dec. 25, Jan. 1. Park units (beaches, monuments, historic areas, and picnic areas) open daily for pedestrians, 7:30 AM–6 PM for vehicles.

HOW TO GET THERE

Guam, the southernmost island of the Mariana Islands, is in the West Pacific, 1,500 mi/2,400 km south of Tokyo and 6,100 mi/9,760 km west of San Francisco. Guam is 15 hours ahead of eastern standard time and doesn't observe daylight saving time. The park consists of seven units, all on the Philippine Sea (west) side of island. The visitor information center and park headquarters are on the beach side of Marine Dr., in the village of Asan.

FOR MORE INFORMATION

Superintendent, War in the Pacific National Historical Park (115 Haloda Bldg., Marine Dr., Asan, Guam 96922, tel. 671/477–9362 or 671/472–7240, fax 671/472–7241; Web site www.nps.gov/wapa). Guam Hotel and Restaurant Association (Box 8565, Tamuning, Guam 96931, tel. 671/649–1447, fax 671/649–8565; Web site www.ghra.org.gu).

See Also

·····················

American Memorial Park, Affiliated Areas in Other National Parklands.

PUERTO RICO

San Juan National Historic Site

In San Juan

The site preserves the Spanish colonial forts of San Felipe del Morro, San Cristobal, El Cañuelo, and the city walls and gate of San Juan. These ancient stone fortifications built along the Atlantic coast protected Spain's possessions and its trade monopoly in the New World. Begun by Spanish troops in the 16th century, the massive masonry defenses are the oldest European-style fortifications within the territory of the United States. The site was established in 1949 and designated a World Heritage Site in 1983.

WHAT TO SEE & DO

Jogging, picnicking, touring forts, watching video. **Facilities:** 2 visitor centers with interpretive exhibits—El Morro and San Cristobal; museum (El Morro), wayside exhibits in forts, furnished troop quarters (San Cristobal). Bookstores. **Programs & Events:** Year-round: ranger-guided tours (San Cristobel: daily at 10 and 2 in English, 11 and 3 in Spanish; El Morro: daily at 10 and 2 in Spanish, 11 and 3 in English), video shown daily (every 15 min., alternating English and Spanish). Living-history programs (occasionally).

PLANNING YOUR VISIT

Lodging: Available in Condado, Isla Verde, and Old San Juan; none at site. **Food & Supplies:** Supplies available at site. Food and supplies also available in Condado, Isla Verde, and Old San Juan. **Tips & Hints:** Surfaces are uneven in forts; wear appropriate walking shoes. Inside forts, surfaces are slippery during rain. Avoid metal sentry boxes during lightning. Busiest in January and February, least crowded in August and September. **Fees, Permits & Limitations:** Entrance fee: $2 per adult, $1 for seniors 62 and older and children 13 to 17, free 12 and under. Fort El Canuelo closed to public. Puerto Rico fishing permit required. No pets in forts, leashed pets only on Fort El Morro grounds. Shirts and shoes required in forts. No smoking in forts. No disturbing of plants and wildlife. No food or drinks in forts. Minors must be with adults. No climbing on walls. Park open daily 9–5. Closed Dec. 25.

HOW TO GET THERE

Fort San Felipe del Morro and Fort San Cristobal are on Norzagaray St. in Old San Juan. Closest airport: Luis Muñoz Marin International (5 mi/8 km).

FOR MORE INFORMATION

San Juan National Historic Site (501 Norzagaray St., Old San Juan, PR
00901-2094, tel. 787/729–6777, fax 787/289–7972; Web site www.
nps.gov/saju). Puerto Rico Tourism Co. (Box 902, 3960 Old San Juan
Station, San Juan, PR 00962-3960, tel. 800/223–6530, fax 787/722–
5208).

VIRGIN ISLANDS

Buck Island Reef National Monument

On St. Croix

A magnificent elkhorn coral barrier reef, shallow-water lagoon, and marine garden encircle this uninhabited 180-acre tropical dry-forest island that rises 328 ft/99 m above the Caribbean waters. The island is a habitat for the endangered brown pelican, hawksbill and leatherback turtle, and the threatened green turtle. Charter boats take visitors to the beach and for a snorkel tour of the underwater interpretive trail. The monument was established December 28, 1961.

WHAT TO SEE & DO

Boating, hiking, picnicking, sailing, scuba diving, snorkeling, swimming. **Facilities:** Beaches, underwater interpretive trail, picnic areas, island trail, dock. Interpretive display boards.

PLANNING YOUR VISIT

Lodging: Available in Christiansted and elsewhere on St. Croix; none at monument. ✗ **Food & Supplies:** Available in Christiansted; none at monument. ☞ **Tips & Hints:** Don't touch the coral because it is easily damaged and it can injure the toucher. Go in December or April for blooms. Take into account rainy seasons in November and March and hurricane season from July to September. Busiest in February and June, least crowded in September and October. **Fees, Permits & Limitations**: Free. Concession trips: $35–$70 (half- or full-day). Reservations recommended. Big Beard Adventures (tel. 340/773–4482); Charis (tel. 340/773–9027); Clyde, Inc. (tel. 340/773–8520); Diva (tel. 340/778–4675); MileMark Water Sports (tel. 340/773–2628); and Terero Charters (tel. 340/773–3161). No spearfishing or pets. No fishing or collecting in marine garden. Island and underwater trail closed at night. Vessels can anchor up to 2 weeks off West Beach. Pit toilets only on island. Park is open daily sunrise–sunset. Information can be obtained from Christiansted National Historic Site (*see separate entry*). Visitor Center in downtown Christiansted, St. Croix, Virgin Islands. Open daily 8–5. Closed Thanksgiving, Dec. 1, Dec. 25.

HOW TO GET THERE

1.5 mi/2.5 km off the northeast side of St. Croix, Virgin Islands. Closest airport: Henry Rohlsen Airport (8 mi/13 km west of Christiansted).

FOR MORE INFORMATION

Buck Island Reef National Monument, National Park Service (Danish Customs House, Kings Wharf #100, Christiansted, St. Croix, VI 00820-4611, tel. 340/773–1460, fax 340/773–5995; e-mail CHRI_Administration@nps.gov; Web site www.nps.gov/buis). Virgin

Islands Department of Tourism (Box 6400, St. Thomas, VI 00804, tel. 800/372–8784). Christiansted Visitors Bureau (Box 4538, Christiansted, St. Croix, VI 00822, tel. 340/773–0495).

Christiansted National Historic Site

In Christiansted, St. Croix

The site protects 18th- and 19th-century buildings in the heart of the historic area of Christiansted, the capital of the former Danish West Indies. Attractions include museums at Fort Christiansvaern and the Steeple Building, and other historic buildings are being renovated. The site was designated Virgin Islands National Historic Site in 1952 and renamed in 1961.

WHAT TO SEE & DO

Self-guided walking tours of historic area, touring museums at fort and steeple. **Facilities:** Visitor contact station at Fort Christiansvaern, Steeple Building Museum. **Programs & Events:** Ranger-led group tours (year-round, by reservation only).

PLANNING YOUR VISIT

Lodging: In town: Caravelle Hotel (tel. 340/773–0687), Danish Manor (340/773–1377), Hotel on the Cay (tel. 340/773–2035), Holger Danske Best Western (tel. 340/773–3600); none at site. **Food & Supplies:** Available in Christiansted; none at site. **Tips & Hints:** Begin tour at fort. Busiest in February and March, least crowded in September and December. **Fees, Permits & Limitations:** Entrance fee: $2 adults 16 and up for Fort and Steeple Building Museum. Site open daily 8–5. Museum open weekdays 8–5, weekends 9–5.

HOW TO GET THERE

The site is in the heart of Christiansted, surrounded by the Christiansted Historic District. The visitor contact station is at Fort Christiansvaern. Park headquarters is in the Danish Customs House. Closest airport: Henry Rohlsen on St. Croix (8 mi/13 km west of Christiansted).

FOR MORE INFORMATION

Christiansted National Historic Site (Box 160, Christiansted, VI 00821, tel. 340/773–1460; Web site www.nps.gov/chri). Virgin Islands Department of Tourism (Box 6400, St. Thomas, VI 00804, tel. 800/372–8784). Christiansted Visitors Bureau (Box 4538, Christiansted, St. Croix, VI 00822, tel. 340/773–0495).

Salt River Bay National Historical Park and Ecological Preserve

On St. Croix

All major cultural periods in the history of the U.S. Virgin Islands are included in this park. It is the only known site where members of the Columbus expedition set foot on what is now U.S. territory. The park contains the only ceremonial prehistoric ball court ever discovered in the lesser Antilles, village middens, and burial grounds. Various European groups, including the Spaniards, French, Dutch, English, and Danish, attempted to colonize the area during the post-Columbian period. The site is marked by Fort Sale, a remaining earthworks fortification from the Dutch period of occupation. The site was authorized on February 24, 1992.

WHAT TO SEE & DO

Scuba diving (rentals, Anchor Dive Center), swimming, touring historic and prehistoric sites. **Facilities:** Visitor center (on wharf in Christiansted), beaches, overviews. **Programs & Events:** Ranger talks (year-round, on request).

PLANNING YOUR VISIT

Lodging: Available in Christiansted and elsewhere on island; none in park. **Food & Supplies:** In the park: meals at Salt River Marina. Food and supplies also available in Christiansted and elsewhere on island. **Fees, Permits & Limitations:** Free. Visitor center open daily 8–5.

HOW TO GET THERE

Visitor center is on the wharf in downtown Christiansted. Closest airport: Henry Rohlsen on St. Croix (8 mi/13 km west of Christiansted).

FOR MORE INFORMATION

Salt River Bay National Historical Park and Ecological Preserve (c/o Christiansted National Historic Site, Danish Custom House, Kings Wharf, 2100 Church St., #100, Christiansted, VI 00820-4611, tel. 340/773–1460; Web site www.nps.gov/sari). Virgin Islands Department of Tourism (Box 6400, St. Thomas, VI 00804, tel. 800/372–8784). Christiansted Visitors Bureau (Box 4538, Christiansted, St. Croix, VI 00822, tel. 340/773–0495).

Virgin Islands National Park

On St. John

The park covers about one half of St. John Island and Hassel Island in St. Thomas harbor and includes quiet coves, white-sand beaches, tropical forests, wildlife, wildflowers, breathtaking views, and offshore coral reefs. Also protected are early Carib Indian relics and the remains of

411

Danish colonial sugar plantations. The park was authorized on August 2, 1956.

WHAT TO SEE & DO

Auto and safari bus touring, bird-watching, boating, fishing, hiking, picnicking, sailing, scuba diving, snorkeling (rentals), swimming, windsurfing. **Facilities:** Visitor center with interpretive exhibits (Cruz Bay, 5-minute walk from public ferry dock), information kiosk (Trunk Bay), bulletin boards, beaches, self-guided underwater trail, trails. Book and map sale area, picnic areas. **Programs & Events:** Year-round: guided island hikes, snorkeling trips, cultural crafts demonstrations, evening programs. Advance registration and transportation fees required in some cases. Black History Month Commemoration (late Feb., Annaberg Sugar Plantation), St. John's Carnival (week of July 4th). Puppet shows, theater companies.

PLANNING YOUR VISIT

⚠ **Camping:** Campground (reservations suggested up to 6 months in advance, tel. 800/539–9998). Private campground available in park at Maho Bay (tel. 800/392–9004). ⌂ **Lodging:** In the park: cottages available at Cinnamon Bay Campground (reservations suggested up to 6 months in advance, tel. 800/539–9998). Lodging also available on island and on St. Thomas. ✕ **Food & Supplies:** In the park: meals at Cinnamon Bay, Cruz Bay, Maho Bay, and Trunk Bay; camp store and cafeteria. Food and supplies also available on island and on St. Thomas. ☞ **Tips & Hints:** Wear light cotton clothes and lightweight trousers to help protect against insect bites. Casual clothes are sufficient for most restaurants. Busiest in March and December, least crowded in September and October. ▦ **Fees, Permits & Limitations:** Free. Make campground reservations for winter months four–six months in advance. Special use permits required for groups of 10 or more using pavilions and picnic areas (tel. 340/776B-6201 ext. 244). Most popular park areas are easily accessed by taxi, otherwise known as safari buses. Rental vehicles are needed to travel to more remote parts of the island. Boat rentals and charters are necessary to visit some of the park bays that do not have road access.Park open daily. Visitor center open daily 8–4:30.

HOW TO GET THERE

The park on St. John is reached via North Shore or Centerline Rds. Hourly ferry service from Red Hood, St. Thomas, is available to St. John and operates 6 AM–midnight. Less frequent ferries make the trip from Charlotte Amalie. Closest airport: St. Thomas.

FOR MORE INFORMATION

Park Headquarters, Virgin Islands National Park (Box 710, Cruz Bay, St. John, VI 00831, tel. 340/776–6201 visitor center; Web site www.nps.gov/viis).

Other National Parklands

SPECIAL-INTEREST PARKS

These National Park sites are included for visitors with interests in a specific aspect of our country's history and culture. These categories may also suggest other sites for visitors to investigate.

African-American History Sites

Booker T. Washington National Monument, Virginia.

Boston African American National Historic Site, Massachussetts.

Brown v. Board of Education National Historic Site, Kansas.

Central High School National Historic Site, Arkansas.

Cumberland Island National Seashore, Georgia.

Dayton Aviation Heritage National Historical Park, Ohio.

Frederick Douglass National Historic Site, District of Columbia.

George Washington Carver National Monument, Missouri.

Harpers Ferry National Historic Park, West Virginia.

Jefferson National Expansion Memorial, Missouri.

Maggie L. Walker National Historic Site, Virginia.

Martin Luther King Jr. National Historic Site, Georgia.

Mary McLeod Bethune Council House National Historic Site, District of Columbia.

Natchez National Historic Park, Mississippi.

New Orleans Jazz National Historical Park, Louisiana.

Nicodemus National Historic Site, Kansas.

Tuskegee Airmen National Historic Site, Alabama.

Tuskegee Institute National Historic Site, Alabama.

Archaeological and Paleontological Sites

Agate Fossil Beds National Monument, Nebraska.

Alibates Flint Quarries National Monument, Texas.

Aztec Ruins National Monument, New Mexico.

Badlands National Park, South Dakota.

Bandelier National Monument, New Mexico.

Canyon de Chelly National Monument, Arizona.

Casa Grande National Monument, Arizona.

Chaco Culture National Historical Park, New Mexico.

Dinosaur National Monument, Colorado.

Effigy Mounds National Monument, Iowa.

Florissant Fossil Beds National Monument, Colorado.

Fossil Butte National Monument, Wyoming.
Gila Cliff Dwellings National Monument, New Mexico.
Hagerman Fossil Beds National Monument, Idaho.
Hopewell Culture National Historical Park, Ohio.
Hovenweep National Monument, Colorado.
John Day Fossil Beds National Monument, Oregon.
Kaloko-Honokohau National Historical Park, Hawaii.
Mesa Verde National Park, Colorado.
Montezuma Castle National Monument, Arizona.
Navajo National Monument, Arizona.
Ocmulgee National Monument, Georgia.
Petroglyph National Monument, New Mexico.
Pipestone National Monument, Minnesota.
Poverty Point National Monument, Louisiana.
Pu'ukohola Heiau National Historic Site, Hawaii.
Theodore Roosevelt National Park, North Dakota.
Tonto National Monument, Arizona.
Tuzigoot National Monument, Arizona.
Walnut Canyon National Monument, Arizona.
Wupatki National Monument, Arizona.
Yucca House National Monument, Colorado.

Battlefields

Big Hole National Battlefield, Montana.
Colonial National Historical Park, Virginia.
Cowpens National Battlefield, South Carolina.
Fort Necessity National Battlefield, Pennsylvania.
Guilford Courthouse National Military Park,
North Carolina.
Horseshoe Bend National Military Park, Alabama.
Jean Lafitte National Historical Park, Louisiana.
Kings Mountain National Military Park, South Carolina.
Little Bighorn Battlefield National Monument, Montana.
Minute Man National Historical Park, Massachusetts.
Moores Creek National Battlefield, North Carolina.
Palo Alto Battlefield National Historic Site, Texas.
Rock Creek Park, District of Columbia.
Saratoga National Historical Park, New York.
War in the Pacific National Historical Park, Guam.
Washita Battlefield National Historic Site, Oklahoma.

Civil War Sites

Andersonville National Historic Site, Georgia.
Antietam National Battlefield, Maryland.

Appomattox Court House National Historical Park, Virginia.

Arkansas Post National Memorial, Arkansas.

Brices Cross Roads National Battlefield Site, Mississippi.

Chickamauga and Chattanooga National Military Park, Georgia.

Fort Donelson National Battlefield, Tennessee.

Fort Pulaski National Monument, Georgia.

Fort Sumter National Monument, South Carolina.

Fredericksburg and Spotsylvania County Battlefields Memorial National Military Park, Virginia.

Gettysburg National Military Park, Pennsylvania.

Harpers Ferry National Historical Park, West Virginia.

Kennesaw Mountain National Battlefield Park, Georgia.

Manassas National Battlefield Park, Virginia.

Monocacy National Battlefield, Maryland.

Pea Ridge National Military Park, Arkansas.

Pecos National Historical Park, New Mexico.

Petersburg National Battlefield, Virginia.

Richmond National Battlefield Park, Virginia.

Shiloh National Military Park, Tennessee.

Stones River National Battlefield, Tennessee.

Tupelo National Battlefield, Mississippi.

Vicksburg National Military Park, Mississippi.

Wilson's Creek National Battlefield, Missouri.

Hispanic Heritage Sites and Sites that Relate to America's Discovery

Amistad National Recreation Area, Texas.

Arkansas Post National Memorial, Arkansas.

Big Bend National Park, Texas.

Biscayne National Park, Florida.

Cabrillo National Monument, California.

Canyon de Chelly National Monument, Arizona.

Castillo de San Marcos National Monument, Florida.

Chamizal National Memorial, Texas.

Channel Islands National Park, California.

Christiansted National Historic Site, Virgin Islands.

Coronado National Memorial, Arizona.

Cumberland Island National Seashore, Georgia.

De Soto National Memorial, Florida.

Dry Tortugas National Park, Florida.

El Morro National Monument, New Mexico.

Fort Caroline National Memorial, Florida.

Fort Clatsop National Memorial, Oregon.

Fort Frederica National Monument, Georgia
Fort Matanzas National Monument, Florida.
Fort Point National Historic Site, California.
Golden Gate National Recreation Area, California.
Grand Portage National Monument, Minnesota.
Gulf Islands National Seashore, Florida and Mississippi.
Knife River Indian Villages National Historic Site,
North Dakota.
Padre Island National Seashore, Texas.
Palo Alto Battlefield National Historic Site, Texas.
Pecos National Historical Park, New Mexico.
Point Reyes National Seashore, California.
Salinas Pueblo Missions National Monument, New Mexico.
Salt River Bay National Historical Park and Ecological
Preserve, Virgin Islands.
San Antonio Missions National Historical Park, Texas.
San Juan National Historic Site, Puerto Rico.
Santa Monica Mountains National Recreation Area,
California.
Timucuan Ecological and Historic Preserve, Florida.
Tumacacori National Monument, Arizona.
Wrangell-St. Elias National Park and Preserve, Alaska.

Presidential History Sites

Abraham Lincoln Birthplace National Historic Site,
Kentucky.
Adams National Historic Site, Massachusetts.
Andrew Johnson National Historic Site, Tennessee.
Eisenhower National Historic Site, Pennsylvania.
Eleanor Roosevelt National Historic Site, New York.
Ford's Theatre National Historic Site, District of Columbia.
Franklin Delano Roosevelt Memorial, District of Columbia.
General Grant National Memorial, New York.
George Washington Birthplace National Monument,
Virginia.
Harry S Truman National Historic Site, Missouri.
Herbert Hoover National Historic Site, Iowa.
Home of Franklin D. Roosevelt National Historic Site,
New York.
James A. Garfield National Historic Site, Ohio.
Jefferson National Expansion Memorial, Missouri.
Jimmy Carter National Historic Site, Georgia.
John Fitzgerald Kennedy National Historic Site,
Massachusetts.
Lincoln Boyhood Home National Monument, Indiana.

Lincoln Home National Historic Site, Illinois.

Lincoln Memorial, District of Columbia.

Lyndon Baines Johnson Memorial Grove on the Potomac, District of Columbia.

Lyndon Baines Johnson National Historical Park, Texas.

Martin Van Buren National Historic Site, New York.

Mount Rushmore National Memorial, South Dakota.

Sagamore Hill National Historic Site, New York.

Shenandoah National Park, Virginia.

Theodore Roosevelt Birthplace National Historic Site, New York.

Theodore Roosevelt Inaugural National Historic Site, New York.

Theodore Roosevelt Island National Memorial, District of Columbia.

Theodore Roosevelt National Park, North Dakota.

Thomas Jefferson Memorial, District of Columbia.

Ulysses S. Grant National Historic Site, Missouri.

Washington Monument, District of Columbia.

White House, District of Columbia.

William Howard Taft National Historic Site, Ohio.

Volcanoes, Caves, and Hot Springs

Capulin Volcano National Monument, New Mexico.

Carlsbad Caverns National Park, New Mexico.

Crater Lake National Park, Oregon.

Craters of the Moon National Monument, Idaho.

Devils Postpile National Monument, California.

Devils Tower National Monument, Wyoming.

El Malpais National Monument, New Mexico.

Great Basin National Park, Nevada.

Haleakala National Park, Hawaii.

Hawaii Volcanoes National Park, Hawaii.

Hot Springs National Park, Arkansas

Jewel Cave National Monument, South Dakota.

Lassen Volcanic National Park, California.

Lava Beds National Monument, California.

Mammoth Cave National Park, Kentucky.

Oregon Caves National Monument, Oregon.

Pinnacles National Monument, California.

Russell Cave National Monument, Alabama.

Sequoia National Park, California.

Sunset Crater Volcano National Monument, Arizona.

Timpanogos Cave National Monument, Utah.

Wind Cave National Park, South Dakota.
Yellowstone National Park, Wyoming.

Women's History Sites

Clara Barton National Historic Site, Maryland.
Eleanor Roosevelt National Historic Site, New York.
Lowell National Historical Park, Masachusetts.
Maggie L. Walker National Historic Site, Virginia.
Mary McLeod Bethune Council House National Historic Site, District of Columbia.
Sewall-Belmont House National Historic Site, District of Columbia.
Whitman Mission National Historic Site, Washington.
Women's Rights National Historical Park, New York.

World Heritage Sites

Carlsbad Caverns National Park, New Mexico.
Chaco Culture National Historical Park, New Mexico.
Everglades National Park, Florida.
Glacier Bay National Park and Preserve, Alaska.
Glacier National Park, Montana.
Grand Canyon National Park, Arizona.
Great Smoky Mountains National Park, Tennessee.
Hawaii Volcanoes National Park, Hawaii.
Independence National Historical Park, Pennsylvania.
Mammoth Cave National Park, Kentucky.
Mesa Verde National Park, Colorado.
Olympic National Park, Washington.
Redwood National Park, California.
San Juan National Historic Site, Puerto Rico.
Statue of Liberty National Monument, New York.
Wrangell-St. Elias National Park and Preserve, Alaska.
Yellowstone National Park, Wyoming.
Yosemite National Park, California.

AFFILIATED AREAS

AIDS Memorial Grove National Memorial

This memorial in Golden Gate Park in San Francisco is dedicated to individuals who have died as a result of acquired immune deficiency syndrome (AIDS). It is also in support of those who are living with AIDS and their loved ones and caregivers. The memorial was authorized on November 12, 1996.

FOR MORE INFORMATION

AIDS Memorial Grove National Memorial (c/o San Francisco Park and Recreation Department, McLaren Lodge, Golden Gate Park, CA 94117).

Aleutian World War II National Historic Area

Preserved here are lands owned by the Ounalaska Corporation on the island of Amaknak. The site interprets the history of the Aleut people and the role they and the Aleutian Islands played in the defense of the United States in World War II. It was authorized on November 12, 1996.

FOR MORE INFORMATION

Aleutian World War II National Historic Area (Box 149, 400 Salmon Way, Unalaska, AK 99685, tel. 907/581–1276; Web site www.ounalashka.com).

American Memorial Park

This site on the island of Saipan in the Northern Mariana Islands honors the sacrifices made during the Mariana Campaign of World War II. Recreational facilities, a World War II museum, and flag monument keep alive the memory of more than 4,000 U.S. military personnel and local islanders who died in June 1944. The park was authorized on August 18, 1978.

FOR MORE INFORMATION

American Memorial Park (Box 5189 CHRB, Saipan, MP 96950).

Benjamin Franklin National Memorial

In the Rotunda of the Franklin Institute, a 20-ft, 30-ton seated statue of Franklin, sculpted by James Earle Fraser, honors the inventor-statesman. The memorial was designated on October 25, 1972, and is owned and administered by the Franklin Institute.

FOR MORE INFORMATION

Benjamin Franklin National Memorial (The Franklin Institute, 20th and Benjamin Franklin Pkwy., Philadelphia, PA 19103, tel. 215/448–1329).

Chicago Portage National Historic Site

A portion of the portage between the Great Lakes and the Mississippi, discovered by French explorers Jacques Marquette and Louis Joliet, is preserved here. The site was designated on January 3, 1952, and is administered by the Forest Preserve District of Cook County.

FOR MORE INFORMATION

Chicago Portage National Historic Site (c/o Forest Preserve District of Cook County, 536 N. Harlem Ave., River Forest, IL 60305).

Chimney Rock National Historic Site

Pioneers traveling west along the Oregon Trail often camped near this famous landmark, which stands 500 ft above the Platte River. The site was designated on August 2, 1956, is owned by Nebraska, and administered by the city of Bayard, the Nebraska State Historical Society, and the National Park Service under a cooperative agreement of June 21, 1956.

FOR MORE INFORMATION

Chimney Rock National Historic Site (Scotts Bluff National Monument, Box 27, Gering, NE 69341).

David A. Berger National Memorial

This monument serves as a reminder of violence which took place in Munich at the 1972 Olympic Games.

FOR MORE INFORMATION

David A. Berger National Memorial (Mayfield Jewish Community Center, 3505 Mayfield Rd., Cleveland Heights, OH 44118, tel. 216/382–4000).

Delaware and Lehigh National Heritage Corridor

The corridor showcases the Delaware, Lehigh, and Wyoming Valleys where anthracite coal was discovered, canals were built and iron was first poured. During the Industrial Revolution, these canals and their associated early railroads gave access to the coal fields of eastern Pennsylvania. The corridor includes museums with displays about the region's cultural and industrial history and two state parks. It is administered by a federal commission appointed by the Secretary of the Interior and the Governor of Pennsylvania working with a consortium of state, county, local, and private landowners. It was designated on November 18, 1988 and reauthorized in 1998.

FOR MORE INFORMATION

Delaware and Lehigh National Heritage Corridor (10 E. Church St., A-208, Bethlehem, PA 18018).

Father Marquette National Memorial

The life and work of Father Jacques Marquette, French priest and explorer, is memorialized here. The site is in Michigan Straits State Park, near St. Ignace, Michigan, where he founded a Jesuit mission in 1671 and was buried in 1678. The memorial was authorized on December 20, 1975.

FOR MORE INFORMATION

Father Marquette National Memorial (Parks Division, Dept. of Natural Resourses, Box 30028, Lansing, MI 48900).

Gloria Del (Old Swedes') Church National Historic Site

This, the second oldest Swedish church in the United States, was founded in 1677. The present structure, a splendid example of 17th-century Swedish church architecture, was erected about 1700. The site was designated on November 17, 1942, and is owned and administered by Corporation of Gloria Del (Old Swedes') Church.

FOR MORE INFORMATION

Gloria Del (Old Swedes') Church National Historic Site (Delaware Ave. and Christian St., Philadelphia, PA 19106).

Green Springs National Historic Landmark District

This portion of Louisa County in Virginia's Piedmont has fine rural manor houses and related buildings (none of which are open to the public) in an unmarred landscape. In 1974 the district was declared a national historic landmark by the Secretary of the Interior.

FOR MORE INFORMATION

Green Springs National Historic Landmark District (c/o Shenandoah National Park, 3655 US 211E, Luray, VA 22835).

Historic Camden

Camden was established in 1732 and at that time was known as Fredericksburg Township. In 1768, the village was named Camden in honor of Charles Pratt, Lord Camden, a British Parliamentary champion of colonial rights. The town was occupied by the British under Lord Cornwallis from June 1, 1780, until May 9, 1781. It was one of the few frontier settlements to have hosted two battles during the American Revolution: the first on August 16, 1780, and the second on April 25, 1781. The Historic Camden Revolutionary War Site was authorized on May 24, 1982.

FOR MORE INFORMATION

Historic Camden (Box 710, Camden, SC 29020, tel. 803/432–9841; Web site www.Historic-camden.org).

Ice Age National Scientific Reserve

This country's first national scientific reserve is home to nationally significant features of continental glaciation. State parks in the area are open to the public. The reserve was authorized on October 13, 1964.

FOR MORE INFORMATION

Ice Age National Scientific Reserve (Wisconsin Dept. of Natural Resources, Box 7921, Madison, WI 53707).

Illinois and Michigan Canal National Heritage Corridor

This canal was built in the 1830s and 1840s along the portage between Lake Michigan and the Illinois River, which had long been used as a Native American trade route. The canal rapidly transformed Chicago from an isolated crossroads into a critical transportation hub between the East and the developing Midwest. A 61-mi/98-km recreational trail follows the canal towpath. The corridor was designated on August 24, 1984.

FOR MORE INFORMATION

Illinois and Michigan Canal National Heritage Corridor (15701 S. Independence Blvd., Lockport, IL 60441).

International Peace Garden

This 2,300 acre park, with its exquisite garden, is located on the North Dakota/Manitoba border. It serves as a unique tribute to the peace and friendship between the people of Canada and the United States.

FOR MORE INFORMATION

International Peace Garden (RR 1, Box 116, Dunseith, ND 58329).

Jamestown National Historic Site

Part of the site of the first permanent British settlement in North America (1607) is on the upper end of Jamestown Island, scene of the first representative legislative government on this continent, July 30,

1619. The site was designated on December 18, 1940, and is owned and administered by Association for the Preservation of Virginia Antiquities. The remainder of Jamestown site and island is part of Colonial National Historical Park.

FOR MORE INFORMATION

Jamestown National Historic Site (c/o Association for the Preservation of Virginia Antiquities, John Marshall House, 2705 Park Ave., Richmond, VA 23220).

John H. Chafee Blackstone River Valley National Heritage Corridor

The American Industrial Revolution began in the mills (including Slater Mill), villages, and associated transportation networks in the Blackstone Valley, which runs along some 46 mi/74 km of river and canals from Worcester, Massachusetts, to Providence, Rhode Island. The corridor was established on November 10, 1986.

FOR MORE INFORMATION

John H. Chafee Blackstone River Valley National Heritage Corridor (1 Depot Sq., Woorsocket, RI 02895, tel. 401/762–0250; Web site www.nps.gov/blac).

McLoughlin House National Historic Site

Dr. John McLoughlin, often called the "Father of Oregon," was prominent in the development of the Pacific Northwest as chief factor of Fort Vancouver. He lived in this house between 1847 and 1857. The site was designated a national historic site on June 27, 1945, and renamed on January 16, 1945. It is owned and administered by McLoughlin Memorial Association.

FOR MORE INFORMATION

McLoughlin House National Historic Site (Oregon City, OR 97045).

New Jersey Coastal Heritage Trail

From the Raritan Bay near New York City south to Cape May and along the Delaware River and Bay, this scenic vehicular trail explores the diverse resources along New Jersey's coast through a series of interpretive themes. Lighthouses, boardwalks, historic communities, wildlife habitats, and migratory flyways are part of the trail. There are fees for some activities sponsored by private and public institutions. Still under development, the trail was authorized on October 20, 1988.

FOR MORE INFORMATION

New Jersey Coastal Heritage Trail Route (389 Fortescue Rd., Box 568, Newport, NJ 08385, tel. 856/447–0103; Web site www.nps.gov/neje).

Pinelands National Reserve

The area is a sandy coastal plain of over 1.1 million acres of low, dense pine and oak forests, streams, wetlands, cranberry bogs and blueberry fields, historic iron and glass factories and small towns. Most facilities are provided within state forests, parks and wildlife management areas. The reserve was authorized on November 10, 1978, and designated a Biosphere Reserve in 1983.

FOR MORE INFORMATION

Pinelands National Reserve (c/o Northeast Regional Office, National Park Service, 200 Chestnut St., Philadelphia, PA 19106-2818).

Port Chicago National Memorial

This memorial, located at the former Concord Naval Weapons Station in Concord, California, recognizes the critical role Port Chicago Naval Magazine played as an important facility for the Pacific Theater in World War II. It also commemorates the July 17, 1944 explosion that occurred at the site, which resulted in the largest stateside disaster of World War II. Open to the public by reservation only. It was authorized on October 8, 1992.

FOR MORE INFORMATION

Port Chicago National Memorial (c/o Eugene O'Neill National Historic Site, PO Box 280, Danville, CA 94526, tel. 925/943–1531).

Quinebaug and Shetucket Rivers Valley National Heritage Corridor

The Quinebaug and Shetucket Rivers Valley in Connecticut is one of the last unspoiled and undeveloped areas in the northeastern U.S. It has remained largely intact, including important aboriginal archaeological sites, excellent water quality, beautiful rural landscapes, architecturally significant mill structures and mill villages, and a large acreage of parks and other permanent open space. The corridor encompasses 850 square mi and includes 25 towns. It was authorized on November 2, 1994.

FOR MORE INFORMATION

Quinebaug and Shetucket Rivers Valley National Heritage Corridor (Quinebaug-Shetucket Heritage Corridor, Inc., Box 161, Putnam, CT 06260).

Red Hill Patrick Henry National Memorial

The law office and grave of the fiery Virginia legislator and orator are preserved at this small plantation along with a reconstruction of Patrick Henry's last home, several dependencies, and a museum. The memorial was authorized on May 13, 1986.

FOR MORE INFORMATION

Red Hill Patrick Henry National Memorial (Patrick Henry Memorial Foundation, Brookneal, VA 24528, tel. 804/376–2044; Web site www.RedHill.org).

Roosevelt Campobello International Park

President Franklin D. Roosevelt spent many vacations at his 34-room summer home on Campobello Island in New Brunswick's Bay of Fundy. The house and grounds include a visitor center, flower gardens and historic furnishings. The park was established on July 7, 1964, and is owned and administered by the United States-Canadian Commission.

FOR MORE INFORMATION

Roosevelt Campobello International Park (c/o Executive Secretary Roosevelt Campobello International Park Commission, Box 129, Lubec, ME 04652, tel. 506/752–2922; Web site www.fdr.net).

Sewall-Belmont House National Historic Site

Rebuilt after fire damage from the War of 1812, this redbrick house is one of the oldest on Capitol Hill. It has been the National Woman's Party Headquarters since 1929 and commemorates the party's founder and woman's suffrage leader, Alice Paul, and associates. Open on a limited basis. The site was authorized on October 26, 1974.

FOR MORE INFORMATION

Sewall-Belmont House National Historic Site (144 Constitution Ave. NE, Washington, DC 20002).

Touro Synagogue National Historic Site

This is the oldest synagogue in the U.S. Designed by colonial architect Peter Harrison and dedicated in 1763, it is a fine example of 18th century Georgian architecture. It was designated on March 5, 1940.

FOR MORE INFORMATION

Touro Synagogue National Historic Site (85 Touro St., Newport, RI 02840; Web site www.tourosynagogue.org).

NATIONAL HERITAGE AREAS

America's Agricultural Heritage Partnership

Sites in this 37-county region of northeastern Iowa illustrate the transformation that took place as mechanization paved the way for a distinctly American system of industrialized agriculture. Tractor design and manufacture, mechanized farming, corn-hog production, dairying, beef cattle feeding, and meat packing continue to characterize this region. The cultural histories of family farming and agribusiness are equally well represented. Primary federal assistance is being provided by the U.S. Department of Agriculture. It was authorized on November 12, 1996.

FOR MORE INFORMATION

America's Agricultural Heritage Partnership (Box 2845, Waterloo, IA 50704).

Augusta Canal National Heritage Area

This 7-mi/11-km corridor follows the full length of the best preserved canal of its kind remaining in the southern United States. The canal transformed Augusta into an important regional industrial area on the eve of the Civil War, and was instrumental in the post-Civil War relocation of much of the nation's textile industry to the south. The area was authorized on November 12, 1996.

FOR MORE INFORMATION

Augusta Canal National Heritage Area (Box 2367, Augusta, GA 30903).

Automobile National Heritage Area

Southeast Michigan, which includes the "Motor Cities" of Detroit, Lansing and Flint, is the region that put the world on wheels. The heritage area consists of six significant corridors. This collection of auto-related museums, attractions, activities and events exists to preserve and interpret the story of the automobile and was authorized Nov. 6, 1998 .

FOR MORE INFORMATION

Automobile National Heritage Area Partnership, Inc. (The University of Michigan-Dearborn Office of Government Relations, 4901 Evergreen Rd., 1130 AB, Dearborn, MI 48128-1491, tel. 313/593–5140).

Cane River National Heritage Area

Before becoming part of the United States, this area at the intersection of the Spanish and French realms in the New World gave rise to the unique Creole culture in a rural setting. The area supports the oldest community in the territory encompassed by the Louisiana Purchase. Historic plantations, Cane River Creole National Historical Park, and three state commemorative areas keep the region's Creole heritage alive. The area was authorized on November 2, 1994.

FOR MORE INFORMATION

Cane River National Heritage Area (c/o Cane River Creole National Historic Park, Box 536, Natchitoches, LA 71457).

Delaware and Lehigh National Heritage Corridor

See Affiliated Areas.

Essex National Heritage Area

Essex County is a 500-square-mi area located directly north of Boston along the Atlantic coast and the Merrimack River. It includes thousands of historic sites that illuminate colonial settlement, the development of the shoe and textile industries, and the growth and decline of the maritime industries—including fishing, privateering, and the China trade. It was authorized on November 12, 1996.

FOR MORE INFORMATION

Essex National Heritage Commission, Inc. (140 Washington St., Salem, MA 01910, tel. 978/740–1650; Web site www.essexheritage.org).

Hudson River Valley National Heritage Area

From Troy to New York City, the Hudson River Valley contains a rich assemblage of natural features and nationally significant cultural and historical sites. The valley has maintained the scenic, rural character that inspired the Hudson Valley School of landscape painting and the Knickerbocker writers. Recreational opportunities are found on the river, in the mountains, parklands, and on greenway trails. The area was authorized on November 12, 1996.

FOR MORE INFORMATION

Hudson River Valley National Heritage Area (Hudson River Valley Greenway and Conservancy, Capitol Bldg., Capitol Station, Room 254, Albany, NY 12224, tel. 518/473–3835; Web site www.HudsonGreenway.state.ny.us).

Illinois and Michigan Canal National Heritage Corridor

See Affiliated Areas.

John H. Chafee Blackstone River Valley National Heritage Corridor

See Affiliated Areas.

National Coal Heritage Area

The cultural geography here has been profoundly influenced over the last 125 years by the pervasive role of the coal mines. The communities in these 11 counties in southern West Virginia reflect their origins as "company towns" formed by local traditions, waves of immigrant workers and the dominance of the mining companies. Ethnic neighborhoods and the physical infrastructure of the mines are still clearly seen throughout the region. The area was authorized on November 12, 1996.

FOR MORE INFORMATION

National Coal Heritage Area (The Cultural Center Capitol Complex, 1900 Kanawha Blvd. E, Charleston, WV 25305, tel. 304/558–0220; Web site www.coalheritage.org).

Ohio and Erie Canal National Heritage Corridor

This area of northeast Ohio celebrates the canal that enabled shipping between Lake Erie and the Ohio River and vaulted Ohio into commercial prominence in the early 1830s. The canal and towpath trail pass through agricultural lands and rural villages into industrial communities such as Akron, Canton, and Cleveland that trace their prosperity to the coming of the canal. (*See also Cuyahoga Valley National Recreation Area.*) The area was authorized on November 12, 1996.

FOR MORE INFORMATION

Ohio and Erie Canal National Heritage Corridor (Ohio and Erie Canal Association, 1556 Boston Mills Rd., Boston, OH 44268).

Quinebaug and Shetucket Rivers Valley National Heritage Corridor

See Affiliated Areas.

Shenandoah Valley Battlefields

This fertile agricultural valley was of strategic value to both sides in the Civil War with the result that it became the site for 15 battles in the conflict. Authorized November 12, 1996.

FOR MORE INFORMATION

Shenandoah Valley Battlefields (National Historic District Commission, PO Box 897, New Market, VA 22844, tel. 540/740–4543).

South Carolina Heritage Corridor

Two routes through 14 counties in western South Carolina begin in the mill villages, waterfalls, and mountains of the Up Country; run through historic courthouse towns and military sites and along the Savannah River; and follow the Edisto River and the South Carolina Railroad to the Low Country's wealth of African-American and antebellum history, centered in and around historic Charleston. The area was authorized on November 12, 1996.

FOR MORE INFORMATION

South Carolina Heritage Corridor (Heritage Tourism Development Office, South Carolina Dept. of Parks, Recreation, and Tourism, 1205 Pendleton St., Columbia, SC 29201).

Southwestern Pennsylvania Industrial Heritage Route

This 500-mi route travels through nine counties of southwestern Pennsylvania and features hundreds of sites relating to the nation's industrial story. Included are the Altoona Railyards, the Johnstown Flood National Memorial and Museum, the steel mills of Johnstown, and Horshoe Curve, a 19th-century engineering marvel built by the Pennsylvania Railroad. Also called the Path of Progress National Heritage Route. The site was authorized on November 19, 1988.

FOR MORE INFORMATION

Southwestern Pennsylvania Industrial Heritage Route (Southwestern Pennsylvania Heritage Preservation Commission, Box 565, 105 Zee Plaza, Hollidaysburg, PA 16648).

Steel Industry American Heritage Area

Steel made a great imprint on the Pittsburgh region in the late 19th and early 20th centuries. The industry made possible railroads, skyscrapers, and shipbuilding while altering corporate practice and labor organization. These are reminders of numerous mills as well as communities founded by mill workers, many of which are linked by hiking trails and riverboat tours. The collection of sites is also known as "Rivers of Steel". It was authorized on November 12, 1996.

FOR MORE INFORMATION

Steel Industry American Heritage Area (Steel Industry Heritage Corporation, 338 E. 9th Ave., 1st Floor, Homestead, PA 15120).

Tennessee Civil War Heritage Area

A number of areas throughout Tennessee preserve and interpret the legacy of the Civil War there. Heritage resources are focused on important events, geographic factors, decisive battles, engagements, and strategic maneuvers of the war; and the impact of the war on Tennessee's residents. The area was authorized on November 12, 1996.

FOR MORE INFORMATION

Tennessee Civil War Heritage Area (Center for Historic Preservation, Middle Tennessee State University, Box 80, Murfreesboro, TN 37132).

NATIONAL TRAILS SYSTEM

Appalachian National Scenic Trail

See the West Virginia chapter for a full description.

FOR MORE INFORMATION

Appalachian National Scenic Trail (Appalachian Trail Conference, Box 807, Harpers Ferry, WV 25425-0807).

California National Historic Trail

The California Trail is a system of overland routes, starting at numerous points along the Missouri River and ending at many locations in California and Oregon. Over these trails passed one of America's great mass migrations, seeking the promise of gold and a new life in California in the late 1840s and 1850s. Traces of their struggles and triumphs are still evident at many trail sites. The trail was established on August 3, 1992.

FOR MORE INFORMATION

California National Historic Trail (National Park Service, Box 45155, 324 S. State St., Salt Lake City, UT 84145-0155).

Continental Divide National Scenic Trail

Runing the length of the Rocky Mountains near the Continental Divide, this trail extends from Canada's Waterton Lake into Montana, along the Idaho border, and on to Wyoming, Colorado, and New Mexico, ending at the U.S.-Mexico border. It was established on November 10, 1978.

FOR MORE INFORMATION

Continental Divide National Scenic Trail (Forest Service, Region 2, 240 Simms St., Golden, CO 80401).

Florida National Scenic Trail

The trail runs the length of Florida from Big Cypress National Preserve near Miami to Gulf Islands National Seashore near Pensacola Beach. It is the only national scenic trail which explores tropical and subtropical regions. More than 600 mi/960 km have been developed for public use. The trail was established on March 28, 1983.

FOR MORE INFORMATION

Florida National Scenic Trail (USDA Forest Service, National Forests in Florida, 325 John Knox Rd., #F-100, Tallahassee, FL 32303, tel. 850/942–9300).

Ice Age National Scenic Trail

Winding over Wisconsin's glacial moraines, the trail links six of the nine units of the Ice Age National Scientific Reserve. It traverses significant features of Wisconsin's glacial heritage. Approximately 500 mi are open to public use; additional miles are being developed. It was authorized on October 3, 1980.

FOR MORE INFORMATION

Ice Age National Scenic Trail (National Park Service, 700 Rayovac Dr., Suite 100, Madison, WI 53711).

Iditarod National Historic Trail

One of Alaska's preeminent Gold Rush Trails, the 2,350-mi/3,760-km Iditarod extends from Seward to Nome and is composed of a network of trails and side trails developed at the turn of the century. It was established on November 20, 1978.

FOR MORE INFORMATION

Iditarod National Historic Trail (Bureau of Land Management, 6881 Abbott Loop Rd., Anchorage, AK 99507).

Juan Bautista de Anza National Historic Trail

This trail commemorates the route of a party of Spanish soldier-settlers and their families, led by Lieutenant-Colonel Juan Bautista de Anza, from Sonora, Mexico, to found a presidio and mission at the port of San Francisco. The trail includes an auto route linking over 100 sites and 150 mi/240 km of trails in Arizona and California for recreational hiking. The 1,200-mi/1,920-km trail was established on August 15, 1990.

FOR MORE INFORMATION

Juan Bautista de Anza National Historic Trail (600 Harrison Street, Suite 600, San Francisco, CA 94107-1372; Web site www.nps.gov/juba).

Lewis and Clark National Historic Trail

The route of the 1804–1806 Lewis and Clark Expedition extends 3,700 mi/5,920 km, from the Mississippi River in Illinois to the Pacific Ocean at the mouth of the Columbia River in Oregon. Water routes, hiking trails, and marked highways follow the explorer's out-bound and return routes. The trail was established on November 10, 1978.

FOR MORE INFORMATION

Lewis and Clark National Historic Trail (National Park Service, 1709 Jackson St., Omaha, NE 68102–2571, tel. 402/221–3471; Web site www.nps.gov/lecl).

Mormon Pioneer National Historic Trail

This 1,300-mi/2,080-km trail follows the route over which Brigham Young led the Mormons from Nauvoo, Illinois, to the site of modern Salt Lake City, Utah, in 1846–1847. An auto tour route has been marked near the trail corridor. It was established on November 10, 1978.

FOR MORE INFORMATION

Mormon Pioneer National Historic Trail (National Park Service, Box 45155, 324 S. State St., Salt Lake City, UT 84154-0155).

Natchez Trace National Scenic Trail

See the Mississippi chapter for a full description.

FOR MORE INFORMATION

Natchez Trace National Scenic Trail (c/o Natchez Trace Parkway, R.R. 1. NT-143, Tupelo, MS 38801-9718).

Nez Perce National Historic Trail

The 1,170-mi/1,872-km Nez Perce trail commemorates the flight of five bands of Nez Perce Indians in 1877. It begins in northeastern Oregon, extends across Idaho and western and central Montana, bisecting Yellowstone National Park in Wyoming and ending near the Bear Paw Mountains. It was established on October 6, 1986.

FOR MORE INFORMATION

Nez Perce National Historic Trail (Forest Service Region 1, Box 7662, Missoula, MT 59807).

North Country National Scenic Trail

The trail connects seven northern tier states extending from Crown Point, New York, to Lake Sakakawea in North Dakota, where it connects with the Lewis and Clark National Historic Trail. Approximately 1,650 mi/2,640 km are open to public use. Additional miles are being developed. The trail was established on March 5, 1980.

FOR MORE INFORMATION

North Country National Scenic Trail (National Park Service, 700 Rayovac Dr., Suite 100, Madison, WI 53711).

Oregon National Historic Trail

Tens of thousands of pioneers followed this 2,170-mi/3,472-km trail west from Independence, Missouri to Oregon City, Oregon, between 1841 and 1860. The trail was established on November 10, 1978.

Oregon National Historic Trail (National Park Service, Box 45155, 324 S. State St., Salt Lake City, UT 84145-0155).

Overmountain Victory National Historic Trail

This 300-mi/480-km route follows the path of American Revolution patriots who mustered in western Virginia and eastern Tennessee and came across the mountains of North Carolina to Kings Mountain, South Carolina, where they defeated British-led Loyalist militia in 1780. The trail was established on September 8, 1980.

FOR MORE INFORMATION

Overmountain Victory National Historic Trail (Southeast Region National Park Service, 1924 Bldg., 100 Alabama St. SW, Atlanta, GA 30303).

Pacific Crest National Scenic Trail

Extending from the Mexican border northward along the Sierra and Cascade peaks of California, Oregon and Washington, the 2,650-mi/4,240-km trail reaches the Canadian border near Ross Lake, Washington. The trail, which is one of the two initial components of the National Trails System, was established on October 2, 1968.

FOR MORE INFORMATION

Pacific Crest National Scenic Trail (U.S. Forest Service, Nature of the Northwest Information Center, 800 NE Oregon St., Rm 177, Portland, OR 97232).

Pony Express National Historic Trail

For 18 months, 1860–1861, riders on horseback carried mail 1,800 mi/2,880 km between St. Joseph, Missouri, and Sacramento, California in just under 10 days, proving that a regular communications link to the Pacific coast was possible. Most of the 150 relay stations no longer exist. The trail was established on August 3, 1992.

FOR MORE INFORMATION

Pony Express National Historic Trail (National Park Service, Box 45155, 324 S. State St., Salt Lake City, UT 84145-0155).

Potomac Heritage National Scenic Trail

See the District of Columbia chapter for a full description.

FOR MORE INFORMATION

Potomac Heritage National Scenic Trail (National Capital Region, National Park Service, 1100 Ohio Dr. SW, Washington, DC 20242-0001).

Santa Fe National Historic Trail

This route of the Santa Fe trail extends from a point near Arrow Rock, Missouri, through Kansas, Oklahoma and Colorado to Santa Fe, New Mexico. To date, 20 certified sites and segments are open for public use.

FOR MORE INFORMATION

Santa Fe National Historic Trail (National Park Service, Long Distance Trails Group, Box 728, Santa Fe, NM 57504-0728).

Selma to Montgomery National Historic Trail

This trail commemorates a 1965 voting rights march led by Dr. Martin Luther King Jr. The marchers walked along US 80 from Brown Chapel A.M.E. Church in Selma, Alabama, to the state capitol in Montgomery. The marched helped inspire passage of voting rights legislation signed by President Johnson on August 6, 1965. The trail was established on November 12, 1965.

FOR MORE INFORMATION

Selma to Montgomery National Historic Trail (National Park Service, Southeast Region, 1924 Bldg., 100 Alabama St. SW, Atlanta, GA 30303).

Trail of Tears National Historic Trail

The Trail of Tears commemorates two of the land and water routes used for the forced removal of more than 15,000 Cherokees from their ancestral lands in North Carolina, Tennessee, Georgia, and Alabama to the Indian Territories of Oklahoma and Arkansas. The journey lasted from June 1838 to March 1839. The trail was established on December 16, 1987.

FOR MORE INFORMATION

Trail of Tears National Historic Trail (National Park Service, Long Distance Trails Group, Box 728, Santa Fe, NM 87504-0728).

WILD AND SCENIC RIVERS SYSTEM

Alagnak Wild River

See the Alaska chapter for a full description.

FOR MORE INFORMATION

Alagnak Wild River (Katmai National Park and Preserve, Box 7, King Salmon, AK 99613-0007).

Alatna Wild River

The stream lies wholly within Gates of the Arctic National Park and Preserve, Alaska, in the Central Brooks Range. Wildlife, scenery, and interesting geologic features abound in the river corridor. The river was authorized on December 2, 1980.

FOR MORE INFORMATION

Alatna Wild River (Gates of the Arctic National Park and Preserve, 201 First Avenue, Fairbanks, Alaska 99701).

Aniakchak Wild River

The river, which lies within Aniakchak National Monument and Preserve, Alaska, flows out of Surprise Lake and plunges spectacularly through "The Gates."

FOR MORE INFORMATION

Aniakchak Wild River (Katmai National Park and Preserve, Box 7, King Salmon, AK 99613-0007).

Bluestone National Scenic River

See the West Virginia chapter for a full description.

FOR MORE INFORMATION

Bluestone National Scenic River (c/o New River Gorge National River, Box 246, Glen Jean, WV 25846-0246).

Cache la Poudre River

The river begins high in the peaks of Colorado's Rocky Mountain National Park. Flowing north and east through Roosevelt National Forest, it tumbles down the slopes of the Front Range and meanders through the city of Fort Collins. From its headwaters to the confluence with the South Platte River east of Greeley, the Cache la Poudre drops

7,000 ft. The river is notable for evidence of Native American occupation and diverse vegetation.

FOR MORE INFORMATION

Cache la Poudre (Arapaho and Roosevelt National Forests, 240 West Prospect, Fort Collins, CO 80526).

Charley Wild River

Lying within Yukon-Charley Rivers National Preserve, Alaska, this stream is known for the exceptional clarity of its water. For the experienced canoer or kayaker, it offers many miles of whitewater challenges. The river was authorized on December 2, 1980.

FOR MORE INFORMATION

Charley Wild River (Yukon-Charley Rivers National Preserve, Box 167, Eagle, AK 99738-0167, tel. 907/547–2234; Web site www.nps.gov/yuch).

Chilikadrotna Wild River

The river lies within Lake Clark National Park and Preserve, Alaska. Long stretches of swift water and outstanding fishing are exceptional features. The river was authorized on December 2, 1980.

FOR MORE INFORMATION

Chilikadrotna Wild River (Lake Clark National Park and Preserve, 4230 University Dr., Suite 311, Anchorage, AK 99508-4626).

Farmington River (West Branch)

The river is an important habitat for wildlife and the Farmington River Valley is currently the only place in Connecticut with nesting bald eagles. Atlantic salmon may return to the river after an absence of decades. Recreational value, rare wildlife, outstanding fisheries and a rich history are some of the features of the Farmington.

FOR MORE INFORMATION

Farmington River (National Park Service, 15 State Street, Boston, MA 02109).

Flathead River

Branches of the Flathead River border the western and southern boundaries of Glacier National Park, Montana. These areas are popular for fishing, floating and recreation.

FOR MORE INFORMATION

Flathead River (Glacier National Park, West Glacier, MT 59936-0128).

Great Egg Harbor
Scenic and Recreational River

See the New Jersey chapter for a full description.

FOR MORE INFORMATION

Great Egg Harbor Scenic and Recreational River (c/o Northeast Region National Park Service, 200 Chestnut St., Philadelphia, PA 19106-2818).

John Wild River

The river flows south through the Anaktuvuk Pass of Alaska's Brooks Range, and its valley is an important migration route for the Arctic Caribou herd. Gates of the Arctic National Park and Preserve contains the wild river. The river was authorized on December 2, 1980.

FOR MORE INFORMATION

John Wild River (Gates of the Arctic National Park and Preserve, 201 First Avenue, Fairbanks, Alaska 99701).

Kern River

This river includes both the North and South Forks of the Kern. The South Fork is totally free-flowing. It descends through deep gorges with large granite outcroppings and domes interspersed with open meadows. The upper 48 mi/77 km of the North Fork flow through Sequoia National Park and Golden Trout Wilderness. The river was authorized on November 24, 1987.

FOR MORE INFORMATION

Kern River (Sequoia National Park, 47050 Generals Hwy., Three Rivers, CA 93271-9651 or Sequoia National Forest, 900 W. Grand Ave., Porterville, CA 93257).

Kings River

The river includes the entire Middle and South Forks, which are largely in Kings Canyon National Park. Beginning in glacial lakes above timberline, the rivers flow through deep, steepsided canyons, over falls and cataracts, eventually becoming an outstanding whitewater rafting river in its lower reaches in Sequoia National Forest. Geology, scenery, recreation, fish, wildlife, and history are all significant aspects. It was authorized on November 3, 1987.

FOR MORE INFORMATION

Kings River (Kings Canyon National Park, 47050 Generals Hwy, Three Rivers, CA 93271-9651).

Klamath River

The Klamath, California's second largest river, flows through the state's northwestern counties and to the ocean through Redwood National Park. The Scott and Salmon, North and South Forks Salmon, and Wooley Creak are included. It is a major salmon producer, particularly coho and chinook. Noted raptor habitats are located along its banks.

FOR MORE INFORMATION

Klamath River (Klamath National Forest, 1312 Fairlane Road, Yreka, CA 96097-9549).

Kobuk Wild River

Kobuk Wild River is contained within Gates of the Arctic National Park and Preserve, Alaska. From its headwaters in the Endicott Mountains, the stream courses south through a wide valley and passes through two scenic canyons. It was authorized on December 2, 1980.

FOR MORE INFORMATION

Kobuk Wild River (Gates of the Arctic National Park and Preserve, 201 First Avenue, Fairbanks, Alaska 99701).

Lamprey Wild and Scenic River

This segment of the Lamprey River, extending from the Bunker Pond Dam in Epping downstream 24 mi/38 km to the confluence with the Picassic river in Newmarket, provides conservation opportunities for associated shorelands, floodplains, and wetlands. The Lamprey is considered the most important anadromous (migrating upriver to breed) fish resource in New Hampshire. It was authorized on November 12, 1996.

FOR MORE INFORMATION

Lamprey Wild and Scenic River (Boston System Support Office, Rivers and Trails Dept., 15 State St., Boston, MA 02109).

Maurice National Scenic and Recreational River

Portions of the Maurice River and three of its main tributaries, the Manumuskim River and the Menantico and Muskee Creeks, were designated to protect critical habitat on the Atlantic Flyway. It was authorized on December 1, 1993.

FOR MORE INFORMATION

Maurice National Scenic and Recreational River (c/o Northeast Region, National Park Service, 200 Chestnut St., Philadelphia, PA 19106-2818).

Merced River

Including the main stem and the South Fork, the Merced flows 81 mi/130 km in alternating pools, cascades, and waterfalls through Yosemite's superlative scenery–from glaciated peaks to lakes, alpine and subalpine meadows, glacially carved valleys and gorges of spectacular proportions. It was authorized on November 2, 1987.

FOR MORE INFORMATION

Merced River (Yosemite National Park, Box 577, Yosemite National Park, CA 95389-0577).

Middle Delaware River

See the Pennsylvania chapter for a full description.

FOR MORE INFORMATION

Middle Delaware River (Delaware Water Gap National Recreation Area, Bushkill, PA 18324-9410).

Missouri National Recreational River

See the Nebraska chapter for a full description.

FOR MORE INFORMATION

Missouri National Recreational River (Box 591, O'Neill, NE 68763).

Mulchatna Wild River

Mulchatna Wild River, which lies within Lake Clark National Park and Preserve, Alaska, is exceptionally scenic as it flows out of the Turquoise Lake with the glacier-clad Chigmit Mountains to the east. Both moose and caribou inhabit the area. The river was authorized on December 2, 1980.

FOR MORE INFORMATION

Mulchatna Wild River (Lake Clark National Park and Preserve, 4230 University Dr., Suite 311, Anchorage, AK 99508-4626).

Niobrara National Scenic Riverway

See the Nebraska chapter for a full description.

FOR MORE INFORMATION

Niobrara National Scenic Riverway (Box 591, O'Neill, NE 68763).

Noatak Wild River

Noatak Wild River is situated in Gates of the Arctic National Park and Preserve and Noatak National Preserve in Alaska. The Noatak drains the largest mountain-ringed river basin in America that is still virtually unaffected by human activities. It was authorized on December 2, 1980.

FOR MORE INFORMATION

Noatak Wild River (Gates of the Arctic National Park and Preserve, 201 First Avenue, Fairbanks, Alaska 99701).

North Fork of the Koyukuk Wild River

The river flows from the south flank of the Arctic Divide through broad, glacially carved valleys beside the rugged Endicott Mountains in Alaska's Central Brooks Range. It was authorized on December 2, 1980.

FOR MORE INFORMATION

North Fork of the Koyukuk Wild River (Gates of the Arctic National Park and Preserve, 201 First Avenue, Fairbanks, Alaska 99701).

Obed Wild and Scenic River

See the Tennessee chapter for a full description.

FOR MORE INFORMATION

Obed Wild and Scenic River (Box 429, Wartburg, TN 37887-0429).

Rio Grande Wild and Scenic River

See the Texas chapter for a full description.

FOR MORE INFORMATION

Rio Grande Wild and Scenic River (Big Bend National Park, Big Bend National Park, TX 79834-0129).

Saint Croix National Scenic Riverway

See the Wisconsin chapter for a full description.

FOR MORE INFORMATION

Saint Croix National Scenic Riverway (Box 708, St. Croix Falls, WI 54024-0708).

Salmon Wild River

Salmon Wild River, located within Kobuk Valley National Park, Alaska, is small but exceptionally beautiful, with deep blue-green pools and many rock outcroppings. It was authorized December 2, 1980.

FOR MORE INFORMATION

Salmon Wild River (Kobuk Valley National Park, Box 1029, Kotzebue, AK 99752-1029).

Sudbury, Assabet and Concord Rivers

Located about 25 mi/40 km west of Boston, the rivers are remarkably undeveloped and provide recreational opportunities in a natural setting. Ten of the river miles lie within the boundary of the Great Meadows National Wildlife Refuge. Historic sites of national importance, including many in the Minute Man National Historical Park, are located near the rivers in Concord.

FOR MORE INFORMATION

Sudbury, Assabet and Concord Rivers (Sudbury Valley Trustees, Box 7, Wayland, MA 01778).

Tinayguk Wild River

Alaska's 44-mi/70-km Tinayguk River is the largest tributary of the North Fork of the Koyukuk. Both lie entirely within the pristine environment of Gates of the Arctic National Park. It was authorized on December 2, 1980.

FOR MORE INFORMATION

Tinayguk Wild River (Gates of the Arctic National Park and Preserve, 201 First Avenue, Fairbanks, Alaska 99701).

Tlikakila Wild River

Located about 100 air miles west of Anchorage in Lake Clark National Park, Alaska, the 51-mi/82-km Tlikakila Wild River is closely flanked by glaciers, 10,000-ft high rock-and-snow-capped mountains and perpendicular cliffs. It was authorized on December 2, 1980.

FOR MORE INFORMATION

Tlikakila Wild River (Lake Clark National Park and Preserve, 4230 University Dr., Suite 311, Anchorage, AK 99508-4626).

Tuolumne River

The Tuolumne originates from snowmelt off Mounts Dana and Lydell in Yosemite National Park and courses 54 mi before crossing into Stanislaus National Forest. The national forest segment contains some of the most noted whitewater in the high Sierras and is an extremely popular rafting stream. It was authorized on September 28, 1981.

FOR MORE INFORMATION

Tuolumne River (Yosemite National Park, Box 577, Yosemite, CA 95389-0577).

Upper Delware River

See the Pennsylvania chapter for a full description.

FOR MORE INFORMATION

Upper Delaware River (Box C, Narrowsburg, NY 12764-0159).

Wekiva River

FOR MORE INFORMATION

Wekiva River (National Park Service, Atlanta Federal Center 1924 Building, 100 Alabama Street, SW, Atlanta, GA 30303, tel. 404/562–3175 x 522).

White Clay Creek

FOR MORE INFORMATION

White Clay Creek (National Park Service, 260 U.S. Custom House, 2nd & Chestnut Streets, Philadelphia, PA 19106, tel 215/597–1655).

Index

INDEX

NOTES

NOTES

NOTES

NOTES

NOTES

NOTES

NOTES

NOTES

NOTES

NOTES

NOTES

NOTES

NOTES